THE HEART OF
THE ANTARCTIC

THE STORY OF THE BRITISH
ANTARCTIC EXPEDITION
1907–1909

Sir Ernest Shackleton

Birlinn

919.9

This edition published in 2000 by
Birlinn Limited
8 Canongate Venture
5 New Street
Edinburgh EH8 8BH

ISBN 1 84158 081 3

British Library Cataloguing in Publication Data
A Catalogue record for this book is available from the British Library

Typesetting and origination by Brinnoven, Livingston
Printed and bound by Creative Print and Design, Ebbw Vale

CONTENTS

PREFACE TO THE BIRLINN EDITION

Ernest Shackleton was born an Anglo-Irishman, the second child of a family of eight, in 1874. In 1884 his family settled in England. He was educated at Dulwich College in London. His academic career was hardly distinguished – his restlessness rendered him ill suited to formal education – and even at an early age he wanted to go to sea. At sixteen he achieved his ambition. One of his teachers wrote that he left behind him the impression of 'a rolling stone who would probably gather no moss'.

Several events now conspired to tug Shackleton in a different direction. Firstly, while he clearly loved the sea, the monotony of a career in the merchant marine seemed to him more and more palpable. Secondly, the lure of the Arctic and Antarctic was seizing the late Victorian mind. In 1895 the brooding, charismatic figure of Fridtjof Nansen had achieved the record for Furthest North in the Fram. His visit to London was a sensation. Thirdly, these frozen regions, *terra incognita* to mankind, seemed to hold the possibility of untold wealth. To Shackleton, the impecunious late Victorian always in need of cash, this was a lure indeed. In fact much of Shackleton's life from then on was spent in the pursuit of cash, either from rich benefactors or through wild business schemes – cash then spent with casual disregard for the trail of angry creditors who pursued him or, as was often the case, those who served under him. His usual solution to these problems was to sail on another expedition, leaving those unfortunates who had to administer his affairs to bear the brunt of the airy promises and financial irresponsibility which kept him perennially on the brink of ruin.

All these factors came together in Shackleton's application to join Sir Clements Markham's National Antarctic Expedition. He was to serve under a young naval lieutenant called Robert Falcon Scott. *The Times* commented that 'As youth is essential, one without actual Polar experience has had to be selected . . .' The expedition was to proceed on the same facile assumption that British pluck and enthusiasm were a match for the professionalism and care of the Scandinavians. This was an assumption that bedevilled all of the British Antarctic expeditions, leading them to heroic and fatal failure. Equally, it proceeded in a welter of intrigue as Markham forced Scott's appointment over the head of other better qualified candidates.

The journey south already began to reveal how ill suited Scott was to command and also how poor a ship *Discovery* was to the task ahead. Nevertheless the expedition drove through the pack ice into the Ross Sea towards Mount Erebus and the magnificent panorama of the Great Ice barrier. The expedition began to move into uncharted waters and prepared to overwinter at the head of McMurdo Sound. It was time to test the road to the South Pole and it was now that the clumsiness and amateurishness of the British attempts began to show themselves most clearly. There were dog teams but no one knew how to drive them. No skis were used – the expedition was going to attempt to trudge south! Shackleton led the first reconnaissance and it was the vision south from an isolated lump of rock that was to fuel his obsession with the Antarctic. For hundreds of miles he gazed at unknown mountains towards the Pole.

As the expedition overwintered, so the tensions within the group grew. While there was no outbreak of hostilities with Scott, the contrast between Shackleton's seething energy and overwhelming personality and the secretive, weaker Scott was storing up trouble for the future. Scurvy – the curse of these long expeditions – broke out and it was Shackleton, the pragmatic problem solver, who found a solution (eating fresh rather than tinned meat), while still not understanding the root cause of the ailment.

Three men started the journey south – Scott, Shackleton and Wilson. Ill equipped, still completely unaware of how to use their dog teams, they slowly staggered south. The tension between Shackleton and Scott broke into open dislike. Travelling light and killing and eating their dogs took them to their Furthest South. As scurvy began to bite and the instability of Scott seemed to increase, so they turned north again. On the return Shackleton started coughing blood, part of a mysterious illness which recurred through his life and which he fought to deny. With no reserves of food, desperately weakened and with a semi-invalid to shepherd home, Scott and Wilson struggled north. Yet even in these desperate times Scott still found time pass remarks on Shackleton's physical weakness. Once again it was the role of Wilson to broker peace. It was on 1 January that they turned back. By the 29th Wilson no longer expected Shackleton to live. Yet somehow his indomitable will asserted itself and 3rd February saw them return to the *Discovery*. While she was still frozen in, a relief ship had arrived, and it was on this that Scott invalided Shackleton home. As he left, he looked back on the receding ice pack:

Ah me it was a sad parting . . . snow was falling, and a dreariness seemed over all things . . . the sun came out in a blaze of glory and bathed the bergs in lights that were more than splendour: the small waves twinkled in the sunlight; waves not seen by me for more than a year . . . It was so familiar my home fading away . . . I turned in and read for a bit but thoughts would go back to those I left on the floe.

Shackleton returned to a mire of intrigue. The expedition was not meant to remain for a second year in the ice, and in any case had run out of money. Sir Clements Markham's enemies pounced and a naval rescue was organised. Shackleton had the opportunity of returning as the rescuer of the man who had attempted to humiliate him. But he now had grander dreams: he wished to lead his own expedition south. But the time was not ripe and a career in journalism beckoned. One of those who took him on recorded:

> Extraordinarily powerful, he moved with the rolling sailor's gait and looked at you with his great humorous dark blue eyes which . . . had often in them the brooding eye of the dreamer . . . he made us see the things he spoke of, and held us all spellbound.

But again his restlessness took charge and he took up a new post – that of secretary to the Royal Geographical Society in Edinburgh. He hit it like a whirlwind, but once again routine began to tire him and the return of Scott – now Captain – acted as a goad to his ambition. He stood (and failed) for parliament as a unionist candidate, and critically won the support of William and Emily Beardmore. Beardmore ran an industrial behemoth and it was under his sheltering wing that Shackleton now found work. For Beardmore, a pillar of Edwardian rectitude, it was to end up as a distinctly uncomfortable relationship. Shackleton (it is rumoured) rapidly began an affair with Emily. One of the reasons for Beardmore money being involved in Shackleton's next expedition was, it is said, to keep him away from Emily.

It was now that one of Shackleton's less attractive sides came to the fore. He was as short of cash as he was full of get-rich schemes for acquiring it. This seems to have been a family trait – his louche brother Frank, denizen of an Edwardian demi-monde, had similar traits. Equally, having begged or borrowed cash for a particular scheme it very rarely returned to the lender. He was both spectacularly naive and shady at the same time, and the swirl of rumour surrounding Frank did not help Shackleton's name. Yet it was now, launched with Beardmore money and with the help of Frank, that Shackleton launched the British Antarctic Expedition of 1907. Three days after Beardmore had committed himself, Shackleton met the two giants of polar exploration – Amundsen and Nansen. Soon afterwards, Shackleton received a tirade from Scott accusing him of standing in the way of his – Scott's – dreams by returning in the path of *Discovery* where he too intended to return. After much acrimony a deal was eventually brokered whereby Shackleton agreed not to use McMurdo Sound as a base.

Shackleton prepared for his expedition with boundless enthusiasm and minimal groundwork. This time he would reject both dogs and skis in favour of horses and a motor car! To the careful, methodical Norwegians, Shackleton must have seemed on the edge of being deranged. Money became a desperate problem, Scott continued to gripe, and a new unexpected threat appeared. Frank was on the edge of bankruptcy and, worse still, was a prime suspect in the theft of the Irish crown jewels. By increasingly threadbare expedients Shackleton managed to get the *Nimrod* away in early August. At Cowes she was boarded by Edward VII and was given a berth – a place of honour amongst the two hundred warships of the Home Fleet – beside the world's mightiest warship, HMS *Dreadnought*. Finally, as the police net closed in on Frank, and with a last loan of £1000 from Beardmore, which Shackleton airily promised to repay before sailing (without having the slighest chance of doing so), *Nimrod* set sail. Nimrod was famous as the mighty hunter of the Bible, but to many on land it must have seemed as if Shackleton was the hunted as the ship slowly slipped beneath the horizon. In Australia his sheer force of personality persuaded the government to make up yet another cash shortfall. He also – and as significantly – persuaded another man who was to become a giant of exploration – Douglas Mawson – to join the expedition. Through appalling weather *Nimrod* thrust south. On 23 January 1908, the gleam of ice appeared on the horizon: 'a hard white line, as if drawn by an enormous ruler, began to materialise out of the blink, becoming sharper . . .'

The great journey to the heart of the Antarctic had begun . . .

PREFACE TO THE ORIGINAL EDITION

The scientific results of the expedition can only be stated generally in the text. The expert members in each branch have contributed other appendices articles which summarise what has been done in the domains of geology, biology, magnetism, meteorology, physics, &c. I will simply indicate here some of the more important features of the geographical work.

We passed the winter 1908 in McMurdo Sound, twenty miles north of the *Discovery* winter quarters. In the autumn a party ascended Mount Erebus and surveyed its various craters. In the spring and summer of 1908–9 three sledging-parties left winter quarters; one went south and attained the most southerly latitude ever reached by man, another reached the South Magnetic Pole for the first time, and a third surveyed the mountain ranges west of McMurdo Sound.

The southern sledge-journey planted the Union Jack in latitude 88° 23′ South, within one hundred geographical miles of the South Pole. This party of four ascertained that a great chain of mountains extends from the 82nd parallel, south of McMurdo Sound, to the 86th parallel, trending in a south-easterly direction; that other great mountain ranges continue to the south and south-west, and that between them flows one of the largest glaciers in the world, leading to an inland plateau, the height of which, at latitude 88° South, is over 11,000 ft. above sea level. This plateau presumably continues beyond the geographical South Pole, and extends from Cape Adare to the Pole. The bearings and angles of the new southern mountains and of the great glacier are shown on the chart, and are as nearly correct as can be expected in view of the somewhat rough methods necessarily employed in making the survey.

The mystery of the Great Ice Barrier has not been solved, and it would seem that the question of its formation and extent cannot be determined definitely until an expedition traces the line of the mountains round its southerly edge. A certain amount of light has been thrown on the construction of the Barrier, in that we were able, from observations and measurements, to conclude provisionally that it is composed mainly of snow. The disappearance of Balloon Bight, owing to the breaking away of a section of the Great Ice Barrier, shows that the Barrier still continues its recession, which has been observed since the voyage of Sir James Ross in 1842. There certainly appears to be a high snow-covered land on the 163rd meridian, where we saw slopes and peaks, entirely snow covered, rising to a height of 800 ft., but we did not see any bare rocks, and did not have an opportunity to take soundings at this spot. We could not arrive at any definite conclusion on the point.

The journey made by the Northern Party resulted in the attainment of the South Magnetic Pole, the position of which was fixed, by observations made on the spot and in the neighbourhood, at latitude 72° 25′ South, longitude 155° 16′ East. The first part of this journey was made along the coast-line of Victoria Land, and many new peaks, glaciers and ice-tongues were discovered, in addition to a couple of small islands. The whole of the coast traversed was carefully triangulated, and the existing map was corrected in several respects.

The survey of the western mountains by the Western Party added to the information of the topographical details of that part of Victoria Land, and threw some new light on its geology.

The discovery of forty-five miles of new coast-line extending from Cape North, first in a south-westerly and then in a westerly direction, was another important piece of geographical work.

During the homeward voyage of the *Nimrod* a careful search strengthened that prevalent idea that Emerald Island, The Nimrod Islands and Dougherty Island do not exist, but I would not advise their removal from the chart without further investigation. There is a remote possibility that they lie at some point in the neighbourhood of their charted positions, and it is safer to have them charted until their non-existence has been proved absolutely.

I should like to tender my warmest thanks to those generous people who supported the expedition in its early days. Miss Dawson Lambton and Miss E. Dawson Lambton made possible the first steps towards the organisation of the expedition, and assisted afterwards in every way that lay in their power. Mr. William Beardmore (Parkhead, Glasgow), Mr. G. A. McLean Buckley (New Zealand), Mr. Campbell McKellar (London), Mr. Sydney Lysaght (Somerset), Mr. A. M. Fry (Bristol), Colonel Alexander Davis (London), Mr. William Bell (Pendell Court, Surrey), Mr. H. H. Bartlett (London), and other friends contributed liberally towards the cost of the expedition. I wish also to thank the people who guaranteed a large part of the necessary expediture, and the Imperial Government for the grant of £20,000, which enabled me to redeem these guarantees. Sir James Mills, managing director of the Union Steam Shipping Company of New Zealand, gave very valuable assistance. The kindness and generosity of the Governments and people of Australia and New Zealand will remain one of the happiest memories of the expedition.

I am also indebted to the firms which presented supplies of various sorts, and to the manufacturers who so readily assisted in the matter of ensuring the highest quality and purity in our foods.

As regards the production of this book, I am indebted to Dr. Hugh Robert Mill for the introduction which he has written; to Mr. Edward Saunders, of New Zealand, who not only acted as my secretary in the writing of the book, but bore a great deal of the labour, advised me on literary points and gave general assistance that was invaluable, and to my publisher, Mr. William Heinemann, for much help and many kindnesses.

I have drawn on the diaries of various members of the expedition to supply information regarding events that occurred while I was absent on journeys. The photographs with which these volumes are illustrated have been selected from some thousands taken by Brocklehurst, David, Davis, Day, Dunlop, Harbord, Joyce, Mackintosh, Marshall, Mawson, Murray, and Wild, secured often under circumstances of exceptional difficulty.

In regard to the management of the affairs of the expedition during my absence in the Antarctic, I would like to acknowledge the work done for me by my brother-in-law, Mr. Herbert Dorman, of London; by Mr. J. J. Kinsey, of Christchurch, New Zealand; and by Mr. Alfred Reid, the manager of the expedition, whose work throughout has been as arduous as it has been efficient.

Finally, let me say that to the members of the expedition, whose work and enthusiasm have been the means of securing the measure of success recorded in these pages, I owe a debt of gratitude that I can hardly find words to express. I realise very fully that without their faithful service and loyal co-operation under conditions of extreme difficulty success in any branch of our work would have been impossible.

ERNEST H. SHACKLETON.
London, *October* 1909.

INTRODUCTION
SOUTH POLAR EXPLORATION IN THE LAST HUNDRED YEARS

by Hugh Robert Mill, DSc, LLD

An outline of the history of recent Antarctic exploration is necessary before the reader can appreciate to the full the many points of originality in the equipment of the expedition of 1907–1909, and follow the unequalled advance made by that expedition into the slowly dwindling blank of the unknown South Polar area.

From the beginning of the sixteenth century it was generally believed that a great continent, equal in area to all the rest of the land of the globe, lay around the South Pole, stretching northward in each of the great oceans far into the tropics. The second voyage of Captain James Cook in 1773–75 showed that if any continent existed it must lie mainly within the Antarctic Circle, which he penetrated at three points in search of the land, and it could be of no possible value for settlement or trade. He reached his farthest south in 71° 10′ South, 1180 miles from the South Pole.

In 1819 Alexander I, Emperor of all the Russias, resolved of his good pleasure to explore the North Polar and the South Polar regions simultaneously and sent out two ships to each destination. The southern expedition consisted of the two ships *Vostok* and *Mirni*, under the command of Captain Fabian von Bellingshausen, with Lieutenant Lazareff as second in command. They made a circumnavigation of the world in a high southern latitude, supplementing the voyage of Cook by keeping south where he went north, but not attempting to reach any higher latitudes. On leaving Sydney in November 1820, Bellingshausen went south in 163° East, a section of the Antarctic which Cook had avoided, and from the eagerness with which the Russian captain apologised for not pushing into the pack it may be inferred that he found the gate leading to Ross Sea only barred by the ice, not absolutely locked. The ships went on in the direction of Cape Horn in order to visit the South Shetlands, recently discovered by William Smith. On the way Bellingshausen discovered the first land yet known within the Antarctic Circle, the little Peter I Island and the much larger Alexander I

Land, which he sighted from a distance estimated at forty miles. A fleet of American sealers was found at work round the South Shetlands and some of the skippers had doubtless done much exploring on their own account, though they kept it quiet for fear of arousing competition in their trade. Bellingshausen returned to Cronstadt in 1821 with a loss of only three men in his long and trying voyage. No particulars of this expedition were published for many years.

In February 1823, James Weddell, a retired Master in the Royal Navy, and part owner of the brig *Jane* of Leith, 160 tons, was sealing round the South Orkneys with the cutter *Beaufoy,* 65 tons, under the command of Matthew Brisbane, in company, when he decided to push south as far as the ice allowed in search of new land where seals might be found. Signs of land were seen in the form of icebergs stained with earth, but Weddell sailed through a perfectly clear sea, now named after him, to 74° 15′ South in 34° 17′ West. This point, reached on February 22, 1823, was 3° South of Cook's farthest and 945 miles from the South Pole. On his return he brought back to Europe the first specimen of the Weddell seal to be seen by any naturalist.

Enderby Brothers, a firm of London shipowners doing a large trade in seal-oil, took a keen interest in discovery, and one of the brothers was an original Fellow of the Royal Geographical Society, founded in 1830. In that very year the firm despatched John Biscoe, a retired Master in the Royal Navy, in the brig *Tula*, with the cutter *Lively* in company, on a two years' voyage, combining exploration with sealing. Biscoe was a man of the type of Cook and Weddell, a first-class navigator, indifferent to comfort, ignorant of fear and keen on exploring the Far South. In January 1831 he commenced a circumnavigation of the Antarctic Regions eastward from the South Atlantic in 60° South. At the meridian of Greenwich he got south of the Circle and pushed on, beating against contrary winds close to the impenetrable pack which blocked advance to the south. At the end of February he sighted a coast-line in 49° 18′ East and about 66° South, which has since been called Enderby Land, but it has never been revisited. He searched in vain for the Nimrod Islands, which had been reported in 56° South, 158° West, and then, crossing the Pacific Ocean well south of the sixtieth parallel, he, ignorant of Bellingshausen's voyage, entered Bellingshausen Sea, and discovered the Biscoe Islands and the coast of Graham Land. On his return in 1833 Biscoe received the second gold medal awarded by the Royal Geographical Society for his discoveries and for his pertinacity in sailing for nearly fifty degrees of longitude south of the Antarctic Circle.

In 1838 the Enderbys sent out John Balleny in the sealing schooner *Eliza Scott,* 154 tons, with the cutter *Sabrina,* 54 tons, and he left Campbell Island, south of New Zealand, on January 17, 1839, to look for new land in the south. On the 29th he reached the Antarctic Circle in 178° East, and got to 69° South before meeting with heavy ice. Turning westward at this point he discovered the group of lofty volcanic islands which bears his name, and there was no mistake as to their existence, as one of the peaks rose to a height of 14,000 ft. An excellent sketch was made of the islands by the mate, and geological specimens were collected from the beach. Proceeding westward Biscoe reported an 'appearance of land in 65° South, and about 121° East', which Mr. Charles Enderby claimed as a discovery and called Sabrina Land after the unfortunate cutter, which was lost with all hands in a gale.

The years 1838 to 1848 saw no fewer than ten vessels bound on exploration to the ice-cumbered waters of the Antarctic, all ostensibly bent on scientific research, but all animated, some admittedly, by the patriotic ambition of each commander to uphold the honour of his flag.

Captain Dumont d'Urville, of the French Navy, was one of the founders of the Paris Geographical Society. He had been sent out on two scientific voyages of circumnavigation, which lasted from 1822 to 1825, and from 1826 to 1829, and he became a great authority on the ethnology of the Pacific Islands. He planned a third cruise to investigate problems connected with his special studies; but, in granting the vessels for this expedition, King Louis Philippe added to the commission, possibly at the suggestion of Humboldt, a cruise to the Antarctic regions in order to out-distance Weddell's farthest south. It was known that an American expedition was on the point of starting with this end in view, and that active steps were also being taken in England to revive southern exploration. Dumont d'Urville got away first with two corvettes, the *Astrolabe*, under his command, and the *Zelée*, under Captain Jacquinot, which sailed from Toulon on September 7, 1837. The two ships reached the pack-ice on January 22, 1888, but were unable to do more than sail to and fro along its edge until February 27, when land was sighted in 63° South and named Louis Philippe Land and Joinville Island. These were, undoubtedly, part of the Palmer Land of the American sealers, and a continuation of Biscoe's Graham Land. Though he did not reach the Antarctic Circle, d'Urville had got to the end of the Antarctic summer and discharged his debt of duty to his instructions.

It was the avowed intention of the American expedition and of the British expedition, since fitted out, to find the South Magnetic Pole, the position of which was believed from the theoretical investigations of Gauss to be near 66° South and 146° East. In December 1839, when d'Urville was at Hobart Town, and the air was full of rumours of these expeditions, he suddenly made up his mind to exceed his instructions and make a dash for the South Magnetic Pole for the honour of France. He left Hobart on January 1, 1840, and on the 21st sighted land on the Antarctic Circle in longitude 138° E. The weather was perfect, the icebergs shone and glittered in the sun like fairy palaces in the streets of a strange southern Venice; only wind was wanting to move the ships. The snow-covered hills rose to a height of about 1500 ft. and received the name of Adelie Land, after Madame Dumont d'Urville. A landing was made on one of a group of rocky islets lying off the icebound shore, and the ships then followed the coast westward for two days. In 135° 30′ West bad weather and a northward bend in the ice drove the corvettes beyond the Circle, and on struggling south again on January 28, in the lift of a fog, the *Astrolabe* sighted a brig flying the American flag, one of Wilkes' squadron. The ships misunderstood each other's intentions; each intended to salute and each thought that the other wished to avoid an interview; and they parted in the fog full of bitterness towards each other without the dip of a flag. All day on the 30th, d'Urville sailed along a vertical cliff of ice 120 to 130 ft. high, quite flat on top, with no sign of hills beyond; but sure that so great a mass of ice could not form except on land he did not hesitate to name it the Clarie coast, after Madame Jacquinot. On February 1, the French ships left the Antarctic in longitude 130° West.

An American man of science, Mr. J. N. Reynolds, had gone to Palmer Land in the early days, and on his return agitated strongly for a national exploring expedition. An Act of Congress in 1836 provided for such an expedition, but there had been controversies giving rise to ill-feeling, and Mr. Reynolds was not allowed to join 'for the sake of harmony'. After one and another of the naval officers designated to command it had resigned or declined the post, Lieutenant Charles Wilkes, U.S.N., was at last persuaded to take charge of the squadron of six ill-assorted vessels manned by half-hearted crews. His instructions were to proceed to Tierra del Fuego with the sloops-of-war *Vincennes* and *Peacock,* the brig *Porpoise,* the store-ship *Belief* and the pilot-boats *Sea Gull* and *Flying Fish*; to leave the larger vessels and the scientific staff – which they carried – and proceed with the *Porpoise* and the tenders 'to explore the southern Antarctic to the southward of Powell's group, and between it and Sandwich Land, following the track of Weddell as closely as practicable, and endeavouring to reach a high southern latitude; taking care, however, not to be obliged to pass the winter there.' He was then with all his squadron to proceed southward and westward as far as Cook's farthest, or 105° West, and then retire to Valparaiso. After surveying in the Pacific they were to proceed to Sydney and then the instructions proceeded: 'You will make a second attempt to penetrate within the Antarctic region, south of Van Diemen's Land, and as far west as longitude 45° East or to Enderby's Land, making your rendezvous on your return at Kerguelen's Land.' Very stringent orders, dated August 11, 1838, were given to Wilkes not to allow any one connected with the expedition to furnish any other persons 'with copies of any journal, charts, plan, memorandum, specimen, drawing, painting or information' concerning the objects and proceedings of the expedition or as to discoveries made. The ships were not fortified for ice navigation; they were not even in sound seaworthy condition; the stores were inadequate and of bad quality; the crews and unhappily some of the officers were disaffected, disliking their commander, and making things very uncomfortable for him. The attempt to navigate Weddell Sea proved abortive; on the side of Bellingshausen Sea one ship reached 68° and another 70° South, but saw nothing except ice.

At Sydney, Wilkes was most unhappy; his equipment was criticised with more justice than mercy by his colonial visitors, and in his narrative he says plainly that he was obliged 'to agree with them that we were unwise to attempt such service in ordinary cruising vessels; we had been ordered to go and that was enough: and go we should.' And they went. On January 16, 1840, land was sighted by three of the ships in longitudes about 1580 East, apparently just on or south of the Antarctic Circle. The ships sailed westwards as best they could along the edge of the pack; sometimes along the face of a barrier of great ice-cliffs, ignorant of the fact that Balleny had been there the year before, but very anxious that they should anticipate any discoveries on the part of the French squadron then in those waters. On January 19, land was reported on the Antarctic Circle both to the south-east and to the south-west, Wilkes being then in 154° 30′ East, and its height was estimated at 3000 ft. The ships were involved all the time in most difficult navigation through drifting floes and bergs, storms were frequent and fogs made life a perpetual misery, as it was impossible to see the icebergs until the ships were almost on them. The *Peacock,* the least seaworthy of the squadron, lay helpless in the ice for three days while the rudder, which had been smashed, was being repaired on deck, and on January 25 she was patched up enough to return to Sydney. Wilkes' ship, the *Vincennes,* got south of the Circle on January 23, and he hoped to reach the land, but the way was barred by ice. On the 28th, land appeared very distinctly in 141° East, but the *Vincennes* was driven off by a gale, the sea being extraordinarily encumbered with icebergs and ice-islands. Two days later land was unquestionably found in 66° 45′ South, 140° 2′ East, with a depth of thirty fathoms; there were bare rocks half a mile from the ship, and the hills beyond rose to 3000 ft.; but the weather was too rough to get boats out. This was the Adelie Land which d'Urville had lighted on nine days before. This also is the only point of land reported by the American expedition, with the very doubtful exception of Sabrina Land, which has been confirmed by another expedition. Against the written remonstrance of the surgeons, who said that longer exposure to the heavy work of ice navigation in the severe conditions of the weather would increase the sicklist to such an extent as to endanger the ships, and in spite of the urgent appeal of a majority of the officers, Wilkes held on to the westward, reporting land in the neighbourhood of the Antarctic Circle every day, observing many earth-stained icebergs and collecting specimens of stones from the floating ice. On February 16, the ice-barrier which Wilkes had been following westward turned towards the north and over it there was 'an appearance of land' which he called Termination Land. He was in 97° 37′ East, and on the 21st, having failed to get farther west, he rejoiced the hearts of all on board by turning northwards and making for Sydney. Ringgold on the *Porpoise* had thought of running to the rendezvous in 1000 East first, and working his way back to the eastward with a favouring wind afterwards, and he accomplished the first part of the programme easily enough, for the wind helped him, passing and disdaining to salute d'Urville's ships on the way. He added nothing material to the information obtained by the *Vincennes*.

Considering the deplorable conditions against which he had to contend both in the seas without and the men within his ships, the voyage of Wilkes was one of the finest pieces of determined effort on record. He erred in not being critical enough of appearances of land; and his charts were certainly faulty, as any charts of land dimly seen through fog were bound to be. Subsequent explorers have sailed over the positions where Wilkes showed land between 164° and 154° East, and if the land he saw there exists, it must be farther south than he supposed. It is certain that Wilkes saw land farther east, and it seems that he was as harshly judged by Ross and as unsympathetically treated by some other explorers and geographers as he was by his own subordinates.

Sir Edward Sabine and other British physicists had been trying from 1885 onward to secure the despatch of a British expedition to study terrestrial magnetism in the Antarctic regions, and pressure was brought to bear on the Royal Society to take the initiative but with little effect. An effort by Captain Washington, the Secretary, to arouse the Royal Geographical Society early in 1887 also failed. In the following year the recently founded British Association for the Advancement of Science memorialised Government on the need for making a series of simultaneous magnetic observations in all parts of the world, particularly by means of a special expedition to high southern latitudes. The Prime Minister, Lord Melbourne, was impressed; he referred the memorial to the Royal Society, which supported it. A naval expedition was decided on and rapidly fitted out on the *Erebus* and *Terror,* two vessels of great strength, designed for firing large bombs from mortars in siege operations, but clumsy craft to navigate, with bluff bows that made them move slowly through the water, and sluggish in answering their helms. The one possible commander was Captain James Clark Ross, a tried Arctic traveller and an enthusiastic student of magnetism, who had reached the North Magnetic Pole in 1831, and whose surpassing fitness for the position had been a potent factor in the minds of the promoters. Captain Crozier was second in command on board the *Terror,* and although all the magnetic and other physical work was to be done by naval officers, the surgeons were appointed with regard to their proficiency in geology, botany and zoology. One of these subsequently took rank amongst the greatest men of science of the nineteenth century, and in 1909 Sir Joseph Hooker retains at the age of ninety-two the same interest in Antarctic exploration which drew him in 1839, as a youth of twenty-one, to join the Navy, in order to accompany the expedition. The ships were of 370 and 850 tons respectively, the whole ship's company of each being seventy-six officers and men, and they were well provisioned for the period, fresh tinned meats and vegetables being available. The instructions of the Admiralty left a good deal of discretion to the commander. He was ordered to land special parties of magnetic observers at St. Helena, the Cape of Good Hope and Van Diemen's Land. On the way he was to proceed south from Kerguelen Land and examine those places where indications of land had been reported. In the following summer he was to proceed southward from Tasmania towards the South Magnetic Pole, which he was to reach if possible, and return to Tasmania. In the following year he was to attain the highest latitude he could reach and proceed eastward to fix the position of Graham Land.

The *Erebus* and *Terror* reached Hobart Town in August 1840, without doing any Antarctic exploration on the way. At Hobart, Ross was in constant communication with Sir John Franklin, the governor of Van Diemen's Land and a great authority on polar exploration in the north. He heard of d'Urville's and Wilkes' discoveries and was very angry that others had taken the track marked out for him. He resolved that he would not, as he somewhat quaintly put it, 'interfere with their discoveries' and in so doing he allowed the haze of uncertainty to rest over the region south of the Indian Ocean to this day; but he also resolved to try to get south on the meridian of 170° East, where Balleny had found open sea in 69° South; and had it not been for the previous French and American voyages causing him to change his plans, Ross might conceivably have missed the great chance of his lifetime. The expedition left Hobart on November 12, 1840, sighted the sea ice on December 31, lying along the Antarctic Circle, and after spending some time searching for the best place to enter it, on January 5, 1841, ships for the first time in the southern hemisphere left the open sea and pushed their way of set purpose into the pack. The vessels having been strengthened after the manner of the northern whalers to resist pressure and Ross himself fortified by long experience in Arctic navigation, the impassable barrier of the earlier explorers had no terrors for him. The pack which all other visitors to the Antarctic had viewed as extending right up to some remote and inaccessible land was found to be a belt about a hundred miles wide, and in four days the *Erebus* and *Terror* passed through it into the open waters of what is now called Ross Sea. The way seemed to lie open to the magnetic pole when a mountain appeared on the horizon. Ross called it Mount Sabine, after the

originator of the expedition, and held on until on January 11 he was within a
few miles of the bold mountainous coast of South Victoria Land; in front of
him lay Cape Adare in latitude 710 South, from which one line of mountains,
the Admiralty Range, ran north-west along the coast to Cape North, another,
the peaks of which he named after the members of the Councils of the Royal
Society and the British Association, ran along the coast to the south. Ross
went ashore on Possession Island on January 12 and took possession of the
first land discovered in the reign of Queen Victoria. The sea swarmed with
whales, in the pursuit of which Ross, probably mistaking the species, thought
that a great trade would spring up. On the 22nd the latitude of 74° South was
passed and the expedition was soon nearer the Pole than any human being
had been before. A few days later Franklin Island was seen and visited; but,
as at Possession Island, no trace of vegetation was found. On the morning
of January 28, a new mountain emitting volumes of smoke appeared ahead;
it was Mount Erebus, named after the leading ship, and on High Island,
as Ross called the land from which it sprung, appeared a lesser and extinct
volcano, called Mount Terror after the second vessel. As the ships drew near,
confident of sailing far beyond the 80th parallel, an icebarrier appeared
similar to that reported by Wilkes on his cruise, but greater. Vast walls of
ice as high as the cliffs of Dover butted on to the new land at Cape Crozier,
its western limit, and formed an absolute bar to further progress. A range
of high land running south was seen over the barrier and this Ross called
the Parry Mountains; to the west around the shores of an ice-girdled bay
(McMurdo Bay) the land seemed to run continuously with the continent,
and Ross accordingly represented Mount Erebus as being on the mainland,
and the coast as turning abruptly in McMurdo Bay from its southerly to
an easterly direction. The ships cruised eastward for two hundred and
fifty miles parallel with the Great Barrier, the remarkable nature of which
impressed all on board, as they recognised its uniform flat-topped extension
and the vast height of the perpendicular ice-cliffs in which it terminated, the
height being something like 200 ft. on the average, though at one point it did
not exceed 50 ft. On February 2, the highest latitude of the trip was reached,
78° 4′ South, or 3° 48′ beyond Weddell's farthest on the opposite side of
the Antarctic Circle. Two days later the pack became so dense that progress
was stopped in 167° West. Ross struggled for a week to get farther east and
then turned to look for a harbour on the coast of Victoria Land in which
he might winter. Passing by McMurdo Bay without examining it closely, he
tried to get a landing nearer the Magnetic Pole, being possessed by a burning
ambition to hoist the flag which he had displayed at the North Magnetic
Pole in 1881 at the South Magnetic Pole in 1841. It was impossible, however,
to get within twelve or fourteen miles of the land on account of the freezing
of the sea locking the pack into a solid mass; it was too late to turn back

and seek a harbour farther south, and after naming the headland at the base of Mount Melbourne, Cape Washington, in honour of the zealous Secretary of the Royal Geographical Society, Ross left the Antarctic regions after having remained south of the Circle for sixty-three days. On the way northward he sighted high islands, which were probably part of the Balleny group, and he sailed across the site of a range of mountains marked on a chart which Wilkes had given him. Wilkes afterwards explained that these mountains were not intended to show one of his discoveries, and an unedifying controversy ensued, which did credit to neither explorer. Ross returned to Hobart on April 6, 1841, after the greatest voyage of Antarctic discovery ever made. Three months later the news reached England, and the Royal Geographical Society at once awarded the Founder's Gold Medal to Captain Ross.

On November 23, 1841, the *Erebus* and *Terror* left the Day of Islands, New Zealand, which had been declared a British possession the year before, to make a new effort to get south in a longitude about 150° West, so as to approach the Great Barrier from a point east of that at which they had been stopped the previous season. The pack was entered about 60° South and 146° West on December 18, and it seemed as if the ships were never to get through it. The Antarctic Circle was reached on New Year's Day, 1842, every effort being made to work the ships through the lanes between the floes. For a time when the wind was favourable the two ships were lashed on each side of a small floe of convenient shape and with all sail set they were able to give it sufficient way to break the lighter ice ahead, using it as a battering-ram and as a buffer to protect their bows. Ross did everything to keep up the spirits of the crews, by instituting sports and keeping up visits between the two ships, as in an Arctic wintering. A terrific storm on January 18 buffeted the ships unmercifully, the huge masses of floating ice being hurled against them in a prodigious swell, and for twenty-four hours the *Erebus* and *Terror* were almost out of control, their rudders having been smashed by the ice, though the stout timbers of the hulls held good. On January 26, after being thirty-nine days in the pack, and boring their way for eight hundred miles through it, the *Erebus* and the *Terror* were only thirty-nine miles farther south than Cook had been in the *Resolution* on the same meridian without entering the ice at all sixty-eight years before. On February 2 the ships escaped from the pack in 159° East, but only one degree south of the Antarctic Circle. The Barrier was not sighted until February 22, and on the 28th the ships at last got within a mile and a half of the face of the ice-wall, which was found to be 107 ft. high at its highest point and the water 290 fathoms deep, in 161° 27′ West and 78° 11′ South. This was the highest latitude reached by Ross, 3° 55′ or 235 miles farther south than Weddell's farthest, and 710 miles from the South Pole. Towards the south-east he saw that the Barrier surface gradually rose with the appearance of mountains of great height, but he could not bring himself to chart this as land, for no sign of bare rock could be seen, and though he felt that 'the presence of land there amounts almost to a certainty' he would not run the risk of any one in the future proving that he had been mistaken, and so charted it as an 'appearance of land' only.

Any other explorer of that period, or of this, would have called it land and given it a name without hesitation, and had Ross only known how to interpret what the numerous rock specimens he dredged up from the bottom had to tell him, he could have marked the land with an easy mind.

It was now time to leave the Far South; the work had been infinitely harder than that of the former season and the result was disappointing. The coast of Victoria Land was not sighted on this cruise, and on March 6, 1842, the *Erebus* and *Terror* crossed the Antarctic Circle northward, after having been sixty-four days within it. Ross Sea was not furrowed by another keel for more than half a century. Once in open water the *Erebus* and *Terror* held an easterly course through the Southern Ocean south of the Pacific, farther north than Biscoe, Bellingshausen or Cook, making passage to the Falkland Islands, by that time a British possession. The greatest danger of the whole cruise occurred suddenly on this passage when the two ships came into collision while attempting to weather an iceberg in a gale and snowstorm during the night; but though for an hour all gave themselves up for lost they came through, and they reached Port Louis in the Falklands on April 5, 1842, one hundred and thirty-seven days out from the Bay of Islands.

Having received authority to spend a third summer in south polar exploration, Ross sailed from the Falklands on December 17, 1842, intending to survey the coasts discovered by d'Urville and follow the land south to a high latitude in Weddell Sea; but though several points on Louis Philippe Land were sighted and mountains named, there was no open way to the south and it was not until March 1, 1843, that the Antarctic Circle was reached by coasting the pack to 12° 20′ West. Here a sounding of the vast depth of 4000 fathoms was obtained, but Dr. W. S. Bruce, with improved and trustworthy apparatus, found sixty years later that the real depth at this point was only 2660 fathoms. Ross proceeded southwards in open water to 71° 30′ South, thirty miles within the ice-pack, but there he was stopped nearly half-way between the positions reached by Bellingshausen in 1820 and by Weddell in 1828; and here his Antarctic exploration ended. On his way to Cape Town, Ross searched for Bouvet Island as unsuccessfully as Cook, though he passed within a few miles of it. Ross' first summer in the Antarctic had brought unexpected and magnificent discoveries, tearing a great gap in the unknown area, and fortune smiled without interruption on the expedition; his second summer brought trouble and danger with but a trifling increase in knowledge, while the third led only to disappointment.

Ross had come triumphantly through a time of unparalleled stress, his personal initiative animated the whole expedition and never were honours more nobly won than those which he received on his return. He was knighted, *fêted*, and presented with many gold medals; and he was offered and begged in the most flattering way to accept the command of the expedition to explore the North-West Passage in his old ships. The position, when he declined it, was given to Sir John Franklin.

Immediately after Ross' return a supplementary cruise for magnetic observations was carried out by Lieutenant T. E. L. Moore, R.N., who had been mate on the *Terror*. He sailed from Cape Town in the hired barque *Pagoda*, 860 tons, on January 9, 1845, and, after the usual fruitless search for Bouvet Island, crossed the Antarctic Circle in 30° 45′ East, but was stopped by the ice in 67° 50′ South. He struggled hard against calms and head winds to reach Enderby Land, but in vain. Moore believed that he saw land in 64° South and about 50° East; but like Ross he stood on a pedantic technicality, 'there was no doubt about it, but we would not say it was land without having really landed on it'. How much controversy and ill-feeling would have been avoided if Wilkes and other explorers had acted on this principle!

In 1850, in one of the Enderbys' ships, the *Brisk*, Captain Tapsell went to the Balleny Islands looking for seals and sailed westward at a higher latitude than Wilkes had reached, as far as the meridian of 148° East, without sighting land; the log of the voyage is lost, and the exact route is not on record.

Though Ross urged the value of the southern whale fishery in strong terms, no one stirred to take it up. Polar enterprise was diverted to the lands within the Arctic Circle by the tragedy of Franklin's fate and the search expeditions. Efforts were made again and again to reawaken interest in the south, notably by the great American hydrographer, Captain Maury, and the eminent German meteorologist, Professor Georg von Neumayer, but without effect.

In 1875, H.M.S. *Challenger*, on her famous voyage of scientific investigation with Captain George Nares, R.N., as commander and Professor Wyville Thomson as scientific director, made a dash south of Kerguelen Land, and on February 16 she had the distinction of being the first vessel propelled by steam across the Antarctic Circle. She went to 66° 40′ South in longitude 78° 22′ East, and pushed eastward in a somewhat lower latitude to within fifteen miles of Wilkes' Termination Land as shown on the charts, but nothing resembling land could be seen. The *Challenger* saw many icebergs, but being an unprotected vessel and bent on other service she could make no serious attempt to penetrate the pack; nevertheless, the researches made on board by sounding and dredging up many specimens of rocks proved beyond doubt that land lay within the ice surrounding the Antarctic Circle and that the land was not insular but a continent.

In the same year a German company sent out the steam whaler *Grönland,* Captain Dallmann, to try whether anything could be made of whaling or sealing in the neighbourbood of the South Shetlands, and he went probably to about 65° South in Bellingshausen Sea on the coast of Graham Land. In the 'eighties of last century Neumayer continued to urge the renewal of Antarctic research in Germany, and Sir John Murray, raising his powerful voice in Great Britain, sketched out a scheme for a fully equipped naval expedition, but refused to have anything to do with any expedition not provided at the outset with funds sufficient to ensure success. The government of Victoria took the matter up and offered to contribute £5000 to an expedition if the Home Government would support it; the British Association, the Royal Society, and the Royal Geographical Society reported in favour of the scheme, but in 1887 the Treasury definitely declined to participate.

In 1892 a fleet of four Dundee whalers set out for Weddell Sea, in order to test Ross' belief that the whalebone whale existed there, and two of them, the *Balaena* and *Active,* were fitted up with nautical and meteorological instruments by the Royal Geographical Society and the Meteorological Office, in the hope that they would fix accurate positions and keep careful records. Dr. W. S. Bruce, an enthusiastic naturalist, accompanied the *Balaena* and Dr. C. W. Donald accompanied the *Active,* commanded by Captain Thomas Robertson. The ships made full cargoes of seals in Weddell Sea, but did not go beyond 65' South, nor did they repeat the venture. A Norwegian whaler, the *Jason,* was sent out at the same time by a company in Hamburg, and her master, Captain Larsen, picked up a number of fossils on Seymour Island, and saw land from Weddell Sea in 64° 40' South. The Hamburg Company sent out three ships in 1893, the *Jason* to Weddell Sea, where Captain Larsen discovered Oscar Land, no doubt the eastern coast of Graham Land, in 66° South and 60° West, and pushing on farther he discovered Foyn Land, the *Jason* being the second steamer to enter the Antarctic regions proper. On his way home along the coast he charted many new islands and discovered active volcanoes near the place where Ross' officers had seen smoke rising from the mountains, though that cautious explorer decided that as it might be only snowdrift he would not claim the discovery of volcanoes there. Meanwhile, in Bellingshausen Sea, Captain Evenson, of the *Hertha,* got beyond 69° 10' South after visiting the Biscoe Islands, and he sighted Alexander I Land for the first time since its discovery.

The next visit to the Antarctic was due to the Norwegian whaler, Svend Foyn, who sent out the *Antarctic,* under Captain Kristensen, with Mr. Bull as agent, to Ross Sea. They had agreed to take Dr. W. S. Bruce, but he found it impossible to reach Melbourne in time to join the ship. A young Norwegian resident in Australia, who was partly English in ancestry, Carstens Egeberg Borchgrevink, shipped as a sailor, having an insatiable desire to see the Antarctic regions and being refused a passage on any other terms. The *Antarctic* sighted the Balleny Islands and was nearly six weeks in working through the pack, but on January 14, 1895, she was the first steamer to enter the open water of Ross Sea. A landing was made on Possession Island, where Borchgrevink discovered a lichen, the first trace of vegetation found within the Antarctic Circle; the ship went as far as 74° South looking for whales and on her way back the first landing on the Antarctic continent was made on a low beach at Cape Adare.

Mr. Borchgrevink described this voyage at the meeting of the Sixth International Geographical Congress in London in 1895, where a great discussion on the possibility of renewing Antarctic exploration had previously been arranged for. Dr. von Neumayer gave an able historical paper on Antarctic exploration, Sir Joseph Hooker spoke as a survivor of Ross' expedition, Sir John Murray as a member of the scientific staff of the *Challenger,* and Sir Clements Markham as President of the Congress. The Congress adopted a resolution to the effect that the exploration of the Antarctic Regions was the greatest piece of geographical exploration remaining to be undertaken, and that it should be resumed before the close of the nineteenth century.

The first result was the expedition of the Belgica under the command of Lieutenant de Gerlache, due to the passionate enthusiasm of the commander, notably aided by Henryk Arçtowski, a Pole, whose ardour in the pursuit of physical science has never been surpassed. Dr. Cook, an American, was surgeon to the expedition; the second in command was Lieutenant Lecointe, a Belgian, the mate, Roald Amundsen, a Norwegian, and the crew were half Belgian and half Norwegian. The scientific staff included, besides Arçtowski, the Belgian magnetician Lieutenant Danco, the Rumanian Racovitza, and the Pole Dobrowolski. The funds were meagre and raised by public subscription with enormous difficulty, and the equipment almost less than the minimum requirement. The ship was small, only two hundred and fifty tons, but in her this cosmopolitan gathering experienced first of all men the long darkness of the Antarctic night. Much valuable time was lost on the outward journey amongst the Fuegian Islands, and much was occupied in the archipelago into which the *Belgica* resolved Palmer Land, between 64° and 65° South. It was February 12, 1898, before the ship proceeded southward along the coast of Graham Land. On the 15th she crossed the Antarctic Circle, on the 16th Alexander I Land was sighted, but could not be approached within twenty miles on account of the ice-pack. The equipment of the ship hardly seems to have justified wintering; prudence called for a speedy retreat, but a gale came down of such severity that Gerlache thrust the ship into the pack for shelter from the heavy breakers on February 28, and finding wide lanes opening under the influence of wind and swell, he pushed southward against the advice of the scientific members of the expedition, determined to make every effort to outdistance all previous explorers towards the pole. On March 3, 1898, the *Belgica* found herself in 71° 30′ South and about 85′ West. An effort to return was unavailing; on the 4th she was fast in the floe, unable to move in any direction, and she remained a prisoner of the ice until February 14, 1899, and then took another month to clear all the pack and reach the open sea. For a year she had been drifting north, west, south and east, in Bellingshausen Sea; even in winter the floe was never at rest, and almost all the time she kept south of the parallel of 70° over water which shallowed from great depths in the north to about two hundred and fifty fathoms in the southern stretches of the drift, evidently on the sloping approach to extensive land. The expedition suffered greatly in health during the winter from inadequate food, and from the absence of proper light in the terrible darkness of the long night. Despite all its difficulties the *Belgica* had done more to promote a scientific knowledge of the Antarctic regions than any of the costly expeditions that went before, and the Belgian Government, coming to the rescue after her return, provided adequate funds for working out the results.

Bellingshausen Sea was visited again in 1904 by Dr. J. B. Charcot in the *Français,* which followed the route of the *Belgica* along the coast of Graham Land, afterwards wintering in Port Charcot, a harbour on Wandel Island in 65′ South. Returning southward in the summer of 1904–5 he discovered land, named Terre Loubet, between Graham Land and Alexander I Land, but its exact position has not been stated. This French cruise was important as a preliminary to the expedition under Charcot, which left in 1908 and is now in those waters with the intention of pushing exploration to the Farthest South, in a ship named with a dash of humour and a flash of hope the *Pourquoi Pas?*

Two voyages of exploration in Weddell Sea may for convenience be referred to here. In October 1901, Dr. Otto Nordenskjold left Gothenberg in the old *Antarctic,* under the command of Captain Larsen, for an expedition which he had got up by his personal efforts. He arrived at the South Shetlands in January 1902, but found it impossible even to reach the Antarctic Circle on the coast of Oscar Land. Allowing the ship to go north for work among the islands, Nordenskjold wintered for two years, 1902 and 1903, in a timber house on Snow Hill Island in 64° 25′ South. Only one year's wintering had been contemplated, but the *Antarctic* was crushed in the ice and sank, fortunately without loss of life. A relief ship was despatched from Sweden, but shortly before she arrived Nordenskjold and his companions had been rescued by the unprotected Argentine naval vessel *Uruguay,* under Captain Irizar.

Dr. W. S. Bruce, who had been to Weddell Sea in the Balaena in 1892, and had since then taken part in several Arctic expeditions, succeeded by dint of hard work and the unceasing advocacy of the further exploration of Weddell Sea, in enlisting the aid of a number of persons in Scotland, and notably of Mr. James Coats, Jr., of Paisley, and Major Andrew Coats, D.S.O., and fitting out an expedition on the *Scotia*. He left the Clyde in November 1902, with Captain Thomas Robertson in command of the ship, Mr. R. C. Mossman, the well-known meteorologist, Mr. Rudmose Brown and Mr. D. W. Wilton as naturalists, and Dr. J. H. H. Pirie as surgeon and geologist. After calling at the South Orkneys, the *Scotia* got south to 70° 25′ South in 17° West on February 22, 1903, not far from the position reached by Ross. Valuable oceanographical work was done, and on returning to the South Orkneys, Mr. Mossman landed there with a party to keep up regular meteorological observations while the ship proceeded to the River Plate. On her return in the following year the Argentine Government took over the meteorological work in the South Orkneys, which has been kept up ever since, to the great advancement of knowledge. The *Scotia* made another dash to the south on the same meridian as before, and on March 2, 1904, when in 72° 18′ South and 18° West, a high ice-barrier was seen stretching from north-east to south-west, the depth of the sea being 1181 fathoms a marked diminution from the prevailing depths. The Barrier was occasionally seen in intervals of mist, and March 6 being a clear day allowed the edge to be followed to the south-west to a point one hundred and fifty miles from the place where it was first sighted. The depth, two and a half miles from the Barrier edge, pack-ice preventing a nearer approach, was 159 fathoms. The description of the appearance of the Barrier given in the 'Cruise of the *Scotia*' is very brief: 'The surface of this great Inland Ice of which the Barrier was the terminal face or sea-front seemed to rise up very gradually in undulating slopes, and faded away in height and distance into the sky, though in one place there appeared to be the outline of distant hills; if so they were entirely ice-covered, no naked rock being visible.' Ross or Moore would certainly have charted this as an appearance of land'; Bruce knew from the shoaling water and the nature of the deposits that he was in the vicinity of land and gave it the name of Coats Land after his principal supporters. He could get no farther and returned from 74° 1′ South in 22° West, a point almost as far south as Weddell had got in his attempt one hundred and eighty miles farther west. The *Scotia* rendered immense service to science by her large biological collections, her unique series of deep-sea soundings in high latitudes and the permanent gain of a sub-Antarctic meteorological station.

The next step in exploration by way of Ross Sea was the fitting-out by Sir George Newnes of an expedition under the leadership of Mr. C. E. Borchgrevink, on board the *Southern Cross*, a stout Norwegian whaler with

Captain Jensen, who had been chief officer in the *Antarctic* when she went to Ross Sea in 1895, as master. Lieutenant Colbeck, R.N.R., went as magnetic observer, Mr. L. C. Bernacchi, a resident in Tasmania, who had arranged to join the *Belgica* if she had gone out by Australia, as meteorologist, and Mr. Nicolai Hanson, of the British Museum, as zoologist. The *Southern Cross* left Hobart on December 19, 1898, and entered the pack about the meridian of the Balleny Islands, 165° East; but after being forced out again on the northern side after six weeks' struggling to get south, she re-entered the pack in 174° East and was through in the clear waters of Ross Sea in six hours on February 11, 1899. A wooden house and stores for the winter were landed at Cape Adare in 71° 15′ South, and there the shore-party went into winter quarters, the ship returning to the north. An important series of meteorological observations was secured during the year of residence, valuable zoological and geological collections were made, and the habits of the penguins were studied; but the few attempts at land exploration were without result. On January 28, 1900, Captain Jensen returned with the *Southern Cross* and on February 2, the Cape Adare colony embarked and set out southward along the coast of Victoria Land. Landings were effected at various points, including the base of Mount Melbourne, where reindeer-moss was found growing, and at Cape Crozier. There was much less ice along the coast than when Ross had visited it. The *Southern Cross*, after sighting Mount Erebus and Mount Terror, ran eastward along the Great Barrier far closer to the ice-cliffs than Ross could go in his sailing-ships, and Colbeck's survey showed that the Barrier had receded on the whole some thirty miles to the south. Parts of the Barrier were quite low, and Borchgrevink landed in 164° West, the ship being laid alongside the ice as if it had been a quay, and made a short journey on ski southward over the surface on February 19, 1900, reaching 78° 50′ South, forty miles beyond Ross' farthest and six hundred and seventy miles from the Pole, the nearest yet attained. The sea was beginning to freeze and the *Southern Cross* made haste for home.

Following on various less weighty efforts set in motion by the resolution of the International Geographical Congress in 1895, all the eminent men of science who had the renewal of Antarctic exploration at heart met in the rooms of the Royal Society in London in February 1898, when Sir John Murray read a stimulating paper. This was followed by a discussion in which part was taken by the veteran Antarctic explorer Sir Joseph Hooker, by the most successful of Arctic explorers Dr. Fridtjof Nansen, by Dr. von Neumayer, who had never ceased for half a century to advocate renewed exploration, and by Sir Clements Markham, President of the Royal Geographical Society. A Joint Committee of the Royal Society and the Royal Geographical Society undertook the equipment of a British expedition and carried it through under the constant stimulus and direction of Sir Clements

Markham, while funds were subscribed by various wealthy individuals, by the Royal Geographical Society, and in largest measure by Government. In Germany a national expedition was got up at the same time under the command of Professor Erich von Drygalski to cooperate by means of simultaneous magnetic and meteorological observations in a different quarter with the British expedition. For the present purpose it is enough to say that the German expedition on board the Gauss descended on the Antarctic Circle by the 90th meridian, and was caught in the pack at the end of February 1902, not far from Wilkes' 'appearance' of Termination Land, and in sight of a hill called the Gaussberg on a land discovered by the expedition and named Kaiser Wilhelm Land. The ship remained fast for a year, and an immense amount of scientific investigation was carried out with characteristic thoroughness. On her release in February 1903, the Gauss tried to push westward in a high latitude, but could not reach the Antarctic Circle and, failing to get permission for another season's work, she returned laden with rich scientific collections and voluminous observations.

The Joint Committee in London built the Discovery at an expense of 952,000, making her immensely strong to resist ice pressure and securing the absence of any magnetic metal in a large area so that magnetic observations of high precision might be carried out. Sir Clements Markham selected as commander Lieutenant Robert F. Scott, R.N., a most fortunate choice, for no one could have been better fitted by disposition and training to ensure success. The second in command was Lieutenant Albert Armitage, R.N.R., who had had Arctic experience, and the other officers were Lieutenants C. Royds, R.N.; M. Barne, R.N.; E. H. Shackleton, R.N.R.; Engineer-Lieutenant Skelton, R.N.; Dr. R. Koettlitz, who had been a comrade of Armitage's in the north, and Dr. E. A. Wilson, an artist of great ability. The scientific staff included, in addition to the surgeons who were also zoologists, Mr. L. C. Bernacchi who had been on the *Southern Cross* expedition, as physicist; as biologist A-fr. T. V. Hodgson, and as geologist Mr. H. T. Ferrar. Meteorological and oceanographical work were undertaken by officers of the ship. The objects of the expedition were primarily magnetic observations, the costly construction of the ship being largely due to the arrangements for this purpose, then meteorological and oceanographical observations and the collection of zoological and geological specimens, and of course geographical exploration. Three pieces of exploration were specified in the instructions, an attempt to reach the land which Ross believed to exist east of the Barrier, though he charted it as an appearance only, a journey westward into the mountains of Victoria Land, and a journey southward. An attempt to reach the Pole was neither recommended nor forbidden. The Royal Geographical Society has always deprecated attempts to attain high latitudes north or south unless as an incident in systematic scientific work. The *Discovery* left

Lyttelton on December 24, 1901, met the pack on January 1, 1902, and got through it into Ross Sea in a week in 1740 East. Landings were made at Cape Adare, at various points along the coast of Victoria Land, and on January 22 at the base of Mount Terror, near Cape Crozier. From this point the Great Barrier was coasted to the east, close along its edge, and on the 29th in 165° East the depth of water was found to be less than a hundred fathoms, a strong indication of the approach to land. The Barrier had receded about thirty miles since Ross was in those seas, and there was much less pack-ice than during his visit; the date also was earlier and Scott was able to penetrate almost to 150° West before being stopped by heavy ice. The land was plainly seen, its higher summits being 2000 to 3000 ft. above the sea, and bare rocks projected from the snow covering of the hills. Thus the first geographical problem set to the expedition was promptly and satisfactorily solved. Although no landing was made on King Edward VII Land, the King's first godchild of discovery, as Victoria Land had been the late Queen's, the *Discovery* was laid alongside a low part of the Barrier in 1640 West, and the captive balloon was raised for a comprehensive view. Returning to McMurdo Bay, Scott showed that the Parry Mountains, running south from Mount Erebus, were not in fact there; Ross had probably seen the southern range across the Barrier. It soon became evident that Ross' original impression that Mount Erebus rose from an island was correct, and this land was named Ross Island.

McMurdo Bay also was found not to be a bay at all, but the opening of a strait leading southward between Ross Island and the mainland. By the middle of February 1902, the *Discovery* had taken up winter quarters on the extreme south of Ross Island, and a large hut had been erected on shore, with smaller huts for the magnetic and other instruments. The winter, four hundred miles farther south than any man had wintered before, was passed pleasantly by all, a great feature being the appearance of the *South Polar Times*, which owed much of its attractiveness to the editorship of E. H. Shackleton and to the art of E. A. Wilson.

With the spring a new era in Antarctic exploration was inaugurated in the series of sledge journeys, for which elaborate preparations had been made. Here Captain Scott showed himself possessed of all the qualities of a pioneer, adapting the methods of Sir Leopold McClintock and Dr. Nansen for Arctic ice travel to the different conditions prevailing in the Antarctic. In preparation for the great effort towards the south a depot had been laid out on the ice, and on November 2, 1902, Scott, Shackleton and Wilson, with four sledges and nineteen dogs, stepped out into the unknown on the surface of the Barrier. It was necessary at first to make the journeys by relays, going over the ground three times to bring up the stores; but the loads were lightened as the food was used and by leaving a depot in 80° 30′ South to be picked up on the return journey. Snowy weather was experienced but the temperature was not excessively low. The dogs, however, rapidly weakened, but by December 30, the little party reached latitude 82° 17′ South, after fifty-nine days' travelling from winter quarters in 77° 49′ South. They had passed over comparatively uniform snow-covered ice, probably afloat, and their track stretched parallel to a great mountain range which rose on their right. Whenever they approached the position of the mountains the surface was always found to be rougher, thrown into ridges or cleft by great crevasses. Failing provisions compelled them to stop at length, and a great chasm in the ice prevented them from reaching the land; but they had made their way to a point 3° 27′ or 297 miles farther south than Borchgrevink and were 468 miles from the Pole. It was the greatest advance ever made over a previous farthest in poleward progress in either hemisphere, and the first long land journey in the Antarctic. Great mountain summits were seen beyond the farthest point reached; one named Mount Markham rose to about 15,000 ft., another, Mount Longstaff, was lower but farther south. The range appeared to be trending southeastward in the distance. The return journey was made in thirty-four days, and the ship was reached on February 8, 1908; the dogs were all dead and had long been useless, the men themselves had been attacked by scurvy, the ancient scourge of polar explorers, and Shackleton's health was in a very serious state; but a journey such as had never been made before had been accomplished, and new methods of travel had been evolved and tested. Meantime shorter expeditions had been sent out from winter quarters, and Armitage had pioneered a way up one of the great glaciers which descended from the western mountains. The relief ship *Morning*, under Captain Colbeck, who had charted the Barrier on the *Southern Cross* expedition, arrived in McMurdo Sound on January 25, 1903; but unbroken sea ice prevented the ship from reaching the Discovery's winter quarters by ten miles. On March 3 she sailed for the north, leaving Lieutenant Mulock, R.N., to take the place of Lieutenant Shackleton, who was a reluctant passenger, invalided home. In the second winter the acetylene gas-plant was brought into use, and by this means the living-rooms were lighted brilliantly, and with the fresh food brought by the *Morning*, the sufferers from scurvy recovered, and the health of all remained excellent throughout the winter. Sledge expeditions set out again early in the spring, the most successful being that led by Captain Scott into the western mountains. Starting on October 26, he ascended the Ferrar Glacier to the summit of a great plateau of which the mountains formed the broken edge, and the party travelled without dogs, hauling their own sledges over a flat surface of compacted snow nine thousand feet above sea-level to the longitude of 146° 33′ East, a distance of 278 statute miles from the ship. This journey proved the existence of a surface beyond the mountains which, although only to be reached by the toilsome and dangerous climbing of a crevassed glacier, and subject to the intensified cold of high altitudes, was as practicable as the Barrier surface itself for rapid travelling, as rapidity is counted in those regions. Thus Scott was able to demonstrate the facility of both kinds of ice travel, over the Antarctic continent as over the Antarctic Sea.

On February 19, 1904, the *Discovery* escaped from the harbour in which she had been frozen for two years. The *Morning* had again come south to meet her with orders to desert the ship if she could not be freed from the ice; and a larger ship, the *Terra Nova,* had been sent by the Admiralty to satisfy the fears of nervous hearts at home. The one thing wanting to round off the expedition was a supply of coal to enable the *Discovery* to follow the track of Wilkes' vessels from the Balleny Islands westward; but the relief ships were only able to spare a trifling quantity and the opportunity was lost. Scott carried on to the west fax south of Wilkes' route to 154° East, showing that the land charted by the American expedition west of that meridian did not exist in the assigned positions; then with barely coal enough left to carry her to New Zealand the *Discovery* left the Antarctic regions and the great South Polar expedition came to an end. It is interesting to note that although no catastrophe such as those which darken the pages of Arctic history has ever happened in the Antarctic, no expedition had gone out without the loss of some of its members by accident or illness. On the *Discovery* the two deaths which occurred were by accident only.

The *Gauss* and the *Discovery* were sold soon after the return of the expeditions; the working up and publication of the scientific results obtained were for the most part entrusted to museums and public institutions; the members of the expeditions returned to their former duties or sought new employments, and the societies which had promoted the expeditions turned their attention to other things. The South Polar regions were left as the arena of private efforts, and in this volume the reader will learn how the enthusiasm and devotion of an individual has once more vindicated the character of the British nation for going far and faring well in the face of difficulties before which it would have been no dishonour to turn back.

LIST OF ILLUSTRATIONS

Plates

Maps

Diagrams in the Text

BRITISH ANTARCTIC EXPEDITION
1907

General Map showing the

EXPLORATIONS AND SURVEYS
OF THE EXPEDITION
1907 - 09.

Scale 1 : 6,000,000

Statute Miles.

Geographical Miles.

Heights in feet above Sea Level.

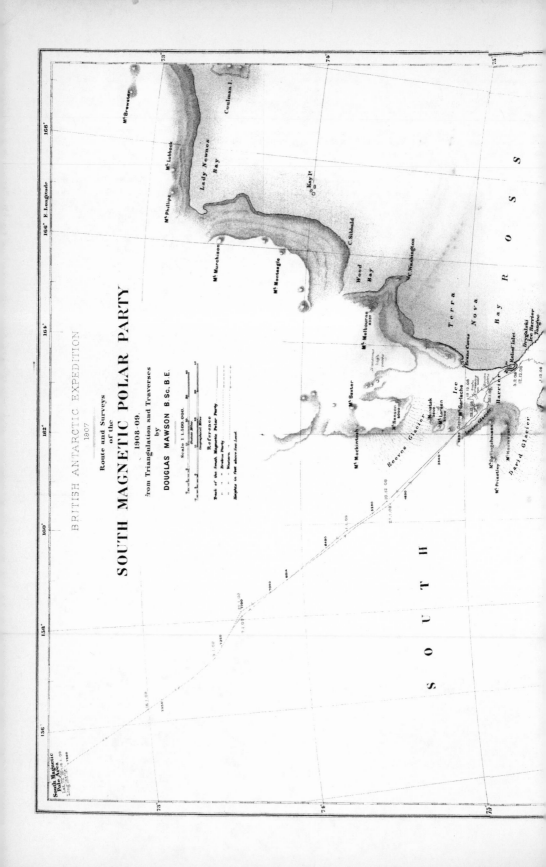

BRITISH ANTARCTIC EXPEDITION
1907

Route and Surveys
of the

SOUTH MAGNETIC POLAR PARTY

1908-09.

from Triangulation and Traverses
by

DOUGLAS MAWSON B.Sc. B.E.

Scale 1:1,500,000.

Statute Miles
Geographical Miles

Reference

Track of the South Magnetic Polar Party
Eastern Party ....
Western „ ....

Heights in Feet above Sea Level

S O U T H

R O S S   S E A

Terra   Nova   Bay

Wood Bay

Lady Newnes Bay

Mt Brewster
Mt Lubbock
Mt Phillips
Coulman I.
Kay I.
Mt Murchison
C. Sibbald
Mt Montagu
Mt Washington
Mt Melbourne
Mt Baxter
Mt Mackintosh
Mt Henson
Reeves Glacier
Nordenskjold Ice Tongue
Mt Larsen
Mt Nansen
Drygalski Ice Barrier Tongue
Mt de Garlache
Mt Eglington
Mt Priestley
Mt Nansen
David Glacier

South Magnetic
Pole Area.

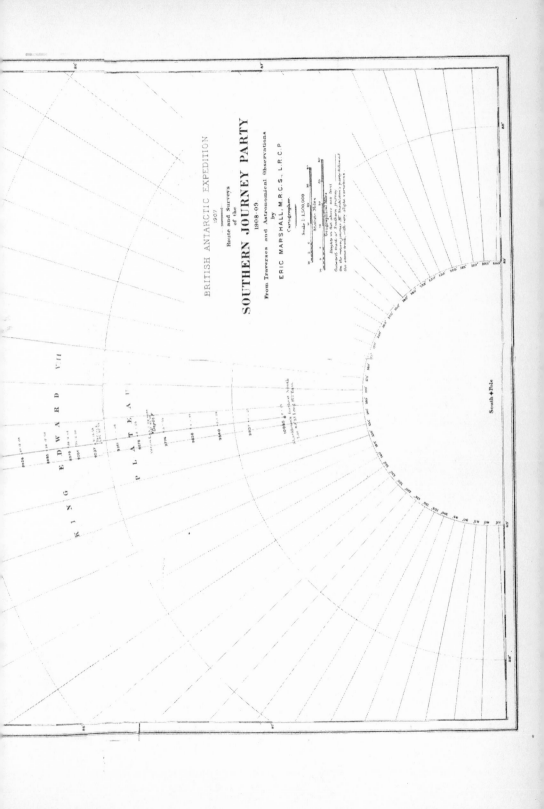

BRITISH ANTARCTIC EXPEDITION

1907

Route and Surveys

of the

SOUTHERN JOURNEY PARTY

1908-09.

From Traverses and Astronomical Observations

by

ERIC MARSHALL, M.R.C.S., L.R.C.P.

Cartographer.

Scale 1:1,500,000

Statute Miles

Geographical Miles

Heights in feet above sea level

KING   EDWARD   VII

PLATEAU

South ✦ Pole

1

THE INCEPTION AND PREPARATION OF THE EXPEDITION

M en go out into the void spaces of the world for various reasons. Some are actuated simply by a love of adventure, some have the keen thirst for scientific knowledge, and others again are drawn away from the trodden paths by the 'lure of little voices', the mysterious fascination of the unknown. I think that in my own case it was a combination of these factors that determined me to try my fortune once again in the frozen south. I had been invalided home before the conclusion of the *Discovery* expedition, and I had a very keen desire to see more of the vast continent that lies amid the Antarctic snows and glaciers. Indeed the stark polar lands grip the hearts of the men who have lived on them in a manner that can hardly be understood by the people who have never got outside the pale of civilisation. I was convinced, moreover, that an expedition on the lines I had in view could justify itself by the results of its scientific work. The *Discovery* expedition had brought back a great store of information, and had performed splendid service in several important branches of science. I believed that a second expedition could carry the work still further.

The *Discovery* expedition had gained knowledge of the great chain of mountains running in a north and south direction from Cape Adare to latitude 82° 17′ south, but whether this range turned to the south-east or eastward for any considerable distance was not known, and therefore the southern limits of the Great Ice Barrier plain had not been defined. The glimpses gained of King Edward VII Land from the deck of the *Discovery* had not enabled us to determine either its nature or its extent, and the mystery of the Barrier remained unsolved. It was a matter of importance to the scientific world that information should be gained regarding the movement of the ice-sheet that forms the Barrier. Then I wanted to find out what lay beyond the mountains to the south of latitude 82° 17′ and whether the Antarctic continent rose to a plateau similar to the one found by Captain Scott beyond the Western Mountains. There was much to be done in the field of meteorology, and this work was of particular importance to Australia and New Zealand, for these countries are affected by weather conditions that have their origin in the Antarctic. Antarctic zoology, though somewhat limited, as regarded the range of species, had very interesting aspects, and I wanted to devote some attention to mineralogy, apart from general geology. The Aurora Australis, atmospheric electricity, tidal movements, hydrography, currents of the air, ice formations and movements, biology and geology, offered an unlimited field for research, and the despatch of an expedition seemed to be justified on scientific grounds quite apart from the desire to gain a high latitude.

The difficulty that confronts most men who wish to undertake exploration work is that of finance, and in this respect I was rather more than ordinarily handicapped. The equipment and despatch of an Antarctic expedition means the expenditure of very many thousands of pounds, without the prospect of any speedy return, and with a reasonable probability of no return at all. I drew up my scheme on the most economical lines, as regarded both ship and staff, but for over a year I tried vainly to raise sufficient money to enable me to make a start. I secured introductions to wealthy men, and urged to the best of my ability the importance of the work I proposed to undertake, but the money was not forthcoming, and it almost seemed as though I should have to abandon the venture altogether.

I persisted, and towards the end of 1906 I was encouraged by promises of support from one or two personal friends. Then I made a fresh effort, and on February 12, 1907, I had enough money promised to enable me to announce definitely that I would go south with an expedition. As a matter of fact some of the promises of support made to me could not be fulfilled, and I was faced by financial difficulties right up to the time when the expedition sailed from England. It was not till I arrived in New Zealand, and the Governments of New Zealand and Australia came to my assistance with ready generosity, that the position became more satisfactory.

In the *Geographical Journal* for March, 1907, I outlined my plan of campaign, but this had to be changed in several respects at a later date owing to the exigencies of circumstances. My intention was that the expedition should leave New Zealand at the beginning of 1908, and proceed to winter quarters on the Antarctic continent, the ship to land the men and stores and then return. By avoiding having the ship frozen in, I would render the use of a relief ship unnecessary, as the same vessel could come south again the following summer and take us off. 'The shore-party of nine or twelve men will winter with sufficient equipment to enable three separate parties to start out in the spring,' I announced. 'One party will go east, and, if possible, across the Barrier to the new land known as King Edward VII Land, follow the coast-line there south, if the coast trends south, or north if north, returning when it is considered necessary to do so. The second party will proceed south over the same route as that of the southern sledge-party of the *Discovery*; this party will keep from fifteen to twenty miles from the coast, so as to avoid any rough ice. The third party will possibly proceed westward over the mountains, and, instead of crossing in a line due west, will strike towards the magnetic Pole. The main changes in equipment will be that Siberian ponies will be taken for the sledge journeys both east and south, and also a specially designed motor-car for the southern journey . . . I do not intend to sacrifice the scientific utility of the expedition to a mere record-breaking journey, but say frankly, all the same, that one of my great efforts will be to reach the southern geographical Pole. I shall in no way neglect to continue the biological, meteorological, geological and magnetic work of the *Discovery*.' I added that I would endeavour to sail along the coast of Wilkes Land, and secure definite information regarding that coast-line.

The programme was an ambitious one for a small expedition, no doubt, but I was confident, and I think I may claim that in some measure my confidence has been justified. Before we finally left England, I had decided that if possible I would establish my base on King Edward VII Land instead of at the *Discovery* winter quarters in McMurdo Sound, so that we might break entirely new ground. The narrative will show how completely, as far as this particular matter was concerned, all my plans were upset by the demands of the situation. The journey to King Edward VII Land over the Barrier was not attempted owing largely to the unexpected loss of ponies before the winter. I laid all my plans very carefully, basing them on experience I had gained with the *Discovery* expedition, and in the fitting out of the relief ships *Terra Nova* and *Morning,* and the *Argentine* expedition that went to the relief of the Swedes. I decided that I would have no committee, as the expedition was entirely my own venture, and I wished to supervise personally all the arrangements.

When I found that some promises of support had failed me and had learned that the Royal Geographical Society, though sympathetic in its attitude, could not see its way to assist financially, I approached several gentlemen and suggested that they should guarantee me at the bank, the guarantees to be redeemed by me in 1910, after the return of the expedition. It was on this basis that I secured a sum of £20,000, the greater part of the money necessary for the starting of the expedition, and I cannot express too warmly my appreciation of the faith shown in me and my plans by the men who gave these guarantees, which could be redeemed only by the proceeds of lectures and the sale of this book after the expedition had concluded its work. These preliminary matters settled, I started to buy stores and equipment, to negotiate for a ship, and to collect round me the men who would form the expedition.

The equipping of a polar expedition is a task demanding experience as well as the greatest attention to points of detail. When the expedition has left civilisation, there is no opportunity to repair any omission or to secure any article that may have been forgotten. It is true that the explorer is expected to be a handy man, able to contrive dexterously with what materials he may have at hand, but makeshift appliances mean increased difficulty and added danger. The aim of one who undertakes to organise such an expedition must be to provide for every contingency, and in dealing with this work I was fortunate in being able to secure the assistance of Mr Alfred Reid, who had already gained considerable experience in connection with previous polar ventures. I appointed Mr Reid manager of the expedition, and I found him an invaluable assistant. I was fortunate, too, in not being hampered by committees of any sort. I kept the control of all the arrangements in my own hands, and thus avoided the delays that are inevitable when a group of men have to arrive at a decision on points of detail.

The first step was to secure an office in London, and we selected a furnished room at 9 Regent Street, as the headquarters of the expedition. The staff at this period consisted of Mr Reid, a district messenger and myself, but there was a typewriting office on the same floor, and the correspondence, which grew in bulk day by day, could be dealt with as rapidly as though I had employed stenographers and typists of my own. I had secured estimates of the cost of provisioning and equipping the expedition before I made any public announcement regarding my intentions, so that there were no delays when once active work had commenced. This was not an occasion for inviting tenders, because it was vitally important that we should have the best of everything, whether in food or gear, and I therefore selected, in consultation with Mr Reid, the firms that should be asked to supply us. Then we proceeded to interview the heads of these firms, and we found that in nearly every instance we were met with generous treatment as to prices, and with ready co-operation in regard to details of manufacture and packing.

Several very important points have to be kept in view in selecting the food-supplies for a polar expedition.

In the first place the food must be wholesome and nourishing in the highest degree possible. At one time that dread disease scurvy used to be regarded as the inevitable result of a prolonged stay in the ice-bound regions, and even the *Discovery* expedition, during its labours in the Antarctic in the years 1902–4, suffered from this complaint, which is often produced by eating preserved food that is not in a perfectly wholesome condition. It is now recognised that scurvy may be avoided if the closest attention is given to the preparation and selection of food-stuffs along scientific lines, and I may say at once that our efforts in this direction were successful, for during the whole course of the expedition we had not one case of sickness attributable directly or indirectly to the foods we had brought with us. Indeed, beyond a few colds, apparently due to germs from a bale of blankets, we experienced no sickness at all at the winter quarters.

In the second place the food taken for use on the sledging expeditions must be as light as possible, remembering always that extreme concentration renders the food less easy of assimilation and therefore less healthful. Extracts that may be suitable enough for use in ordinary climates are little use in the polar regions, because under conditions of very low temperature the heat of the body can be maintained only by use of fatty and farinaceous foods in fairly large quantities. Then the sledging-foods must be such as do not require prolonged cooking, that is to say, it must be sufficient to bring them to the boiling-point, for the amount of fuel that can be carried is limited. It must be possible to eat the foods without cooking at all, for the fuel may be lost or become exhausted.

More latitude is possible in the selection of foods to be used at the winter quarters of the expedition, for the ship may be expected to reach that point, and weight is therefore of less importance. My aim was to secure a large variety of foods for use during the winter night. The long months of darkness impose a severe strain on any men unaccustomed to the conditions, and it is desirable to relieve the monotony in every way possible. A variety of food is healthful, moreover, and this is especially important at a period when it is difficult for the men to take much exercise, and when sometimes they are practically confined to the hut for days together by bad weather.

All these points were taken into consideration in the selection of our food-stuffs, and the list that I append shows the more important items of our provisions. I based my estimates on the requirements of twelve men for two years, but this was added to in New Zealand when I increased the staff. Some important articles of food were presented to the expedition by the manufacturers, and others, such as the biscuits and pemmican, were specially manufactured to my order. The question of packing presented some difficulties, and I finally decided to use 'Venesta' cases for the food-stuffs and as much as possible of the equipment. These cases are manufactured from composite boards prepared by uniting three layers of birch or other hard wood with waterproof cement. They are light, weather-proof and strong, and proved to be eminently suited to our purposes. The cases I ordered measured about two feet six inches by fifteen inches, and we used about 2500 of them. The saving of weight, as compared with an ordinary packing-case, was about four pounds per case, and we had no trouble at all with breakages, in spite of the rough handling given our stores in the process of landing at Cape Royds after the expedition had reached the Antarctic regions.

FOOD-SUPPLIES FOR THE SHORE-PARTY FOR TWO YEARS

6720 lb. Colman's wheaten flour.
6000 lb. various tinned meats.
600 lb. ox and lunch tongues.

800 lb. roast and boiled fowl, roast turkey, curried fowl, chicken and ham pâté, &c.

1000 lb. York hams.

1400 lb. Wiltshire bacon.

1400 lb. Danish butter.

1000 lb. milk.

1000 lb. 'Glaxo' milk powder.

1700 lb. lard, beef suet and beef marrow.

1000 lb. moist sugar.

700 lb. Demerara sugar.

500 lb. granulated sugar.

260 lb. lump sugar.

2600 lb. assorted tinned fish: haddocks, herrings, pilchards, salmon, sardines, mackerel, lobster, whitebait, mullet.

500 lb. Rowntree's elect cocoa.

350 lb. Lipton's tea.

1000 lb. cheese, mainly Cheddar.

70 lb. coffee.

1900 lb. assorted jams and marmalade.

336 lb. golden syrup.

3600 lb. cereals such as oatmeal, quaker oats, rice, barley, tapioca, sago, semolina, cornflour, petit pois, haricots verts, marrow-fat peas, split peas, lentils, dried haricot beans.

3400 lb. assorted soups in tins.

660 lb. assorted fruits: apricots, pears and pine-apple chunks.

1150 bottles bottled fruit.

1000 lb. dried fruit: prunes, peaches, apricots, raisins, sultanas, currants, apples.

500 lb. salt.

80 doz. assorted pickles, relishes, chutneys, sauces, &c., &c.

120 lb. plum puddings.

2800 lb. assorted dried vegetables (equivalent to about 30,000 lb. of fresh vegetables): potatoes, cabbage, carrots, oinions, Brussels-sprouts, cauliflower, celery, spinach, Scotch kale, parsnips, parsley, mint, rhubarb, mushrooms, beetroot, artichokes.

1000 lb. pemmican (best beef with 60 per cent of fat added). The best pemmican was that supplied by J. D. Beauvais, of Copenhagen.

2240 lb. of wholemeal biscuits with 25 per cent of Plasmon added.

12 doz. tins beef Plasmon.

6 doz. tins Plasmon powder.

6 doz. tins Plasmon cocoa.

448 lb. wholemeal biscuits.

448 lb. Garibaldi biscuits.

224 lb. ginger nuts.

150 lb. whole-egg powder.

20 lb. albumen.

900 lb. of Oxo, Lemeo and other brands of meat extract.

The following firms presented us with food-stuffs, all of which proved entirely satisfactory:

Messrs. J. and J. Colman, Ltd., of Norwich.
  9 tons wheat flour.
  ??ton self-raising flour.
  1/2 ton wheat meal.
  1 cwt. cornflour.
  84 lb. best mustard.
  13/4 gross mixed mustard.
Messrs. Rowntree and Co., Ltd., York.
  1700 lb. elect cocoa (28 per cent. of fat).
  200 lb. Queen's chocolate.
Messrs. Alfred Bird and Sons, Ltd., Birmingham.
  120 doz. custard, baking, egg, crystal jelly, and blanc-mange powders.
  Liebig's Extract of Meat Co., Ltd., London.
  'Oxo', Service oxo emergency food'. 'Lemco', and Fray Bentos ox tongues.
Evans, Sons, Lescher and Webb, Ltd., London.
  27 cases Montserrat lime-juice.
Messrs. Lipton, Ltd.
  350 lb. Ceylon tea.

Some additions were made to our food-supplies after the arrival of the *Nimrod* in New Zealand. Messrs. Nathan and Company, of Wellington, presented the expedition with sixty-eight cases of 'Glaxo' dried milk, and this preparation, which consists of the solid constituents of fresh milk, was a valuable addition to our food-stuffs. The same firm presented us with 192 lb. of New Zealand butter and two cases of New Zealand cheese. Some farmers generously provided thirty-two live sheep, which were killed in the Antarctic and allowed to freeze for winter consumption. Several other acceptable gifts were made to us before the *Nimrod* left Lyttelton.

It was arranged that supplies for thirty-eight men for one year should be carried by the *Nimrod* when the vessel went south for the second time to bring back the shore party. This was a precautionary measure in case the *Nimrod* should get caught in the ice and compelled to spend a winter in the Antarctic, in which case we would still have had one year's provisions in hand. I append a list showing the principal items of the relief supplies.

RELIEF FOOD-SUPPLIES, THIRTY-EIGHT MEN FOR ONE YEAR

  3800 lb. assorted New Zealand tinned meats.
  1300 lb. New Zealand butter.
  100 lb. tea.
  50 lb. coffee.
  1000 lb. Rowntree's elect cocoa.

60 doz. bottles bottled fruit.

16 doz. jars jam.

220 lb. assorted tinned fish.

510 lb. sardines.

280 lb. New Zealand cheese.

1440 fresh New Zealand eggs packed in salt.

250 lb. dried figs.

11,200 lb. Colman's wheat flour.

560 lb. Colman's wheat meal.

28 lb. Colman's mustard.

1 gross Colman's mixed mustard.

800 lb. assorted meats.

1600 lb. York hams.

2600 lb. bacon.

560 lb. beef suet.

1600 lb. milk.

2900 lb. sugar.

2800 lb. assorted tinned fish.

450 tins baked beans and tomato sauce.

3000 lb. assorted jams and marmalade.

540 lb. golden syrup.

5800 lb. cereals: oatmeal, quaker oats, rice, barley, sago, tapioca, semolina, cornflour, haricot verts, marrowfat peas, split peas, lentils, dried haricot beans.

1050 lb. assorted tinned soups.

1050 lb. pears, apricots, and pine-apple chunks in syrup. 1500 lb. dried fruits.

80 doz. pints assorted pickles, sauces, chutneys, &c. 240 lb. plum puddings.

3700 lb. assorted dried vegetables equal to about 40,000 lb. fresh vegetables.

After placing some of the principal orders for food-supplies, I went to Norway with Mr Reid in order to secure the sledges, fur boots and mits, sleeping-bags, ski, and some other articles of equipment. I was fortunate, on the voyage from Hull to Christiania, in making the acquaintance of Captain Pepper, the commodore captain of the Wilson Line of steamers. He took a keen interest in the expedition, and he was of very great assistance to me in the months that followed, for he undertook to inspect the sledges in the process of manufacture. He was at Christiania once in each fortnight, and he personally looked to the lashings and seizings as only a sailor could. We arrived at Christiania on April 22, and then learned that Mr C. S. Christiansen, the maker of the sledges used on the *Discovery* expedition, was in the United States. This was a disappointment, but after consultation with Scott-Hansen, who was the first lieutenant of the *Fram* on Nansen's famous expedition, I decided to place the work in the hands of Messrs. L. H. Hagen and Company. The sledges were to be of the Nansen pattern, built of specially selected timber, and of the best possible workmanship. I ordered ten twelve-foot sledges, eighteen eleven-foot sledges and two seven-foot sledges. The largest ones would be suitable for pony-haulage. The eleven-foot ones could be drawn by either ponies or men, and the small pattern would be useful for work around the winter quarters and for short journeys such as the scientists of the expedition were likely to undertake. The timbers used for the sledges were seasoned ash and American hickory, and in addition to Captain Pepper, Captain Isaachsen and Lieutenant Scott-Hansen, both experienced Arctic explorers, watched the work of construction on my behalf. Their interest was particularly valuable to me, for they were able in many little ways hardly to be understood by the lay reader to ensure increased strength and efficiency. I had formed the opinion that an eleven-foot sledge was best for general work, for it was not so long as to be unwieldy, and at the same time was long enough to ride over sastrugi and hummocky ice. Messrs. Hagen and Company did their work thoroughly well, and the sledges proved all that I could have desired.

The next step was to secure the furs that the expedition would require, and for this purpose we went to Drammen and made the necessary arrangements with Mr W. C. Möller. We selected skins for the sleepingbags, taking those of young reindeer, with short thick fur, less liable to come out under conditions of dampness than is the fur of the older deer. Our furs did not make a very large order, for after the experience of the *Discovery* expedition I decided to use fur only for the feet and hands and for the sleeping-bags, relying for all other purposes on woollen garments with an outer covering of wind-proof materials. I ordered three large sleeping-bags, to hold three men each, and twelve one-man bags. Each bag had the reindeer fur inside, and the seams were covered with leather, strongly sewn. The flaps overlapped about eight inches, and the head of the bag was sewn up to the top of the fly. There were three toggles for fastening the bag up when the man was inside. The toggles were about eight inches apart. The one-man bags weighed about ten pounds when dry, but of course the weight increased as they absorbed moisture when in use.

The foot-gear I ordered consisted of eighty pairs of ordinary finnesko, or reindeer fur boots, twelve pairs of special finnesko and sixty pairs of ski boots of various sizes. The ordinary finnesko is made from the skin of the reindeer stag's head, with the fur outside, and its shape is roughly that of a very large boot without any laces. It is large enough to hold the foot, several pairs of socks, and a supply of sennegrass, and it is a wonderfully comfortable and warm form of footgear. The special finnesko are made from the skin of the reindeer stag's legs, but they are not easily secured, for the reason that the native tribes, not unreasonably, desire to keep the best goods for themselves. I had a man sent to Lapland to barter for finnesko of the best kind, but he only succeeded in getting twelve pairs. The ski boots are made of soft leather, with the upper coming right round under the sole, and a flat piece of leather sewn on top of the upper. They are made specially for use with ski, and are very useful for summer wear. They give the foot plenty of play and do not admit water. The heel is very low, so that the foot can rest firmly on the ski. I bought five prepared reindeer skins for repairing, and a supply of repairing gear, such as sinew, needles and waxed thread.

I have mentioned that sennegrass is used in the finnesko. This is a dried grass of long fibre, with a special quality of absorbing moisture. I bought fifty kilos (109.37 lb.) in Norway for use on the expedition. The grass is sold in wisps, bound up tightly, and when the finnesko are being put on, some of it is teased out and a pad placed along the sole under the foot. Then when the boot has been pulled on more grass is stuffed round the heel. The grass absorbs the moisture that is given off from the skin, and prevents the sock freezing to the sole of the boot, which would then be difficult to remove at night. The grass is pulled out at night, shaken loose, and allowed to freeze. The moisture that has been collected congeals in the form of frost, and the greater part of it can be shaken away before the grass is replaced on the following morning. The grass is gradually used up on the march, and it is necessary to take a fairly large supply, but it is very light and takes up little room.

I ordered from Mr Möller sixty pairs of wolfskin and dogskin mits, made with the fur outside, and sufficiently long to protect the wrists. The mits had one compartment for the four fingers and another for the thumb, and they were worn over woollen gloves. They were easily slipped off when the use of the fingers was required, and they were hung round the neck with lamp-wick in order that they might not get lost on the march. The only other articles of equipment I ordered in Norway were twelve pairs of ski, which were supplied by Messrs. Hagen and Company. They were not used on the sledging journeys at all, but were useful around the winter quarters. I stipulated that all the goods were to be delivered in London by June 15, for the *Nimrod* was to leave England on June 30.

At this time I had not finally decided to buy the *Nimrod,* though the vessel was under offer to me, and before I left Norway I paid a visit to Sandyfjord in order to see whether I could come to terms with Mr C. Christiansen, the owner of the *Bjorn.* This ship was specially built for polar work, and would have suited my purposes most admirably. She was a new vessel of about 700 tons burthen and with powerful triple-expansion engines, better equipped in every way than the forty-year-old *Nimrod,* but I found that I could not afford to buy her, much as I would have wished to do so. Finally, I placed orders with some of the Norwegian food-preserving companies for special tinned foods such as fish balls, roast reindeer and roast ptarmigan, which were very attractive luxuries during the winter night in the south.

When I returned to London I purchased the *Nimrod*, which was then engaged on a sealing venture, and was expected to return to Newfoundland within a short time. The ship was small and old, and her maximum speed under steam was hardly more than six knots, but on the other hand, she was strongly built, and quite able to face rough treatment in the ice. Indeed, she had already received a good many hard knocks in the course of a varied career. The *Nimrod* did not return to Newfoundland as soon as I had hoped, and when she did arrive she proved to be somewhat damaged from contact with the ice, which had overrun her and damaged her bulwarks. She was inspected on my behalf and pronounced sound, and, making a fairly rapid passage, arrived in the Thames on June 15. I must confess that I was disappointed when I first examined the little ship, to which I was about to commit the hopes and aspiration of many years. She was very dilapidated and smelt strongly of seal-oil, and an inspection in dock showed that she required caulking and that her masts would have to be renewed. She was rigged only as a schooner and her masts were decayed, and I wanted to be able to sail her in the event of the engine breaking down or the supply of coal running short. There was only a few weeks to elapse before the date fixed for our departure, and it was obvious that we would have to push the work ahead very quickly if she was to be ready in time. I had not then become acquainted with the many good qualities of the *Nimrod*, and my first impression hardly did justice to the plucky old ship.

I proceeded at once to put the ship in the hands of Messrs. R. and H. Green, of Blackwall, the famous old firm that built so many of Britain's 'wooden walls', and that had done fitting and repair work for several other polar expeditions. She was docked for the necessary caulking, and day by day assumed a more satisfactory appearance. The signs of former conflicts with the ice-floes disappeared, and the masts and running-gear were prepared for the troubled days that were to come. Even the penetrating odour of seal-oil ceased to offend after much vigorous scrubbing of decks and holds, and I began to feel that after all the *Nimrod* would do the expedition no discredit. Later still I grew really proud of the sturdy little ship.

In the meantime Mr Reid and myself had been very busy completing the equipment of the expedition, and I had been gathering round me the men who were to compose the staff. As I had indicated when making the first announcement regarding the expedition, I did not intend that the *Nimrod* should remain in the Antarctic during the winter. The ship was to land a shore-party, with stores and equipment, and then to return to New Zealand, where she would wait until the time arrived to bring us back to civilisation. It was therefore very necessary that we should have a reliable hut in which to live during the Antarctic night until the sledging journeys commenced. The hut would be our only refuge from the fury of the blizzards and the

Section, showing Interior of "Nimrod"

1. Forecastle. 2. Stores. 3. Chain locker. 4. Fore hold. 5. Lower hold. 6. Stoke hold. 7. Carpenter's shop. 8. Cook's galley. 9. Engine room.
10. Engine room. 11. Boiler. 12. After hold. 13. Lower hold. 14. After Bridge. 15. Officers' quarters. 16. Captain's quarters. 17. Oyster Alley.

intense cold of the winter months. I thought then that the hut would have to accommodate twelve men, though the number was later increased to fifteen, and I decided that the outside measurements should be thirty-three feet by nineteen feet by eight feet to the caves. This was not large, especially in view of the fact that we would have to store many articles of equipment and some of the food in the hut, but a small building meant economy in fuel. The hut was specially constructed to my order by Messrs. Humphreys, of Knightsbridge, and after being erected and inspected in London was shipped in sections in the *Nimrod*.

It was made of stout fir timbering of best quality in walls, roofs, and floors, and the parts were all morticed and tenoned to facilitate erection in the Antarctic. The walls were strengthened with iron cleats bolted to main posts and horizontal timbering, and the roof principals were provided with strong iron tie rods. The hut was lined with match-boarding, and the walls and roof were covered externally first with strong roofing felt, then with one-inch tongued and grooved boards, and finally with another covering of felt. In addition to these precautions against the extreme cold the four-inch space in framing between the match-boarding and the first covering of felt was packed with granulated cork, which assisted materially to render the wall non-conducting. The hut was to be erected on wooden piles let into the ground or ice, and rings were fixed to the apex of the roof so that guy ropes might be used to give additional resistance to the gales. The hut had two doors, connected by a small porch, so that ingress and egress would not mean the admission of a draught of cold air, and the windows were double, in order that the warmth of the hut might be retained. There were two louvre ventilators in the roof, controlled from the inside. The hut had no fittings, and we took little furniture, only some chairs. I proposed to use cases for the construction of benches, beds and other necessary articles of internal equipment. The hut was to be lit with acetylene gas, and we took a generator, the necessary piping, and a supply of carbide.

The cooking-range we used in the hut was manufactured by Messrs. Smith and Wellstead, of London, and was four feet wide by two feet four inches deep. It had a fire chamber designed to burn anthracite coal continuously day and night and to heat a large superficial area of outer plate, so that there might be plenty of warmth given off in the hut. The stove had two ovens and a chimney of galvanised steel pipe, capped by a revolving cowl. It was mounted on legs. This stove was erected in the hut at the winter quarters, and with it we heated the building and did all our cooking while we were there. We took also a portable stove on legs, with a hot-water generator at the back of the fire, connected with a fifteen-gallon tank, but this stove was not erected, as we did not find that a second stove was required.

For use on the sledging expeditions I took six 'Nansen' cookers made of aluminium, and of the pattern that has been adopted, with slight modifications, ever since Nansen made his famous journey in 1893–96. The sledging-tents, of which I bought six, were made of light Willesden rot-proof drill, with a 99 spout' entrance of Burberry garberdine. They were green in colour, as the shade is very restful to the eyes on the white snow plains, and weighed thirty pounds each, complete with five poles and floorcloth.

Each member of the expedition was supplied with two winter suits made of heavy blue pilot cloth, lined with Jaeger fleece. A suit consisted of a double-breasted jacket, vest and trousers, and weighed complete fourteen and three-quarter pounds. The underclothing was secured from the Dr Jaeger Sanitary Woollen Company, and I ordered the following articles:

48 double-breasted vests.
48 double-fronted pants.
24 pyjama suits.
96 double-breasted shirts.
24 colic belts.
12 cardigans.
12 lined slippers.
48 travelling-caps lined with zanella.
48 felt mits.
144 pairs socks.
144 pairs stockings.
48 sweaters.
144 pairs fleece wool bed-socks.
48 pairs mits.
48 pairs gloves.
48 pairs mittens.
12 Buxton fleece boots.
12 under-waistcoats with sleeves.

An outer suit of wind-proof material is necessary in the polar regions, and I secured twenty-four suits of Burberry gaberdine, each suit consisting of a short blouse, trouser overalls and a helmet cover. For use in the winter quarters we took four dozen Jaeger camel-hair blankets and sixteen camel-hair triple sleeping-bags.

I decided to take ponies, dogs, and a motor-car to assist in hauling our sledges on the long journeys that I had in view, but my hopes were based mainly on the ponies. Dogs had not proved satisfactory on the Barrier surface, and I did not expect my dogs to do as well as they actually did. The use of a motor-ear was an experiment which I thought justified by my experience of the character of the Barrier surface, but I knew that it would not do to place much reliance on the machine in view of the uncertainty of the conditions. I felt confident, however, that the hardy ponies used in Northern China and Manchuria would be useful if they could be landed on the ice in good condition. I had seen these ponies in Shanghai, and I had heard of the good work they did on the Jackson-Harmsworth expedition. They are accustomed to hauling heavy loads in a very low temperature, and they are hardy, sure-footed and plucky. I noticed that they had been used with success for very rough work during the Russo-Japanese War, and a friend who had lived in Siberia gave me some more information regarding their capabilities.

I therefore got into communication with the London manager of the Hong Kong and Shanghai Bank (Mr C. S. Addis), and he was able to secure the services of a leading firm of veterinary surgeons in Shanghai. A qualified man went to Tientsin on my behalf, and from a mob of about two thousand of the ponies, brought down for sale from the northern regions, he selected fifteen of the little animals for my expedition. The ponies chosen were all over twelve and under seventeen years in age, and had spent the early part of their lives in the interior of Manchuria. They were practically unbroken, were about fourteen hands high, and were of various colours. They were all splendidly strong and healthy, full of tricks and wickedness, and ready for any amount of hard work over the snow-fields. The fifteen ponies were taken to the coast and shipped by direct steamer to Australia. They came through the test of tropical temperatures unscathed, and at the end of October 1908 arrived in Sydney, where they were met by Mr Reid and at once transferred to a New Zealand bound steamer. The Colonial Governments kindly consented to suspend the quarantine restrictions, which would have entailed exposure to summer heat for many weeks, and thirty-five days after leaving China the ponies were landed on Quail Island in Port Lyttelton, and were free to scamper about and feed in idle luxury.

I decided to take a motor-car because I thought it possible, from my previous experience, that we might meet with a hard surface on the Great Ice Barrier, over which the first part at any rate of the journey towards the south would have to be performed. On a reasonably good surface the machine would be able to haul a heavy load at a rapid pace. I selected a 12–15 horse-power New Arrol-Johnston car, fitted with a specially designed air-cooled four-cylinder engine and Simms Bosch magneto ignition. Water could not be used for cooling, as it would certainly freeze. Round the carburetter was placed a small jacket, and the exhaust gases from one cylinder were passed through this in order that they might warm the mixing chamber before passing into the air. The exhaust from the other cylinders was conveyed into a silencer that was also to act as a foot-warmer. The frame of the car was of the standard pattern, but the manufacturers had taken care to secure the maximum of strength, in view of the fact that the car was likely to experience severe strains at low temperature. I ordered a good supply of spare parts in order to provide for breakages, and a special non-freezing oil was prepared for me by Messrs. Price and Company. Petrol was taken in the ordinary tins. I secured wheels of several special patterns as well as ordinary wheels with rubber tyres, and I had manufactured wooden runners to be placed under the front wheels for soft surfaces, the wheels resting in chocks on top of the runners. The car in its original form had two bracket seats, and a large trough behind for carrying stores. It was packed in a large case and lashed firmly amidships on the *Nimrod*, in which position it made the journey to the Antarctic continent in safety.

I placed little reliance on the dogs, as I have already stated, but I thought it advisable to take some of these animals. I knew that a breeder in Stewart Island, New Zealand, had dogs descended from the Siberian dogs used on the Newnes-Borchgrevink expedition, and I cabled to him to supply as many as he could up to forty. He was only able to let me have nine, but this team proved quite sufficient for the purposes of the expedition, as the arrival of pups brought the number up to twenty-two during the course of the work in the south.

The equipment of a polar expedition on the scientific side involved the expenditure of a large sum of money and I felt the pinch of necessary economics in this branch. I approached the Royal Society with a view to securing the loan of the Eschen-Hagen magnetic instruments that had been used by the *Discovery*, but that body was unable to lend them, as they had been promised in connection with some other work. I was lent three chronometer watches by the Royal Geographical Society, which very kindly had them thoroughly overhauled and examined. I bought one chronometer watch, and three wardens of the Skinners' Company gave me one which proved the most accurate of all and was carried by me on the journey towards the Pole.

The Geographical Society was able to send forward an application made by me for the loan of some instruments and charts from the Admiralty, and that body generously lent me the articles contained in the following list:

3 Lloyd-Creak dip circles.
3 marine chronometers.
1 station pointer 6 ft.
1 set of charts, England to Cape and Cape to New Zealand.
1 set of Antarctic charts.
1 set of charts from New Zealand through Indian Ocean to Aden.
1 set of charts, New Zealand to Europe via Cape Horn.
12 deep-sea thermometers.
2 marine standard barometers.
1 navy-pattern ship's telescope.
1 ship's standard compass.
2 azimuth mirrors (Lord Kelvin's type).

1 deep-sea sounding-machine.
8 heeling error instruments.
1 3-in. portable astronomical telescope.

I placed an order for further scientific instruments with Messrs. Cary, Porter and Company, Limited, of London, and amongst other instruments I took the following:

16-in. theodolite transit with micrometers to circle and limb, reading to 5″.
1 electric thermometer complete with 440 yards of cable, including recorder, battery, and 100 recorder sheets, recording-drum to record every twenty-five hours.
3 3-in. alt-azimuth theodolites, portable, complete with sliding leg-stand.
1 small observing sextant.
6 explorers' compasses with luminous dial and shifting needle.
3 3-in. surveying aneroids with altitude scale to 15,000 ft.
3 pocket aneroids.
4 standard thermometers.
12 deep-sea thermometers, Admiralty.
12 deep-sea registering Admiralty pattern.
4 prismatic compasses (R.G.S.) pattern.
1 portable artificial horizon, aluminium.
2 small plane tables complete with alidade.
2 barographs.
2 thermographs.
1 Oertling balance and one set of weights.
1 Robinson anemometer.
75 various thermometers.
1 5-in. transit theodolite reading to 20″ with short tripod stand. 15 magnifiers.
1 pair night binoculars.
1 pair high-power binoculars.
Quantity of special charts, drawing materials and instruments, steel chains and tapes, levelling staves, ranging poles, &c.
2 microscopes.

Amongst other instruments that we had with us on the expedition was a four-inch transit theodolite, with Reeve's micrometers fitted to horizontal and vertical circles. The photographic equipment included nine cameras by various makers, plant for the darkroom, and a large stock of plates, films and chemicals. We took also a cinematograph machine in order that we might place on record the curious movements and habits of the seals and penguins, and give the people at home a graphic idea of what it means to haul sledges over the ice and snow.

The miscellaneous articles of equipment were too numerous to be mentioned here in any detail. I had tried to provide for every contingency, and the gear ranged from needles and nails to a Remington typewriter and two Singer sewing machines. There was a gramophone to provide us with music, and a printing press, with type, rollers, paper and other necessaries, for the production of a book during the winter night. We even had hockey sticks and a football.

SNOW GOGGLES

2

THE STAFF

The personnel of an expedition of the character I proposed is a factor on which success depends to a very large extent. The men selected must be qualified for the work, and they must also have the special qualifications required to meet polar conditions. They must be able to live together in harmony for a long period without outside communication, and it must be remembered that the men whose desires lead them to the untrodden paths of the world have generally marked individuality. It was no easy matter for me to select the staff, although over four hundred applications arrived from persons wishing to join the expedition.

I wanted to have two surgeons with the shore-party, and also to have a thoroughly capable biologist and geologist, for the study of these two branches of science in the Antarctic seemed to me to be of especial importance. After much consideration I selected eleven men for the shore-party. Three of them only, Adams, Wild and Joyce, had been known to me previously, while only Wild and Joyce had previous experience of polar work, having been members of the *Discovery* expedition. Every man, however, was highly recommended, and this was the case also with the officers whom I selected for the *Nimrod*. The names of the men appointed with their particular branches of work, were as follows:

Shore-Party

Lieutenant J. B. Adams, R.N.R., meteorologist.
Sir Philip Brocklehurst, Bart., assistant geologist, and in charge of current observations.
Bernard Day, electrician and motor expert.
Ernest Joyce, in charge of general stores, dogs, sledges and zoological collections.
Dr A. F. Mackay, Surgeon.
Dr Eric Marshall, surgeon, cartographer.
G. E. Marston, artist.
James Murray, biologist.

RAYMOND PRIESTLEY, geologist.
WILLIAM ROBERTS, cook.
FRANK WILD, in charge of provisions.

After the expedition had reached New Zealand and the generous assistance of the Australian and New Zealand Governments had relieved me from some financial anxiety, I was able to add to the strength of the staff. I engaged Douglas Mawson, lecturer of mineralogy and petrology at the Adelaide University, as physicist, and Bertram Armytage as a member of the expedition for general work. Professor Edgeworth David, F.R.S., of Sydney University, consented to accompany us as far as the winter quarters, with the idea of returning in the *Nimrod,* but I persuaded him eventually to stay in the Antarctic, and his assistance in connection with the scientific work, and particularly the geology, was invaluable. Leo Cotton, a young Australian, arranged to come south with us and help with the preliminary work before the *Nimrod* returned to New Zealand, and at the last moment George Buckley, residing in New Zealand, accompanied us on the voyage South, returning in the steamer that towed the *Nimrod.*

The members of the ship's staff, at the time when the *Nimrod* left Great Britain, were as follows:

LIEUTENANT RUPERT ENGLAND, R.H.R., master.
JOHN K. DAVIS, first officer.
A. L. A. MACKINTOSH, second officer.
Dr W. A. R. MICHELL, surgeon.
H. J. L. DUNLOP, chief engineer.
ALFRED CHEETHAM, third officer and boatswain.

Captain England, whom I placed in command of the *Nimrod,* had been first officer of the *Morning* when that vessel proceeded to the relief of the *Discovery* expedition, and had therefore had previous experience of work in the Antarctic. Immediately before joining the *Nimrod* he had been in the Government service on the west coast of Africa.

Davis, first officer and later captain, had not been in the Antarctic before, but he was a first-class seaman.

Mackintosh came from the service of the Peninsular and Oriental Steam Navigation Company. He was transferred to the shore-party at a later date, but an unfortunate accident finally prevented his remaining in the Antarctic with us. Dr Michell, the ship's surgeon, was a Canadian, and Dunlop, the chief engineer, was an Irishman. Cheetham, the third officer and boatswain, had served on the *Morning* and some of the men had also Antarctic experience.

After the *Nimrod* reached New Zealand, A. E. Harbord, an Englishman, joined as second officer in place of Mackintosh, whom I intended to transfer to the shore-party.

The following brief notes regarding the members of the shore-party may be of interest to readers:

ERNEST HENRY SHACKLETON, commander of the expedition. Born 1874, and educated at Dulwich College. Went to sea in the merchant service at the age of sixteen, became a lieutenant in the Royal Naval Reserve, and in 1901 joined the British National Antarctic expedition. Was a member of the party which established a 'furthest south' record, and on return to the winter quarters was invalided. Fitted out the *Discovery* relief expeditions under the Admiralty Committee, and also assisted fitting out the Argentine expedition that went to the relief of the Swedish Antarctic expedition. Married in 1904, and became secretary and treasurer of the Royal Scottish Geographical Society. Resigned to contest the Dundee seat as a Unionist at the election of 1906, and after being defeated became personal assistant to Mr William Beardmore, head of the Glasgow firm of battleship builders and armour plate manufacturers. Then decided to take an expedition to the Antarctic.

JAMESON BOYD ADAMS, born in 1880 at Rippingale, Lincolnshire. Went to sea in the merchant service in 1893, served three years as a lieutenant in the Royal Naval Reserve, and joined the expedition in March, 1907. Appointed second in command in February 1908. Unmarried.

BERTRAM ARMYTAGE, born in Australia in 1869. Educated at Melbourne Grammar School and Jesus College, Cambridge. After serving for several years with the Victorian Militia and one year with the Victorian Permanent Artillery, he was appointed to the Carabiniers, 6th Division Guards, when on active service in South Africa (Queen's medal and three clasps, King's medal and two clasps). Joined the expedition in Australia. Married.

SIR PHILIP LEE BROCKLEHURST, Bart., born at Swythamley Park, Staffordshire, in 1887, educated at Eton and Trinity Hall, Cambridge. Holds a commission in the Derbyshire Yeomanry, represented Cambridge in the light weight boxing competitions for 1905 and 1906. Unmarried.

THOMAS W. EDGEWORTH DAVID, F.R.S., Professor of Geology at the Sydney University, is a Welshman by birth, and is fifty years of age. He was educated at New College, Oxford, and afterwards studied geology at the Royal College of Science. He went to Australia to take up the post of Geological Surveyor to the New South Wales Government, and for the past eighteen years has held his present appointment. He is an authority on dynamical geology and glaciation, and has made a study of Australian coalfields. Married.

BERNARD C. DAY, born at Wymondham, Leicestershire, in August 1884, educated at Wellingborough Grammar School. He was connected with engineering from 1903 until September 1907, when he left the service of the New Arroll Johnston MotorCar Company in order to join the expedition. Unmarried.

ERNEST JOYCE, born in 1875, entered the Navy from the Greenwich Royal Hospital School in 1891, became a first-class petty officer, and served in South Africa with the Naval Brigade (medal and clasp). Joined the *Discovery* expedition from the Cape, and served in the Antarctic (polar medal and clasp, Geographical Society's silver medal). Served in the Whale Island Gunnery School. Left the Navy in December 1905, rejoined in August 1906, and left by purchase in order to join the expedition in May 1907. Unmarried.

ALISTAIR FORBES MACKAY, born in 1878, son of the late Colonel A. Forbes Mackay, of the 92nd Gordon Highlanders. Educated in Edinburgh, and then did biological work under Professors Geddes and D'Arcy Thompson at Dundee. Served in South Africa as a trooper in the C.I.V. (Queen's medal and clasps), and later with Baden Powell's police, then returned to pass his final examinations in medicine, and went to the front again as a civil surgeon. Entered the Navy as a surgeon, retired after four years' service, and then joined the expedition. Unmarried.

AENEAS LIONEL ACTON MACKINTOSH, born in Tirhoot, Bengal, India, in 1881, and educated at the Bedford Modern School. Went to sea in 1894 in the merchant service, and in 1899 entered the service of the Peninsular and Oriental Steam Navigation Company. Was lent to the expedition in 1907. Received commission in the Royal Naval Reserve in July 1908. Unmarried.

ERIC STEWART MARSHALL, born in 1879, educated at Monckton Combe School and at Emmanual College, Cambridge. Represented his college in rowing and football. Studied for the Church. Entered St Bartholomew's Hospital in 1899, and qualified as a surgeon in 1906. Was captain St Bartholomew's Hospital Rugby football team, 1903–4, and played for the Richmond Club, 1903–4–5. Joined the expedition as surgeon and cartographer. Unmarried.

GEORGE EDWARD MARSTON was born at Portsmouth in 1882, and received the greater part of his art education at the Regent Street Polytechnic. He is a qualified art teacher, and joined the expedition as artist. Unmarried.

DOUGLAS MAWSON was born in Australia in 1880, his parents coming from the Isle of Man. He was educated in Australia and is lecturer in mineralogy and petrology at the Adelaide University and honorary curator of the South Australian Museum. He joined the expedition in Australia. Unmarried.

JAMES MURRAY was born in Glasgow in 1865. In early life was occupied in various branches of art work. Was interested in natural history, especially botany, and in 1901 turned his attention to microscopic zoology. In 1902 was engaged by Sir John Murray as biologist on Scottish Lake Survey. Was still engaged in this work when he joined the expedition as biologist. Married in 1892.

RAYMOND E. PRIESTLEY, born 1886, and educated at Tewkesbury School. Matriculated in London in 1903, and held mastership at Tewkesbury until 1905. Then became a student at the Bristol University College, and passed the intermediate examination in science in 1906. He was taking the final course when appointed geologist to the expedition.

WILLIAM C. ROBERTS, born in London in 1872, and has worked as cook on sea and land. Engaged as cook for the expedition. Married.

FRANK WILD, born in Yorkshire in 1873. His mother was a direct descendant of Captain Cook, and one of his uncles was three times in the Arctic regions. Entered the merchant service in 1889, and in 1900 joined the Navy. He was a member of the National Antarctic expedition between 1901 and 1904 (polar medal and clasp, Royal Geographical Society's silver medal). Was at the Sheerness Gunnery School when the Admiralty consented to his appointment to the British Antarctic expedition.

3

THE FIRST STAGE

The work of preparing for the expedition made rapid progress towards completion, and as the end of July approached, the stores and equipment were stowed away in the holds of the *Nimrod* in readiness for the voyage to New Zealand. The final departure for the south was to be made from Lyttelton, a well-equipped port at which I felt sure, from the experience of the three vessels of the *Discovery* expedition, that I should receive every assistance that lay in the power of the authorities. Early in July we exhibited in a room in Regent Street samples of our stores and equipment, and some thousands of people paid us a visit. The days were all too short for scores of details demanded attention and small difficulties of all sorts had to be overcome, but there were no delays, and on July 30, 1907, the *Nimrod* was able to sail from the East India Docks for Torquay, the first stage of the journey of sixteen thousand miles to New Zealand. Most of the members of the shore staff, including myself, intended to make this journey by steamer, but I left the docks with the *Nimrod,* intending to travel as far as Torquay.

We anchored for the first night at Greenhithe, and on the morning of the 31st continued on our way to Torquay, landing Mr Reid at Tilbury in order that he might return to London for letters. When he reached London that afternoon, he found at the office a telegram from the King's equerry, commanding the *Nimrod* to visit Cowes in order to enable their Majesties the King and Queen to come on board and inspect the ship and equipment on Sunday, August 4. Mr Reid had considerable difficulty in delivering this message to me, but the Admiral Superintendent at Sheerness kindly despatched a tug which overtook the *Nimrod* off Ramsgate, and conveyed the news that an alteration in our plans was necessary. We sailed in the night for Cowes, and on the morning of August 1 stopped for an hour off Eastbourne in order to enable some of the supporters of the expedition to pay us a farewell visit. On the Sunday we were anchored at Cowes, and their Majesties the King and Queen, their Royal Highnesses the Prince of Wales, the Princess Victoria, Prince Edward and the Duke of Connaught came on board. The King graciously conferred upon me the Victorian Order, and the Queen entrusted me with a Union Jack, to carry on the southern sledge journey.

The *Nimrod* sailed for Torquay early on the following morning, and arrived there on August 6. We drank success to the expedition at a farewell dinner that evening, and on the morning of Wednesday, August 7, the ship sailed for New Zealand, and after calling at St Vincent and Capetown, arrived at Lyttelton on November 23, the voyage having occupied three months and a half. Mr Reid reached Australian waters a month ahead of the *Nimrod,* in order to make the necessary arrangements and meet the Manchurian ponies, and I arrived early in December, my intention being to leave Lyttelton on January 1, 1908.

The people of New Zealand and Australia took a keen and sympathetic interest in the expedition from the first. The Commonwealth Government gave me £5000 and the New Zealand Government £1000, and this sum of money placed me in a position to increase the number of the shore-party, to add to the stores and equipment in certain directions and to strengthen the ship still further, which I could not afford to do earlier. The New Zealand Government also agreed to pay half the cost of towing the *Nimrod* down to the Antarctic Circle, so that coal might be saved for the heavy work amongst the ice, and in many other ways assisted us. The Postmaster-General of the Dominion had printed off for me a small issue of special stamps, and constituted me a postmaster for the period of my stay in the Antarctic, an arrangement that much simplified the handling of the correspondence sent back from the winter quarters with the *Nimrod.*

The ponies were enjoying their holiday on Quail Island and were becoming sleek and fat, and it was necessary that they should be broken to handling and sledge-hauling. Mr C. Tubman undertook this work, with the assistance of Dr Mackay, and there were some exciting moments on the island. The ponies were very wild, and more than once Mackay and Tubman had to make a rapid retreat from the animal they were schooling at the time. The white ponies, which later proved the most hardy, were the least tractable, and there was one white pony in particular that was left behind, because, though a splendid specimen physically, it could not be brought to a reasonable state of docility in the time at our disposal. I intended to take only ten ponies out of the fifteen, having allowed a margin for losses on the voyage to New Zealand, and Tubman and Mackay devoted their attention to the most promising animals. All the ponies had names, although I do not know from whom they received them, and we finally left New Zealand with 'Socks', 'Quan', 'Grisi', 'Chinaman', 'Billy', 'Zulu', 'Doctor', 'Sandy', 'Nimrod', and 'Mac'.

I had secured in London twenty tons of maize and ten hundredweight of compressed Maujee ration for the feeding of the ponies in the Antarctic. The maize was packed in about seven hundred tin-lined, air-tight cases, and the ration was in one-pound, air-tight tins. This ration consists of dried beef, carrots, milk, currants and sugar, and it provides a large amount of nourishment with comparatively little weight. One pound of the ration will absorb four pounds of water, and the ponies were very fond of it. We also secured in Australia ten tons of compressed fodder, consisting of oats, bran and chaff. This fodder was packed in two hundred and fifty small bales. I purchased for the dogs one ton and a half of dog biscuits, and proposed to make up their rations with seal meat.

The final preparations involved an enormous amount of work, but by December 31 everything was ready. Quarters were provided on the *Nimrod* for the scientific staff by enclosing a portion of the after-hold, and constructing cabins which were entered by a steep ladder from the deck-house. The quarters were certainly small, in fact there was just room for the bunks and nothing else, and they were promptly named 'Oyster Alley', for some reason not on record. As the day of departure approached and the scientists brought their personal belongings, the alley reached a state of congestion that can hardly be imagined. The ponies were to be carried on deck, and ten stout stalls were built for them. The motor-car was enclosed in a large case and made fast with chains on the after-hatch from whence it could be transferred easily on to the ice when the occasion arose. The deck load was heavy and included cases of maize, tins of carbide for the manufacture of acetylene gas, a certain quantity of coal and the sledges. The *Nimrod* was low in the water as a result, and when we left Lyttelton the little ship had only three feet six inches of freeboard. Some live sheep presented to us by New Zealand farmers were placed on board the *Koonya*, the steamer which was to tow the *Nimrod* to the south.

I had been anxious to have the *Nimrod* towed south in order to save coal. The ship could not take in a large quantity of coal after our provisions and equipment had been placed on board, for she was considerably overloaded, and it was important that there should be enough coal to take the ship through the ice and back to New Zealand, and also to provide for the warming of the hut during the winter. The Government of the Dominion consented to pay half the cost of the tow, and Sir James Mills, chairman of the Union Steamship Company, offered to pay the other half. The *Koonya*, a steel-built steamer of about 1100 tons, was chartered and placed under the command of Captain F. P. Evans. The wisdom of this selection was proved by after events. The pressure of work was at this time tremendous, and I owed a very great deal to the assistance and advice I received from Mr J. J. Kinsey, of Christchurch. Before my departure I placed the conduct of the affairs of the expedition in New Zealand in his hands.

December 31 was the last day of our stay in New Zealand, for as I had stated when announcing the expedition, we were to leave Lyttelton on the first day of the new year. The stores and equipment were on board and were as complete as we could make them, and I had written my final letters, both business and personal. The ponies and the dogs were to be placed on board the *Nimrod* early the following morning.

4

LYTTELTON TO THE
ANTARCTIC CIRCLE

January 1, 1908, arrived at last! Warm, fine, and clear broke the morning
of our last day in civilisation. Before sunset we were to sever all ties with
the outer world and more than a year must elapse ere we could look again on
the scenes familiar to ordinary daily life. For me this day brought a feeling of
relief, after all the strenuous work of the previous year, though the new work
I was entering upon was fraught with more anxiety and was more exacting
than any that had gone before. We all looked forward eagerly to our coming
venture, for the glamour of the unknown was with us and the South was
calling.

My personal belongings were gathered out of the chaos of papers and odds
and ends in my office at the hotel; I knew that the legacy of unanswered
letters, requests for special stamps, and the hundred and one things that
collect under such circumstances would be faithfully administered by Mr
Reid. Orders had been given to Captain England to have all in readiness for
casting off at 4 p.m., and early in the afternoon most of us were on board.
It was Regatta day and Lyttelton was crowded with holiday-makers, many
thousands of whom had come to see the *Nimrod*. All day the deck of our
little vessel was thronged by the general public, who evinced the greatest
interest in everything connected with the ship and her equipment. Naturally
the ten ponies, now safely housed in their stalls on the forward deck, were a
special attraction. Our nine dogs also claimed a share of attention, although
it was a gymnastic feat to climb through the supports of the pony structure,
stretching across the decks, in order to reach the forecastle, where the dogs
lay panting in the hot sun. To the uninitiated the number and size of the
beams belonging to the pony structure seemed excessive, but we knew we
might encounter heavy weather which would tax their strength to the utmost.
The *Nimrod* was deep in the water, for every available corner had been
stowed with stores and coal and, if we could have carried it, we would have
added at least another fifty tons to our two hundred and fifty; but the risk
was too great. Indeed I was somewhat anxious as to the weather she might
make, though I knew she was a good sea boat and had great confidence in

her. There were many whose criticisms were frankly pessimistic as to our chances of weathering an Antarctic gale; and as I stood on deck I could hear the remarks of these Job's comforters. Such criticisms, however, did not disturb us, for we were confident in the ship.

Oyster Alley was crammed with the personal belongings of at least fourteen of the shore party; it was the temporary resting-place for many of the scientific instruments, so that both ingress and egress were matters of extreme difficulty. The entrance to this twentieth-century Black Hole was through a narrow doorway and down a ladder, which ushered one into almost complete darkness, for the doorway was practically filled up with cases, and the single narrow deck light generally covered by the feet of sightseers. The shore party's fourteen bunks were crammed with luggage, which also occupied the whole of the available floor space. It was in this uncomfortable place that the spirit of romance, the desire for the wind-whitened Southern Seas, and the still whiter wastes of the silent Antarctic grew stronger in the heart of George Buckley, as he sat there talking over the days and doings before us, longing for a share in the work, even though he might only go as far as the Antarctic circle. He knew that time would not permit him to do more than this. Suddenly he jumped up, came to me, and asked if I would take him as far as the ice. I was only too glad to consent, for his interest in the expedition showed that his heart was in our venture, and his personality had already appealed to us all. It was 2 p.m. when the decision was made, and the *Nimrod* was to sail at 4 p.m. He managed to catch a train to Christchurch, dashed into his club, gave his power of attorney to a friend; slung his tooth-brush and some underclothing into a bag; struggled through one seething crowd at Christchurch Station and another at the wharf, and arrived on board the *Nimrod,* a few minutes before sailing time, equipped for the most rigorous weather in the world with only the summer suit he was wearing: surely a record in the way of joining a Polar Expedition.

Time was passing quickly, it was nearing four o'clock, and all our party were on board save Professor David. I had seen him earlier in the afternoon, struggling along the crowded wharf, bending under the weight of one end of a long iron pipe, a railway porter attached to the other. This precious burden, he had informed me, when it was safely on board, was part of the boring gear to be used in obtaining samples of ice from the Great Ice Barrier; he had found it at the railway station, where it had been overlooked. Doubtless he was having a last skirmish round in case there was anything else that had been left, and just as I was getting anxious, for I did not want to delay the departure of the ship, he appeared. His arms were filled with delicate glass apparatus and other scientific paraphernalia. As he was gingerly crossing the narrow gangway he was confronted by a stout female, of whom the Professor afterwards said. 'She was for the shore, let who would be for the Pole.' They met in the middle of the gangway. Hampered by the things he was carrying, the Professor could not move aside; he was simply charged down by superior weight, and clutching his precious goods, fell off the gangway on to the heads of some of our party. Wonderful to relate nothing was broken.

At one minute to four orders were given to stand by the engines, at 4 p.m. the lines were cast off from the wharf and the *Nimrod* moved slowly ahead. Cheer after cheer broke from the watching thousands as we moved towards the harbour entrance, with the Queen's flag flying at the fore and our ensign dipping farewell at the stern. The cheering broke out afresh as we passed the United States' magnetic survey ship *Galilee*. She also was engaged in a scientific mission, but her lines were laid in warmer climes and calmer seas. Hearty as was this send-off it seemed mild compared to that which we received on passing the pier-head lighthouse. The air trembled with the crash of guns, the piercing steam whistles and sirens of every steamship in the port, and a roar of cheering from the throats of the thirty thousand people who were watching the little black-hulled barque moving slowly towards the open sea. With our powerful ally, the Koonya, steaming in front, and on each side passenger boats of the Union Company carrying some six or seven thousand persons, we passed down the Roads, receiving such a farewell and 'God-speed' from New Zealand as left no man of us unmoved. The farewells were not over, for we were to receive one more expression of goodwill, and one that came nearer to the hearts of those of us who were sailors than any other could. Lying inside the Heads were three of his Majesty's ships of the Australian Squadron, the flagship *Powerful,* the *Pegasus* and the *Pioneer.* As we steamed past the last-named her crew mustered on the forecastle head and gave us three hearty cheers; we received the same from the *Pegasus* as we came abeam of her, our party of thirty-nine returning the cheers as we passed each ship in turn. Then we drew abreast of the flagship and from the throats of the nine hundred odd bluejackets on board her we got a ringing farewell, and across the water came the sound of her band playing 'Hearts of oak are our ships', followed by 'Auld Lang Syne'. We responded with three cheers and gave another cheer for Lady Fawkes, who had taken a kindly interest in the expedition.

Shortly after passing the *Powerful,* we stopped to pick up our tow-line from the *Koonya,* but before doing this we transferred to the tug-boat *Canterbury* the few personal friends who had accompanied some of the members of the expedition down the harbour. We then came close up to the stern of the *Koonya* and hauled in the 4-inch wire cable she was to tow us with. A 4-inch wire is measured not as 4 inch diameter, but 4 inches in circumference, and is made of the finest steel. We passed a shackle through the eye at the end of this wire and shackled on to the free ends of both our chain cables. We then let out thirty fathoms of each cable one on each side of the bow, and made the inner ends fast round the foremast in the 'tween decks. This cable acted as a 'spring', to use a nautical term: that is to say, it lessened the danger of the wire snapping if a sudden strain were put upon it, for the cable hung down in the water owing to its weight, even when the ship was being towed at seven or eight knots. This operation being completed we signalled the *Koonya* to go ahead and we were soon in the open sea. There was a slight breeze and a small choppy sea. Before we had been under way for an hour water began to come in at the scupper holes and through the wash ports. This looked ominous to us, for if the *Nimrod* was going to be wet in such fine weather, what was she going to be like when we got a southerly gale! She moved through the water astern of the *Koonya* like a reluctant child being dragged to school; she seemed to have no vitality of her own. This was due to her deeply loaded condition, and more especially to the seven tons of cable and the weight of the wire on her bows dragging her nose down into the sea. No Antarctic exploring ship had been towed to the ice before, but it meant the saving of coal to us for a time when the tons saved in this manner might prove the salvation of the expedition.

Night came down on us, and the last we saw of New Zealand was a bold headland growing fainter and fainter in the gathering gloom. The occupants of Oyster Alley, after a somewhat sketchy meal in the wardroom, were endeavouring to reduce the chaos of their quarters to some sort of order. The efforts of some of the scientific staff were interrupted at times by sudden attacks of seasickness, and indeed one would not have been surprised if the seafaring portion of the staff had also succumbed, for the atmosphere of the alley, combined with the peculiar motion of the ship, was far from pleasant. A few of the members of the party preferred to sleep on deck in any odd corner they could find, and one man in particular was so overcome by the sea that for three days and nights he lay prostrate amongst the vegetables and cases of butter and carbide, on the unused fore-bridge of the ship. He seemed to recover at meal-times, and as his lair was just above the galley, he simply appeared from under his sodden blankets, reached down his hand, and in a plaintive voice asked for something to fill the yawning cavern that existed in his interior. Professor David was given Dr Michell's cabin, the latter taking up his abode in Oyster Alley. The cabin measured about 5 ft. 10 in. by 3 ft., and as the Professor had nearly a quarter of a ton of scientific instruments, books and cameras, one can imagine that he had not much room for himself. The wardroom of the *Nimrod* was about 12 ft. long and 9 ft. broad, and as there were twenty-two mouths to feed there three times a day, difficulties were present from the beginning of the voyage. Dunlop's cabin came into service as the largest overflow diningroom, for it accommodated three people. Davis and Mackintosh each found room for another hungry explorer in his cabin. When the food arrived it was passed along to the outside dining-rooms first. Then people in the main room were served. All went well that first night out, for there was comparatively little movement, but later on the story of an ordinary meal became a record of adventure. I took up my quarters in the captain's cabin, and fluctuated between the bunk and the settee for a resting-place, until the carpenter made me a plank bed about four inches off the deck. We did not know that we were not to take our clothes off for the next two weeks, but were to live in a constant state of wetness, wakefulness, and watchfulness until the *Nimrod* arrived in the neighbourhood of the winter quarters.

Bad weather was not long delayed. As the night of January 1 wore on, the wind began to freshen from the south-west, and the following morning the two vessels were pitching somewhat heavily and steering wildly. The *Koonya* signalled us to veer, that is, to slack out thirty more fathoms on each of our two cables, and with great difficulty we managed to do this. The ship was pitching and rolling, flinging the cables from one side of the deck to the other, and with our forty-year-old windlass it was no light task to handle the heavy chains. Then I felt one of the first real pinches of the stringent economy that had to be practised from the inception of the expedition. How I wished for the splendid modern gear of the *Discovery*, the large specially built vessel that we had on the previous expedition. During the afternoon the wind and sea increased greatly, and the *Nimrod* pitched about, shifting everything that could be moved on deck. The seas began to break over her, and we were soon wet through, not to be properly dry again for the next fortnight. The decks were flooded with heavy seas, which poured, white-capped, over the side, and even the topsail yards were drenched with the spray of breaking waves. Life-lines were stretched along the deck, and it was a risky thing to go forward without holding on.

Our chief anxiety was the care of the ponies, and looking back now to those days, it remains a matter of wonder to me how they survived the hardships that fell to their lot. That night I arranged for a two-hour watch, consisting of two members of the shore staff, to be always in attendance on the ponies. The pony shelter had five stalls on the port side and five on the starboard side of the deck, with the fore hatch between them. The watch keepers named this place 'The Cavalry Club', and here in the bleak and bitter stormy nights, swept off their feet every now and then by the seas washing over the forehatch, the members of the shore party passed many a bad quarter of an hour. They bore all the buffeting and discomfort cheerfully, even as those men of old, who 'ever with a frolic welcome took the thunder and the sunshine.' Night in the pony-stables was a weird experience, with inky blackness all round, save only where the salt-encrusted hurricane lamp, jerking to and fro, made a glimmer of light. The roar of the tempest rose into a shriek as the wind struck the rigid rigging, the creaking and swaying of the roof of the stable and the boat-skids, which partly rested their weight on it, seemed to threaten a sudden collapse with each succeeding and heavier roll, and the seas crashed dully as they fell on board. The swirling waters, foam-white in the dim rays of the lamp, rushed through the stable and over the hatch, and even from the bridge far aft, we could hear the frightened whinnies of the animals, as they desperately struggled to keep their feet in the water that flooded the rolling stables. Every now and then some wave, larger and fiercer than the one before, would sweep the decks, tear the mats from under the feet of the ponies, and wash the watch-keepers almost under the struggling beasts. When the bulk of the water had passed, the mats were nailed down again with difficulty, and the two watchers resumed their seats on a bag of fodder that had been fastened to the hatch. One can imagine that after a two-hours' watch a rest was welcome. Oyster Alley was wet enough, and the beds were soaking, while the atmosphere was thick and heavy; but these conditions did not prevent the wearied men from falling asleep after wedging themselves into their bunks, lest some extra heavy lurch should send them to keep company with the miscellaneous collection of articles careering up and down the deck of the alley.

All during our second night out, the weather was so bad that we kept going slow, having requested the *Koonya* to slacken speed late in the afternoon. Next morning found us plunging, swerving, and rolling in a high sea, with a dull grey stormy sky overhead, and apparently no prospect of the weather becoming settled. We were moving little more than a mile an hour towards the south, and the ship seemed to be straining herself on account of the heavy pull on her bows, and the resulting lack of buoyancy. The weather moderated somewhat in the afternoon, and we signalled the *Koonya* to 'increase speed'. By midnight the improvement in the weather was much more marked. The following morning, January 4, we set loose the carrier pigeon which one of the New Zealand sailors had brought with him. We attached a message to the bird, briefly describing our passage so far, and hoped it would safely accomplish the three hundred odd miles to the land. On releasing our messenger it made one or two wide circles round the ship, and then set off in a bee-line towards its home. We wondered at the time whether any of the albatrosses, which were now fairly numerous about our stern, especially at meal times, would attack the stranger, and we heard afterwards that the pigeon had not reached its home.

The hope that we were going to keep finer weather was dispelled in the afternoon, for the wind began to increase and the rising sea to break on board again, and within a couple of hours we were bearing the full brunt of another furious gale. The sea-going qualities of the *Nimrod* were severely taxed, but the little vessel rose to the occasion. As the gale increased in vehemence, she seemed to throw off the lethargy, one might almost say the sulkiness, which possessed her when she found herself outward bound at the end of a tow-line, for the first time in her strenuous life of forty years. Now that the towline, in the fury of the gale, was but of little use, save to steady us, the *Nimrod* began to play her own hand. It was wonderful to see how she rose to the largest oncoming waves. She was flung to and fro, a tiny speck in this waste of waters, now poised on the summit of a huge sea, whence we got almost a bird's-eye view of the gallant *Koonya* smashing into the turmoil ahead; now dipping into the wave valleys, from which all we could discern of our consort was in very truth 'just a funnel and a mast lurching through the spray'.

As the afternoon wore on, those of us who were not still in the clutches of sea-sickness watched the grandeur of the gale. I shall always remember Buckley, who stood for hour after hour on the *Nimrod*'s poop, revelling in the clash and strife of the elements. Keen yachtsman that he was, his admiration was aroused by the way the two ships battled with the storm. Professor David also, hanging to the dripping rails, was fascinated by the wild scene, and between the gusts, we spoke of many things. Somehow or another the conversation turned to one's favourite poets, and it is but natural that, under these circumstances of stress and strain, Browning's verse was often the subject of conversation. Night drew on, sullen and black, our only light the lamp we steered by on the *Koonya*'s mast. We could imagine the stalwart figure of that splendid seaman, Captain Evans, as he stood on his spray-drenched bridge, alert, calm and keen, doing his best to ease the little ship astern. We had nothing but admiration for the consummate seamanship that anticipated our every need and wish. All that night it blew harder than ever; on the morning of the 5th I told Captain England to signal the *Koonya* and ask her to pour oil on the water in the hope that it might help us. To a certain extent I think it did, but not enough to prevent the heaviest seas from breaking on board. I thought that the gale had reached its height on the previous day, but certainly this evening it was much stronger. The *Nimrod* rolled over fifty degrees from the perpendicular to each side; how much more than that I cannot say, for the indicator recording the roll of the ship was only marked up to fifty degrees, and the pointer had passed that mark. Let the reader hold a pencil on end on a table, and then incline it fifty degrees one way, and back again till it reaches fifty degrees on the other side, and he will realise the length of arc through which the masts and deck of the *Nimrod* swung. It was only natural, under these circumstances, that the sturdy little ponies had their strength taxed to the utmost to keep their footing at all. It was impracticable to sling them, for they were only half broken, and the attempt to put a sling under one drove it nearly crazy with fright. All we could do was to try and soothe them, and the animals evidently appreciated the human voice and touch. Buckley had a wonderful way with them, and they seemed to understand that he was trying to help them.

Occasionally there were clear patches of sky to the south and east between the squalls. We had sleet for the first time on January 5, and the wind, ranging between west, south, and south-west, was chilly for the height of summer, the temperature being about 46° Fahr. We passed large masses of floating kelp, which may have torn from the islands to the south-west of us, for at noon on January 5, we were still north of the fiftieth parallel, a latitude corresponding to the South of England. Our course lay practically south, for I wanted to enter tile pack ice somewhere about the 178th meridian east, previous experience having shown that the pack is less dense about that meridian than it is further west. About 9 p.m. that night, during an extra heavy roll, one of the ponies slipped down in its stall, and when the ship rolled the opposite way, turned right over on its back, as it could not regain its footing. We tried everything in our power to get the poor beast up again, but there was no room to work in the narrow stall, and in the darkness and rushing water it would have been madness to have tried to shift the other ponies out of the adjacent stalls in order to take down the partition, and so give the poor animal room to get up itself. We had perforce to leave it for the night, trusting that when daylight came the weather might have moderated, and that with the light we might be able to do more. It speaks wonders for the vitality of the animal that in spite of its cramped position and the constant washing of the cold seas over it during the whole night, it greedily ate the handfuls of hay which were given it from time to time. Every now and then the pony made frantic efforts to get on to its feet again, but without avail, and before the morning its struggles gradually grew weaker and weaker. The morning of January 6 broke with the gale blowing more strongly than ever. There was a mountainous sea running, and at ten o'clock, after having made another futile attempt to get 'Doctor', as he was called, on his legs, and finding that he had no strength of his own, I had regretfully to give orders to have him shot. One bullet from a heavy service revolver ended his troubles. During the morning the gale moderated somewhat, and at noon we were in latitude 50° 58′ South, and longitude 175° 19′ East.

During the afternoon of January 6 the wind increased again, the squalls being of hurricane force, and the wind shifting to between west and north-west. The *Koonya* ahead was making bad weather of it, but was steaming as fast as practicable, for with the wind and sea coming more abeam she was able to make better headway than when she was plunging into a head sea with the weight and bulk of the towing cable and the *Nimrod* astern of her, factors in the situation that made the handling and steering of the steamer very difficult. The temperature of the air that day was up to 49° Fahr., but the sea temperature had dropped to 44°. This continuous bad weather was attributed by some on board to the fact that we had captured an albatross on the second day out. It is generally supposed by seamen to be unlucky to kill this bird, but as we did it for the purposes of scientific collections and not with the wantonness of the 'Ancient Mariner', the superstitious must seek for some other reason for the weather. By this time most of the scientific staff had recovered from sea-sickness, so to employ their time when they were not on pony-guard meteorological observations were taken every hour. There sometimes was an inclination to obtain the temperature of the sea-water from the never-failing stream which poured over the deck, but to the observer's credit this feeling was sternly suppressed, and the more legitimate and accurate, if less simple means, that of drawing it from over the side, was adopted. It is not at all an easy operation to draw water in this way from the sea when a ship is under way, and in our particular circumstances, the observer often got premature knowledge of the temperature by the contents of the bucket, or the top of a sea, drenching him. On this day we began to feel the serious effects of the towing strain on the ship. For days the sailors' quarters below the fore-deck had been in a state of constant wetness from the leaking of the fore-deck, and the inhabitants of Oyster Alley had come to the conclusion that it might more suitably be named 'Moisture Alley'. But when Dunlop, the chief engineer, came on the poop bridge that afternoon and reported that the ship was making about three feet of water in an hour, matters assumed a more serious complexion. I had not expected that we would get off scot free, as the ship had to endure a very severe strain, and was old, but three feet of water in an hour showed that she was feeling the effects of the towing very much. It was necessary to rig the hand-pump to help the steam-pumps to keep the water under, and this became, as the Professor remarked, the occasion for an additional scientific instrument to be used by the shore party. A watch was set to use this pump, and two members of the staff worked it for two hours, or as long as occasion demanded, and at the end of that time were relieved by two more. The weather grew steadily worse, and by midnight the squalls were of hurricane force. Even the mastheads of the *Koonya* disappeared from you at times, and the light we were steering by would only be seen for a few seconds, and would then disappear behind the mounting wall of waters that separated the two ships. A moderate estimate of the height of the waves is forty-two feet. During the squalls, which were accompanied by hail and sleet, the tops of the seas were cut off by the force of the wind and flung in showers of stinging spray against our faces, drenching even the topsail yards of the *Nimrod*. Each green wave rushed at us as though it meant to swamp the ship, but each time the *Nimrod* rose bravely, and, riding over the seemingly overwhelming mass, steadied for a moment on the other side as it passed on, seething and white, baffled of its prey. All night there were squalls of terrific force, and the morning of

January 7 brought no abatement of the storm. The seas now came on board with increasing frequency, finding out any odd article that had escaped our vigilance and survived the rolling of the ship. A sack of potatoes was washed on to the deck, and the contents were floating in two or three feet of water. But standing on the poop bridge I heard one of the crew, in no way disheartened, singing, as he gathered them up, 'Here we go gathering nuts in May'.

At noon we were in latitude 53° 26′ South and longitude 172° 42′ East. In the afternoon the weather moderated slightly, though there was a heavy, lumpy sea. Albatrosses were becoming much more numerous, especially the sooty species, the death of which, on Shelvoche's voyage, inspired Coleridge's memorable 'Rival'. I noticed one, flying low between the two ships, strike its wings against the wire tow-line, which had suddenly emerged from the waves owing to the lift of the *Koonya*'s stern upon a sea. The weather became fairly moderate during the night and remained so next morning, with the wind in the north-west. After the second day out we had shifted the dogs from the forecastle head to the fore bridge, and one of these in its struggles to get down on to the main deck, strangled itself before we knew that it was in trouble.

There was constant rain during the morning of January 8, but it did not beat the sea down much, and during the evening, with the wind shifting to the south-southwest, the gale increased again. It was so bad, owing to the confused sea, that we had to signal the *Koonya* to heave to. We did this with the sea on our starboard quarter. Suddenly one enormous wave rushed at us, and it appeared as though nothing could prevent our decks, being swept, but the ship rose to it, and missed the greater part, though to us it seemed as if the full weight of water had come on board. We clung tightly to the poop rails, and as soon as the water had passed over us we wiped the salt from our eyes and surveyed the scene. The sea had smashed in part of the starboard bulwarks and destroyed a small house on the upper deck, pieces of this house and the bulwarks floating out to the leeward; the port washport was torn from its hinges, so that water now surged on board and swept away at its own sweet will, and the stout wooden rails of the poop deck, to which we had been clinging, were cracked and displaced, but no vital damage was done. The look of disgust on the faces of the dripping pony watch-keepers, as they emerged from the water-logged 'Cavalry Club', was eloquent of their feelings. The galley was washed out and the fire extinguished. This happened more than once, but so pluckily did the members of the cooking-department work, that never during the whole of this very uncomfortable time had we been without a warm meal. This means far more than one is apt to think, for the galley was only five feet square, and thirty-nine persons blessed with extremely hearty appetites had to be provided for.

In a large measure, this unbroken routine of hot meals, the three oases of what I might call pleasure in the daily desert of discomfort, was due to Roberts, who besides being assistant zoologist to the expedition, was going to act as cook. Seeing that the ship's staff would have more work to do than they could well carry out in providing for the thirty-nine people on board, he volunteered the first day out to assist the ship's cook, and the result was that we were always provided with fresh bread and hot cocoa and tea. Montague, the ship's cook, was ever at work, though the galley was in a constant state of flood. The stewards, Handcock and Ansell, worked wonders in getting the food across the danger zone between the galley and the wardroom. Ansell, with ten plates in one hand, overlapping one another up his arm, would arrive safely at his destination, though his boots were often filled with water on the way aft. Of course there were times when he was not so successful, and he would emerge from a sea with his clothes, hair, and face plentifully sprinkled with food. As a rule the accidents occurred in the wardroom, after the arrival of the food. The tablecloth, after two or three days, assumed an écru colour, owing to the constant upsetting of tea and coffee. Some of the staff had perforce to take their meals standing, from lack of seating accommodation, and the balancing of a plate of soup when the ship was rolling heavily required skill and experience. The meal was generally accompanied by the spurting of seawater through the wardroom door, or through cracks in the skylight, and the water washed to and fro unheeded until the meal was ended, and the indefatigable Ansell turned his attention to it. It was in the wardroom that I salved a small wooden case from the water, and found that it contained a patent mixture for extinguishing fires. The rooms of the ship's officers, opening out of the wardroom, were in a similar state of dampness, and when an officer finished his watch and turned in for a well-earned sleep, he merely substituted for clothes that were soaked through, others which were a little less wet.

The water, however, did not damp the spirits of those on board, for nearly every night extemporary concerts were held, and laughter and mirth filled the little wardroom. It is usual on Saturday nights at sea to drink the toasts, 'Absent Friends', and 'Sweethearts and Wives'. I was generally at this time in the after cabin or on the bridge, and if, as sometimes happened, I had forgotten that particular day, a gentle hint was conveyed to me by Wild or Dunlop starting a popular song, entitled ' Sweethearts and Wives', the chorus of which was heartily rendered by all hands. This hint used to bring my neglect to my mind, and I would procure the necessary bottle.

On January 10 we had a clear sky during the morning until about ten o'clock, and then, with a westerly wind, the breeze became heavier, and rain commenced. Most of us that day, taking advantage of the comparative steadiness of the ship, managed to wash our saltencrusted faces and hair; we had become practically pickled during the past week. About midnight we had a light wind from the north-north-east, and the most continual rain of the previous twelve hours had flattened the sea considerably.

At noon on January 11, we were in latitude 57° 38′ South, and longitude 178° 39′ East, and during the day the wind and sea increased again from the north-west. The nature of this particular sea made it necessary for us to keep the ship away, altering our course from south to south-east, and before midnight the gale had reached its now customary force and violence. As I was standing on the bridge at 2 a.m., peering out to windward through a heavy snow-squall that enveloped us, I saw, in the faint light of breaking day, a huge sea, apparently independent of its companions, rear itself up alongside the ship. Fortunately only the crest of the wave struck us, but away went the starboard bulwarks forward and abreast of the pony stalls, leaving a free run for the water through the stables. When we left port it was our augean problem how best to clean out the stables, but after the first experience of the herculean waves, the difficulty was to try and stop the flushing of them by every sea that came on board forward, and now not only each wave that fell on board, but the swell of the ocean itself swept the stables clean. This particular sea shifted the heavy starboard whaleboat from its chocks, landing it almost amidships on top of the 'Cavalry Club', and swept some of our bales of fodder down on to the main deck, where they mingled with the drums of oil and cases of carbide torn from their lashings. Our position at noon on the 12th was latitude 59° 28′ South and longitude 179° 30′ East. The squalls of sleet and snow gave place later to clearer weather with a mackerel sky, which was of special interest to the meteorologists, as indicating the trend of the upper currents of the air.

During the afternoon the strength of the expedition was increased by Possum, one of our dogs, giving birth to six fine puppies. The mother and family were found a warm bed on the engine room skylight, where a number of our cases were stowed. We signalled the happy event to the *Koonya* by flags, and received Captain Evans' congratulations. Signalling by flags is necessarily a somewhat slow operation, especially as the commercial code of signals is not exactly adapted for this particular sort of information, and we could see by the length of time they took to verify each signal that they were at a loss as to the subject-matter of our communication, the incident of a birth naturally being farthest removed from their thoughts at such a time. Whenever the weather moderated at all the two ships always held short conversations by flags, and the commander of the *Koonya* used to make inquiries in particular after the health of the scientific staff.

January 13 brought with it a gentle breeze from the eastward, the heavy leaden sky broke into blue, flecked with light cirrus clouds, and the day seemed warmer and more pleasant than any we had experienced since we left Lyttelton, though the temperature of the air and sea water were down to 34° and 37° Fahr. respectively. The warm sun tempted those who had not before been much in evidence on to the poop deck, and the whole vessel began to look like a veritable Petticoat Lane. Blankets, coats, boots, bags that might once have been leather but which now looked like lumps of dilapidated brown paper; pyjamas that had been intended to be worn when the owners first came aboard the *Nimrod;* books that had parted with their covers after sundry adventures in dripping Oyster Alley, but whose leaves evinced the strongest disinclination to separate; pillows of pulp that had once been pillows of feathers; carpet slippers, now merely bits of carpet; in short, all the personal belongings of each member of the expedition, including their most sacred Penates and Lares, were lying in a heterogeneous mass on the poop deck, in order that they might dry. A few of us ventured on baths, but it was chilly work in the open air, with the temperature only two degrees above freezing-point.

Some of our party, who were old sailors, had not much impedimenta to look after and to dry, the hard-won experience of other days having taught them the lesson that the fewer things you have to get wet, the fewer you have to get dry. Adams in particular observed this rule, for he wore the flannel trousers in which he came on board the ship at Lyttleton through all this weather, allowing them to dry on him after each successive wetting. He fondly clung to them throughout the period we were navigating in the ice, and whilst working the ship at winter quarters, and would doubtless have worn them on the ascent of Erebus if they had not practically come to pieces.

We were now keeping a sharp look-out for icebergs and pack; we had been steering a little more to the east, as I felt, that our delay owing to bad weather would give us little time for navigation if we had to pass through much pack-ice, and a few degrees more casting might perhaps give us a more open sea. The meeting with the pack-ice was to terminate the *Koonya's* tow, and that also meant our parting with Buckley, who had endeared himself to every man on board, from able seaman upwards, and had been of the greatest assistance to us in the matter of the ponies. It was due to his prompt action on one occasion that the life of 'Zulu' was saved. We decided to give a farewell dinner to our friend that night, and Marston designed special menu cards for the occasion. At noon this day we were in latitude 61° 29' South, longitude 179° 53' East. During the afternoon the weather kept fine, and we set some square sail. Occasionally during the bad weather of the previous week we had put 'fore and afters' on to try and steady the ship, but the wind had carried them away. The *Koonya* had done the same, with a similar result. Our dinner that night was a great success, and it was early in the morning before we turned in.

Next morning, January 14, we sighted our first iceberg, and passed it at a distance of about two and a half miles. It had all the usual characteristics of the Antarctic bergs, being practically tabular in form, and its sides being of a dead white colour. The sight of this, the first sentinel of the frozen south, increased Buckley's desire to stay with us, and it was evident that the thought of leaving our little company was not a pleasant one to him. There was a remarkable belt of clouds across the sky during the morning, and their direction indicated the movement of the upper air, so the Professor and Cotton made several estimates of the height of this belt of cloud to try to determine the lower limit of the higher current. The mean measurements were taken, partly with a sextant and partly with an Abney level, to the edge of the belt of mackerel sky. The result of the observations was that the height of this belt was fixed at about thirteen thousand feet. The belt of cloud was travelling in an east-north-east direction at the rate of about fourteen miles an hour. The surface wind, at this time, was blowing lightly from the west. Our latitude at noon was 63° 59′ South and the longitude 179° 47′ West, so we had crossed the 180th meridian.

During the afternoon we passed two more icebergs with their usual tails of brash ice floating out to leeward. The sea had changed colour from a leaden blue to a greenish grey. Albatrosses were not nearly so numerous, and of those following the ship the majority were the sooty species. The Cape pigeon and Wilson's petrel were occasionally to be seen, also a small grey-coloured bird, which is generally found near the pack, the name of which I do not know. We called them 'ice-birds'. Another sign of the nearness of the ice was that the temperature of the air and water had dropped to 32° Fahr. Everything pointed to our proximity to the pack, so we signalled the *Koonya* that we were likely to sight the ice at any moment. I also asked Captain Evans to kill and skin the sheep he was carrying for our supplies, as they would be much more easily transported when the time came to cast off. The weather remained fine with light winds during the night.

Next morning it was fairly thick with occasional light squalls of snow, and about 9 a.m. we saw the ice looming up through the mist to the southward. It seemed to stretch from south-west to south-east, and was apparently the forerunner of the pack. Now had come the time for the *Koonya* to drop us, after a tow of 1510 miles – a record in towage for a vessel not built for the purpose. Before the *Koonya* finally cast off from us, she had achieved another record, by being the first steel vessel to cross the Antarctic Circle.

About 10 a.m. I decided to send Captain England across to the *Koonya* with Buckley and the mail. Our letters were all stamped with the special stamp given by the New Zealand Government. The sea was rising again, and the wind increasing, so we lost no time in making the necessary communication by boat between the two ships. During a favourable roll the whale-boat was dropped into the water, and Buckley, with his weekend handbag, jumped into her. We gave him three cheers as the boat pushed off on its boisterous journey, to the *Koonya*. With his usual forethought, to make matters lighter for the boat crew, Captain Evans had floated a line astern, attached to a life-buoy, and after about twenty-five minutes' hard pulling against wind and sea, the buoy was picked up, and the boat hauled alongside the steamer. I was glad to see the boat coming back again shortly afterwards, for the wind kept increasing and the sea was rising every moment, but in a lull, after pouring oil on the water, we hauled the boat up safely.

A thin line had been brought back from the *Koonya,* and at a signal from us Captain Evans paid out a heavier one, which we hauled on board. He then manoeuvred his ship, so as to get her as near as possible to us, in order that we might haul the carcasses of the sheep on board. Ten of these were lashed on the line, and by dint of pulling hard, we got them on board. Meanwhile the greater part of our crew were working the old-fashioned windlass, getting in slowly, link by link, the port-towing cable, whilst the *Koonya* took in as much of her wire hawser as she conveniently could. Our heavy line was carried away, owing to a sudden strain, before we received the second instalment of water-logged mutton. Captain Evans brought the *Koonya* round our stern, and a heaving-line, to which the sheep were attached, was thrown on board, but as soon as we began to haul in, it broke, and we had the chagrin of seeing our fresh mutton floating away on the billows. It was lost to sight shortly afterwards, but we could locate its position by the albatrosses hovering above, doubtless surprised and delighted with this feast.

About a quarter to one Captain Evans signalled that he was going to cut his hawser, for in the rising sea the two vessels were in dangerous proximity to each other. We saw the axe rise and fall, rise and fall again, and the tie was severed. The *Koonya*'s work was done, and the *Nimrod* was dependent on her own resources at last.

Our consort steamed round us, all hands on both ships cheering, then her bows were set north and she vanished into a grey, snowy mist, homeward bound. We spent a long afternoon struggling to get on board the one hundred and forty fathoms of cable and thirty fathoms of wire that were hanging from our bows. The windlass was worked by means of levers, and all hands were divided into two parties, one section manning the port levers, the other the starboard. All that afternoon, and up to seven o'clock in the evening, they unremittingly, toiled at getting the cable in link by link. At last we were able to proceed, the ship's head was put due south, and we prepared to work our way through the floating belt of pack that guards the approach to the Ross Sea. The weather had cleared, and we passed the ice which we had seen in the morning. It was a fairly loose patch of what appeared to be thick land ice. We gradually made our way through similar streams of ice and small hummocky bergs, most of them between forty and fifty feet in height, but a few reaching a hundred feet.

By 2 a.m. on the morning of January 16, the bergs were much more numerous; perhaps they could hardly be classed as bergs, for their average height was only about twenty feet, and I am of opinion, from what I saw later, that this ice originally formed part of an icefoot from some coast line. None of the ice that we passed through at this time had the slightest resemblance to ordinary pack-ice. About 3 a.m., we entered an area of tabular bergs, varying from eighty to one hundred and fifty feet in height, and all the morning we steamed in beautiful weather with a light northerly wind, through the lanes and streets of a wonderful snowy Venice. Tongue and pen fail in attempting to describe the magic of such a scene. As far as the eye could see from the crow's-nest of the *Nimrod*, the great, white, wall-sided bergs stretched east, west and south, making a striking contrast with the lanes of blue-black water between them. A stillness, weird and uncanny, seemed to have fallen upon everything when we entered the silent water streets of this vast unpeopled white city. Here there was no sign of life, except when one of the little snow petrels, invisible when flying across the glistening bergs, flashed for a moment into sight as it came against the dark water, its pure white wings just skimming the surface. The threshing of our screw raised a small wave astern of the ship, and at times huge masses of ice and snow from the bergs, disturbed by the unaccustomed motion, fell thundering in our wake. Some of these bergs had been weathered into the fantastic shapes more characteristic of the Arctic regions, and from peak and spire flashed out the new caught rays of the morning sun. Beautiful as this scene was, it gave rise to some anxiety in my mind, for I knew that if we were caught in a breeze amidst this maze of floating ice, it would go hard with us. Already an ominous dark cloud was sweeping down from the north, and a few flakes of falling snow heralded the approach of the misty northerly wind. I was unfeignedly thankful, when, about three in the afternoon, I saw from the crow's-nest open water ahead. A few more turnings and twistings through the devious water lanes, and we entered the ice free Ross Sea. This was the first time that a passage had been made into the Ross Sea without the vessel having been held up by pack-ice. I think our success was due to the fact that we were away to the eastward of the pack, which had separated from the land and the barrier, and had drifted in a northwest direction. All my experience goes to prove that the easterly route is the best. Behind us lay the long line of bergs through which we had threaded our way for more than eighty miles from north to south, and which stretched east and west for an unknown distance, but far enough for me to say without exaggeration that there must have been thousands of these floating masses of ice. Whence they had come was open to conjecture; it was possible for them to have drifted from a barrier edge to the eastward of King Edward the Seventh Land. If that were so, the barrier must be much lower than the Great Ice Barrier, and also much more even in height, for the vast majority of the bergs we passed were not more than one hundred and thirty feet high, and seemed to be of a fairly uniform thickness. The lights and shadows on the bergs to the eastward at times almost gave them the appearance of land, but as they were congregated most thickly in this direction, we did not venture to make closer acquaintance with them. Of one thing I am certain, this ice had not long left the parent barrier or coast-line, for there was no sign of weathering or wind action on the sides; and if they had been afloat for even a short period they must infallibly have shown some traces of weathering, as the soft snow was at least fifteen to twenty feet thick. This was apparent when pieces broke off from the bergs, and in one or two cases, where sections had been sheared off the top of particular bergs, evidently by collision with their fellows. There were no indications or signs of embedded rocks or earthly material on the bergs, so I am led to believe that this great mass of ice must have been set free only a short time previously from some barrier edge at no great distance. Our latitude at noon on the 16th was 68° 6′ South, and the longitude 179° 21′ West.

Before we entered the actual line of bergs a couple of seals appeared on the floe ice. I did not see them myself, but from descriptions I gathered that one was a crab-eater, and the other a Weddell seal. A few of the Adelie penguins were observed also, and their quaint walk and insatiable curiosity afforded great amusement to our people, the surprise of the birds on seeing the ship was so thoroughly genuine. Marston, our artist, whose sense of the ludicrous is very fully developed, was in ecstasies at their solemn astonishment and profound concern, and at the way they communicated their feelings to one another by flapping their makeshift wings, craning their necks forward with ruffled feathers, and uttering short squawks. Marston's imitation of the penguin was perfect, and he and the rest of us always responded eagerly to the call on deck whenever we were passing a group of these polar inhabitants.

When we were clear of the icebergs a distinct swell was felt coming from the south, and for once the movement of the ocean was welcome to us, for it showed that we might expect open water ahead. I was fairly confident that we had managed to elude the pack, and without doubt for a ship, well found and capable of fair speed, the passage between the bergs on the meridian down which we steered is preferable to the slower progress through the ordinary pack farther west. I doubt if I would, except under similar circumstances, when time and coal were very precious, risk an old vessel like the *Nimrod*, which steams but slowly in this labyrinth of heavy ice, but a better vessel could make the passage with safety. It may be that in future seasons the Antarctic Ocean in this particular part will be found to be quite ice-free, and a later expedition may be able to work more to the eastward, and solve the riddle as to the existence of land in that neighbourhood.

It was fortunate that we cleared the ice that afternoon, for shortly afterwards the wind increased from the north, and the weather became thick with falling snow.

The temperature was just at freezing-point, and the snow melted on the decks when it fell. Altogether about an inch of snow fell between 2 p.m. and midnight. We saw no ice until eight o'clock next morning (January 17), and then only one small berg. The wind shifted to the south-east, the sky cleared somewhat, and with an open horizon all round we observed no sign of ice at all.

FINNESKO

5

THE ATTEMPT TO REACH
KING EDWARD VII LAND

We were now in the Ross Sea, and it was evident that we had avoided the main pack. Our position at noon was 70° 43′ South latitude, and 178° 58′ East longitude. We were now steering a little more westerly, so as to strike the Barrier well to the east of Barrier Inlet, and also to avoid the heavy pack that previous expeditions had encountered to the east of meridian 160° West, where the ice has always proved impenetrable. In the afternoon the wind blew fresh, and the sky became overcast again, and snow began to fall. This snow differed from that brought by the northerly wind; the northerly snow had consisted of flakes about a quarter of an inch in diameter, while that now met with was formed of small round specks, hard and dry, like sago – the true Antarctic type. Birds now became more numerous. Large numbers of Antarctic petrels circled round and round the ship. Their numbers were so great that as the flights passed close by, the whirring of their wings could be distinctly heard on board.

Towards evening we began to pass a number of small floe-bergs and pack ice. We could not see very far ahead, as the weather was thick, so we steered more to the west to skirt this mass of ice. One berg had evidently been overturned, and also showed signs of having been aground. The Adelie penguins had become much more numerous, and we saw an occasional seal, but too far off to distinguish the species. During the early hours of January 18 we passed a few large bergs, and as morning progressed the wind increased, ranging between south by west and south by east. The ship was pitching to a short sea and as the water coming on board froze on deck and in the stables, we made shift to keep it out by nailing canvas over the gaping holes in the bulwarks. Adams and Mackay were engaged in this very chilly job; Adams, slung in a rope over the side, every now and then got soaked up to the middle when the ship dipped into the sea, and as the temperature of the air was four degrees below freezing-point, his tennis trousers were not of much value for warmth in the circumstances. When he got too cold to continue outside, Mackay took his place, and between them they made a very creditable jury bulwark, which prevented the bulk of the water rushing into the stable. The wind continued with a force of about forty miles an hour, up till midday of the 19th, when it began to take off a little, and the sky broke blue to the northeast; the decks were thickly coated with soft ice, and the fresh water-pumps had frozen up hard.

We were now revelling in the indescribable freshness of the Antarctic that seems to permeate one's being, and which must be responsible for that longing to go again which assails each returned explorer from polar regions. Our position at noon on January 19 was latitude 73° 44′ South and longitude 177° 19′ East. The wind had decreased somewhat by midnight, and though the air remained thick and the sky overcast during the whole of the 20th, the weather was better. We passed through occasional masses of floating ice and large tabular bergs, and at noon were in latitude 74° 45′ South, longitude 179° 21′ East.

On the 21st, the weather grew clear, the temperature was somewhat higher, and the wind light. We observed small flights of snow petrels and Antarctic petrels, and saw a single giant petrel for the first time. There were also several whales spouting in the distance. The same sort of weather continued throughout the day, and similar weather, though somewhat clearer, was experienced on the 22nd. On the morning of the 23rd we saw some very large icebergs, and towards evening these increased in number. They were evidently great masses broken off the Barrier; early in the morning we passed a large tilted berg, yellow with diatoms. On our port side appeared a very heavy pack, in which a number of large bergs were embedded. Our course for these three days was about due south, and we were making good headway under steam.

We were now keeping a sharp look-out for the Barrier, which we expected to see at any moment. A light southeasterly wind blew cold, warning us that we could not be very far away from the ice-sheet. The thermometer registered some twelve degrees of frost, but we hardly felt the cold, for the wind was so dry. At 9.30 a.m. on the 23rd a long, low straight line appeared ahead of the ship. It was the Barrier. After half an hour it disappeared from view, having evidently been only raised into sight as an effect of mirage, but by eleven o'clock the straight line stretching out east and west was in full view, and we rapidly approached it. I had hoped to make the Barrier about the position of what we call the Western Bight, and at noon we could see a point on our starboard, from which the Barrier dropped back. This was evidently the eastern limit of the Western Bight. Shortly after noon we were within a quarter of a mile of the ice-face, and exclamations of wonder and astonishment at the stupendous bulk of the Barrier were drawn from the men who had not seen it before.

We slowly steamed along, noting the various structures of the ice, and were thankful that the weather promised to keep fine, for the inlet to which we were bound could not easily have been picked up in thick weather. The height of the Barrier about this point ranged from a hundred and fifty feet to two hundred feet. In the afternoon, about half past one, we passed an opening in the Barrier trending in a south-easterly direction, but its depth was only about three-quarters of a mile. The eastern point had the form of the bows of a gigantic man-of-war, and reached a height of about two hundred and thirty feet. It was appropriately called 'The Dreadnought'.

As we steamed close in to the Barrier, watching carefully for any sign of an opening, we were able to observe accurately the various changes in the ice-face. In places the wall was perfectly smooth, clean cut from the top to the water-line, in other places it showed signs of vertical cracks, and sometimes deep caverns appeared, which, illuminated by the reflected light, merged from light translucent blue into the deepest sapphire. At times great black patches appeared on the sides of the Barrier in the distance, but as we neared them they were resolved into huge caverns, some of which cut the waterline. One was so large that it would have been possible to have steamed the *Nimrod* through its entrance without touching either side or its top by mast or yard. Looking at the Barrier from some little distance, one would imagine it to be a perfectly even wall of ice; when steaming along parallel with it, however, the impression it gave was that of a series of points, each of which looked as though it might be the horn of a bay. Then when the ship came abeam of it, one would see that the wall only receded for a few hundred yards, and then new points came into view as the ship moved on. In some places a cornice of snow overhung the Barrier top, and again in others the vertical cracks had widened so that some portions of the ice-wall seemed in immediate danger of falling. The vagaries of light and shadow made appearances very deceptive. One inlet we passed had the sides thrown up in little hummocks, not more than ten or fifteen feet high, but until we were fairly close, these irregularities had the appearance of hills.

The weather continued fine and calm. During the voyage of the *Discovery* we always encountered a strong westerly current along the Barrier, but there was absolutely no sign of this here, and the ship was making a good five knots. To the northward of us lay a very heavy pack, interspersed with large ice-bergs, one of which was over two miles long and one hundred and fifty feet high. This pack-ice was much heavier and more rugged than any we had encountered on the previous expedition. Evidently there must have been an enormous breaking away of ice to the eastward, for as far as we could see from the crow's-nest, to the north and east, this ice continued.

About mid-night we suddenly came to the end of a very high portion of the Barrier, and found as we followed round that we were entering a wide shallow bay. This must have been the inlet where Borchgrevink landed in 1900, but it had greatly changed since that time. He describes the bay as

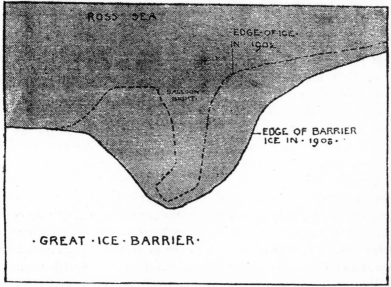

ROSS SEA

EDGE OF ICE. IN 1902

BALLOON BIGHT

EDGE OF BARRIER ICE IN · 1908 ·

· GREAT · ICE · BARRIER ·

BARRIER INLET: DOTTED LINE SHOWS POSITION OF ICE IN 1902

being a fairly narrow inlet. On our way east in the *Discovery* in 1902 we passed an inlet somewhat similar, but we did not see the western end as it was obscured by fog at the time. There seems to be no doubt that the Barrier had broken away at the entrance of this bay or inlet, and so had made it much wider and less deep than it was in previous years. About half a mile down the bay we reached fast ice. It was now about half-past twelve at night, and the southerly sun shone in our faces. Our astonishment was great to see beyond the six or seven miles of flat bay ice, which was about five or six feet thick, high rounded icecliffs, with valleys between, running in an almost east and west direction. About four miles to the south we saw the opening of a large valley, but could not say where it led. Due south of us, and rising to a height of approximately eight hundred feet, were steep and rounded cliffs, and behind them sharp peaks. The southerly sun being low, these heights threw shadows which, for some time, had the appearance of bare rocks. Two dark patches in the face of one of the further cliffs had also this appearance, but a careful observation taken with a telescope showed them to be caverns. To the east rose a long snow slope which cut the horizon at the height of about three hundred feet. It had every appearance of ice-covered land, but we could not stop then to make certain, for the heavy ice and bergs lying to the northward of us were setting down into the bay, and I saw that if we were not to be beset it would be necessary to get away at once. All round us were numbers of great whales showing their dorsal fins as they occasionally sounded, and on the edge of the bay-ice half a dozen Emperor penguins stood lazily observing us. We named this place the Bay of Whales, for it was a veritable playground for these monsters.

We tried to work to the eastward so as once more to get close to the Barrier, which we could see rising over the top of the small bergs and pack-ice, but we found this impossible, and so struck northwards through an open lead and came south to the Barrier again about 2 a.m. on the 24th. We coasted eastward along the wall of ice always on the look-out for the inlet. The lashings had been taken off the motor-car, and the tackle rigged to hoist it out directly we got alongside the ice-foot, to which the *Discovery* had been moored; for in Barrier Inlet we proposed to place our winter quarters.

I must leave the narrative for a moment at this point and refer to the reasons that made me decide on this inlet as the site for the winter quarters. I knew that Barrier Inlet was practically the beginning of King Edward VII Land, and that the actual bare land was within an easy sledge journey of that place, and it had the great advantage of being some ninety miles nearer to the South Pole than any other spot that could be reached with the ship. A further point of importance was that it would be an easy matter for the ship on its return to us to reach this part of the Barrier, whereas King Edward VII Land itself might quite conceivably be unattainable if the season was adverse. Some of my *Discovery* comrades had also considered Barrier Inlet a good place at which to winter. After thinking carefully over the matter I had decided in favour of wintering on the Barrier instead of on actual land, and on the *Koonya*'s departure I had sent a message to the headquarters of the expedition in London to the effect that, in the event of the *Nimrod* not returning at the usual time in 1908, no steps were to be taken to provide a relief ship to search for her in 1909, for it was only likely under those circumstances that she was frozen in; but that if she did not turn up with us in 1909, then the relief expedition should start in December of that year. The point to which they should first direct their search was to be Barrier Inlet, and if we were not found there they were to search the coast of King Edward VII Land. I had added that it would only be by stress of most unexpected circumstances that the ship would be unable to return to New Zealand.

However, the best-laid schemes often prove impracticable in Polar exploration, and within a few hours our first plan was found impossible of fulfilment. Within thirty-six hours a second arrangement had to be abandoned. We were steaming along westward close to the Barrier, and according to the chart we were due to be abreast of the inlet about 6 a.m., but not a sign was there of the opening. We had passed Borchgrevink's Bight at 1 a.m., and at 8 p.m. were well past the place where Barrier Inlet ought to have been. The Inlet had disappeared, owing to miles of the Barrier having calved away, leaving a long wide bay joining up with Borchgrevink's Inlet, and the whole was now merged into what we had called the Bay of Whales. This

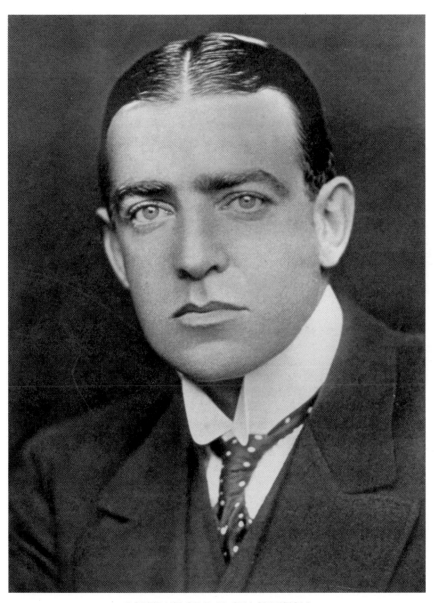

PORTRAIT OF E. H. SHACKLETON

MARSTON   DAVID   MAWSON   MACKAY

SHACKLETON   ADAMS   WILD   MARSHALL

MURRAY   ARMYTAGE   ROBERTS   MACKINTOSH

JOYCE   BROCKLEHURST   DAY   PRIESTLEY

THEIR MAJESTIES THE KING AND QUEEN INSPECTING THE EQUIPMENT
ON THE *NIMROD* AT COWES

TRAINING THE PONIES ON QUAIL ISLAND, PORT LYTTELTON

A PHOTOGRAPH TAKEN FROM THE *NIMROD* AS THE EXPEDITION WAS
LEAVING LYTTELTON. OVER 30, 000 PEOPLE WATCHED THE DEPARTURE.

THE *NIMROD* PASSING H.M.S *POWERFUL,* FLAGSHIP OF THE AUSTRALASIAN
SQUADRON, IN LYTTELTON HARBOUR

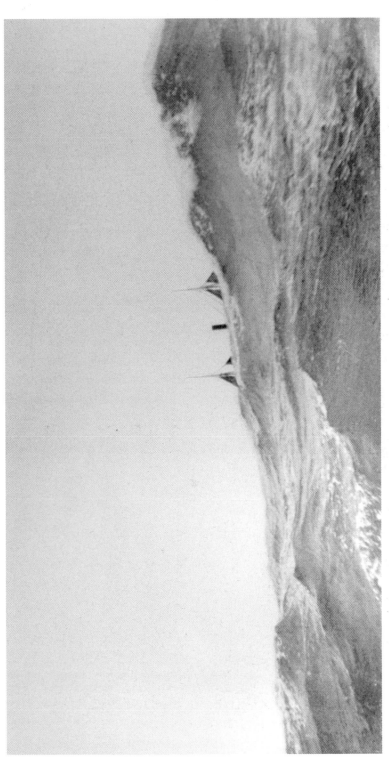

THE TOWING STEAMER *KOONYA*, AS SEEN FROM THE *NIMROD*, IN A HEAVY SEA. THIS PARTICULAR WAVE CAME ABOARD THE *NIMROD* AND DID CONSIDERABLE DAMAGE.

MOUNTAINOUS SEAS

HAULING MUTTON FROM THE *KOONYA* TO THE *NIMROD* BEFORE THE
VESSELS PARTED COMPANY WITHIN THE ANTARCTIC CIRCLE

THE *NIMROD* PUSHING THROUGH HEAVY PACK ICE ON HER WAY SOUTH

TWO VIEWS OF THE GREAT ICE BARRIER. THE WALL OF ICE WAS 90 FEET
AT THE POINT SHOWN IN THE FIRST PICTURE, AND 120 FEET HIGH AT
THE POINT WHERE THE SECOND VIEW WAS TAKEN

THE *NIMROD* PUSHING HER WAY THROUGH MORE OPEN PACK TOWARDS KING EDWARD VII LAND

SOUNDING ROUND A STRANDED BERG IN ORDER TO SEE WHETHER THE
SHIP COULD LIE THERE

THE *NIMROD* MOORED TO THE STRANDED BERG, ABOUT A MILE FROM
THE WINTER QUARTERS. THE *NIMROD* SHELTERED IN THE LEE OF
THIS BERG DURING BLIZZARDS.

THE FIRST LANDING-PLACE, SHOWING BAY ICE BREAKING OUT AND
DRIFTING AWAY NORTH

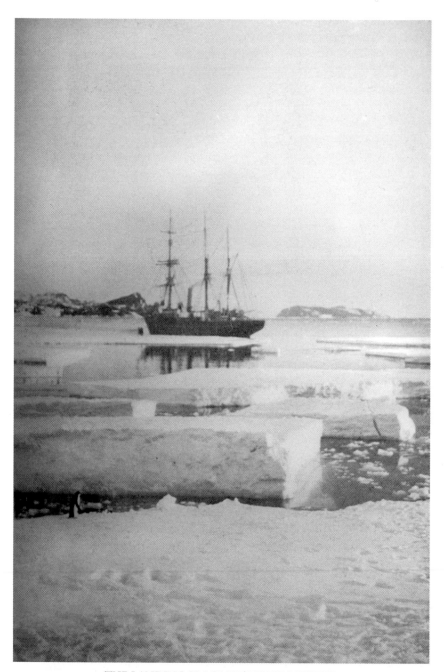

THE LANDING-PLACE WHARF BROKEN UP

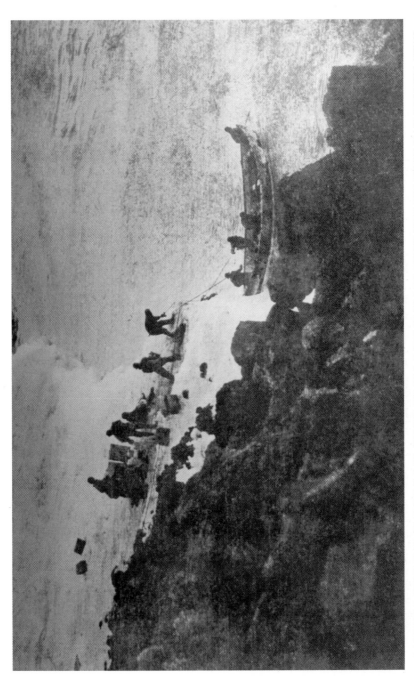

LANDING STORES FROM THE BOAT AT THE FIRST LANDING-PLACE AFTER THE ICE-FOOT HAD BROKEN AWAY

DERRICK POINT, SHOWING THE METHOD OF HAULING STORES
UP THE CLIFF

was a great disappointment to us, but we were thankful that the Barrier had broken away before we had made our camp on it. It was bad enough to try and make for a port that had been wiped off the face of the earth, when all the intending inhabitants were safe on board the ship, but it would have been infinitely worse if we had landed there whilst the place was still in existence, and that when the ship returned to take us off she should find the place gone. The thought of what might have been made me decide then and there that under no circumstances would I winter on the Barrier, and that wherever we did land we would secure a solid rock foundation for our winter home.

We had two strings to our bow, and I decided to use the second at once and push forward towards King Edward VII Land. Just after eight a.m. on the 24th we turned a corner in the Barrier, where it receded about half a mile, before continuing to the eastward again. The line of its coast here made a right angle and the ice sloped down to sea-level at the apex of the angle, but the slope was too steep and too heavily crevassed for us to climb up and look over the surface if we had made landing.

We tied the ship up to a fairly large floe, and I went down to England's cabin to talk the matter over. In the corner where we were lying there were comparatively few pieces of floe ice, but outside us lay a very heavy pack, in which several large bergs were locked. Our only chance was to go straight on, keeping close to the Barrier, as a lane of open water was left between the Barrier and the edge of the pack to the north of us. Sights were taken for longitude by four separate observers, and the positions calculated showed us we were not only well to the eastward of the place where Barrier Inlet was shown on the chart, but also that the Barrier had receded at this particular point since January 1902.

About nine o'clock we cast off from the floe and headed the ship to the eastward, again keeping a few hundred yards off the Barrier, for just here the cliff overhung, and if a fall of ice had occurred while we were close in the results would certainly have been disastrous for us. I soon saw that we would not be able to make much casting in this way, for the Barrier was now trending well to the north-east, and right ahead of us lay an impenetrably close pack, set with huge icebergs. By 10 a.m. we were close to the pack and found that it was pressed hard against the Barrier edge, and, what was worse, the whole of the northern pack and bergs at this spot were drifting in towards the Barrier. The seriousness of this situation can be well realised by the reader if he imagines for a moment that he is in a small boat right under the vertical white cliffs of Dover; that detached cliffs are moving in from seaward slowly but surely, with stupendous force and resistless power, and that it would only be a question of perhaps an hour or two before the two masses came into contact with his tiny craft between.

There was nothing for it but to retrace our way and try some other route.

Our position was latitude 78° 20′ South and longitude 162° 14′ West when the ship turned. The pack had already moved inside the point of the cliff where we had lain in open water at eight o'clock, but by steaming hard and working in and out of the looser floes we just managed to pass the point at 11.20 a.m. with barely fifty yards of open water to spare between the Barrier and the pack.

I breathed more freely when we passed this zone of immediate danger, for there were two or three hundred yards of clear water now between us and the pack. We were right under the Barrier cliff, which was here over two hundred and fifty feet high, and our course lay well to the south of west, being roughly south-west true; so as we moved south more quickly than the advancing ice we were able to keep close along the Barrier, which gradually became lower, until about three o'clock we were abreast of some tilted bergs at the eastern entrance of the Bay of Whales. There was a peculiar light which rendered distances and the forms of objects very deceptive, and a great deal of mirage, which made things appear much higher than they actually were. This was particularly noticeable in the case of the pack-ice; the whole northern and western sea seemed crowded with huge icebergs, though in reality there was only heavy pack. The penguins that we had seen the previous night were still at the same place, and when a couple of miles away from us they loomed up as if they were about six feet high. This bay ice, on which many seals were lying, was cracking, and would soon float away, with one or two large icebergs embedded in it.

Skirting along the seaward edge we came to the high cliff of ice at the westerly end, and passed safely out of the bay' at ten minutes to four. We then continued to the westward, still having the heavy pack to the north. One berg that we passed was a temporary resting-place for hundreds of Antarctic and snow petrels, and these took flight as we approached. About 6 p.m. the pack-ice seemed to loosen somewhat, and by half-past seven, from the crow's-nest, I could see a lead of open water to the north through the belt of pack, and beyond that there appeared to be a fairly open sea. About eight o'clock the ship's head was put north, and we soon gained a fairly open sea, occasionally having to make *détours* round the heavier packed floes, though we were able to push aside the lighter pieces. At midnight, our easterly progress was arrested by a line of thick conglomerated pack, and we had to steer north for nearly an hour before we could again set the course easterly. It is remarkable how limited one's horizon is at sea, for from the crow's-nest, after passing this belt of pack, there appeared to be open water for an indefinite distance, yet by two o'clock we were up against the rigid ice again. Low pack-ice is not visible at any great distance, and one could not trust an appearance of open water, even with the wide horizon obtained from the crow's-nest. All night long we followed a zig-zag course in the endeavour to penetrate to the east, at times steering due west, practically doubling on our tracks, before we could find an opening which would admit of our pursuing the direction we desired to follow. During the night it had been somewhat cloudy towards the south, but about 3 a.m. it became quite clear over the Barrier, and we saw to our disappointment that we had made hardly any progress to the eastward, for we were at that hour only just abeam of the Bay of Whales. About half-past seven in the morning we passed a huge berg, nearly three miles in length and over two hundred feet in height, and at eight o'clock the sea became much more open; indeed, there was no ice in sight to the east at all. It was a bright, sunny morning, and things looked much more hopeful as I left the bridge for a sleep, after having been on deck all night.

When I came up again, just before noon on January 25, I found that my hopes for a clear run were vain. Our noon observations showed that we were well to the north of the Barrier, and still to the westward of the point we had reached the previous morning before we had been forced to turn round. The prospect of reaching King Edward VII Land seemed to grow more remote every ensuing hour. There was high hummocky pack interspersed with giant icebergs to the east and south of the ship, and it was obvious that the whole sea between Cape Colbeck and the Barrier at our present longitude must be full of ice. To the northward the strong ice blink on the horizon told the same tale. It seemed as if it would be impossible to reach the land, and the shortness of coal, the leaky condition of the ship, and the absolute necessity of landing all our stores and putting up the hut before the vessel left us made the situation an extremely anxious one for me. I had not expected to find Barrier Inlet gone, and, at the same time, the way to King Edward VII Land absolutely blocked by ice, though the latter condition was not unusual, for every expedition in this longitude up till 1901 had been held up by the pack; indeed Ross, in this locality, sailed for hundreds of miles to the northward along the edge of a similar pack on this meridian. It is true that we had steam, but the *Discovery*, or even the *Yermak*, the most powerful ice-breaker ever built, would have made no impression upon the cemented field of ice.

I decided to continue to try and make a way to the east for at least another twenty-four hours. We altered the course to the north, skirting the ice as closely as possible, and taking advantage of the slightest trend to the eastward, at times running into narrow *culs-de-sac* in the main pack, only to find it necessary to retrace our way again. The wind began to freshen from the west, and the weather to thicken. A little choppy sea washed over the edges of the floes, and the glass was falling. About five o'clock some heavy squalls of snow came down, and we had to go dead slow, for the horizon was limited at times to a radius of less than one hundred yards. Between the squalls it was fairly clear, and we could make out great numbers of long, low bergs, one of which was over five miles in length, though not more than forty feet high. The waves were splashing up against the narrow end as we passed within a couple of cables' length of the berg, and almost immediately afterwards another squall swept down upon us. The weather cleared again shortly, and we saw the western pack moving rapidly towards us under the influence of the wind; in some places it had already met the main pack. As it was most likely that we would be caught in this great mass of ice, and that days, or even weeks might elapse before we could extricate ourselves, I reluctantly gave orders to turn the ship and make full speed out of this dangerous situation. I could see nothing for it except to steer for McMurdo Sound, and there make our winter quarters. For many reasons I would have preferred landing at King Edward VII Land, as that region was absolutely unknown. A fleeting glimpse of bare rocks and high snow slopes was all that we obtained of it on the *Discovery* expedition, and had we been able to establish our winter quarters there, we could have added greatly to the knowledge of the geography of that region. There would perhaps have been more difficulty in the attempt to reach the South Pole from that base, but I did not expect that the route from there to the Barrier surface, from which we could make a fair start for the Pole, would have been impracticable. I did not give up the destined base of our expedition without a strenuous struggle, as the track of the ship given in the sketch-map shows; but the forces of these uncontrollable ice-packs are stronger than human resolution, and a change of plan was forced upon us.

6

THE SELECTION OF
WINTER QUARTERS

It was with a heavy heart that I saw our bows swinging round to the west, and realised that for a year at least we would see nothing of the land which we had hoped to have made our winter quarters. We turned to the westward about eight o'clock that night, watching the ice carefully as we went along, and up to one o'clock on the morning of January 26 there was not a break in the close-set pack to the northward of us. We then lost sight of the ice in the mist. The glass was unsteady, and the wind somewhat gusty from the south-west, with a choppy sea. About six o'clock on the morning of the 26th, the ship's head was put south, for I wanted to pick up the Barrier and follow it along at least as far as the Western Bight, before setting the course direct for Mount Erebus. We passed the inlet we had seen on our way east, and about twelve o'clock were abreast of the eastern point of Western Bight. We now laid our course for Mount Erebus, and as I hoped to examine the Barrier more closely in the following year we made a direct course west, which took us some distance off the edge of the ice. The weather was fine and clear, excepting for a low stratus cloud over the Barrier; this lifted later in the day, but before evening we had entirely lost sight of the ice-face. There was an extraordinary absence of bird-life of any description, but whales were blowing all round us, some coming right alongside the ship. We had so far seen fewer of the snow petrels and many more of the Antarctic petrels than during the previous expedition. On this day we saw one albatross of the sooty species, and a couple of giant petrels. The wind was westerly all day, and towards the evening there were one or two slight snow squalls. Our position at noon on the 26th was latitude 78° 9′ South, and longitude 178° 43′ West, and the air temperature had risen to 28° Fahr.

On the 28th, the weather kept fine, though the sky was practically covered with cloud. A great arch of clear sky rose in the south about noon; shortly before this a curious whitish appearance gave one the impression of land, and as the sky cleared this became more distinct, and proved to be Erebus and Terror, the two huge mountains we were approaching. By 2 p.m. they had grown much more distinct, and were evidently raised by mirage to even statelier altitudes than their own. We could plainly see the smoke from Mount Erebus, which from our point of view showed to the south of Mount Terror. We altered the course a little so as to make Cape Crozier. I had some thoughts of placing a depot there to be handy for any party that might go over from winter quarters to study penguin life, but on second thoughts decided not to delay the ship. Our noon position put us in latitude 77° 6′ South, and longitude 175° 35′ East. We passed Cape Crozier, where the Barrier meets the land some distance off, about ten o'clock that night. The weather was beautifully fine and clear, and except for an occasional berg and a few pieces of heavy floe, there was no ice visible. We steamed fairly close in along the coast, and at 3 a.m. were abreast of Erebus Bay. To the north-west of us was Beaufort Island showing a precipitous rock face on its eastern side; Cape Bird was just on our port bow. The weather was overcast and snowy as we turned Cape Bird at 5.30 a.m. on January 29. We hoped to reach our new winter quarters without more opposition from the ice. As we steamed down McMurdo Sound we passed through occasional loose patches of pack-ice, on which immense numbers of penguins were congregated.

There was a great deal more ice to the west, and a strong ice blink gave indication that it must be heavily packed right up to the western shore. Passing down the sound, and keeping well to the east and close under the land, we observed a long, low sandy beach, terminating landwards in a steep slope, the whole place for an area of about two square miles yellow and pink with penguin guano. It was a large penguin rookery.

We passed but little ice till about ten o'clock, but within an hour after that we could see the fast ice ahead of us, and by half-past eleven we were brought up against it. It was now January 29, and some twenty miles of frozen sea separated us from Hut Point, where we hoped to make our winter quarters. The ice at the spot at which we were first stopped by it was very much decayed and covered with about a foot of snow. We tried to break through it by ramming, but the attempt was not a success, for the ship entered about half her length into the sludgy mass, and then stuck, without producing a crack in front. We backed out again, and, when some little distance away, put on full speed, ramming the ship up against the ice-edge. This second attempt was equally futile, so the ice anchor was made fast to the floe, while we considered some better plan of action.

The weather had cleared somewhat, and we were able to see our surroundings. To the south lay the Delbridge Islands, and beyond appeared the sharp peak of Observation Hill under which lay the winter quarters of the last expedition. Castle Rock, towering above other local heights, seemed like an old friend, and White Island was dimly seen beneath the rising pall of cloud. To the south-west Black Island and Brown Island showed up distinctly, and behind the former we could trace the rounded lines of Mount

Discovery. To the west were the gigantic peaks of the western mountains with their huge amphitheatres and immense glaciers. About seven miles to the eastward lay a dark mass of rock, Cape Royds, named after the first lieutenant of the *Discovery*. So familiar were they that it seemed as though it were only yesterday that I had looked on the scene, and yet six years had gone by.

During the day we had occasional falls of light, dry snow, and the air temperature at times went down to 11° Fahr., although this was the height of summer. The wind continued southerly but with no great force, and now we would have welcomed even a heavy blizzard to break- up the ice. A northerly swell would have been better still, for a few hours of this would make short work of the miles of ice that now formed an impenetrable bar to our ship. When the SY *Morning*, the first relief ship to the *Discovery*, arrived about January 23, 1902, there was a similar amount of ice in the sound, and it was not till February 28 that she got within five miles of Hut Point, and the ice did not break out up to the Point at all during that year. The following year both the *Terra Nova* and the *Morning* arrived at the ice-face about January 4, and found that the sound was frozen over for twenty miles out from Hut Point. Yet by February 15, the ice had broken away to the south of Hut Point, and the *Discovery* was free. With only these two diverse experiences on which to base any theory as to the probable action of the ice, it will easily be seen that the problem was a difficult one for me. If I kept the ship for two weeks in the hope of the ice breaking up, and it did not do so, we would then be in a very serious position, for it would take nearly a fortnight to land all the stores and get the hut up, and this could only be done after selecting new winter quarters somewhere in the neighbourhood, either on the west coast or on one of the bare patches of rocks lying to the eastward of us. The outlook to the west was not promising, for about five or six miles to the west of where we were lying the ice was heavily packed. To the eastward it seemed more hopeful.

I decided to lie off the ice-foot for a few days at least, and give Nature a chance to do what we could not with the ship, that is, to break up the miles of ice intervening between us and our goal. We seemed fated to meet with obstacles in every attempt we made to carry out our plans, but remembered in these somewhat anxious times that obstacles are the common lot of Polar explorers, and that indeed the game would not be worth playing if there were not difficulties. My chief anxiety was due to the fact that each day's delay at the ice-foot would mean a diminution of our scanty stock of coal, for it was necessary to keep up steam that we might be ready to move at a moment's notice in the event of the ice packing down on us from the north, or the breaking away of the floe to which we were fast. The latter circumstance indeed was a constant occurrence; either the ice broke bodily away, or a slight breeze would catch the ship and draw the anchor out of the floe. Then we had to steam up and get a fresh grip. The plan of sledging the stores across the distance intervening between us and Hut Point I soon dismissed as impracticable, for even if the ponies had been in perfect condition, and it had been possible to use the motor-car, we could never have shifted the hundred and eighty odd tons of equipment in the time available.

I was troubled at this time in regard to the health of Captain England; he did not seem at all well, and it was evident that the strain of the bad weather we had encountered, and more especially of the difficulties in the ice had told upon him. Our circumstances at the time were not likely to afford him much rest. He was naturally anxious to get the ship away as soon as possible, as he felt that she could not be much depended on for sailing, but I could not see my way to fixing an actual date for the *Nimrod*'s departure, especially in view of the fact that I did not even know where our winter quarters were to be.

On the evening of January 29 we took the sides and top off the motor-car case and put the wheels on the car, for I hoped to try it on the floe. The member of the staff in charge was Day, who soon had the engine running, and the following morning, the 30th, though the temperature was low, it seemed to go without any hitch. Its behaviour on the floe, where the snow was lying deep, had yet to be tested. We put on the light wheels and Dunlop tyres and the non-skid chains, for we had hopes that it might be unnecessary to use the heavier wheels, and we wished to have everything ready.

During the day a fresh breeze sprang up from the south-east with drifting snow, and the vessel soon assumed a wintry appearance. At meal times on this day everybody crowded into the wardroom for warmth, as it was no longer possible to take one's food standing by the galley door. The ship broke from her anchors two or three times, and the ice to which she had been attached drifted away to the north, and though the pieces were only about a hundred yards long our hopes were raised, for we felt that the ice was beginning to break up, though we realised that if only a few hundred yards shifted in a day it would take too long for a mass of ice, twenty miles broad, to go out, and enable us to get to Hut Point in time to discharge her stores.

All day long Killer whales in large numbers had been rising and blowing near the ice. They came right alongside the ship, and every now and then we could see one rear itself on end and poke its head over the ice-edge on the lookout for a seal. On one occasion we saw a seal suddenly shoot out of the water on to the floe-edge and hurry into safety with almost incredible speed for an animal of such unwieldy proportions. It travelled at least a quarter of a mile over the firm ice before pausing for breath. A minute or two later the cause of this extreme haste became evident, for the huge sinister head of a Killer slowly reared itself out of the water and gazed round for its intended victim. We have never seen a seal captured by one of these monsters, but undoubtedly they must fall victims sometimes, for the Killer is always hanging round the ice, poking his head up amongst the loose floes, and the manifest alarm of seals lying there, and their quick retreat to a more secure position away from the water can only be explained as the struggle to escape from a known danger. There were many Adelie penguins about, and it was amusing to watch them forming up in line on the edge of the ice, and then diving in turn into the sea, like swimmers in a handicap race. A couple of minutes might elapse before they appeared again.

We unfastened most of the beams of the pony shelter, so that there would be no difficulty in getting the ponies out at a moment's notice, and removed a lot of the top hamper from the skids. Most of the poor beasts were in bad condition. Those which were white all over seemed, for some reason, to have stood the rough weather better than the parti-coloured ones, but all were enjoying the steadiness of the ship after the terrible rolling. The flanks of most of the horses had been skinned by the constant knocking and rubbing against the sides of their stalls, and Zulu was in such a bad condition from this cause that I decided to have him shot at once. This left us with eight ponies, and we considered ourselves fortunate in reaching winter quarters with the loss of only two animals.

So far the voyage had been without accident to any of the staff, but on the morning of the 31st, when all hands were employed getting stores out of the after-hatch, preparatory to landing them, a hook on the tackle slipped and, swinging suddenly across the deck, struck Mackintosh in the right eye. He fell on the deck in great pain, but was able, in a few minutes, to walk with help to England's cabin, where Marshall examined him. It was apparent that the sight of the eye was completely destroyed, so he was put under chloroform, and Marshall removed the eye, being assisted at the operation by the other two doctors, Michell and Mackay. It was a great comfort to me to know that the expedition had the services of thoroughly good surgeons. Mackintosh felt the loss of his eye keenly; not so much because the sight was gone, but because it meant that he could not remain with us in the Antarctic. He begged to be allowed to stay, but when Marshall explained that he might lose the sight of the other eye, unless great care were taken, he accepted his ill-fortune without further demur, and thus the expedition lost, for a time, one of its most valuable members.

Whilst we were waiting at the ice I thought it as well that a small party should proceed to Hut Point, and report on the condition of the hut left there by the *Discovery* expedition, for it was possible that, after five years' disuse, it might be drifted up with snow. I decided to send Adams, Joyce and Wild, giving Adams instructions to get into the hut, and then return the next day to the ship. We were then about sixteen miles from Hut Point, and the party started off the next morning with plenty of provisions in case of being delayed, and a couple of spades with which to dig out the hut. It was Adams' first experience of sledging, and a fifteen or sixteen-mile march with a fairly heavy load was a stiff proposition for men who had been cooped up in the ship for over a month. They started at a good swinging pace. The Professor and Cotton met the party some two or three miles away from the ship, and accompanied them for another mile. On their return they reported that the sledge-party had got on to old ice that had not broken out the previous year. The ice across which the party had started was about four feet thick, and much more solid than that which stopped the ship on our first arrival. It was one-year ice, but I think it quite possible that it had broken out earlier and frozen in again.

During the previous night we had moved somewhat further west and tied up to the floe, after another ineffectual attempt to break through to the south. Shortly after the sledge-party started we hoisted the motor-car over the side and landed it safely on the sea-ice. Day immediately got in, started the engine, and off the car went with the throbbing sound which has become so familiar in the civilised world, and was now heard for the first time in the Antarctic. The run was but a short one, for within a hundred yards the wheels clogged in the soft snow. With all hands pushing and pulling we managed to get the car across a crack in the ice, which we momentarily expected would open out, and allow the floe to drift away to the north. Once over the crack the engine was started again, and for a short distance the car went ahead under its own power, but it was held up again by the snow. By dint of more pushing and pulling, and with the help of its own engine, the car reached a point about half a mile south of the ship, but our hopes as to the future practical utility of the machine were considerably damped. We could not accurately judge of the merits of the car on this trial, for it had not been fitted with the proper wheels for travelling in snow, and the engine was not tuned up to working efficiency. There was no difficulty with the ignition, for it sparked at once, in spite of there being at the time 17° of frost. We left the car at one o'clock and went on board to lunch, and, on coming back, found a couple of Adelie penguins on the ice solemnly eyeing the strange arrival. More cracks had opened up near the car, and as there was no prospect of it helping us to reach the land at this time I decided to have it hauled back to the ship and hoisted on board at once, to await a more favourable opportunity for a thorough test. Ignominiously it was hauled through the snow until it got within a hundred yards of the ship where the ice was harder. Then, with a puff and a snort, it ran up alongside. In the morning I had had dreams of mounting the car with Day and gaily overtaking the sledge-party as they toiled over the ice, but these dreams were short-lived.

In the afternoon we hauled our anchor in and steamed west to have a look at the situation of the ice on the western coast, but we had not gone four miles before we were brought up by ice, and we returned to our old moorings. That evening most of our staff tasted skua gull for dinner for the first time, and pronounced it delicious. The method of catching these birds was simple and efficient, if not exactly sporting. A baited hook and line was thrown on to the floe, and in a couple of minutes a skua would walk up to the bait and swallow it, only to find himself being dragged towards the ship. His companions did not seem to realise that their comrade was in any difficulty, but appeared to think rather that he had some particularly dainty morsel of which they were being deprived, for they at once proceeded to attack him in the hope of making him disgorge. About ten or twelve skuas were caught in this way before they began to suspect that anything was amiss, but when they did realise the situation, the lure of the most dainty bits of meat proved ineffectual. In the afternoon we also killed a couple of Weddell seals and next morning had bacon and fresh seal liver for breakfast.

There was no perceptible change in the state of the ice on February 2, though occasional floes were breaking off, and as the weather kept fine a party consisting of Professor David, Mawson, Cotton, Priestly and Armytage started off across the ice bound for Inaccessible Island. I went out with England towards the south on ski to examine the ice for cracks, but the result of our walk was not at all satisfactory, for the ice was firm and the only cracks were those alongside the ship. I therefore decided to wait no longer at the ice-face, but, when the sledge-party returned, to seek for winter quarters on the east coast of Ross Island. Early in the afternoon a breeze sprang up from the eastward, the sky became overcast, and a slight drift blew across the fast ice. The loose ice drifted rapidly from the eastward, so the ship was backed into clear water, and it was well that this was done, for shortly afterwards the loose ice over-rode the solid floe and would have given the ship a nasty squeeze had she been lying at her former moorings. On the wind springing up in the afternoon, the recall flag had been hoisted as a signal to the party ashore, but they did not see it, and it was nearly five o'clock before they turned up. We had, by that time, remoored the ship about a mile to the eastward of our former position. The Professor reported that they had been unable to land on the island, as about fifty yards of water intervened between the ice and the bare land. They found a sea urchin on the ice, and Murray at once claimed it for his collection. They had learned the first lesson of the Antarctic, which is, that distances are very deceptive, and that land is always much more distant than it appears to be.

This evening we kept a lookout for the return of the sledge travellers, but there was no sign of them by bedtime. I knew that Adams would be sure to return unless his party had found much difficulty in effecting an entrance into the hut. At half-past one in the morning Harboard came down and reported that he could see the party coming along in the distance. Of course at this time we had perpetual daylight and there was practically no difference between day and night. I had some cocoa and sardines prepared for them, for I knew from experience how comforting is this fare to a way-worn sledger. Adams, on his arrival, reported that they had had a very heavy march on the way to the hut, and had not reached it till a quarter to twelve at night, having been going since 10 a.m. The surface for the last two miles had been smooth ice, clear of snow, and a large pool of open water lay off the end of Hut Point. The bay in which the *Discovery* had been frozen in was covered with clear blue ice, showing that in the previous season the sea-ice had not broken out. They were so tired that they turned into their sleeping-bags inside the hut directly they made an entrance which was easily done through one of the lee windows. They found the hut practically clear of snow, and the structure quite intact. There was a small amount of ice inside on the walls, evidently the result of a summer thaw, but even after five years' desertion, the building was in excellent preservation. A few relics of the last expedition were lying about, including bags containing remnants of provisions from various sledging-parties. Amongst these provisions was an open tin of tea, and the following morning the party made an excellent brew from the contents. It speaks volumes for the dryness of the climate that the tea should retain its flavour after exposure to the air for five years. A sledging-tin of petroleum was also used and was found to be in perfect condition. The ice on the end of Hut Point was cracked and crevassed, but in all other respects things seemed to be the same as when the *Discovery* steamed away to the north in February 1904. The cross put up in memory of Vince, who lost his life close by in a blizzard, was still standing, and so were the magnetic huts. At 1 p.m. the following day the three sledgers set out for the ship, and though they had the assistance of an extemporised sail, rigged to take advantage of the southerly wind, they found the travelling very heavy, and were heartily glad to get on board the *Nimrod* again.

In the morning we moved close in towards Inaccessible Island, as the ice seemed to have broken out right up to it, but on getting near we saw there was still a large amount stretching between the ship and the island. Soundings here gave us 298 fathoms, with a bottom of volcanic pebbles. We tied up again to the ice, and during the afternoon the shore-party filled the little tank on top of the boiler-room grating with snow, and the resulting water made the tea much more pleasant than the water from the ship's tanks to which we had been accustomed.

About four o'clock we got under way and started towards Cape Barne on the lookout for a suitable landing-place. About two miles off the point, at 6 p.m., a sounding of seventy-nine fathoms was obtained, and half a mile further in the depth was forty-four fathoms. The arming of the lead was covered with sponge spicules, suggesting that this place would be a fine hunting-ground for the biologist. Steaming slowly north along the coast we saw across the bay a long, low snow-slope, connected with the bare rock of Cape Royds, which appeared to be a likely place for winter quarters.

About eight o'clock, accompanied by Adams and Wild in the whale boat, and taking the hand lead with us, I left the ship and went in towards the shore. After about ten minutes' pulling, with frequent stops for soundings, we came up against fast ice. This covered the whole of the small bay from the corner of Flagstaff Point, as we afterwards named the seaward cliff at the southern end of Cape Royds, to Cape Barne to the southward. Close up to the Point the ice had broken out, leaving a little natural dock. We ran the boat into this, and Adams and I scrambled ashore, crossing a well-defined tide-track and going up a smooth snow-slope about fifteen yards wide, at the top of which was bare rock. Hundreds of penguins were congregated on the bay ice, and hundreds more on the top of the slope, and directly we reached the bare land our nostrils were greeted with the overbearing stench of the rookery where were many hundreds of the Adelie penguins. These were moving to and fro, and they greeted us with hoarse squawks of excitement. Above them were flying many of their natural enemies, the rapacious skua gulls. These birds had young, for as we walked along, evidently nearing the nestlings, they began to swoop down on us, almost touching our heads, and the sharp whirr of their rapidly moving wings told us how strongly they resented our intrusion.

A very brief examination of the vicinity of the ice-foot was sufficient to show us that Cape Royds would make an excellent place on which to land our stores. We therefore shoved off in the boat again, and, skirting along the ice-foot to the south, sounded the bay, and found that the water deepened from two fathoms close in shore to about twenty fathoms four hundred yards further south. After completing these soundings we pulled out towards the ship, which had been coming in very slowly. We were pulling along at a good rate when suddenly a heavy body shot out of the water, struck the seaman who was pulling stroke, and dropped with a thud into the bottom of the boat. The arrival was an Adelie penguin. It was hard to say who was the most astonished – the penguin, at the result of its leap on to what it had doubtless thought was a rock, or we, who so suddenly took on board this curious passenger. The sailors in the boat looked upon this incident as an omen of good luck. There is a tradition amongst seamen that the souls of old sailors, after death, occupy the bodies of penguins, as well as of albatrosses; this idea, however, does not prevent the mariners from making a hearty meal off the breasts of the former when opportunity offers. We arrived on board at 9 p.m., and by 10 p.m. on February 3 the *Nimrod* was moored to the bay ice, ready to land the stores.

Immediately after securing the ship I went ashore, accompanied by the

Professor, England, and Dunlop, to choose a place for building the hut. We passed the penguins, which were marching solemnly to and fro, and on reaching the level land, made for a huge boulder of kenyte, the most conspicuous mark in the locality. I thought that we might build the hut under the lee of this boulder, sheltered from the south-east wind, but the situation had its drawbacks, as it would have entailed a large amount of levelling before the foundation of the hut could have been laid. We crossed a narrow ridge of rock just beyond the great boulder, and, turning a little to the right up a small valley, found an ideal spot for our winter quarters. The floor of this valley was practically level and covered with a couple of feet of volcanic earth; at the sides the bed rock was exposed, but a rough eye measurement was quite sufficient to show that there would be not only ample room for the hut itself, but also for all the stores, and for a stable for the ponies. A hill right behind this little valley would serve as an excellent shelter to the hut from what we knew was the prevailing strong wind, that is, the southeaster. A glance at the illustrations will give the reader a much better idea of this place than will a written description, and he will see how admirably Nature had provided us with a protection against her own destructive forces.

After deciding on this place as our home for the winter we went round a ridge to the south, and on a level piece of ground overlooking the bay we came across the camp where Captain Scott and Dr Wilson spent some days in January, 1904, whilst they were waiting for the arrival of the relief ship. The camp had been placed in a splendid position, with an uninterrupted view of the sea to the north and the great panorama of the Western Mountains. We found all the camp gear and cooking utensils just as they had been left, and, considering the exposed position of the camp, it appeared as though this spot could not have been subjected to very violent storms, otherwise the tent cloths, empty boxes, and other things lying about would have been blown away. From the top of the ridge we could see a small bay inside the wide one in which the ship was lying, and a little more to the eastward was a smaller bay, the end of which formed the sea limit to this part of the coast. A number of seals lying on the bay ice gave promise that there could be no lack of fresh meat.

With this ideal situation for a camp, and everything else satisfactory, including a supply of water from a lake right in front of our little valley, I decided that we could not do better than start getting our gear ashore at once. There was only one point that gave me any anxiety, and that was as to whether the sea would freeze over between this place and Hut Point in ample time for us to get across for the southern and western journeys in the following spring. It was also obvious that nothing could be done in the way of laying out depots for the next season's work, as directly the ship left we would be cut off from any communication with the lands to the south of us, by sea and by land, for the heavily crevassed glaciers fringing the coast were an effectual bar to a march with sledges. However, time was pressing, and we were fortunate to get winter quarters as near as this to our starting-point for the south.

COOKER AND PRIMUS STOVE

7

THE LANDING OF STORES
AND EQUIPMENT

We returned to the ship to start discharging our equipment, and with this work commenced the most uncomfortable fortnight, and the hardest work, full of checks and worries, that I or any other member of the party had ever experienced. If it had not been for the whole-hearted devotion of our party, and their untiring energy, we would never have got through the long toil of discharging. Day and night, if such terms of low latitudes can be used in a place where there was no night, late and early, they were always ready to turn to, in face of most trying conditions, and always with a cheerful readiness. If a fresh obstacle appeared there was no time lost in bemoaning the circumstance, but they all set to work at once to remove the obstruction. The first thing to be landed was the motorcar, and after that came the ponies, for it was probable that any day might see the break-up of the bay ice, and there being only two fathoms of water along the shore, as we had ascertained by sounding down the tide crack, the ship could not go very close in. It would have been practically impossible to have landed the ponies in boats, for they were only half-broken in, and all in a highly strung, nervous condition. At 10.30 p.m. on February 3 we swung the motor over on to the bay ice, and all hands pulled it up the snow slope across the tide-crack and left it safe on the solid ground. This done, we next landed one of the lifeboats which we intended to keep down there with us. Joyce ran the dogs ashore and tied them up to rocks, all except Possum, who was still engaged with her little puppies. Then followed the foundation pieces of the hut, for it was desirable that we should be safely housed before the ship went north. Meanwhile, the carpenter was busily engaged in unbolting the framework of the pony-stalls, and the animals became greatly excited, causing us a lot of trouble. We worked till 3 a.m., landing pony fodder and general stores, and then knocked off and had some cocoa and a rest, intending to turn to at 6 a.m.

We had hardly started work again when a strong breeze sprung up with drifting snow. The ship began to bump heavily against the ice-foot and twice dragged her anchors out, so, as there seemed no possibility of getting ahead with the landing of the stores under these conditions, we steamed out and tied up at the main iceface, about six miles to the south, close to where we had lain for the past few days. It blew fairly hard all day and right through the evening, but the wind went down on the afternoon of the 5th, and we returned to the bay that evening. The poor dogs had been tied up all this time without any shelter or food, so directly we made fast, Joyce was off ashore with a steaming hot feed for them. Scamp came running down to meet him, and Queenie had got loose and played havoc amongst the penguins. They had killed over a hundred, and the skuas were massed in great numbers, taking full advantage of this disaster. We never saw Queenie again. She must have fallen over a cliff into the sea.

We lost no time in getting the ponies ashore. This was by no means an easy task, for some of the animals were very restive, and it required care to avoid accident to themselves or to us. Some time before we had thought of walking them down over a gang-plank on to the ice, but afterwards decided to build a rough horsebox, get them into this, and then sling it over the side by means of the main gaff. We covered the decks with ashes and protected all sharp projections with bags and bales of fodder. The first pony went in fairly quietly, and in another moment or two had the honour of being the pioneer horse on the Antarctic ice. One after another the ponies were led out of the stalls into the horsebox and were slung over on to the ice. Presently it came to Grisi's turn, and we looked for a lively time with this pony, for he was the most spirited and in the best condition of all. Our anticipations proved correct, and there were a few lively minutes before he was secured in the horse-box, the door of which was fastened with a rope. It was only by Mackay exerting all his strength at the most critical moment that we got the pony in. As the box was being hoisted up, his violent kicking threatened to demolish the somewhat frail structure, and it was with a devout feeling of thankfulness that I saw him safe on the ice. They all seemed to feel themselves at home, for they immediately commenced pawing at the snow as they are wont to do in their own far-away Manchurian home, where, in the winter, they scrape away the snow to get out the rough tussocky grass that lies underneath. It was 3.30 a.m. on the morning of the 6th before we got all the ponies off the ship, and they were at once led up on to the land. The poor beasts were naturally stiff after the constant buffeting they had experienced in their narrow stalls on the rolling ship for over a month, and they walked very stiffly ashore.

They negotiated the tide-crack all right, the fissure being narrow, and were soon picketed out on some bare earth at the entrance to a valley which lay about fifty yards from the site of our hut. We thought that this would be a good place, but the selection was to cost us dearly in the future. The tide-crack played an important part in connection with the landing of the stores.

In the polar regions, both north and south, when the sea is frozen over there always appears between the fast ice, which is the ice attached to the land, and the sea ice, a crack which is due to the sea ice moving up and down with the rise and fall of the tide. When the bottom of the sea slopes gradually from the land, sometimes two or three tide-cracks appear running parallel to each other. When no more tide-cracks are to be seen landwards, the snow or ice-foot has always been considered as being a permanent adjunct to the land, and in our case this opinion was further strengthened by the fact that our soundings in the tide-crack showed that the ice-foot on the landward side of it must be aground. I have explained this fully, for it was after taking into consideration these points that I, for convenience sake, landed the bulk of the stores just below the bare rocks on what I considered to be the permanent snow-slope.

About 9 a.m. on the morning of February 6 we started work with sledges, hauling provisions and pieces of the hut to the shore. The previous night the foundation posts of the hut had been sunk and frozen into the ground with a cement composed of volcanic earth and water. The digging of the foundation holes, on which job Dunlop, Adams, Joyce, Brocklehurst, and Marshall were engaged, proved hard work, for in some cases where the hole had to be dug the bed-rock was found a few inches below the coating of the earth, and this had to be broken through or drilled with chisel and hammer. Now that the ponies were ashore it was necessary to have a party living ashore also, for the animals would require looking after if the ship were forced to leave the ice-foot at any time, and, of course, the building of the hut could go on during the absence of the ship. The first shore party consisted of Adams, Marston, Brocklehurst, Mackay and Murray, and two tents were set up close to the hut, with the usual sledging requisites, sleeping-bags, cookers, &c. A canvas cover was rigged on some oars to serve as a cooking-tent, and this, later on, was enlarged into a more commodious house, built out of bales of fodder.

The first things landed this day were bales of fodder for the ponies, and sufficient petroleum and provisions for the shore party in the event of the ship having to put to sea suddenly owing to bad weather. For facility in landing the stores, the whole party was divided into two gangs. Some of the crew of the ship hoisted the stores out of the hold and slid them down a wide plank on to the ice, others of the ship's crew loaded the stores on to the sledges, and these were hauled to land by the shore party, each sledge having three men harnessed to it. The road to the shore consisted of hard, rough ice, alternating with very soft snow, and as the distance from where the ship was lying at first to the tide-crack was nearly a quarter of a mile, it was strenuous toil, especially when the tide-crack was reached and the sledges had to be pulled up the slope. After the first few sledge-loads had been hauled right up on to the land, I decided to let the stores remain on the snow slope beyond the tidecrack, where they could be taken away at leisure. The work was so heavy that we tried to substitute mechanical haulage in place of man haulage, and to achieve this end we anchored a block in the snow slope just over the tide-crack, and having spliced together practically all the running gear and all the spare line in the ship, we rove one end of the rope through the block and brought it back to the ship. The other end was brought round the barrel of the steam winch, and after the first part had been made fast to the loaded sledges, orders were given to heave away on the winch, and the sledges were, in this manner, hauled ashore. This device answered well enough in principle, but in actual practice we found that the amount of time that would be occupied in doing the work would be too great, especially because of the necessity for hauling back the rope to the ship each time, as in our present position we could not make an endless haulage. We therefore reverted to our original plan, and all that morning did the work by man haulage. During the lunch hour we shifted the ship about a hundred yards nearer the shore alongside the ice-face, from which a piece had broken out during the morning, leaving a level edge where the ship could be moored easily.

Just as we were going to commence work at 2 p.m. a fresh breeze sprung up from the south-east, and the ship began to bump against the ice-foot, her movement throwing the water over the ice. We were then lying in a rather awkward position in the apex of an angle in the bay ice, and as the breeze threatened to become stronger, I sent the shore-party on to the ice, and, with some difficulty, we got clear of the ice-foot. The breeze freshening we stood out to the fast ice in the strait about six miles to the south and anchored there. It blew a fresh breeze with drift from the south-east all that afternoon and night, and did not ease up till the following afternoon. During this time, Cape Royds, Mount Erebus, and Mount Bird were quite obscured, and from where we were lying there appeared to be bad weather ashore, but when we returned to the bay the following night at 10 p.m. we heard that, except for a little falling snow, the weather had been quite fine, and that the wind which had sprung up at two o'clock had not continued for more than an hour. Thus, unfortunately, two valuable working days were lost.

When I went ashore I found that the little party left behind had not only managed to get up to the site of the hut all the heavy timber that had been landed, but had also stacked on the bare land the various cases of provisions which had been lying on the snow slope by the tide-crack. We worked till 2 a.m. on the morning of the 9th, and then knocked off till 9 a.m. Then we commenced again, and put in one of the hardest day's work one could imagine, pulling the sledges to the tidecrack and then hauling them bodily over. Hour after hour all hands toiled on the work, the crossing of the tide-crack becoming more difficult with each succeeding sledge-load, for the ice in the bay was loosening, and it was over floating, rocking pieces of floe with gaps several feet wide between them that we hauled the sledges. In the afternoon the ponies were brought into action, as they had had some rest, and their arrival facilitated the discharge, though it did not lighten the labours of the perspiring staff. None of our party were in very good condition, having been cooped up in the ship, and the heavy cases became doubly heavy to their arms and shoulders by midnight.

Next day the work continued, the ice still holding in, but threatening every minute to go out. If there had been sufficient water for the ship to he right alongside the shore we would have been pleased to see the ice go out, but at the place where we were landing the stores there was only twelve feet of water, and the *Nimrod*, at this time, drew fourteen. We tried to anchor one of the smaller loose pieces of bay ice to the ice-foot, and this answered whilst the tide was setting in. As a result of the tidal movement, the influx of heavy pack in the bay where we were lying caused some anxiety, and more than once we had to shift the ship away from the landing-place because of the heavy floes and hummocky ice which pressed up against the bay ice. One large berg sailed in from the north and grounded about a mile to the south of Cape Royds, and later another about the same height, not less than one hundred and fifty feet, did the same, and these two bergs were frozen in when they grounded and remained in that position through the winter. The hummocky pack that came in and out with the tide was over fifteen feet in height, and, being of much greater depth below water, had ample power and force to damage the ship if a breeze sprang up.

When we turned to after lunch, and before the first sledge-load reached the main landing-place, we found that it would be impossible to continue working there any longer, for the small floe which we had anchored to the ice had dragged out the anchor and was being carried to sea by the ebbing, tide. Some three hundred and fifty yards further along the shore of the bay was a much steeper ice-foot at the foot of the cliffs, and a snow slope narrower than the one on which we had been landing the provisions. This was the nearest available spot at which to continue discharging. We hoped that when the ship had left we could hoist the stores up over the cliff; they would then be within a hundred yards of the hut, and, after being carried for a short distance they could be rolled down the steep snow slope at the head of the valley where it was being built. At this time the hut-party were working day and night, and the building was rapidly assuming an appearance of solidity. The uprights were in, and the brace ties were fastened together, so that if it came on to blow there was no fear of the structure being destroyed.

The stores had now to be dragged a distance of nearly three hundred yards from the ship to the landing-place, but this work was greatly facilitated

Scale of Yards

0   220   440   880

Dotted Line - Ice
• - Coal Depot
✧ - Places of Landing

Ice at time of 1st Landing

Cape Royds

Derrick Pt.

1st D.
1st G.

Coal Depot

2nd. Store Depot

Coal Pit

3rd. Store Depot

Hut

4th. Store & Coal Landing

Coal Depot

S **PLAN OF ICE EDGE**

WITH DEPOTS & STORES

E ———— W

N

by our being able to use four of the ponies, working two of them for an hour, and then giving these a spell whilst two others took their place. The snow was very deep, and the ponies sank in well above the knees; it was heavy going for the men who were leading them. A large amount of stores were landed in this way, but a new and serious situation arose through the breaking away of the main ice-foot.

On the previous day an ominous-looking crack had been observed to be developing at the end of the ice-foot nearest to Flagstaff Point, and it became apparent that if this crack continued to widen, it would cut right across the centre of our stores, with the result that, unless removed, they would be irretrievably lost in the sea. Next day (the 10th) there was no further opening of the crack, but at seven o'clock that night another crack formed on the ice-foot inside of Derrick Point, where we were now landing stores. There was no immediate danger to be apprehended at this place, for the bay ice would have to go out before the ice-foot could fall into the sea. Prudence suggested that it would be better to shift the stores already landed to a safer place before discharging any more from the ship, so at eight p.m. on the 10th we commenced getting the remainder of the wood for the hut and the bales of cork for the lining up on to the bare land. This took till about midnight, when we knocked off for cocoa and a sleep.

We turned to at six o'clock next morning, and I decided to get the stores up the cliff face at Derrick Point before dealing with those at Front Door Bay, the first landing-place, for the former ice-foot seemed in the greater peril of collapse than did the latter. Adams, Joyce, and Wild soon rigged up a boom and tackle from the top of the cliff, making the heel of the boom fast by placing great blocks of volcanic rocks on it. A party remained below on the ice-foot to shift and hook on the cases, whilst another party on top, fifty feet above, hauled away when the word was given from below, and on reaching the top of the cliff, the cases were hauled in by means of a guy rope. The men were hauling on the thin rope of the tackle from eight o'clock in the morning till one o'clock the following morning with barely a spell for a bit to eat.

We now had to find another and safer place on which to land the rest of the coal and stores. Further round the bay from where the ship was lying was a smaller bight where a gentle slope led on to bare rocks, and Back Door Bay, as we named this place, became our new depot. The ponies were led down the hill, and from Back Door Bay to the ship. This was a still longer journey than from Derrick Point, but there was no help for it, and we started landing the coal, after laying a tarpaulin on the rocks to keep the coal from becoming mixed with the earth. By this time there were several ugly looking cracks in the bay ice, and these kept opening and closing, having a play of seven or eight inches between the floes. We improvised bridges out of the bottom and sides of the motor-car case, so that the ponies could cross the cracks, and by eleven o'clock were well under way with the work. Mackay had just taken ashore a load with a pony, Armytage was about to hook on another pony to a loaded sledge at the ship, and a third pony was standing tied to our stern anchor rope waiting its turn for sledging, when suddenly, without the slightest warning, the greater part of the bay ice opened out into floes, and the whole mass that had opened started to drift slowly out to sea. The ponies on the ice were now in a perilous position. The sailors rushed to loosen the one tied to the stern rope, and got it over the first crack, and Armytage also got the pony he was looking after off the floe nearest the ship on to the next floe. Just at that moment Mackay appeared round the corner from Back

Door Bay with a third pony attached to an empty sledge on his way back to the ship to load up. Orders were shouted to him not to come any further, but he did not at first grasp the situation, for he continued advancing over the ice, which was now breaking away more rapidly. The party working on the top of Derrick Point, by shouting and waving, made him realise what had occurred. He accordingly left his sledge and pony and rushed over towards where the other two ponies were adrift on the ice, and, by jumping the widening cracks, he reached the moving floe on which they were standing. This piece of ice gradually drew closer to a larger piece, from which the animals would be able to gain a place of safety. Mackay started to try and get the pony Chinaman across the crack when it was only about six inches wide, but the animal suddenly took fright, reared up on his hind legs, and backing towards the edge of the floe, which had at that moment opened to a width of a few feet, fell bodily into the ice-cold water. It looked as if it was all over with poor Chinaman, but Mackay hung on to the head rope, and Davis, Mawson, Michell and one of the sailors who were on the ice close by, rushed to his assistance. The pony managed to get his fore feet on to the edge of the ice-floe. After great difficulty a rope sling was passed underneath him, and then by tremendous exertion he was lifted up far enough to enable him to scramble on to the ice. There he stood, wet and trembling in every limb. A few seconds later the floe closed up against the other one. It was providential that it had not done so during the time that the pony was in the water, for in that case the animal would inevitably have been squeezed to death between the two huge masses of ice. A bottle of brandy was thrown on to the ice from the ship, and half its contents were poured down Chinaman's throat. The ship was now turning round with the object of going bow on to the floe, in order to push it ashore, so that the ponies might cross on to the fast ice, and presently, with the engine at full speed, the floe was slowly but surely moved back against the fast ice. Directly the floe was hard up against the unbroken ice, the ponies were rushed across and taken straight, ashore, and the men who were on the different floes took advantage of the temporary closing of the crack to get themselves and the stores into safety. I decided, after this narrow escape, not to risk the ponies on the sea ice again. The ship was now backed out, and the loose floes began to drift away to the west.

By 1 p.m. most of the ice had cleared out, and the ship came in to the edge of the fast ice, which was now abreast of Back Door Bay. Hardly were the ice-anchors made fast before new cracks appeared, and within a quarter of an hour the ship was adrift again. As it was impossible to discharge under these conditions, the *Nimrod* stood off. We had now practically the whole of the wintering party ashore, so when lunch was over, the main party went on with the work at Derrick Point, refreshed by the hot tea and meat, which they hastily swallowed.

I organised that afternoon a small party to shift the main stores into safety. We had not been long at work before I saw that it would need the utmost despatch and our most strenuous endeavours to save the valuable cases; for the crack previously observed opened more each hour. Perspiration poured down our faces and bodies as we toiled in the hot sun. After two hours' work we had shifted into a place of safety all our cases of scientific instruments, and a large quantity of fodder, and hardly were they secured when, with a sharp crack, the very place where they had been lying fell with a crash into the sea. Had we lost these cases the result would have been very serious, for a great part of our scientific work could not have been carried out, and if the fodder had been lost, it would have meant the loss of the ponies also. The breaking of this part of the ice made us redouble our efforts to save the rest of the stores, for we could not tell when the next piece of ice might break off, though no crack was yet visible. The breaking up of the bay ice that morning turned out to he after all for the best, for I would not otherwise have gone on so early with this work. I ran up the hill to the top of Flagstaff Point, as we called the cliff at the southern extremity of Cape Royds, to call the ship in, in order to obtain additional help from the crew; she had been dodging about outside of the point since one o'clock, but she was beyond hailing distance, and it was not till about seven o'clock that I saw her coming close in again. I at once hailed England and told him to send every available man ashore immediately. In a few minutes a boat came off with half a dozen men, and I sent a message back by the officer in charge for more members of the ship's crew to be landed at once, and only enough men left on board to steer the ship and work the engines. I had previously knocked off the party working on the hut, and with the extra assistance we 'smacked things about', in a lively fashion. The ice kept breaking off in chunks, but we had the satisfaction of seeing every single package safe on the rocks by midnight.

Our party then proceeded to sledge the heavier cases and the tins of oil at the foot of Derrick Point round the narrow causeway of ice between the perpendicular rocks and the sea to the depot at Back Door Bay. I was astonished and delighted on arriving at the derrick to find the immense amount of stores that had been placed in safety by the efforts of the Derrick Point party, and by 1 a.m. on February 13 all the stores landed were in safety. About a ton of flour in cases remained to be hauled up, but as we already had enough ashore to last us for a year, and knowing that at Hut Point there were large quantities of biscuit left by the last expedition, which would be available if needed, we just rolled the cases on the ice-foot into a hollow at the foot of the cliff, where they were in comparative safety, as the ice there would not be likely to break away immediately. We retrieved these after the ship left.

As I stated in the chapter on the equipment of the expedition, I tried to get the bulk of the stores into cases of uniform size and weight, averaging fifty to sixty pounds gross, and thus allow of more easy handling than would have been the case if the stores were packed in the usual way. The goods packed in Venesta cases could withstand the roughest treatment without breakage or damage to the contents. These Venesta cases are made of three thin layers of wood, fastened together by a patent process; the material is much tougher than ordinary wood, weighs much less than a case of the same size made of the usual deal, and, being thinner, takes up much less room, a consideration of great moment to a Polar expedition. The wood could not be broken by the direct blow of a heavy hammer, and the empty cases could be used for the making of the hundred and one odds and ends that have to be contrived to meet requirements in such an expedition as this.

At 1 a.m. on the morning of February 13 I signalled the ship to come in to take off the crew, and a boat was sent ashore. There was a slight breeze blowing, and it took them some time to pull off to the *Nimrod*, which lay a long way out. We on shore turned in, and we were so tired that it was noon before we woke up. A glance out to sea showed that we had lost nothing by our sleep, for there was a heavy swell running into the bay, and it would have been quite impossible to have landed any stores at all. In the afternoon the ship came in fairly close, but I signalled England that it was useless to send the boat. This northerly swell, which we could hear thundering on the ice-foot, would have been welcome a fortnight before, for it would have broken up a large amount of fast ice to the south, and I could not help imagining that probably at this date there was open water up to Hut Point. Now, however, it was the worst thing possible for us, as the precious time was slipping by, and the still more valuable coal was being used up by the continual working of the ship's engines. Next day the swell still continued, so at 4 p.m. I signalled England to proceed to Glacier Tongue and land a depot there. Glacier Tongue is a remarkable formation of ice which stretches out into the sea from the south-west slopes of Mount Erebus. About five miles in length, running east and west, tapering almost to a point at its seaward end, and having a width of about a mile where it descends from the land, cracked and crevassed all over and floating in deep water, it is a phenomenon which still remains a mystery. It lies about eight miles to the northward of Hut Point, and about thirteen to the southward of Cape Royds, and I thought this would be a good place at which to land a quantity of sledging stores, as by doing so we would be saved haulage at least thirteen miles, the distance between the spot on the southern route and Cape Royds. The ship arrived there in the early evening, and landed the depot on the north side of the Tongue. The Professor took bearings so that there might be no difficulty in finding the depot when the sledging season commenced. The sounding at this spot gave a depth of 157 fathoms. From the seaward end of the glacier it was observed that the ice had broken away only a couple of miles further south, so the northerly swell had not been as far reaching in its effect as I had imagined. The ship moored at the Tongue for the night.

During this day we, ashore at Cape Royds, were variously employed; one party continued the building of the hut, whilst the rest of us made a more elaborate temporary dwelling and cook house than we had had up to that time. The walls were constructed of bales of fodder, which lent themselves admirably for this purpose; the cook-tent tarpaulin was stretched over these for a roof and was supported on planks, and the outer walls were stayed with uprights from the pony-stalls. As the roof was rather low and people could not stand upright, a trench was dug at one end, where the cook could move about without bending his back the whole time. In this corner were concocted the most delicious dishes that ever a hungry man could wish for. Wild acted as cook till Roberts came ashore permanently, and it was a sight to see us in the dim light that penetrated through the door of the fodder hut as we sat in a row on cases, each armed with a spoon manufactured out of tin and wood by the ever-inventive Day, awaiting with eagerness our bowl of steaming hoosh or rich dark-coloured penguin breast, followed by biscuit, butter and jam; tea and smokes ended up the meal, and, as we lazily stretched ourselves out for the smoke, regardless of a temperature of 16 or 18 degrees of frost, we felt that things were not so bad.

The same day that we built the fodder hut we placed inside it some cases of bottled fruit, hoping to save them from being cracked by the severe frost outside. The bulk of the cases containing liquid we kept on board the ship till the last moment so that they could be put into the main hut when the fire was lighted. We turned in about midnight, and got up at seven next morning. The ship had just come straight in, and I went off on board. Marshall also came off to attend to Mackintosh, whose wound was rapidly healing. He was now up and about. He was very anxious to stay with us, but Marshall did not think it advisable for him to risk it. During the whole of this day and the next, the 15th, the swell was too great to admit of any stores being landed, but early on the morning of the 16th we found it possible to get ashore at a small ice-foot to the north of Flagstaff Point, and here, in spite of the swell, we managed to land six boatloads of fruit, some oil, and twenty-four bags of coal. The crew of the boat, whilst the stores were being taken out, had to keep to their oars, and whenever the swell rolled on the shelving beach, they had to back with all their might to keep the bow of the boat from running under the overhanging ice-foot and being crushed under the ice by the lifting wave. Davis, the chief officer of the *Nimrod*, worked like a Titan. A tall, red-headed Irishman, typical of his country, he was always working and always cheerful, having no time-limit for his work. He and Harboard, the second officer, a quiet, self-reliant man, were great acquisitions to the expedition.

These two officers were ably supported by the efforts of the crew. They had nothing but hard work and discomfort from the beginning of the voyage, and yet they were always cheerful, and worked splendidly. Dunlop, the chief engineer, not only kept his department going smoothly on board but was the principal constructor of the hut. A great deal of the credit for the work being so cheerfully performed was due to the example of Cheetham, who was an old hand in the Antarctic, having been boatswain of the *Morning* on both the voyages she made for the relief of the *Discovery*. He was third mate and boatswain on this expedition.

When I had gone on board the previous day I found that England was still poorly and that he was feeling the strain of the situation. He was naturally very anxious to get the ship away and concerned about the shrinkage of the coal supply. I also would have been glad to have seen the *Nimrod* on her way north, but it was impossible to let her leave until the wintering party had received their coal from her. In view of the voyage home, the ship's main topmast was struck to lessen her rolling in bad weather. It was impossible to ballast the ship with rock, as the time needed for this operation would involve the consumption of much valuable coal, and I was sure that the heavy iron-bark and oak hull, and the weight of the engine and boiler filled with water would be sufficient to ensure the ship's safety.

We found it impossible to continue working at Cliff Point later on in the day, so the ship stood off whilst those on shore went on with the building of the hut. Some of the shore-party had come of in the last boat to finish writing their final letters home, and during the night we lay to waiting for the swell to decrease. The weather was quite fine, and if it had not been for the swell we could have got through a great deal of work. February is by no means a fine month in the latitude we were in, and up till now we had been extremely fortunate, as we had not experienced a real blizzard.

The following morning, Monday, February 17, the sea was breaking heavily on the ice-foot at the bottom of Cliff Point. The stores that had been landed the previous day had been hoisted up the overhanging cliff and now formed the fourth of our scattered depots of coal and stores. The swell did not seem so heavy in Front Door Bay, so we commenced landing the stores in the whale-boat at the place where the ice-foot had broken away, a party on shore hauling the bags of coal and the cases up the ice-face, which was about fourteen feet high. The penguins were still round us in large numbers. We had not had any time to make observations on them, being so busily employed discharging the ship, but just at this particular time our attention was called to a couple of these birds which suddenly made a spring from the water and landed on their feet on the ice-edge, having cleared a vertical height of twelve feet. It seemed a marvellous jump for these small creatures to have made, and shows the rapidity with which they must move through the water to gain the impetus that enables them to clear a distance in vertical height four times greater than their own, and also how unerring must be their judgment in estimation of the distance and height when performing this feat. The work of landing stores at this spot was greatly hampered by the fact that the bay was more or less filled with broken floes, through which the boat had to be forced. It was impossible to use the oars in the usual way, so, on arriving at the broken ice, they were employed as poles. The bow of the boat was entered into a likely looking channel, and then the crew, standing up, pushed the boat forward by means of the oars, the ice generally giving way on each side, but sometimes closing up and nipping the boat, which, if it had been less strongly built, would assuredly have been crushed. The Professor, Mawson, Cotton, Michell and a couple of seamen formed the boat's crew, and with Davis or Harboard in the stern, they dodged the ice very well, considering the fact that the swell was rather heavy at the outside edge of the floes. When alongside the icefoot one of the crew hung on to a rope in the bow, and another did the same in the stern, hauling in the slack as the boat rose on top of the swell, and easing out as the water swirled downwards from the ice-foot. There was a sharp-pointed rock, which, when the swell receded, was almost above water, and the greatest difficulty was experienced in preventing the boat from crashing down on the top of this. The rest of the staff in the boat and on shore hauled up the cases and bags of coal at every available opportunity. The coal was weighed at the top of the ice-foot, and the bags emptied on to a heap which formed the main supply for the winter months. We had now three depots of coal in different places round the winter quarters. In the afternoon the floating ice at this place became impassable, but fortunately it had worked its way out of Black Door Bay, where, in spite of the heavy swell running against the ice-foot, we were able to continue adding to the heap of coal until nearly eight tons had been landed. It was a dull and weary job except when unpleasantly enlivened by the imminent danger of the boat being caught between heavy pieces of floating ice and the solid ice-foot. These masses of ice rose and fell on the swell, the water swirling round them as they became submerged, and pouring off their top and sides as they rose to the surface. It required all Harboard's watchfulness and speediness of action to prevent damage to the boat. It is almost needless to observe that all hands were as grimy as coal-heavers', especially the boat's crew who were working in the half-frozen slushy coal-dust and sea spray. The Professor, Mawson, Cotton, and Michell still formed part of the crew. They had, by midnight, been over twelve hours in the boat, excepting for about ten minutes' spell for lunch, and after discharging each time had a long pull back to the ship. When each boat-load was landed, the coal and stores had to be hauled up on a sledge over a very steep gradient to a place of safety, and after this was accomplished, there was a long wait for the next consignment.

Work was continued all night, though every one was nearly dropping with fatigue; but I decided that the boat returning to the ship at 5 a.m. (the 18th) should take a message to England that the men were to knock off for breakfast and turn to at seven o'clock. Meanwhile Roberts had brewed some hot coffee in the hut, where we now had the stove going, and, after a drink of this, our weary people threw themselves down on the sleeping-bags in order to snatch a short rest before again taking up the weary work. At 7 a.m. I went to the top of Flagstaff Point, but instead of seeing the ship close in, I spied her hull down on the horizon, and could see no sign of her approaching the winter quarters to resume discharging. After watching her for about half an hour, I returned to the hut, woke up those of the staff who from utter weariness had dropped asleep, and told them to turn into their bags and have a proper rest. I could not imagine why the ship was not at hand, but at a quarter to eleven Harboard came ashore and said that England wanted to see me on board; so, leaving the others to sleep, I went off to the *Nimrod*. On asking England why the ship was not in at seven to continue discharging, he told me that all hands were so dead-tired that he thought it best to let them have a sleep. The men were certainly worn out. Davis' head had dropped on the wardroom table, and he had gone sound asleep with his spoon in his mouth, to which he had just conveyed some of his breakfast. Cotton had fallen asleep on the platform of the engine-room steps, whilst Mawson, whose lair was a little store-room in the engine-room, was asleep on the floor. His long legs, protruding through the doorway, had found a resting-place on the cross-head of the engine, and his dreams were mingled with a curious rhythmical motion which was fully accounted for when he woke up, for the ship having got under way, the up-and-down motion of the piston had moved his limbs with every stroke. The sailors also were fast asleep; so, in the face of this evidence of absolute exhaustion, I decided not to start work again till after one o'clock, and told England definitely that when the ship had been reduced in coal to ninety-two tons as a minimum I would send her north. According to our experiences on the last expedition, the latest date to which it would be safe to keep the *Nimrod* would be the end of February, for the young ice forming about that time on the sound would seriously hamper her getting clear of the Ross Sea. Later observations of the ice conditions of McMurdo Sound at our winter quarters showed us that a powerfully-engined ship could have gone north later in the year, perhaps even in the winter, for we had open water close to us all the time.

About 2 p.m. the *Nimrod* came close in to Flagstaff Point to start discharging again. I decided that it was time to land the more delicate instruments, such as watches, chronometers, and all personal gear. The members of the staff who were on board hauled their things out of Oyster Alley, and, laden with its valuable freight, we took the whale boat into Front

Door Bay. Those who had been ashore now went on board to collect their goods and finish their correspondence. This party consisted of Day, Wild, Adams and Marshall. Mackintosh and the carpenter were ashore, the latter being still busily engaged on the construction of the hut, which was rapidly approaching completion. During the afternoon we continued boating coal to Front Door Bay, which was again free of ice, and devoted our attention almost entirely to this work.

8

A BLIZZARD: THE DEPARTURE
OF THE *NIMROD*

About five o'clock on the afternoon of February 18 snow began to fall, with light wind from the north, and as at times the boat could hardly be seen from the ship, instructions were given to the boat's crew that whenever the *Nimrod* was not clearly visible they were to wait alongside the shore until the snow squall had passed and she appeared in sight again. At six o'clock, just as the boat had come alongside for another load, the wind suddenly shifted to the south-east and freshened immediately. The whaler was hoisted at once, and the *Nimrod* stood off from the shore, passing between some heavy ice-floes, against one of which her propeller struck, but fortunately without sustaining any damage. Within half an hour it was blowing a furious blizzard, and every sign of land, both east and west, was obscured in the scudding drift. I was aboard the vessel at the time. We were then making for the fast-ice to the south, but the *Nimrod* was gaining but little headway against the terrific wind and short, rising sea; so to save coal I decided to keep the engines just going slow and maintain our position in the sound as far as we could judge, though it was inevitable that we should drift northward to a certain extent. All night the gale raged with great fury. The speed of the gusts at times must have approached a force of a hundred miles an hour. The tops of the seas were cut off by the wind, and flung over the decks, mast, and rigging of the ship, congealing at once into hard ice, and the sides of the vessel were thick with the frozen sea water. 'The masts were grey with the frozen spray, and the bows were a coat of mail.' Very soon the cases and sledges lying on deck were hard and fast in a sheet of solid ice, and the temperature had dropped below zero. Harboard, who was the officer on watch, on whistling to call the crew aft, found that the metal whistle stuck to his lips, a painful intimation of the low temperature. I spent most of the night on tile bridge, and hoped that the violence of the gale would be of but short duration. This hope was not realised, for next morning, February 19, at 8 a.m., it was blowing harder than ever. During the early hours of the day the temperature was −16° Fahr., and consistently kept below −12° Fahr. The motion of the ship was sharp and jerky, yet, considering the nature of the sea and the trim of the vessel, she was remarkably steady. To a certain extent this was due to the fact that the main topmast had been lowered. We had constantly to have two men at the wheel, for the rudder, being so far out of the water, received the blows of the sea as they struck the quarter and stern; and the steersman having once been flung right over the steering-chains against the side of the ship, it was necessary to have two always holding on to the kicking wheel. At times there would be a slight lull, the seas striking less frequently against the rudder, and the result would be that the rudder-well soon got filled with ice, and it was found impossible to move the wheel at all. To overcome this dangerous state of things the steersman had to keep moving the wheel alternately to port and starboard, after the ice had been broken away from the well. In spite of this precaution, the rudder-well occasionally became choked, and one of the crew, armed with a long iron bar, had to stand by continually to break the frozen sea water off the rudder. In the blinding drift it was impossible to see more than a few yards from the ship, and once a large iceberg suddenly loomed out of the drift close to the weather bow of the *Nimrod*; fortunately the rudder had just been cleared, and the ship answered her helm, thus avoiding a collision.

All day on the 20th, through the night, and throughout the day and night of the 21st, the gale raged. Occasionally the drift ceased, and we saw dimly bare rocks, sometimes to the east and sometimes to the west, but the upper parts of them being enveloped in snow clouds, it was impossible to ascertain exactly what our position was. At these times we were forced to wear ship; that is, to turn the ship round, bringing the wind first astern and then on to the other side, so that we could head in the opposite direction. It was impossible in face of the storm to tack, i.e., to turn the ship's head into the wind, and round, so as to bring the wind on the other side. About midnight on the 21st, whilst carrying out this evolution of wearing ship, during which the *Nimrod* always rolled heavily in the trough of the waves, she shipped a heavy sea, and, all the release-water ports and scupper holes being blocked with ice, the water had no means of exit, and began to freeze on deck, where, already, there was a layer of ice over a foot in thickness. Any more weight like this would have made the ship unmanageable. The ropes, already covered with ice, would have been frozen into a solid mass, so we were forced to take the drastic step of breaking holes in the bulwarks to allow the water to escape. This had been done already in the forward end of the ship by the gales we experienced on our passage down to the ice, but as the greater part of the weight in the holds was aft, the water collected towards the middle and stern, and the job of breaking through the bulwarks was a tougher one than we had imagined; it was only by dint of great exertions that Davis and Harboard accomplished it. It was a sight to see Harboard, held by his legs, hanging over the starboard side of the *Nimrod,* and wielding a heavy axe, whilst Davis, whose length of limb enabled him to lean over without being held, did the same on the other side. The temperature at this time was several degrees below zero. Occasionally on this night, as we approached the eastern shore, the coast of Ross Island, we noticed the sea covered with a thick yellowish-brown scum. This was due to the immense masses of snow blown off the mountain sides out to sea, and this scum, to a certain extent, prevented the tops of the waves from breaking. Had it not been for this unexpected protection we would certainly have lost our starboard boat, which had been unshipped in a sea and was hanging in a precarious position for the time being. It was hard to realise that so high and so dangerous a sea could possibly have risen in the comparatively narrow waters of McMurdo Sound. The wind was as strong as that we experienced in the gales that assailed us after we first left New Zealand, but the waves were not so huge as those which had the whole run of the Southern Ocean in which to gather strength before they met us. At 2 a.m. the weather suddenly cleared, and though the wind still blew strongly and gustily, it was apparent that the force of the gale had been expended. We could now see our position clearly. The wind and current, in spite of our efforts to keep our position, had driven us over thirty miles to the north, and at this time we were abeam of Cape Bird. The sea was rapidly decreasing in height, enabling us to steam for Cape Royds.

We arrived there in the early morning, and I went ashore at Back Door Bay, after pushing the whale boat through pancake ice and slush, the result of the gale.

Hurrying over to the hut I was glad to see that it was intact, and then I received full details of the occurrences of the last three days on shore. The report was not very reassuring as regards the warmth of the hut, for the inmates stated that, in spite of the stove being alight the whole time, no warmth was given off. Of course the building was really not at all complete. It had not been lined, and there were only makeshift protections for the windows, but what seemed a grave matter was the behaviour of the stove, for on the efficiency of this depended not only our comfort but our very existence. The shore-party had experienced a very heavy gale indeed. The hut had trembled and shaken the whole time, and if the situation had not been so admirable I doubt whether there would have been a hut at all after the gale. A minor accident had occurred, for our fodder hut had failed to withstand the gale, and one of the walls had collapsed, killing one of Possum's pups. The roof had been demolished at the same time.

On going down to our main landing-place, the full effect of the blizzard became apparent. There was hardly a sign to be seen of the greater part of our stores. At first it appeared that the drifting snow had covered the cases and bales and the coal, but a closer inspection showed that the real disappearance of our stores from view was due to the sea. Such was the force of the wind blowing straight on to the shore from the south that the spray had been flung in sheets over everything and had been carried by the wind for nearly a quarter of a mile inland, and consequently in places, our precious stores lay buried to a depth of five or six feet in a mass of frozen sea water. The angles taken up by the huddled masses of cases and bales had made the surface of this mass of ice assume a most peculiar shape, as may be seen from the illustrations. We feared that it would take weeks of work to get the stores clear of the ice. It was probable also that the salt water would have damaged the fodder, and worked its way into cases that were not tin-lined or made of Venesta wood, and that some of the things would never be seen again. No one would have recognised the landing-place as the spot on which we had been working during the past fortnight, so great was the change wrought by the furious storm. Our heap of coal had a sheet of frozen salt water over it, but this was a blessing in disguise, for it saved the smaller pieces of coal from being blown away.

There was no time then to do anything about releasing the stores from the ice; the main thing was to get the remainder of the coal ashore and send the ship north. We immediately started landing coal at the extreme edge of Front Door Bay. The rate of work was necessarily very slow, for the whole place was both rough and slippery from the newly formed ice that covered everything. In spite of the swell we worked all the morning, and in the early afternoon, as the bay became full of ice, instructions were sent to the ship to proceed to Glacier Tongue, deposit five tons of coal there, and then report at Flagstaff Point. The sea went down greatly about half an hour after the ship left, and we were much pleased, about 6 p.m., to see the *Nimrod* returning, for it was greatly to our advantage to land the coal at winter quarters instead of having to sledge it thirteen miles from Glacier Tongue.

On the *Nimrod*'s return, England reported that loose floe-ice surrounded Glacier Tongue, so that it was impossible to make a depot there. We now proceeded to continue discharging, and shortly before 10 p.m. on February 22, the final boatload of coal arrived. We calculated that we had in all only about eighteen tons, so that the strictest economy would be required to make this amount spin out until the sledging commenced in the following spring. I should certainly have liked more coal, but the delays that had occurred in finding winter quarters, and the difficulties encountered in landing the stores had caused the *Nimrod* to be kept longer than I had intended already. We gave our final letters and messages to the crew of the last boat, and said good-bye. Cotton, who had come south just for the trip, was among them, and never had we a more willing worker. At 10 p.m. the *Nimrod*'s bows were pointed to the north, and she was moving rapidly away from the winter quarters with a fair wind. Within a month I hoped she would be safe in New Zealand, and her crew enjoying a well-earned rest. We were all devoutly thankful that the landing of the stores had been finished at last, and that the state of the sea would no longer be a factor in our work, but it was with something of a pang that we severed our last connection with the world of men. We could hope for no word of news from civilisation until the *Nimrod* came south again in the following summer, and before that we had a good deal of difficult work to do, and some risks to face.

There was scant time for reflection, even if we had been moved that way. We turned in for a good night's rest as soon as possible after the departure of the ship, and the following morning we started digging the stores out of the ice, and transporting everything to the vicinity of the hut. It was necessary that the stores should be close by the building, partly in order that there might be no difficulty in getting what goods we wanted during the winter, and partly because we would require all the protection that we could get from the cold, and the cases would serve to keep off the wind when piled around our little dwelling. We hoped, as soon as the stores had all been placed in position, to make a start with the scientific observations that were to be an important part of the work of the expedition.

The next four or five days were spent in using pick and shovel and iron crowbars on the envelope of ice that covered our cases, corners of which only peeped out from the mass. The whole had the appearance of a piece of the sweet known as almond rock, and there was as much difficulty in getting the cases clear of the ice as would be experienced if one tried to separate almonds from that sticky conglomerate without injury. Occasionally the breaking out of a case would disclose another which could be easily extracted, but more often each case required the pick or crowbars. A couple of earnest miners might be seen delving and hewing the ice off a case, of which only the corner could be seen, and after ten minutes' hard work it would be hauled up, and the stencilled mark of its contents exposed to view. Brocklehurst took great interest in the recovery of the chocolate, and during this work took charge of one particular case which had been covered by the ice. He carried it himself up to the hut so as to be sure of its safety, and he was greeted with joy by the Professor, who recognised in the load some of his scientific instruments which were playing the part of the cuckoo in an old chocolate box. Needless to say Brocklehurst's joy was not as heartfelt as the Professor's.

After about four days' hard work at the Front Door Bay landing-place, the bulk of the stores was recovered, and I think we may say that there was not much lost permanently, though, as time went on, and one or two cases that were required did not turn up, we used to wonder whether they had been left on board the ship, or were buried under the ice. We do know for certain that our only case of beer lies to this day under the ice, and it was not until a few days before our final departure that one of the scientists of the expedition dug out some volumes of the Challenger reports, which had been intended to

WINTER QUARTERS

provide us with useful reading-matter during the winter nights. A question often debated during the long, dark days was which of these stray sheep, the Challenger reports or the case of beer, any particular individual would dig for if the time and opportunity were available. In moving up the recovered stores, as soon as a load arrived within fifteen yards of the hut, where, at this time of the year, the snow ended, and the bare earth lay uncovered, the sledges were unpacked, and one party carried the stuff up to the south side of the hut, whilst the sledges returned to the landing-place for more. We were now utilising the ponies every day, and they proved of great assistance in moving things to and fro. The stores on the top of the hill at Derrick Point were fortunately quite clear of snow, so we did not trouble to transport them, contenting ourselves with getting down things that were of immediate importance. Day by day we continued collecting our scattered goods, and within ten days after the departure of the ship we had practically everything handy to the hut, excepting the coal. The labour had been both heavy and fertile in minor accidents. Most of us at one time or another had wounds and bruises to be attended to by Marshall, who was kept busy part of every day dressing the injuries. Adams was severely cut in handling some iron-bound cases, and I managed to jamb my fingers in the motor-car. The annoying feature about these simple wounds was the length of time it took for them to heal in our special circumstances. The irritation seemed to be more pronounced if any of the earth got into the wound, so we always took care after our first experiences to go at once to Marshall for treatment, when the skin was broken. The day after the ship left we laid in a supply of fresh meat for the winter, killing about a hundred penguins and burying them in a snow-drift close to the hut. We now felt assured that, with the penguins as well as the mutton given us by friends in New Zealand, we would have ample fresh meat during the winter months. By February 28 we were practically in a position to feel contented with ourselves, and to look further afield and explore the neighbourhood of our winter quarters.

9
AROUND THE WINTER QUARTERS: COMPLETION OF THE HUT

From the door of our hut, which faced the north-west, we commanded a splendid view of the sound and the western mountains. Right in front of us, at our door, lay a small lake, which came to be known as Pony Lake; to the left of that was another sheet of ice that became snow-covered in the autumn, and it was here in the dark months that we exercised the ponies, and also ourselves. Six times up and down the 'Green Park', as it was generally called, made a mile, and it was here, before darkness came on, that we played hockey and football. To the left of Green Park was a gentle slope leading down between two cliffs to the sea, and ending in a little bay known as Dead Horse Bay. On either side of this valley lay the penguin rookery, the slopes being covered with guano, and during the fairly high temperatures that held sway up to April, the smell from these deserted quarters of the penguins was extremely unpleasant. On coming out of the hut one had only to go round the corner of the building in order to catch a glimpse of Mount Erebus, which lay directly behind us. Its summit was about fifteen miles from our winter quarters, but its slopes and foothills commenced within three-quarters of a mile of the hut. Our view was cut off in all directions from the east to the south-west by the ridge at the head of the valley where the hut stood. On ascending this ridge, one looked over the bay to the south-east, where lay Cape Barne. To the right was Flagstaff Point, and to the left lay, at the head of the Bay, the slopes of Erebus. There were many localities which became favourite places for walks, and these are shown on the accompanying map. Sandy Beach, about a mile away to the north-west of the hut, was generally the goal of any one taking exercise, when the uncertainty of the weather warned us against venturing further afield, and while the dwindling light still permitted us to go so far. It was here that we sometimes exercised the ponies, and they much enjoyed rolling in the soft sand. The beach was formed of black volcanic sand, blown from the surrounding hills, and later on the pressed-up ice, which had been driven ashore by the southward movement of the pack, also became covered with the wind-borne dust and sand. The coast-line from Flagstaff Point right round to Horse Shoe Bay, on the north side of Cape Royds, was jagged and broken up. At some points ice-cliffs, in others bare rocks, jutted out into the sea, and here and there small beaches composed of volcanic sand were interposed. Our local scenery, though not on a grand scale, loomed large in the light of the moon as the winter nights lengthened. Fantastic shadows made the heights appear greater and the valleys deeper, casting a spell of Unreality around the place, which never seemed to touch it by day. The greatest height of any of the numerous sharp-pointed spurs of volcanic rock was not more than three hundred feet, but we were infinitely better off as regards the interest and the scenery of our winter quarters than the expedition which wintered in McMurdo Sound between 1901 and 1904. Our walks amongst the hills and across the frozen lakes were a great source of health and enjoyment, and as a field of work for geologists and biologists, Cape Royds far surpassed Hut Point. The largest lake, which lay about half a mile to the north-east, was named Blue Lake, from the intensely vivid blue of the ice. This lake was peculiarly interesting to Mawson, who made the study of ice part of his work. Beyond Blue Lake, to the northward, lay Clear Lake, the deepest inland body of water in our vicinity. To the left as one looked north, close to the coast, was a circular basin which we called Coast Lake, where, when we first arrived, hundreds of Skua gulls were bathing and flying about. Following the coast from this point back towards winter quarters was another body of water called Green Lake. In all these various lakes something of interest to science was discovered, and though they were quite small, they were very important to our work and in our eyes, and were a source of continuous interest to us during our stay in the vicinity. Beyond Blue Lake, to the east, rose the lower slopes of Mount Erebus, covered with ice and snow. After passing one or two ridges of volcanic rocks, there stretched a long snow plain, across which sledges could travel without having their runners torn by gravel. The slope down to Blue Lake was picked out for ski-ing and it was here, in the early days, when work was over, that some of our party used to slide from the top of the slope for about two hundred feet, arriving at the bottom in a few seconds, and shooting out across the frozen surface of the Lake, until brought up by the rising slope on the other side. To the north of Clear Lake the usual hills of volcanic rock separated by valleys filled more or less with snow-drifts, stretched for a distance of about a mile. Beyond this lay the coast, to the right of which, looking north, was Horse Shoe Bay, about four miles from our winter quarters; further to the right of the northern end of Cape Royds the slopes of Erebus were reached again. From the northern coast a good view could be obtained of Cape Bird, and from the height we could see Castle Rock to the south, distant about eighteen miles from the winter quarters. The walk from Hut Point to Castle Rock was familiar to us on the last expedition. It seemed much nearer than it really was, for in the Antarctic the distances are most deceptive, curiously different effects being produced by the variations of light and the distortion of mirage.

As time went on we felt more and more satisfied with our location, for there was work of interest for every one. The Professor and Priestley saw open before them a new chapter of geological history of great interest, for Cape Royds was a happier hunting-ground for the geologist than was Hut Point. Hundreds of erratic boulders lay scattered on the slopes of the adjacent hills, and from these the geologists hoped to learn something of the past conditions of Ross Island. For Murray, the lakes were a fruitful field for new research. The gradually deepening bay was full of marine animal life, the species varying with the depth, and here also an inexhaustible treasure-ground stretched before the biologist. Adams, the meteorologist, could not complain, for Mount Erebus was in full view of the meteorological station, and this fortunate proximity to Erebus and its smokecloud led, in a large measure, to important results in this branch. For the physicist the structure of the ice, varying on various lakes, the different salts in the earth, and the magnetic conditions of the rocks claimed investigation, though, indeed, the magnetic nature of the rocks proved a disadvantage in carrying out magnetic observations, for the delicate instruments were often affected by the local attraction. From every point of view I must say that we were extremely fortunate in the winter quarters to which we had been led by the state of the sea-ice, for no other spot could have afforded more scope for work and exercise.

Before we had been ten days ashore the hut was practically completed, though it was over a month before it had been worked up from the state of an empty shell to attain the fully furnished appearance it assumed after every one had settled down and arranged his belongings. It was not a very spacious dwelling for the accommodation of fifteen persons, but our narrow quarters were warmer than if the hut had been larger. The coldest part of the house when we first lived in it was undoubtedly the floor, which was formed of inch tongue-and-groove boarding, but was not double-lined. There was a space of about four feet under the hut at the north-west end, the other end resting practically on the ground, and it was obvious to us that as long as this space remained we would suffer from the cold, so we decided to make an airlock of the area under the hut. To this end we decided to build a wall round the south-east and southerly sides, which were to windward, with the bulk of the provision cases. To make certain that no air would penetrate from these sides we built the first two or three tiers of cases a little distance out from the walls of the hut, pouring in volcanic earth until no gaps could be seen, and the earth was level with the cases; then the rest of the stores were piled up to a height of six or seven feet. This accounted for one side and one end.

PLAN OF THE HUT AT WINTER QUARTERS

On either side of the porch two other buildings were gradually erected. One, built out of biscuit cases, the roof covered with felt and canvas, was a store-room for Wild, who looked after the issue of all food-stuffs. The building on the other side of the porch was a much more ambitious affair, and was built by Mawson, to serve as a chemical and physical laboratory. It was destined, however, to be used solely as a store-room, for the temperature within its walls was practically the same as that of the outside air, and the warm, moist atmosphere rushing out from the hut covered everything inside this store-room with fantastic ice crystals.

The lee side of the hut ultimately became the wall of the stables, for we decided to keep the ponies sheltered during the winter. During the blizzard we experienced on February 18, and for the three following days, the animals suffered somewhat, mainly owing to the knocking about they had received whilst on the way south in the ship. We found that a shelter, not necessarily warmed to a high temperature, would keep the ponies in better condition than if they were allowed to stand in the open, and by February 9 the stable building was complete. A double row of cases of maize, built at one end to a height of five feet eight inches, made one end, and then the longer side of the shelter was composed of bales of fodder. A wide plank at the other end was cemented into the ground, and a doorway left. Over all this was stretched the canvas tarpaulin which we had previously used in the fodder hut, and with planks and battens on both sides to make it windproof, the stable was complete. A wire rope was stretched from one end to the other on the side nearest to the hut, and the ponies' head-ropes were made fast to this. The first night that they were placed in the stable there was little rest for any of us, and during the night some of the animals broke loose and returned to their valley. Shortly afterwards Grisi, one of the most high-spirited of the lot, pushed his head through a window, so the lower halves of the hut windows had to be boarded up. The first strong breeze we had shook the roof of the stable so much that we expected every moment it would blow away, so after the gale all the sledges except those which were in use were laid on the top of the stable, and a stout rope passed from one end to the other. The next snowfall covered the sledges and made a splendid roof, upon which no subsequent wind had any effect. Later, another addition was made to the dwellings outside the hut in the shape of a series of dog-houses for those animals about to pup, and as that was not an uncommon thing down there, the houses were constantly occupied.

On the south-east side of the hut a store-room was built, constructed entirely of cases, and roofed with hammocks sewn together. Here we kept the toolchest, shoe-makers' outfit, which was in constant requisition, and any general stores that had to be issued at stated times. The first heavy blizzard found this place out, and after the roof had been blown off, the wall fell down, and we had to organise a party, when the weather got fine, to search for anything that might be lost, such as mufflers, woollen helmets, and so on. Some things were blown more than a mile away. I found a Russian felt boot, weighing five pounds, lying three-quarters of a mile from the crate in which it had been stowed, and it must have had a clear run in the air for the whole of this distance, for there was not a scratch on the leather; if it had been blown along the rocks, which lay in the way, the leather would certainly have been scratched all over. The chimney, which was an iron pipe, projecting two or three feet above the roof of the hut, and capped by a cowl, was let through the roof, at the south-east end, and secured by numerous rope stays supporting it at every point from which the wind could blow.

We were quite free from the trouble of down draughts or choking with snow, such as had been of common occurrence in the large hut on the *Discovery* expedition. Certainly the revolving cowl blew off during the first blizzard, and this happened again in the second, so we took the hint and left it off for good, without detriment, as it happened, to the efficiency of the stove.

The dog kennels were placed close to the porch of the hut, but only three of the dogs were kept constantly chained up. The meteorological station was on the weather side of the hut on the top of a small ridge, about twenty feet above the hut and forty feet above sealevel, and a natural path led to it. Adams laid it out, and the regular readings of the instruments began on March 22. The foundation of the thermometer screen consisted of a heavy wooden case resting on rocks. The case was three-quarters filled with rock, and round the outside were piled more blocks of kenyte; the crevices between them were filled with volcanic earth on to which water was poured, the result being a structure as rigid as the ground itself. On each side of the box a heavy upright was secured by the rocks inside the case and by bolts at the sides, and to these uprights the actual meteorological screen, one of the Stevenson pattern and of standard size, was bolted. As readings of the instruments were to be taken day and night at intervals of two hours, and as it was quite possible that the weather might be so thick that a person might be lost in making his way between the screen and the hut, a line was rigged up on posts which were cemented into the ground by ice, so that in the thickest weather the observer could be sure of finding his way by following this very substantial clue.

10

FIRST DAYS IN WINTER QUARTERS

The inside of the hut was not long in being fully furnished, and a great change it was from the bare shell of our first days of occupancy. The first thing done was to peg out a space for each individual, and we saw that the best plan would be to have the space allotted in sections, allowing two persons to share one cubicle. This space for two men amounted to six feet six inches in length and seven feet in depth from the wall of the hut towards the centre. There were seven of these cubicles, and a space for the leader of the expedition; thus providing for the fifteen who made up the shore party. The accompanying photographs will give an idea of the hut as finished. One of the most important parts of the interior construction was the darkroom for the photographers. We were very short of wood, so cases of bottled fruit, which had to be kept inside the hut to prevent them freezing, were utilised for building the walls. The dark-room was constructed in the left-hand corner of the hut as one entered, and the fruit-cases were turned with their lids facing out, so that the contents could be removed without demolishing the walls of the building. These cases, as they were emptied, were turned into lockers, where we stowed our spare gear and so obtained more room in the little cubicles. The interior of the dark-room was fitted up by Mawson and the Professor. The sides and roof were lined with the felt left over after the hut was completed. Mawson made the fittings complete in every detail, with shelves, tanks, &c., and the result was as good as any one could desire in the circumstances.

On the other side of the doorway, opposite the darkroom, was my room, six feet long, seven feet deep, built of boards and roofed, the roof being seven feet above the floor. I lined the walls inside with canvas, and the bed-place was constructed of fruit boxes, which, when emptied, served, like those outside, for lockers. My room contained the bulk of our library, the chronometers, the chronometer watches, barograph, and the electric recording thermometer; there was ample room for a table, and the whole made a most comfortable cabin. On the roof we stowed those of our scientific instruments which were not in use, such as theodolites, spare thermometers, dip circles, &c. The gradual accumulation of weight produced a distinct sag in the roof, which sometimes seemed to threaten collapse as I sat inside, but no notice was taken, and nothing happened. On the roof of the dark-room we stowed all our photographic gear and our few cases of wine, which were only drawn upon on special occasions, such as Mid-winter Day. The acetylene gas-plant was set up on a platform between my room and the dark-room. We had tried to work it from the porch, but the temperature was so low there that the water froze and the gas would not come, so we shifted it inside the hut, and had no further trouble. Four burners, including a portable standard light in my room, gave ample illumination. The simplicity and portability of the apparatus and the high efficiency of the light represented the height of luxury under polar conditions and did much to render our sojourn more tolerable than would have been possible in earlier days. The particular form that we used was supplied by Mr Morrison, who had been chief engineer on the *Morning* on her voyage to the relief of the *Discovery*. The only objectionable feature, due to having the generating-plant in our livingroom, was the unpleasant smell given off when the carbide tanks were being recharged, but we soon got used to this, though the daily charging always drew down strong remarks on the unlucky head of Day, who had the acetylene plant especially under his charge. He did not have a hitch with it all the time. Flexible steel tubes were carried from the tank, and after being wound round the beams of the roof, served to suspend the lights at the required positions.

A long ridge of rope wire was stretched from one end of the hut to the other on each side, seven feet out from the wall; then at intervals of six feet another wire was brought out from the wall of the hut, and made fast to the fore and aft wire. These lines marked the boundaries of the cubicles, and sheets of duck sewn together hung from them, making a good division. Blankets were served out to hang in the front of the cubicle, in case the inhabitants wanted at any time to 'sport their oak'. As each of the cubicles had distinctive features in the furnishing and general design, especially as regards beds, it is worth while to describe them fully. This is not so trivial a matter as it may appear to some readers, for during the winter months the inside of the hut was the whole inhabited world to us. The wall of Adams' and Marshall's cubicle, which was next to my room, was fitted with shelves made out of Venesta cases, and there was so much neatness and order about this apartment that it was known by the address, 'No. 1 Park Lane'. In front of the shelves hung little gauze curtains, tied up with blue ribbon, and the literary tastes of the occupants could be seen at a glance from the bookshelves. In Adams' quarter the period of the French Revolution and the Napoleonic era filled most of his bookshelves, though a complete edition of Dickens came in a good second.

Marshall's shelves were stocked with bottles of medicine, medical works, and some general literature. The dividing curtain of duck was adorned by Marston with life-sized coloured drawings of Napoleon and Joan of Arc. Adams and Marshall did Sandow exercises daily, and their example was followed by other men later on, when the darkness and bad weather made open-air work difficult. The beds of this particular cubicle were the most comfortable in the hut, but took a little longer to rig up at night than most of the others. This disadvantage was more than compensated for by the free space gained during the day, and by permission of the owners it was used as consulting-room, dispensary, and operating theatre. The beds consisted of bamboos lashed together for extra strength, to which strips of canvas were attached, so that each bed looked like a stretcher. The wall end rested on stout cleats screwed on to the side of the hut, the other ends on chairs, and, so supported, the occupants slept soundly and comfortably.

The next cubicle on the same side was occupied by Marston and Day, and as the former was the artist and the latter the general handy man of the expedition, one naturally found an ambitious scheme of decoration. The shelves were provided with beading, and the Venesta boxes were stained brown. This idea was copied from No. 1 Park Lane, where they had stained all their walls with Condy's Fluid. Marston's and Day's cubicle was known as 'The Gables', presumably from the gabled appearance of the shelves. Solid wooden beds, made out of old packing-cases and upholstered with wood shavings covered with blankets, made very comfortable couches, one of which could be pushed during meal times out of the way of the chairs. The artist's curtain was painted to represent a fireplace and mantelpiece in civilisation; a cheerful fire burned in the grate, and a bunch of flowers stood on the mantelpiece. The dividing curtain between it and No. 1 Park Lane, on the other side of the cubicle, did not require to be decorated, for the colour of Joan of Arc, and also portions of Napoleon, had oozed through the canvas. In 'The Gables' was set up the lithographic press, which was used for producing pictures for the book which was printed at our winter quarters.

The next cubicle on the same side belonged to Armytage and Brocklehurst. Here everything in the way of shelves and fittings was very primitive. I lived in Brocklehurst's portion of the cubicle for two months, as he was laid up in my room, and before I left it I constructed a bed of empty petrol cases. The smell from these for the first couple of nights after rigging them up was decidedly unpleasant, but it disappeared after a while. Next to Brocklehurst's and Armytage's quarters came the pantry. The division between the cubicle and the pantry consisted of a tier of cases, making a substantial wall between the food and the heads of the sleepers. The pantry, bakery, and store-room, all combined, measured six feet by three, not very spacious, certainly, but sufficient to work in. The far end of the hut constituted the other wall of the pantry, and was lined with shelves up to the slope of the roof. These shelves were continued along the wall behind the stove, which stood about four feet out from the end of the house, and an erection of wooden battens and burlap or sacking concealed the biological laboratory. The space taken up by this important department was four feet by four, but lack of ground area was made up for by the shelves, which contained dozens of bottles soon to be filled with Murray's biological captures.

Beyond the stove, facing the pantry, was Mackay's and Roberts' cubicle, the main feature of which was a ponderous shelf, on which rested mostly socks and other light articles, the only thing of weight being our gramophone and records. The bunks were somewhat feeble imitations of those belonging to No. 1 Park Lane, and the troubles that the owners went through before finally getting them into working order afforded the rest of the community a good deal of amusement. I can see before me now the triumphant face of Mackay, as he called all hands round to see his design. The inhabitants of No. 1 Park Lane pointed out that the bamboo was not a rigid piece of wood, and that when Mackay's weight came on it the middle would bend and the ends would jump off the supports unless secured. Mackay undressed before a critical audience, and he got into his bag and expatiated on the comfort and luxury he was experiencing, so different to the hard boards he had been lying on for months. Roberts was anxious to try his couch, which was constructed on the same principle, and the audience were turning away disappointed at not witnessing a catastrophe, when suddenly a crash was heard, followed by a strong expletive. Mackay's bed was half on the ground, one end of it resting at a most uncomfortable angle. Laughter and pointed remarks as to his capacity for making a bed were nothing to him; he tried three times that night to fix it up, but at last had to give it up for a bad job. In due time he arranged fastenings, and after that he slept in comfort.

Between this cubicle and the next there was no division, neither party troubling about the matter. The result was that the four men were constantly at war regarding alleged encroachments on their ground. Priestley, who was long-suffering, and who occupied the cubicle with Murray, said he did not mind a chair or a volume of the *Encyclopaedia Britannica* being occasionally deposited on him while he was asleep, but that he thought it was a little too strong to drop wet boots, newly arrived from the stables, on top of his belongings. Priestley and Murray had no floor-space at all in their cubicle, as their beds were built of empty dog-biscuit boxes. A division of boxes separated the two sleepingplaces, and the whole cubicle was garnished on Priestley's side with bits of rock, ice-axes, hammers and chisels, and on Murray's with biological requisites.

Next came one of the first cubicles that had been built. Joyce and Wild occupied the 'Rogues' Retreat', a painting of two very tough characters drinking beer out of pint mugs, with the inscription *The Rogues' Retreat* painted underneath, adorning the entrance to the den. The couches in this house were the first to be built, and those of the opposite dwelling, 'The Gables', were copied from their design. The first bed had been built in Wild's store-room for secrecy's sake; it was to burst upon the view of every one, and to create mingled feelings of admiration and envy, admiration for the splendid design, envy of the unparalled luxury provided by it. However, in building it, the designer forgot the size of the doorway he had to take it through, and it had ignominiously to be sawn in half before it could be passed out of the store-room into the hut. The printing press and type case for the polar paper occupied one corner of this cubicle.

The next and last compartment was the dwellingplace of the Professor and Mawson. It would be difficult to do justice to the picturesque confusion of this compartment; one hardly likes to call it untidy, for the things that covered the bunks by daytime could be placed nowhere else conveniently. A miscellaneous assortment of cameras, spectroscopes, thermometers, microscopes, electrometers and the like lay in profusion on the blankets. Mawson's bed consisted of his two boxes, in which he had stowed his scientific apparatus on the way down, and the Professor's bed was made out of kerosene cases. Everything in the way of tin cans or plug-topped, with straw wrappers belonging to the fruit bottles was collected by these two scientific men. Mawson, as a rule, put his possessions in his store-room outside, but the Professor, not having any retreat like that, made a pile of glittering tins and coloured wrappers at one end of his bunk, and the heap looked like the nest of the Australian bower bird. The straw and the tins were generally cleared away when the Professor and Priestley went in for a day's packing of geological specimens; the straw wrappers were utilised for wrapping round the rocks, and the tins were filled with paper wrapped round the more delicate geological specimens. The name given, though not by the owners, to this cubicle was 'The Pawn Shop', for not only was there always a heterogeneous mass of things on the bunks, but the wall of the darkroom and the wall of the hut at this spot could not be seen for the multitude of cases ranged as shelves and filled with a varied assortment of note-books and instruments. in order to give as much free space as possible in the centre of the hut we had the table so arranged that it could he hoisted up over our heads after meals were over. This gave ample room for the various earpentering and engineering efforts that were constantly going on. Murray built the table out of the lids of packing-cases, and though often scrubbed, the stenciling on the cases never came out. We had no table-cloth, but this was an advantage, for a wellscrubbed table had a cleaner appearance than would be obtained with such washing as could be done in an Antarctic laundry. The legs of the table were detachable, being after the fashion of trestles, and the whole affair, when meals were over, was slung by a rope at each end about eight feet from the floor. At first we used to put the boxes containing knives, forks, plates and bowls on top of the table before hauling it up, but after these had fallen on the unfortunate head of the person trying to get them down, we were content to keep them on the floor.

I had been very anxious as regards the stove, the most important, part of the hut equipment, when I heard that, after the blizzard that kept me on board the *Nimrod*, the temperature of the hut was below zero, and that socks put to dry in the baking-ovens came out as damp as ever the following morning. My anxiety was dispelled after the stove had been taken to pieces again, for it was found that eight important pieces of its structure had not been put in. As soon as this omission was rectified the stove acted splendidly, and the makers deserve our thanks for the particular apparatus they picked out as suitable for us. The stove was put to a severe test, for it was kept going day and night for over nine months without once being out for more than ten minutes, when occasion required it to be cleaned. It supplied us with sufficient heat to keep the temperature of the hut sixty to seventy degrees above the outside air. Enough bread could be baked to satisfy our whole hungry party of fifteen every day; three hot meals a day were also cooked, and water melted from ice at a temperature of perhaps twenty degrees below zero in sufficient quantity to afford as much as we required for ourselves, and to water the ponies twice a day, and all this work was done on a consumption not exceeding five hundredweight of coal per week. After testing the stove by running it on an accurately measured amount of coal for a month, we were reassured about our coal-supply being sufficient to carry us through the winter right on to sledging time.

As the winter came on and the light grew faint outside, the hut became more and more like a workshop, and it seems strange to me now, looking back to those distant days, to remember the amount of trouble and care that was taken to furnish and beautify what was only to be a temporary home. One of our many kind friends had sent us a number of pictures, which were divided between the various cubicles, and these brightened up the place wonderfully. During our first severe blizzard, the hut shook and trembled so that every moment we expected the whole thing to carry away, and there is not the slightest shadow of a doubt that if we had been located in the open, the hut and everything in it would have been torn up and blown away. Even with our sheltered position I had to lash the chronometers to the shelf in my room, for they were apt to be shaken off when the walls trembled in the gale. When the storm was over we put a stout wire cable over the hut, burying the ends in the ground and freezing them in, so as to afford additional security in case heavier weather was in store for us in the future.

11

SLEDGING EQUIPMENT,
PONIES AND DOGS

At the commencement of this narrative I gave some general information regarding our equipment and provisioning, but it will now be necessary to describe more fully the sledging outfits used by the various expeditions that left our winter quarters. The first, and one of the most important of the items was, of course, the sledge, though, indeed, everything taken on a sledge journey is absolutely essential; one does not load up odds and ends on the chance of their proving useful, for the utmost reduction of weight compatible with efficiency is the first and last thing for the polar explorer to aim at. The sledge which we used is the outcome of the experience of many former explorers, but it is chiefly due to Nansen that it has become the very useful vehicle that it is at the present day. On the *Discovery* expedition we had sledges of various lengths, seven feet, nine feet, eleven feet and twelve feet. Our experience on that occasion showed that the eleven-foot sledge was the best for all-round use, but I had taken with me a certain number of twelve-foot sledges as being possibly more suitable for pony traction. A good sledge for Antarctic or Arctic travelling must be rigid in its upright and cross-bars, and yet give to uneven surfaces, so that in travelling over sastrugi the strain will not come on the whole of the sledge. A well-constructed sledge, travelling over an uneven surface, appears to have an undulating, snake-like movement, and the attainment of this suppleness without interfering with the strength of the structure as a whole, is the main point to be aimed at; in our case there was nothing wanting in this respect.

The wooden runners were about four inches wide and made of hickory, split from the tree with the grain of the wood and not sawn. Many pieces were inspected and rejected and only those passed as perfect were used. This method of preparing the runners, it can easily be seen, allows much greater scope for bending than would be the case if the wood were sawn regardless of the run of the grain. In pulling the sledge the direction of the grain on the snow surface has to be observed, and it is wonderful what a difference it makes whether one is pulling with or against the grain of the runner. The second point to consider is the height of the framework of the sledge above the surface of the snow. Naturally, with a low framework there is less chance of the sledge-load capsizing when passing over rough ground, and the aim of the explorer is therefore to keep the load as low as possible on the sledge. It has been found that a clearance of six inches is ample in all ordinary circumstances, so the uprights of our sledges were only about six inches high. These uprights were fastened at intervals into holes on the upper side of the runners, and instead of being fastened on the underside of the latter, other holes were bored in the ridge on the upper side and raw hide lashings passed through them and through the upright. Crosspieces were fastened by a sort of dovetailing process, supplemented by marlin lashings, and the angle made by the vertical upright and horizontal cross-piece was crossed by a short iron stay. This junction of crosspiece and upright was the only absolutely rigid part of the whole sledge. Every other portion of a good sledge gives somewhat as it takes up the various strains, and it entirely depends on good workmanship and sailor-like lashings whether, on the strain being removed, the sledge returns to its normal shape or is permanently distorted. Two long runners or bearers, about an inch square, rested on the uprights, and crosspieces projecting the whole length of the sledge and fastened by extra strong marlin lashings, covered with leather to protect them from the chafing of the equipment stowed on top, formed a sort of platform on which the stores were placed. The fore end of the sledge had a bow of wood, forming practically a semicircle, the two ends being fastened to the slightly upturned ends of the runners. The upper bearers were pressed down, and also lashed to this bow. This upturning at the forward end of the sledge allowed for the meeting of unequal surfaces, and the shape of the bow was intended to prevent the ends of the sledge being driven into snow or ice obstructions. The rear end of the sledge was also slightly turned up, and the top bearers bent down and lashed to the bare ends. Of course, a bow was not necessary at that end. At each end of the sledge, made fast round the first two uprights and the last two on both sides, were two pieces of Alpine rope, which combines strength with lightness. The bight of this rope was formed into a becket, and by this means a toggle attached to the sledge harness could be readily put in. When sledges are running in line, one behind the other, particular care has to be taken with these ropes, so that the tracks of the second sledge coincide with the first. By doing this the amount of friction on the runners of the second sledge is greatly reduced, for the forward sledge does practically all the work of breaking the trail, and the following ones run lightly over the made track. An eleven-foot sledge, fully loaded, is at its best working weight with about 650 lb. on it, but this by no means represents its actual strength capacity, for we tested ours most rigorously during the unloading of the ship, often placing over a thousand pounds' weight on a sledge without it sustaining the slightest damage. After our experience on the barrier surface during the *Discovery* expedition, I had decided to dispense with metal runners, so only a few sets of detachable steel underrunners were provided, to be used for work on ground bare of snow or on rough glacier-ice. In order to fasten the stores on the sledge we riveted straps on to the bearers, and thus formed a handy and trustworthy means of fastening things with the least possible loss of time.

Another vitally important article of equipment for the polar explorer is the cooker and cooking-stove. Here again we were indebted to the practical genius of Nansen, who designed the form of cooker that is now invariably used in polar work. The stove was the ordinary 'primus', burning kerosene, vapourised in the usual way. This stove is highly efficient, and, with strict economy, one gallon of oil will last three men for ten days, allowing three hot meals per day. This economy is due, in a large measure, to the qualities of the cooker. The form we used consisted of an outer cover of aluminium drawn out of one piece, inside which was a ring-shaped vessel so designed that the heated air could circulate round it. Inside this vessel was the centre cooking-pot, and these pots were all mounted on a concave plate of aluminium which fitted over the top of the primus lamp. The middle cooker was first filled with snow or ice, pressed tightly down, the lid was put on and this vessel placed inside the outer, ring-shaped cooker, which was also filled with snow; over all this apparatus the aluminium outside cover was placed, inverted. The heated gases from the stove, after heating the bottom of the centre cooker, mounted into the space between the two vessels, and were then forced down the outside of the ring-shaped cooker by the cover, finally escaping at the lower edge. Experiments showed that about 92 per cent. of the heat generated by the lamp was used in the cooker, a most satisfactory result, for economy in fuel is of great importance when the oil has to be carried on sledges. I did not have draw-off taps on the cookers, but they were so arranged that the boiling-pot in the centre lifted in and out easily. Such was the efficiency of the cooker and stove that, in a temperature of forty or fifty degrees below zero, the snow or ice, which would be at this temperature, could be melted and a hot meal prepared within half an hour from the time the cooker was first placed on the primus. The whole apparatus, including the primus, did not weigh more than fifteen pounds. When the cooker was empty after meals, our feeding-utensils were placed inside. They consisted of pannikins and spoons only. The former were made of aluminium in pairs, and fitted one into another. The outer pannikin, for holding the hot tea or cocoa, was provided with handles, and the other fitted over the top of this and was used for the more solid food. There was no 'washing up' on the march, for spoons were licked clean and pannikins scraped assiduously when sledging appetites had been developed.

The next important item was the tent. The usual unit for sledging consists of three men, and our tents were designed to contain that number. The tent cloth was thin Willesden duck, with a 'snow cloth' of thicker material round the lower edge. This snow cloth was spread out on the ground and snow or ice piled on it so that the form of the tent was like that of an inverted convolvulus. Instead of a single tent pole we used five male bamboo rods, eight feet six inches in length, fastened together at one end in a cap, over which the apex of the tent fitted. The bamboos were stretched out, and the tent was slung over the top, with the door, which took the form of a sort of spout of Burberry material, on the lee side. This Burberry spout was loose and could be tied up by being gathered together when the occupants were inside the tent, or could be left open when desired. Inside the tent was placed on the snow a circle of thick Willesden waterproof canvas to protect the sleeping bags from actual contact with the ground. The material of which the tents were constructed appeared flimsy and the bamboos were light, but one could trust them with absolute confidence to encounter successfully the fiercest blizzards of this exceptionally stormy part of the world. There was no instance of damage to a tent owing to bad weather during the expedition.

The next important item of our equipment was the sleeping-bag. It has been generally assumed by polar explorers, despite our experience with the *Discovery* expedition, that it is absolutely necessary for sledge travellers to wrap themselves up in furs. We have found this to be quite unnecessary, and I think that I am justified, from my experience during two expeditions in what is, undoubtedly, a more rigorous climate than exists in the north polar regions, in stating that, except for the hands and feet, in the way of personal clothing, and the sleeping-bags for camping, furs are entirely unnecessary. Our sleeping-bags, as I have already stated, were made of hides of young reindeer. The hide of the young reindeer is the most comfortable fur that can be used for this purpose, being very close and thick. The term 'bag' literally describes this portion of the sledging-gear. It is a long bag, with closely sewn seams, and is entered by means of a slit at the upper end. A flap comes down over the head of the occupant, and a toggle on the flap fastens into an eye at the mouth of the bag; thus secured, one can sleep in more or less comfort, according to the temperature.

The clothing usually worn for sledging-work consisted of thick Jaeger underclothing, heavy blue pilotcloth trousers, a Jaeger pyjama jacket for coat, and over this, as our main protection against cold and wind, the Burberry blouse and trousers. On the hands we wore woollen gloves and then fur mits, and on the feet several pairs of heavy woollen socks and then finnesko. Any one feeling the texture and lightness of the Burberry material would hardly believe that it answers so well in keeping out the cold and wind and in offering, during a blizzard, a complete protection against the fine drifting snow that permeates almost anything. Some of our party wore a pair of

Burberry trousers over the Jaeger underclothing throughout the winter, and did not feel the need of the cloth trousers at all. The head-gear, which is another item of one's equipment especially important as regards comfort, was a matter upon which there were marked differences of opinion. The most general method of keeping the head and ears warm was to wrap a woollen muffler twice round the chin and head, thus forming protection for the ears, which are the first part of the body to show signs of frost-bite; the muffler was then brought round one's neck, and over the muffler was pulled what is known as a fleecy travelling cap, a woollen helmet, in appearance something like an old-time helmet without the visor. If a blizzard were blowing the muffler was discarded, the helmet put on, and over this the Burberry helmet, which has a stiff flap in front that can be buttoned into a funnel shape. The helmet and the fur mits were made fast to a length of lamp-wick which was tied round the neck, so that they could be removed temporarily without fear of being lost. The sledge traveller wearing this gear could be assured that his features and body would be exempt from frost-bite under all ordinary circumstances. Of course, in very low temperatures, or with a moderately low temperature and a breeze blowing, it was necessary occasionally to inspect each other's faces for the sign of frost-bite, and if the white patch which denotes this was visible, it had to be attended to at once.

Having considered the clothing, camping and cookinge-quipment of a sledge-party we now come to the important item of food. The appetite of a man who has just come to camp after a five-hours' march in a low temperature is a thing that the ordinary individual at home would hardly understand, and, indeed, the sledger himself has moments of surprise when, after finishing his ration, he feels just about as hungry as when he started. Much has been written on the subject of food in most books on polar exploration, and in Captain Scott's account of the *Discovery* expedition this matter is dealt with in an interesting and exhaustive manner. In selecting our supplies I had based my plans on the experience gained by the previous expedition, and for the sledging journeys I had tried to provide the maximum amount of heat-giving and flesh-forming materials, and to avoid as far as possible foods containing a large amount of moisture, which means so much dead weight to be carried. Our cuisine was not very varied, but a voracious appetite has no nice discernment and requires no sauce to make the meal palatable; indeed, all one wants is more, and this is just what cannot be allowed if a party is to achieve anything in the way of distance whilst confined to man-haulage. It is hard for a hungry man to rest content with the knowledge that the particular food he is eating contains so much nourishment and is sufficient for his needs, if at the same time he does not feel full and satisfied after the meal and if, within an hour or so, the aching void again makes itself felt, and he has to wait another five hours before he can again temporarily satisfy the craving. One of the main items of our food-supply was pemmican, which consisted of the finest beef powdered with 60 per cent of fat added. This is one of the staple foods in polar work, and the fat has properties specially tending to promote heat. Our pemmican for use on the long sledge journeys was obtained from Messrs. Beauvais, of Copenhagen, and was similar to the pemmican we had on the *Discovery* expedition. Biscuits are a standard food also, and in this matter I had made a departure from the example of the previous expedition. We found then that the thin wholemeal biscuits which we used in sledging work were apt to break, and it was difficult to make out the exact allowance for each day, the result being that sometimes we used up our supply for the week too early. I secured thicker biscuits, but the principal change was in the composition itself. The Plasmon Company supplied a ton of the best wholemeal biscuit, containing 25 per cent. of plasmon; the plasmon tended to harden the biscuit, and, as is well known, it is an excellent food. These biscuits were specially baked, and, with an allowance of one pound for each man per day, were a distinct advance on the farinaceous food of the previous expedition. This allowance, I may mention, was reduced very considerably when food began to run short on the southern and northern journeys, but we had no fault to find with the quality of the biscuits. The addition of the plasmon certainly increased their food-value. Tea and cocoa were selected as our beverages for use on the march. We used tea for breakfast and lunch, and cocoa, which tends to produce sleepiness, for dinner at night. Sugar is a very valuable heat-forming substance, and our allowance of this amounted to about a third of a pound for each man for a day. We also took chocolate, cheese and oatmeal, so that, though there was not very much variety, we felt we were getting the most nutritious food possible. We had a much more varied selection of foods at the winter quarters, and the supplies taken on the sledging journeys could be varied to some extent according to the necessities of the occasion.

In considering the various methods of haulage in the Antarctic the experience of the National Antarctic Expedition proved of very great value. Until the *Discovery* wintered at the head of McMurdo Sound no sledge journey had been made over the surface of the Great Ice Barrier, and, indeed, when the *Discovery* left England there was an idea amongst many of the best authorities that very little sledging would be necessary. It was thought that the main part of the exploration would be undertaken by the ship itself. Preparations had been made in the event of a landing, and the equipment, as far as the sledges, harness, and so on, were concerned, was excellent. The expedition was dependent, however, on dogs for haulage purposes, and the use of these animals on the Barrier was not at all successful. Only twenty dogs were taken with the *Discovery*, and the trouble they gave and their eventual collapse and failure are matters of common knowledge amongst those interested in Antarctic exploration. The knowledge I gained of the Barrier surface on that occasion suggested to me the feasibility of using ponies for traction purposes, for I had heard that in Siberia and Northern Manchuria ponies of a peculiarly hardy and sturdy stock did excellent work in hauling sledges and carrying packs over snow and ice at very low temperatures and under very severe weather conditions.

It seems to be generally assumed that a Manchurian pony can drag a sledge over a broken trail at the rate of twenty to thirty miles a day, pulling not less than twelve hundred pounds. Some authorities even put the weight to be hauled at eighteen hundred pounds, but this is, I think, far too heavy a load. It was a risk to take ponies from the far north through the tropics and then across two thousand miles of stormy sea on a very small ship, but I felt that if it could be done it would be well worth the trouble, for, compared with the dog, the pony is a far more efficient animal, one pony doing the work of at least ten dogs on the food allowance for ten dogs, and travelling a longer distance in a day.

We established ourselves at the winter quarters with eight ponies, but unfortunately we lost four of them within a month of our arrival. The loss was due, in the case of three of the four, to the fact that they were picketed when they first landed on sandy ground, and it was not noticed that they were eating the sand. I had neglected to see that the animals had a supply of salt given to them, and as they found a saline flavour in the volcanic sand under their feet, due to the fact that the blizzards had sprayed all the land near the shore with sea water, they ate it at odd moments. All the ponies seem to have done this, but some were more addicted to the habit than the others. Several of them became ill, and we were quite at a loss to account for the trouble until Sandy died. Then a post-mortem examination revealed the fact that his stomach contained many pounds of sand, and the cause of the illness of the other ponies became apparent. We shifted them at once from the place where they were picketed, so that they could get no more sand, and gave them what remedial treatment lay in our power, but two more died in spite of all our efforts. The loss of the fourth pony was due to poisoning. The Manchurian ponies will eat anything at all that can be chewed, and this particular animal seems to have secured some shavings in which chemicals had been packed. The post-mortem examination showed that there were distinct signs of corrosive poisoning. The losses were a matter of deep concern to us.

We were left with four ponies, Quan, Socks, Grisi and Chinaman, and it is a rather curious fact that the survivors were the white or light-coloured animals, while disaster had befallen all the dark animals.

The four ponies were very precious in our eyes, and they were watched and guarded with keen attention. At first we exercised them daily by walks across the hills, and later in the season, when it became too dark to go across the rough ground with safety, they were exercised up and down the snow-covered lake known as Green Park close to the hut. Before day-light grew faint the usual morning walk was over the hills along the sea-coast to Sandy Beach, where they always had a roll on the soft volcanic sand, and after this a circuit was made homewards round the further side of Blue Lake and Back Door Bay. For a change sometimes they were taken on to the snow slopes and foothills of Mount Erebus on the level stretches of which they were ridden, but this was stopped as soon as there was any fear of them stumbling in the fading daylight.

During the winter months those of us who generally took the ponies out for exercise got to learn the different traits and character of each individual animal. Every one of them seemed to possess more cunning and sense than the ordinary broken-in horse at home, and this cunning, when put into practice to gain any end of their own, was a constant source of petty annoyance to us. Quan was the worst offender, his particular delight being to bite through his head rope and attack the bales of fodder stacked behind him; then, when we put a chain on to prevent this, he deliberately rattled it against the side of the hut, which kept us awake. The wall of the hut was sheathed with galvanised iron, and shortly after the ponies entered the stable, as they started to gnaw the ropes, a line of wire had been stretched fore and aft along the stables to which to make fast the head rope. Quan used to take this line between his teeth and pull back as far as possible and then let it go with a bang. We tried keeping his nose-bag on, but within a few hours he would have worked a hole in this and started again on the rope. On going into the stables to try and stop his mischief, one's annoyance invariably passed away on seeing the intelligent look on the delinquent's face, as he rolled his eye round and leered at one as though to say: 'Ha! Got the best of you again.' At last old Quan was tethered by his fore and hind legs, the ridge rope was taken away, and peace reigned, as a rule, in the stables. He had at first suffered from eating sand, and we had to use great care to prevent him getting at it again, he being greatly addicted to the practice; if he were given the smallest opportunity down would go his head and he would be crunching a mouthful of the loose volcanic material.

Grisi was our best-looking pony, with a very pretty action and in colour a dapple grey; his conduct in the stables, however, was not friendly to the other ponies and we had to build him a separate stall in the far corner, as on the slightest provocation he would lash out with his hind feet. He became rather nervous and high-strung during the dark months, though we kept a lamp continually burning in the ponies' quarters. Socks was a pretty little pony, shaped something like a miniature Clydesdale, very willing to work and always very fiery. After leading him along when out walking, it seemed a

great change to take great raw-boned good-natured old Quan, who, in spite
of his ugly appearance, was a general favourite. The last of our remaining
ponies, Chinaman, was a strong beast, sulky in appearance, but in reality
one of the best of the horses; he also had a penchant for biting through his
head rope, but a chain stopped this. When we first landed we had an idea
of not building a stable, as information from people in Siberia suggested that
the ponies were able to resist cold unsheltered, but after the first blizzard it
was quite obvious that if they were to keep any sort of condition it would be
necessary to stable them. It was not till nearly August that we were forced
to take away part of their house to feed them with. Our windows on that
side of the hut where the stable stood had been planked over last, the weather
side of the hut having been done much earlier. The lower half of the lee
side windows had been boarded up, which Grisi put his head through, but
the tops had been left. Amongst the duties of the night watchman was a
two-hourly inspection of the stables, and if he heard any suspicious noises
between inspection time, he had to go out and investigate the cause. After
a couple of months these precautions became unnecessary, for a little army
of pups used to sleep in the stables during the cold weather, and if by any
means a pony got adrift, they at once surrounded him, barking furiously, and
the noise conveyed to the watchman that the outside watchers had observed
something wrong. I remember one night that Grisi got free and dashed out of
the stables, followed by the whole party of pups, who rounded him up on the
Green Park, and after a struggle Mackay secured the truant and brought him
back, the dogs following with an air of pride as though conscious of having
done their duty.

We had been able to obtain only nine dogs, five bitches and four dogs, but
so prolific were they that before mid-winter we had a young family of nine
pups, five of these being born on the *Nimrod*. There were many more births,
but most of the puppies came to an untimely end, there being a marked
difference between the mothers as regards maternal instincts. Gwendoline,
known as the 'mad bitch', took no care at all of her pups, whilst Daisy
not only mothered her own but also a surviving puppy belonging to Gwen,
which was taken from her when the culpable carelessness she had exhibited
in the rearing of her offspring had resulted in the death of the remainder.
The younger pups born at winter quarters did not attain the same size when
grown up as did Possum's pups, born on the *Nimrod*. This may be due either
to the very cold world they were born into or to the fact that their mothers
were much smaller than Possum. The old dogs that we brought were kept
tied up except when out for exercise or training in a sledge, for not only
did they chase and kill penguins when we had these birds with us, and
hunt placid, stupid Weddell seals, but two of the best dogs had a violent
antipathy towards each other, and more than once fierce fights took place

in consequence. Trip, one of our dogs, was pure white in colour, and was a fine upstanding beast of a very affectionate disposition. Adams looked after Trip, taking him for his sledge-training, whilst Marshall fancied Scamp, who was an older dog, more set in his bones and with a black-and-white coat. It was between these two that the battles raged, and I think there was little to choose between them as far as strength and courage were concerned. On the occasion of a fight the combatants were surrounded by all the puppies and a couple of the bitches, the latter observing the fight with the keenest interest, and I think some of these battles must be put down to the desire to gain the approval of the females.

The presence of the dogs around winter quarters and on our walks was very cheerful, and gave a homelike feeling to the place, and our interest in the pups was always fresh, for as they gradually grew up each one developed characteristics and peculiarities of its own. Names were given to them regardless of their sex. Roland, for example, did not belong to the sterner sex, and was in her earlier days a very general favourite. She had a habit of watching for the door to be opened, and then launching herself, a white furry ball, into the midst of the party in the hut. Ambrose, a great big sleepy dog, was so named by Adams, perhaps owing to his portly proportions, which might bear resemblance to the well-favoured condition of a monk. Somehow or another the name Ambrose seemed to suit him. He had a trick of putting his head between one's legs whenever we were standing about outside, so when in the dark we felt a dog about our knees, we knew it was Ambrose. Ambrose had a brother and sister, but they were nameless, shining only in the reflected glory of the great Ambrose, being known as 'Ambrose's brother' or ' Ambrose's sister'. Another white dog was called Sissy, and this particular animal affected the company of Priestley during his ice-digging expeditions. Sissy would lie on the ice alongside the hole that was being dug and was generally rewarded by getting a biscuit when the scientist did not return to the hut for lunch, taking it in the open instead. Another popular puppy, also a female, was called Mercury, because of its rapidity of movement.

All the pups were white or would have been white if some of them had not elected to sleep in the dustbin where the warm ashes were thrown at night time; indeed, the resting-places these little creatures found were varied and remarkable. In cold weather they always gravitated to the light and heat of the stables, but if the temperature was not much below zero, they slept outside, three or four bundled together inside a cork bale, another squeezed into an empty tin, another in the dust-bin, and so on. Most of them learnt by sad experience the truth of the ancient words:

Such are the perils that environ
The man who meddles with cold iron.

for sometimes an agonising wail would proceed from a puppy and the poor little beast would be found with its tongue frozen fast to a tin in which it had been searching for some succulent remains. I have mentioned the puppies' usefulness in keeping watch on the ponies. They did the same service as regards the older dogs, which were tied up, for if by chance one of these dogs got adrift, he was immediately pursued by a howling mob of puppies; when the larger puppies were eventually chained up, the smaller ones watched them, too, with jealous eye. After enjoying some months of freedom, it seemed to be a terrible thing to the young dogs when first a collar was put on and their freedom was taken from them, and even less did they enjoy the experience of being taken to the sledge and there taught to pull. I remember that on the first day the dogs simply lay down in front of the sledge, so another method was adopted, Ambrose and his brother being made fast to the rear of the sledge, and pulled willy-nilly after it. After the training had gone on some time on Green Park, the dogs were taken further afield and a favourite run was to Cape Barne and back. The Cape lay about two miles and a quarter to the south-east of our winter quarters, and with a light load the dogs would traverse this distance and back again in an hour.

Our experience on the *Discovery* expedition, specially during the long southern journey when we had so much trouble with our mixed crowd of dogs, rather prejudiced me against these animals as a means of traction, and we only took them as a stand-by in the event of the ponies breaking down. Since we were reduced to four ponies, it became necessary to consider the dogs as a possible factor in our work, and so their training was important. Peary's account of his expeditions shows that in the Arctic regions dogs have been able to traverse long distances very quickly. In one instance over ninety miles were accomplished in twenty-three hours, but this evidently had been done on smooth sea ice or on the smooth glaciated surface of the land, for it would be impossible to accomplish such a feat on the Antarctic Barrier surface, where the travelling alternates between hard sastrugi and soft snow. We were agreeably surprised with the dogs, for it must be remembered that their forebears had not lived under polar conditions since 1899 and that none of the animals had experienced Arctic weather nor were they trained for the work they had to perform on the ice. Scamp, indeed, had been a sheep-dog, and when out for a walk with the other animals it was interesting to watch how he retained the habits learnt in civilisation. He was always 'rounding up' the other dogs, and I think that they enjoyed their walks much more when Scamp was absent.

I have described our first attempt to make the motorcar go on the sea ice. After that we made similar experiments ashore, and there was no difficulty in starting the engine at a temperature of ten degrees below zero, but the driving-wheels were a great source of trouble, and the weight of the car itself made it almost impossible to travel over the snow; the heavy rear wheels sank into even the hardest snow and then spun round in the hole they had made for themselves. The car went splendidly on the bare earth, even up the steep gradient of Pony Glen, and we decided that when the spring came we would try an alteration of the wheels. If the car had only been able to travel over the Barrier surface all our difficulties would have been solved, for a hundred miles a day would not have been too much to have expected of it.

12

THE CONQUEST OF MOUNT EREBUS

The arrangement of all the details relating to settling in our winter quarters, the final touches to the hut, the building of the pony stables, and the meteorological screen, and the collection of stores, engaged our attention up to March 3. Then we began to seek some outlet for our energies that would be useful in advancing the cause of science, and the work of the expedition. I was very anxious to make a depot to the south for the furtherance of our southern journey in the following summer, but the sheet of open water that intervened between us and Hut Point forbade all progress in that direction, neither was it possible for us to make a journey towards the western mountains, where the geology might have been studied with the probability of most interesting results.

There was one journey possible, a somewhat difficult undertaking certainly, yet gaining an interest and excitement from that very reason, and this was an attempt to reach the summit of Mount Erebus. For many reasons the accomplishment of this work seemed to be desirable. In the first place, the observations of temperature and wind currents at the summit of this great mountain would have an important bearing on the movements of the upper air, a meteorological problem as yet but imperfectly understood. From a geological point of view the mountain ought to reveal some interesting facts, and apart from scientific considerations, the ascent of a mountain over 13,000 ft. in height, situated so far south, would be a matter of pleasurable excitement both to those who were selected as climbers and to the rest of us who wished for our companions' success. After consideration I decided that Professor David, Mawson and Mackay should constitute the party that was to try to reach the summit, and they were to be provisioned for ten days. A supporting-party, consisting of Adams, Marshall and Brocklehurst, was to assist the main-party as far as feasible. The whole expedition was to be under Adams' charge until he decided that it was time for his party to return, and the Professor was then to be in charge of the advance-party. In my written instructions to Adams, he was given the option of going on to the summit if he thought it feasible for his party to push on, and he actually did so, though the supporting-party was not so well equipped for the mountain work as the advance-party, and was provisioned for six days only. Instructions were given that the supporting-party was not to hamper the main-party, especially as regarded the division of provisions, but as a matter of fact, instead of hampering, the three men became of great assistance to the advance division, and lived entirely on their own stores and equipment during the whole trip. No sooner was it decided to make the ascent, which was arranged for, finally, on March 4, than the winter quarters became busy with the bustle of preparation. There were crampons to be made, food-bags to be prepared and filled, sleeping-bags to be overhauled, ice-axes to be got out and a hundred and one things to be seen to; yet such was the energy thrown into this work that the men were ready for the road and made a start at 8.30 a.m. on the 5th.

In a previous chapter I have described the nature and extent of equipment necessary for a sledging trip, so that it is not necessary now to go into details regarding the preparations for this particular journey, the only variation from the usual standard arrangement being in the matter of quantity of food. In the ascent of a mountain such as Erebus it was obvious that a limit would soon be reached beyond which it would be impossible to use a sledge. To meet these circumstances the advance-party had made an arrangement of straps by which their single sleeping-bags could be slung in the form of a knapsack upon their backs, and inside the bags the remainder of their equipment could be packed. The men of the supporting-party, in case they should journey beyond ice over which they could drag the sledge, had made the same preparations for transferring their load to their shoulders. When they started I must confess that I saw but little prospect of the whole party reaching the top, yet when, from the hut, on the third day out, we saw through Armytage's powerful telescope six tiny black spots slowly crawling up the immense deep snow-field to the base of the rugged rocky spurs that descended to the edge of the field, and when I saw next day out on the skyline the same small figures, I realised that the supporting-party were going the whole way. On the return of this expedition Adams and the Professor made a full report, with the help of which I will follow the progress of the party, the members of which were winning their spurs not only on their first Antarctic campaign, but in their first attempt at serious mountaineering.

Mount Erebus bears a name that has loomed large in the history of polar exploration both north and south. Sir James Clark Ross, on January 28, 1841, named the great volcano at whose base our winter quarters were placed after the leading ship of his expedition. The final fate of that ship is linked with the fate of Sir John Franklin and one of the most tragic stories of Arctic exploration, but though both the *Erebus* and *Terror* have sunk far from the scenes of their first exploration, that brilliant period of Antarctic discovery will ever be remembered by the mountains which took their names from those stout ships. Standing as a sentinel at the gate of the Great Ice Barrier, Erebus forms a magnificent picture. The great mountain rises from sea-level to an altitude of over 13,000 ft., looking out across the Barrier, with its enormous snow-clad bulk towering above the white slopes that run up from the coast. At the top of the mountain an immense depression marks the site of the old crater, and from the side of this rises the active cone, generally marked by steam or smoke. The ascent of such a mountain would be a matter of difficulty in any part of the world, hardly to be attempted without experienced guides, but the difficulties were accentuated by the latitude of Erebus, and the party started off with the full expectation of encountering very low temperatures. The men all recognised, however, the scientific value of the achievement at which they were aiming, and they were determined to do their utmost to reach the crater itself. How they fared and what they found will be told best by extracts from the report which was made to me.

Erebus, as seen from our winter quarters, showed distinctly the traces of the three craters observed from a distance by the scientific staff of the *Discovery* expedition. From sea-level up to an altitude of about 5500 ft. the lower slopes ascend in a gentle but gradually steepening curve to the base of the first crater; they are largely covered with snow and glacier-ice down to the shore, where the ice either breaks off to form a cliff or, as at Glacier Tongue, spreads out seawards in the form of a narrow blue pier about five miles in length. Near Cape Royds, however, there are long smooth ridges of brown glacial gravels and moraines, mostly bare of snow. These are interspersed with masses of black volcanic rock, and extend to an altitude of about 1000 ft. Above this and up to about 5000 ft. above the sea, all is snow and ice, except for an occasional outcrop of dark lava or a black parasitic cone sharply silhouetted against the light background of snow or sky. At a level of about 6000 ft. and just north of the second or main crater, rises a huge black fang of rock, the relic of the oldest and lowest crater. Immediately south of this the principal cone sweeps upwards in that graceful double curve, concave below, convex above, so characteristic of volcanoes. Rugged buttresses of dark volcanic rock, with steep snow slopes between, jut out at intervals and support the rim of this second crater, which reaches an altitude of fully 11,400 ft. From the north edge of this crater the ground ascends, at first gradually, then somewhat abruptly, to the third crater, further south. It is above this last crater that there continually floats a huge steam cloud. At the time of Ross' expedition this cloud was reddened with the glow of molten lava, and lava streams descending from the crater are also described. On the *Discovery* expedition we saw a glow once or twice during the winter months, but we were then situated about twenty-eight miles from the summit, so that possibly there were at times faint glows which we did not see, and, besides,

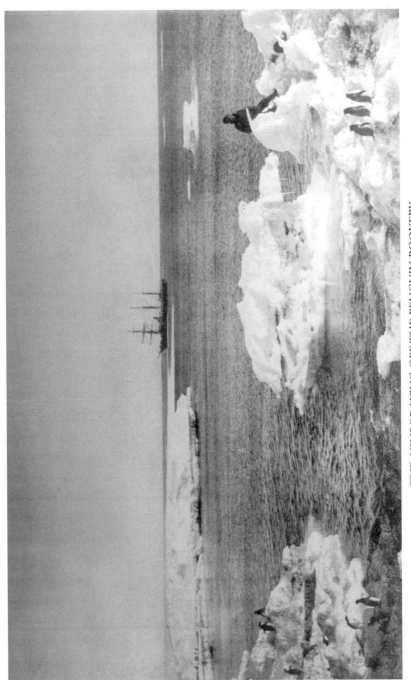

THE *NIMROD* LYING OFF THE PENGUIN ROOKERY

THE PONY 'QUAN' ABOUT TO DRAW A SLEDGE-LOAD OF STORES FROM THE ICE-FOOT TO THE HUT

FLAGSTAFF POINT, WITH THE SHORE PARTY'S BOAT HAULED UP ON THE ICE

THE VICINITY OF CAPE ROYDS. A SCENE OF DESOLATION.

PREPARING A SLEDGE DURING THE WINTER

CAPE BARNE. THE PILLAR IN THE RIGHT FOREGROUND IS VOLCANIC

A VIEW OF THE HUT LOOKING NORTHWARDS. ON THE LEFT IS SHOWN JOYCE'S HUT, MADE OF CASES. THE STABLE AND GAR-AGE ARE ON THE RIGHT SIDE OF THE HUT, AND ON THE EXTREME RIGHT IS THE SNOW GAUGE. THE INSTRUMENT FOR RECORDING ATMOSPHERIC ELECTRICITY PROJECTS FROM A CORNER ON THE ROOF. OPEN WATER CAN BE SEEN ABOUT A MILE AWAY. THIS WATER ALTERNATELY FROZE AND BROKE UP DURING THE WINTER.

A GROUP OF THE SHORE PARTY AT THE WINTER QUARTERS

STANDING (FROM LEFT): JOYCE, DAY, WILD, ADAMS, BROCKLEHURST, SHACKLETON, MARSHALL, DAVID, ARMITAGE, MARSTON

SITTING: PRIESTLEY, MURRAY, ROBERTS

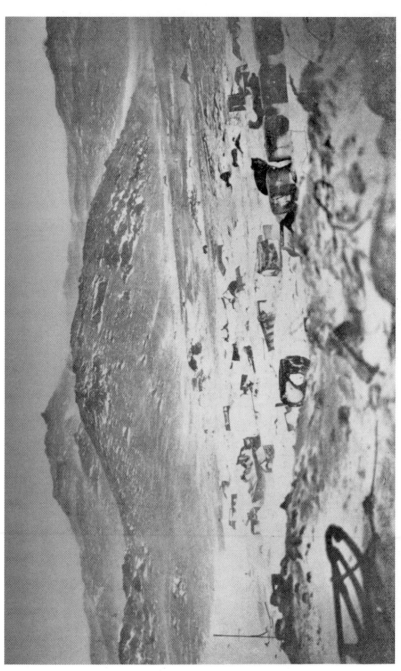

THE START OF A BLIZZARD AT THE WINTER QUARTERS, THE FUZZY APPEARANCE BEING DUE TO DRIFTING SNOW

MOUNT EREBUS AS SEEN FROM THE WINTER QUARTERS, THE OLD CRATER ON THE LEFT, AND THE ACTIVE CONE RISING ON THE RIGHT

THE FIRST SLOPES OF EREBUS

THE PARTY PORTAGING THE SLEDGE OVER A PATCH OF BARE ROCK

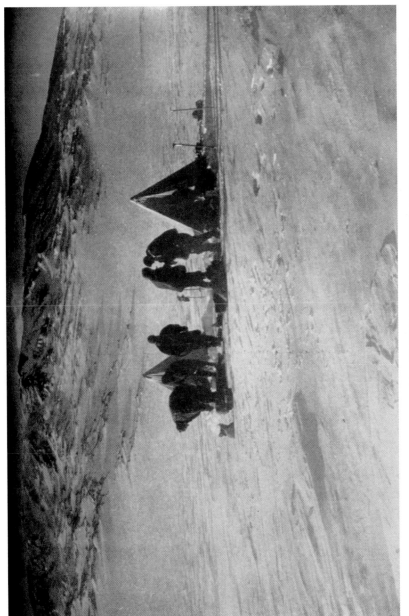

THE CAMP 7000 FEET UP MOUNT EREBUS. THE STEAM FROM THE ACTIVE CRATER CAN BE SEEN.

BROCKLEHURST LOOKING DOWN FROM A POINT 9000 FEET UP MOUNT EREBUS. THE CLOUDS LIE BELOW, AND CAPE ROYDS CAN BE SEEN.

THE OLD CRATER OF EREBUS, WITH AN OLDER CRATER IN THE BACKGROUND. ALTITUDE 11, 000 FEET. THE ACTIVE CONE IS HIGHER STILL.

A REMARKABLE FUMAROLE IN THE OLD CRATER, IN THE FORM OF A COUCHANT LION. THE MEN (FROM THE LEFT)
ARE: MACKAY, DAVID, ADAMS, MARSHALL.

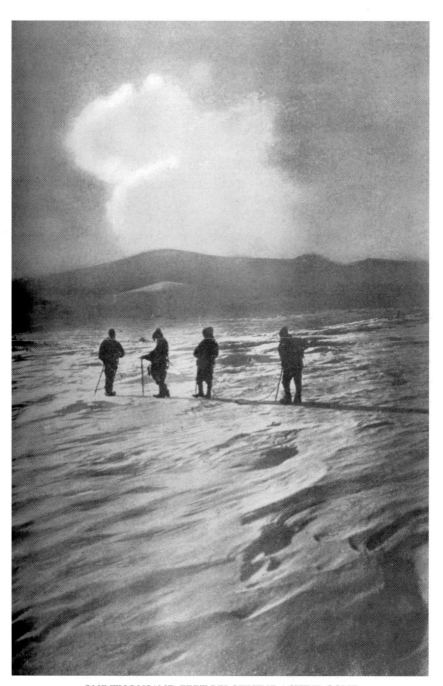

ONE THOUSAND FEET BELOW THE ACTIVE CONE

THE CRATER OF EREBUS, 900 FEET DEEP AND HALF A MILE WIDE.
STEAM IS SEEN RISING ON THE LEFT. THE PHOTOGRAPH WAS TAKEN
FROM THE LOWER PART OF THE CRATER EDGE.

it was necessary to go two or three hundred yards from the ship before the mountain, which was hidden by the local foot-hills, appeared in view. In our winter quarters on the present occasion we had a far better opportunity for observing the summit of the volcano, for we were only about fifteen miles off and from our point of view the slope of the mountain was more gentle towards the summit. Immediately we stepped outside the door of the hut we were in full view of the greater part of the mountain. The observer taking the meteorological observations every two hours had the mountain in sight, and as Erebus was our high-level meteorological observatory, to the crown of which we always looked for indications of wind-currents at that elevation, we naturally saw every phase of activity produced by the fires within. It was for this reason, no doubt, that during the period of our stay in these regions, more especially through the winter months, we were able to record a fairly constant condition of activity on the mountain. It became quite an ordinary thing to hear reports from men who had been outside during the winter that there was a 'strong glow on Erebus'. These glows at times were much more vivid than at others. On one particular occasion, when the barometer showed a period of extreme depression, the glow was much more active, waxing and waning at intervals of a quarter of an hour through the night, and at other times we have seen great bursts of flame crowning the crater.

The huge steam column that rises from the crater into the cold air shot up at times to a height of 3000 or 4000 ft. before spreading out and receiving its line direction from the air-currents at that particular hour holding the upper atmosphere. There were occasions when the view of this steam cloud became much more vivid, and we found that the best view that could be obtained was when the moon, rising in the eastern sky, passed behind the summit of the mountain. Then, projected on the disc of the moon, we could see the great cloud travelling upwards, not quietly, but impelled by force from below. There were times also when it was obvious that the molten lava in the crater could not have been very far from the lip of the cup, for we could see the deep-red glow reflected strongly on the steam cloud. We often speculated as to the course the lava stream would take and its probable effect on the great glaciers and snow-fields flanking the sides of the mountain, should it ever overflow. These sudden uprushes were obviously the result of a vast steam explosion in the interior of the volcano and were sufficient proofs that Erebus still possesses considerable activity.

On March 5, after the busy day and night of preparation, the start was made. Breakfast was served at 6 a.m., and one of the eleven-foot sledges was packed and lashed, the total weight of the load and sledge being 560 lb. I took a photograph of the party as they started off. They got under way from the hut at a quarter to nine, all hands accompanying them across the rocky ridge at the back of the hut, lifting the sledge and load bodily over this, and then helping the party to pull along the slopes of Back Door Bay across Blue Lake up the eastern slope to the first level. There we said farewell to the mountain party. They first steered straight up a snow slope and skirted closely some rocky ridges and moraines in order to avoid crevassed glaciers. About a mile out and four hundred feet above sea-level a glacial moraine barred their path, and they had to portage the sledge over it by slipping ice-axes under the load between the runners and bearers of the sledge and lifting it over the obstruction. On the further side of the moraine was a sloping surface of ice and névé on which the sledge capsized for the first time. Light snow was falling, and there was a slight wind. The report supplied to me by Professor David and Adams depicts in a graphic manner these first experiences of this party in sledging.

Pulling the sledge proved fairly heavy work in places; at one spot, on the steep slope of a small glacier, the party had a hard struggle, mostly on their hands and knees, in their efforts to drag the sledge up the surface of smooth blue ice thinly coated with loose snow. This difficulty surmounted, they encountered some sastrugi, which impeded their progress somewhat. 'Sastrugi' means wind furrow, and is the name given to those annoying obstacles to sledging, due to the action of the wind on the snow. A blizzard has the effect of scooping out hollows in the snow, and this is especially the case when local currents are set up owing to some rock or point of land intercepting the free run of the wind. These sastrugi vary in depth from two or three inches to three or four feet, according to the position of any rock masses that may be near and to the force of the wind forming them. The raised masses of snow between the hollows are difficult to negotiate with a sledge, especially when they run more or less parallel to the course of the traveller. Though they have many disadvantages, still there are times when their presence is welcome; especially is this the case when the sky is overcast and the low stratus cloud obliterates all landmarks. At these times a dull grey light is over everything, and it is impossible to see the way to steer unless one takes the line of sastrugi and notes the angle it makes with the compass course, the compass for the moment being placed on the snow to obtain the direction. In this way one can steer a fairly accurate course, occasionally verifying it by calling a halt and laying off the course again with the compass, a precaution that is very necessary, for at times the sastrugi alter in direction.

The sledgers, at this particular juncture, had much trouble in keeping their feet, and the usual equanimity of some of the men was disturbed, their remarks upon the subject of sastrugi being audible above the soft pad of the finnesko, the scrunch of the ski-boots, and the gentle sawing sound of the sledge-runners on the soft snow. About 6 p.m. the party camped at a small nunatak of black rock, about 2750 ft. above sea level and a distance of seven miles from winter quarters.

After a good hot dinner they turned into their sleeping-bags in the tents and were soon sound asleep. The following morning when the men got up for breakfast, the temperature was 10° below zero Fahr., whilst at our winter quarters at the same time it was zero.

They found, on starting, that the gradient was becoming much steeper, being 1 in 5, and sastrugi, running obliquely to their course, caused the sledge to capsize frequently. The temperature was 8° below zero Fahr., but the pulling was heavy work and kept the travellers warm. They camped that night, March 6, at an altitude of 5630 ft., having travelled only three miles during the whole day, but they had ascended over 2800 ft. above their previous camp. The temperature that night was 28° below zero Fahr. The second camp was in a line with the oldest crater of Erebus, and from the nature of the volcanic fragments lying around, the Professor was of the opinion that Erebus had been producing a little lava within its crater quite recently.

On the following morning Adams decided that the supporting-party should make the attempt with the forward-party to reach the summit. I had left the decision in this matter to his discretion, but I myself had not considered there would be much chance of the three men of the supporting-party gaining the summit, and had not arranged their equipment with that object in view. They were thus handicapped by having a three-man sleeping-bag, which bulky article one man had to carry; they also were not so well equipped for carrying packs, bits of rope having to act as substitutes for the broad straps provided for the original advance-party. The supporting-party had no crampons, and so found it more difficult, in places, to get a grip with their feet on the slippery surface of the snow slopes. However, the Professor, who had put bars of leather on his ski-boots, found that these answered as well as crampons, and lent the latter to Marshall. Both Adams and the Professor wore ski-boots during the whole of the ascent. Ski could not be used for such rough climbing, and had not been taken. All the men were equipped with both finnesko and ski-boots and with the necessaries for camping, and individual tastes had been given some latitude in the matter of the clothing worn and carried.

The six men made a depot of the sledge, some of the provisions and part of the cooking-utensils at the second camp, and then resumed the climb again. They started off with tent-poles amongst other equipment, but after going for half a mile they realised it would be impossible to climb the mountain with these articles, which were taken back to the depot. Each man carried a weight of about 40 lb., the party's gear consisting chiefly of sleeping-bags, two tents, cooking apparatus, and provisions for three days. The snow slopes became steeper, and at one time Mackay, who was cutting steps on the hard snow with his ice axe, slipped and glissaded with his load for about a hundred feet, but his further downward career was checked by a projecting ledge of snow, and he was soon up again. On the third evening, March 7, the party camped about 8750 ft. above sea-level, the temperature at that time being 20° below zero Fahr.

Between 9 and 10 p.m. that night a strong wind sprang up, and when the men awoke the following morning they found a fierce blizzard blowing from the south-east. It increased in fury as the day wore on, and swept with terrific force down the rocky ravine where they were camped. The whirling snow was so dense and the roaring wind so loud that, although the two sections were only about ten yards apart, they could neither see nor hear each other. Being without tent-poles, the tents were just doubled over the top ends of the sleeping-bags so as to protect the openings from the drifting snow, but, in spite of this precaution, a great deal of snow found its way into the bags. In the afternoon Brocklehurst emerged from the threeman sleeping-bag, and instantly a fierce gust whirled away one of his wolfskin mits; he dashed after it, and the force of the wind swept him some way down the ravine. Adams, who had left the bag at the same time as Brocklehurst, saw the latter vanish suddenly, and in endeavouring to return to the bag to fetch Marshall to assist in finding Brocklehurst he also was blown down by the wind. Meanwhile, Marshall, the only remaining occupant of the bag, had much ado to keep himself from being blown, sleeping-bag and all, down the ravine. Adams had just succeeded in reaching the sleeping-bag on his hands and knees when Brocklehurst appeared, also on his hands and knees, having, by desperate efforts, pulled himself back over the rocks. It was a close call, for he was all but completely gone, so biting was the cold, before he reached the haven of the sleeping-bag. He and Adams crawled in, and then, as the bag had been much twisted up and drifted with snow while Marshall had been holding it down, Adams and Marshall got out to try and straighten it out. The attempt was not very successful, as they were numb with cold and the bag, with only one person inside, blew about, so they got into it again. Shortly afterwards Adams made another attempt, and whilst he was working at it the wind got inside the bag, blowing it open right way up. Adams promptly got in again, and the adventure thus ended satisfactorily. The men could do nothing now but lie low whilst the blizzard lasted. At times they munched a plasmon biscuit or some chocolate. They had nothing to drink all that day, March 8, and during the following night, as it would have been impossible to have kept a lamp alight to thaw out the snow. They got some sleep during the night in spite of the storm. On awaking at 4 a.m. the following day, the travellers found that the blizzard was over, so, after breakfast, they started away again at about 5.30 a.m.

The angle of ascent was now steeper than ever, being thirty-four degrees, that is, a rise of 1 in 1½. As the hard snow slopes were much too steep to climb without cutting steps with an ice-axe, they kept as much as possible to the bare rocks. Occasionally the arête would terminate upwards in a large snow slope, and when this was the case they cut steps across the slope to any other bare rocks which seemed to persist for some distance in an upward direction. Brocklehurst, who was wearing ski-boots, began to feel the cold attacking his feet, but did not think it was serious enough to change into finnesko. At noon they found a fair camping-ground, and made some tea. They were, at this time, some 800 ft. below the rim of the old crater and were feeling the effects of the high altitude and the extreme cold. Below them was a magnificent panorama of clouds, coast and Barrier snow, but they could not afford to spend much time admiring it. After a hasty meal they tackled the ascent again. When they were a little distance from the top of the rim of the main crater, Mackay elected to work his way alone with his ice-axe up a long and very steep névé slope instead of following the less difficult and safer route by the rocks where the rest of the party were proceeding. He passed out of sight, and then the others heard him call out that he was getting weak and did not think he could carry on much longer. They made haste to the top of the ridge, and Marshall and the Professor dropped to the point where he would be likely to be. Happily, they found him coming toward them, and Marshall took his load, for he looked very done up. It appeared that Mackay had found the work of cutting steps with his heavy load more difficult than he had anticipated, and he only just managed to reach safety when he fell and fainted. No doubt this was due, in part, to mountain sickness, which, under the severe conditions and at the high altitude the party had attained, also affected Brocklehurst.

Having found a camping-place, they dropped their loads, and the members of the party were at leisure to observe the nature of their surroundings. They had imagined an even plain of névé or glacier ice filling the extinct crater to the brim and sloping up gradually to the active cone at its southern end, but instead of this they found themselves on the very brink of a precipice of black rock, forming the inner edge of the old crater. This wall of dark lava was mostly vertical, while, in some places, it overhung, and was from eighty to a hundred feet in height. The base of the cliff was separated from the snow plain beyond by a deep ditch like a huge dry moat, which was evidently due to the action of blizzards. These winds, striking fiercely from the south-east against the great inner wall of the old crater, had given rise to a powerful back eddy at the edge of the cliff, and it was this eddy which had scooped out the deep trench in the hard snow. The trench was from thirty to forty feet deep, and was bounded by more or less vertical sides. Around our winter quarters any isolated rock or cliff face that faced the south-east blizzard-wind exhibited a similar phenomenon, though, of course, on a much smaller scale. Beyond the wall and trench was an extensive snowfield with the active cone and crater at its southern end, the latter emitting great volumes of steam, but what surprised the travellers most were the extraordinary structures which rose here and there above the surface of the snow-field. They were in the form of mounds and pinnacles of the most varied and fantastic appearance. Some resembled beehives, others were like huge ventilating cowls, others like isolated turrets, and others again in shape resembled various animals. The men were unable at first sight to understand the origin of these remarkable structures, and as it was time for food, they left the closer investigation for later in the day.

As they walked along the rampart of the old crater wall to find a camping-ground, their figures were thrown up against the sky-line, and down at our winter quarters they were seen by us, having been sighted by Armytage with his telescope. He had followed the party for the first two days with the glasses, but they were lost to view when they began to work through the rocky ground, and it was just on the crater edge that they were picked up by the telescope again.

The camp chosen for the meal was in a little rocky gully on the north-west slope of the main cone, and about fifty feet below the rim of the old crater. Whilst some cooked the meal, Marshall examined Brocklehurst's feet, as the latter stated that for some time past he had lost all feeling in them. When his ski-boots and socks had been taken off, it was found that both his big toes were black, and that four more toes, though less severely affected, were also frost-bitten. From their appearance it was evident that some hours must have elapsed since this had occurred. Marshall and Mackay set at work at once to restore circulation in the feet by warming and chafing them. Their efforts were, under the circumstances, fairly successful, but it was clear that ultimate recovery from so severe a frost-bite would be both slow and tedious. Brocklehurst's feet, having been thoroughly warmed, were put into dry socks and finnesko stuffed with sennegrass, and then all hands went to lunch at 3.30 p.m. It must have required great pluck and determination on his part to have climbed almost continuously for nine hours up the steep and difficult track they had followed with his feet so badly frost-bitten. After lunch Brocklehurst was left safely tucked up in the three-man sleeping-bag, and the remaining five members of the party started off to explore the floor of the old crater. Ascending to the crater rim, they climbed along it until they came to a spot where there was a practicable breach in the crater wall and where a narrow tongue of snow bridged the névé trench at its base.

They all roped up directly they arrived on the hard snow in the crater and advanced cautiously over the snow-plain, keeping a sharp look-out for crevasses.

They steered for some of the remarkable mounds already mentioned, and when the nearest was reached and examined, they noticed some curious hollows, like partly roofed-in drains, running towards the mound. Pushing on slowly, they reached eventually a small parasitic cone, about 1000 ft. above the level of their camp and over a mile distant from it. Sticking out from under the snow were lumps of lava, large felspar crystals, from one to three inches in length, and fragments of pumice; both felspar and pumice were in many cases coated with sulphur. Having made as complete an examination as time permitted, they started to return to camp, no longer roped together, as they had not met any definite crevasses on their way out. They directed their steps towards one of the ice mounds, which bore a whimsical resemblance to a lion couchant and from which smoke appeared to be issuing. To the Professor the origin of these peculiar structures was now no longer a mystery, for he recognised that they were the outward and visible signs of fumaroles. In ordinary climates, a fumarole, or volcanic vapour-well, may be detected by the thin cloud of steam above it, and usually one can at once feel the warmth by passing one's hand into the vapour column, but in the rigour of the Antarctic climate the fumaroles of Erebus have their vapour turned into ice as soon as it reaches the surface of the snow-plain. Thus ice mounds, somewhat similar in shape to the sinter mounds formed by the geysers of New Zealand, of Iceland, and of Yellowstone Park, are built up round the orifices of the fumaroles of Erebus. Whilst exploring one of these fumaroles, Mackay fell suddenly up to his thighs into one of its concealed conduits, and only saved himself from falling in deeper still by means of his ice-axe. Marshall had a similar experience at about the same time.

The party arrived at camp shortly after 6 p.m., and found Brocklehurst progressing as well as could be expected. They sat on the rocks after tea admiring the glorious view to the west. Below them was a vast rolling sea of cumulus cloud, and far away the western mountains glowed in the setting sun. Next morning, when they got up at 4 a.m., they had a splendid view of the shadow of Erebus projected on the field of cumulus cloud below them by the rising sun. Every detail of the profile of the mountain as outlined on the clouds could be readily recognised. After breakfast, while Marshall was attending to Brocklehurst's feet, the hypsometer, which had become frozen on the way up, was thawed out and a determination of the boiling-point made. This, when reduced and combined with the mean of the aneroid levels, made the altitude of the old crater rim, just above the camp, 11,400 ft. At 6 a.m. the party left the camp and made all speed to reach the summit of the present crater. On their way across the old crater, Mawson photographed the fumarole that resembled the lion and also took a view of the active crater about one and a half miles distant, though there was considerable difficulty in taking photographs owing to the focal plane shutter having become jammed by frost. Near the furthest point reached by the travellers on the preceding afternoon they observed several patches of yellow ice and found on examination that the colour was due to sulphur. They next ascended several rather steep slopes formed of alternating beds of hard snow and vast quantities of large and perfect felspar crystals, mixed with pumice. A little further on they reached the base of the volcano's active cone. Their progress now was painfully slow, as the altitude and cold combined to make respiration difficult. The cone of Erebus is built up chiefly of blocks of pumice, from a few inches to a few feet in diameter. Externally these were grey or often yellow owing to incrustations of sulphur, but when broken they were of a resinous brown colour. At last, a little after 10 a.m., on March 10, the edge of the active crater was reached, and the little party stood on the summit of Erebus, the first men to conquer perhaps the most remarkable summit in the world. They had travelled about two and a half miles from the last camp, and had ascended just 2000 ft., and this journey had taken them over four hours. The report describes most vividly the magnificent and awe-inspiring scene before them.

'We stood on the verge of a vast abyss, and at first could see neither to the bottom nor across it on account of the huge mass of steam filling the crater and soaring aloft in a column 500 to 1000 ft. high. After a continuous loud hissing sound, lasting for some minutes, there would come from below a big dull boom, and immediately great globular masses of steam would rush upwards to swell the volume of the snowwhite cloud which ever sways over the crater. This phenomenon recurred at intervals during the whole of our stay at the crater. Meanwhile, the air around us was extremely redolent of burning sulphur. Presently a pleasant northerly breeze fanned away the steam cloud, and at once the whole crater stood revealed to us in all its vast extent and depth. Mawson's angular measurement made the depth 900 ft. and the greatest width about half a mile. There were at least three well-defined openings at the bottom of the cauldron, and it was from these that the steam explosions proceeded. Near the south-west portion of the crater there was an immense rib in the rim, perhaps 300 to 400 ft. deep. The crater wall opposite the one at the top of which we were standing presented features of special interest. Beds of dark pumiceous lava or pumice alternated with white zones of snow. There was no direct evidence that the snow was bedded with the lava, though it was possible that such may have been the case. From the top of one of the thickest of the lava or pumice beds, just where it touched the belt of snow, there rose scores of small steam jets all in a row. They were too numerous and too close together to have been each an independent fumarole; the appearance was rather suggestive of the snow being converted into steam by the heat of the layer of rock immediately below it.'

While at the crater's edge the party made a boilingpoint determination by the hypsometer, but the result was not so satisfactory as that made earlier in the morning at the camp. As the result of averaging aneroid levels, together with the hypsometer determination at the top of the old crater, Erebus may be calculated to rise to a height of 13,370 ft. above sealevel. As soon as the measurements had been made and some photographs had been taken by Mawson, the party returned to the camp, as it had been decided to descend to the base of the main cone that day, a drop of 8000 ft.

On the way back a traverse was made of the main crater, and levels taken for constructing a geological section. Numerous specimens of the unique felspar crystals and of the pumice and sulphur were collected. On arriving in camp the travellers made a hasty meal, packed up, shouldered their burdens once more and started down the steep mountain slope. Brocklehurst insisted on carrying his own heavy load in spite of his frost-bitten feet. They followed a course a little to the west of the one they took when ascending. The rock was rubbly and kept slipping under their feet, so that falls were frequent. After descending a few hundred feet they found that the rubbly spur of rock down which they were floundering ended abruptly in a long and steep névé slope. Three courses were now open to them: they could retrace their steps to the point above them where the rocky spur had deviated from the main arête; cut steps across the névé slope; or glissade down some five or six hundred feet to a rocky ledge below. In their tired state preference was given to the path of least resistance, which was offered by the glissade, and they therefore rearranged their loads so that they would roll down easily. They were now very thirsty, but they found that if they gathered a little snow, squeezed it into a ball and placed it on the surface of a piece of rock, it melted at once almost on account of the heat of the sun and thus they obtained a makeshift drink. They launched their loads down the slope and watched them as they bumped and bounded over the wavy ridges of névé. Brocklehurst's load, which contained the cooking-utensils, made the noisiest descent, and the aluminium cookers were much battered when they finally fetched up against the rocks below. Then the members of the party, grasping their ice-axes firmly, followed their gear. As they gathered speed on the downward course and the chisel-edge of the ice-axe bit deeper into the hard névé, their necks and faces were sprayed with a shower of ice. All reached the bottom of the slope safely, and they repeated this glissade down each succeeding snow slope towards the foot of the main cone. Here and there they bumped heavily on hard sastrugi and both clothes and equipment suffered in the rapid descent; unfortunately, also, one of the aneroids was lost and one of the hypsometer thermometers broken. At last the slope flattened out to the gently inclined terrace where the depot lay, and they reached it by walking. Altogether they had dropped down 5000 ft. between three in the afternoon and seven in the evening.

Adams and Marshall were the first to reach the depot, the rest of the party, with the exception of Brocklehurst, having made a *détour* to the left in consequence of having to pursue some lost luggage in that direction. At the depot they found that the blizzard of the 8th had played havoc with their gear, for the sledge had been overturned and some of the load scattered to a distance and covered partly with drift-snow. After dumping their packs, Adams and Marshall went to meet Brocklehurst, for they noticed that a slight blizzard was springing up. Fortunately, the wind soon died down, the weather cleared, and the three were able to regain the camp. Tea was got ready, and the remainder of the party arrived about 10 p.m. They camped that night at the depot and at 3 a.m. next day got up to breakfast. After breakfast a hunt was made for some articles that were still missing, and then the sledge was packed and the march homewards commenced at 5.30 a.m. They now found that the sastrugi caused by the late blizzard were very troublesome, as the ridges were from four to five feet above the hollows and lay at an oblique angle to the course. Rope brakes were put on the sledge-runners, and two men went in front to pull when necessary, while two steadied the sledge, and two were stationed behind to pull back when required. It was more than trying to carry on at this juncture, for the sledge either refused to move or suddenly it took charge and overran those who were dragging it, and capsizes occurred every few minutes. Owing to the slippery nature of the ground, some members of the party who had not crampons or barred ski-boots were badly shaken up, for they sustained innumerable sudden falls. One has to experience a surface like this to realise how severe a jar a fall entails. The only civilised experience that is akin to it is when one steps unknowingly on a slide which some small street boy has made on the pavement. Marshall devised the best means of assisting the progress of the sledge. When it took charge he jumped on behind and steered it with his legs as it bumped and jolted over the sastrugi, but he found sometimes that his thirteen-stone weight did not prevent him from being bucked right over the sledge and flung on the névé on the other side.

They reached the nunatak where they had made their first camp on the way up, six miles distant from Cape Royds, at about 7.30 a.m. By this time there was every symptom of the approach of a blizzard, and the snow was beginning to drift before a gusty south-easterly wind. This threatened soon to cut them off from all view of the winter quarters. They were beginning to feel very tired, one of the tents had a large hole burnt in it, the oil-supply was almost done, and one of the primus stoves had been put out of action as the result of the glissade; so, in the circumstances, they decided to make a dash for Cape Royds, leaving their sledge and equipment to be picked up later. In the grey uncertain light the sastrugi did not show up in relief, and every few feet some member of the party stumbled and fell, sprawling over the snow. At last their eyes were gladdened by the shining surface of the Blue Lake only half a mile distant from winter quarters. Now that the haven was at hand,

and the stress and strain over, their legs grew heavy and leaden, and that last half-mile seemed one of the hardest they had covered. It was fortunate that the weather did not become worse.

Meanwhile, at winter quarters, we had been very busy opening cases and getting things ship-shape outside, with the result that the cubicles of the absentees were more or less filled with a general accumulation of stores. When Armytage reported that he saw the party on their way down the day before they arrived at the hut, we decided to make the cubicles tidy for the travellers. We had just begun on the Professor's cubicle when, about 11 a.m., I left the hut for a moment and was astonished to see within thirty yards of me, coming over the brow of the ridge by the hut, six slowly moving figures. I ran towards them shouting: 'Did you get to the top?' There was no answer, and I asked again. Adams pointed with his hand upwards, but this did not satisfy me, so I repeated my question. Then Adams said: 'Yes', and I ran back to the hut and shouted to the others, who all came streaming out to cheer the successful venturers. We shook hands all round and opened some champagne, which tasted like nectar to the way-worn people. Marshall prescribed a dose to us stay-at-home ones, so that we might be able to listen quietly to the tale the party had to tell.

Except to Joyce, Wild and myself, who had seen similar things on the former expedition, the eating and drinking capacity of the returned party was a matter of astonishment. In a few minutes Roberts had produced a great saucepan of Quaker oats and Ula, the contents of which disappeared in a moment, to be followed by the greater part of a fresh-cut ham and home-made bread, with New Zealand fresh butter. The six had evidently found on the slopes of Erebus six fully developed, polar sledging appetites. The meal at last ended, came more talk, smokes and then bed for the weary travellers.

After some days' delay on account of unfavourable weather, a party, consisting of Adams, the Professor, Armytage, Joyce, Wild and Marshall, equipped with a seven-foot sledge, tent and provisions, as a precaution against possible bad weather, started out to fetch in the eleven-foot sledge with the explorer's equipment. After a heavy pull over the soft, new-fallen snow, in cloudy weather, with the temperature at mid-day 20° below zero Fahr., and with a stiff wind blowing from the south-east, they sighted the nunatak, recovered the abandoned sledge and placing the smaller one on top, pulled them both back as far as Blue Lake. I went out to meet the party, and we left the sledge at Blue Lake until the following day, when two of the Manchurian ponies were harnessed to the sledges and the gear was brought into winter quarters.

13

RESULTS OF THE EREBUS JOURNEY

In closing the report the Professor and Adams mention the impression made upon them by the scenes that unfolded themselves during the journey. 'The glorious sunsets, the magic of the sunrise seen from our camp above the clouds when the great shadow of Erebus swept across McMurdo Sound, and touched the far-off Western Mountains, the weird shapes of the green and white ice mounds built around the fumaroles of the old crater, with its pavement of sparkling crystals interspersed with snow and pumice; the hissing and booming cauldron of the modern crater with its long line of steam jets and its snow-white pillow of steam, are all memories that will never fade from our minds.'

It must be said that, considering the time of year, the party were extremely fortunate in the weather encountered on their journey. In the first place the route followed proved satisfactory, for while it gave a good snow surface for the sledge it kept the party entirely free from any dangerously crevassed ice. Next, the blizzard, though very trying while it lasted on account of its violence and low temperature, commencing at 30° below zero Fahr., really proved a blessing in disguise, for it lasted just long enough to raise the temperature considerably, as well as to check the high-level south-westerly wind, and so produce a calm. Naturally I was much pleased to have all our party back after so fine a piece of work and without any serious accident, though, indeed, Brocklehurst's foot did not look at all promising, for two of the toes on the right foot were very much swollen and discoloured, whilst the big toe remained black and Marshall was of the opinion that part would have to be amputated later. Except for this accident every one was in the best of health. I asked the Professor to give me a short summary of the scientific results of the ascent, and I think they will not be out of place in this narrative, for the object of the ascent was mainly to gather scientific information, though, of course, there was a strong desire to reach the summit of a hitherto unclimbed mountain, of great height and unknown nature.

Among the scientific results [wrote Professor David] may be mentioned in the first place the calculation of the height of the mountain. Sir James Clark Ross, in 1841, estimated the height to be 12,367 ft. The

National Antarctic Expedition of 1901 determined its height at first to be 13,120 ft., but this was subsequently altered to 12,922 ft., the height now given on the Admiralty chart of the region. Our observations for altitude were made partly with aneroids and partly with a hypsometer. All the aneroid levels and hypsometer observations have been calculated by means of simultaneous readings of the barometer taken at our winter quarters, Cape Royds. These observations show that the rim of the second or main crater of Erebus is about 11,350 ft. above sea-level, and that the height of the summit of the active crater is about 13,350 ft. above sea-level. The fact may be emphasised that in both the methods adopted by us for estimating the altitude of the mountain, atmospheric pressure was the sole factor on which we relied. The determination arrived at by the *Discovery* expedition was based on measurements made with a theodolite from sea-level. It is, of course, quite possible that Ross' original estimate of the height of Erebus may have been correct, and this active volcano may have gained in height by about a thousand feet during the sixty-seven years which have elapsed since the time of his expedition. In the next place among features of geological interest may be mentioned the fact that the old moraines left by a former gigantic ancestor of the great ice barrier, ascend the western slopes of Erebus to a height of fully 1000 ft. above sea-level. As the adjacent McMurdo Sound is at least three hundred fathoms deep, this ice sheet when at its maximum development must have been at least 2800 ft. in thickness. We noticed that in addition to these old ice barrier moraines, there were moraines newer than the period of greatest glaciation. They had evidently been formed by glaciers radiating from Erebus.

As regards the geological structure of Erebus, we have concluded provisionally that there is evidence of the existence of four superimposed craters. The oldest and lowest and, at the same time, the largest of these attained an altitude of between 6000 and 7000 ft. above sea-level, and was fully six miles in diameter. The second rises to a height of 11,350 ft. and has a diameter of over two miles; its rim is bounded inwards by a vertical cliff, which no doubt descended originally into a crater of vast depth. This second crater has now been filled up almost to the brim, partly with snow, partly with large crystals of felspar and fragments of pumice, and partly with the numerous funnel-shaped ice mounds already described. The third crater rises to a height of fully 12,200 ft. above sea-level, and its former outline has now been almost obliterated by the material of the modern active cone and crater. The latter, which rises about 800 ft. above the former, is composed chiefly of fragments of pumice. These vary in size from an inch or so up to

ASCENT OF EREBUS

MARCH 6ᵀᴴ TO 12ᵀᴴ 1908

Route followed :– ------------

SCALE OF GEOGRAPHICAL MILES

CRATER OF MOUNT EREBUS AND SECTION

a yard in diameter. Quantities of felspar crystals are interspersed with them, and both are incrusted with sulphur. The fumes rising from the crater at the time of our visit smelt strongly of sulphur, and this fact, considered in conjunction with the yellow coating of sulphur round the rim of the active crater, shows that the volcano is partly in a solfataric stage. At the same time the frequent glows on the steam cloud above the crater, and at the actual edge, as seen from our winter quarters during the winter months, prove that molten lava still wells up into the crater. The fresh volcanic bombs picked up by us at spots four miles distant from the crater and lying on the surface of comparatively new snow are evidence that Erebus has recently been projecting lava to great heights.

As regards size, as already mentioned, the active crater measures about half a mile by one-third of a mile in diameter, and is about 900 ft. in depth. If the active crater of Erebus be compared with that of Vesuvius it will be found that the former is about three times as deep as that of the latter. One of the most striking features observed at the summit was the long row of steam jets about 300 ft. below the inside rim of the crater. There were many scores of these developed at the upper surface of a thick bed of dark lava or pumice, which projected slightly into the crater. Possibly the horizon of the steam jets represented a highwater mark, so to speak, of lava within the crater, and the steam may have been due to the vapourising of snow in contact with the hot rock; certainly there was a white band of snow above the zone of dark rock which gave origin to the steam jets, but whether this snow formed a definite bed intercalated in the pumice beds or whether it was a superficial layer caught in the projecting ledge of dark rock is uncertain. It is evident from the mineralogical character of the recently erupted pumice of the active crater that Erebus is still producing that rare type of lava known as kenyte. Two features on the geology of Erebus which are specially distinctive are the vast quantities of large and perfect felspar crystals, and the ice fumaroles. The crystals are from two to three inches in length. Many of them have had their angles and edges slightly rounded by attrition, through clashing against one another when they were originally projected from the funnel of the volcano, but numbers of them are beautifully perfect. The fluid lava which once surrounded them has been blown away in the form of fine dust by the force of steam explosions, and the crystals have been left behind intact.

The ice fumaroles are specially remarkable. About fifty of these were visible to us on the track which we followed to and from the crater, and doubtless there were numbers that we did not see. These unique ice-mounds have resulted from the condensation of vapour around the orifices of the fumaroles. It is only under conditions of very low temperature that such structures could exist. No structures like them are known in any other part of the world.

It would be hard to overestimate the scientific importance of knowledge of the meteorological conditions obtaining at Erebus. Erebus is the Pisgah of the meteorologist. The details of the phenomena observed there will, of course, be given in the meteorological memoirs of this expedition, but they are too bulky to quote here. Mention, however, may be made of four phenomena which specially impressed themselves upon us during our ascent of Erebus. In the first place we noticed that the whole of the snow-field lying within the rim of the second crater is strongly ridged with sastrugi, which trend from west by south to east by north. These sastrugi have a sharp edge directed towards the west. The latter is the quarter from which the prevalent wind blows near the summit of Erebus. This is the return current of air blowing back from the South Pole towards the Equator. Next our experience on Erebus showed that the south-easterly blizzard sometimes extends from sea-level up to at least as high as the top of the second crater, that is to over 11,000 ft. in height. Thirdly, it may be noticed that on the day we reached the summit of Erebus, March 10, we found ourselves, at a level of 13,300 ft., within the lower limit of the upper wind which at that time was blowing gently from a northerly direction. It may be remembered that this date was one and a half days after a strong south-east blizzard. These conditions seem to indicate that after a blizzard, and probably during its later phases, the great middle air current normally travelling from near the South Pole towards the Equator, is temporarily abolished, having become absorbed into the immense stream of the blizzard.

Fourthly, it may be recorded that the temperatures taken by us demonstrate the following fact, obviously of considerable importance: From sea-level at Cape Royds, up to the summit of Erebus, for the first 6000 ft., the temperature falls at the rate of about 4° Fahr. per thousand feet, but above the altitude the fall is much less rapid, being at the rate of less than 1° Fahr. per thousand feet, and in one case the temperature curve on Erebus was found to be inverted.

Finally, we had an opportunity, when in our camp on Erebus on the morning of March 10, of seeing an explanation of the remarkable phenomena called 'earth shadows' by Captain Scott. On that occasion we saw that the rising sun projected across McMurdo Sound a great conical shadow of Erebus some forty miles wide on to the western mountains. If now an observer were to stand within, or near to the base of this shadow, and looking towards the apex of it westwards, he would see a conic section like that of a slightly inverted cone, seen very obliquely. We noticed subsequently when viewing the earth shadows from our winter quarters at Cape Royds that the two barbs of the broad arrow of the earth shadows were not equally inclined to the vertical, but that their relative angles of slope were directly proportional to the angles of slope of the north and south side respectively of Erebus. It is evident, therefore, that these dark barbs are a shadow projection of the cone of Erebus. The central vertical dark beam figured by Captain Scott has not yet been definitely observed by us.

From the above brief notes it will be obvious that Erebus is very interesting geologically on account of its unique fumaroles, its remarkable felspar crystals and rare lavas, as well as on account of its having served as a gigantic tide gauge to record the flood level of the greatest recent glaciation of Antarctica, when the whole of Ross Island was but a nunatak in a gigantic field of ice. From a meteorological point of view, its situation between the belt of polar calms and the South Pole; its isolation from the disturbing influence of large land masses; its great height, which enables it to penetrate the whole system of atmospheric circulation, and, above all, the constant steam cloud at its summit, swinging to and fro like a huge wind vane, combine to make Erebus one of the most interesting places on earth to the meteorologist.

14
LIFE AND WORK IN WINTER QUARTERS

After the journey to the summit of Erebus we began to settle down and prepare for the long winter months that were rapidly approaching. Already the nights were lengthening and stars becoming familiar objects in the sky. Our main work was to secure the hut firmly against possible damage from the south-east blizzards. After everything had been made safe as far as it lay in our power, we felt that if anything untoward happened it would not be our fault, so we turned our attention to the scientific studies that lay to our hand. As we were only a small party, it was impossible for all of us to carry on scientific work and, at the same time, attend to what I might call the house-hold duties. It was most important for the geologists of the expedition to get as far afield as practicable before the winter night closed in on us, so every day both the Professor and Priestley were out early and late, with their collecting-bags and geological hammers, finding on every successive trip they made within a radius of three or four miles of the winter quarters new and interesting geological specimens, the examination of which would give them plenty of work in the winter months. Scattered around Cape Royds were large numbers of granite boulders of every size and colour, deposited there by the great receding ice-sheet that once filled McMurdo Sound and covered the lower slopes of Erebus. The geologists were full of delight that circumstances should have placed our winter quarters at a spot so fruitful for their labours. Murray was equally pleased at the prospect of the biological work which lay before him, for hardly a day passed without some one bringing in a report of the existence of another lake or tarn, and soon we realised that around us lay more than a dozen of these lakelets, which might possibly prove a fruitful field for biological study. To Mawson the many varied forms of ice and snow, both in the lakes and on the surrounding hills, gave promise of encouraging results in that branch of physics in which he was particularly interested. The lengthening nights also gave us indications that the mysterious Aurora Australis would soon be waving its curtains and beams over our winter quarters, and as information on this phenomenon was greatly needed, Mawson made preparations for recording the displays.

I have already stated that the meteorological screen had been set up and observations begun before the Erebus party left. Now that all hands were back at the hut, a regular system of recording the observations was arranged. Adams, who was the meteorologist of the expedition, took all the observations from 8 a.m. to 8 p.m. The night-watchman took them from 10 p.m. till 6 a.m. These observations were taken every two hours, and it may interest the reader to learn what was done in this way, though I do not wish to enter here into a lengthy dissertation on meteorology. The observations on air temperature, wind and direction of cloud have an important bearing on similar observations taken in more temperate climes, and in a place like the Antarctic, where up till now our knowledge has been so meagre, it was most essential that every bit of information bearing on meteorological phenomena should be noted. We were in a peculiarly favourable position for observing not only the changes that took place in the lower atmosphere but also those which took place in the higher strata of the atmosphere. Erebus, with steam and smoke always hanging above it indicated by the direction assumed by the cloud what the upper air-currents were doing, and thus we were in touch with an excellent high-level observatory.

The instruments under Adams' care were as complete as financial considerations had permitted. The meteorological screen contained a maximum thermometer, that is, a thermometer which indicates the highest temperature reached during the period elapsing between two observations. It is so constructed that when the mercury rises in the tube it remains at its highest point, though the temperature might fall greatly shortly afterwards. After reading the recorded height, the thermometer is shaken, and this operation causes the mercury to drop to the actual temperature obtaining at the moment of observation; the thermometer is then put back into the screen and is all ready for the next reading taken two hours later. A minimum thermometer registered the lowest temperature that occurred between the two-hourly readings, but this thermometer was not a mercury one, as mercury freezes at a temperature of about 39° below zero, and we therefore used spirit thermometers. When the temperature drops the surface of the column of spirit draws down a little black indicator immersed in it, and if the temperature rises and the spirit advances in consequence, the spirit flows past the indicator, which remains at the lowest point, and on the observations being taken its position is read on the graduated scale. By these instruments we were always able to ascertain what the highest temperature and what the lowest temperature had been throughout the two hours during which the observation screen had not been visited.

In addition to the maximum and minimum thermometers, there were the wet and dry bulb thermometers. The dry bulb records the actual temperature of the air at the moment, and we used a spirit thermometer for this purpose. The wet bulb consisted of an ordinary thermometer, round the bulb of which was tied a little piece of muslin that had been dipped in water and of course froze at once on exposure to the air. The effect of the evaporation from the ice which covered the bulb was to cause the temperature recorded to be lower than that recorded by the dry bulb thermometer in proportion to the amount of water present in the atmosphere at the time. To ensure accuracy the wet bulb thermometers were changed every two hours, the thermometer which was read being brought back to the hut and returned to the screen later freshly sheathed in ice. It was, of course, impossible to wet the exposed thermometer with a brush dipped in water, as is the practice in temperate climates, for water could not be carried from the hut to the screen without freezing into solid ice. To check the thermometers there was also kept in the screen a self-recording thermometer, or thermograph. This is a delicate instrument fitted with metal discs, which expand or contract readily with every fluctuation of the temperature. Attached to these discs is a delicately poised lever carrying a pen charged with ink, and the point of this pen rests against a graduated roll of paper fastened to a drum, which is revolved by clock-work once in every seven days. The pen thus draws a line on the paper, rising and falling in sympathy with the changes in the temperature of the air.

All these instruments were contained inside the meteorological screen, which was so constructed that while there was free access of air, the wind could not strike through it with any violence, neither could the sun throw its direct beams on the sensitive thermometers inside. On the flat top of the screen were nailed two pieces of wood in the form of a cross, the long axis of which lay in the true meridian, that is, one end pointing due south, the other end due north. On a small rod attached to the fore end of the screen was a vane that floated out in the opposite direction to that from which the wind was blowing, and by reference to the vane and the cross the direction of the wind was ascertained and noted when the other observations were taken. To record the force of the wind and the number of miles it travelled between each observation, there was an instrument called an anemometer, which rested on one of the uprights supporting the meteorological screen; the type of anemometer used by the expedition is known as the 'Robinson'. It consists of four cups or hemispheres revolving on a pivot which communicates by a series of cogs with a dial having two hands like the hands of a watch. The long hand makes one revolution and records five miles, and the smaller hand records up to five hundred miles. At a glance we could thus tell the number of miles the wind had blown during the time elapsing between successive observations. In ordinary climates the work of reading these instruments was a matter of little difficulty and only took a few minutes, but in the Antarctic, especially when a blizzard was blowing, the difficulty was much increased and the strong wind often blew out the hurricane lamp which was used to read the instruments in the darkness. On these occasions the unfortunate observer had to return to the hut, relight the lamp and again struggle up the windy ridge to the screen. In order to try and facilitate the reading of the various instruments during the long polar night the dry cells from the motor-car were connected with a cable from the hut to the screen, but the power was not sufficient to give a satisfactory light.

In addition to the meteorological screen, there was another erection built on the top of the highest ridge by Mawson, who placed there an anemometer of his own construction to register the strength of the heaviest gusts of wind during a blizzard. We found that the squalls frequently blew with a force of over a hundred miles an hour. There remained still one more outdoor instrument connected with weather observation, that was the snow gauge. The Professor, by utilising some spare lengths of stove chimney, erected a snow gauge into which was collected the falling snow whenever a blizzard blew. The snow was afterwards taken into the hut in the vessel into which it had been deposited, and when it was melted down we were able to calculate fairly accurately the amount of the snowfall. This observation was an important one, for much depends on the amount of precipitation in the Antarctic regions.

It is on the precipitation in the form of snow, and on the rate of evaporation, that calculations regarding the formation of the huge snow-fields and glaciers depend. We secured our information regarding the rate of evaporation by suspending measured cubes of ice and snow from rods projecting at the side of the hut, where they were free from the influence of the interior warmth. Inside the hut was kept a standard mercurial barometer, which was also read every two hours, and in addition to this there was a barograph which registered the varying pressure of the atmosphere in a curve for a week at a time. Every Monday morning Adams changed the paper on both thermograph and barograph, and every day recorded the observations in the meteorological log. It will be seen that the meteorologist had plenty to occupy his time, and generally when the men came in from a walk they had some information as to the movement of the smoke cloud on Erebus or the observation of a parhelion or parselene to record.

As soon as the ice was strong enough to bear in the bay, Murray commenced his operations there. His object was the collection of the different marine creatures that rest on the bottom of the sea or creep about there, and he made extensive preparations for their capture. A hole was dug through the ice, and a trap let down to the bottom; this trap was baited with a piece of penguin or seal, and the shell-fish, crustacea and other marine animals found their way in through the opening in the top, and the trap was usually left down for a couple of days. When it was hauled up, the contents were transferred to a tin containing water, and then taken to the hut and thawed out, for the contents always froze during the quarter of a mile walk homeward. As soon as the animals thawed out they were sorted into bottles and then killed by various chemicals, put into spirits and bottled up for examination when they reached England. Later on Murray found that the trap business was not fruitful enough, so whenever a crack opened in the bay ice, a line was let down, one end being made fast at one end of the crack, and the length of the line allowed to sink in the water horizontally for a distance of sixty yards. A hole was dug at each end of the line and a small dredge was let down and pulled along the bottom, being hauled up through the hole at the far end. By this means much richer collections were made, and rarely did the dredge come up without some interesting specimens. When the crack froze over again, the work could still be continued so long as the ice was broken at each end of the line, and Priestley for a long time acted as Murray's assistant, helping him to open the holes and pull the dredge.

When we took our walks abroad, every one kept their eyes open for any interesting specimen of rock or any signs of plant-life, and Murray was greatly pleased one day when we brought back some moss. This was found in a fairly sheltered spot beyond Back Door Bay and was the only specimen that we obtained in the neighbourhood of the winter quarters before the departure of the sun. Occasionally we came across a small lichen and some curious algae growing in the volcanic earth, but these measured the extent of the terrestrial vegetation in this latitude. In the north polar regions, in a corresponding latitude, there are eighteen different kinds of flowering plants, and there even exists a small stunted tree, a species of willow.

Although terrestrial vegetation is so scanty in the Antarctic, the same cannot be said of the sub-aqueous plant-life. When we first arrived and some of us walked across the north shore of Cape Royds, we saw a great deal of open water in the lakes, and a little later, when all these lakes were frozen over, we walked across them, and looking down through the clear ice, could see masses of brilliantly coloured algae and fungi. The investigation of the plant-life in the lakes was one of the principal things undertaken by Murray, Priestley and the Professor during the winter months. The reader has the plan of our winter quarters and can follow easily the various places that are mentioned in the course if this narrative.

After the Erebus party returned, a regular winter routine was arranged for the camp. Brocklehurst took no part in the duties at this time, for his frostbitten foot prevented his moving about, and shortly after his return Marshall saw that it would be necessary to amputate at least part of the big toe. The rest of the party all had a certain amount of work for the common weal, apart from their own scientific duties. From the time we arrived we always had a night-watchman, and now took turns to carry out this important duty. Roberts was exempt from night-watchman's duties, as he was busy with the cooking all day, so for the greater part of the winter every thirteenth night each member took the night watch. The ten-o'clock observations was the night-watchman's first duty, and from that hour till nine o'clock next morning he was responsible for the well-being and care of the hut, ponies and dogs. His most important duties were the two-hourly meteorological observations, the upkeep of the fire and the care of the acetylene gas-plant. The fire was kept going all through the night, and hot water was ready for making the breakfast when Roberts was called at 7.30 in the morning. The night watch was by no means an unpleasant duty, and gave us each an opportunity, when our turn came round, of washing clothes, darning socks, writing and doing little odd jobs which could not receive much attention during the day. The night-watchman also generally took his bath either once a fortnight, or once a month as his inclination prompted him.

Some individuals had a regular programme which they adhered to strictly. For instance, one member, directly the rest of the staff had gone to bed, cleared the small table in front of the stove, spread a rug on it and settled down to a complicated game of patience, having first armed himself with a supply of coffee against the wiles of the drowsy god. After the regulation numbers of games had been played, the despatch box was opened and letters, private papers and odds and ends were carefully inspected and replaced in their proper order, after which the journal was written up. These important matters over, a ponderous book on historical subjects received its share of attention.

Socks were the only articles of clothing that had constantly to be repaired and various were the expedients used to replace the heels, which, owing to the hard footgear, were always showing gaping holes. These holes had to be constantly covered, for we were not possessed of an unlimited number of any sort of clothes, and many and varied were the patches. Some men used thin leather, others canvas, and others again a sort of coarse flannel to sew on instead of darning the heels of the socks. Towards the end of the winter, the wardrobes of the various members of the expedition were in a very patched condition.

During the earlier months the night-watchman was kept pretty busy, for the ponies took a long time to get used to the stable and often tried to break loose and upset things out there generally. These sudden noises took the watchman out frequently during the night, and it was a comfort to us when the animals at last learned to keep fairly quiet in their stable. Every two hours the observations and the fire and acetylene gas required attention. The individual was fortunate who obtained a good bag of coal for his night watch, with plenty of lumps in it, for there was then no difficulty in keeping the temperature of the hut up to 40° Fahr., but a great deal of our coal was very fine and caused much trouble during the night. To meet this difficulty we had recourse to lumps of seal blubber, the watchman generally laying in a stock for himself before his turn came for night duty. When placed on top of the hot coal the blubber burned fiercely, and it was a comfort to know that with the large supply of seals that could easily be obtained in these latitudes, no expedition need fear the lack of emergency fuel. There was no perceptible smell from the blubber in burning, though fumes came from the bit of hairy hide generally attached to it. The thickness of the blubber varied from two to four inches. Some watchmen during the night felt disinclined to do anything but read and take the observations, and I was amongst this number, for though I often made plans and resolutions as to washing and other necessary jobs, when the time came these plans fell through, with the exception of the bath.

Towards the middle of winter some of our party stayed up later than during the time when there was more work outside, and there gradually grew into existence an institution known as eleven o'clock tea. The Professor was greatly attached to his cup of tea and generally undertook the work of making it for men who were still out of bed. Some of us preferred a cup of hot fresh milk, which was easily made from the excellent dried milk of which we had a large quantity. By one o'clock in the morning, however, nearly all the occupants of the hut were wrapped in deep and more or less noisy slumber. Some had a habit of talking in their sleep, and their fitful phrases were carefully treasured up by the night-watchman for retailing at the breakfast-table next morning; sometimes also the dreams of the night before were told by the dreamer to his own great enjoyment, if not to that of his audience. About five o'clock in the morning came the most trying time for the watchman. Then one's eyes grew heavy and leaden, and it took a deal of effort to prevent oneself from falling fast asleep. Some of us went in for cooking more or less elaborate meals. Marshall, who had been to a school of cookery before we left England, turned out some quite respectable bread and cakes.

Though people jeered at the latter when placed on the table, one noticed that next day there was never any left. At 7.30 a.m. Roberts was called, and the watchman's night was nearly over. At this hour also Armytage or Mackay was called to look after the feeding of the ponies, but before mid-winter day Armytage had taken over the entire responsibility of the stables and ponies, and he was the only one to get up. At 8.30 a.m. all hands were called, special attention being paid to turning out the messman for the day, and after some minutes of luxurious half-wakefulness, people began to get up, expressing their opinions forcibly if the temperature of the hut was below freezing-point, and informing the night-watchman of his affinity to Jonah if his report was that it was a windy morning. Dressing was for some of the men a very simple affair, consisting merely in putting on their boots and giving themselves a shake; others, who undressed entirely, got out of their pyjamas into their cold underclothing.

At a quarter to nine the call came to let down the table from its position near the roof, and the messman then bundled the knives, forks and spoons on to the board, and at nine o'clock sharp every one sat down to breakfast.

The night-watchman's duties were over for a fortnight, and the messman took on his work. The duties of the messman were more onerous than those of the night-watchman. He began, as I have stated, by laying the table – a simple operation owing to the primitive conditions under which we lived. He then garnished this with three or four sorts of hot sauces to tickle the tough palates of some of our party. At nine o'clock, when we sat down, the messman passed up the bowls of porridge and the big jug of hot milk, which was the standing dish every day. Little was heard in the way of conversation until this first course had been disposed of. Then came the order from the messman, 'up bowls', and reserving our spoons for future use, the bowls were passed along. If it were a 'fruit day', that is a day when the second course consisted of bottled fruit, the bowls were retained for this popular dish.

At twenty-five minutes to ten breakfast was over and we had had our smokes. All dishes were passed up, the table hoisted out of the way, and the messman started to wash up the breakfast-things, assisted by his cubicle companion and by one or two volunteers who would help him to dry up. Another of the party swept out the hut; and this operation was performed three times a day, so as to keep the building in a tidy state. After finishing the breakfast-things, the duty of the man in the house was to replenish the melting-pots with ice, empty the ashes and tins into the dust-box outside and get in a bag of coal. By half-past ten the morning work was accomplished and the messman was free until twenty minutes to one, when he put the water on for the mid-day tea. At one o'clock tea was served and we had a sort of counter lunch. This was a movable feast, for scientific and other duties often made some of our party late, and after it was over there was nothing for the messman to do in the afternoon except to have sufficient water ready to provide tea at four o'clock. At a quarter past six the table was brought down again and dinner, the longest meal of the day, was served sharp at 6.30. One often heard the messman anxiously inquiring what the dinner dishes were going to consist of, the most popular from his point of view being those which resulted in the least amount of grease on the plates. Dinner was over soon after seven o'clock and then tea was served. Tobacco and conversation kept us at table until 7.30, after which the same routine of washing up and sweeping out the hut was gone through. By 8.30 the messman had finished his duties for the day, and his turn did not come round again for another thirteen days. The state of the weather made the duties lighter or heavier, for if the day happened to be windy, the emptying of dish-water and ashes and the getting in of fresh ice was an unpleasant job. In a blizzard it was necessary to put on one's Burberries even to walk the few yards to the ice-box and back.

In addition to the standing jobs of night-watchman and messman there were also special duties for various members of the expedition who had particular departments to look after. Adams every morning, directly after breakfast, wound up the chronometers and chronometer watches, and rated the instruments. He then attended to the meteorological work and took out his pony for exercise. If he were going far afield he delegated the readings to some members of the scientific staff who were generally in the vicinity of winter quarters. Marshall, as surgeon, attended to any wounds, and issued necessary pills, and then took out one of the ponies for exercise. Wild, who was store-keeper, was responsible for the issuing of all stores to Roberts, and had to open the cases of tinned food and dig out of the snow drifts in which it was buried the meat required for the day, either penguin, seal or mutton. Joyce fed the dogs after breakfast, the puppies getting a dish of scraps over from our meals after breakfast and after dinner. When daylight returned after our long night, he worked at training the dogs to pull a sledge every morning. The Professor generally went off to 'geologise' or to continue the plane-table survey of our winter quarters, whilst Priestley and Murray worked on the floe dredging or else took the temperatures of the ice in shafts which the former had energetically sunk in the various lakes around us. Mawson was occupied with his physical work, which included auroral observations and the study of the structure of the ice, the determination of atmospheric electricity and many other things. In fact, we were all busy, and there was little cause for us to find the time hang heavy on our hands; the winter months sped by and this without our having to sleep through them, as has often been done before by polar expeditions. This was due to the fact that we were only a small party and that our household duties, added to our scientific work, fully occupied our time. In another chapter the reader will find a short summary of the scientific work of each department, and will see from this that in a practically unknown country and under such peculiar weather conditions, there were many things of interest in natural science to be studied.

It would only be repetition to chronicle our doings from day to day during the months that elapsed from the disappearance of the sun until the time arrived when the welcome daylight came back to us. We lived under conditions of steady routine, affected only by short spells of bad weather, and found amply sufficient to occupy ourselves in our daily work, so that the spectre known as 'polar ennui' never made its appearance. Mid-winter's Day and birthdays were the occasions of festivals, when our teetotal *regime* was broken through and a sort of mild spree indulged in. Before the sun finally went hockey and football were the outdoor games, while indoors at night some of us played bridge, poker and dominoes. Joyce, Wild, Marston and Day during the winter months spent much time in the production of the 'Aurora Australis', the first book ever written, printed, illustrated and bound in the Antarctic. Through the generosity of Messrs. Joseph Causton and Sons, Limited, we had been provided with a complete printing outfit and the necessary paper for the book, and Joyce and Wild had been given instruction in the art of type-setting and printing, Marston being taught etching and lithography. They had hardly become skilled craftsmen, but they had gained a good working knowledge of the branches of the business. When we had settled down in the winter quarters, Joyce and Wild set up the little hand-press and sorted out the type, these preliminary operations taking up all their spare time for some days, and then they started to set and print the various contributions that were sent in by members of the expedition. The early days of the printing department were not exactly happy, for the two amateur type-setters found themselves making many mistakes, and when they had at last 'set up' a page, made all the necessary corrections, and printed off the necessary required number of copies, they had to undertake the laborious work of 'dissing', that is, of distributing the type again.

They plodded ahead steadily, however, and soon became more skilful, until at the end of a fortnight or three weeks they could print two pages in a day. A lamp had to be placed under the type-rack to keep it warm, and a lighted candle was put under the inking-plate, so that the ink would keep reasonably thin in consistency. The great trouble experienced by the printers at first was in securing the right pressure on the printing-plate and even inking of the page, but experience showed them where they had been at fault. Day meanwhile prepared the binding by cleaning, planing, and polishing wood taken from the Venesta cases in which our provisions were packed. Marston reproduced the illustrations by algraphy, or printing from aluminium plates. He had not got a proper lithographing press, so had to use an ordinary etching press, and he was handicapped by the fact that all our water had a trace of salt in it. This mineral acted on the sensitive plates, but Marston managed to produce what we all regarded as creditable pictures. In its final form the book had about one hundred and twenty pages, and it had at least assisted materially to guard us from the danger of lack of occupation during the polar night.

15

THE POLAR NIGHT

On March 13 we experienced a very fierce blizzard. The hut shook and rocked in spite of our sheltered position, and articles that we had left lying loose outside were scattered far and wide. Even cases weighing from fifty to eighty pounds were shifted from where they had been resting, showing the enormous velocity of the wind. When the gale was over we put everything that was likely to blow away into positions of greater safety. It was on this day also that Murray found living microscopical animals on some fungus that had been thawed out from a lump of ice taken from the bottom of one of the lakes. This was one of the most interesting biological discoveries that had been made in the Antarctic, for the study of these minute creatures occupied our biologist for a great part of his stay in the south, and threw a new light on the capability of life to exist under conditions of extreme cold and in the face of great variations of temperature. We all became vastly interested in the rotifers during our stay, and the work of the biologist in this respect was watched with keen attention. From our point of view there was an element of humour in the endeavours of Murray to slay the little animals he had found. He used to thaw them out from a block of ice, freeze them up again, and repeat this process several times without producing any result as far as the rotifers were concerned. Then he tested them in brine so strongly saline that it would not freeze at a temperature above minus 7° Fahr., and still the animals lived. A good proportion of them survived a temperature of 200° Fahr. It became a contest between rotifers and scientist, and generally the rotifers seemed to triumph. The biologist will tell his own story in another chapter.

I noted in my diary that in the middle of March, when daylight lasted eight hours, we still had the skua gulls with us. The young birds were now nearly all flying, but in some cases there were backward youngsters that had not yet gained the use of their wings and were still under the protection of their parents. The Adelie penguins had practically deserted us, only about thirty remaining in the rookery at this time. These birds had been moulting, but all except six had finished the operation. We observed that when moulting the penguin does not enter the sea for food, and seems to live on its own blubber, taking no food but eating large quantities of snow. On March 17, after snow had been falling all night, Murray walked over to the rookery and saw only half the penguins remaining, as he thought, but suddenly the others rose up from under his feet. They had been lying down and had been covered with snow, their bills only protruding. There were large numbers of Weddel seals about at this time, and from the top of the cliff we saw one lying asleep in the water, with his nostrils just showing above the surface. There was still open water close to our winter quarters, but young ice was beginning to form in the bay again, and beautiful ice flowers appeared on the surface of this young ice. About this time on the slopes of Erebus, a mile and a half from the hut, a most interesting find of marine, serpulae was made on a moraine about 320 ft. above sea-level and near this deposit was some yellow earth containing diatoms. We could not at the time determine the cause of this peculiar deposit, but it was certainly not what one might expect on such a place as Ross Island, and both to geologists and biologists was a matter of interest. So far we had not had any dearth of animal life when viewed from the standpoint of the replenishing of our larder, but towards the end of March the seals became less numerous and the appearance of one of these was generally followed by its death. Towards the end of the month Erebus became very active, shooting out huge clouds of steam, which rose to the height of 2000 ft. above the crater and were then caught by the upper winds, giving us very definite information as to the trend of the upper air-currents.

About the same time we began to see the aurora, and night after night, except when the moon was at its full or the sky overcast, the waving mystic lines of light were thrown across the heavens, waxing and waning rapidly, falling into folds and curtains, spreading out into great arches and sometimes shooting vertical beams almost to the zenith. Sometimes, indeed often, the aurora hovered over Mount Erebus, attracted no doubt by this great isolated mass of rock, sometimes descending to the lower slopes and always giving us an interest that never failed. When the familiar cry of 'aurora' was uttered by some one who had been outside, most of us rushed out to see what new phase this mysterious phenomenon would take, and we were indeed fortunate in the frequency and brilliancy of the displays. Mawson, as physicist, obtained a number of interesting notes which throw new light on this difficult subject.

At the end of March there was still open water in the bay and we observed a Killer whale chasing a seal. About this time we commenced digging a trench in Clear Lake and obtained, when we came to water, samples of the bottom mud and fungus, which were simply swarming with living organisms. The sunsets at the beginning of April were wonderful; arches of prismatic colours, crimson and golden-tinged clouds, hung in the heavens nearly all day, for time was going on and soon the sun would have deserted us. The days grew shorter and shorter, and the twilight longer. During these sunsets the Western Mountains stood out gloriously and the summit of Erebus was wrapped in crimson when the lower slopes had faded into grey. To Erebus and the Western Mountains our eyes turned when the end of the long night grew near in the month of August, for the mighty peaks are the first to catch up and tell the tale of the coming glory and the last to drop the crimson mantle from their high shoulders as night draws on. Tongue and pencil would sadly fail in attempting to describe the magic of the colouring in the days when the sun was leaving us. The very clouds at this time were irridescent with rainbow hues. The sunsets were poems. The change from twilight into night, sometimes fit by a crescent moon, was extraordinarily beautiful, for the white cliffs gave no part of their colour away, and the rocks beside them did not part with their blackness, so the effect of deepening night over these contrasts was singularly weird. In my diary I noted that throughout April hardly a day passed without an aurora display. On more than one occasion the aurora showed distinct lines of colour, merging from a deep red at the base of the line of light into a greenish hue on top. About the beginning of April the temperature began to drop considerably, and for some days in calm, still weather the thermometer often registered 40° below zero.

On April 6, Marshall decided that it was necessary to amputate Brocklehurst's big toe, as there was no sign of it recovering like the other toes from the frostbite he had received on the Erebus journey. The patient was put under chloroform and the operation was witnessed by an interested and sympathetic audience. After the bone had been removed, the sufferer was shifted into my room, where he remained till just before Mid-winter's Day, when he was able to get out and move about again. We had about April 8 one of the peculiar southerly blizzards so common during our last expedition, the temperature varying rapidly from minus 23° to plus 4° Fahr. This blizzard continued till the evening of the 11th, and when it had abated we found the bay and sound clear of ice again. I began to feel rather worried about this and wished for it to freeze over, for across the ice lay our road to the south. We observed occasionally about this time that peculiar phenomenon of McMurdo Sound called 'earth shadows'. Long dark bars, projected up into the sky from the Western Mountains, made their appearance at sunrise. These lines are due to the shadow of the giant Erebus being cast across the Western Mountains. Our days were now getting very short and the amount of daylight was a negligible quantity. We boarded up the remainder of the windows, and depended entirely upon the artificial light in the winter quarters. The light given by the acetylene gas was brilliant, four burners lighting the whole of the hut.

We saw only two sea-leopards during the whole period of our stay in the Antarctic, and both these specimens were secured. The first was killed soon after the sun left us. A seal was reported to have been seen on the ice near the winter quarters, and Joyce went down to kill it, as we wanted fresh meat and blubber. When he got close he found that the animal was a sea-leopard. He was armed only with a club, and came running for a pistol, for the sea-leopards are savage and aggressive, and can move very rapidly on the ice. When he got back, carrying a heavy revolver, the animal was still in the same position, and he shot it twice through the heart, and then twice through the skull. It had remarkable tenacity of life, for it still struggled, and even after a fifth ball had been put through its brain some minutes elapsed before it turned over and lay still. Joyce skinned the carcase, and he found that the first two bullets had actually gone through the heart. He also reported that it seemed to have two hearts, one of which had not been injured, but unfortunately the organs that he brought back to the hut were found and promptly devoured by some of the dogs, so that it is not possible to produce evidence on the point. The specimen was a very fine one, and was a welcome addition to our zoological collection. Soon after the sun returned in the spring I sighted a seal that seemed to be out of the ordinary off Cape Barne, about two miles and a half from the hut. I found that it was a young sea-leopard, apparently suffering from starvation and I sent Joyce down to kill it. I fancy that it had got on to the ice and had been unable to find its way into the water again. Joyce killed it, and found that the stomach was quite empty.

When daylight returned and sledging began about the middle of August, on one of our excursions on the Cape Royds peninsula, we found growing under volcanic earth a large quantity of fungus. This was of great interest to Murray, as plant-life of any sort is extremely rare in the Antarctic. Shortly after this a strong blizzard cast up a quantity of seaweed on our ice-foot; this was another piece of good fortune, for on the last expedition we obtained very little seaweed.

16
SPRING SLEDGING JOURNEYS

When Mid-winter's Day had passed and the twilight that presaged the return of the sun began to be more marked day by day, I set on foot the arrangements for the sledging work in the forthcoming spring. It was desirable that, at as early a date as possible, we should place a depot of stores at a point to the south, in preparation for the departure of the Southern Party, which was to march towards the Pole. I hoped to make this depot at least one hundred miles from the winter quarters. Then it was desirable that we should secure some definite information regarding the condition of the snow surface on the Barrier, and I was also anxious to afford the various members of the expedition some practice in sledging before the serious work commenced. Some of us had been in the Antarctic before, but the majority of the men had not yet had any experience of marching and camping on snow and ice in low temperatures.

The ponies had been kept in good training by means of regular exercise and constant attention during the winter, but although they were thoroughly fit, and, indeed, apparently anxious for an opportunity to work off some of their superfluous energy, I did not propose to take them on the preliminary sledging journeys. It seemed to be unwise to take any unnecessary risk of further loss now that we had only four ponies left, few enough for the southern journey later in the season. Sledging work in the spring, when the temperature is very low, the light bad, and the weather uncertain, is a rather severe strain on man and beast. For this reason, manhauling was the order for the first journeys.

During the winter I had given a great deal of earnest consideration to the question of the date at which the party that was to march towards the Pole should start from the hut. The goal that we hoped to attain lay over 880 statute miles to the south, and the brief summer was all too short a time in which to march so far into the unknown and return to winter quarters. The ship would have to leave for the north about the end of February, for the ice would then be closing in, and, moreover, we could not hope to carry on our sledges much more than a three months' supply of provisions, or anything like full rations. I finally decided that the Southern Party should leave the winter quarters about October 28, for if we started earlier it was probable that the ponies would suffer from the severe cold at nights, and we would gain no advantage from getting away early in the season if, as a result, the ponies were incapacitated before we had made much progress. The ponies would be sure to sweat when pulling their heavy loads during the day, and a very low temperature when they were resting would be dangerous in view of the fact that we could not hope to provide them with shelter from the winds.

The date for the departure of the Southern Party having been fixed, it became necessary to arrange for the laying of the depot during the early spring, and I thought that the first step towards this should be a preliminary journey on the Barrier surface, in order to gain an idea of the conditions that would be met with, and to ascertain whether the motor-car would be of service, at any rate, for the early portion of the journey. The sun had not yet returned and the temperature was very low indeed, but we had proved in the course of the *Discovery* expedition that it is quite possible to travel under these conditions. I therefore started on this preliminary journey on August 12, taking with me Professor David, who was to lead the Northern Party towards the South Magnetic Pole, and Bertram Armytage, who was to take charge of the party that was to make a journey into the mountains of the west later in the year. The reader can imagine that it was not with feelings of unalloyed pleasure that we turned our backs on the warm, well-found hut and faced our little journey out into the semi-darkness and intense cold, but we did get a certain amount of satisfaction from the thought that at last we were actually beginning the work we had come south to undertake.

We were equipped for a fortnight with provisions and camp gear, packed on one sledge, and had three gallons of petroleum in case we should decide to stay out longer. A gallon of oil will last a party of three men for about ten days under ordinary conditions, and we could get more food at Hut Point if we required it. We took three one-man sleeping-bags, believing that they would be sufficiently warm in spite of the low temperature. The larger bags, holding two or three men, certainly give greater warmth, for the occupants warm one another, but, on the other hand, one's rest is very likely to be disturbed by the movements of a companion. We were heavily clothed for this trip, because the sun would not rise above the horizon until another ten days had passed.

Our comrades turned out to see us off, and the pony Quan pulled the sledge with our camp gear over the sea ice until we got close to the glacier south of Cape Barne, about five miles from the winter quarters. Then he was sent back, for the weather was growing thick, and, as already explained, I did not want to run any risk of losing another pony from our sadly diminished team. We proceeded close in by the skuary, and a little further on pitched camp for lunch. Professor David, whose thirst for knowledge could not be quenched, immediately went off to investigate the geology of the neighbourhood. After lunch we started to pull our sledge round the coast towards Hut Point, but the weather became worse, making progress difficult, and at 6 p.m. we camped close to the tide-crack at the south side of Turk's Head. We slept well and soundly, although the temperature was about forty degrees below zero, and the experience made me more than ever convinced of the superiority of one-man sleeping-bags.

On the following morning, August 13, we marched across to Glacier Tongue, having to cross a wide crack that had been ridged up by ice-pressure between Tent Island and the Tongue. As soon as we had crossed we saw the depot standing up clear against the sky-line on the Tongue. This was the depot that had been made by the ship soon after our first arrival in the Sound. We found no difficulty in getting on to the Tongue, for a fairly gentle slope led up from the sea-ice to the glacier surface. The snow had blown over from the south during the winter and made a good way. We found the depot intact, though the cases, lying on the ice, had been bleached to a light yellow colour by the wind and sun. We had lunch on the south side of the Tongue, and found there another good way down to the sea ice. There is a very awkward crack on the south side, but this can hardly be called a tide-crack. I think it is due to the fact that the tide has more effect on the sea ice than on the heavy mass of the Tongue, though there is no doubt this also is afloat; the rise and fall of the two sections of ice are not coincident, and a crack is produced. The unaccustomed pulling made us tired, and we decided to pitch a camp about four miles off Hut Point, before reaching Castle Rock. Castle Rock is distant three miles and a half from Hut Point, and we had always noticed that after we got abeam of the rock the final march on to the hut seemed very long, for we were always weary by that time. The temperature was now about forty-five degrees below zero Fahr., and my two companions were feeling for the first time the discomfort of using metal utensils in this extreme cold. The Professor's fingers seemed to have a wonderful power of resisting frost-bite. We were travelling in a light that resembled broad twilight, but as the sun was still below the horizon there were no shadows, and we stumbled a great deal amongst the rough ice.

We reached the old *Discovery* winter quarters at Hut Point on the morning of August 14, and after a good breakfast I took the Professor and Armytage over all the familiar ground. It was very interesting to me to revisit the old scenes. There was the place where, years before, when the *Discovery* was lying fast in the ice close to the shore, we used to dig for the ice that was required for the supply of fresh water. The marks of the picks and shovels were still to be seen. I noticed an old case bedded in the ice, and remembered

the day when it had been thrown away. Round the hut was collected a very
large amount of *debris,* including sealskins and the skeletons of seals and
penguins. Some of the seal-skins had still blubber attached, though the skuas
had evidently been at work on them. We went up towards the Gap and had
a look at the only lake, or rather pool, that lay near these winter quarters. It
was quite a tiny sheet of water in comparison with the large lakes at Cape
Royds, and I realised more fully the special advantages we had at our winter
quarters as far as biological and zoological work were concerned. Through
the Gap we saw the Barrier stretched out before us – the long white road that
we were shortly to tread. The fascination of the unknown was strong upon
me, and I longed to be away towards the south on the journey that I hoped
would lay bare the mysteries of the place of the Pole.

We climbed to the top of Crater Hill with a collectingbag and the
Professor's camera, and here we took some photographs and made an
examination of the cone. Professor David expressed the opinion that the
icesheet had certainly passed over this hill, which is about 1100 ft. high,
for there was distinct evidence of glaciation. We climbed along the ridge to
Castle Rock, about four miles to the north, and made an examination of the
formation there. Then we returned to the hut to have a square meal and get
ready for our journey across the Barrier.

The old hut had never been a very cheerful place, even when we were
camped alongside it in the *Discovery,* and it looked doubly inhospitable now,
after having stood empty and neglected for six years. One side was filled with
cases of biscuit and tinned meat and the snow that had found its way in
was lying in great piles around the walls. There was no stove, for this had
been taken away with the *Discovery,* and coal was scattered about the floor
with other *debris* and rubbish. Besides the biscuits and the tinned beef and
mutton there was some tea and coffee stored in the hut. We cleared a spot on
which to sleep, and decided that we would use the cases of biscuit and meat
to build, another hut inside the main one, so that the quarters would be a
little more cosy. I proposed to use this hut as a stores depot in connection
with the southern journey, for if the ice broke out in the Sound unexpectedly
early, it would be difficult to convey provisions from Cape Royds to the
Barrier, and, moreover, Hut Point was twenty miles further south than our
winter quarters. We spent that night on the floor of the hut, and slept fairly
comfortably, though not as well as on the previous night in the tent, because
we were not so close to one another.

On the morning of the following day (August 15) we started away about
9 a.m., crossed the smooth ice to Winter Harbour, and passed close round
Cape Armitage. We there found cracks and pressed-up ice, showing that
there had been Barrier movement, and about three miles further on we
crossed the spot at which the sea ice joins the Barrier, ascending a slope about

eight feet high. Directly we got on to the Barrier ice we noticed undulations on the surface. We pushed along and got to a distance of about twelve miles from Hut Point in eight hours. The surface generally was hard, but there were very marked sastrugi, and at times patches of soft snow. The conditions did not seem favourable for the use of the motor-car because we had already found that the machine could not go through soft snow for more than a few yards, and I foresaw that if we brought it out on to the Barrier it would not be able to do much in the soft surface that would have to be traversed. The condition of the surface varied from mile to mile, and it would be impracticable to keep changing the wheels of the car in order to meet the requirements of each new surface.

The temperature was very low, although the weather was fine. At 6 p.m. the thermometer showed fifty-six degrees below zero, and the petroleum used for the lamp had become milky in colour and of a creamy consistency. That night the temperature fell lower still, and the moisture in our sleeping-bags, from our breath and Burberrys, made us very uncomfortable when the bags had thawed out with the warmth of our bodies. Everything we touched was appallingly cold, and we got no sleep at all. The next morning (August 16) the weather was threatening, and there were indications of the approach of a blizzard, and I therefore decided to march back to Hut Point, for there was no good purpose to be served by taking unnecessary risks at that stage of the expedition. We had some warm food, of which we stood sorely in need after the severe night, and then started at 8 a.m. to return to Hut Point. By hard marching, which had the additional advantage of warming us up, we reached the old hut again at three o'clock that afternoon, and we were highly delighted to get into its shelter. The sun had not yet returned, and though there was a strong light in the sky during the day, the Barrier was not friendly under winter conditions.

We reached the hut none too soon, for a blizzard sprang up, and for some days we had to remain in shelter. We utilised the time by clearing up the portion of the hut that we proposed to use, even sweeping it with an old broom we found, and building a shelter of the packing-cases, piling them right up to the roof round a space about twenty feet by ten; and thus we made comparatively cosy quarters. We rigged a table for the cooking-gear, and put everything neatly in order. My two companions were, at this time, having their first experience of polar life under marching conditions as far as equipment was concerned, and they were gaining knowledge that proved very useful to them on the later journeys.

On the morning of August 22, the day on which the sun once more appeared above the horizon, we started back for the winter quarters, leaving Hut Point at 5 a.m. in the face of a bitterly cold wind from the north-east, with low drift. We marched without a stop for nine miles, until we reached-

Glacier Tongue, and then had an early lunch. An afternoon march of fourteen miles took us to the winter quarters at Cape Royds, where we arrived at 5 p.m. We were not expected at the hut, for the weather was thick and windy, but our comrades were delighted to see us, and we had a hearty dinner and enjoyed the luxury of a good bath.

The chief result of this journey was to convince me that we could not place much reliance on the motor-car for the southern journey. Professor David and Armytage had received a good baptism of frost, and as it was very desirable that all the members of the expedition should have personal experience of travelling over the ice and snow in low temperatures before the real work began, I arranged to despatch a small party every week to sledge stores and equipment south to Hit Point. These journeys were much alike in general character, though they all gave rise to incidents that were afterwards related in the winter quarters, and it will be sufficient if I describe briefly one trip as a specimen.

On September 1, Wild, Day and Priestley started for Hut Point via Glacier Tongue with 450 lb. of gear and provisions, their instructions being to leave 230 lb. of provisions at the *Discovery* hut in readiness for the southern journey. They made a start at 10.20 a.m., being accompanied by Brocklehurst with a pony for the first five miles. The weather was fine, but a very low barometer gave an indication that bad weather was coming. I did not hesitate to let these parties face bad weather, because the road they were to travel was well known, and a rough experience would be very useful to the men later in the expedition's work. The party camped for lunch at Inaccessible Island, with a temperature at seventeen degrees below zero Fahr., and a fresh wind blowing from the north, with light drift. At 2.30 p.m. they left the island and started for Glacier Tongue, the weather growing thicker, but they had no trouble with the tide-cracks, and at the Tongue depot had a short rest, breaking a bottle of frozen preserved cherries. Then they crossed the Tongue, but as the drift was obscuring all landmarks, decided to camp in the snow close to the south side of the Tongue.

Next morning the weather was still bad, and they were not able to make a start until after noon. At 1.20 p.m. they ran out of the northerly wind into light southerly airs with intervals of calm, and they noticed that at the meeting of the two winds the clouds of drift were formed into whirling columns, some of them over forty feet high. They reached the *Discovery* hut at 4.30 p.m., and soon turned in, the temperature being forty degrees below zero. When they dressed at 5.30 a.m. the next day they found that a southerly wind with heavy drift rendered a start on the return journey inadvisable. After breakfast they walked over to Observation Hill, where they examined a set of stakes which Ferrar and Wild had placed in the Gap glacier in 1902. The stakes showed that the movement of the glacier during the six years since the stakes had been put into position had amounted to a few inches only. The middle stake had advanced eight inches and those next it on either side about six inches. At noon the wind dropped, and although the drift was still thick, the party started back, steering by the sastrugi till the Tongue was reached. At the point at which they had run out of the north wind on the outward journey, they again picked up a strong northerly breeze. They did not sight Glacier Tongue till they were close to it, and they found that owing to their fear of going outside it, they had got too far east, and were about a mile and a half from the depot. They started to march alongside the Tongue towards the depot, but a strong south easterly wind came up, with heavy drift, so they decided to cross the Tongue, and managed to climb up a drift after just missing a twenty-foot drop into a hollow scooped out by the wind in the snow. By this time the men could not see more than a yard or two before them, and they hurried across the Tongue, taking the small crevasses in their stride, and after travelling three quarters of a mile pulled up the sledge within half a dozen yards of the other edge of the Tongue, at a point where they afterwards found there was a forty-foot precipice. Wild felt his way along the edge with the ice-axe until he came to a steep slope that seemed to promise a means of descent, and then all three tobogganed down on the sledge and camped for the night in the lee of the glacier, with a blizzard blowing over them and the temperature rising, the result being that everything was uncomfortably wet. They managed to sleep, however, and when they awoke the next morning the weather was clear, and they had an easy march in, being met beyond Cape Barne by Joyce, Brocklehurst and the dogs. They had been absent four days.

Each party came back with adventures to relate, experiences to compare, and its own views on various matters of detail connected with sledge-travelling.

The conversation in the hut after the return of a party would become very animated, for each man had definite opinions, born of experience, on such important questions as how to dress and how to get into a sleeping-bag with the minimum of discomfort. Curiously enough, every one of the parties encountered bad weather, but there were no accidents, and all the men seemed to enjoy the work.

Early in September a party consisting of Adams, Marshall and myself started for Hut Point, and we decided to make one march of the twenty-three miles, and not camp on the way. We started at 8 a.m., and when we were nearly at the end of the journey, and were struggling slowly through bad snow towards the hut, close to the end of Hut Point, a strong blizzard came up. Fortunately I knew the bearings of the hut, and how to get over the ice-foot. We abandoned the extra weights we were pulling for the depot, and managed to get to the hut at 10 p.m. in a sorely frostbitten condition, almost too tired to move. We were able to get ourselves some hot food, however, and were soon all right again. I mention the incident merely to show how constantly one has to be on guard against the onslaughts of the elements in the inhospitable regions of the south.

17

SOUTHERN DEPOT JOURNEY

By the middle of September a good supply of provisions, oil, and gear had been stored at Hut Point in preparation for the sledge journeys. All the supplies required for the southern journey had been taken there, in order that the start might be made from the most southern base available. During this period, while the men were gaining experience and getting into training, the ponies were being exercised regularly along the sea ice from winter quarters across to Cape Barne, and I was more than satisfied with the way in which they did their work. I felt that the little animals were going to justify the confidence I had reposed in them when I had brought them all the way from Manchuria to the bleak Antarctic. I tried the ponies with loads of varying weights in order to ascertain as closely as possible how much they could haul with maximum efficiency, and after watching the results of the experiments very carefully came to the conclusion that a load of 650 lb. per pony should be the maximum. It was obvious that if the animals were overloaded their speed would be reduced, so that there would be no gain to us, and if we were to accomplish a good journey to the south it was important that they should not be tired out in the early stages of the march over the Barrier surface. The weight I have mentioned was to include that of the sledge itself, which I have already stated was about 60 lb. When I came to consider the question of weight, I realised the full seriousness of the loss the expedition had sustained when the other four ponies were lost during the winter, for I saw that we would not be able to take with us towards the Pole as much food as I should have liked.

The dogs, whose numbers had been increased by births until we had a fairly large team, were trained, but I did not see much scope for them on the southern journey. I knew from past experience that dogs would not travel when low drift was blowing in their faces, and such drift was to be expected fairly often on the Barrier surface, even in the summer.

During the month of May Day had taken the engine out of the motor-car, a task of no little difficulty in a temperature below zero, and after cleaning every part thoroughly, had packed it away in a case for the winter. On September 14, when the light was beginning to get stronger, he got the engine back into the car, working in a temperature of minus 10° Fahr., and began preparations for the journeys over the ice. The car made its first journey of importance on September 19, and by that time experiments had proved that an extensive reduction in weight was necessary if the machine was to accomplish anything at all. Day therefore proceeded to strip it of every bit of wood or metal not absolutely essential to running efficiency. In its final form the bare chassis carried the engine and one seat for the driver. No great difficulties were experienced in connection with the engine, even when the temperature was many degrees below zero. The mixing chamber and inlet pipes were warmed up by burning petrol in a small dish rigged round the carburetter just below the throttle, the carburetter being flooded at the same time. By the time the petrol had burned out the engine would start with a few turns of the crank. The petrol tank carried twenty-three gallons, and fed the carburetter by pressure from a small hand-pump. Accumulator ignition was found to be impossible, as the acid and water froze solid, but the magneto gave no trouble. A second petrol tank, which fed the carburetter by gravity, was taken off in order to save weight. The car had a drip-feed lubricator for oiling the crank-ease, but as the oil got frozen in the pipes it was not at all reliable, so oil was poured into the case through holes every five miles or so. Ordinary heavy oil got thick at a temperature of 20° Fahr., and solid at zero Fahr., but a special Antarctic oil supplied by Messrs. Price and Co. gave good results even at a temperature of minus 30° Fahr.

The power was transmitted to the gear-box through a leather-faced case clutch, and the gears, which were specially low, were four speeds forward and one reverse. When Day first tried to get the car under way he found that he could not declutch, as the leather had frozen to the metal, and it was necessary to warm up the parts and dry them off with a sponge. We had wheels of several types, but soon found that ordinary wheels with rubber tyres and non-skid chains gave the best results. At a temperature of minus 30° Fahr. the tyres became quite hard, with no spring in them, but we had no tyre troubles at all, even when the ice was very rough.

On September 19 the motor-car took Day, Brocklehurst and Adams, with a sledge on which were packed 750 lb. of stores, to lay a depot at Glacier Tongue for the southern journey. There was a stiff breeze blowing, with a temperature of minus 23° Fahr., but the car ran well for eight miles as far as Inaccessible Island over the sea ice. Then it got into the heavy sastrugi caused by the wind blowing between Inaccessible Island and Tent Island, and was stopped by soft snow, into which it ploughed deeply. An easier route was found about a mile further north, at a point where the sastrugi were less marked. The car reached a point a quarter of a mile distant from the Tongue, and the sledge was hauled the rest of the way by the men, as the surface was very soft. The return journey presented fewer difficulties, for Day was able to drive in the outward tracks. The total distance covered by the car that day was at least thirty miles, and the speed had ranged from three to fifteen miles an hour. The three men left the winter quarters at 9.30 a.m., and arrived back at 6.45 p.m., having accomplished an amount of work that would have occupied six men for two or three days without the assistance of the car.

It was always a matter of difficulty to get the car from the hut to the sea ice, and this was often the most formidable part of a journey. A short slope at an angle of about forty-five degrees, led down to the large tide-crack, and beyond this were some smaller cracks and one large crack with hummocky ice on either side of it and big drifts. Sometimes the car got stuck altogether, and then the assistance of all hands would be required to pull and push. The car could not be left on the sea ice because no shelter could be provided there, and a blizzard might sweep down at very short notice.

About September 14 we started to make active preparations for the depot journey. I decided to place a depot one hundred geographical miles south of the *Discovery* winter quarters, the depot to consist of pony maize. If by any chance we were not able to pick it up when going south on our attempt to reach the Pole, the loss of the maize would be a less serious matter than the loss of any portion of the provisions for our own consumption. I did not anticipate that there would be much difficulty in picking up the depot again, but there was the possibility that severe weather might bury the stores and obliterate any marks set up for our guidance. I picked a depot party consisting of Adams, Marshall, Wild, Joyce and Marston, with myself as the sixth man. I did not propose to take either ponies or dogs, for reasons I have already explained. We took two tents, three men going in each, and two three-man sleeping-bags, for we expected to meet with very low temperatures. The disadvantages of these bags, as I have already stated, is that one's sleep is liable to be disturbed, but this would not matter so much on a comparatively short journey, and we would probably need the additional warmth derived from one another's bodies. There is no doubt in my mind that for extended journeys in the polar regions the use of one-man bags is desirable. Apart from all other considerations, it is a great comfort to have a little home of one's own into which to retire when the day's work is done, secure from all interruptions. The opening can be adjusted just as the occupant pleases, whereas if there are two or three men in the one bag, one may think the atmosphere suffocating, while another objects to the draught.

The depot party left Cape Royds on September 22, with a load of about 170 lb. per man, and made the first part of the journey in the motor-car. Day was able to get the machine, with the sledges towed behind and all the members of the party either on the car or the sledges, as far as Inaccessible Island, moving at a speed of about six miles an hour. I heard afterwards that the car ran back to the hut, a distance of eight miles, in twenty minutes. We took the sledges on ourselves over a fairly good surface, and spent the first night at the *Discovery* hut. Three of the puppies had followed the car when we started away from the winter quarters, and they had firmly refused to go back with it, apparently because Joyce had been in the habit of feeding them, and they were not willing to leave him. They followed us right to Hut Point, the first long march of their short lives, and after devouring all the meat and biscuits we would give them, they settled down in a corner of the hut for the night. We could not take the poor little animals out on to the Barrier with us, though they would have followed us readily enough, and we decided that the only thing to do was to shut them up in the hut until we came back. There was plenty of snow there, so that they would not want for water, and we opened a box of biscuits and some tinned meat, and left the food where they could reach it. Their anxious barks and whines followed us as we moved off southwards.

The journey was a severe one, for the temperature got down to fifty-nine degrees below zero Fahr., with blizzard winds, but as we travelled over ground that had become fairly familar in the course of the previous expedition, I will not deal with our experiences in any great detail. The first blizzard struck us when we were south of White Island. We started off in the morning, though there was a stiff breeze blowing and the weather looked threatening, and marched until about 10.30 a.m. Then the gusts became more fierce, and the drift got so thick that we had to camp. We only put up one tent at first, in the hope that we would be able to start again in a few hours, but the wind continued, so we erected the other tent and abandoned hope of marching farther that day. We were able to make an early start on the following morning, the 26th. The petroleum for our stoves was practically frozen at times, refusing to run at all. We got into pressure ridges when some distance north of Minna Bluff, but fortunately we were having good weather at this time. Most of us had the experience at one time or other of dropping into a crevasse to the length of our harness. Adams, Marshall and Marston had not yet become accustomed to the little misadventures incidental to travel in the Antarctic, but it did not take them long to become inured. I remember one night hearing Marston asking whether it would be safe to have a look round outside. 'Well, you can play "perhaps" if you like', remarked some one. Marston did not understand, and the other man explained that the 'game' was played on the basis of 'perhaps you go down and perhaps you don't'. Marston was making sketches and taking notes of colours, and his work was rendered very difficult by the extreme cold. There were wonderful lights in the sky at dawn and dusk, and the snow and ice presented the gradations of delicate colour that can hardly be realised by those who have never seen a polar landscape, but heavy mits, with one compartment for the four fingers and another for the thumb, are hardly designed for the handling of pencil or crayons, and the use of bare hands was out of the question. Marston persisted in the face of his various troubles, and managed to secure a good deal of interesting and valuable material.

We left one bag of maize at a depot on the way out, but we never picked this up again. The main depot was laid in latitude 79.36° South, longitude 168o East, a distance of about one hundred and twenty geographical miles from the winter quarters. We reached it on October 6. This depot was out of sight of land, and was marked with an upturned sledge and a black flag on a bamboo rod. We left there a gallon tin of oil and 167 lb. of pony maize, so that our load would be lightened considerably for the first portion of the journey when we started south. This southern depot was called Depot A.

The weather was bad and the temperature low on the journey back, and I decided to take the outside course in order to avoid the crevasses as much as possible. The disturbed condition of the ice in this neighbourhood is caused by the Barrier impinging on the Bluff, and by the glaciers coming down from Mount Discovery. As had been the case on the outward journey, we were delayed a good deal by blizzards, and owing to this fact we had to make very long marches when the weather was fine, for we had brought food for twenty days only. We experienced a very severe blizzard before we reached White Island. We had got away from camp at 4 a.m. that morning, and had been marching for about an hour and a half when the wind that was following us began to approach blizzard strength. Four men kept the traces taut while two men held the sledge from behind, but even then the sledge sometimes caught up to the men in front. As the wind increased the drifting snow got thicker and finer, and after a short time we could not see more than ten or fifteen yards ahead. Then we found that we were amongst crevasses, for first one man and then another put his foot through a snow lid, and we therefore stopped and camped. The wind increased rapidly, and it took about an hour and a half of hard work to get the tents pitched. The snow blew into our faces and formed masks of ice, and several members of the party got bad frost-bites. When we finally got the tents up, we had to be in them for thirty hours. As a result of such delays, we did not reach the old *Discovery* winter quarters until October 13. We had been twenty-one days out, and our food was finished, though we had been able to keep on full rations until the last day. We had been able to march only on fourteen and a half days, but we had made some good journeys on the way back, having covered as much as twenty-five miles in a day.

We found our little friends, the puppies, safe and sound in the hut, and their delight at seeing us again was simply huge. Directly they heard us approaching they started to make every effort in their power to attract attention, and the moment the door was opened they rushed out and fairly threw themselves upon us. They twined their fat little bodies round our boots and yelped in an ecstasy of welcome. Poor little dogs, they had, no doubt, been lonely and frightened during the three weeks they had spent in the hut, though physically they seemed to have been comfortable enough. They had eaten all the meat left for them, but they still had biscuits, and they had put on flesh. Their coats were quite black owing to their having lain amongst the fragments of coal on the floor.

The next day we started for Cape Royds, and had the good fortune to meet the motor-car, driven by Day, at a point about a mile and a half south of Cape Barne. The sledges were soon hitched on behind, and we drove back triumphantly to the winter quarters. It was October 13 and we had travelled 320 statute miles since we left the hut twenty-two days before. We arrived hungry and rather tired, and were able to appreciate at their full value the warmth and comfort of our little hut. The adventurous puppies were outside doing their best to convince their friends and relatives that they were not three strangers trying to force their way into the community.

During our absence the Northern Party, consisting of Professor David, Mawson and Mackay, had started on the journey that was to result in the attainment of the South Magnetic Pole. I had instructed the Professor, who was in command of this party, to get away on October 1, or as soon after that date as weather and other circumstances would permit. On September 25 Professor David, Priestley and Day took 850 lb. of stores for the northern journey out into the middle of the sound, a distance of about fourteen miles, by means of the motor-car. Day had intended to go to Dinley isles, but sastrugi that stretched right across the ice of the sound prevented this. The sastrugi were in places two feet deep, and the wheels could get no grip in the soft snow, into which they sank deeply. Some very bad cracks were encountered, including one two feet wide, but the machine humped over without damage. A second load of stores was taken out by the car on October 3, some bad weather having intervened. Professor David, Day, Priestley and Mackay went out on this occasion, and the journey produced a larger crop of minor accidents than usual, though men were always liable to sustain cuts and bruises when handling the car at a low temperature and in difficult situations. Priestley got a nail torn off, the Professor jammed a finger in the front wheel, and Mackay suffered a Colles' fracture of the wrist from the starting handle. One crack that lay across the course delayed the party for two hours, and the front axle was bent by another crack, into which the wheels dropped when the car was travelling at a speed of about twelve miles an hour.

The Northern Party finally left the winter quarters on October 5, picked up their stores where the motor-car had deposited them, and began their long journey over the sea ice along the coast. Day carried them in the car for the first three miles, but then had to return as the weather was becoming very thick and the temperature was failing. Mackay's wrist was troublesome, but it did not prevent him hauling in harness. I had said goodbye to Professor David and his two companions on September 22, 1908, and I did not see them again until March 1, 1909.

18
PREPARATION FOR THE SOUTHERN JOURNEY

The southern sledging-party was to leave the winter quarters on October 29, and immediately on the return of the depot party we started to make the final preparations for the attempt to reach the South Pole. I decided that four men should go south, I myself to be one of them, and that we should take provisions for ninety-one days; this amount of food, with the other equipment, would bring the load per pony up to the weight fixed as a result of experiments as the maximum load. It will be remembered that in outlining the scheme of the expedition in the early part of 1907 I had proposed that a party should travel to the east across the Barrier surface towards King Edward VII Land, with the object of solving, if possible, the mystery of the Barrier itself, and securing some information about the land on the other side of it. The accidents that had left us with only four ponies caused me to abandon this project. The ponies would have to go south, the motor-car would not travel on the Barrier, and the dogs were required for the southern depot journey. I deemed it best to confine the efforts of the sledging-parties to the two Poles, Geographical and Magnetic, and to send a third party into the Western Mountains with the object of studying geological conditions and, in particular, of searching for fossils.

The men selected to go with me on the southern journey were Adams, Marshall and Wild. A supporting-party was to accompany us for a certain distance in order that we might start fairly fresh from a point beyond the rough ice off Minna Bluff, and we would take the four ponies and four sledges. It was with some regret that I decided that the motor-car would have to stay behind. The trials that we had made in the neighbourhood of the winter quarters had proved that the car could not travel over a soft snow surface, and the depot journey had shown me that the surface of the Barrier was covered with soft snow, much softer and heavier than it had been in 1902, at the time of the *Discovery* expedition. In fact I was satisfied that, with the Barrier in its then condition, no wheeled vehicle could travel over it. The wheels would simply sink in until the body of the car rested on the snowy surface. We had made alterations in the wheels and we had reduced the weight of the car to an absolute minimum by the removal of every unnecessary part, but still it could do little on a soft surface, and it would certainly be quite useless with any weight behind, for the driving wheels would simply scoop holes for themselves. The use of sledge-runners under the front wheels, with broad, spiked driving-wheels, might have enabled us to get the car over some of the soft surfaces, but this equipment would not have been satisfactory on hard, rough ice, and constant changes would occupy too much time. I had confidence in the ponies, and I thought it best not to attempt to take the car south from the winter quarters.

The provisioning of the Southern Party was a matter that received long and anxious consideration. Marshall went very carefully into the question of the relative food-values of the various supplies, and we were able to derive much useful information from the experience of previous expeditions. We decided on a daily ration of 34 oz. per man; the total weight of food to be carried, on the basis of supplies for ninety-one days, would therefore be 77½ lb. The staple items were to be biscuits and pemmican. The biscuits, as I have stated, were of wheatmeal with 25 per cent. of plasmon added, and analysis showed that they did not contain more than 3 per cent. of water. The pemmican had been supplied by Beauvais, of Copenhagen, and consisted of the finest beef, dried and powdered, with 60 per cent. of beef-fat added. It contained only a small percentage of water. The effort of the polar explorer is to get his foods as free from water as possible, for the moisture represents so much useless weight to be carried.

The daily allowance of food for each man on the journey, as long as full rations were given, was to be as follows:

	Oz
Pemmican	7.5
Emergency ration	1.5
Biscuit	16.0
Cheese or chocolate	2.0
Cocoa	.7
Plasmon	1.0
Sugar	4.3
Quaker Oats	1.0
	34.0

Tea, salt and pepper were extras not weighed in with the daily allowance. We used about two ounces of tea per day for the four men. The salt and pepper were carried in small bags, each bag to last one week. Some of the biscuit had been broken up, and 1 lb. per week for each man was intended to be used for thickening the hoosh, the amount so used to be deducted from the ordinary allowance of biscuit.

It may be interesting to compare this allowance with the scale used on the *Discovery* sledging journey over the Barrier. The daily allowance of food for each man on that journey was as follows:

	Oz
Pemmican	7.6
Red ration (corresponding to emergency ration)	1.1
Biscuit	12.0
Cheese	2.0
Chocolate	1.1
Cocoa	.7
Plasmon	2.0
Sugar	3.8
Oatmeal	1.5
Pea flour	1.5
	33.3

The following list shows the provisions taken for the southern journey, tea, salt and pepper being omitted:

	lb.	Oz
Pemmican	170	10
Emergency ration	34	2
Biscuit	364	0
Cheese	22	12
Chocolate	22	12
Cocoa	15	14.8
Plasmon	22	12
Sugar	97	13.2
Quaker Oats	22	12
	773	8

We left the winter quarters with ten pounds of tea, but took an additional pound from the *Discovery* hut before we moved on to the Barrier. The allowance of salt amounted to two ounces per week per man, and that of pepper to two ounces per fortnight for the four men.

The biscuits were packed in 25-lb. tins, and they weighed about fourteen to the pound. All the other foods we packed in calico bags, each bag holding one week's supply of the particular article. Larger bags in turn contained a fortnight's rations, from which a week's food would be taken as required. The weight of one of the fortnightly bags, which did not include the biscuit, was 98 lb.

The clothing worn by each man when we started on the southern journey was very light. We had experimented on the spring sledging journey, and had proved that it was quite possible, even in very low temperatures, to abandon the heavy pilot cloth garments, which tire the wearer by their own weight, and to march in woollen undergarments and windproof overalls. The personal equipment of the members of the Southern Party was as follows:

> Woollen pyjama trousers.
> Woollen singlet.
> Woollen shirt.
> Woollen guernsey.
> Two pairs thick socks.
> One pair finnesko.
> Burberry overalls.
> Balaclava.
> Burberry head covering.
> Woollen mits.
> Fur mits.

Each man had his spare clothing and his personal belongings in a bag, the total weight of which was about seventeen pounds. The contents of each of these bags, in addition to diaries, letters and similar personal possessions, was as follows:

> Pyjama sleeping-jacket.
> Pyjama trousers, spare.
> Eight pairs woollen socks.
> Three pairs finnesko.
> Supply sennegrass.
> Three pairs mittens.
> Spare woollen helmet.
> One pair spiked ski-boots.
> Woollen muffler.
> Two pairs goggles, one smoked, one coloured.
> Roll lamp-wick, for tying on mits and finnesko.
> Sledge flag.
> Tobacco and matches.

There was also a small repair bag, with spare pieces of Burberry cloth for patching our wind clothes, needles, thread and buttons. The other items of our equipment were as follows:

> Two tents, with poles and floorcloths, each weighing complete 30 lb.
> Four sleeping-bags, each weighing 10 lb. when dry.
> One cooker, with spare inner pot.
> Two primus lamps, with spare parts.
> Thirteen gallons paraffin oil.
> One gallon methylated spirits.
> Two heavy knives.
> One .450 revolver, with twelve cartridges, weighing 4 lb.
> Four ice-axes (each 8 lb.).

Two shovels (each 6 lb.).
Eight 12-ft. bamboos.
Eight depot flags.
Two sledge-meters.
Four pony rugs.
Wire tether.
Four nose-bags.
Spare straps and rivets for repairing harness.
Roll of creosoted hemp rope.
Charts.
Ten fathoms of Alpine rope.
Two Union Jacks (Queen's flag and another).
Brass cylinder containing small Union Jack stamps and documents, for furthest
   south point.

Adams, Marshall and myself each carried a large pocket-knife. The
scientific equipment had to be cut down as far as was reasonably possible in
order to save weight, but we were not badly off in this respect. We had:

One 3-in. theodolite on stand.
Three chronometer watches.
Three compasses (pocket).
Six thermometers.
One hypsometer and two thermometers.
One camera and three dozen plates (quarter-plate by Newman and Guardia).
One case surveying instruments, dividers, &c.
Two prismatic compasses.
One sextant and artificial horizon.
Two volumes of *Hints to Travellers*.
One chart and spare paper.

The medical chest took the form of a small brown leather bag, and it
contained the following items, the chemicals being in compressed forms:

One tube laxative pills.
One tube boric acid.
One tube perchloride of mercury.
One tube iron and arsenic composition.
One tube quinine bisulphate.
One tube eye sololds.
One tube hemesins (adrenalin).
Two tubes cocaine hydrochloride.
Two tubes zinc sulphate.
One tube aloin compound.
One tube crete aromat cum opio.
One tube chlorodyne.
One tube ulphonal.

One tube soda mint.
One tube bismuth pepsin charcoal.
One tube potassium chlorate.
One tube ammonium bromide.
One tube ginger essence.
One tube sodium salicylate.
One tube morphine sulphate.
Two clinical thermometers.

We had also the following medical stores:

Four first field dressings.
Two compressed bandages.
Two triangular bandages.
Two ounces compressed absorbent wool.
Two ounces compressed cyanide gauze.
Two pieces wood splinting.
One reel adhesive plaster.
Packet court plaster.
One tube gold-beaters'-skin.
One pocket surgical dressing-case.
Two pairs spare goggles and spare glasses.
One pair molar dental forceps.
Two bottles Newskin.
Six hundred tabloids Easton's syrup (1 dr.).
Six ounces Emergency Oxo.

The total weight of the drugs and medical stores was seven pounds.

Four eleven-foot sledges were to be taken, one for each pony. Each sledge was fitted with straps, five placed at intervals along its length, so that the stores and equipment might be made fast. The buckle end of a strap was on one side and the hauling end on the other alternately. At either end of each sledge was fixed a box. These boxes contained the instruments, burning oil, primus lamps, medical stores and other small articles and on top of one of them was lashed the cooker. The sledge harness for manhauling was attached to a becket at the bow of the sledge.

The harness for the ponies was made with a broad leather band round the chest and traces of Alpine rope running from this. There was a strap over the neck to support the hauling band and a strap across the back, with a girth. The traces were toggled to a swingle-tree, which was attached to the sledge bow in the centre. Our great fear was that the ponies would chafe from the rubbing of the harness when they perspired and the moisture congealed from the cold, but we had very little trouble from this source. All the buckles were leather-covered in order that no metal might touch the ponies, and we took great care to keep the harness free from ice and dirt.

The food for the ponies on the march consisted of maize and Maujee ration, with a little of the Australian compressed fodder. Each pony was to have 10 lb. of food per day, and we took in all 900 lb. of food for the animals. The maize was carried in linen bags weighing about eighty pounds each, as was also the Maujee ration. I had decided that Murray should be in charge of the expedition during the absence of the Southern Party, and I left with him instructions covering, as far as I could see, all possible contingencies. Priestley was to be given facilities for examining the geological conditions on the north slope of Erebus, and at the beginning of December Armytage, Priestley and Brocklehurst were to be sent to lay a depot for the Northern Party and then to proceed into the Western Mountains. All the routine scientific work was to be carried on, and stores were to be transported to Glacier Tongue and Hut Point in case the ice broke up in the sound and cut off the winter quarters from the points further south. On January 15 a depot party was to proceed south in order to place at a point off Minna Bluff sufficient stores to provide for the return journey of the Southern Party from that point. The depot party, which was to be under the command of Joyce, was to return to Hut Point, reload its sledge, and march out to the depot a second time, to await the arrival of the Southern Party there until February 10. If we had then not arrived, they were to go back to Hut Point and thence to the ship.

If the ice in the sound broke out, the ship, which should reach the winter quarters late in December or early in January, was to watch for the Northern and Western Parties, which would signal from Butter Point. If nothing had been heard of Professor David, Mawson and Mackay by February 1, the *Nimrod* was to proceed to Granite Harbour and search for record on the north side of the entrance to the harbour. If there was no record the ship was to proceed north as far as the low beach on the north side of the Drygalski Barrier, keeping as close as practicable to the shore and making a thorough search for the party. The *Nimrod* was to return to winter quarters not later than February 10. In the event of the non-return of the Southern Party, the *Nimrod* was to make another search for the Northern Party, examining the coast as thoroughly as was compatible with the safety of the ship. The return of the Southern Party was to be expected after the first week in February, and the men at the winter quarters were to watch for a flash signal from Glacier Tongue between noon and 1 p.m. each day. If the ice had broken out south of the Tongue, the ship was to be sent down to Hut Point occasionally to look for the party. In the meantime all the collections and gear were to be placed on board the ship in preparation for the final departure.

It was necessary to prepare for the non-return of the Southern Party, although we were taking no gloomy view of our prospects, and I therefore left full instructions for the conduct of the expedition in the event of accident. My instructions to Murray on this point were as follows:

In the event of the non-arrival of the Southern Party by February 25 you are to land sufficient coal and provisions to support a party of seven men for one year at Cape Royds. You are then to pick three men to stay behind, and you will pick these men from volunteers. If there are no volunteers, which is highly improbable, you are to select three men and order them to stay. You will give these three men instructions to proceed at once to the south on the 168th meridian in search of the Southern Party, the leader using discretion as to the time they should take over the search. You are to leave all the dogs ashore to assist this party. You will instruct them to search for the remains of the Southern Party in the following summer. You are to use your discretion as to any other orders you may think it desirable to issue. The *Nimrod* is to land as much sugar, fruit and jam as possible. There are ample provisions otherwise, but anything in the way of dainties or special vegetables should be landed. There are sufficient ordinary vegetables. The *Nimrod* is also to land any clothing that you may think necessary for the party of three men remaining behind. . . . In the event of J. B. Adams returning and my non-return, he is in full command of the whole expedition, and has my instructions in the matter. The ship must on the 1st of March steam to the entrance of McMurdo Sound to see the ice conditions, and if there is no heavy pack likely to hold her up, she can return to Cape Royds again; but I think that the utmost Emit for the date to which you should remain is the 10th of March, 1909, as if we have not returned by then something very serious must have happened.'

My instructions provided for the conclusion of the work of the expedition in its various branches, and for the steps to be taken for the relief of the men left in the Antarctic in the case of the non-return of the Southern Party. Everything was ready for the start of the journey towards the Pole as the end of October approached, and we looked forward with keen anticipation to the venture. The supporting-party was to consist of Joyce, Marston, Priestley, Armytage and Brocklehurst, and was to accompany us for ten days. Day was to have been a member of this party, but he damaged his foot while toboganning down a slope at the winter quarters, and had to stay behind. The weather was not very good during our last days at the hut, but there were signs that summer was approaching. The ponies were in good condition. We spent the last few days overhauling the sledges and equipment, and making sure that everything was sound and in its right place. In the evenings we wrote letters for those at home, to be delivered in the event of our not returning from the unknown regions into which we hoped to penetrate.

19

FIRST DAYS OF THE SOUTHERN MARCH

The events of the southern journey were recorded day by day in the diary I wrote during the long march. I read this diary when we had got back to civilisation, and arrived at the conclusion that to rewrite it would be to take away the special flavour which it possesses. It was written under conditions of much difficulty, and often of great stress, and these conditions I believe it reflects. I am therefore publishing the diary with only such minor amendments to the phraseology as were necessary in order to make it easily understood. The reader will understand that when one is writing in a sleeping-bag, with the temperature very low and food rather short, a good proportion of the 'of's', 'and's', and 'the's' get left out. The story will probably seem bold, but it is at any rate a faithful record of what occurred. I will deal more fully with some aspects of the journey in a later chapter. The altitudes given in the diary were calculated at the time, and were not always accurate. The corrected altitudes are given on the map and in a table at the end of the book. The distances were calculated by means of a sledge-meter, checked by observations of the sun, and are approximately accurate.

October 29, 1908. A glorious day for our start; brilliant sunshine and a cloudless sky, a fair wind from the north, in fact, everything that could conduce to an auspicious beginning. We had breakfast at 7 a.m., and at 8.30 the sledges that the motor was to haul to Glacier Tongue were taken down by the penguin rookery and over to the rough ice. At 9.30 a.m. the supporting party started and was soon out of sight, as the motor was running well. At 10 a.m. we four of the Southern Party followed. As we left the hut where we had spent so many months in comfort, we had a feeling of real regret that never again would we all be together there. It was dark inside, the acetylene was feeble in comparison with the sun outside, and it was small compared to an ordinary dwelling, yet we were sad at leaving it. Last night as we were sitting at dinner the evening sun entered through the ventilator and a circle of light shone on the picture of the Queen. Slowly it moved across and lit up the photograph of his Majesty the King. This seemed an omen of good luck, for only on that day and at that particular time could this have happened, and today we started to strive to plant the Queen's flag on the last spot of the world. At 10 a.m. we met Murray and Roberts, and said good-bye, then went on our way. Both of these, who were to be left, had done for me all that men could do in their own particular line of work to try and make our little expedition a success. A clasp of the hands means more than many words, and as we turned to acknowledge their cheer and saw them standing on the ice by the familiar cliffs, I felt that we must try to do well for the sake of every one concerned in the expedition.

Hardly had we been going for an hour when Socks went dead lame. This was a bad shock, for Quan had for a full week been the same. We had thought that our troubles in this direction were over. Socks must have hurt himself on some of the sharp ice. We had to go on, and I trust that in a few days he will be all right. I shall not start from our depot at Hut Point until he is better or until I know actually what is going to happen. The lameness of a pony in our present situation is a serious thing. If we had eight, or even six, we could adjust matters more easily, but when we are working to the bare ounce it is very serious.

At 1 p.m. we halted and fed the ponies. As we sat close to them on the sledge Grisi suddenly lashed out, and striking the sledge with his hoof, struck Adams just below the knee. Three inches higher and the blow would have shattered his knee-cap and ended his chance of going on. As it was the bone was almost exposed, and he was in great pain, but said little about it. We went on and at 2.30 p.m. arrived at the sledges which had gone on by motor yesterday, just as the car came along after having dragged the other sledges within a quarter of a mile of the Tongue. I took on one sledge, and Day started in rather soft snow with the other sledges, the car being helped by the supporting party in the worst places. Pressure ridges and drift just off the Tongue prevented the car going further, so I gave the sledge Quan was dragging to Adams, who was leading Chinaman, and went back for the other. We said good-bye to Day, and he went back, with Priestley and Brocklehurst helping him, for his foot was still very weak.

We got to the south side of Glacier Tongue at 4 p.m., and after a cup of tea started to grind up the maize in the depot. It was hard work, but we each took turns at the crusher, and by 8 p.m. had ground sufficient maize for the journey. It is now 11 p.m., and a high warm sun is shining down, the day calm and clear. We had hoosh at 9 p.m. Adams' leg is very stiff and sore. The horses are fairly quiet, but Quan has begun his old tricks and is biting his tether. I must send for wire rope if this goes on.

At last we are out on the long trail, after four years' thought and work. I pray that we may be successful, for my heart has been so much in this.

There are numbers of seals lying close to our camp. They are nearly all females, and will soon have young. Erebus is emitting three distinct columns of steam today, and the fumaroles on the old crater can be seen plainly. It is a mercy that Adams is better tonight. I cannot imagine what he would have done if he had been knocked out for the southern journey, his interest in the expedition has been so intense. Temperature plus 2° Fahr., distance for the day, 14½ miles.

October 30. At Hut Point. Another gloriously fine day. We started away for Hut Point at 10.30 a.m., leaving the supporting party to finish grinding the maize. The ponies were in good fettle and went away well, Socks walking without a sledge, while Grisi had 500 lb., Quan 430 lb., and Chinaman 340 lb. Socks seems better today. It is a wonderful change to get up in the morning and put on ski-boots without any difficulty, and to handle cooking vessels without 'burning' one's fingers on the frozen metal. I was glad to see all the ponies so well, for there had been both wind and drift during the night. Quan seems to take a delight in biting his tether when any one is looking, for I put my head out of the tent occasionally during the night to see if they were all right, and directly I did so Quan started to bite his rope. At other times they were all quiet.

We crossed one crack that gave us a little trouble, and at 1.30 p.m. reached Castle Rock, travelling at one mile and three-quarters per hour. There I changed my sledge, taking on Marshall's sledge with Quan, for Grisi was making hard work of it, the surface being very soft in places. Quan pulled 500 lb. just as easily and at 3 p.m. we reached Hut Point, tethered the ponies, and had tea. There was a slight north wind. At 5 p.m. the supporting party came up. We have decided to sleep in the hut, but the supporting party are sleeping in the tent at the very spot where the *Discovery* wintered six years ago. Tomorrow I am going back to the Tongue for the rest of the fodder. The supporting party elected to sleep out because it is warmer, but we of the Southern Party will not have a solid roof over our heads for some months to come, so will make the most of it. We swept the *debris* out. Wild killed a seal for fresh meat and washed the liver at the seal hole, so tomorrow we will have a good feed. Half a tin of jam is a small thing for one man to eat when he has a sledging appetite, and we are doing our share, as when we start there will be no more of these luxuries. Adams' leg is better, but stiff. Our march was nine and a half miles today. It is now 10 p.m.

October 31. This day started with a dull snowy appearance, which soon developed into a snowstorm, but a mild one with little drift. I wanted to cross to Glacier Tongue with Quan, Grisi and Chinaman.

During the morning we readjusted our provision weights and unpacked the bags. In the afternoon it cleared, and at 3.30 p.m. we got under way, Quan pulling our sleeping equipment. We covered the eight miles and a half to Glacier Tongue in three hours, and as I found no message from the hut, nor the gear I had asked to be sent down, I concluded it was blowing there also, and so decided to walk on after dinner. I covered the twelve miles in three hours, arriving at Cape Royds at 11.30, and had covered the twenty-three miles between Hut Point and Cape Royds in six hours, marching time. They were surprised to see me, and were glad to hear that Adams and Socks were better.

I turned in at 2 a.m. for a few hours' sleep. It had been blowing hard with thick drift, so the motor had not been able to start for Glacier Tongue. On my way to Cape Royds I noticed several seals with young ones, evidently just born. Murray tells me that the temperature has been plus 22° Fahr.

November 1. Had breakfast at 6 a.m., and Murray came on the car with me, Day driving. There was a fresh easterly wind. We left Cape Royds at 8 a.m., and arrived off Inaccessible Island at twenty minutes past eight, having covered a distance of eight miles. The car was running very well. Then off Tent Island we left the car, and hauled the sledge, with the wire rope, &c., round to our camp off Glacier Tongue. Got under way at 10 a.m. and reached Hut Point at 2 p.m., the ponies pulling 500 and 550 lb. each. Grisi bolted with his sledge, but soon stopped. The ponies pulled very well, with a bad light and a bad surface. We arranged the packing of the sledges in the afternoon, but we are held up because of Socks. His foot is seriously out of order. It is almost a disaster, for we want every pound of hauling power. This evening it is snowing hard, with no wind. Adams' leg is much better. Wild noticed a seal giving birth to a pup. The baby measured 3 ft. 10 in. in length, and weighed 50 lb. I turned in early tonight, for I had done thirty-nine miles in the last twenty-four hours.

November 2. Dull and snowy during the early hours of today. When we awoke we found that Quan had bitten through his tether and played havoc with the maize and other fodder. Directly he saw me coming down the ice foot, he started off, dashing from one sledge to another, tearing the bags to pieces and trampling the food out. It was ten minutes before we caught him. Luckily, one sledge of fodder was untouched.

He pranced round, kicked up his heels, and showed that it was a deliberate piece of destructiveness on his part, for he had eaten his fill. His distended appearance was obviously the result of many pounds of maize.

In the afternoon three of the ponies hauled the sledges with their full weights across the junction of the sea and the Barrier ice, and in spite of the soft snow they pulled splendidly. We are now all ready for a start the first thing tomorrow. Socks seems much better, and not at all lame. The sun is now (9 p.m.) shining gloriously, and the wind has dropped, all auguring for a fine day tomorrow. The performance of the ponies was most satisfactory, and if they will only continue so for a month, it will mean a lot to us. Adams' leg is nearly all right.

November 3. Started at 9.30 from Hut Point, Quan pulling 660 lb., Grisi 615 lb., Socks 600 lb., and Chinaman 600 lb. Five men hauled 660 lb., 153 lb. of this being pony feed for our party. It was a beautifully fine day, but we were not long under way when we found that the surface was terribly soft, the ponies at times sinking in up to their bellies and always over their hocks.

We picked up the other sledges at the Barrier junction, and Brocklehurst photographed us all, with our sledgeflags flying and the Queen's Union Jack. At 10.50 we left the sea ice, and instead of finding the Barrier surface better, discovered that the snow was even softer than earlier in the day. The ponies pulled magnificently, and the supporting party toiled on painfully in their wake. Every hour the pony leaders changed places with the sledge haulers. At 1 p.m. the advance party with the ponies pitched camp and tethered out the ponies, and soon lunch was under way, consisting of tea with plasmon, plasmon biscuits and cheese. At 2.30 we struck camp, the supporting party with the man-sledge going on in advance, while the others with the ponies did the camp work. By 4 p.m. the surface had improved in places, so that the men did not break through the crust so often, but it was just as hard work as ever for the ponies. The weather kept beautifully fine, with a slight south-east wind. The weather sides of the ponies were quite dry, but their lee sides were frosted with congealed sweat. Whenever it came to our turn to pull, we perspired freely. As the supporting party are not travelling as fast as the ponies, we have decided to take them on only for two more days, and then we of the Southern Party will carry the remainder of the pony feed from their sledge on our backs. So, tomorrow morning we will depot nearly 100 lb. of oil and provisions, which will lighten the load on the supporting party's sledge a good deal.

We camped at 6 p.m., and, after feeding the ponies, had our dinner, consisting of pemmican, emergency ration, plasmon biscuits and plasmon cocoa, followed by a smoke, the most ideal smoke a man could wish for after a day's sledging. As there is now plenty of biscuit to spare, we gave the gallant little ponies a good feed of them after dinner. They are now comfortably standing in the sun, with the temperature plus 14° Fahr., and occasionally pawing the snow. Grisi has dug a large hole already in the soft surface. We have been steering a south-east course all day, keeping well to the north of White Island to avoid the crevasses. Our distance for the day is 12 miles (statute) 300 yards.

November 4. Started at 8.30 this morning; fine weather but had light. Temperature plus 9° Fahr. We wore goggles, as already we are feeling the trying light. The supporting party started first, and with an improved surface during the morning they kept ahead of the ponies, who constantly broke through the crust. As soon as we passed the end of White Island, the surface became softer, and it was trying work for both men and ponies. However, we did 9 miles 500 yards (statute) up to 1 p.m., the supporting party going the whole time without being relieved. Their weights had been reduced by nearly

100 lb., as we depoted that amount of oil and provisions last night. In the afternoon the surface was still softer, and when we came to camp at 6 p.m. the ponies were plainly tired. The march for the day was 16 miles 500 yards (statute), over fourteen miles geographical, with a bad surface, so we have every reason to be pleased with the ponies. The supporting party pulled hard. The cloud rolled away from Erebus this evening, and it is now warm, clear and bright to the north, but dark to the south. I am steering about east-south-east to avoid the crevasses off White Island, but tomorrow we go southeast. We fixed our position tonight from bearings, and find that we are thirty-four miles south of Cape Royds. Every one is fit and well.

November 5. On turning out this morning, we found the weather overcast, with slight snow falling and only a few landmarks visible to the north, nothing to the south. We got under way at 8.15 a.m., steering by compass. The light was so bad that the sastrugi could not be seen, though of the latter there was not much, for there was a thick coating of fallen snow. The surface was very bad for ponies and men. The ponies struggled gamely on through the tiring morning, and we camped for lunch at 1 p.m., having done 8 miles 1200 yards. After lunch we started at 2.15 p.m. in driving snow, but our steering was very wild. We had been making a south-east course all the morning, but in the afternoon the course was a devious one. Suddenly Marshall, who was leading Grisi, got his legs into a crevasse, and Grisi also; they recovered themselves, and Marshall shouted out to me. I stopped my horse and went to his assistance in getting the sledge off the snow-bridge covering the chasm. The crevasse was about 3 ft. wide, with the sides widening out below. No bottom could be seen. The line of direction was north-west by south-east. I at once altered the course to east, but in about a quarter of an hour Wild, Adams and Marshall got into a narrow crevasse, so I stopped and pitched camp, to wait until the weather cleared and we could get some idea of our actual position. This was at 3 p.m., the sledge meter recording 9 miles 1200 yards (statute) for the day. At 4 p.m. it commenced to drift and blow, and it is blowing hard and gustily now. It is very unfortunate to be held up like this, but I trust that it will blow itself out tonight and be fine tomorrow. The ponies will be none the worse for the rest. We wore goggles today, as the light was so bad and some of us got a touch of snow-blindness.

November 6. Lying in our sleeping-bags all day except when out feeding the ponies, for it has been blowing a blizzard, with thick drift, from south by west. It is very trying to be held up like this, for each day means the consumption of 40 lb. of pony feed alone. We only had a couple of biscuits each for lunch, for I can see that we must retrench at every set-back if we are going to have enough food to carry us through. We started with ninety-one days' food, but with careful management we can make it spin out to 110 days. If we have not done the job in that time it is God's will. Some of the supporting party did not turn out for any meal during the last twenty-four hours. Quan and Chinaman have gone their feeds constantly, but Socks and Grisi not so well. They all like Maujee ration and eat that up before touching the maize. They have been very quiet, standing tails to the blizzard, which has been so thick that at times we could not see them from the peep-holes of our tents. There are great drifts all round the tents, and some of the sledges are buried. This evening about 5.30 the weather cleared a bit and the wind dropped. When getting out the feed-boxes at 6 p.m. I could see White Island and the Bluff, so I hope that tomorrow will be fine. The barometer has been steady all day at 28.60 in., with the temperature up to 18° Fahr., so it is quite warm, and in our one-man sleeping-bags each of us has a little home, where he can read and write and look at the Penates and Lares brought with him. I read *Much Ado About Nothing* during the morning. The surface of the Barrier is better, for the wind has blown away a great deal of the soft snow, and we will, I trust, be able to see any crevasses before we are on to them. This is our fourth day out from Hut Point, and we are only twenty miles south. We must do better than this if we are to make much use of the ponies. I would not mind the blizzard so much if we had only to consider ourselves, for we can save on the food, whereas the ponies must be fed full.

November 7. Another disappointing day. We got up at 5 a.m. to breakfast, so as to be in time to start at 8 a.m. We cleared all the drift off our sledges, and, unstowing them, examined the runners, finding them to be in splendid condition. This work, with the assistance of the supporting party, took us till 8.30 a.m. Shortly afterwards we got under way, saying goodbye to the supporting party, who are to return today. As we drew away, the ponies pulling hard, they gave us three cheers. The weather was thick and overcast, with no wind. Part of White Island could be seen, and Observation Hill, astern, but before us lay a dead white wall, with nothing, even in the shape of a cloud, to guide our steering. Almost immediately after we left we crossed a crevasse, and before we had gone half a mile we found ourselves in a maze of them, only detecting their presence by the ponies breaking through the crust and saving themselves, or the man leading a pony putting his foot through. The first one Marshall crossed with Grisi was 6 ft. wide, and when I looked down, there was nothing to be seen but a black yawning void. Just after this, I halted Quan on the side of one, as I thought in the uncertain light, but I found that we were standing on the crust in the centre, so I very gingerly unharnessed him from the sledge and got him across. Then the sledge, with our three months' provisions, was pulled out of danger. Following this, Adams crossed another crevasse, and Chinaman got his forefoot into the hole at the side. I, following with Quan, also got into difficulties, and so I decided that it was too risky to proceed, and we camped between two large crevasses.

We picketed the ponies out and pitched one tent, to wait till the light became better for we were courting disaster by proceeding in that weather. Thus ended our day's march of under a mile, for about 1 p.m. it commenced to snow, and the wind sprang up from the south-west with drift. We pitched our second tent and had lunch, consisting of a pot of tea, some chocolate and two biscuits each. The temperature was plus 12° Fahr. at noon.

It blew a little in the afternoon, and I hope to find it clear away this pall of dead white stratus that stops us. The ponies were in splendid trim for pulling this morning, but, alas! we had to stop. Grisi and Socks did not eat up their food well at lunch or dinner. The temperature this evening is plus 9° Fahr., and the ponies feel chilly. Truly this work is one demanding the greatest exercise of patience, for it is more than trying to have to sit here and watch the time going by, knowing that each day lessens our stock of food. The supporting party got under way about 9.30 a.m., and we could see them dwindling to a speck in the north. They will, no doubt, be at Hut Point in a couple of days. We are now at last quite on our own resources, and as regards comfort in the tents are very well off, for with only two men in each tent, there is ample room. Adams is sharing one with me, whilst Marshall and Wild have the other. Wild is cook this week, so they keep the cooker and the Primus lamp in their tent, and we go across to meals, after first feeding the ponies. Next week Adams will be cook, so the cooking will be done in the tent I am in. We will also shift about so that we will take turns with each other as tent-mates. On the days on which we are held up by weather we read, and I can only trust that these days may not be many. I am just finishing reading *The Taming of the Shrew*. I have Shakespeare's *Comedies*, Marshall has Borrow's *The Bible in Spain*, Adams has Arthur Young's *Travels in France*, and Wild has *Sketches by Boz*. When we have finished we will change round. Our allowance of tobacco is very limited, and on days like these it disappears rapidly, for our anxious minds are relieved somewhat by a smoke. In order to economise my cigarettes, which are my luxury, I whittled out a holder from a bit of bamboo today, and so get a longer smoke, and also avoid the paper sticking to my lips, which have begun to crack already from the hot metal pot and the cold air.

NOTE. The difficulties of travelling over snow and ice in a bad light are very great. When the light is diffused by clouds or mist, it casts no shadows on the dead white surface, which consequently appears to the eye to be uniformly level. Often as we marched the sledges would be brought up all standing by a sastrugi, or snow mound, caused by the wind, and we would be lucky if we were not tripped up ourselves. Small depressions would escape the eye altogether, and when we thought that we were marching along on a level surface, we would suddenly step down two or three feet. The strain on the eyes under these conditions is very great, and it is when the sun is covered and the weather is thickish that snow blindness is produced. Snow blindness, with which we all become acquainted during the southern journey, is a very painful complaint. The first sign of the approach of the trouble is running at the nose; then the sufferer begins to see double, and his vision gradually becomes blurred. The more painful symptoms appear very soon. The blood-vessels of the eyes swell, making one feel as though sand had got in under the lids, and then the eyes begin to water freely and gradually close up. The best method of relief is to drop some cocaine into the eye, and then apply a powerful astringent, such as sulphate of zinc, in order to reduce the distended blood-vessels. The only way to guard against an attack is to wear goggles the whole time, so that the eyes may not be exposed to the strain caused by the reflection of the light from all quarters. These goggles are made so that the violet rays are cut off, these rays being the most dangerous, but in warm weather, when one is perspiring on account of exertion with the sledges, the glasses fog, and it becomes necessary to take them off frequently in order to wipe them. The goggles we used combined red and green glasses, and so gave a yellow tint to everything and greatly subdued the light. When we removed them, the glare from the surrounding whiteness was intense, and the only relief was to get inside one of the tents, which were made of green material, very restful to the eyes. We noticed that during the spring journey, when the temperature was very low and the sun was glaring on us, we did not suffer from snow blindness. The glare of the light reflected from the snow on bright days places a very severe strain on the eyes, for the rays of the sun are flashed back from millions of crystals. The worst days, as far as snow blindness was concerned, were when the sun was obscured, so that the light came equally from every direction, and the temperature was comparatively high.

November 8. Drawn blank again! In our bags all day, while outside the snow is drifting hard and blowing freshly at times. The temperature was plus 8° Fahr. at noon. The wind has not been really strong; if it had been I believe that this weather would have been over sooner. It is a sore trial to one's hopes and patience to lie and watch the drift on the tentside, and to know that our valuable pony food is going, and this without benefiting the animals themselves. Indeed, Socks and Grisi have not been eating well, and the hard maize does not agree with them. At lunch we had only a couple of biscuits and some chocolate, and used our oil to boil some Maujee ration for the horses, so that they had a hot hoosh. They all ate it readily, which is a comfort. This standing for four days in drift with 24° of frost is not good for them, and we are anxiously looking for finer weather. Tonight it is clearer, and we could see the horizon and some of the crevasses. We seem to be in a regular nest of them. The occupants of the other tent have discovered that it is pitched on the edge of a previously unseen one. We had a hot hoosh tonight, consisting of pemmican, with emergency ration and the cocoa. This warmed us up, for to lie from breakfast time at 6 a.m. for twelve or thirteen hours without hot food in this temperature is chilly work. If only we could get under way and put some good marches in, we would feel more happy. It is 750 miles as the crow flies from our winter quarters to the Pole, and we have done only fifty-one miles as yet. But still the worst will turn to the best, I doubt not. That a polar explorer needs a large stock of patience in his equipment there is no denying. The sun is showing thin and pale through the drift this evening, and the wind is more gusty, so we may have it really fine tomorrow. I read some of Shakespeare's comedies today.

November 9. A different story today. When we woke up at 4.30 a.m. it was fine, calm and clear, such a change from the last four days. We got breakfast at 5 a.m., and then dug the sledges out of the drift. After this we four walked out to find a track amongst the crevasses, but unfortunately they could only be detected by probing with our ice-axes, and these disclosed all sorts, from narrow cracks to great ugly chasms with no bottom visible. A lump of snow thrown down one would make no noise, so the bottom must have been very far below. The general direction was southeast and north-west, but some curved round to the south and some to the east. There was nothing for it but to trust to Providence, for we had to cross them somewhere. At 8.30 a.m. we got under way, the ponies not pulling very well, for they have lost condition in the blizzard and were stiff. We got over the first few crevasses without difficulty, then all of a sudden Chinaman went down a crack which ran parallel to our course. Adams tried to pull him out and he struggled gamely, and when Wild and I, who were next, left our sledges and hauled along Chinaman's sledge, it gave him more scope, and he managed to get on to the firm ice, only just in time, for three feet more and it would have been all up with the southern journey. The three-foot crack opened out into a great fathomless chasm, and down that would have gone the horse, all our cooking gear and biscuits and half the oil, and probably Adams as well. But when things seem the worst they turn to the best, for that was the last crevasse we encountered, and with a gradually improving surface, though very soft at times, we made fair headway. We camped for lunch at 12.40 p.m., and the ponies ate fairly well. Quan is pulling 660 lb., and had over 700 lb. till lunch; Grisi has 590 lb., Chinaman 570 lb., and Socks 600 lb. In the afternoon the surface further improved, and at 6 p.m. we camped, having done 14 miles 600 yards, statute. The Bluff is showing clear, and also Castle Rock miraged up astern of us. White Island is also clear, but a stratus cloud overhangs Erebus, Terror and Discovery. At 6.20 p.m. we suddenly heard a deep rumble, lasting about five seconds, that made the air and the ice vibrate. It seemed to come from the eastward, and resembled the sound and had the effect of heavy guns firing. We conjecture that it was due to some large mass of the Barrier breaking away, and the distance must be at least fifty miles from where we are. It was startling, to say the least of it. Tonight we boiled some

Maujee ration for the ponies, and they took this feed well. It has a delicious smell, and we ourselves would have enjoyed it. Quan is now engaged in the pleasing occupation of gnawing his tether rope. I tethered him up by the hind leg to prevent him attacking this particular thong, but he has found out that by lifting his hind-leg he can reach the rope, so I must get out and put a nose-bag on him. The temperature is now plus 5° Fahr., but it feels much warmer, for there is a dead calm and the sun is shining.

NOTE. On my return to the winter quarters I made inquiries as to whether the rumbling sound we had heard had been heard at Cape Royds, but I found that no member of the party there had noticed anything out of the ordinary. Probably Mounts Erebus and Terror had intercepted the sound. There is no doubt that the Barrier ice breaks away in very large masses. We had an illustration of that fact in the complete disappearance of Barrier Inlet, the spot at which I had proposed to place the winter quarters. It is from the edge of the Barrier, not only in our quadrant locality, but also on the other side of the Antarctic area, that the huge tabular bergs found in the Antarctic waters are calved off. Fractures develop as the ice is influenced by the open water, and these fractures extend until the breaking-point is reached. Then a berg, or perhaps a series of bergs, is left free to float northwards. At the time when we heard and felt the concussion of a break, we were some fifty miles from the Barrier edge, so that the disturbance in the ice must have been very extensive.

SKI BOOTS

20
STEADY PROGRESS: THE SIGHTING OF NEW LAND

November 10. Got up to breakfast at 6 a.m., and under way at 8.15 a.m. During the night we had to get out to the ponies. Quan had eaten away the straps on his rug, and Grisi and Socks were fighting over it. Quan had also chewed Chinaman's tether, and the latter was busy at one of the sledges, chewing rope. Happily he has not the same mischievous propensities as Quan, so the food-bags were not torn about. All these things mean work for us when the day's march is over, repairing the damage done. The ponies started away well, with a good hard surface to travel on, but a bad light, so we, being in finnesko, had frequent falls over the sastrugi. I at last took my goggles off, and am paying the penalty tonight, having a touch of snow-blindness. During the morning the land to the west became more distinct, and the going still better, so that when we camped for lunch, we had covered nine and a half statute miles. All the ponies, except Quan, showed the result of the Maujee ration, and are quite loose. Directly we started, after lunch, we came across the track of an Adelie penguin. It was most surprising, and one wonders how the bird came out here. It had evidently only passed a short time before, as its tracks were quite fresh. It had been travelling on its stomach a good way, and its course was due east towards the sea, but where it had come from was a mystery, for the nearest water in the direction from which it came was over fifty miles away, and it had at least another fifty miles to do before it could reach food and water. The surface in the afternoon became appallingly soft, the ponies sinking in up to their hocks, but there was hard snow underneath. At 6 p.m. we camped, with a march for the day of 15 miles 1550 yards statute. The sun came out in the afternoon, so we turned our sleepingbags inside out and dried them. Today's temperature ranged from plus 3° Fahr. in the morning to plus 12° Fahr. at noon. At 8 p.m. it was plus 5° Fahr. There is now a light north wind, and I expect Erebus will be clear soon; bearings and angles put us sixty miles from our depot, where lies 167 lb. of pony food.

November 11. It was 8.40 before we got under way this morning, for during the night the temperature dropped well below zero, and it was minus 12°

when we got up and found our finnesko and all our gear frozen hard, just like spring sledging times. We had to unpack the sledges and scrape the runners, for the sun had melted the snow on the upper surfaces, and the water had run down and frozen hard during the night on the under sides. The surface was again terribly soft, but there were patches of hard sastrugi beneath, and on one of these Quan must have stepped, for, to our great anxiety, he suddenly went lame about 11 a.m. I thought it was just the balling of the snow on his feet but on scraping this off he still was lame.

Fortunately, however, he improved greatly and was practically all right after lunch. During the night, the snow always balls on the ponies' feet, and it is one of our regular jobs to scrape it off, before we harness up in the morning. The snow was not so thick on the surface in the afternoon, only about 5 in., and we got on fairly well. The Bluff is now sixteen miles to the north-west of us, and all the well-known land is clear, Erebus sending out a huge volume of steam, that streams away to the south-west right past Mount Discovery, fifty miles from its crater. Again this afternoon we passed an Adelie penguin track. The bird was making the same course as the one we had passed before. At 6.30 p.m. we camped, having done fifteen statute miles. After dinner we got bearings which put us forty-seven miles from our depot. I do trust that the weather will hold up till we reach it. It is cold tonight writing, the temperature being minus 9° Fahr. The land to the south-south-west is beautifully clear.

November 13. No diary yesterday, for I had a bad attack of snow-blindness, and am only a bit better tonight. We did a good march yesterday of over fifteen miles over fair surface, and again today did fifteen miles, but the going was softer. The ponies have been a trouble again. I found Quan and Chinaman enjoying the former's rug. They have eaten all the lining. The weather has been beautifully fine, but the temperature down to 12° below zero. The others' eyes are all right. Wild, who has been suffering, has been better today. Snow-blindness is a particularly unpleasant thing. One begins by seeing double, then the eyes feel full of grit; this makes them water and eventually one cannot see at all. All yesterday afternoon, though I was wearing goggles, the water kept running out of my eyes, and, owing to the low temperature, it froze on my beard. However, the weather is beautiful, and we are as happy as can be, with good appetites, too good in fact for the amount of food we are allowing ourselves. We are on short rations, but we will have horse meat in addition when the ponies go under. We have saved enough food to last us from our first depot into the Bluff, where, on the way back, we will pick up another depot that is to be laid out by Joyce during January next. I trust we will pick up the depot tomorrow night and it will be a relief, for it is a tiny speck in this snowy plain, and is nearly sixty miles from the nearest land. It is much the same as picking up a buoy in the North Sea with only distant mountains for bearings. We are now clear of the pressure round the Bluff, and the travelling should be good until we reach the depot.

On the spring journey we got into the crevasses off the Bluff, these crevasses being due to the movement of the ice-sheet impinging against the long arm of the Bluff reaching out to the eastward. Close in the pressure is much more marked, the whole surface of the Barrier rising into hillocks and splitting into chasms. When the summer sun plays on these and the wind sweeps away the loose snow, a very slippery surface is presented, and the greatest care has to be exercised to prevent the sledges skidding into the pits, often over 100 ft. deep. As one gets further away from the area of disturbance the ridges flatten out, the pits disappear, and the crevasses become cracks. We are now on to level going, clear of any dangers.

November 14. Another beautiful day, but with a low temperature (minus 7° Fahr. at 6 p.m.). During the morning there was a wind from the west-south-west, bitterly cold on our faces and burst lips, but the sun was warm on our backs. The ponies pulled well, and in spite of somewhat deep snow they got on very well. We stopped at noon for bearings, and to get the sun's altitude for latitude, and at lunch worked out our position. We expected to see the depot tonight or tomorrow morning, but during the afternoon, when we halted for a spell, we found that our 'ready use' tin of kerosene had dropped off a sledge, so Adams ran back three miles and found it. This caused a delay, and we camped at 6 p.m. We were just putting the position on the chart after dinner when Wild, who was outside looking through the Goertz glasses, shouted out that he could see the depot, and we rushed out. There were the flag and sledge plainly to be seen through the glasses. It is an immense relief to us, for there is stored at the depot four days' pony feed and a gallon of oil. We will sleep happily tonight. The Barrier surface now is covered with huge sastrugi, rounded off and running west-south-west and east-north-east, with soft snow between. We have never seen the surface alike for two, consecutive days. The Barrier is as wayward and as changeful as the sea.

November 15. Another beautiful day. We broke camp at 8 a.m., and reached our depot at 9.20 a.m. We found everything intact, the flag waving merrily in the breeze, the direction of which was about west-south-west. We camped there and at once proceeded to redistribute weights and to parcel our provisions to be left there. We found that we had saved enough food to allow for three days' rations, which ought to take us into the Bluff on our return, so we made up a bag of provisions and added a little oil to the tin we had been using from, leaving half a gallon to take us the fifty odd miles to the Bluff on the way back. We then depoted our spare gear and finnesko, and our tin of sardines and pot of black currant jam. We had intended these provisions for Christmas Day, but the weight is too much; every ounce is of importance.

We took on the maize, and the ponies are now pulling 449 lb. each. Quan was pulling 469 lb. before the depot was reached, so he had nothing added to his load. All this arranging took time, and it was nearly noon before we were finished. We took an observation for latitude and variation, and found the latitude to be 79° 36´ South, and the variation 1550 East. Had lunch at noon and started due south at 1.15 p.m., the ponies pulling well. As the afternoon went on the surface of the Barrier altered to thick, crusty snow, with long rounded sastrugi about 4 ft. high, almost looking like small undulations, running south-west to north-west, with small sastrugi on top running west and east. Camped at 6 p.m., having done 12 miles 1500 yards (statute) today. There are some high, stratified, light clouds in the sky, the first clouds we have had for nearly a week. The sun now, at 9 p.m., is beautifully warm, though the air temperature is minus 2° Fahr. It is dead calm. We are going to build a snow mound at each camp as a guide to our homeward track, and as our camps will only be seven miles apart, these marks ought to help us. The mystery of the Barrier grips us, and we long to know what lies in the unknown to the south. This we may do with good fortune in another fortnight.

NOTE. I wrote that the provisions left at the depot would suffice for three days, but as a matter of fact there was not more than a two days' supply. We felt that we ought to take on every ounce of food that we could, and that if we got back to the depot we would be able to manage as far as the Bluff all right. During the winter we had thought over the possibility of making the mounds as a guide for the return march, and had concluded that though they would entail extra work, we might be well repaid if we picked up only one or two of them at critical times. We had with us two shovels, and ten minutes' work was sufficient to raise a mound 6 or 7 ft. high. We wondered whether the mounds would disappear under the influence of wind and sun, and our tracks remain, whether the tracks would disappear and the mounds remain, whether both tracks and mounds would disappear, or whether both would remain. As we were not keeping in towards the land, but were making a bee-line for the south, it was advisable to neglect no precaution, and as events turned out, the mounds were most useful. They remained after the sledge tracks had disappeared, and they were a very great comfort to us during the journey back from our furthest south point.

November 16. We started again this morning in gloriously fine weather, the temperature minus 15° Fahr. (down to minus 25° Fahr. during the night). The ponies pulled splendidly. All the western mountains stood up, miraged into the forms of castles. Even the Bluff could be seen in the far distance, changed into the semblance of a giant keep. Before starting, which we did at 7.40 a.m., we made a mound of snow, 6 ft. high, as a guide to us on our homeward way, and as it was built on a large sastrugi, we saw it for two and a half statute miles after starting. At twenty minutes to twelve, we halted for latitude observations, and found that we had reached 79° 50′ South. After lunch the surface changed somewhat, but the going was fairly good, in fact we covered 17 miles 200 yards (statute), a record day for us. This evening it is cloudy, high cumulus going from south-east to north-west. The temperature tonight is minus 5° Fahr., but it being dead calm we feel quite warm. A hot sun during the day dried our reindeer skin sleeping-bags, the water, or rather ice, all drying out of them, so we sleep in dry bags again. It has been a wonderful and successful week, so different to this time six years ago, when I was toiling along five miles a day over the same ground. Tonight one can see the huge mountain range to the south of Barne Inlet. In order to further economise food we are saving three lumps of sugar each every day, so in time we will have a fair stock. The great thing is to advance our food-supply as far south as possible before the ponies give out. Every one is in splendid health, eyes all right again, and only minor troubles, such as split lips, which do not allow us to laugh. Wild steered all day, and at every hourly halt I put the compass down to make the course we are going straight as a die to the south. Chinaman, or 'The Vampire', as Adams calls him, is not so fit; he is stiff in the knees and has to be hauled along. Quan, alias 'Blossom', is A1, but one cannot leave him for a moment, otherwise he would have his harness chewed up. Within the last week he has had the greater part of a horse-cloth, about a fathom of rope, several pieces of leather, and odds and ends such as a nose-bag buckle, but his digestion is marvellous, and he seems to thrive on his strange diet. He would rather eat a yard of creosoted rope than his maize and Maujee, indeed he often, in sheer wantonness, throws his food all over the snow.

November 17. A dull day when we started at 9.50 a.m., but the mountains abeam were in sight till noon. The weather then became completely overcast, and the light most difficult to steer in; a dead white wall was what we seemed to be marching to, and there was no direct light to cast even the faintest shadow on the sastrugi. I steered from noon to 1 p.m., and from lunch till 6 p.m., but the course was most erratic, and we had to stop every now and then to put the compass down to verify our course and alter it if necessary. Our march for the day was 16 miles 200 yards (statute) through a bad surface, the ponies sinking in up to their hocks. This soft surface is similar to that we experienced last trip south, for the snow had a crust easily broken through and about 6 in. down an airspace, then similar crusts and air-spaces in layers. It was trying work for the ponies, but they all did splendidly in their own particular way. Old 'Blossom' plods stolidly through it; Chinaman flounders rather painfully, for he is old and stiff nowadays; Grisi and Socks take the soft places with a rush; but all get through the day's work and feed up at night, though Quan evinces disgust at not having more Maujee ration and flings his maize out of his nose-bag. One wonders each night what trouble they will get into. This morning on turning out, we found Grisi lying down unable to get up. He had got to the end of his tether, and could not draw back his leg. He was shivering with cold, though the temperature was only minus 5°. Today we had a plus temperature, for the first time since leaving – plus 9° Fahr. at noon, and plus 5° Fahr. at 6 p.m. The pall of cloud no doubt acts as a blanket, and so we were warm, too warm in fact for marching.

November 18. Started at 8 a.m. in clearer weather, and the sun remained visible all day, though during the morning it was snowing from the south, and made the steering very difficult. The surface has been simply awful. We seem to have arrived at a latitude where there is no wind and the snow remains where it falls, for we were sinking in well over our ankles, and the poor ponies are having a most trying time. They break through the crust on the surface and flounder up to their hocks, and at each step they have to pull their feet out through the brittle crust. It is telling more on Chinaman than on the others, and he is going slowly. The chafing of the snow crust on his fetlocks has galled them, so we will have to shoot him at the next depot in about three days' time. The ponies are curious animals. We give them full meals, and yet they prefer to gnaw at any odd bits of rope. Quan got my jacket in his teeth this morning as I was scraping the snow off his hind feet, and I had to get out last night to stop Socks biting and swallowing lumps out of Quan's tail. If we had thought that they would have been up to these games, we would have had a longer wire to tether them, so as to keep them apart. It is possible that we have reached the windless area around the Pole, for the Barrier is a dead, smooth, white plain, weird beyond description, and having no land in sight, we feel such tiny specks in the immensity around us. Overhead this afternoon, when the weather cleared, were wonderful lines of clouds, radiating from the south-west, travelling very fast to the north-east.

It seems as though we were in some other world, and yet the things that concern us most for the moment are trivial, such as split lips and big appetites. Already the daily meals seem all too short, and we wonder what it will be like later on, when we are really hungry. I have had that experience once, and my companions will soon have it again with me. All the time we are moving south to our wished-for goal, and each day we feel that another gain has been made. We did 15 miles 500 yards today.

November 19. Started at 8.15 this morning with a fresh southerly breeze and drift. The temperature was plus 2° Fahr., and this was the temperature all day, making it cold travelling, but good for the ponies, who, poor beasts, had to plough through a truly awful surface, sinking in 8 or 10 in. at every step. This does not seem very deep, but when one goes on hour after hour it is a strain on man and horse, for we have to hold the ponies up as they stumble along. In spite of the surface and the wind and drift, we covered 15 miles 200 yards (statute) by 6 p.m., and were glad to camp, for our beards and faces were coated in ice, and our helmets had frozen stiff on to our faces. We got sights for latitude at noon, and found that we were in latitude 80° 32′ South. On the last journey I was not in that latitude till December 16, though we left Hut Point on November 2, a day earlier than we did this time.

The ponies have truly done well. I wrote yesterday that we seemed to be in a windless area, but today alters that opinion. The sastrugi are all pointing clearly due south, and if we have the wind on our way back it will be a great help. The same radiant points in the clouds south-east to northwest were visible again today, and at times when it cleared somewhat a regular nimbus cloud, similar to the rain clouds in the 'doldrums', could be seen. At the base of the converging point of the south-east part of cloud there seemed to rise other clouds to meet the main body. The former trended directly from the horizon at an angle of 30° to meet the main body, and did not seem to be more than a few miles off. The drift on the Barrier surface was piled up into heaps of very fine snow, with the smallest grains, and on encountering these the sledges ran heavily. The crust that has formed, when broken through discloses loose-grained snow, and the harder crust, about 8 in. down, is almost even. I suppose that the top 8 in. represents the year's snowfall.

November 20. Started at 8.55 a.m. in dull, overcast weather again, but the sun broke through during the morning, so we had something to steer by. The surface has been the worst we have encountered so far terribly soft, but we did 15 miles 800 yards (statute) for the day. The latter part of the afternoon was better. It seems to savour of repetition to write each day of the heavy going and the soft surface, but these factors play a most important part in our daily work, and it causes us a great deal of speculation as to what we will eventually find as we get further south. The whole place and conditions seem so strange and so unlike anything else in the world in our experience, that one cannot describe them in fitting words. At one moment one thinks of Coleridge's 'Ancient Mariner': 'Alone, alone; all, all alone, alone on a wide, wide sea,' and then when the mazy clouds spring silently from either hand and drift quickly across our zenith, not followed by any wind, it seems uncanny. There comes a puff of wind from the north, another from the south, and anon one from the east or west, seeming to obey no law, acting on erratic impulses. It is as though we were truly at the world's end, and were bursting in on the birthplace of the clouds and the nesting home of the four winds, and one has a feeling that we mortals are being watched with a jealous eye by the forces of nature. To add to these weird impressions that seem to grow on one in the apparently limitless waste, the sun tonight was surrounded by mock suns and in the zenith was a bow, turning away from the great vertical circle around the sun. These circles and bows were the colour of the rainbow.

We are all fairly tired tonight, and Wild is not feeling very fit, but a night's rest will do him good. The ponies are all fit except poor old Chinaman, and he must go tomorrow. He cannot keep up with the others, and the bad surface has played him out. The temperature is zero Fahr.

November 21. Started at 7.30 a.m. as we had to come to camp early tonight, and we wanted to get a good latitude observation at noon. Although we got away early, however, all morning we were steering through thick weather with driving ice-crystals, and at noon there was no chance of getting the sun for latitude. We came to camp at 12.30 p.m., just as the weather cleared a little, and we could see land on our right hand, but only the base of the mountains, so could not identify them. Chinaman came up at last, struggling painfully along, so when we made our depot this evening he was shot. We will use the meat to keep us out longer, and will save on our dried stores. The temperature at noon was only plus 8° Fahr., and the little wind that there was has been extremely cold. The wind veers round and round the compass, and the clouds move in every direction. The surface of the Barrier was better today, but still the ponies sank in 8 in. at least. The sastrugi point towards the south-east, this being the direction of the most usual wind here. This evening it cleared, and we could see land almost ahead, and the great mass of land abaft the beam to the north of Barne Inlet. Our day's march was 15 miles 450 yards. We are now south of the 81st parallel, and feel that we are well on the road to our wished-for goal. This is now our second depot, and we intend to leave about 80 lb. of pony meat, one tin of biscuits (27 lb.), some sugar and one tin of oil to see us back to Depot A. It is late now, for all arrangements for the depot took time. There was a lot of work in the arranging of the sledges for the remaining three ponies: packing stores, skinning Chinaman and cutting him up, all in a low temperature.

NOTE. The killing of the ponies was not pleasant work, but we had the satisfaction of knowing that the animals had been well fed and well treated up to the last, and that they suffered no pain. When we had to kill a pony, we threw up a snow mound to leeward of the camp, so that no smell of blood could come down wind, and took the animal behind this, out of sight of the others. As a matter of fact, the survivors never displayed any interest at all in the proceedings, even the report of the revolver used in the killing failing to attract their attention. The sound did not travel far on the wide open plain. The revolver was held about 3 in. from the forehead of the victim and one shot was sufficient to cause instant death. The throat of the animal was cut immediately and the blood allowed to run away. Then Marshall and Wild would skin the carcass, and we took the meat off the legs, shoulders and back. In the case of Chinaman the carcase was opened and the liver and undercut secured, but the job was such a lengthy one that we did not repeat it in the case of the other animals. Within a very short time after killing the carcass would be frozen solid, and we always tried to cut the meat up into as small pieces as possible before this occurred, for the cutting became very much more difficult after the process of freezing was complete. On the following days, whenever there was time to spare, we would proceed with the cutting until we had got all the meat ready for cooking. It was some time before we found out that it was better merely to warm the meat through when we wanted to eat it, and not attempt to cook it properly. It was fairly tender when only warmed, but if it were boiled it became very tough, and we would not spare enough oil to stew it in order to soften it thoroughly. Our supply of oil had been cut down very fine in order to save weight. The only meat that we cooked thoroughly was that from Grisi, because we found, at a later stage of the journey, that this meat was not good, and we thought that cooking might make it less liable to cause attacks of dysentery. We used the harness from the dead pony to make stays for the sledge which would be left at the depot. The sledge was reared on to its end, about 3 ft. being sunk into the snow, and a bamboo with a black flag stuck on the top, so that we might be able to find the little 'cache' of food on the return journey. Stays were required lest a blizzard should blow down the whole erection.

November 22. A beautiful morning. We left our depot with its black flag flying on the bamboo lashed to a discarded sledge, stuck upright in the snow, at 8.20 a.m. We now have three ponies dragging 500 lb. each, and they did splendidly through the soft snow. The going, I am thankful to say, is getting better, and here and there patches of harder surface are to be met with. The outstanding feature of today's march is that we have seen new land to the south – land never seen by human eyes before. The land consists of great snow-clad heights rising beyond Mount Longstaff, and also far inland to the north of Mount Markham. These heights we did not see on our journey south on the last expedition, for we were too close to the land or, rather, foothills, but now at the great distance we are out they can be seen plainly. It has been a beautifully clear day, and all the well-known mountains are clearly visible. The coast trends about south by east, so that we are safe for a good long way south. We camped at noon and got a good meridian altitude and azimuth. We found our latitude to be 81° 8′ South. In the afternoon we steered a little to the east of south, and camped at 6 p.m. with 15 miles 250 yards (statute) to the credit of the day. This is good, for the ponies have a heavy load, but they are well fed. We were rather long at lunch camp, for we tried to pull out Adams' tooth, which has given him great pain, so much that he has not slept at night at all. But the tooth broke and he has a bad time now. We were not equipped on this trip for tooth-pulling. Wild is better today, but fatty food is not to his taste just now, so he had a good feed of horse-flesh. We all liked it, for it filled us well, in spite of being somewhat tough. The flavour was good and it means a great saving of our other food. The temperature has risen to plus 7° Fahr., and the surface of the Barrier is good for sledgehauling.

November 23. Our record march today, the distance being 17 miles 1650 yards statute. It has been a splendid day for marching, with a cool breeze from the south and the sun slightly hidden. The horses did very well indeed, and the surface has improved, there being fairly hard sastrugi from the south. We are gradually rising the splendid peaks of Longstaff and Markham. The former, from our present bearing, has several sharp peaks, and the land fades away in the far distance to the south, with numbers of peaks showing, quite new to human eyes. All the old familiar mountains, towards which I toiled so painfully last time I was here, are visible, and what a difference it is now! Tonight there is a fresh wind from what appears at this distance to be a strait between Longstaff and Markham, and a low drift is flying along. Wild is better tonight, but he was tired after the long march. We made him a cup of our emergency Oxo for lunch, and that bucked him up for the afternoon. He has not eaten much lately, but says that he feels decidedly better tonight. Marshall has just succeeded in pulling out Adams' tooth, so now the latter will be able to enjoy horse-meat. This evening we had it fried, and so saved all our other food except biscuits and cocoa. It is my week as cook now, and Wild is my tent companion.

November 24. Started this morning at 7.55, and made a good march of 10 miles 600 yards (statute) up to 1 p.m., when we camped for lunch. We marched from 2.30 to 6 p.m., and camped then for the night. When we started there was a searching breeze in our faces, which gradually increased during the day with low drift, and it was blowing a summer blizzard when we camped this evening, the temperature up to plus 17° Fahr., and the drift melting in the tent and on all our gear. The ponies did splendidly again, in spite of soft surface, our day's run being 17 miles 680 yards statute. The Barrier surface is still as level as a billiard table, with no sign of any undulation or rise; but if the Barrier shows no sign of change it is otherwise with the mountains. Each mile shows us new land, and most of it consists of lofty mountains, whose heights at present we cannot estimate. They are well over 10,000 ft. The great advantage of being out from the coast is now obvious, for we can see a long range of sharp-peaked mountains running to the westward from Mounts Markham, and forming the south side of Shackleton Inlet on the east side of Mounts Markham, and other peaks and one table-topped mountain standing away to the south between Longstaff and Markham. There appears to be a wide strait or inlet between Longstaff and the new land east of Markham. Then trending about south-east from Longstaff is a lofty range of mountains which we will see more closely as we move south. I trust that the blizzard will blow itself out tonight, so that we may have easy going tomorrow. Wild is much better today, and went his ordinary food. We had fried pony for dinner tonight, and raw pony frozen on the march. The going is very good, but we can only afford a little oil to cook up the meat for meals.

November 25. Started at 8 a.m. this morning in fairly good weather. The wind has gone during the night, leaving our tents drifted up with fine snow. The land was obscured nearly all day, but towards the evening it cleared and we could see the details of the coast. There appears to be a series of inlets and capes opening at all angles, and with no fixed coast-line, though the lofty range of mountains continues to the south with a very slight trend to the eastward. The surface of the Barrier was very trying today, for the snow had no consistency and slipped away as one trod on it. It was not so trying for the ponies, and they did 17 miles 1600 yards. We had frozen raw pony meat to eat on the march, and a good hoosh of pony meat and pemmican for dinner. Wild is practically all right, and Adams finds a wisdom tooth growing in place of the one he lost. Our eyes are not too comfortable just now. It is a wonderful place we are in, all new to the world, and yet I feel that I cannot describe it. There is an impression of limitless solitude about it all that makes us feel so small as we trudge along, a few dark specks on the snowy plain, and watch the new land appear.

21

BEYOND ALL FORMER FOOTSTEPS

November 26. A day to remember, for we have passed the 'furthest South' previously reached by man. Tonight we are in latitude 82° 18½′ South, longitude 168° East, and this latitude we have been able to reach in much less time than on the last long march with Captain Scott, when we made latitude 82° 16½′ our 'furthest South'. We started in lovely weather this morning, with the temperature plus 19° Fahr., and it has been up to plus 20° Fahr. during the day, giving us a chance to dry our sleeping-bags. We were rather anxious at starting about Quan, who had a sharp attack of colic, the result no doubt of his morbid craving for bits of rope and other odds and ends in preference to his proper food. He soon got well enough to pull, and we got away at 7.40 a.m., the surface still very soft. There are abundant signs that the wind blows strongly from the south-south-east during the winter, for the sastrugi are very marked in that direction. There are extremely large circular crystals of snow on the Barrier surface, and they seem hard and brittle. They catch the light from the sun, each one forming a reflector that dazzles the eyes as one glances at the million points of light. As each hour went on today, we found new interest to the west, where the land lies, for we opened out Shackleton Inlet, and up the inlet lies a great chain of mountains, and far in to the west appear more peaks; to the west of Cape Wilson appears another chain of sharp peaks about 10,000 ft. high, stretching away to the north beyond the Snow Cape, and continuing the land on which Mount A. Markham lies. To the south-south-east ever appear new mountains. I trust that no land will block our path. We celebrated the breaking of the 'furthest South' record with a four-ounce bottle of Curaçoa, sent us by a friend at home. After this had been shared out into two tablespoonfuls each, we had a smoke and a talk before turning in. One wonders what the next month will bring forth. We ought by that time to be near our goal, all being well.

NOTE. It falls to the lot of few men to view land not previously seen by human eyes, and it was with feelings of keen curiosity, not unmingled with awe, that we watched the new mountains rise from the great unknown that lay ahead of us. Mighty peaks they were, the eternal snows at their bases, and their rough-hewn forms rising high towards the sky. No man of us could tell what we would discover in our march south, what wonders might not be revealed to us, and our imaginations would take wings until a stumble in the snow, the sharp pangs of hunger, or the dull ache of physical weariness brought back our attention to the needs of the immediate present. As the days wore on, and mountain after mountain came into view, grimly majestic, the consciousness of our insignificance seemed to grow upon us. We were but tiny black specks crawling slowly and painfully across the white plain, and bending our puny strength to the task of wresting from nature secrets preserved inviolate through all the ages. Our anxiety to learn what lay beyond was none the less keen, however, and the long days of marching over the Barrier surface were saved from monotony by the continued appearance of new land to the south-east.

November 27. Started at 8 a.m., the ponies pulling well over a bad surface of very soft snow. The weather is fine and clear save for a strong mirage, which throws all the land up much higher than it really is. All day we have seen new mountains arise, and it is causing us some anxiety to note that they trend more and more to the eastward, for that means an alteration of our course from nearly due south. Still they are a long way off, and when we get up to them we may find some strait that will enable us to go right through them and on south. One speculates greatly as we march along, but patience is what is needed. I think that the ponies are feeling the day-in, day-out drudgery of pulling on this plain. Poor beasts, they cannot understand, of course, what it is all for, and the wonder of the great mountains is nought to them, though one notices them at times looking at the distant land. At lunch-time I took a photograph of our camp, with Mount Longstaff in the background. We had our sledge flags up to celebrate the breaking of the southern record. The long snow cape marked on the chart as being attached to Mount Longstaff is not really so. It is attached to a lower bluff mountain to the north of Mount Longstaff. The most northerly peak of Mount Longstaff goes sheer down into the Barrier, and all along this range of mountains are very steep glaciers, greatly crevassed. As we pass along the mountains the capes disappear, but there are several well-marked ones of which we have taken angles. Still more mountains appeared above the horizon during the afternoon, and when we camped tonight some were quite clearly defined, many, many miles away. The temperature has been up to plus 22° Fahr. today, and we took the opportunity of drying our sleeping-bags, which we turned inside out and laid on the sledges. Tonight the temperature is plus 13° Fahr. We find that raw frozen pony meat cools one on the march, and during the ten minutes' spell after an hour's march we all cut up meat for lunch or dinner; in the hot sun it thaws well. This fresh meat ought to keep away scurvy from us. Quan seems much better today, but Grisi does not appear fit at all. He seems to be snow-blind. Our distance today was 16 miles 1200 yards.

November 28. Started at 7.50 a.m. in beautiful weather, but with a truly awful surface, the ponies sinking in very deeply. The sledges ran easily, as the temperature was high, plus 17° to plus 20° Fahr., the hot sun making the snow surface almost melt. We halted at noon for a latitude observation, and found our latitude to be 82° 38′ South. The land now appears more to the east, bearing south-east by south, and some very high mountains a long way off, with lower foothills, can be seen in front, quite different to the land abeam of us, which consists of huge sharp-pointed mountains with crevassed glaciers moving down gullies in their sides. Marshall is making a careful survey of all the principal heights. All day we have been travelling up and down long undulations, the width from crest to crest being about one and a half miles, and the rise about 1 in 100. We can easily see the line by our tracks sometimes being cut off sharp when we are on the down gradient and appearing again a long way astern as we rise. The first indication of the undulation was the fact of the mound we had made in the morning disappearing before we had travelled a quarter of a mile. During the afternoon the weather was very hot. A cool breeze had helped us in the forenoon, but it died away later. Marshall has a touch of snow-blindness, and both Grisi and Socks were also affected during the day. When we camped tonight Grisi was shot. He had fallen off during the last few days, and the snow-blindness was bad for him, putting him off his feed. He was the one chosen to go at the depot we made this evening. This is Depot C, and we are leaving one week's provisions and oil, with horsemeat, to carry us back to Depot B. We will go on tomorrow with 1200 lb. weight (nine weeks' provisions), and we four will pull with the ponies, two on each sledge. It is late now, 11 p.m., and we have just turned in. We get up at 5.30 a.m. every morning. Our march for the day was 15 miles 1500 yards statute.

November 29. Started at 8.45 a.m. with adjusted loads of 630 lb. on each sledge. We harnessed up ourselves, but found that the ponies would not pull when we did, and as the loads came away lightly, we untoggled our harness. The surface was very soft, but during the morning there were occasional patches of hard sastrugi, all pointing south-south-east. This is the course we are now steering, as the land is trending about south-east by east. During the day still more great mountains appeared to the south-east, and to the west we opened up several huge peaks, 10,000 to 15,000 ft. in height. The whole country seems to be made up of range after range of mountains, one behind the other. The worst feature of today's march was the terribly soft snow in the hollows of the great undulations we were passing. During the afternoon one place was so bad that the ponies sank in right up to their bellies, and we had to pull with might and main to get the sledges along at all. When we began to ascend the rise on the southern side of the undulation it got better. The ponies were played out by 5.45 p.m., especially old Quan, who nearly collapsed, not from the weight of the sledge, but from the effort of lifting his feet and limbs through the soft snow. The weather is calm and clear, but very hot, and it is trying to man and beast. We are on a short allowance of food, for we must save all we can, so as to help the advance as far as possible. Marshall has taken the angles of the new land today. He does this regularly. The hypsometer readings at 1 p.m. are very high now if there is no correction, and it is not due to weather. We must be at about sea-level. The undulations run about east by south, and west by west, and are at the moment a puzzle to us. I cannot think that the feeding of the glaciers from the adjacent mountains has anything to do with their existence. There are several glaciers, but their size is inconsiderable compared to the vast extent of Barrier affected. The glaciers are greatly crevassed. There are enormous granite cliffs at the foot of the range we are passing, and they stand vertically about 4000 to 6000 ft. without a vestige of snow upon them. The main bare rocks appear to be like the schists of the western mountains opposite our winter quarters, but we are too far away, of course, to be able to tell with any certainty. Down to the south are mountains entirely clear of snow, for their sides are vertical, and they must be not less than 8000 or 9000 ft. in height. Altogether it is a weird and wonderful country. The only familiar thing is the broad expanse of Barrier to the east, where as yet no land appears. We did 14 miles 900 yards (statute) today, and are tired. The snow came well above our ankles, and each step became a labour. Still we are making our way south, and each mile gained reduces the unknown. We have now done 300 miles due south in less than a month.

November 30. We started at 8 a.m. this morning. Quan very shaky and seemingly on his last legs, poor beast. Both he and Socks are snow-blind, so we have improvised shades for their eyes, which we trust will help them a little. We took turns of an hour each hauling at Quan's sledge, one at each side, to help him. Socks, being faster, always gets ahead and then has a short spell, which eases him considerably. We advanced very slowly today, for the surface was as bad as ever till the afternoon, and the total distance covered was 12 miles 150 yards. Quan was quite played out, so we camped at 5.45 p.m. We give the ponies ample food, but they do not eat it all, though Quan whinnies for his every meal-time. He is particularly fond of the Maujee ration, and neglects his maize for it. Again today we saw new land to the south, and unfortunately for our quick progress in that direction, we find the trend of the coast more to the eastward. A time is coming, I can see, when we will have to ascend the mountains, for the land runs round more and more in an easterly direction. Still after all we must not expect to find things cut and dried and all suited to us in such a place. We will be thankful if we can keep the ponies as far as our next depot, which will be in latitude 84° South. They are at the present moment lying down in the warm sun. It

GOING OUT TO BRING IN THE EREBUS PARTY'S SLEDGE

THE HUT IN THE EARLY WINTER

HAULING SEAL MEAT FOR THE WINTER QUARTERS

AN ICE CAVERN IN THE WINTER. PHOTOGRAPHED BY THE LIGHT OF
HURRICANE LAMPS.

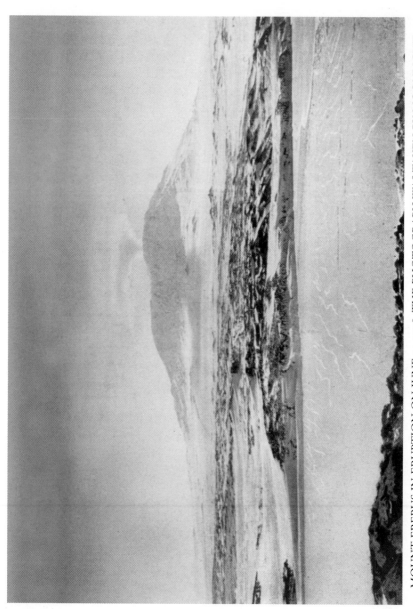

MOUNT EREBUS IN ERUPTION ON JUNE 14, 1908. THE PHOTOGRAPH WAS TAKEN BY MOONLIGHT.

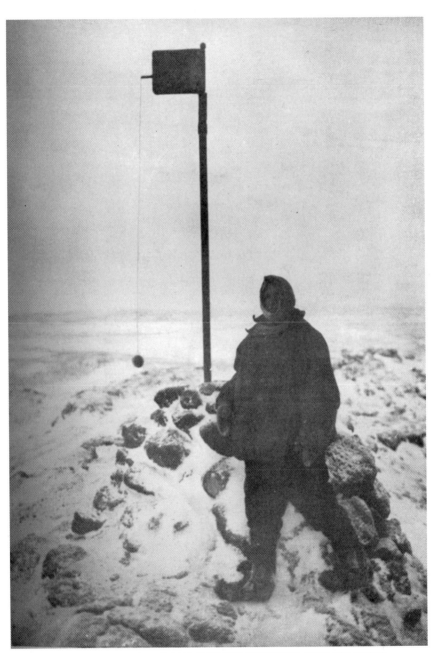

PROFESSOR DAVID STANDING BY MAWSON'S ANEMOMETER

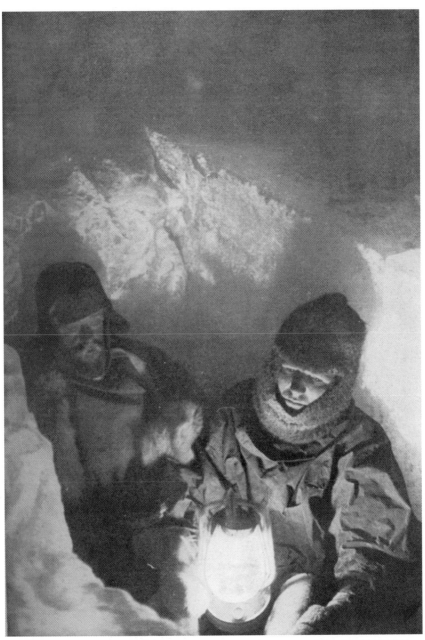

MURRAY AND PRIESTLEY GOING DOWN A SHAFT DUG IN GREEN LAKE
DURING THE WINTER

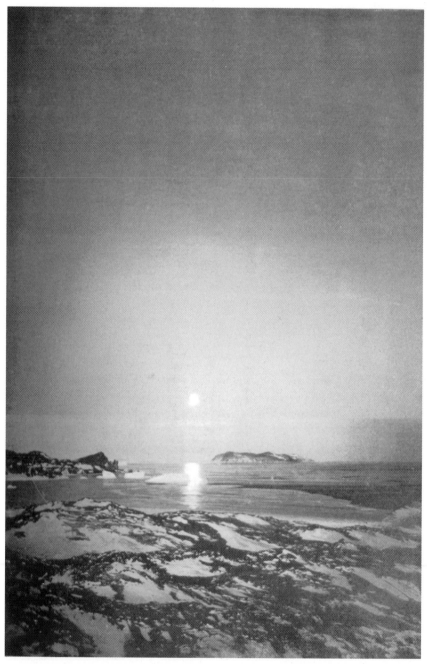

THE FULL MOON IN THE TIME OF AUTUMN TWILIGHT. CAPE BARNE
ON THE LEFT. INACCESSIBLE ISLAND ON THE RIGHT.

MAWSON'S CHEMICAL LABORATORY. THE BOTTLES WERE COATED WITH
ICE BY CONDENSATION FROM THE WARM, MOIST AIR OF THE HUT.

THE CUBICLE OCCUPIED BY PROFESSOR DAVID AND MAWSON:
IT WAS NAMED 'THE PAWN-SHOP'

THE TYPE-CASE AND PRINTING PRESS FOR THE PRODUCTION OF
THE 'AURORA AUSTRALIS' IN JOYCE'S AND WILD'S CUBICLE,
KNOWN AS 'THE ROGUES' RETREAT'

THE MIDWINTER'S DAY FEAST

THE STOVE IN THE HUT

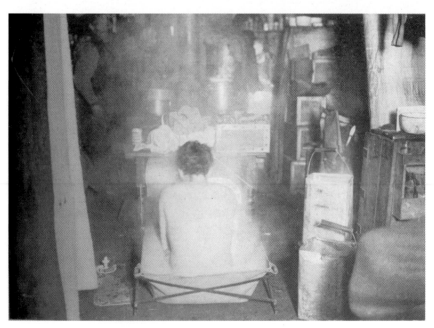

A MEMBER OF THE EXPEDITION TAKING HIS BATH

MARSTON IN HIS BED

MARSTON TRYING TO REVIVE MEMORIES OF OTHER DAYS

THE ACETYLENE GAS PLANT, OVER THE DOOR. MARSHALL STANDING
BY THE BAROMETER.

THE LEADER OF THE EXPEDITION IN WINTER GARB

is a beautifully calm, clear evening; indeed as regards weather we have been wonderfully fortunate, and it has given Marshall the chance to take all the necessary angles for the survey of these new mountains and coast-line. Wild is cook this week, and my week is over so I am now living in the other tent. We are all fit and well, but our appetites are increasing at an alarming rate. We noticed this tonight after the heavy pulling today. A great deal of the land we are passing seems to consist of granite in huge masses, and here and there are much crevassed glaciers, pouring down between the mountains, perhaps from some inland ice-sheet similar to that in the north of Victoria Land. The mountains show great similarity in outline, and there is no sign of any volcanic action at all so far. The temperature for the day has ranged between plus 16° and plus 12° Fahr., but the hot sun has made things appear much warmer.

December 1. Started at 8 a.m. today. Quan has been growing weaker each hour, and we practically pulled the sledge. We passed over three undulations, and camped at 1 p.m. In the afternoon we only did four miles, Quan being led by Wild. He also led Socks with one sledge, whilst Adams, Marshall and I hauled 200 lb. each on the other sledge over a terribly soft surface. Poor old Quan was quite finished when we came to camp at 6 p.m., having done 12 miles 200 yards, so he was shot. We all felt losing him, I particularly, for he was my special horse ever since he was ill last March. I had looked after him, and in spite of all his annoying tricks he was a general favourite. He seemed so intelligent. Still it was best for him to go, and like the others he was well fed to the last. We have now only one pony left, and are in latitude 83° W 16′ South. Ahead of us we can see the land stretching away to the east, with a long white line in front of it that looks like a giant Barrier, and nearer a very crusted-up appearance, as though there were great pressure ridges in front of us. It seems as though the Barrier end had come, and that there is now going to be a change in some gigantic way in keeping with the vastness of the whole place. We fervently trust that we will not be delayed in our march south. We are living mainly on horsemeat now, and on the march, to cool our throats when pulling in the hot sun, we chew some raw frozen meat. There was a slight breeze for a time today, and we felt chilly, as we were pulling stripped to our shirts. We wear our goggles all the time, for the glare from the snow surface is intense and the sky is cloudless. A few wisps of fleecy cloud settle on the tops of the loftiest mountains, but that is all. The surface of the Barrier still sparkles with the million frozen crystals which stand apart from the ordinary surface snow. One or two new peaks came in sight today, so we are ever adding to the chain of wonderful mountains that we have found.

At one moment our thoughts are on the grandeur of the scene, the next on what we would have to eat if only we were let loose in a good restaurant.

We are very hungry these days, and we know that we are likely to be for another three months. One of the granite cliffs we are nearing is over 6000 ft. sheer, and much bare rock is showing, which must have running water on it as the hot sun plays down. The moon was visible in the sky all day and it was something familiar, yet far removed from these days of hot sunshine and wide white pathways. The temperature is now plus 160 Fahr., and it is quite warm in the tent.

December 2. Started at 8 a.m., all four of us hauling one sledge, and Socks following behind with the other. He soon got into our regular pace, and did very well indeed. The surface during the morning was extremely bad and it was heavy work for us. The sun beat down on our heads and we perspired freely, though we were working only in shirts and pyjama trousers, whilst our feet were cold in the snow. We halted for lunch at 1 p.m., and had some of Quan cooked, but he was very tough meat, poor old beast. Socks, the only pony left now, is lonely. He whinnied all night for his lost companion. At 1 p.m. today we had got close enough to the disturbance ahead of us to see that it consisted of enormous pressure ridges, heavily crevassed and running a long way east, with not the slightest chance of our being able to get southing that way any longer on the Barrier. So after lunch we struck due south in toward the land, which is now running in a southeast direction, and at 6 p.m. we were close to the ridges off the coast. There is a red hill about 3000 ft. in height, which we hope to ascend tomorrow, so as to gain a view of the surrounding country. Then we will make our way, if possible, with the pony up a glacier ahead of us on to the land ice, and on to the Pole if all goes well. It is an anxious thing for us, for time is precious and food more so; we will be greatly relieved if we find a good route through the mountains. Now that we are close to the land we can see more clearly the nature of the mountains. From Mount Longstaff in a southeast direction, the land appears to be far more glaciated than further north, and since the valleys are very steep, the glaciers that they contain are heavily crevassed. These glaciers bear out in a north-east direction into the Barrier. Immediately opposite our camp the snow seems to have been blown off the steep mountain sides. The mountain ahead of us, which we are going to climb tomorrow, is undoubtedly granite, but very much weathered. In the distance it looked like volcanic rock, but now there can be no doubt that it consists of granite. Evidently the great ice sheet has passed over this part of the land, for the rounded forms could not have been caused by ordinary weathering. Enormous pressure ridges that run out from the south of the mountain ahead must be due to a glacier far greater in extent than any we have yet met. The glacier that comes out of Shackleton Inlet makes a disturbance in the Barrier ice, but not nearly as great as the disturbance in our immediate neighbourhood at the present time. The glacier at Shackleton Inlet is quite a short one. We have now closed in to the land, but before we did so we could see the rounded tops of great mountains extending in a south-easterly direction. If we are fortunate enough to reach the summit of the mountain tomorrow, we should be able to see more clearly the line of these mountains to the south-east. It would be very interesting to follow along the Barrier to the south-east, and see the trend of the mountains, but that does not enter into our programme. Our way lies to the south. How one wishes for time and unlimited provisions! Then indeed we could penetrate the secrets of this great lonely continent. Regrets are vain, however, and we wonder what is in store for us beyond the mountains if we are able to get there. The closer observation of these mountains ought to give geological results of importance. We may have the good fortune to discover fossils, or at any rate to bring back specimens that will determine the geological history of the country and prove a connection between the granite boulders lying on the slopes of Erebus and Terror and the land lying to the far south. Our position tonight is latitude 83° 28′ South, longitude 171° 30′ East. If we can get on the mountain tomorrow it will be the pioneer landing in the far south. We travelled 11 miles 1450 yards (statute) today, which was not bad, seeing that we were pulling 180 lb. per man on a bad surface. We got a photograph of the wonderful red granite peaks close to us, for now we are only eight miles or so off the land. The temperature is plus 20°, with a high barometer. The same fine weather continues, but the wind is cold in the early morning, when we turn out at 5.30 a.m. for breakfast.

December 4. Unable to write yesterday owing to bad attack of snow-blindness, and not much better tonight, but I must record the events of the two most remarkable days that we have experienced since leaving the winter quarters. After breakfast at 5.30 a.m. yesterday, we started off from camp, leaving all camp gear standing and a good feed by Socks to last him the whole day. We got under way at 9 a.m., taking four biscuits, four lumps of sugar and two ounces of chocolate each for lunch. We hoped to get water at the first of the rocks when we landed. Hardly had we gone one hundred yards when we came to a crevasse, which we did not see very distinctly, for the light was bad, and the sun obscured by clouds. We roped up and went on in single file, each with his ice-pick handy. I found it very difficult to see clearly with my goggles, and so took them off, and the present attack of snowblindness is the result, for the sun came out gloriously later on. We crossed several crevasses filled with snow except at the sides, the gaps being about 2 ft. wide, and the whole crevasses from 10 to 20 ft. across. Then we were brought up all standing by an enormous chasm of about 80 ft. wide and 300 ft. deep which lay right across our route. This chasm was similar to only larger than the one we encountered in latitude 80° 30′ South when on the southern journey with Captain Scott during the *Discovery* Expedition.

By making a *détour* to the right we found that it gradually pinched out and became filled with snow, and so were able to cross and resume our line to the land, which very deceptively appeared quite close but was really some miles away.

Crossing several ridges of ice-pressure and many more crevasses, we eventually at 12.30 p.m. reached an area of smooth blue ice in which were embedded several granite boulders, and here we obtained a drink of delicious water formed by the sun playing on the rock face and heating the ice at the base. After travelling for half a mile, we reached the base of the mountain which we hoped to climb in order to gain a view of the surrounding country. This hill is composed of granite, the red appearance being no doubt due to iron. At 1 p.m. we had a couple of biscuits and some water, and then started to make our way up the precipitous rock face. This was the most difficult part of the whole climb, for the granite was weathered and split in every direction, and some of the larger pieces seemed to be just nicely balanced on smaller pieces, so that one could almost push them over by a touch. With great difficulty we clambered up this rock face, and then ascended a gentle snow slope to another rocky bit, but not so difficult to climb. From the top of this ridge there burst upon our view an open road to the South, for there stretched before us a great glacier running almost south and north between two huge mountain ranges. As far as we could see, except towards the mouth, the glacier appeared to be smooth, yet this was not a certainty, for the distance was so great. Eagerly we clambered up the remaining ridges and over a snowslope, and found ourselves at the top of the mountain, the height being 3350 ft. according to aneroid and hypsometer. From the summit we could see the glacier stretching away south inland till at last it seemed to merge in high inland ice. Where the glacier fell into the Barrier about north-east bearing, the pressure waves were enormous, and for miles the surface of the Barrier was broken up. This was what we had seen ahead of us the last few days, and we now understood the reason of the commotion on the Barrier surface. To the south-east we could see the lofty range of mountains we had been following still stretching away in the same direction, and we can safely say that the Barrier is bounded by a chain of mountains extending in a south-easterly direction as far as the 86th parallel South. The mountains to the west appear to be more heavily glaciated than the ones to the eastward. There are some huge granite faces on the southern sides of the mountains, and these faces are joined up by cliffs of a very dark hue. To the south-south-east, towards what is apparently the head of the glacier, there are several sharp cones of very black rock, eight or nine in all. Beyond these are red granite faces, with sharp, needle-like spurs, similar in appearance to the 'cathedral' rocks described by Armitage in connection with the *Discovery* Expedition to the western mountains. Further on to the south the mountains have a bluff appearance, with long lines of stratification running almost horizontally. This bluff mountain range seems to break about sixty miles away, and beyond can be seen dimly other mountains. Turning to the west, the mountains on that side appeared to be rounded and covered with huge masses of ice, and glaciers showing the lines of crevasses. In the far distance there is what looked like an active volcano. There is a big mountain with a cloud on the top, bearing all the appearance of steam from an active cone. It would be very interesting to find an active volcano so far south. After taking bearings of the trend of the mountains, Barrier and glacier, we ate our frugal lunch and wished for more, and then descended. Adams had boiled the hypsometer and taken the temperature on the top, whilst Marshall, who had carried the camera on his back all the way up, took a couple of photographs. How we wished we had more plates to spare to get a record of the wonderful country we were passing through. At 4 p.m. we began to descend, and at 5 p.m. we were on the Barrier again. We were rather tired and very hungry when, at 7 p.m., we reached our camp. After a good dinner, and a cupful of Maujee ration in the hoosh as an extra, we turned in.

Today, December 4, we got under way at 8 a.m. and steered into the land, for we could see that there was no question as to the way we should go now. Though on the glacier, we might encounter crevasses and difficulties not to be met with on the Barrier, yet on the latter we could get no further than 86° South, and then we have had to turn in towards the land and get over the mountains to reach the Pole. We felt that our main difficulty on the glacier route would be with the pony Socks, and we could not expect to drag the full load ourselves as yet without relay work. Adams, Marshall and I pulled one sledge with 680 lb. weight, and Wild followed with Socks directly in our wake, so that if we came to a crevasse he would have warning. Everything went on well except that when we were close in to land, Marshall went through the snow covering of a crevasse. He managed to hold himself up by his arms. We could see no bottom to this crevasse. At 1 p.m. we were close to the snow-slope up which we hoped to reach the interior of the land and thence get on to the glacier. We had lunch and then proceeded, finding, instead of a steep, short slope, a long, fairly steep gradient. All the afternoon we toiled at the sledge, Socks pulling his load easily enough and eventually, at 5 p.m., reached the head of the pass, 2000 ft. above sea-level. From that point there was a gentle descent towards the glacier, and at 6 p.m. we camped close to some blue ice with granite boulders embedded in it, round which were pools of water. This water saves a certain amount of our oil, for we have not to melt snow or ice. We turned in at 8 p.m., well satisfied with the day's work. The weather now is wonderfully fine, with not a breath of wind, and a warm sun beating down on us. The temperature was up to plus 22° Fahr. at noon, and is now plus 18° Fahr. The pass through which we have come is flanked by great granite pillars at least 2000 ft. in height and making a magnificent entrance to the 'Highway to the South'. It is all so interesting and everything is on such a vast scale that one cannot describe it well. We four are seeing these great designs and the play of nature in her grandest moods for the first time, and possibly they may never be seen by man again. Poor Marshall had another four miles' walk this evening, for he found that he had lost his Jaeger jacket off the sledge. He had therefore to tramp back uphill for it, and found it two miles away on the trail. Socks is not feeding well. He seems lonely without his companions. We gave him a drink of thaw water this evening, but he did not seem to appreciate it, preferring the snow at his feet.

22

ON THE GREAT GLACIER

December 5. Broke camp sharp at 8 a.m. and proceeded south down an icy slope to the main glacier. The ice was too slippery for the pony, so Wild took him by a circuitous route to the bottom on snow. At the end of our ice slope, down which the sledge skidded rapidly, though we had put on rope brakes and hung on to it as well as we could, there was a patch of soft snow running parallel with the glacier, which here trended about south-west by south. Close ahead of us were the massed-up, fantastically shaped and split masses of pressure across which it would have been impossible for us to have gone, but, fortunately, it was not necessary even to try, for close into the land was a snow slope free from all crevasses, and along this gentle rise we made our way. After a time this snow slope gave place to blue ice, with numberless cracks and small crevasses across which it was quite impossible for the pony to drag the sledge without a serious risk of a broken leg in one of the many holes, the depth of which we could not ascertain. We therefore unharnessed Socks, and Wild took him over this bit of ground very carefully, whilst we others first hauled our sledge and then the pony sledge across to a patch of snow under some gigantic granite pillars over 2000 ft. in height, and here, close to some thaw water, we made our lunch camp. I was still badly snow-blind, so stayed in camp whilst Marshall and Adams went on to spy out a good route to follow after lunch was over. When they returned they informed me that there was more cracked-up blue ice ahead, and that the main pressure of the glacier came in very close to the pillar of granite that stood before us, but that beyond that there appeared to be a snow slope and good going. The most remarkable thing they reported was that as they were walking along a bird, brown in colour with a white line under each wing, flew just over their heads and disappeared to the south. It is, indeed, strange to hear of such an incident in latitude 83° 40′ South. They were sure it was not a skua gull, which is the only bird I could think of that would venture down here, and the gull might have been attracted by the last dead pony, for when in latitude 80° 30′ South, on my last southern trip, a skua gull arrived shortly after we had killed a dog.

After lunch we started again, and by dint of great exertions managed, at 6 p.m., to camp after getting both sledges and then the pony over another couple of miles of crevassed blue ice. We then went on and had a look ahead, and saw that we are going to have a tough time tomorrow to get along at all. I can see that it will, at least, mean relaying three or four times across nearly half a mile of terribly crevassed ice, covered in places with treacherous snow, and razor-edged in other places, all of it sloping down towards the rock *débris* strewn shore on the cliff side. We are camped under a wonderful pillar of granite that has been rounded by the winds into a perfectly symmetrical shape, and is banded by lines of gneiss. There is just one little patch of snow for our tents, and even that bridges some crevasses. Providence will look over us tonight, for we can do nothing more. One feels that at any moment some great piece of rock may come hurtling down, for all round us are pieces of granite, ranging from the size of a hazel-nut to great boulders twenty to forty tons in weight, and on one snow slope is the fresh track of a fallen rock. Still we can do no better, for it is impossible to spread a tent on the blue ice, and we cannot get any further tonight. I guess we will sleep soundly enough. My eyes are my only trouble, for their condition makes it impossible for me to pick out the route or do much more than pull. The distance covered today was 9 miles, with 4 miles relay.

December 6. Started at 8 a.m. today in fine weather to get our loads over the half-mile of crevassed ice that lay between us and the snow slope to the south-southwest. We divided up the load and managed to get the whole lot over in three journeys, but it was an awful job, for every step was a venture, and I, with one eye entirely blocked up because of snow blindness, felt it particularly uncomfortable work. However, by 1 p.m. all our gear was safely over, and the other three went back for Socks. Wild led him, and by 2 p.m. we were all camped on the snow again. Providence has indeed looked after us. At 3 p.m. we started south-southwest up a long slope to the right of the main glacier pressure. It was very heavy going, and we camped at 5 p.m. close to a huge crevasse, the snow bridge of which we crossed. There is a wonderful view of the mountains, with new peaks and ranges to the southeast, south and south-west. There is a dark rock running in conjunction with the granite on several of the mountains. We are now over 1700 ft. up on the glacier, and can see down on to the Barrier. The cloud still hangs on the mountain ahead of us; it certainly looks as though it were a volcano cloud, but it may be due to condensation. The lower current clouds are travelling very fast from south-south-east to north-north-west. The weather is fine and clear, and the temperature plus 17° Fahr.

December 7. Started at 8 a.m., Adams, Marshall and self pulling one sledge. Wild leading Socks behind. We travelled up and down slopes with very deep snow, into which Socks sank up to his belly, and we plunged in and out continuously, making it very trying work. Passed several crevasses on our right hand and could see more to the left. The light became bad at 1 p.m., when we camped for lunch, and it was hard to see the crevasses, as most were more or less snow covered. After lunch the light was better, and as we marched along we were congratulating ourselves upon it when suddenly we heard a shout of 'help' from Wild.

We stopped at once and rushed to his assistance, and saw the pony sledge with the forward end down a crevasse and Wild reaching out from the side of the gulf grasping the sledge. No sign of the pony. We soon got up to Wild, and he scrambled out of the dangerous position, but poor Socks had gone. Wild had a miraculous escape. He was following up our tracks, and we had passed over a crevasse which was entirely covered with snow, but the weight of the pony broke through the snow crust and in a second all was over. Wild says he just felt a sort of rushing wind, the leading rope was snatched from his hand, and he put out his arms and just caught the further edge of the chasm. Fortunately for Wild and us, Socks' weight snapped the swingle-tree of the sledge, so it was saved, though the upper bearer is broken. We lay down on our stomachs and looked over into the gulf, but no sound or sign came to us; a black bottomless pit it seemed to be. We hitched the pony sledge to ourselves and started off again, now with a weight of 1000 lb. for the four of us. Camped at 6.20 p.m., very tired, having to retreat from a maze of crevasses and rotten ice on to a patch where we could pitch our tents. We are indeed thankful for Wild's escape. When I think over the events of the day I realise what the loss of the sledge would have meant to us. We would have had left only two sleeping-bags for the four of us, and I doubt whether we could have got back to winterquarters with the short equipment. Our chance of reaching the Pole would have been gone. We take on the maize to eat ourselves. There is one ray of light in this bad day, and that is that anyhow we could not have taken Socks on much further. We would have had to shoot him tonight, so that although his loss is a serious matter to us, for we had counted on the meat, still we know that for traction purposes he would have been of little further use. When we tried to camp tonight we stuck our ice-axes into the snow to see whether there were any more hidden crevasses, and everywhere the axes went through. It would have been folly to have pitched our camp in that place, as we might easily have dropped through during the night. We had to retreat a quarter of a mile to pitch the tent. It was very unpleasant to turn back, even for this short distance, but on this job one must expect reverses.

December 8. Started at 8 a.m. and immediately began dodging crevasses and pits of unknown depth. Wild and I were leading, for, thank heaven, my eyes are fit and well again. We slowly toiled up a long crevassed slope, and by lunch time were about 1900 ft. up the glacier and had covered 6 miles 150 yards of an uphill drag, with about 250 lb. per man to haul. After lunch we still travelled up, but came on to blue glacier ice almost free from crevasses, so did much better, the sledges running easily. We camped at 6 p.m., the day's journey having been 12 miles 150 yards. The slope we went up in the morning was not as bad as we had anticipated, but quite bad enough for us to be thankful that we are out, at any rate for a time, from the region of hidden crevasses. The hypsometer tonight gave our height as 2300 ft. above sea-level. It is beautifully fine still. We have been wonderfully fortunate in this, especially in view of the situation we are in.

December 9. Another splendid day as far as the weather is concerned, and much we needed it, for we have had one of our hardest day's work and certainly the most dangerous so far. We started at 7.45 a.m. over the blue ice, and in less than an hour were in a perfect maze of crevasses, some thinly bridged with snow and others with a thicker and therefore more deceptive covering. Marshall went through one and was only saved by his harness. He had quite disappeared down below the level of the ice, and it was one of those crevasses that open out from the top, with no bottom to be seen, and I daresay there was a drop of at least 1000 ft. Soon after, Adams went through, then I did. The situation became momentarily more dangerous and uncertain. The sledges, skidding about, came up against the sheer, knife-like edges of some of the crevasses, and thus the bow of the second sledge, which had been strained when Socks fell, gave way.

We decided to relay our gear over this portion of the glacier until we got on to safer ground, and it was well past eleven o'clock before we had got both sledges on to better ice. We camped at 11.45 a.m. to get the sun's meridian altitude, and, to save time while watching the sun's rise and fall, decided to lunch at noon. The latitude we found to be 84° 2′ South, which is not so bad, considering that we have been hauling our heavy load of 250 lb. per man uphill for the last two days. At noon we were nearly 2500 ft. above sea level. In the afternoon we had another heavy pull, and now are camped between two huge crevasses, but on a patch of hard snow. We pitched camp at 6 p.m., very tired and extremely hungry after dragging uphill all the afternoon for over five hours. It is 8 p.m. now, and we are nearly 3000 ft. above sea-level. Low cumulus clouds are hanging to the south of us, as they have done for many days past, obscuring any view in that direction. We are anxiously hoping to find soon a level and inland ice-sheet so that we can put on more speed. The distance today was 11 miles 1450 yards plus 2 miles relay. The talk now is mainly about food and the things we would like to eat, and at meal-times our hoosh disappears with far too great speed. We are all looking forward to Christmas Day, for then, come what may, we are going to be full of food.

December 10. Falls, bruises, cut shins, crevasses, razor-edged ice, and a heavy upward pull have made up the sum of the day's trials, but there has been a measure of compensation in the wonderful scenery, the marvellous rocks and the covering of a distance of 11 miles 860 yards towards our goal. We started at 7.30 a.m. amongst crevasses, but soon got out of them and pulled up a long slope of snow. Our altitude at noon was 3250 ft. above sea-level. Then we slid down a blue ice slope, after crossing crevasses. Marshall and I each went down one. We lunched at 1 p.m. and started at 2 p.m. up a long ridge by the side moraine of the glacier. It was heavy work, as the ice was split and presented knife-like edges between the cracks, and there were also some crevasses. Adams got into one. The going was terribly heavy, as the sledges brought up against the ice-edges every now and then, and then there was a struggle to get them started again. We changed our foot-gear, substituting ski-boots for the finnesko, but nevertheless had many painful falls on the treacherous blue ice, cutting our hands and shins. We are all much bruised. We camped on a patch of snow by the land at 6 p.m. The rocks of the moraine are remarkable, being of every hue and description. I cannot describe them, but we will carry specimens back for the geologists to deal with. The main rocks of the 'Cloud Maker', the mountain under which we are camped, appear to be slates, reef-quartz and a very hard, dark brown rock, the name of which I do not know. The erratics of marble conglomerate and breccia are beautiful, showing a great mass of wonderful colours, but these rocks we cannot take away. We can only take with us small specimens of the main rocks, as weight is of importance to us, and from these small specimens the geologists must determine the general character of the land. This mountain is the one we thought might be an active volcano when we saw it from the mountain at the foot of the glacier, but the cloud has blown away from its head today, and we can see definitely that it is not a volcano. It is a remarkable sight as it towers above us with the snow clinging to its sides. Tonight there is a cold north wind. I climbed about 600 ft. up the mountain and got specimens of the main rocks in situ. The glacier is evidently moving very slowly and not filling as much of the valley as it did at some previous date, for the old moraines lie higher up in terraces. Low cumulus clouds to the south are hiding some of the new land in that direction. We are all very hungry and tired tonight after the day's fight with glacier. Whilst I went up the mountain to spy out the land the others ground up the balance of the maize, brought for pony feed, between flat stones, in order that we may use it ourselves to eke out our supply of food. The method of preparation was primitive, but it represented the only way of getting it fit to cook without the necessity of using more oil than we can spare for lengthy boiling. The temperature was plus 12° Fahr. at noon today, and is plus 14° now at 8 p.m. We are getting south, and we hope to reach the inland ice in a couple of days; then our marching will be faster. The weather is still fine.

December 11. A heavy day. We started away at 7.40 a.m. and tried to keep alongside the land, but the ice of the glacier sloped so much that we had to go on to the ridge, where the sledges could run without side-slipping. This slipping cuts the runners very badly. We crossed the medial moraine, and found rock there with what looked like plant impressions. We collected some specimens.

In the afternoon we found the surface better, as the cracks were nearly all filled up with water turned to ice. We camped for lunch on rubbly ice. After lunch we rounded some pressure ridges fairly easily, and then pulled up a long ice-slope with many sharp points. All the afternoon we were passing over ice in which the cracks had been closed up, and we began to have great hopes that the end of the glacier was in sight, and that we would soon be able to put in some good marches on the plateau. At 5 p.m. we found more cracks and a mass of pressure ice ahead, and land appeared as the clouds ahead lifted. I cannot tell what it means, but the position makes us anxious. The sledges will not stand much more of this ice work, and we are still 340 geographical miles away from the Pole. Thank God the weather is fine still. We camped at 6 p.m. on hard ice between two crevasses. There was no snow to pack round the tents, so we had to put the sledges and the provision bags on the snow cloths. We made the floor level inside by chipping away the points of ice with our ice-axes. We were very hungry after hoosh tonight. An awkward feature about the glacier are the little pits filled with mud, of which I collected a small sample.* It seems to be ground-down rock material, but what the action has been I cannot tell. The hot sun, beating down on this mud, makes it gradually sink into the body of the glacier, leaving a rotten ice covering through which we often break. It is like walking over a cucumber frame, and sometimes the boulders that have sunk down through the ice can be seen 3 or 4 ft. below the surface. The ice that has formed above the sunken rocks is more clear than the ordinary glacier ice. We are 3700 ft. up, and made 8 miles 900 yards to the good today. We have the satisfaction of feeling that we are getting south, and perhaps tomorrow may see the end of all our difficulties. Difficulties are just things to overcome after all. Every one is very fit.

December 12. Our distance – 3 miles for the day – expresses more readily than I can write it the nature of the day's work. We started at 7.40 a.m. on the worst surface possible, sharp-edged blue ice full of chasms and crevasses, rising to hills and descending into gullies; in fact, a surface that could not be equalled in any polar work for difficulty in travelling. Our sledges are suffering greatly, and it is a constant strain on us both to save the sledges from breaking or going down crevasses, and to save ourselves as well. We are a mass of bruises where we have fallen on the sharp ice, but, thank God, no one has even a sprain. It has been relay work today, for we could only take on one sledge at a time, two of us taking turns at pulling the sledge whilst

---

*These pits are known as 'cryoconite holes'.

the others steadied and held the sledge to keep it straight. Thus we would advance one mile, and then return over the crevasses and haul up the other sledge. By repeating this today for 3 miles we marched 9 miles over a surface where many times a slip meant death. Still we have advanced 3 miles to the south, and tonight we are camped on a patch of névé. By using our ice-axes we made a place for the tent. The weather is still splendidly fine, though low clouds obscure our horizon to the south. We are anxiously hoping to cross the main pressure tomorrow, and trust that we will then have better travelling. Given good travelling, we will not be long in reaching our goal. Marshall is putting in the bearings and angles of the new mountains. They still keep appearing to the west and east. Distance 3 miles 500 yards, with relays 9 miles 1500 yards.

December 13. We made a start at 8 a.m. and once again went up hill and down dale, over crevasses and blue, ribbed ice, relaying the sledges. We had covered about a mile when we came to a place where it seemed almost impossible to proceed. However, to our right, bearing about south-west by south, there seemed to be better surface and we decided to make a detour in that direction in order, if possible, to get round the pressure. While returning for one of the sledges I fell on the ice and hurt my left knee, which was a serious matter, or rather might have been. I have had a bandage on all the afternoon while pulling, and the knee feels better now, but one realises what it would mean if any member of our party were to be damaged under these conditions and in this place. This afternoon we came on to a better surface, and were able to pull both sledges instead of relaying. We are still gradually rising, and tonight our hypsometer gives 203.7 or 4370 feet up. There is a cool southerly wind; indeed, more than we have had before, and as we have only a patch of névé on the glacier for our tents, we had to take the provision bags and gear off the sledges to keep the tent cloths down. The temperature is plus 19° Fahr. New mountains are still appearing to the west-south-west as we rise. We seem now to be going up a long yellow track, for the ice is not so blue, and we are evidently travelling over an old moraine, where the stones have sunk through the ice when its onward movement has been arrested. I am sure that the bulk of the glacier is growing less, but the onward movement still continues, though at a much slower pace than at some previous period. The gain for the day was 5 miles, and in addition we did 4 miles relay work.

December 14. This has been one of our hardest day's work so far. We have been steering all day about south-south-west up the glacier, mainly in the bed of an ancient moraine, which is full of holes through which the stones and boulders have melted down long years ago. It has been snowing all day with a high temperature, and this has made everything very wet. We have ascended over 1000 ft. today, our altitude at 6 p.m. being 5600 ft. above sea-level, so the mountains to the west must be from 10,000 to 15,000 ft. in height, judging from their comparative elevation. My knee is better today. We have had a heavy pull and many falls on the slippery ice. Just before camping, Adams went through some snow, but held up over an awful chasm. Our sledges are much the worse for wear, and the one with the broken bow constantly strikes against the hard, sharp ice, pulling us up with a jerk and often flinging us down. At this high altitude the heavy pulling is very trying, especially as we slip on the snow covering the blue ice. There has evidently been an enormous glaciation here, and now it is dwindling away. Even the mountains show signs of this. Tonight our hopes are high that we are nearly at the end of the rise and that soon we will reach our longed-for plateau. Then southward indeed! Food is the determining factor with us. We did 7½ miles today.

December 15. Started at 7.40 a.m. in clear weather. It was heavy going uphill on the blue ice, but gradually we rose the land ahead, and it seemed as though at last we were going to have a change, and that we would see something new. At lunch-time we were on a better surface, with patches of snow, and we could see stretching out in front of us what was apparently a long, wide plain. It looked as though now really we were coming to the level ground for which we have longed, especially as the hypsometer gave us an altitude to 7230 ft., but this altitude at night came down to 5830 ft., so the apparent height may be due to barometric pressure and change of weather, for in the afternoon a stiff breeze from the south-west sprang up. The temperature was plus 18° Fahr. at noon, and when the wind came up it felt cold, as we were pulling in our pyjama trousers, with nothing underneath. We have been going steadily uphill all the afternoon, but on a vastly improved surface, consisting of hard névé instead of blue ice and no cracks only covered-in crevasses, which are easily seen. Ahead of us really lies the plateau. We can also see ahead of us detached mountains, piercing through the inland ice, which is the road to the south for us. Huge mountains stretch out to the east and west. After last week's toil and anxiety the change is delightful. The distance covered today was 13 miles 200 yards.

December 16. We started at 7 a.m., having had breakfast at 5.30 a.m. It was snowing slightly for the first few hours, and then the weather cleared. The surface was hard and the going good. We camped at noon and took sights for latitude, and ascertained that our position was 84° 50′ South. Ahead of us we could see a long slope, icy and crevassed, but we did 13 miles 1650 yards for the day. We camped at 5.30 p.m., and got ready our depot gear. We have decided to travel as lightly as possible, taking only the clothes we are wearing, and we will leave four days' food, which I calculate should get us back to the last depot on short ration. We have now traversed nearly one hundred miles of crevassed ice, and risen 6000 ft. on the largest glacier in the world. One more crevassed slope, and we will be on the plateau, please God. We are all fit and well. The temperature tonight is plus 15° Fahr., and the wind is blowing freshly from the south-west. There are splendid ranges of mountains to the west-south-west, and we have an extended view of glacier and mountains. Ahead of us lie three sharp peaks, connected up and forming an island in what is apparently inland ice or the head of the glacier. The peaks lie due south of us. To the eastward and westward of this island the ice bears down upon the inland ice-sheet, and joins the head of the glacier proper. To the westward the mountains along the side of the glacier are all of the bluff type, and the lines of stratification can be seen plainly. Still further to the westward, behind the frontal range, lie sharper peaks, some of them almost perfect cones. The trend of the land from the 'Cloud-Maker' is about south-south-west. We are travelling up the west side of the glacier. On the other side, to the east, there is a break in the bluff mountains, and the land beyond runs away more to the south-east. The valley is filled with pressure ice, which seems to have come from the inland ice-sheet. The mountains to the south-east also show lines of stratification. I hope that the photographs will be clear enough to give an idea of the character of this land. These mountains are not beautiful in the ordinary acceptance of the term, but they are magnificent in their stern and rugged grandeur. No foot has ever trod on their mighty sides, and until we reached this frozen land no human eyes had seen their forms.

December 17. We made a start at 7.20 a.m. and had an uphill pull all the morning over blue ice with patches of snow, which impeded our progress until we learned that the best way was to rush the sledges over them, for it was very difficult to keep one's footing on the smooth ice, and haul the sledges astern over the snow. By 1 p.m. we had done 8 miles of this uphill work, and in the afternoon we did four more. We had worked from 7.23 a.m. until 6.40 p.m. with one hour's rest for lunch only and it seems as though 12 miles was not much, but the last two hours' going was very stiff. We had to take on one sledge at a time up the icy slope, and even then we had to cut steps with our ice-axes as we went along. The work was made more difficult by the fact that a strong southerly wind was dead in our faces. The second sledge we hauled up the rise by means of the Alpine rope. We made it fast to the sledge, went on with the first sledge till the rope was stretched out to its full length, then cut a place to stand on, and by our united efforts hauled the sledge up to where we stood. We repeated this until we had managed to reach a fairly level spot with both the sledges, and we pitched our tents on a small patch of snow. There was not enough of the snow to make fast the snow-cloths of the tents, and we had to take the gear off the sledges and pile that round to supplement the snow. We have burned our boats behind us now as regards warm clothing, for this afternoon we made a depot in by the rocks of the island we are passing, and there left everything except the barest necessaries. After dinner tonight Wild went up the hill-side in order to have a look at the plateau. He came down with the news that the plateau is in sight at last, and that tomorrow should see us at the end of our difficulties. He also brought down with him some very interesting geological specimens, some of which certainly look like coal. The quality may be poor, but I have little doubt that the stuff is coal. If that proves to be the case, the discovery will be most interesting to the scientific world. Wild tells me that there are about six seams of this dark stuff, mingled with sandstone, and that the seams are from 4 in. to 7 or 8 ft. in thickness. There are vast quantities of it lying on the hill-side. We took a photograph of the sandstone, and I wish very much that we could spare time to examine the rocks more thoroughly. We may be able to do this on the way back. We have but little time for geological work, for our way is south and time is short, but we found that the main rock is sandstone and on our way back we will collect some. I expect that this will be the most southerly rock that we shall obtain, for we ought to reach the plateau tomorrow, and then there will be no more land close to us. It is gusty tonight, but beautifully clear. The altitude, according to the hypsometer, is 6100 ft.

> NOTE. When I showed the specimens to Professor David after our return to the *Nimrod*, he stated definitely that some of them were coal and others 'mother of coal'. The notes on geological matters in another chapter will deal more fully with this very interesting discovery.

23

ON THE PLATEAU TO
THE FURTHEST SOUTH

December 18. Almost up! The altitude tonight is 7400 ft. above sea-level. This has been one of our hardest days, but worth it, for we are just on the plateau at last. We started at 7.30 a.m., relaying the sledges, and did 6 miles 600 yards, which means nearly 19 miles for the day of actual travelling. All the morning we worked up loose, slippery ice, hauling the sledges up one at a time by means of the Alpine rope, then pulling in harness on the less stiff rises. We camped for lunch at 12.45 p.m. on the crest of a rise close to the pressure and in the midst of crevasses, into one of which I managed to fall, also Adams. Whilst lunch was preparing I got some rock from the land, quite different to the sandstone of yesterday. The mountains are all different just here. The land on our left shows beautifully clear stratified lines, and on the west side sandstone stands out, greatly weathered. All the afternoon we relayed up a long snow slope, and we were hungry and tired when we reached camp. We have been saving food to make it spin out, and that increases our hunger; each night we all dream of foods. We save two biscuits per man per day, also pemmican and sugar, eking out our food with pony maize, which we soak in water to make it less hard. All this means that we have now five weeks' food, while we are about 300 geographical miles from the Pole, with the same distance back to the last depot we left yesterday, so we must march on short food to reach our goal. The temperature is plus 16° Fahr. tonight, but a cold wind all the morning cut our faces and broken lips. We keep crevasses with us still, but I think that tomorrow will see the end of this. When we passed the main slope today more mountains appeared to the west of south, some with sheer cliffs and others rounded off, ending in long snow slopes. I judge the southern limit of the mountains to the west to be about latitude 86° South.

December 19. Not on the plateau level yet, though we are tonight 7888 ft. up, and still there is another rise ahead of us. We got breakfast at 5. a.m. and started at 7 a.m. sharp, taking on one sledge. Soon we got to the top of a ridge, and went back for the second sledge, then hauled both together all the rest of the day. The weight was about 200 lb. per man, and we kept going until 6 p.m., with a stop of one hour for lunch. We got a meridian altitude at noon, and found that our latitude was 85° 5′ South. We seem unable to get rid of the crevasses, and we have been falling into them and steering through them all day in the face of a cold southerly wind, with a temperature varying from plus 15° to plus 9° Fahr. The work was very heavy, for we were going uphill all day, and our sledge runners, which have been suffering from the sharp ice and rough travelling, are in a bad way. Soft snow in places greatly retarded our progress, but we have covered our 10 miles, and now are camped on good snow between two crevasses. I really think that tomorrow will see us on the plateau proper. This glacier must be one of the largest if not the largest in the world. The sastrugi seem to point mainly to the South, so we may expect head winds all the way to the Pole. Marshall has a cold job tonight, taking the angles of the new mountains to the west, some of which appeared today. After dinner we examined the sledge runners and turned one sledge end for end, for it had been badly torn while we were coming up the glacier, and in the soft snow it clogged greatly. We are still favoured with splendid weather, and that is a great comfort to us, for it would be almost impossible under other conditions to travel amongst these crevasses, which are caused by the congestion of the ice between the headlands when it was flowing from the plateau down between the mountains. Now there is comparatively little movement, and many of the crevasses have become snow-filled. Tonight we are 290 geographical miles from the Pole. We are thinking of our Christmas dinner. We will be full that day, anyhow.

December 20. Not yet up, but nearly so. We got away from camp at 7 a.m., with a strong head wind from the south, and this wind continued all day, with a temperature ranging from plus 7° to plus 5°. Our beards coated with ice. It was an uphill pull all day around pressure ice, and we reached an altitude of over 8000 ft. above sea-level. The weather was clear, but there were various clouds, which were noted by Adams. Marshall took bearings and angles at noon, and we got the sun's meridian altitude, showing that we were in latitude 85° 17′ South. We hope all the time that each ridge we come to will be the last, but each time another rises ahead, split up by pressure, and we begin the same toil again. It is trying work and as we have now reduced our food at breakfast to one pannikin of hoosh and one biscuit, by the time the lunch hour has arrived, after five hours' hauling in the cold wind up the slope, we are very hungry. At lunch we have a little chocolate, tea with plasmon, a pannikin of cocoa and three biscuits. Today we did 11 miles 950 yards (statute) having to relay the sledges over the last bit, for the ridge we were on was so steep that we could not get the two sledges tip together. Still, we are getting on; we have only 279 more miles to go, and then we will have reached the Pole. The land appears to run away to the south-east now, and soon we will be just a speck on this great inland waste of snow and ice. It is cold tonight. I am cook for the week, and started tonight. Every one is fit and well.

December 21. Midsummer Day, with 28° of frost! We have frost-bitten fingers and ears, and a strong blizzard wind has been blowing from the south all day, all due to the fact that we have climbed to an altitude of over 8000 ft. above sea-level. From early morning we have been striving to the south, but 6 miles is the total distance gained, for from noon, or rather from lunch at 1 p.m., we have been hauling the sledges up, one after the other, by standing pulls across crevasses and over great pressure ridges. When we had advanced one sledge some distance, we put up a flag on a bamboo to mark its position, and then roped up and returned for the other. The mind, no doubt, has a great deal to do with the low temperature, and we feel the cold, as we are going on short commons. The altitude adds to the difficulties, but we are getting south all the time. We started away from camp at 6.45 a.m. today, and except for an hour's halt at lunch, worked on until 6 p.m. Now we are camped in a filled-up crevasse, the only place where snow to put round the tents can be obtained, for all the rest of the ground we are on is either névé or hard ice. We little thought that this particular pressure ridge was going to be such an obstacle; it looked quite ordinary, even a short way off, but we have now decided to trust nothing to eyesight, for the distances are so deceptive up here.

It is a wonderful sight to look down over the glacier from the great altitude we are at, and to see the mountains stretching away east and west, some of them over 15,000 ft. in height. We are very hungry now, and it seems as cold almost as the spring sledging. Our beards are masses of ice all day long. Thank God we are fit and well and have had no accident, which is a mercy, seeing that we have covered over 130 miles of crevassed ice.

December 22. As I write of today's events, I can easily imagine I am on a spring sledging journey for the temperature is minus 5° Fahr. and a chilly southeasterly wind is blowing and finds its way through the walls of our tent, which are getting worn. All day long, from 7 a.m., except for the hour when we stopped for lunch, we have been relaying the sledges over the pressure mounds and across crevasses. Our total distance to the good for the whole day was only 4 miles southward, but this evening our prospects look brighter, for we must now have come to the end of the great glacier. It is flattening out, and except for crevasses there will not be much trouble in hauling the sledges tomorrow. One sledge today, when coming down with a run over a pressure ridge, turned a complete somersault, but nothing was damaged, in spite of the total weight being over 400 lb. We are now dragging 400 lb. at a time up the steep slopes and across the ridges, working with the Alpine rope all day, and roping ourselves together when we go back for the second sledge, for the ground is so treacherous that many times during the day we are saved only by the rope from falling into fathomless pits. Wild describes the sensation of walking over this surface, half ice and half snow, as like walking over the glass roof of a station. The usual query when one of us falls into a crevasse is: 'Have you found it?' One gets somewhat callous as regards the immediate danger, though we are always glad to meet crevasses with their coats off, that is, not hidden by the snow covering. Tonight we are camped in a filled-in crevasse. Away to the north down the glacier a thick cumulus cloud is lying, but some of the largest mountains are standing out clearly. Immediately behind us lies a broken sea of pressure ice. Please God, ahead of us there is a clear road to the Pole.

December 23. Eight thousand eight hundred and twenty feet up, and still steering upwards amid great waves of pressure and ice-falls, for our plateau, after a good morning's march, began to rise in higher ridges, so that it really was not the plateau after all. Today's crevasses have been far more dangerous than any others we have crossed, as the soft snow hides all trace of them until we fall through. Constantly today one or another of the party has had to be hauled out from a chasm by means of his harness, which had alone saved him from death in the icy vault below. We started at 6.40 a.m. and worked on steadily until 6 p.m., with the usual lunch hour in the middle of the day. The pony maize does not swell in the water now, as the temperature is very low and the water freezes. The result is that it swells inside after we have eaten it. We are very hungry indeed, and talk a great deal of what we would like to eat. In spite of the crevasses, we have done 13 miles today to the south, and we are now in latitude 85° 41′ South. The temperature at noon was plus 6° Fahr. and at 6 p.m. it was minus 10 Fahr., but it *is* much lower at night. There was a strong southeast to south-south-east wind blowing all day, and it was cutting to our noses and burst lips. Wild was frost-bitten. I do trust that tomorrow will see the end of this bad travelling, so that we can stretch out our legs for the Pole.

December 24. A much better day for us; indeed, the brightest we have had since entering our Southern Gateway. We started off at 7 a.m. across waves and undulations of ice, with some one or other of our little party falling through the thin crust of snow every now and then. At 10.30 a.m. I decided to steer more to the west, and we soon got on to a better surface, and covered 5 miles 250 yards in the forenoon. After lunch, as the surface was distinctly improving, we discarded the second sledge, and started our afternoon's march with one sledge. It has been blowing freshly from the south and drifting all day, and this, with over 40° of frost, has coated our faces with ice. We get superficial frostbites every now and then. During the afternoon the surface improved greatly, and the cracks and crevasses disappeared, but we are still going uphill, and from the summit of one ridge saw some new land, which runs south-south-east down to latitude 86° South.

We camped at 6 p.m., very tired and with cold feet. We have only the clothes we stand up in now, as we depoted everything else, and this continued rise means lower temperatures than I had anticipated. Tonight we are 9095 ft. above sea-level, and the way before us is still rising. I trust that it will soon level out, for it is hard work pulling at this altitude. So far there, is no sign of the very hard surface that Captain Scott speaks of in connection with his journey on the Northern Plateau. There seem to be just here regular layers of snow, not much wind-swept, but we will see better the surface conditions in a few days. Tomorrow will be Christmas Day, and our thoughts turn to home and all the attendant joys of the time. One longs to hear 'the hansoms slurring through the London mud'. Instead of that we are lying in a little tent, isolated high on the roof of the end of the world, far, indeed, from the ways trodden of men. Still, our thoughts can fly across the wastes of ice and snow and across the oceans to those whom we are striving for and who are thinking of us now. And, thank God, we are nearing our goal. The distance covered today was 11 miles 250 yards.

December 25. Christmas Day. There has been from 45° to 48° of frost, drifting snow and a strong biting south wind, and such has been the order of the day's march from 7 a.m. to 6 p.m. up one of the steepest rises we have yet done, crevassed in places. Now, as I write, we are 9500 ft. above sea-level, and our latitude at 6 p.m. was 85° 55′ South. We started away after a good breakfast, and soon came to soft snow, through which our worn and torn sledge-runners dragged heavily. All morning we hauled along, and at noon had done 5 miles 250 yards. Sights gave us latitude 85° 51′ South. We had lunch then, and I took a photograph of the camp with the Queen's flag flying and also our tent flags, my companions being in the picture. It was very cold, the temperature being minus 16° Fahr., and the wind went through us. All the afternoon we worked steadily uphill, and we could see at 6 p.m. the new land plainly trending to the south-east. This land is very much glaciated. It is comparatively bare of snow, and there are well-defined glaciers on the side of the range, which seems to end up in the south-east with a large mountain like a keep. We have called it 'The Castle'. Behind these the mountains have more gentle slopes and are more rounded. They seem to fall away to the south-east, so that, as we are going south, the angle opens and we will soon miss them. When we camped at 6 p.m. the wind was decreasing.

It is hard to understand this soft snow with such a persistent wind, and I can only suppose that we have not yet reached the actual plateau level, and that the snow we are travelling over just now is on the slopes, blown down by the south and south-east wind. We had a splendid dinner. First came hoosh, consisting of pony ration boded up with pemmican and some of our emergency Oxo and biscuit. Then in the cocoa water I boiled our little plum pudding, which a friend of Wild's had given him. This, with a drop of medical brandy, was a luxury which Lucullus himself might have envied; then came cocoa, and lastly cigars and a spoonful of *creme de menthe* sent us by a friend in Scotland. We are full tonight, and this is the last time we will be for many a long day. After dinner we discussed the situation, and we have decided to still further reduce our food. We have now nearly 500 miles, geographical, to do if we are to get to the Pole and back to the spot where we are at the present moment. We have one month's food, but only three weeks' biscuit, so we are going to make each week's food last ten days. We will have one biscuit in the morning, three at mid-day, and two at night. It is the only thing to do. Tomorrow we will throw away everything except the most absolute necessities. Already we are, as regards clothes, down to the limit, but we must trust to the old sledge-runners and dump the spare ones. One must risk this. We are very far away from all the world, and home thoughts have been much with us today, thoughts interrupted by pitching forward into a hidden crevasse more than once. Ah, well, we shall see all our own people when the work here is done. Marshall took our temperatures tonight. We are all two degrees subnormal, but as fit as can be. It is a fine open-air life and we are getting south.

December 26. Got away at 7 a.m. sharp, after dumping a lot of gear. We marched steadily all day except for lunch, and we have done 14 miles 480 yards on an uphill march, with soft snow at times and a bad wind. Ridge after ridge we met, and though the surface is better and harder in places, we feel very tired at the end of ten hours' pulling. Our height tonight is 9590 ft. above sea-level according to the hypsometer. The ridges we meet with are almost similar in appearance. We see the sun shining on them in the distance, and then the rise begins very gradually. The snow gets soft, and the weight of the sledge becomes more marked. As we near the top the soft snow gives place to a hard surface, and on the summit of the ridge we find small crevasses. Every time we reach the top of a ridge we say to ourselves: 'Perhaps this is the last,' but it never is the last; always there appears away ahead of us another ridge. I do not think that the land lies very far below the ice-sheet, for the crevasses on the summits of the ridges suggest that the sheet is moving over land at no great depth. It would seem that the descent towards the glacier proper from the plateau is by a series of terraces. We lost sight of the land today, having left it all behind us, and now we have the waste of snow all around. Two more days and our maize will be finished. Then our hooshes will be more woefully thin than ever. This shortness of food is unpleasant, but if we allow ourselves what, under ordinary circumstances, would be a reasonable amount, we would have to abandon all idea of getting far south.

December 27. If a great snow plain, rising every 7 miles in a steep ridge, can be called a plateau, then we are on it at last, with an altitude above the sea of 9820 ft. We started at 7 a.m. and marched till noon, encountering at

11 a.m. a steep snow ridge which pretty well cooked us, but we got the sledge up by noon and camped. We are pulling 150 lb. per man. In the afternoon we had good going till 5 p.m. and then another ridge as difficult as the previous one, so that our backs and legs were in a bad way when we reached the top at 6 p.m., having done 14 miles 930 yards for the day. Thank heaven it has been a fine day, with little wind. The temperature is minus 90 Fahr. This surface is most peculiar, showing layers of snow with little sastrugi all pointing south-south-east. Short food make us think of plum puddings, and hard half-cooked maize gives us indigestion, but we are getting south. The latitude is 86° 19′ South tonight. Our thoughts are with the people at home a great deal.

December 28. If the Barrier is a changing sea, the plateau is a changing sky. During the morning march we continued to go up hill steadily, but the surface was constantly changing. First there was soft snow in layers, then soft snow so deep that we were well over our ankles, and the temperature being well below zero, our feet were cold through sinking in. No one can say what we are going to find next, but we can go steadily ahead. We started at 6.55 a.m., and had done 7 miles 200 yards by noon, the pulling being very hard. Some of the snow is blown into hard sastrugi, some that looks perfectly smooth and hard has only a thin crust through which we break when pulling; all of it is a trouble. Yesterday we passed our last crevasse, though there are a few cracks or ridges fringed with shining crystals like diamonds, warning us that the cracks are open. We are now 10,199 ft. above sealevel, and the plateau is gradually flattening out, but it was heavy work pulling this afternoon. The high altitude, and a temperature of 48° of frost made breathing and work difficult. We are getting south-latitude 86° 31′ South tonight. The last sixty miles we hope to rush, leaving everything possible, taking one tent only and using the poles of the other as marks every ten miles, for we will leave all our food sixty miles off the Pole except enough to carry us there and back. I hope with good weather to reach the Pole on January 12, and then we will try and rush it to get to Hut Point by February 28. We are so tired after each hour's pulling that we throw ourselves on our backs for a three minutes' spell. It took us over ten hours to do 14 miles 450 yards today, but we did it all right. It is a wonderful thing to be over 10,000 ft. up at the end of the world almost. The short food is trying, but when we have done the work we will be happy. Adams had a bad headache all yesterday, and today I had the same trouble, but it is better now. Otherwise we are all fit and well. I think the country is flattening out more and more, and hope tomorrow to make 15 miles, at least.

December 29. Yesterday I wrote that we hoped to do 15 miles today, but such is the variable character of this surface that one cannot prophesy with any certainty an hour ahead. A strong southerly wind, with from 44° to 49° of frost, combined with the effect of short rations, made our distance 12 miles 600 yards instead. We have reached an altitude of 10,310 ft., and an uphill gradient gave us one of the most severe pulls for ten hours that would be possible. It looks serious, for we must increase the food if we are to get on at all, and we must risk a depot at 70 miles off the Pole and dash for it then. Our sledge is badly strained, and on the abominably bad surface of soft snow is dreadfully hard to move. I have been suffering from a bad headache all day, and Adams also was worried by the cold. I think that these headaches are a form of mountain sickness, due to our high altitude. The others have bled from the nose, and that must relieve them. Physical effort is always trying at a high altitude, and we are straining at the harness all day, sometimes slipping in the soft snow that overlies the hard sastrugi. My head is very bad. The sensation is as though the nerves were being twisted up with a corkscrew and then pulled out. Marshall took our temperatures tonight, and we are all at about 94°, but in spite of this we are getting south. We are only 198 miles of our goal now. If the rise would stop the cold would not matter, but it is hard to know what is man's limit. We have only 150 lb. per man to pull, but it is more severe work than the 250 lb. per man up the glacier was. The Pole is hard to get.

December 30. We only did 4 miles 100 yards today. We started at 7 a.m., but had to camp at 11 a.m., a blizzard springing up from the south. It is more than annoying. I cannot express my feelings. We were pulling at last on a level surface, but very soft snow, when at about 10 a.m. the south wind and drift commenced to increase, and at 11 a.m. it was so bad that we had to camp. And here all day we have been lying in our sleeping-bags trying to keep warm and listening to the threshing drift on the tent-side. I am in the cooking-tent, and the wind comes through, it is so thin. Our precious food is going and the time also, and it is so important to us to get on. We lie here and think of how to make things better, but we cannot reduce food now, and the only thing will be to rush all possible at the end. We will do, and are doing all humanly possible. It is with Providence to help us.

December 31. The last day of the old year, and the hardest day we have had almost, pushing through soft snow uphill with a strong head wind and drift all day. The temperature is minus 70 Fahr., and our altitude is 10,477 ft. above sea-level. The altitude is trying. My head has been very bad all day, and we are all feeling the short food, but still we are getting south. We are in latitude 86° 54′ South tonight, but we have only three weeks' food and two weeks' biscuit to do nearly 500 geographical miles. We can only do our best. Too tired to write more tonight. We all get iced-up about our faces, and are on the verge of frost-bite all the time. Please God the weather will be fine during the next fourteen days. Then all will be well. The distance today was 11 miles.

NOTE. If we had only known that we were going to get such cold weather as we were at this time experiencing, we would have kept a pair of scissors to trim our beards. The moisture from the condensation of one's breath accumulated on the beard and trickled down on to the Burberry blouse. Then it froze into a sheet of ice inside, and it became very painful to pull the Burberry off in camp. Little troubles of this sort would have seemed less serious to us if we had been able to get a decent feed at the end of the day's work, but we were very hungry. We thought of food most of the time. The chocolate certainly seemed better than the cheese, because the two spoonfuls of cheese per man allowed under our scale of diet would not last as long as the two sticks of chocolate. We did not have both at the same meal. We had the bad luck at this time to strike a tin in which the biscuits were thin and overbaked. Under ordinary circumstances they would probably have tasted rather better than the other biscuits, but we wanted bulk. We soaked them in our tea so that they would swell up and appear larger, but if one soaked a biscuit too much, the sensation of biting something was lost, and the food seemed to disappear much too easily.

January 1. Head too bad to write much. We did 11 miles 900 yards (statute) today, and the latitude at 6 p.m. was 87° 6½′ South, so we have beaten North and South records. Struggling uphill all day in very soft snow. Every one done up and weak from want of food. When we camped at 6 p.m. fine warm weather, thank God. Only 172½ miles from the Pole. The height above sea-level., now 10,755 ft., makes all work difficult. Surface seems to be better ahead. I do trust it will be so tomorrow.

January 2. Terribly hard work today. We started at 6.45 a.m. with a fairly good surface, which soon became very soft. We were sinking in over our ankles, and our broken sledge, by running sideways, added to the drag. We have been going uphill all day, and tonight are 11,034 ft. above sea-level. It has taken us all day to do 10 miles 450 yards, though the weights are fairly light. A cold wind, with a temperature of minus 14° Fahr., goes right through us now, as we are weakening from want of food, and the high altitude makes every movement an effort, especially if we stumble on the march. My head is giving me trouble all the time. Wild seems the most fit of us. God knows we are doing all we can, but the outlook is serious if this surface continues and the plateau gets higher, for we are not travelling fast enough to make our food spin out and get back to our depot in time. I cannot think of failure yet. I must look at the matter sensibly and consider the likes of those who are with me. I feel that if we go on too far it will be impossible to get back over this surface, and then all the results will be lost to the world. We can now definitely locate the South Pole on the highest plateau in the world, and our geological work and meteorology will be of the greatest use to science; but all this is not the Pole. Man can only do his best, and we have arrayed against us the strongest forces of nature. This cutting south wind with drift plays the mischief with us, and after ten hours of struggling against it one pannikin of food with two biscuits and a cup of cocoa does not warm one up much. I must think over the situation carefully tomorrow, for time is going on and food is going also.

January 3. Started at 6.55 a.m., cloudy but fairly warm. The temperature was minus 8° Fahr. at noon. We had a terrible surface all the morning, and did only 5 miles 100 yards. A meridian altitude gave us latitude 87° 22′ South at noon. The surface was better in the afternoon, and we did 6 geographical miles. The temperature at 6 p.m. was minus 11° Fahr. It was an uphill pull towards the evening, and we camped at 6.20 p.m., the altitude being 11,220 ft. above the sea. Tomorrow we must risk making a depot on the plateau, and make a dash for it, but even then, if this surface continues, we will be two weeks in carrying it through.

January 4. The end is in sight. We can only go for three more days at the most, for we are weakening rapidly. Short food and a blizzard wind from the south, with driving drift, at a temperature of 47° of frost, have plainly told us today that we are reaching our limit, for we were so done up at noon with cold that the clinical thermometer failed to register the temperature of three of us at 94 degrees. We started at 7.40 a.m. leaving a depot on this great wide plateau, a risk that only this case justified, and one that my comrades agreed to, as they have to every one so far, with the same cheerfulness and regardlessness of self that have been the means of our getting as far as we have done so far. Pathetically small looked the bamboo, one of the tent poles, with a bit of bag sown on as a flag, to mark our stock of provisions, which has to take us back to our depot, 150 miles north. We lost sight of it in half an hour, and are now trusting to our footprints in the snow to guide us back to each bamboo until we pick up the depot again. I trust that the weather will keep clear. Today we have done 12½ geographical miles, and with only 70 lb. per man to pull it is as hard, even harder, work than the 100 odd lb. was yesterday, and far harder than the 250 lb. were three weeks ago, when we were climbing the glacier. This, I consider, is a clear indication of our failing strength. The main thing against us is the altitude of 11,200 ft. and the biting wind. Our faces are cut, and our feet and hands are always on the verge of frostbite. Our fingers, indeed, often go, but we get them round more or less. I have great trouble with two fingers on my left hand. They have been badly jammed when we were getting the motor up over the ice face at winter quarters, and the circulation is not good. Our boots now are pretty well worn out, and we have to halt at times to pick the snow out of the soles. Our stock of sennegrass is nearly exhausted, so we have to use the same frozen stuff day after day. Another trouble is that the lamp-wick with which we tie the finnesko is chafed through, and we have to tie knots in it. These knots catch the snow under our feet, making a lump that has to be cleared every now and then. I am of the opinion that to sledge even in the height of summer on this plateau we should have at least forty ounces of food a day per man, and we are on short rations of the ordinary allowance of thirty-two ounces. We depoted our extra underclothing to save weight about three weeks ago, and are now in the same clothes night and day. One suit of underclothing, shirt and guernsey, and our thin Burberries, now all patched. When we get up in the morning, out of the wet bag, our Burberries become like a coat of mail at once, and our heads and beards get iced-up with the moisture when breathing on the march. There is half a gale blowing dead in our teeth all the time. We hope to reach within 100 geographical miles of the Pole; under the circumstances we can expect to do very little more. I am confident that the Pole lies on the great plateau we have discovered, miles and miles from any outstanding land. The temperature tonight is minus 24° Fahr.

January 5. Today head wind and drift again, with 50° of frost, and a terrible surface. We have been marching through 8 in. of snow, covering sharp sastrugi, which plays hell with our feet, but we have done 13 1–3 geographical miles, for we increased our food, seeing that it was absolutely necessary to do this to enable us to accomplish anything. I realise that the food we have been having has not been sufficient to keep up our strength, let alone supply the wastage caused by exertion, and now we must try to keep warmth in us, though our strength is being used up. Our temperatures at 5 a.m. were 94° Fahr. We got away at 7 a.m. sharp and marched till noon, then from 1 p.m. sharp till 6 p.m. All being in one tent makes our camp-work slower, for we are so cramped for room, and we get up at 4.40 a.m. so as to get away by 7 a.m. Two of us have to stand outside the tent at night until things are squared up inside, and we find it cold work. Hunger grips up hard, and the food-supply is very small. My head still gives me great trouble. I began by wishing that my worst enemy had it instead of myself, but now I don't wish even my worst enemy to have such a headache; still, it is no use talking about it. Self is a subject that most of us are fluent on. We find the utmost difficulty in carrying through the day, and we can only go for two or three more days. Never once has the temperature been above zero since we got on to the plateau, though this is the height of summer. We have done our best, and we thank God for having allowed us to get so far.

January 6. This must be our last outward march with the sledge and camp equipment. Tomorrow we must leave camp with some food, and push as far south as possible, and then plant the flag. Today's story is 57° of frost, with a strong blizzard and high drift; yet we marched 13¼ geographical miles through soft snow, being helped by extra food. This does not mean fun rations, but a bigger ration than we have been having lately. The pony maize is all finished. The most trying day we have yet spent, our fingers and faces being frost-bitten continually. Tomorrow we will rush south with the flag. We are at 88° 7′ South tonight. It is our last outward march. Blowing hard tonight. I would fail to explain my feelings if I tried to write them down, now that the end has come. There is only one thing that lightens the disappointment, and that is the feeling that we have done all we could. It is the forces of nature that have prevented us from going right through. I cannot write more.

January 7. A blinding, shrieking blizzard all day, with the temperature ranging from 60° to 70° of frost. It has been impossible to leave the tent, which is snowed up on the lee side. We have been lying in our bags all day, only warm at food time, with fine snow making through the walls of the worn tent and covering our bags. We are greatly cramped. Adams is suffering from cramp every now and then. We are eating our valuable food without marching. The wind has been blowing eighty to ninety miles an hour. We can hardly sleep. Tomorrow I trust this will be over. Directly the wind drops we march as far south as possible, then plant the flag, and turn homeward. Our chief anxiety is lest our tracks may drift up, for to them we must trust mainly to find our depot; we have no land bearings in this great plain of snow. It is a serious risk that we have taken, but we had to play the game to the utmost, and Providence will look after us.

January 8. Again all day in our bags, suffering considerably physically from cold hands and feet, and from hunger, but more mentally, for we cannot get on south, and we simply lie here shivering. Every now and then one of our party's feet go, and the unfortunate beggar has to take his leg out of the sleeping-bag and have his frozen foot nursed into life again by placing it inside the shirt, against the skin of his almost equally unfortunate neighbour. We must do something more to the south, even though the food is going, and we weaken lying in the cold, for with 72° of frost, the wind cuts through our thin tent, and even the drift is finding its way in and on to our bags, which are wet enough as it is. Cramp is not uncommon every now and then, and the drift all round the tent has made it so small that there is hardly room for us at all. The wind has been blowing hard all day; some of the gusts must be over seventy or eighty miles an hour. This evening it seems as though it were going to ease down, and directly it does we shall be up and away south for a rush. I feel that this march must be our limit. We are so short of food, and at this high altitude, 11,600 ft., it is hard to keep any warmth in our bodies between the scanty meals. We have nothing to read now, having depoted our little books to save weight, and it is dreary work lying in the tent with nothing to read, and too cold to write much in the diary.

January 9. Our last day outwards. We have shot our bolt, and the tale is latitude 88° 23′ South, longitude 162° East. The wind eased down at 1 a.m., and at 2 a.m. were up and had breakfast. At 4 a.m. started south, with the

Queen's Union Jack, a brass cylinder containing stamps and documents to place at the furthest south point, camera, glasses and compass. At 9 a.m. we were in 88° 23′ South, half running and half walking over a surface much hardened by the recent blizzard. It was strange for us to go along without the nightmare of a sledge dragging behind us. We hoisted her Majesty's flag and the other Union Jack afterwards, and took possession of the plateau in the name of his Majesty. While the Union Jack blew out stiffly in the icy gale that cut us to the bone, we looked south with our powerful glasses, but could see nothing but the dead white snow plain. There was no break in the plateau as it extended towards the Pole, and we feel sure that the goal we have failed to reach lies on this plain. We stayed only a few minutes, and then, taking the Queen's flag and eating our scanty meal as we went, we hurried back and reached our camp about 3 p.m. We were so dead tired that we only did two hours' march in the afternoon and camped at 5.30 p.m. The temperature was minus 19° Fahr. Fortunately for us, our tracks were not obliterated by the blizzard; indeed, they stood up, making a trail easily followed. Homeward bound at last. Whatever regrets may be, we have done our best.

24

THE RETURN MARCH

January 10. We started at 7.30 a.m. with a fair wind, and marched all day, with a stop of one hour for lunch, doing over 18½ geographical miles to the north. It has, indeed, been fortunate for us that we have been able to follow our outward tracks, for the force of the gale had torn the flags from the staffs. We will be all right when we pick up our depot. It has been a big risk leaving our food on the great white plain, with only our sledge tracks to guide us back. Tonight we are all tired out, but we have put a good march behind us. The temperature is minus 9° Fahr.

January 11. A good day. We have done nearly 17 geographical miles. We have picked up our depot and now are following the sledge tracks to the north. The temperature has been minus 15° Fahr. There has been tremendous wind here, and the sastrugi are enormous.

January 12. We did 14 miles 100 yards today with little wind to help us. The surface was very heavy and we found enormous sastrugi. The wind is getting up tonight. I hope for a good breeze behind us tomorrow.

January 13. It was heavy pulling all day, but we did a good distance in spite of it, getting 15 miles 1650 yards to the north. We have the sail up continually, but I cannot say that it has been very much help today. The temperature, minus 18° Fahr. nearly all the time, makes things very cold, and we ourselves slept badly last night. I did not sleep at all, for both my heels are frost-bitten and have cracked open, and I also have cracks under some of my toes; but we can march all right, and are moving over the ground very fast. We must continue to do so, for we have only about 20 lb. of biscuit to last us over 140 miles, and I expect there will be little in the locker by the time we strike our glacier head depot. The surface has been very severe today.

January 14. A strong following blizzard all day gave us our best day's run of the whole trip, 20 miles 1600 yards in ten hours. We decided to cut down the rations by another biscuit, as we have only six days' biscuit left on short ration, and 120 miles to go before we reach the depot, so we feel very hungry, and with the temperature minus 18° Fahr. to minus 21° Fahr. all day in the wind, one easily gets frost-bitten.

January 15. Started in a strong blizzard at 7.30 a.m. with a temperature of minus 23° Fahr., and marched steadily till noon, doing 9½ miles; then marched from 1.30 p.m. till 6 p.m., making a total distance for the day of 20 miles, statute. It has been thick, with a pale sun only shining through, but we are still able to follow our old sledge tracks, though at times they are very faint. Unfortunately, when we halted at 3.30 p.m. for a spell, we found that the sledge meter had disappeared, and discovered that it had broken off short at the brass fitting. This is a serious loss to us, for all our Barrier distances between depots are calculated on it, and although we have another depoted at the foot of the glacier we do not know the slip. We now must judge distance till we get a sight of land.

January 16. With a strong following blizzard, we did 18½ miles to the north today. My burst heels gave me great pain all day. Marshall dressed them tonight. We saw the land again today after being out of sight of it for three weeks nearly.

January 17. Started sharp at 7 a.m., and in a fresh blizzard wind, with a temperature of minus 23° Fahr., we did our best march, for it was mainly downhill and we covered 22½ miles. At 10 a.m. we came up to our Christmas camp and there took on a bamboo we had left, and which now comes in useful for our sail. This sail is now our great help. We dropped over 500 ft. today, and in three days ought to reach our depot at this rate.

January 18. Our best day, 26½ miles downhill, with a strong following wind. We have nearly got to the end of the main icefall The temperature has risen sensibly, it being minus 14° Fahr. tonight, and the hypsometer, 196.50, shows a good rise. With luck we may reach our depot tomorrow night. With food now in hand, we had a decent feed tonight. I have been very unlucky today, falling into many crevasses and hurting my shoulder badly. I have also had many falls, besides the trouble with the bad heels on the hard stuff.

January 19. Another record day, for we have done about 29 miles to the north, rushing under sail down icefalls and through crevasses, till, at 6 p.m., we picked up our sledge tracks of December 18 outwards. We camped, dead beat, at 6.30 p.m., and had a good hoosh. We have descended to 7500 ft., and the temperature tonight is minus 14° Fahr. We are now only 8½ miles from our depot, which we will reach tomorrow morning, all being well. This strong blizzard wind has been an immense help this way, though not outwards for us.

January 20. Although we have not covered so much ground today, we have had an infinitely harder time. We started at 7 a.m. on our tracks of December 19, and at 7.30 passed the camp of the evening of the 18th. For two hours we were descending a snow-slope, with heavy sastrugi, and then struck a patch of badly crevassed névé, about half a mile across. After that we got on to blue slippery ice, where our finnesko had no hold. A gale was blowing, and often fierce gusts came along, sweeping the sledge sideways, and knocking us off our feet. We all had many falls, and I had two specially heavy ones which shook me up severely. When we reached the steep slopes where we had roped the sledges up on our outward journey, we lowered the sledge down by means of the Alpine rope, using an ice-axe as a bollard to lower by. On several occasions one or more of us lost our footing, and were swept by the wind down the ice-slope, with great difficulty getting back to our sledge and companions. We arrived at our depot at 12.30 p.m. with sore and aching bodies. The afternoon was rather better, as, after the first hour, we got off the blue ice on to snow. However bad as the day has been, we have said farewell to that awful plateau, and are well on our way down the glacier.

January 21. Started at 7.45 a.m. with a fresh southerly breeze, so we still have valuable assistance from our sail. The heavy falls I had yesterday have so shaken me that I have been very ill today. I harnessed up for a while. but soon had to give up pulling and walk by the sledge; but, as the course has been downhill nearly all day and a fair wind has been assisting, the others have had no difficulty in getting along at a good pace, and we have covered 17 miles. The weather is much warmer, the temperature tonight being about minus 1° Fahr.

January 22. Started at 7.80 a.m. on a good surface that changed to crevassed ice slopes in the afternoon, down which we made fair progress. Am still too ill to harness up, but as the pull was not much it did not matter. Indeed, we had another man out of harness guiding the sledge. The distance today was 15½ miles.

January 23. Similar weather, surface and work. Fine and warm; temperature plus 8° Fahr.

January 24. One of our hardest day's work, and certainly the longest, for we started at 6.45 a.m., went on till 12.50 p.m., had lunch, started at 2 p.m., went on till 6 p.m., had a cup of tea, and went on till 9 p.m. Then we had our single pot of hoosh and one biscuit, for we have only two days' food left and one day's biscuit on much reduced ration, and we have to cover 40 miles of crevasses to reach our depot before we can get any more food. I am now all right again, though rather weak. We had a terribly hard time in the crevassed ice this morning, and now our sledge has not much more than half a runner on one side, and is in a very shaky state. However, I believe we are safe now. The distance today was 16 miles, statute.

January 25. We started away from camp at 6.45 a.m., marched till noon, when we had a cup of tea, and then marched till 3 p.m., when we had lunch, consisting of a cup of tea, two biscuits, two spoonfuls of cheese. Then we marched till 9 p.m., when we had one pot of hoosh and one biscuit. We did 26 miles; fine weather. The food is all finished but one meal. No biscuit, only cocoa, tea, salt and pepper left, very little of these also. Must reach depot tomorrow. It was fairly good going today till the last two hours, and then we were falling into most dangerous crevasses and were saved only by our harness. Very tired indeed. Thank God warm and fine weather. We can see our depot rock in the distance, so hope to reach it tomorrow. Turning in now, 11 p.m.; breakfast as usual 5 a.m. The temperature is plus 12° Fahr.

January 26 and 27. Two days written up as one, and they have been the hardest and most trying we have ever spent in our lives, and will ever stand in our memories. Tonight (the 27th) we have had our first solid food since the morning of the 26th. We came to the end of all our provisions except a little cocoa and tea, and from 7 a.m. on the 26th till 2 p.m. on the 27th we did 16 miles over the worst surfaces and most dangerous crevasses we have ever encountered, only stopping for tea or cocoa till they were finished, and marching twenty hours at a stretch, through snow 10 to 18 in. thick as a rule, with sometimes 2½ ft. of it. We fell into hidden crevasses time after time, and were saved by each other and by our harness. In fact, only an all-merciful Providence has guided our steps to tonight's safety at our depot. I cannot describe adequately the mental and physical strain of the last forty-eight hours. When we started at 7 a.m. yesterday, we immediately got into soft snow, an uphill pull with hidden crevasses. The biscuit was all finished, and with only one pannikin of hoosh, mostly pony maize, and one of tea, we marched till noon. Then we had one pannikin of tea and one ounce of chocolate, and marched till 4.45 p.m. We had one pannikin of tea. There was no more food. We marched till 10 p.m., then one small pannikin of cocoa. Marched till 2 a.m., when we were played out. We had one pannikin of cocoa, and slept till 8 a.m. Then a pannikin of cocoa, and we marched till 1 p.m. and camped, about half a mile from the depot. Marshall went on for food, and we got a meal at 2 p.m. We turned in and slept. Adams fell exhausted in his harness, but recovered and went on again. Wild did the same the night before.

January 28. Thank God we are on the Barrier again at last. We got up at 1 a.m. this morning, had breakfast, consisting of tea and one biscuit, and got under way at 3 a.m. We reached the depot in half an hour without any difficulty. The snow here was deep enough to carry us over the crevasses that had impeded our progress so much on the outward march. We had proper breakfast at 5 a.m. then dug out our depot. The alternate falls of snow and thaws had frozen solidly in a great deal of our gear, and our spare sledge meter was deeply buried. We marched along till we were close to the Gap, then had lunch. At 1 p.m. we were through the Gap and on to the crevassed and ridged Barrier surface. We are now safe, with six days' food and only 50 miles to the depot, but Wild has developed dysentery. We are at a loss to know what is the cause of it. It may possibly be due to the horse-meat. The weather has been fairly fine all day, though clouding up from the south towards noon, and we were assisted by a fresh southerly breeze up the slope to the head of the Gap. Indeed, we needed it, for the heavy surface and our dilapidated sledge made the hauling extremely hard. Just before we left the glacier I broke through the soft snow, plunging into a hidden crevasse. My harness jerked up under my heart, and gave me rather a shake up. It seemed as though the glacier were saying: ' There is the last touch for you; don't you come up here again.' It was with a feeling of intense relief that we left this great glacier, for the strain has been hard, and now we know that except for blizzards and thick weather, which two factors can alone prevent us from finding our depots in good time, we will be all right. The light became bad this evening when we were on the last hour before camping, and we cannot say for certain whether we are clear of the main chasm by the land or not, so must give its line of direction a wide berth. The temperature is well up, plus 26° Fahr., and it is warm indeed after the minus temperatures which have been our lot for the last month or so.

January 29. We are having a most unfriendly greeting from the Barrier. We got up as usual and had breakfast at 5.30 a.m., the weather thick and overcast, but the land showing enough for us to steer by. We got away at 7.20 a.m., and soon after it began to snow, which in a temperature of plus 30° Fahr. melted on the sledge and all our gear, making everything into a miserably wet state. We had to put the compass down every now and then, for it became too thick to see any landmarks, and at 9.30 the wind suddenly sprang up from the east, cold and strong, freezing solid all our wet clothes, and the various things on the sledge. It was blowing a blizzard with snow and heavy drift in less than five minutes from the time the wind started, and with difficulty we managed to get up one tent and crawl into it, where we waited in the hope that the weather would clear. As there was no sign of an improvement at noon we pitched the other tent, had food, and lay in our bags patching our worn-out clothes. All day the blizzard has continued to blow hard, with extra violent gusts at times. Our tents get snowed up, and we have to clear them by kicking at the snow every now and then.

January 30. We made a start at 8.15 a.m., after spending three-quarters of an hour digging out our sledges and tents from the drift of the blizzard, which stopped at 1 a.m. It was clear over part of the land as we started, but soon snow began to fall again and the weather became very thick; yet, steering on a course, we came through the crevasses and drift without even touching one, though before, in good light, we have had to turn and twist to avoid them. The surface was heavy for pulling on, owing to the fine snow from the blizzard, but we did 13 miles for the day, working a full ten hours till 7.50 p.m. The weather cleared right up in the afternoon, and we made a good course. Wild is seedy today, but we hope that as soon as he reaches Grisi depot he will be better. We have no variety of food, and only have four miserably thin biscuits a day to eke out the horse-meat. The plasmon is all finished and so are we ourselves by the end of the day's march. The sledge also is in a terribly bad state, but as soon as we reach the depot all will be well. The surface in the afternoon improved, and is much better than we had hoped for. The temperature is plus 24° Fahr., fine and warm. A heavy day's pull, but we were assisted by the wind in the afternoon. Wild is still seedy, just walking in harness. The surface is good, and we are rapidly nearing the depot. Short of food, down to twenty ounces a day. Very tired. Good weather.

January 31. Started at 7 a.m., Wild bad with dysentery. Picked up mound 4 p.m., and camped at 6 p.m. Very bad surface. Did 13½ miles.

February 1. Started 7 a.m.; awful surface at times. Wild very bad. Picked up mound. Camped 6 p.m., having done nearly 14 miles.

February 2. Started at 6.40 a.m. and camped 7 p.m. at depot. Wild and self dysentery; dead tired, bad surface, with undulations. Did 13½ miles. Ray's birthday, celebrated with two lumps of sugar, making five each in cocoa.

February 3. Started with new sledge and 150 lb. more weight at 8.40 a.m.; camped 5.30 p.m. Only five miles; awfully soft snow surface. All acute dysentery due to meat. Trust that sleep will put us right. Could go no further tonight. Wild very bad, self weaker, others assailed also. Bad light, short food, surface worse than ever. Snow one foot deep. Got up 4.30 a.m. after going to bed 11 p.m. No more tonight. Temperature plus 5° Fahr. Dull.

February 4. Cannot write more. All down with acute dysentery; terrible day. No march possible; outlook serious . . . Fine weather.

February 5. Eight miles today; dead tired. Dysentery better, but Adams not too right. Camped at 5.30 p.m. We are picking up the mounds well. Too weak on half ration to write much. Still hanging on to geological specimens. Please God we will get through all right. Great anxiety.

February 6. Did 10 miles today. All better and a better surface. Terribly hungry. Six biscuits per day and one pannikin horse-meat each meal. Picked up November 28 mound and made camp. I do trust this hunger will not weaken us too much. It has been great anxiety. Thank God the dysentery stopped and the surface better. We may do more tomorrow, as there are signs of wind from the south-east. Temperature plus 9° Fahr.

February 7. Blowing hard blizzard. Kept going till 6 p.m. Adams and Marshall renewed dysentery. Dead tired. Short food; very weak.

February 8. Did 12 miles. We had fine weather after 10 a.m. Started from camp in blizzard. Adams and Marshall still dysentery; Wild and I all right. Feel starving for food. Talk of it all day. Anyhow, getting north, thank God. Sixty-nine miles to Chinaman depot.

February 9. Strong following blizzard, and did 14½ miles to north. Adams not fit yet. All thinking and talking of food.

February 10. Strong following wind. Did 20 miles 300 yards. Temperature plus 22° Fahr. All thinking and talking of food.

February 11. We did 16½ miles today, and continued to pick up the mounds, which is a great comfort. The temperature is plus 20° Fahr. tonight. All our thoughts are of food. We ought to reach the depot in two days. Now we are down to half a pannikin of meat and five biscuits a day. Adams not all right yet, and Wild shaky tonight. Good surface and following wind. We were up at 4.45 a.m. and camped at 6 p.m.

February 12. Fine day, with no wind. We were up at 4.30 a.m., and marched till 6 p.m., doing 14½ miles. Adams sighted the depot flag at 6 p.m. The temperature has ranged from plus 5° to plus 20° Fahr. Passed sastrugi running south-south-east in the afternoon. Slight westerly wind. Very tired.

February 13. Breakfast at 4.40 a.m. We packed up, with a cold wind blowing, and reached the depot, with all our food finished, at 11.30 a.m. There we got Chinaman's liver, which we have had tonight. It tasted splendid. We looked round for any spare bits of meat, and while I was digging in the snow I came across some hard red stuff, Chinaman's blood frozen into a solid core. We dug it up, and found it a welcome addition to our food. It was like beef-tea when boiled up. The distance today was 12 miles, with a light wind.

February 14. A good surface today, but no wind. The pulling was hard, and the temperature plus 10° to plus 18° Fahr. We did 11¾ miles. We are still weak, but better, the horse-blood helps. Burst lips are our greatest trouble.

February 15. My birthday today. I was given a present of a cigarette made out of pipe tobacco and some coarse paper we had with us. It was delicious. A hard pull today, and my head is very bad again. The distance was 12¼ miles, with a fairly good surface and fine weather. We are picking up our mounds with great regularity. The land can be seen faintly through the haze in the distance. We have found undulations even out here, but not very marked, running in the usual direction. Temperature minus 3° Fahr. at noon.

February 16. A fair surface today, but no wind. The sastrugi are disappearing. We are appallingly hungry. We are down to about half a pannikin of halfcooked horse-meat a meal and four biscuits a day. We covered 13 miles today, with the temperature from zero to minus 7° Fahr. There are appearances of wind from the south, long windy streamers of torn stratus. We are so weak now that even to lift our depleted provision bag is an effort. When we break camp in the morning we pull the tent off the poles and take it down before we move the things inside, for the effort of lifting the sleeping-bags, &c., through the doorway is too great. At night when we have come to camp we sometimes have to lift our legs one at a time with both hands in getting into the tent. It seems a severe strain to lift one's feet without aid after we have stiffened from the day's march. Our fingers are extremely painful. Some of us have big blisters that burst occasionally.

February 17. I thought we were in for it and was not wrong. Today we have been marching in a blinding blizzard, with 42° of frost, but, thank heaven, the wind was behind us and we have done 19 miles, the sledge with the sail up often overrunning us, and then at other times getting into a patch of soft snow and bringing us up with a jerk. The harness round our weakened stomachs gives us a good deal of pain when we are brought up suddenly. We started at 6.40 a.m. and marched till 6 p.m., and today we had three pannikins of semi-cooked horse-meat and six biscuits on the strength of the good march. We all have tragic dreams of getting food to eat, but rarely have the satisfaction of dreaming that we are actually eating. Last night I did taste bread and butter. We look at each other as we eat our scanty meals and feel a distinct grievance if one man manages to make his hoosh last longer than the rest of us. Sometimes we do our best to save a bit of biscuit for the next meal, but it is a much debated question whether it is best to eat all the food at once or to save. I eat all my lunch biscuit, but keep a bit from dinner to eat in the bag so as to induce sleep. The smaller the quantity of biscuits grows the more delicious they taste.

February 18. The wind dropped during the night, and at 4.40 a.m. we got up, picked our buried sledge out of the drift, and were under way by 7 a.m. There was little wind, and the temperature was minus 20° Fahr. at noon. This afternoon we sighted old Discovery. What a home-like appearance it has. Its big, bluff form showed out in the north-west, and we felt that the same mountain might at that very moment be drawing the eyes of our own people at winter quarters. It seemed to be a connecting link. Perhaps they will be wondering whether we are in sight of it.

February 19. A very cold south wind today, but we turned out at 4.40 a.m., with a temperature minus 20° Fahr. We have been hungry and cold all day, but did 14¼ miles on a good surface. We sighted Mount Erebus in the morning. The old landmarks are so pleasant. Camped at 6 p.m., temperature minus 100 Fahr. We ought to reach Depot A tomorrow. We have picked up the last mound except one. If we had food all would be well, but we are now at the end of our supplies again, except for some scraps of meat scraped off the bones of Grisi after they had been lying on the snow in the sun for all these months. We dare not risk it until the worst comes. Still in five days more we ought to be in the land of plenty.

February 20. Started to get up at 4.40 a.m. It is almost a farce to talk of getting up to 'breakfast' now, and there is no call of 'Come on, boys; good hoosh.' No good hoosh is to be had. In less time than it has taken me to write this the food is finished, and then our hopes and thoughts lie wholly in the direction of the next feed, so called from force of habit. It was dull and overcast today, and we could see only a little way. Still we made progress, and at 4 p.m. we reached depot A. The distance for the day was 14 miles, with 52° of frost. We sighted the depot at 2.30 p.m., and now we have enough food to carry us to the Bluff Depot. We had run out of food when we reached the depot today, and we have had a good hoosh tonight. The unaccustomed pemmican fat made me feel quite queer, but I enjoyed the pudding we made out of biscuits and the tin of jam which we originally intended to have for Christmas Day, but which we left behind when on the way south in order to save weight. Our depoted tobacco and cigarettes were here, and it is difficult to describe the enjoyment and luxury of a good smoke. I am sure that the tobacco will make up for the shortage of food. I do not doubt but that the Bluff Depot will have been laid all right by Joyce. Anyhow we must stake on it, for we have not enough food to carry us to the ship. Joyce knows his work well, and we talk now of nothing but the feeds that we will have when we reach, the Bluff. That depot has been the bright beacon ahead through these dark days of hunger. Each time we took in another hole in our belts we have said that it will be all right when we get to the Bluff Depot, and now we are getting towards it.

February 21. We got up at 4.40 a.m., just as it commenced to blow, and the wind continued all day, a blizzard with as low as 67° of frost. We could not get warm, but we did twenty miles. In ordinary polar work one would not think of travelling in such a severe blizzard, but our need is extreme, and we must keep going. It is neck or nothing with us now. Our food lies ahead, and death stalks us from behind. This is just the time of the year when the most bad weather may be expected. The sun now departs at night, and the darkness is palpable by the time we turn in, generally about 9.30 p.m. We are so thin that our bones ache as we lie on the hard snow in our sleeping-bags, from which a great deal of the hair has gone. Tonight we stewed some of the scraps of Grisi meat, and the dish tasted delicious. Too cold to write more. Thank God, we are nearing the Bluff.

February 22. A splendid day. We did 20½ miles and on the strength of the distance had a good feed. About 11 a.m. we suddenly came across the tracks of a party of four men, with dogs. Evidently the weather has been fine and they have been moving at a good pace towards the south. We could tell that the weather has been fine, for they were wearing ski-boots instead of finneskoe, and occasionally we saw the stump of a cigarette. The length of the steps showed that they were going fast. We are now camped on the tracks, which are fairly recent, and we will try to follow them to the Bluff, for they must have come from the depot. This assures us that the depot was laid all right. I cannot imagine who the fourth man can be, unless it was Buckley, who might be there now that the ship is in. We passed their noon camp, and I am certain that the ship is in, for there were tins lying round bearing brands different from those of the original stores. We found three small bits of chocolate and a little bit of biscuit at the camp after carefully searching the ground for such unconsidered trifles, and we 'turned backs' for them. I was unlucky enough to get the bit of biscuit, and a curious unreasoning anger took possession of me for a moment at my bad luck. It shows how primitive we have become, and how much the question of even a morsel of food affects our judgment. We are near the end of our food, but as we have staked everything on the Bluff Depot, we had a good feed tonight. If we do not pick up the depot there will be absolutely no hope for us.

25

THE FINAL STAGE

February 23. Started at 6.45 a.m. in splendid weather, and at 11 a.m., while halting for a spell, Wild saw the Bluff Depot miraged up. It seemed to be quite close, and the flags were waving and dancing as though to say. 'Come, here I am, come and feed.' It was the most cheerful sight our eyes have ever seen, for we had only a few biscuits left. These we at once devoured. The Grisi meat had given Wild renewed dysentery. After a short camp we pushed on. A flashing light appeared to be on the depot, and when we reached it at 4 p.m., this turned out to be a biscuit tin, which had been placed in the snow so as to catch the light of the sun. It was like a great cheerful eye twinkling at us. The depot had appeared much closer than it really was, because we were accustomed to judging from the height of an ordinary depot, whereas this one was built on a snow mound over 10 ft. high, with two bamboos lashed together on top, and three flags. It was a splendid mark. Joyce and his party have done their work well. Now we are safe as regards food, and it only remains for us to reach the ship. I climbed up on top of the depot, and shouted out to those below of the glorious feeds that awaited us. First, I rolled down three tins of biscuits, then cases containing luxuries of every description, many of them sent by friends. There were Carlsbad plums, eggs, cakes, plum puddings, gingerbread and crystallized fruit, even fresh boiled mutton from the ship. After months of want and hunger, we suddenly found ourselves able to have meals fit for the gods, and with appetites that the gods might have envied. Apart from the luxuries there was an ample supply of ordinary sledging rations. Tonight we improvised a second cooking-stand out of a biscuit tin, and used our second Primus to cook some of the courses. Our dream of food has come true, and yet after we had eaten biscuits and had two pannikins of pemmican, followed by cocoa, our contracted bodies would not stand the strain of more food, and reluctantly we had to stop. I cannot tell what a relief it has been to us. There is nothing much in the way of news from the ship, only just a letter saying that she had arrived on January 5, and that all was well. This letter, dated January 20, is signed by Evans, who evidently is the Evans who towed us down in the *Koonya*. We now only have to catch the ship, and I hope we will do that. Wild is better tonight. The temperature is plus 10° Fahr., fine and warm. I am writing in my bag with biscuits beside me, and chocolate and jam.

February 24. We got up at 5 a.m., and at 7 a.m. had breakfast, consisting of eggs, dried milk, porridge and pemmican, with plenty of biscuits. We marched until 1 p.m., had lunch and then marched until 8 p.m., covering a distance of 15 miles for the day. The weather was fine. Though we have plenty of weight to haul now we do not feel it so much as we did the smaller weights when we were hungry. We have good food inside us, and every now and then on the march we eat a bit of chocolate or biscuit. Warned by the experience of Scott and Wilson on the previous southern journey, I have taken care not to over-eat. Adams has a wonderful digestion, and can go on without any difficulty. Wild's dysentery is a bit better today. He is careful of his feeding and has only taken things that are suitable. It is a comfort to be able to pick and choose. I cannot understand a letter I received from Murray about Mackintosh getting adrift on the ice, but no doubt this will be cleared up on our return. Anyhow every one seems to be all right. There was no news of the northern party or of the western party. We turned in full of food tonight.

February 25. We turned out at 4 a.m. for an early start, as we are in danger of being left if we do not push ahead rapidly and reach the ship. On going into the tent for breakfast I found Marshall suffering from paralysis of the stomach and renewed dysentery, and while we were eating a blizzard came up. We secured everything as the Bluff showed masses of ragged cloud, and I was of opinion that it was going to blow hard. I did not think Marshall fit to travel through the blizzard. During the afternoon, as we were lying in the bags, the weather cleared somewhat, though it still blew hard. If Marshall is not better tonight, I must leave him with Adams and push on, for time is going on, and the ship may leave on March 1, according to orders, if the Sound is not clear of ice. I went over through the blizzard to Marshall's tent. He is in a bad way still, but thinks that he could travel tomorrow.

February 27 (1 a.m.). The blizzard was over at midnight, and we got up at 1 a.m., had breakfast at 2, and made a start at 4. At 9.30 a.m. we had lunch, at 3 p.m. tea, at 7 p.m. hoosh, and then marched till 11 p.m. Had another hoosh, and turned in at 1 a.m. We did 24 miles. Marshall suffered greatly but stuck to the march. He never complains.

March 5. Although we did not turn in until 1 a.m. on the 27th, we were up again at 4 a.m. and after a good hoosh, we got under way at 6 a.m. and marched until 1 p.m. Marshall was unable to haul, his dysentery increasing, and he got worse in the afternoon, after lunch. At 4 p.m. I decided to pitch camp, leave Marshall under Adams' charge, and push ahead with Wild, taking one day's provisions and leaving the balance for the two men at the camp. I hoped to pick up a relief party at the ship. We dumped everything

off the sledge except a prismatic compass, our sleepingbags and food for
one day, and at 4.30 p.m. Wild and I started, and marched till 9 p.m. Then
we had a hoosh, and marched until 2 a.m. of the 28th, over a very hard
surface. We stopped for one hour and a half off the north-east end of White
Island, getting no sleep, and marched till 11 a.m., by which time our food was
finished. We kept flashing the heliograph in the hope of attracting attention
from Observation Hill, where I thought that a party would be on the look-
out, but there was no return flash. The only thing to do was to push ahead,
although we were by this time very tired. At 2.30 p.m. we sighted open
water ahead, the ice having evidently broken out four miles south of Cape
Armitage, and an hour and a half later a blizzard wind started to blow, and
the weather got very thick. We thought once that we saw a party coming
over to meet us, and our sledge seemed to grow lighter for a few minutes, but
the 'party' turned out to be a group of penguins at the ice-edge. The weather
was so thick that we could not see any distance ahead, and we arrived at
the ice edge suddenly. The ice was swaying up and down, and there was
grave risk of our being carried out. I decided to abandon the sledge, as I
felt sure that we would get assistance at once when we reached the hut, and
time was becoming important. It was necessary that we should get food
and shelter speedily. Wild's feet were giving him a great deal of trouble. In
the thick weather we could not risk making Pram Point, and I decided to
follow another route seven miles round by the other side of Castle Rock. We
clambered over crevasses and snow slopes, and after what seemed an almost
interminable struggle reached Castle Rock, from whence I could see that
there was open water all round the north. It was indeed a different home-
coming from what we had expected. Out on the Barrier and up on the
plateau our thoughts had often turned to the day when we would get back
to the comfort and plenty of the winter-quarters, but we had never imagined
fighting our way to the back-door, so to speak, in such a cheerless fashion.
We reached the top of Ski Slope at 7.45 p.m., and from there we could see
the hut and the bay. There was no sign of the ship, and no smoke or other
evidence of life at the hut. We hurried on to the hut, our minds busy with
gloomy possibilities, and found not a man there. There was a letter stating
that the Northern Party had reached the Magnetic Pole, and that all the
parties had been picked up except ours. The letter added that the ship would
be sheltering under Glacier Tongue until February 26. It was now February
28, and it was with very keen anxiety in our minds that we proceeded to
search for food. If the ship was gone, our plight, and that of the two men left
out on the Barrier, was a very serious one.

We improvised a cooking vessel, found oil and a Primus lamp, and had
a good feed of biscuit, onions and plum pudding, which were amongst the
stores left at the hut. We were utterly weary, but we had no sleeping-gear, our

bags having been left with the sledge, and the temperature was very low. We found a piece of roofing felt, which we wrapped round us and then we sat up all night, the darkness being relieved only when we occasionally lighted the lamp in order to secure a little warmth. We tried to burn the magnetic hut in the hope of attracting attention from the ship, but we were not able to get it alight. We tried, too, to tie the Union Jack to Vince's cross, on the hill, but we were so played out that our cold fingers could not manage the knots. It was a bad night for us, and we were glad indeed when the light came again. Then we managed to get a little warmer, and at 9 a.m. we got the magnetic hut alight, and put up the flag. All our fears vanished when in the distance we saw the ship, miraged up. We signalled with the heliograph, and at 11 a.m. on March 1 we were on board the *Nimrod* and once more safe amongst friends. I will not attempt to describe our feelings. Every one was glad to see us, and keen to know what we had done. They had given us up for lost, and a search-party had been going to start that day in the hope of finding some trace of us. I found that every member of the expedition was well, that the plans had worked out satisfactorily, and that the work laid down had been carried out. The ship had brought nothing but good news from the outside world. It seemed as though a great load had been lifted from my shoulders.

The first thing was to bring in Adams and Marshall, and I ordered out a relief party at once. I had a good feed of bacon and fried bread, and started at 2.30 p.m. from the Barrier edge with Mackay, Mawson and McGillon, leaving Wild on the *Nimrod*. We marched until 10 p.m., had dinner and turned in for a short sleep. We were up again at 2 a.m. the next morning (March 2), and travelled until 1 p.m., when we reached the camp where I had left the two men. Marshall was better, the rest having done him a lot of good, and he was able to march and pull. After lunch we started back again, and marched until 8 p.m. in fine weather. We were under way again at 4 a.m. the next morning, had lunch at noon,, and reached the ice-edge at 3 p.m. There was no sign of the ship, and the sea was freezing over. We waited until 5 p.m., and then found that it was possible to strike land at Pram Point. The weather was coming on bad, clouding up from the south-east, and Marshall was suffering from renewed dysentery, the result of the heavy marching. We therefore abandoned one tent and one sledge at the ice-edge, taking on only the sleeping-bags and the specimens. We climbed up by Crater Hill, leaving everything but the sleeping-bags, for the weather was getting worse, and at 9.35 p.m. commenced to slide down towards Hut Point. We reached the winter-quarters at 9.50, and Marshall was put to bed. Mackay and I lighted a carbide flare on the hill by Vince's cross, and after dinner all hands turned in except Mackay and myself. A short time after Mackay saw the ship appear. It was now blowing a hard blizzard, but Mackintosh had seen our flare from a distance of nine miles. Adams and I went on board the *Nimrod,* and Adams, after surviving all the dangers of the interior of the Antarctic continent, was nearly lost within sight of safety. He slipped at the ice-edge, owing to the fact that he was wearing new finnesko, and only just saved himself from going over. He managed to hang on until rescued by a party from the ship.

A boat went back for Marshall and the others, and we were all safe on board at 1 a.m. on March 4.

NOTE. Subsequent calculations have shown that the distances given in my diary of the Southern journey were not always quite accurate. The calculations were made under circumstances of special difficulty, and were not checked until after my return to civilisation. The reader will notice that some of the distances are given in statute miles and others in geographical miles. After the last meridian altitude was taken at the plateau depot and until the return to the same depot the distances were noted in geographical miles. I have thought it best to let the diary figures stand, but in the construction of the map certain corrections have been made, and at the end of the book will be found a table showing the actual distances travelled day by day.

26

SOME NOTES ON THE SOUTHERN JOURNEY

We brought back with us from the journey towards the Pole vivid memories of how it feels to be intensely, fiercely hungry. During the period from November 15, 1908, to February 23, 1909, we had but one full meal, and that was on Christmas Day. Even then we did not keep the sense of repletion for very long, for within an hour or two it seemed to us that we were as hungry as ever. Our daily allowance of food would have been a small one for a city worker in a temperate climate, and in our case hunger was increased by the fact that we were performing vigorous physical labour in a very low temperature. We looked forward to each meal with keen anticipation, but when the food was in our hands it seemed to disappear without making us any the less ravenous. The evening meal at the end of ten hours' sledging used to take us a long time to prepare. The sledges had to be unpacked and the camp pitched. Then the cooker was filled with snow and the Primus lamp lit, often no easy matter with our cold, frost-bitten fingers. The materials for the thin hoosh would be placed in the boilingpot, with the addition, perhaps, of some pony maize, and the allowance of tea was placed in the outer boiler. The tea was always put in a strainer, consisting of a small tin in which we had punched a lot of holes, and it was removed directly the water had come to the boil. We used to sit round the cooker waiting for our food, and at last the hoosh would be ready and would be ladled into the pannikins by the cook of the week. The scanty allowance of biscuit would be distributed and we would commence the meal. In a couple of minutes the hot food would be gone, and we would gnaw carefully round the sides of our biscuits, making them last as long as possible. Marshall used sometimes to stand his pannikin of hoosh in the snow for a little while, because it got thicker as it cooled, but it was a debatable point whether this paid. One seemed to be getting more solid food, but there was a loss of warmth, and in the minus temperatures on the plateau we found it advisable to take our hoosh very hot. We would make the biscuits last as long as possible, and sometimes we tried to save a bit to eat in the sleeping-bag later on, but it was hard to do this. If one of us dropped a crumb, the others would point it out, and the owner would wet his finger in his mouth and pick up the morsel. Not the smallest fragment was allowed to escape.

We used to 'turn backs' in order to ensure equitable division of the food. The cook would pour the hoosh into the pannikins and arrange the biscuits in four heaps. Perhaps some one would suggest that one pannikin had rather less in it than another, and if this view was endorsed by the others there would be a readjustment. Then when we were all satisfied that the food had been divided as fairly as possible, one man would turn his back, and another, pointing at one pannikin or group of biscuits, would say, 'Whose?' The man who had his back turned, and therefore could not see the food, would give a name, and so the distribution would proceed, each of us always feeling sure that the smallest share had fallen to our lot. At lunch-time there would be chocolate or cheese to distribute on alternate days, and we much preferred the chocolate days to the cheese days. The chocolate seemed more satisfying, and it was more easily divided. The cheese broke up into very small fragments on the march, and the allowance, which amounted to two spoonfuls per man, had to be divided up as nearly as possible into four equal heaps. The chocolate could be easily separated into sticks of equal size. It can be imagined that the cook for the week had no easy task. His work became more difficult still when we were using pony-meat, for the meat and blood, when boiled up, made a delightful broth, while the fragments of meat sunk to the bottom of the pot. The liquor was much the better part of the dish, and no one had much relish for the little dice of tough and stringy meat, so the cook had to be very careful indeed. Poor old Chinaman was a particularly tough and stringy horse.

We found that the meat from the neck and rump was the best, the most stringy portions coming from the ribs and legs. We took all the meat we could, tough or tender, and as we went south in the days when horse-meat was fairly plentiful, we used to suck frozen, raw fragments as we marched along. Later we could not afford to use the meat except on a definite allowance. The meat to be used during the day was generally cut up when we took a spell in the morning, and the bag containing the fragments was hung on the back of the sledge in order that the meat might be softened by the sun. It cut more easily when frozen than when partially thawed, but our knives gradually got blunt, and on the glacier we secured a rock on which to sharpen them. During the journey back, when every ounce of weight was of great importance, we used one of our geological specimens, a piece of sandstone, as a knife-sharpener. The meat used to bulk large in the pot, but as fresh meat contains about 60 per cent. of moisture, it used to shrink considerably in the process of cooking, and we did not have to use very much snow in the pot.

We used the meat immediately we had started to kill the ponies in order to save the other food, for we knew that the meat contained a very large percentage of water, so that we would be carrying useless weight with it. The pemmican and biscuits, on the other hand contained very little moisture, and it was more profitable to keep them for the march further south, when we were likely to want to reduce the loads as far as possible. We left meat at each depot, to provide for the march back to the coast, but always took on as much as possible of the prepared foods. The reader will understand that the loss of Socks, which represented so many pounds of meat, was a very severe blow to us, for we had after that to use sledging stores at the depots to make up for the lost meat. If we had been able to use Socks for food, I have no doubt that we would have been able to get further south, perhaps even to the Pole itself, though in that case we could hardly have got back in time to catch the ship before she was forced to leave by the approach of winter.

When we were living on meat our desire for cereals and farinacious foods became stronger; indeed any particular sort of food of which we were deprived seemed to us to be the food for which nature craved. When we were short of sugar we would dream of sweet-stuffs, and when biscuits were in short supply our thoughts were concerned with crisp loaves and all the other good things displayed in the windows of the bakers' shops. During the last weeks of the journey outwards, and the long march back, when our allowance of food had been reduced to twenty ounces per man a day, we really thought of little but food. The glory of the great mountains that towered high on either side, the majesty of the enormous glacier up which we travelled so painfully, did not appeal to our emotions to any great extent. Man becomes very primitive when he is hungry and short of food, and we learned to know what it is to be desperately hungry. I used to wonder sometimes whether the people who suffer from hunger in the big cities of civilisation felt as we were feeling, and I arrived at the conclusion that they did not, for no barrier of law and order would have been allowed to stand between us and any food that had been available. The man who starves in a city is weakened, hopeless, spiritless, and we were vigorous and keen. Until January 9 the desire for food was made the more intense by our knowledge of the fact that we were steadily marching away from the stores of plenty.

We could not joke about food, in the way that is possible for the man who is hungry in the ordinary sense. We thought about it most of the time, and on the way back we used to talk about it, but always in the most serious manner possible. We used to plan out the enormous meals that we proposed to have when we got back to the ship and, later, to civilisation. On the outward march we did not experience really severe hunger until we got on the great glacier, and then we were too much occupied with the heavy and dangerous climbing over the rough ice and crevasses to be able to talk much. We had to keep some distance apart in case one man fell into a crevasse.

Then on the plateau our faces were generally coated with ice, and the blizzard wind blowing from the south made unnecessary conversation out of the question. Those were silent days, and our remarks to one another were brief and infrequent. It was on the march back that we talked freely of food, after we had got down the glacier and were marching over the barrier surface. The wind was behind us, so that the pulling was not very heavy, and as there were no crevasses to fear we were able to keep close together. We would get up at 5 a.m. in order to make a start at 7 a.m., and after we had eaten our scanty breakfast, that seemed only to accentuate hunger, and had begun the day's march, we could take turns in describing the things we would eat in the good days to come. We were each going to give a dinner to the others in turn, and there was to be an anniversary dinner every year, at which we would be able to eat and eat and eat. No French chef ever devoted more thought to the invention of new dishes than we did.

It is with strange feelings that I look back over our notes, and see the wonderful meals that we were going to have. We used to tell each other, with perfect seriousness, about the new dishes that we had thought of, and if the dish met with general approval there would be a chorus of, 'Ah! That's good.' Sometimes there would be an argument as to whether a suggested dish was really an original invention, or whether it did not too nearly resemble something that we had already tasted in happier days. The 'Wild roll' was admitted to be the high-water mark of gastronomic luxury. Wild proposed that the cook should take a supply of well-seasoned minced meat, wrap it in rashers of fat bacon, and place around the whole an outer covering of rich pastry, so that it would take the form of a big sausage-roll. Then this roll would be fried with plenty of fat. My best dish, which I must admit I put forward with a good deal of pride as we marched over the snow was a sardine pasty, made by placing well-fried sardines inside pastry. At least ten tins of sardines were to be emptied on to a bed of pastry, and the whole then rolled up and cooked, preparatory to its division into four equal portions. I remember one day Marshall came forward with a proposal for a thick roll of suet pudding with plenty of jam all over it, and there arose quite a heated argument as to whether he could fairly claim this dish to be an invention, or whether it was not the jam roll already known to the housewives of civilisation. There was one point on which we were all agreed, and that was that we did not want any jellies or things of that sort at our future meals. The idea of eating such elusive stuff as jelly had no appeal to us at all.

On a typical day during this backward march we would leave camp at about 6.40 a.m., and half an hour later would have recovered our frost-bitten fingers, while the moisture on our clothes, melted in the sleepingbags, would have begun to ablate, after having first frozen hard. We would be beginning to march with some degree of comfort, and one of us would remark, 'Well, boys, what are we going to have for breakfast today?' We had just finished our breakfast as a matter of fact, consisting of half a pannikin of semi-raw horse-meat, one biscuit and a half and a pannikin of tea, but the meal had not taken the keenness from our appetites. We used to try to persuade ourselves that our half-biscuit was not quite a half, and sometimes we managed to get a little bit more that way. The question would receive our most serious and careful consideration at once, and we would proceed to weave from our hungry imaginations a tale of a day spent in eating. 'Now we are on board ship,' one man would say. 'We wake up in a bunk, and the first thing we do is to stretch out our hands to the side of the bunk and get some chocolate, some Garibaldi biscuits and some apples. We eat those in the bunk, and then we get up for breakfast. Breakfast will be at eight o'clock, and we will have porridge, fish, bacon and eggs, cold ham, plum pudding, sweets, fresh roll and butter, marmalade and coffee. At eleven o'clock we will have hot cocoa, open jam tarts, fried cods' roe and slices of heavy plum cake. That will be all until lunch at one o'clock. For lunch we will have Wild roll, shepherd's pie, fresh soda-bread, hot milk, treacle pudding, nuts, raisins and cake. After that we will turn in for a sleep, and we will be called at 3.45, when we will reach out again from the bunks and have dough-nuts and sweets. We will get up then and have big cups of hot tea and fresh cake and chocolate creams. Dinner will be at six, and we will have thick soup, roast beef and Yorkshire pudding, cauliflower, peas, asparagus, plum pudding, fruit, apple-pie with thick cream, scones and butter, port wine, nuts, and almonds and raisins. Then at midnight we will have a really big meal, just before we go to bed. There will be melon, grilled trout and butter-sauce, roast chicken with plenty of livers, a proper salad with eggs and very thick dressing, green peas and new potatoes, a saddle of mutton, fried suet pudding, peaches a' la Melba, egg curry, plum pudding and sauce, Welsh rarebit, Queen's pudding, angels on horseback, cream cheese and celery, fruit, nuts, port wine, milk and cocoa. Then we will go to bed and sleep till breakfast time. We will have chocolate and biscuits under our pillows, and if we want anything to eat in the night we will just have to get it.' Three of us would listen to this programme and perhaps suggest amendments and improvements, generally in the direction of additional dishes, and then another one of us would take up the running and sketch another glorious day of feeding and sleeping.

I daresay that all this sounds very greedy and uncivilised to the reader who has never been on the verge of starvation, but as I have said before, hunger makes a man primitive. We did not smile at ourselves or at each other as we planned wonderful feats of over-eating. We were perfectly serious about the matter, and we noted down in the back pages of our diaries details of the meals that we had decided to have as soon as we got back to the places where food was plentiful. All the morning we would allow our imaginations to run riot in this fashion. Then would come one o'clock, and I would look at my watch and say, 'Camp!' We would drop the harness from our tired bodies and pitch the tent on the smoothest place available, and three of us would get inside to wait for the thin and scanty meal, while the other man filled the cooker with snow and fragments of frozen meat. An hour later we would be on the march again, once more thinking and talking of food, and this would go on until the camp in the evening. We would have another scanty meal, and turn into the sleeping-bags, to dream wildly of food that somehow we could never manage to eat.

The dysentery from which we suffered during the latter part of the journey back to the coast was certainly due to the meat from the pony Grisi. This animal was shot one night when in a greatly exhausted condition, and I believe that his flesh was made poisonous by the presence of the toxin of exhaustion, as is the case with animals that have been hunted. Wild was the first to suffer, at the time when we started to use Grisi meat with the other meat, and he must have been unfortunate enough to get the greater part of the bad meat on that occasion. The other meat we were using then came from Chinaman, and seemed to be quite wholesome.

A few days later we were all eating Grisi meat, and we all got dysentery. The meat could not have become affected in any way after the death of the pony, because it froze hard within a very short time. The manner in which we managed to keep on marching when suffering, and the speed with which we recovered when we got proper food, were rather remarkable, and the reason, no doubt, was that the dysentery was simply the result of the poison, and was not produced by organic trouble of any sort. We had a strong wind behind us day after day during this period, and this contributed in a very large measure to our safety, for in the weakened condition we had then reached we could not have made long marches against a head-wind, and without long marches we would have starved between the depots. We had a sail on the sledge, formed of the floorcloth of a tent, and often the sledge would overrun us, though at other times it would catch in a drift and throw us heavily.

When we were travelling along during the early part of the journey over the level Barrier surface, we felt the heat of the sun severely, though as a matter of fact the temperature was generally very low, sometimes as low as zero Fahr. though the season was the height of summer. It was quite usual to feel one side of the face getting frozen while the other side was being sunburned. The ponies would have frozen perspiration on their coats on the sheltered side, while the sun would keep the other side hot and dry, and as the day wore on and the sun moved round the sky the frosted area on the animals would change its position in sympathy. I remember that on December 4 we were marching stripped to our shirts, and we got very much sunburned, though at noon that day the air temperature showed ten degrees of frost. When we started to climb the glacier and marched close to the rocks, we felt the heat much more, for the rocks acted as radiators, and this experience weighed with me in deciding to leave all the spare clothing and equipment at the Upper Glacier Depot, about seven thousand feet up. We did not expect to have to climb much higher, but, as the reader knows, we did not reach the plateau until we had climbed over ten thousand feet above sea-level, and so we felt the cold extremely. Our wind-proof Burberry clothing had become thin by this time, and had been patched in many places in consequence of having been torn on the sharp ice. The wind got in through a tear in my Burberry trousers one day and I was frost-bitten on the under part of the knee. This frost-bite developed into an open wound, into which the wool from my underclothing worked, and I had finally to perform a rather painful operation with a knife before the wound would heal. We were continually being frost-bitten up on the plateau, and when our boots had begun to give out and we were practically marching on the sennegrass inside the finnesko, our heels got frost-bitten. My heels burst when we got on to hard stuff, and for some time my socks were caked with blood at the end of every day's march. Finally Marshall put some 'Newskin' on a pad, and that stuck on well until the cracks had healed. The scars are likely to remain with me. In the very cold days, when our strength had begun to decrease, we found great difficulty in hoisting the sail on our sledge, for when we lifted our arms above our heads in order to adjust the sail, the blood ran from our fingers and they promptly froze. Ten minutes or a quarter of an hour sometimes elapsed before we could get the sledge properly rigged. Our troubles with frostbite were no doubt due in a measure to the lightness of our clothing, but there was compensation in the speed with which we were able to travel. I have no doubt at all that men engaged in polar exploration should be clothed as lightly as is possible, even if there is a danger of frost-bite when they halt on the march.

The surface over which we travelled during the southern journey changed continually. During the first few days we found a layer of soft snow on top of a hard crust, with more soft snow underneath that again. Our weight was sufficient to break through the soft snow on top, and if we were pulling the increased pressure would cause the crust to break also, letting us through into the second layer of soft snow. This surface made the travelling very heavy. Until we had got beyond Minna Bluff we often passed over high, sharp sastrugi, and beyond that we met with ridges four to six feet high. The snow generally was dry and powdery, but some of the crystals were large, and showed in reflected light all the million colours of diamonds. After we had passed latitude 80° South the snow got softer day by day, and the ponies would often break through the upper crust and sink in right up to their bellies. When the sun was hot the travelling would be much better, for the surface snow got near the melting-point and formed a slippery layer not easily broken. Then again a fall in the temperature would produce a thin crust, through which one broke very easily. Between latitude 80° South and 83° South there were hard sastrugi under the soft snow, and the hoofs of the horses suffered in consequence. The surface near the land was broken up by the pressure from the glaciers, but right alongside the mountains there was a smooth plain of glassy ice, caused by the freezing of water that had run off the rocky slopes when they were warm under the rays of the sun. This process had been proceeding on the snow slopes that we had to climb in order to reach the glacier. Here at the foot of the glacier there were pools of clear water round the rocks, and we were able to drink as much as we wanted, though the contact of the cold water with our cracked lips was painful.

The glacier itself presented every variety of surface, from soft snow to cracked and riven blue ice, by-and-by the only constant feature were the crevasses, from which we were never free. Some were entirely covered with a crust of soft snow, and we discovered them only when one of us broke through, and hung by his harness from the sledge. Others occurred in mazes of rotten ice, and were even more difficult to negotiate than the other sort. The least unpleasant of the crevasses were those that were wide open and easily seen, with firm ice on either side. If these crevasses were not too wide, we would pull the sledges up to the side then jump over, and pull them after us. This was more difficult than it sounds from the fact that the ice gave only a very uncertain footing, but we always had the harness as a safeguard in case of a fall. If the crevasses were wide we had to make a *détour*. The sledges, owing to their length, were not liable to slip down a crevasse, and we felt fairly safe when we were securely attached to them by the harness. When the surface was so bad that relay work became necessary we used to miss the support of a sledge on the back journeys. We would advance one sledge half a mile or a mile, put up a bamboo pole to mark the spot, and then go back for the other. We were roped together for the walk back to the second sledge, but even then we felt a great deal less secure than when harnessed to one of the long, heavy sledges. On some days we had to travel up steep slopes of smooth ice, and often it became necessary to cut steps WITH our ice-axes, and haul the sledges after us with the Alpine rope. When we had gone up about sixty feet, the length of the rope, we would haul up the sledge to which we had attached the lower end, and jamb it so that it could not slide back. Then one of us would slide down in order to fix the rope to the other sledge.

One of the curious features of the glacier was a yellow line, evidently an old moraine, extending for thirty or forty miles. The rocks of the moraine had gradually sunk in out of sight, the radiation of the sun's heat from them causing the ice to melt and let them through, and there had remained enough silt and dust to give the ice a dirty yellow appearance. The travelling along this old moraine was not so bad, but on either side of it there was a mass of pressure ice, caused by the constriction of the glacier between the mountains to the east and west. Unfortunately we brought back no photographs of this portion of the glacier. The number of plates at our disposal was limited, and on the outward march we decided not to take many photographs in case we found interesting land or mountains in the far south nearer the Pole. We thought that we would be able to secure as many photographs of the glacier as we wanted on the way back if we had the plates to spare, but as a matter of fact when we did get on to the glacier a second time we were so short of food that we could not afford the time to unpack the camera, which had to be stowed away carefully on the sledge in order to avoid damage to it.

Many nights on the glacier there was no snow on which to pitch the tents, and we had to spend perhaps an hour smoothing out a space on a rippled, sharp-pointed sea of ice. The provision bags and sledges had to be packed on the snow cloths round the tents, and it was indeed fortunate for us that we did not meet with any bad weather while we were marching up the glacier. Had a blizzard come on while we were asleep, it would have scattered our goods far and wide, and we would have been faced with a very serious position. All the time that we were climbing the glacier we had a northerly wind behind us, although the direction of the sastrugi showed clearly that the prevailing wind was from the south; when we were coming back later in the season the wind was behind us all the time. We encountered a strong wind on the outward journey when near the top of the glacier, and as the ice slopes were covered with snow it was difficult to pull the sledges up them. When we reached the same slopes on the way back, the summer sun had cleared the snow from them, leaving clear ice, and we simply glissaded down all but the steepest slopes, although one of the sledge runners was very badly torn. We had to travel carefully on the steep slopes, for if we had let the sledge get out of hand it would have run away altogether, and would probably have been smashed up hundreds of feet below.

The Upper Glacier Depot was overhung by great cliffs of rock, shattered by the frosts and storms of countless centuries, and many fragments were poised in such a fashion that scarcely more than a touch seemed needed to bring them hurtling down. All around us on the ice lay rocks that had recently fallen from the heights, and we wondered whether some boulder would come down upon us while we were in camp. We had no choice of a camping-ground, as all around was rough ice. The cliffs were composed largely of weathered sandstone, and it was on the same mountains, higher up the glacier, that the coal was found, at a point where the slope was comparatively gentle.

Looking down from this height, we could see the glacier stretching away to the point of junction with the Barrier, the mountains rising to east and west. Many of the mountains to the west of the glacier were more or less dome-shaped, but there were some sharp conical peaks to the westward of the particular mountain under which the Upper Glacier Depot had been placed. There were three distinct peaks, as the photographs show, and the plateau ice sweeping down made a long moraine on the west side of the glacier. To the eastward there was a long ridge of high mountains, fairly uniform in shape and without any sharp peaks, but with ridges, apparently of granite, projecting towards the west and so constricting the glacier. The mountains were distant about twenty-five miles, but well-defined stratification lines could plainly be seen. Below us, as we looked from the depot, could be seen the cumulus clouds that always hung above the 'Cloud-Maker'.

When we looked to the south from this depot we saw no clouds; there was nothing but hard clear sky. The sky gave no indication of the blizzard winds that were to assail us when we reached the plateau, and after we had gone as far south as we could and retraced our footsteps to the depot, we looked back and saw the same clear sky, with a few wisps of fleecy cloud in it. We had no doubt that below those clouds the pitiless gale was still raging across the great frozen plain, and that the wind which followed us during our march back to the coast was coming from the vicinity of the Pole. As we advanced from the Upper Glacier Depot we came upon great ice falls. The surface looked smooth from a distance, and we thought that we were actually on the plateau, but as we advanced we saw that before us lay enormous ridges rising abruptly. We had to relay our gear over these ridges, and often at the tops there would be a great crevasse, from which would radiate smaller crevasses fringed with crystals and showing ghastly depths below. We would creep forward to see what lay on the other side, and perhaps would find a fall of fifty feet, with a grade of about 1 in 3. Many times we risked our sledge on very severe slopes, allowing it to glissade down, but other times the danger of a smash was too great, and we had to lower the sledge slowly and carefully with the rope. The ice was safe enough to walk upon at this time except at the ridges, where the crevasses were severe, for the smaller crevasses in the hollows and slopes could be passed without difficulty.

The ice falls delayed us a good deal, and then we got into soft snow, over which the sledge dragged heavily. We thought that we were finally on the plateau level, but within a few days we came to fresh ridges and waves of pressure ice. The ice between the waves was very rotten, and many times we fell through when we put our weight on it. We fastened the Alpine rope to the sledge harness, and the first man pulled at a distance of about eighteen feet from the sledge, while the whole party was so scattered that no two men could fall into a crevasse together. We got on to better ground by steering to the westward, but this step was rather dangerous, for by taking this course we travelled parallel with the crevasses and were not able to meet them at right angles. Many times we nearly lost the sledge and ourselves when the ice started to break away into an unseen crevasse running parallel with our course. We felt very grateful to Providence that the weather remained clear, for we could not have moved a yard over this rotten ice in thick weather without courting disaster. I do not know whether the good weather we experienced in that neighbourhood was normal. We generally had about seven miles of easy going after we had passed one ridge in this area, and then another ridge would rise up ahead of us, and we would start to climb again. There were always crevasses at the top of the ridges, suggesting that the ice was moving over land at no great depth.

We passed the last ridge at last, and reached the actual plateau, but instead of hard névé, such as the *Discovery* expedition had encountered in the journey to the plateau beyond the mountains west of McMurdo Sound, we found soft snow and hard sastrugi. All the sastrugi pointed to the south, and the wind blew strongly nearly all the time from the south or south-east, with an occasional change to the south-west. Sometimes we marched on hard sastrugi, and at other times we had soft snow under our feet, but could feel the sastrugi on which the snow was lying. I formed the opinion that during the winter on the plateau the wind must blow with terrible violence from the south, and that the hard sastrugi are produced then. Still further south we kept breaking through a hard crust that underlay the soft surface snow, and we then sank in about eight inches. This surface, which made the marching heavy, continued to the point at which we planted the flag. After the long blizzard, from the night of January 6 until the morning of January 9, we had a better surface over which to make our final march southwards, for the wind had swept the soft snow away and produced a fairly hard surface, over which, unencumbered with a sledge as we were, we could advance easily.

We found the surface generally to be improved on the march back. The blizzard winds had removed the soft surface snow, and incidentally uncovered many of the crevasses. We were following our outward tracks, and often I noticed the tracks lead us to the edge of a crevasse which had been covered previously and over which we had passed in ignorance of our danger on the march southwards. When we got to the head of the glacier we tried to take a short cut to the point where we had left the Upper Glacier Depot, but we got enmeshed in a maze of crevasses and pressure ridges to the eastward, and so had to steer in a westerly direction again in order to get clear. The dangers that we did know were preferable to those that we did not know. On the way down the glacier we found all the snow stripped away by the wind and sun for nearly one hundred miles, and we travelled over slippery blue ice, with innumerable cracks and sharp edges. We had many painful falls during this part of the journey. Then when about forty miles from the foot of the glacier we got into deep soft snow again, over which rapid progress was impossible. There had evidently been a heavy snowfall in this area while we were further south, and for days, while our food was running short, we could see ahead of us the rocks under which the depot had been placed. We toiled with painful slowness towards the rocks, and as the reader has already learned, we were without any food at all for the last thirty hours of that march. We found the Barrier surface to be very soft when we got off the Glacier, but after we had passed Grisi Depot there was an improvement. The surface remained fairly good until we reached the winter quarters, and in view of our weakened condition it was fortunate for us that it did so.

In reviewing the experience gained on the southern journey, I do not think that I could suggest any improvement in equipment for any future expedition. The Barrier surface evidently varies in a remarkable fashion, and its condition cannot be anticipated with any degree of certainty. The traveller must be prepared for either a hard surface or a very soft one, and he may get both surfaces in the course of one day's march. The eleven-foot sledge is thoroughly suitable for the work, and our method of packing the stores and hauling the sledges did not develop any weak points. We would have been glad to have had crampons for use on the glacier; what would be better still would be heavy Alpine boots with nails all round, for very often the surface would give little grip to crampons, which would only touch the rough ice at one or two points. The temperature is too cold to permit of the explorer wearing ordinary leather boots, and some boot would have to be designed capable of keeping the feet warm and carrying the nails all round. A mast consisting of a bamboo lashed to the forward oil-box proved as efficient as could be required for use in connection with a sail on the sledges. It was easily rigged and had no elaborate stays. I would suggest no change in the clothing, for the light woollen underclothing, with thin windproof material outside, proved most satisfactory in every way. We could certainly not have travelled so fast had we been wearing the regulation pilot cloth garment generally used in polar exploration. Our experience made it obvious that a party which hopes to reach the Pole must take more food per man than we did, but how the additional weight is to be provided for is a matter for individual consideration. I would not take cheese again, for although it is a good food, we did not find it as palatable as chocolate, which is practically as sustaining. Our other foods were all entirely satisfactory.

Each member of the Southern Party had his own particular duties to perform. Adams had charge of the meteorology, and his work involved the taking of temperatures at regular intervals, and the boiling of the hypsometer, sometimes several times in a day. He took notes during the day, and wrote up the observations at night in the sleeping-bag. Marshall was the cosmographer and took the angles and bearings of all the new land; he also took the meridian altitudes and the compass variation as we went south. When a meridian altitude was taken, I generally had it checked by each member of the party, so that the mean could be taken.

Marshall's work was about the most uncomfortable possible, for at the end of a day's march, and often at lunch-time, he would have to stand in the biting wind handling the screws of the theodolite. The map of the journey was prepared by Marshall, who also took most of the photographs. Wild attended to the repair of the sledges and equipment, and also assisted me in the geological observations and the collection of specimens. It was he who found the coal close to the Upper Glacier Depot. I kept the courses and distances, worked out observations and laid down our directions. We all kept diaries. I had two, one my observation book, and the other the narrative diary, reproduced in the first volume.

27

SUMMER AT THE WINTER QUARTERS

We were distant about thirty-two miles from Hut Point when I decided to send the supporting-party back. The men watched us move off across the white plain until we became mere dots on the wide expanse, and then loaded up their gear and started north. Joyce was left in charge of the party, and he decided to make one forced march to Hut Point. They had to cross a good deal of crevassed ice, but a special effort would enable them to make their next camp under shelter. They got under way at 7 a.m. and marched till noon, making good progress in spite of the surface. In the afternoon they marched from two till five o'clock, and then a final march, from 7 p.m. till 1.30 a.m., took them to the old *Discovery* hut. The only incident of the day had been the succumbing of Brocklehurst's feet to another attack of frost-bite, he having worn ski-boots when the other men had put on finnesko. The damage was not serious, although the sufferer himself had trouble with his feet for some time after. The party had covered thirty-two miles in fourteen hours and a half, very good marching in view of the soft and broken character of the surface.

The party left Hut Point on the morning of November 12, and had a hard pull to Glacier Tongue. They at first thought of camping on the southern side of the Tongue, but, fortunately, kept on, for on the other side they met Day, Murray and Roberts, who had brought out stores with the motor-car. I had left orders that about 1800 lb. of provisions and gear should be taken to the depot there, as a provision for the sledging-parties, in case they should be cut off from Cape Royds by open water on their return. Day had succeeded in running the car right up to the Tongue, about twelve miles from winter quarters. After a good meal of biscuits, jam, lobscouse, tongue and cods' roe, the two parties joined in getting the stores up to the depot. Then they all went back to the winter quarters on the car and the light sledges it had in tow, leaving the heavy sledge that had been used by the supporting-party to be brought in at some later opportunity. They reached the hut in the small hours of the morning, and after another meal turned in for a good sleep.

Routine work occupied the men at the hut for some time after the return of the supporting-party. The scientific members were more than a little grieved to find that during the days when the hut had been untenanted, for Murray, Day and Roberts had been away too on a small expedition, some of the dogs had managed to get loose, and had killed thirty or forty penguins. We had from the first tried very hard to avoid any accidents of this sort, for we did not want to cause any unnecessary destruction of animal life. The penguins were now laying, and the men found that the eggs were very good to eat. The egg of the penguin is about the same size as that of a duck, and it has a transparent, jelly-like white and a small yolk. It takes about eight minutes' boiling to cook the egg nicely, and ten minutes if it is required set hard to the centre. The shell is the most beautiful dark-green inside, while the outer shell is chalky and white, though generally stained prettily by guano. Murray set aside a certain portion of the rookery for the supply of eggs for 'domestic purposes', partly in order to ensure freshness and partly in order to ascertain how many eggs the penguins would lay. The other portion of the rookery was left untouched in order that the development and education of the young penguins might be studied.

The scientific work in its various branches was carried on by the men at the winter quarters, and they made a series of small expeditions to points of interest in the surrounding country. 'Today we motored to Tent Island via Inaccessible Island,' wrote Priestley on November 14. 'The main object of the expedition was to enable Joyce to kill and skin some young seals, but we did geological work as well. Day, Joyce, Murray and myself were the party, and when the motor was pulled up opposite Inaccessible Island three of us strolled over to look at its western slopes. We did not have time to climb, but the island from that side consists entirely of a flow of massive basalt, with small porphyritic felspars, which show out best in the weathered specimens. The sheet of basalt appeared to be dipping to the south. Day endeavoured to join us, but he chose a bad place, and got so deep in the drift that his axle was aground, so he was obliged to reverse engines and back out. From there we proceeded to Tent Island, and after Joyce had picked out a young seal and started operations, Murray, Day and I climbed up a water-worn gully on the island and had a cursory look at the rocks, which are an agglomerate with very coarse fragments; capping the agglomerate there is a massive flow of kenyte . . . Day photographed the lower slopes of the gully while Murray and I climbed the rock-slopes till they ended, and then cut steps up a snow slope, at the top of which I came across a snow cornice and nearly got into trouble getting through it. On reaching the top we walked along the ridge, and photographed a splendid weathered kenyte boulder, hollowed out like a summer-house, and studded with felspars as an old-fashioned church door is studded with nails. After taking these photographs we climbed down the other side of the island, and walked round to join the others. The rock-climbing here, on any slopes at all steep, is very difficult because of the weathered fragments, which, owing to lack of powerful natural agents of transportation and to the fact that the wind carries all the lightest soil away, are left lying just at their angle of repose; a false step may send mountaineer and mountain surface hurtling down fifty or a hundred feet – no agreeable sensation, as I know from frequent experience. The sun was very hot today, and the gully was occupied by a little stream which was carrying quite a quantity of light soil down with it.'

Day had an exciting experience with the car during this journey. He encountered a big crack in the ice near Cape Barne, and steering at right angles to its course, put on speed in order to 'fly' it in the usual way. When only a few yards from it and travelling at a speed of about fifteen miles an hour, he found that the crack made a sudden turn, so as to follow the line he was taking, and an instant later his right-hand front wheel dropped in. Any weak points in the car would have been discovered by the sudden strain, but happily nothing broke, and the crack making another turn, the wheel bounded out at the elbow, and the car was on sound ice again.

On November 16 Priestley made an interesting trip up the slopes of Erebus. Beyond the lower moraines and separated from them by a snow-field of considerable size, he found a series of kenyte ridges and cones, covered by very little *débris*. The ridges continued for some distance to the edge of the main glacier, where they terminated in several well-marked nunataks. 'One which I visited, and which was the nearest to the large parasitic cone, was eighty feet high, of massive kenyte of brown colour and close texture, jointed into very large cubical joints by a very complete series of masterjoints. From this nunatak I obtained nine kinds of lichen, including four or five new species, and one piece of moss. One of the lichens was so much larger than the others and branched so much that it might well be called a forest-lichen, and Murray considers it to be very closely allied to the reindeer-moss, or ice-moss.'

Joyce was engaged at this time in making zoological collections, and with the aid of the motor-car he was able to cover a great deal of ground. The motor-car, driven by Day, would take him fifteen or sixteen miles over the sea-ice to some suitable locality, generally near the Cathedral Rocks on the north side of Glacier Tongue, and leave him there to kill seals and penguins. In order to kill young seals, some specimens of which were required, he had first to drive the mothers away, and this often took a long time, as the female seal becomes aggressive when interfered with in this manner. The work was not at all pleasant, but Joyce killed and prepared for preservation five young Weddell seals and four adult specimens. He had taken lessons in taxidermy before leaving England in order to be ready for this duty. Joyce and Day also killed and skinned twenty Emperor penguins, twelve Adelie penguins and twelve skua gulls, and all the men at the winter quarters assisted in collecting eggs.

Murray was looking after the scientific work, paying special attention to his own particular domain, that of biology, and Marston was devoting as much time as he could to sketching and painting. He had taken oils, water-colours and pastels to the south with him. He found that the water-colours could not be used in the open at all, for they froze at once. Oils could be used fairly comfortably in the summer, though it was always chilly work to sit still for any length of time; during the spring the oils froze after they had been in the open air for about an hour, so that steady work was not possible. The pastels could always be used for making 'colour notes'. Mits had to be worn for all outside work, and this made sketching difficult.

Marston found, as other artists have found, that Nature's colour-schemes in the Antarctic are remarkably crude, though often wondrously beautiful. Bright blues and greens are seen in violent contrast with brilliant reds, and an accurate record of the colours displayed in a sunset, as seen over broken ice, would suggest to many people an impressionistic poster of the kind seen in the London streets. Words fail one in an attempt to describe the wildly bizarre effects observed on days when the sky was fiery red and pale green, merging into a deep blue overhead, and the snow-fields and rocks showed violet, green and white under the light of the moon. Marston used to delight in, the 'grey days', when there was no direct sunlight and the snow all around showed the most subtle tones of grey; there would be no shadows anywhere, perhaps light drifts of snow would be blowing about, and the whole scene became like a frozen fairyland. The snow-bergs and snow-fields were white under direct light, but any hollows showed a vivid blue, deepening almost to black in the depths. There was an unlimited amount of interesting work for an artist, and Marston suffered to some extent, as did the other specialists on the expedition, from the fact that the number of men available was so small that every one, in addition to his own work, had to take a share in the routine duties.

Joyce devoted what spare time he could find to the completion of the volumes of the 'Aurora Australis'. Practice had made him more skilful in the handling of type, and he was able to make a good deal of progress, Day assisting with the preparation of the Venesta boards in which the volumes were to be bound. Some of the contributions towards the literary part of the work had come in late, so that there was plenty of work left to do. Marston went on with the lithographing for the illustrations.

Instructions had been left for a geological reconnaisance to be made towards the northern slopes of Mount Erebus, to examine, if possible, some parasitic cones and the oldest main crater of the mountain. Threatening weather prevented the carrying out of this plan for some time, yet for nearly a fortnight after the return of the southern supporting-party the expected blizzard did not come, while the weather was not propitious for the journey.

At length no further delay was possible if the trip was to be made, as Priestly, the geologist, had to leave for the western mountains, so on November 23 the trip was begun, though with misgivings as to the long overdue blizzard.

The party consisted of Priestley, Marston, Joyce, Murray and Brocklehurst, and they took seventy pounds of food – a week's supply on the ordinary basis of thirty-two ounces per day for each man – but carried only one tent, intended to hold three men, their idea being that one or two men could sleep in the bags outside the tent. The weather was fine when they left the hut, but in the afternoon a strong southerly wind sprang up, and they had to march through low drift. They camped for the night close to a steep nunatak about five miles from the hut and nearly two thousand feet above sea-level. There was difficulty in getting a good snowy camping-ground, and they had to put up the tent on smooth blue glacier ice, having a thin coating of snow, and sloping gently down till it terminated in an ice-cliff overlooking the sea not many hundreds of yards below. After dinner Priestley, Murray and Joyce climbed over the nunataks, and found several new lichens, but the specimens collected were lost in the blizzard later on. Priestley also found a number of very perfect felspar crystals weathered out of the kenyte, and collected a couple of handfuls of the best. The members of the party retired to their sleeping-bags at eight o'clock on Monday night, and before midnight a blizzard swept down upon them, and proved to be an exceptionally severe one, with dense drift. Priestley had volunteered to sleep outside that night, and had taken his sleeping-bag to a nook in the rocks some distance away. When the other men heard the roaring of the blizzard they looked out, and were reassured to find that he had come down while there was time and had lain down close by the tent. The first night the light snow round the tent was blown away leaving one side open to the wind, but the occupants were able to find a few bits of rock close by, and secured it with those.

'Inside the tent for the next three days we were warm enough in our sleeping-bags,' wrote Murray in his report. 'Though we could not cook anything we ate the dry biscuit and pemmican. The little snow under the floorcloth was squeezed in the hand till it became ice, and we sucked this for drink. We were anxious about Priestley, and occasionally opened the door-flap and hailed him, when he always replied that he was all right. Joyce had managed to pass him some food early in the storm, so there was no fear of starving, but as we learned afterwards he could get nothing to drink and so could not eat. No one could offer to change places with him, as in doing so the sleeping-bag would have filled with snow, and might have blown away. On Wednesday Marston dressed in his Burberries and crawled down to Priestley, who reported "All well," but he had had no food for twenty-four hours. Marston gave him some biscuits and chocolate. On Thursday morning he replied to the hail, but he was getting further and further from the tent, as every time he moved he slipped a little bit down the smooth glacier. At midday there was no reply to our hail, and we thought of the precipitious ice-foot and imagined things. Joyce and I dressed and went out to seek him. The drift was so thick that nothing whatever could be seen, and when the head was lifted to try and look the whole face and eyes were instantly covered by a sheet of ice. We crept about on hands and knees looking for the lost man. The only chance of getting back to the tent again was to steer by the wind, down the wind looking for Priestley, up the wind home again. At one side the sledge lay, forming a landmark, and Priestley had been not very far from the far-away end. Creeping along the sledge to where he had lain, I found that he was not there. Joyce went a little further to the right and came upon him, all alive.'

Priestley's experiences during this period are related in his diary. 'I had volunteered to sleep in the bag outside the tent,' he wrote, 'and by the time I was ready to turn in the drift had started again pretty badly, and the only sheltered spot I could find was at the top of the hill, so I told Joyce where he would find me in the morning and camped down, first luckily taking the precaution to put a few cubic feet of kenyte on my Burberry trousers and jacket outside the bag. A few hours later I woke up to find that the wind had increased to the dimensions of a blizzard, and that the drift was sweeping in a steady cloud over my head. I realised that those in the tent would have trouble in reaching me in the morning, so I got out of the bag and dressed, getting both the bag and my clothes full of snow in the process. Then, after some trouble, I got the bag down the steep slope of the nunatak to the sledge, where I wrapped myself up in the tent-cloth and lay athwart the wind. In about two hours I got drifted up so close that I was forced to get my shoulders out of the bag and lever myself out of the drift, and I then tried the experiment of lying head to wind on the opening of the sleeping-bag. This answered very well, and it was in this position that I spent the next seventy-two hours, getting shifted down a yard or two at a time at every change in the direction of the wind, and being gradually pushed along the wind-swept surface of the glacier until I was some twenty or thirty yards from the tent, and in some danger of getting swept, as the wind increased in violence, either on to some rocks a quarter of a mile below or else straight down the glacier and over a hundred-foot drop into Horseshoe Bay.

'Three times the people in the tent managed to pass me over some biscuits and raw pemmican, and Marston got my chocolate from the rucksack and brought it to me. My chief difficulty, however, was want of water. I had had a little tea before I turned in, but from that time for nearly eighty hours I had nothing to drink but some fragments of ice that I could prise up with the point of a small safety-pin. The second time Joyce came down, I believe about the beginning of the third day, he reported that the lashings at the top of the tent-poles had given way and that a rent had been torn in the material by the corner of a biscuit-tin. He added that it was impossible to keep any snow on the skirt of the tent, and that, as the snowcloth was kept down only by a few rocks, the occupants of the tent were in constant expectation of seeing the tent leave them altogether. When Joyce left me on this occasion the drift was so thick that he could see nothing, and had to find his way back by shouting and listening for the return shouts of his tent-mates. He had gone only a quarter of the distance when both his eyes were filled with drift and immediately choked with ice, and when he reached the tent his face was a mask of ice and both feet were frost-bitten. He was helped inside and his feet brought round with rubbing, but no further attempt could be made to reach me. He had brought me some biscuit and raw pemmican. Cooking was not possible in the tent owing to the impossibility of reaching the sledge to get the oil-filler. It may sound like an exaggeration to say that we could not reach the sledge, which was four yards or less from the tent, but it must be remembered that we were lying on the slopes of a clean-swept glacier, on which finnesko could get no hold. The snow that had covered the ice when we pitched camp had all disappeared before the fury of the blizzard. Our spiked ski-boots were on the iceaxes round the sledge, where they had been hung to dry, but in any case it would have been impossible to wear them in a blizzard when feet were getting badly frost-bitten even in finnesko. A slip on the ice meant very serious danger of destruction.

'A slight decrease in the wind at the close of the third day gave me hope of getting up to the tent, and I prepared to move by putting on my outdoor clothing, no easy task in a sleeping-bag; then, rolling over on my side, I tried to get out. I found that there was less wind and less drift, and that I was able for the first time to see where I was with regard to surrounding objects. I was unable, however, to get out of the bag without being blown further down the slippery glacier, and I could see that it would be impossible to crawl up the slopes with the cumbrous bag. If I lost the bag I might as well have let myself slide.'

About two hours after this Marston ventured forth from the tent in one of the remarkable intervals of calm occasionally experienced in the course of an Antarctic blizzard. On either side of the spot on which the camp had been pitched he could see the drift flying along with the full force of the wind, but he was able to make his way down to Priestley before the blizzard swept down on them again. They dragged the bag up the glacier by kneeling on it and jerking it along, and both got into the tent. 'Four men in a threemen tent is a big squeeze,' continued Priestley, 'but five was fearful, and it was some time before I managed to get even sitting room. The first thing to do was to examine and attend frost-bitten feet, and the examination showed as big a crop as could be expected, for Marston and I each had both feet frost-

THE WINTER QUARTERS OF THE DISCOVERY EXPEDITION AT HUT POINT,
AFTER BEING DESERTED FOR SIX YEARS

THE SUPPORTING PARTY AT GLACIER TONGUE

THE CAMP AT HUT POINT

THE START FROM THE ICE-EDGE SOUTH OF HUT POINT

THE SOUTHERN PARTY MARCHING INTO THE WHITE UNKNOWN

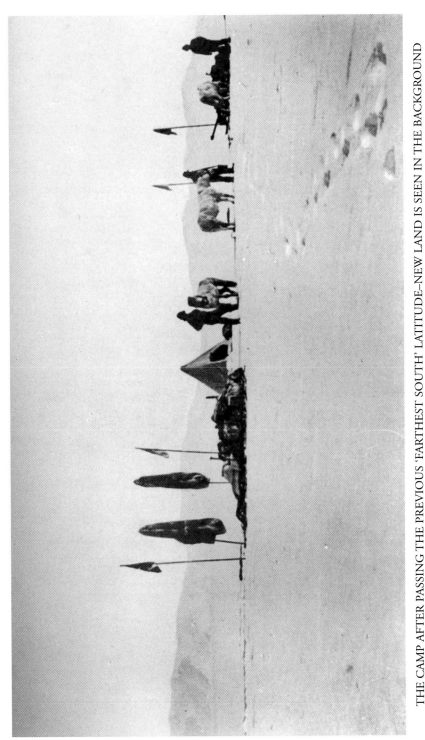

THE CAMP AFTER PASSING THE PREVIOUS 'FARTHEST SOUTH' LATITUDE–NEW LAND IS SEEN IN THE BACKGROUND

MOUNT HOPE   THE GAP

NEW LAND. THE PARTY ASCENDED MOUNT HOPE AND SIGHTED THE GREAT GLAC
THE BARRIER

HICH THEY MARCHED THROUGH THE GAP. THE MAIN BODY OF THE GLACIER JOINS
TO THE LEFT.

THE VIEW FROM THE SUMMIT OF MOUNT HOPE, LOOKING SOUTH. DEPOT D, ON
THE MOUNTAIN CALLED "THE CLOUDM

...ACIER DEPOT, WAS UNDER THE ROCK, CASTING A LONG SHADOW TO THE RIGHT. ...EN IN THE CENTRE OF THE HORIZON.

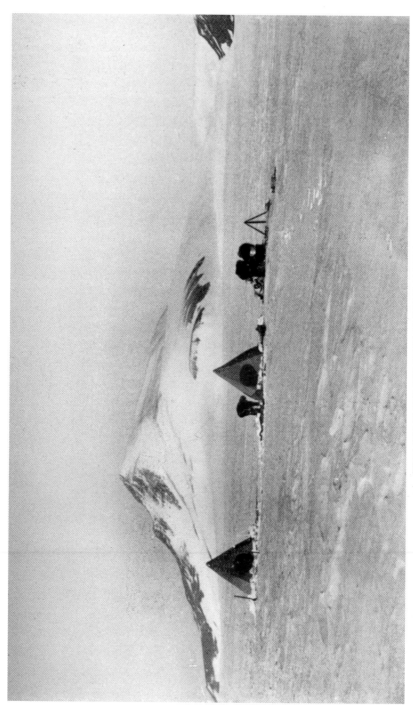

THE CAMP BELOW 'THE CLOUDMAKER'

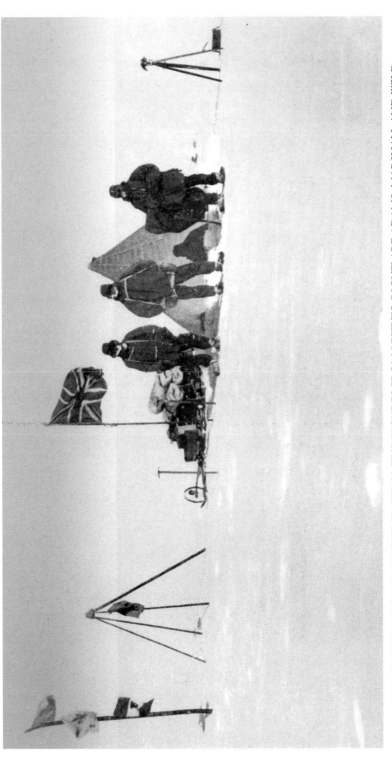

THE CHRISTMAS CAMP ON THE PLATEAU. THE FIGURES FROM LEFT TO RIGHT ARE ADAMS, MARSHALL AND WILD. THE FROST CAN BE SEEN ON THE MEN'S FACES.

4th Jan.

The end is in sight. We can only go
for 3 more days at the most for
we are weakening rapidly. Short
food and a blizzard wind from
the South with driving drift has
at a temp. 47° ... ...
Hardly told us today that we are
reaching our limit for we
were so done up at noon with
cold that the chemical thermometer
refused to register our temp.
[3] was at 94°. We started at
[...] leaving a depot on the
great inland plateau a risk
that only this case justified
and one that my companions
agreed to as they have always
done with the same cheerfulness
and regardless of self.
this has been the means of
our getting as far as we have
done so far, Pathetically

FACSIMILE OF PAGE OF SHACKLETON'S DIARY

FARTHEST SOUTH

THE CAMP UNDER THE GRANITE PILLAR, HALF A MILE FROM THE LOWER
GLACIER DEPOT, WHERE THE PARTY CAMPED ON JANUARY 27

LOWER GLACIER DEPOT. THE STORES WERE BURIED IN THE SNOW NEAR THE ROCK IN THE FOREGROUND.

SHACKLETON AND WILD WAITING AT HUT POINT TO BE PICKED
UP BY THE SHIP

THE START OF THE RELIEF PARTY, WHICH BROUGHT IN ADAMS
AND MARSHALL

bitten. A course of massage brought them round, and I got into Marston's bag while he made tea . . . After tea I got into my own bag and lay down on top of Murray and Marston, and by dint of much wriggling we managed to get fairly settled, though our positions were so cramped that sleep was impossible.

'At about half-past four in the morning we cooked some pemmican in the tent and had a proper breakfast. as for the first time the wind had really begun to die away. Owing to the cold, the long period of semistarvation in our cramped quarters, and the fact that oil had got mixed up with the food, we were unable to do justice either to the hoosh or to the cocoa which followed it, and were still fairly empty when the drift ceased and we turned out to face the blizzard, pack the sledge and start for home. The ascent of the mountain had, of course, to be abandoned. I put on my damp finnesko and went out to help, but in less than five minutes, though the temperature was plus 22° Fahr., I was back in the tent with the front portions of both feet frozen, and we took half an hour to bring them round by beating, massaging and rubbing with snow. This latter remedy, Marston's favourite, is a very drastic one, and as painful as any I know, for the Antarctic snow is invariably in small sharp crystals, very brittle and hard. We all chafed very much at the unavoidable delay, as there was every sign of a renewal of the blizzard and the drift, but fortunately we got under way before any drift rose, and the wind was rather in our favour. We left all the provisions there, and unanimously named the nunatak "Misery Nunatak," and we were about as glad to leave the place as a soul would be to leave purgatory. We also left a tin of biscuits and some oil with a view to a future attempt at an ascent, to be made by Murray, Day, Marston and Joyce.

'There was a remarkable contrast between the wind-swept surface of the glacier and the surface over which we had toilsomely dragged the sledges during our day's journey outward. Instead of a uniform carpet, six inches deep, of soft snow, varied with drifts up to one's knees, we found patches of glacier ice, larger stretches of névé, and hard drifts of snow, on which neither our weight nor the weight of the sledge made the slightest impression; these drifts were deeply undercut on the south-east side, and were frequently a foot to eighteen inches in height. It was no easy matter to direct the sledge across the strong wind then blowing, although we had two men pulling and two others guiding the sledge, and we ascended about half a mile to the north of Horseshoe Bay in what was, for a long time, totally unfamiliar country, and through a series of moraines which had not yet been explored. I was, unfortunately, of no use in the pulling, being only just able to get along myself, and we were all extremely glad to get the sledge to the Back Door Bay end of Blue Lake, where it was left till the next day. We reached the hut and started on a course of feeding and recuperating, having been five days out.'

Mount Erebus was noticed to be in eruption when the party was marching back to the hut on November 27. Huge diverging columns of steam were rising from the crater, and behind could be seen curious clouds of feathery cirrus. The temperature during the blizzard had not fallen below 12° Fahr., and been above 20° Fahr. during most of the time, so that the frost-bites sustained by the men must have been due mainly to lowered vitality, caused by the cramped situation and the lack of hot food.

The experience had been rather a severe one, but the men were none the worse for it after a day or two at the winter quarters, and they commenced at once to make preparations for the western journey. I had left instructions that on December 1 Armytage, Priestley and Brocklehurst should start for Butter Point with 600 lb. of stores in order to lay a depot for the Northern Party which might be expected to reach that point on its journey back from the Magnetic Pole. Then the three men were to secure what stores they required for their own purposes, and proceed up the Ferrar Glacier as far as the Depot Nunatak in order that Priestley might search for fossils in the sandstones of the western mountains. They were to get back to Butter Point early in January in order to meet Professor David, Mawson and Mackay, and if a junction was effected, Mawson, Priestley and Brocklehurst were to carry on geological work in Dry Valley and the surrounding country, while Professor David, Armytage and Mackay were to return to the winter quarters. The fact that the Northern Party did not arrive upset this arrangement to some extent, but the other three men did some very useful work. The mountains to the west of McMurdo Sound had been explored by Lieutenant Armytage and Captain Scott during the *Discovery* expedition, Armitage having climbed the mountains and penetrated west to an altitude of 9000 ft. on the ice-cap, while Scott had reached longitude 146° 33′ East, on the western plateaux. Further information was required, however, in regard to the geology of the mountains.

Armytage, Priestley and Brocklehurst accordingly left the winter quarters on December 1, taking with them about 1200 lb. of gear and stores. The motor-car carried them for the first sixteen miles, although the sea ice was by this time in a very bad condition. The season was well advanced, the sun was above the horizon all the time, and there were cracks and pools in all directions. Day and Marston took the car out, and when they were coming back after leaving the Western Party the car got stuck firmly in a crack that ran across the course. They spent two hours cutting away the ice sufficiently to get the car out, and then had to make a *détour* of five miles in order to get round the crack. This was the last journey of the car in the Antarctic, for it was laid up when it got back to the hut.

The Western Party, after some heavy sledging, camped on December 4 at the foot of the Ferrar Glacier. Armytage was, at this time, suffering from an attack of snow-blindness. Priestley found moss and a species of fungus at the stranded moraines and also some kenyte. The men had been looking forward with pleasurable anticipation to securing skuas' eggs, which would have been a welcome change from pemmican and biscuit, but the birds had apparently not begun to lay and no eggs were secured. 'A good deal of water denudation and transportation is taking place along the sea-cliffs of these moraines,' wrote Priestley in his diary. 'Quite a thick alluvial deposit, bearing a strong resemblance to a series of miniature deltas, is to be seen along the icefoot awaiting the breaking up of the ice and its removal to the sea. The dust from the moraines had made a remarkable surface for two miles this side of them. Some winds had evidently been strong enough to remove a considerable quantity of the gravel with the snow, and the drifts which had contained this gravel had melted away, undercutting the edges of the cleaner snowdrifts, and thus giving a surface of bare ice with patchy snowdrifts undercut on all sides.'

The party reached Butter Point, about thirty-five miles as the crow flies from the winter quarters, on December 5, and found a small depot left there by the Northern Party on its way to the Magnetic Pole. Professor David and his companions had placed some final letters in a milk-tin. The stores brought for the purpose were placed at the depot, and then Armytage, Priestley and Brocklehurst proceeded back to the winter quarters, arriving there on December 7 at 11.30 p.m. On December 9 they started for Butter Point again, taking five weeks' provisions for three men, in order to proceed up the Ferrar Glacier, and later to try to effect a junction with the Northern Party.

Only five men – Murray, Joyce, Day, Marston and Roberts – were now at the winter quarters. The heat of the Antarctic summer being at its height, the snowdrifts were melting rapidly, and the trickling of running water was everywhere to be heard. A large drift remained on the hill behind the hut, leading up to Mawson's anemometer. On December 1 it was melting in several little trickles, and next day it was found that one of these had got under the hut and made a pool about a foot in depth at the lower end. Many valuable things were stored under the hut, and the only opening was occupied by the pool of water. A hole had to be made at one side of the house, where the ground was higher, and into this Joyce crawled and spent some hours wriggling about in a space hardly more than one foot in height, rescuing valuable boxes of printing material and printed matter.

In the succeeding days the men at the hut had an illustration of the contrasts which the Antarctic climate presents. The heat of the sun melted the snow, and indeed made the weather oppressively warm, yet the water which ran below the house where the sunshine could not penetrate and the air temperature never rose above 32° Fahr., froze at night and never thawed again, so that the water each day added a layer to the accumulation beneath the hut till it reached nearly up to the floor.

After the final departure of the Western Party on December 9, life at the winter quarters was uneventful until the arrival of the *Nimrod*. The members of the expedition remaining at Cape Royds were busy collecting skua eggs, preparing skins, carrying on the routine scientific observations, and watching the doings of the Adelie penguins. Many photographs were taken, especially by Day, of penguins in every variety of attitude, and of other subjects of interest. Experiments were made in photographing microscopic animals, and many pictures of them from life were obtained.

28

RETURN OF THE *NIMROD*

After leaving us on February 22, the *Nimrod* had an uneventful voyage back to New Zealand. Fair winds were encountered all the way, and the ice gave no difficulty, the coast of New Zealand being sighted twelve days after the departure from Cape Royds. During the winter the *Nimrod* had been laid up in Port Lyttelton waiting till the time arrived to bring us back to civilisation. The little ship had been docked and thoroughly overhauled, so that all effects of the severe treatment she received during the first voyage down to the ice had been removed, and she was once more ready to battle with the floes. Towards the end of the year stores were taken on board, for there was a possibility that a party might have to spend a second winter at Cape Royds, if the men comprising one of the sledging expeditions had not returned, and, of course, there was always the possibility of the *Nimrod* herself being caught in the ice and frozen in for the winter. Sufficient stores were taken on board to provide for any such eventualities, and as much coal as could be stowed away was also carried. Captain P. F. Evans, who had commanded the *Koonya* at the time she towed the *Nimrod* down to the Antarctic Circle, was appointed master of the *Nimrod* under my power of attorney, Captain England having resigned on account of ill-health after reaching New Zealand earlier in the year.

The *Nimrod* left Lyttelton on December 1, 1908, and encountered fine weather for the voyage southwards. On the evening of the 3rd, the wind being favourable, the propeller was disconnected, and the vessel proceeded under sail alone until the 20th, when she was in latitude 66° 30′ South, longitude 178° 28′ West. The 'blink' of ice was seen ahead and the ship was hove to until steam had been raised and the propeller connected. Then Captain Evans set sail again, and proceeded towards the pack. The vessel was soon in brash ice, and after pushing through this for a couple of hours reached the pack, and made her way slowly through the lanes. Numerous seals were basking on the floes, regarding the ship with their usual air of mild astonishment. On the following day the pack was more congested, and the progress southward was slow, so much so that the crew found time to kill and skin several crabeater seals. Open water was reached again that evening, and at noon on the 22nd the *Nimrod* was in latitude 68° 20′ South, longitude 175° 23′ East, and proceeding under sail through the open water of Ross Sea. The belt of pack-ice had been about sixty miles wide.

On December 26 the *Nimrod* reached latitude 70° 42′ South, longitude 173° 4′ West, the position in which, in 1843, Sir James Ross sighted 'compact, hummocky ice', but found only drift ice, with plenty of open water. A sounding gave no bottom with 1575 fathoms of wire, so that the theory that the ice seen by Ross was resting on land was completely disproved. At noon on the 27th the *Nimrod,* which was proceeding in a south-east direction, was brought up by thick floes in latitude 72° 8′ South, longitude 173° 1′ West. Progress became possible again later in the day, and at four o'clock on the following morning the *Nimrod* was in open water, with the blink of pack to the eastward.

Captain Evans had kept east with the hope of sighting King Edward VII Land, but the pack seemed to be continuous in that direction, and on the 30th he therefore shaped a course for Cape Bird, and on January 1, 1909, Mount Erebus was sighted. The experience of Captain Evans on this voyage confirms my own impression that, under normal conditions, the pack that stretches out from the Barrier to the eastward of the Ross Sea is not penetrable, and that the *Discovery* was able to push to within sight of King Edward VII Land in 1902 for the reason that the ice was unusually open that season.

The progress of the *Nimrod* towards the winter quarters was blocked by ice off Beaufort Island, and after manoeuvring about for three hours Captain Evans made the vessel fast to a floe with ice anchors. The next morning he cast off from the floe, and with the help of the current, which seems to set constantly to the west between Cape Bird and Beaufort Island, and by taking advantage of lanes of open water, gradually proceeded in two days to a point only twenty-eight miles from Cape Royds. Some heavy bumps against the floes tested the strength of the vessel, and finally what appeared to be fast ice was encountered, so that no further progress towards the south was possible for the time.

There seemed to be no immediate possibility of the *Nimrod* reaching Cape Royds, and Captain Evans therefore decided to send Mackintosh with three men to convey a mail-bag and the news of the ship's arrival to the winter quarters. The party was to travel over the sea ice with a sledge, and it did not seem that there would be any great difficulties to be encountered. A start was made at 10.15 a.m. on January 3, the party consisting of Mackintosh, McGillan, Riches and Paton, with one sledge, a tent, sleeping-bags, cooking equipment and a supply of provisions. The distance to be covered was about twenty-five miles. In the afternoon Mackintosh sent Riches and Paton back to the ship, and he reduced the load on the sledge by leaving fifty pounds of provisions in a depot. The travelling became very rough, the two men encountering both bad ice and soft snow. They camped at 7.50 p.m., and started for Cape Royds again at 1.55 a.m. on the following day. They soon got on to a better surface, and made good progress until 5.30 a.m., when they met with open water, with pressure ice floating past. This blocked the way. They walked for two hours in a westerly direction to see how far the open water extended, but did not reach the end of it. The whole of the ice to the southward seemed to be moving, and the stream at the spot at which they were then standing was travelling at the rate of about three miles an hour. They breakfasted at 7.30 a.m., and then started back for the ship, as there seemed to be no chance of reaching Cape Royds in consequence of the open water.

Presently Mackintosh found that there was open water ahead, blocking the way to the ship, and a survey of the position from a hummock revealed the unpleasant fact that the floe-ice was breaking up altogether, and that they were in most serious danger of drifting out into the sound. Safety lay in a hurried dash for the shore to the east, and they proceeded to drag their sledge across rough ice and deep snow with all possible speed. At places they had to lift the sledge bodily over the ice-faces, and when, after an hour's very heavy work, they arrived off the first point of land, they found an open lane of water barring their way. 'We dragged on to the next point, which appeared to be safe,' wrote Mackintosh in his diary. 'The floes were small and square in shape. Every two hundred yards we had to drag our sledge to the edge of a floe, jump over a lane of water, and then with a big effort pull the sledge after us. After an hour of this kind of work our hands were cut and bleeding, and our clothes, which, of course, froze as stiff as boards, had been wet through to the waist, for we had frequently slipped and fallen when crossing from floe to floe. At 2.30 p.m. we were near to the land, and came to a piece of glacier ice that formed a bridge. The floe that we were on was moving rapidly, so we had to make a great effort and drag our sledge over a six-foot breach. Our luck was in, and we pulled our sledge a little way up the face of the fast ice, and unpacked it. We were in a safe position again, and none too soon, for fifteen minutes later there was open water where we had gained the land.'

Mackintosh decided to go into camp near the spot where they had landed, as a journey across the rocks and the glaciers of the coast was not a thing to be undertaken lightly, and would probably be impossible unless the mailbag was left behind. McGillan, moreover, had developed snow-blindness, and both men were very tired. I will quote from Mackintosh's report on the subsequent experience of this little party.

'Early the next morning I found McGillan in great pain,' wrote Mackintosh. 'His eyes were closed up completely, and his face was terribly swollen. The only remedy I could apply was to bathe them, and this seemed to give him some relief. From an elevated position I had a good look round for the ship, and could not see a trace of her. As the day wore on my own eyes became painful. I fervently hoped I was not going to be as bad as my companion, for we would then be in a very difficult position. The morning of January 6 found us both blind. McGillan's face was frightfully swollen, and his eyes completely and tightly shut, so that he did not know that I was attacked too. At first I refrained from telling him, but the pain was very severe, and I had to tell him. By the painful process of forcing my eyelids apart with my fingers I could see a little, but I was not able to do this for long. I continued to bathe McGillan's eyes, and then suffered six hours' agony, ending in a good long sleep, from which I awoke refreshed and much better. I was able to see without effort. McGillan was also much better, and our relief, after the anxiety we had felt, was very great. By midnight we had improved so much that we walked to the penguin rookery, where we had great fun with the birds and found several eggs.'

The men stayed in camp for several days, seeing no sign of the ship, and after their eyes were better spent a good deal of time studying the neighbourhood and especially the bird-life. They cut down their food to two meals a day, as their supply of food was not large. Finally, Mackintosh decided that he would leave the mail-bag in the tent, it being too heavy to carry for any distance, and march into Cape Royds. They made a start on the morning of January 11, carrying forty pounds each, including food for three meals, and expected to be able to reach the winter quarters within twenty-four hours. The first portion of the journey lay over hills of basaltic rock, at the base of Mount Bird, and they thought it best to get as high as possible in order to avoid the valleys and glaciers. They went up about five thousand feet, and had fairly easy travelling over slopes until they got well on to the glaciers. Then their troubles commenced. They were wearing ski-boots without spikes, and had many heavy falls on the slippery ice. 'We were walking along, each picking his own tracks, and were about fifty yards apart, foolishly not roped, when I happened to look round to speak to my companion, and found that he had disappeared,' wrote Mackintosh. 'Suddenly I heard my name called faintly from the bowels of the glacier, and immediately rushed towards the place from which the sound proceeded. I found McGillan in a yawning chasm, many feet beneath me, and held up on a projection of ice. I took off my straps from my pack and to them tied my waist lashing, and lowered this extemporised rope down to him. It just reached his hand, and with much pulling on my part and kneeclimbing on his, he got safely to the surface of the glacier again. The Primus stove and our supply of food had gone further down the crevasse. We tried to hook them up, and in doing so I lost my straps and line which I had attached to a ski-stick, so we were left almost without equipment. As soon as McGillan had recovered from the shock he had received we started off again, with the spare strap tying the two of us together. We crossed over many snow-bridges that covered the dangers underneath, but soon we were in a perfect hot-bed of crevasses. They were impassable and lay right across our path, so that we could look down into awful depths. We turned and climbed higher in order to get a clear passage round the top. We were roped together and I was in the lead, with McGillan behind, so that when I fell, as I often did, up to my waist in a crevasse, he could pull me out again. We found a better surface higher up, but when we began to descend we again got into crevassed regions. At first the crevasses were ice-covered gaps, but later we came to huge open ones, whose yawning depths made us shudder. It was not possible to cross them. We started to ascend again, and soon came to a bridge of ice across a huge crevasse about twenty feet wide. We lashed up tighter, and I went off in the lead, straddlelegged across the narrow bridge. We both reached the other side in safety, but one slip, or the breaking of the bridge would have precipitated us into those black depths below.'

The two men found their way blocked by crevasses in whichever direction they turned, and at last reached a point from which ascent was out of the question, while below lay a steep slope running down for about three thousand feet. They could not tell what lay at the bottom of the slope, but their case was desperate, and they decided to glissade down. Their knives, which they attempted to use as brakes, were torn from their grasp, but they managed to keep their heels in the snow, and although they passed crevasses, none lay directly in their path. They reached the bottom in safety at 4 p.m. on the 11th. They were very hungry and had practically no food, but they could get forward now, and at 6 p.m. they could see Cape Royds and were travelling over a smooth surface. They ate a few biscuit crumbs and half a tin of condensed milk, the only other food they had being a little chocolate. Soon snow commenced to fall, and the weather became thick, obscuring their view of the Cape. They could not see two yards ahead, and for two hours they stumbled along in blinding snow. They rested for a few minutes, but their clothes were covered with ice, icicles hung from their faces, and the temperature was very low. In a temporary clearing of the blizzard Mackintosh thought that he could make out the Cape and they dashed off, but at lunch-time on the 12th they were still wandering over the rocks and snow, heavy snow cutting off all view of the surrounding country. Soon after this the snow ceased to fall, though the drift-snow, borne along by the blizzard wind, still made the weather thick. Several times they thought that they saw Cape Royds, but found that they had been mistaken. As a matter of fact they were quite close to the winter quarters when, at about 7 p.m., they were found by Day. They were in a state of complete exhaustion, and were just managing to stagger along because they knew that to stop meant death.

Within a few minutes they were in the hut, where warm food, dry clothes and a good rest soon restored them. They had a narrow escape from death, and would probably have never reached the hut had not Day happened to be outside watching for the return of the ship.

Mackintosh and McGillan reached the hut on January 12, but in the meantime the *Nimrod* had arrived at Cape Royds and had gone north again in search of the missing men. Murray had sailed in the *Nimrod,* and as events turned out, he was not able to get back to the hut for about ten days. 'We were having tea on the afternoon of January 5, and Marston happening to open the door, there was the *Nimrod* already moored to the edge of the fast ice, not more than a mile away,' wrote Murray in a report on the summer work. 'We ran towards the ship, over the rotten sea ice, in boots or slippers as chanced, with the one idea that is uppermost in these circumstances – to get "letters from home". We were doomed to disappointment. Before we had finished greeting our old friends, the officers asked us, "Has Mackintosh arrived?" and we learned to our horror that he and a companion had left the ship two days before and thirty miles north of Cape Royds, to try to bring the letters sooner to us over the sea ice, over the bay where only a few days ago we saw a broad sheet of open water to the horizon, and which was even now only filled with loose pack! So we got no home letters, and had good reason to believe that our friends had lost their lives in the endeavour to bring them. We knew that they must have embarked on a large floe, and little expected to see them again. On January 7 the *Nimrod* left Cape Royds to seek for the lost men, on the chance that they might have got ashore near Cape Bird. Within a few hours she was caught by the pack which was drifting rapidly southward along the shore of Ross Island. Driven almost on shore near Horseshoe Bay, the ship, by dint of hard steaming, got a little way off the land, and was there beset by the ice and so remained from the 7th to the 15th, with only a few hours' ineffectual steaming during the first day or two. At length she was rigidly jammed and was carried helplessly by a great eddy of the pack away towards the western side of the sound, and gradually northward.

On January 12 she was as tight as though frozen in for the winter. In the afternoon sudden pressure affected all the ice from the *Nimrod* as far as we could see. Great blocks of ice, six or eight feet in thickness, were tossed and piled on the surface of the floes. These pressure heaps were formed on each side of the ship's bow, but she took no harm, and in about an hour the pressure ceased. On the morning of January 15 there was not the slightest sign of slacking of the pack, but in the early afternoon Harbord, from the crow's-nest, saw lanes of water at no great distance to the east. Steam was got up and in a few hours we had left our prison and got into a broad lane, with only thin ice which the ship could charge, and the open water was in sight. Shortly after midnight we got clear of the ice. When released we were not very far from the Nordenskjold Ice-Barrier.

The deceptive appearance of loose pack was impressed upon us. For many hours there was blue water apparently only a mile or two ahead, but it never appeared to get any nearer for hours, and we could not be sure it was really near till we were within a few hundred yards of the edge. All this time in the pack we were in doubt as to the fate of Mackintosh, or rather, we had not much doubt about it, for we had given him up for lost, but we were helpless to do anything. On the afternoon of the 16th, on which day we cleared the ice, we had passed Beauford Island and were approaching through very loose pack the only piece of shore on which there was any chance of finding the lost men. Near the end of this stretch of beach, where it is succeeded by hopeless cliffs, a small patch of greenish colour was seen, and the telescope showed the details of a deserted camp, a tent torn to ribbons and all the camp gear lying around. A boat was sent ashore in charge of Davis, who found the bag of letters, and a note from Mackintosh pinned to the tent, telling of his risky attempt to cross the mountains nearly a week before. Knowing the frightfully crevassed character of the valley between Mount Bird and Mount Erebus, there seemed to us little hope that they would get through. The crevassed slope extends right to the top of Mount Bird, and is very steep towards the Erebus side. When we reached Cape Royds about midnight, only two men came out to meet the ship. One of the men was Mackintosh's comrade in all his adventures, and we soon learned that all had ended well.

In the meantime the Bluff Depot party had started off to place a supply of provisions off Minna Bluff in readiness for the return of the Southern Party. The crew of the *Nimrod* proceeded to take on board the geological and zoological specimens collected by the expedition and stored at the hut, so that all might be in readiness for the final departure when the parties had been picked up. Then followed weeks of uncertainty as to the fate of the men who were away.

29

THE BLUFF DEPOT JOURNEY

I had left instructions at the winter quarters that a party should proceed to Minna Bluff at the beginning of the new year, and place at a point opposite the Bluff a depot of stores for the use of the Southern Party on its return journey. Joyce was to take charge of this work, and it was of very considerable importance, since we four of the Southern Party would be depending on the depot to supply us with the provisions necessary for the last hundred miles or so of the journey back to the winter quarters. Joyce was accompanied by Mackintosh, Day and Marston, and he found that as the snow surface was very soft it would be necessary to make two journeys to the Bluff, one with ordinary sledging provisions, and the other with special luxuries from the ship. The party left the winter quarters at Cape Royds on January 15, with one sledge and 500 lb. of provisions, drawn by eight dogs. Early in the afternoon they encountered soft ice, sticky with salt, and the travelling became very heavy. They kept well away from the land, but Joyce, Mackintosh and Marston all fell through at different times, the soft surface giving away under them, and they got wet up to their waists. Their clothing froze stiff at once. They camped for the night at Glacier Tongue, and the next morning found the weather so bad that they were unable to march. There was a strong southerly wind, with drift, and this soon turned into a howling blizzard. A calm succeeded at midnight, and on the morning of the 18th they got under way again. The dogs had been buried under the drift by the blizzard, only their noses showing at the surface, and it was necessary to dig them out before they could be harnessed up. A seven-foot sledge was loaded with 300 lb. of store from the depot at the Tongue, and the four men took on the two sledges, with a total weight of 800 lb. They had a heavy day's work, over soft ice and snow-drift, but reached the old *Discovery* winter quarters at Hut Point at midnight. The dogs pulled very well, and seemed to be enjoying their work after the long spell of semi-idleness at Cape Royds.

On the morning of the 19th the party proceeded on to the Barrier. The surface was fairly good, and the dogs ran practically all the time, Joyce finding it necessary to put two men on the sledge in order to reduce the speed, for the men would not travel at the pace set by the dogs. The weight per dog was well over 100 lb., though only one sledge had been taken on from Hut Point. The temperature was low during the days that followed, and the men's beards were constantly coated with ice, but their progress was rapid. On January 23, when they were travelling over a deep snow surface covering sastrugi, they sighted a depot about three miles to the west of their course. This was the depot at which some pony fodder had been left in the spring. Soon after this the party came upon crevasses running at right angles to their course, and the travelling became difficult. Joyce had the members of the party roped together, as the crevasses were hidden by treacherous snow lids and were therefore dangerous. The crevasses became worse in the following two days. Some of the pressure ridges were over thirty feet in height, running in an east-south-east and west-north-west direction, with enormous crevasses between them, and they all had the experience of falling through, to be hauled out again by means of the rope, after they had dropped to the length of their harness with a heavy jerk. On one occasion the four centre dogs fell through a snowlid into a crevasse, and were got out with great difficulty. Day and Joyce, with two leaders, were on one side of the crevasse, and Mackintosh and Marston, with the two rear dogs, were on the other side. Day and Joyce had to unharness and ease the dogs, while the other two men pulled them back to the sledge. The dogs meanwhile were hanging over the abyss, and evidently did not like their position. Joyce had to keep altering his course in order to avoid these crevasses, but after steering in a south-west direction for about six hours he reached a better surface. The crevasses were getting smaller, although the surface of névé caused many falls. An attempt to steer south, straight for the spot at which the depot was to be laid, resulted in the party getting into the badly crevassed area again, and once more Joyce had to steer east-south-east. Finally they got clear of the crevasses, and at midnight on January 25, reached the spot at which it had been decided to place the depot, about fourteen miles off Minna Bluff.

An early start was made on the 26th, and for seven hours the party laboured erecting a mound of snow ten feet high. On top of the mound they put two eleven-foot bamboos, lashed together and carrying three black flags. The total height of the depot was twenty-two feet, and it could be seen at a distance of eight miles. The bearing of this depot I had arranged with Joyce during the spring depot journey, before my departure for the southern journey. It was on a line drawn through a sharp peak on the Bluff well-known to Joyce, and the top of Mount Discovery, with a cross bearing secured by getting the centre peak of White Island in line with a peak of Mount Erebus.

The party started north again on the morning of the 27th, and after they had travelled a short distance Day sighted a pole projecting from the snow, some distance to the west of their course. Joyce was able to identify this as the depot laid out for the *Discovery's* Southern Party in the spring of 1902. There was a bamboo pole about eight feet high projecting from the snow, with a tattered flag attached to it, and a food tin on top. The guys to which the pole was attached were completely buried under the snow. The men dug down for about five feet with the idea of ascertaining how deeply the depot had been covered by snow, but as the bottom had not been reached and time was limited, they put fresh flags on the pole and proceeded on their way, intending to visit the depot on the second journey. A fresh southerly wind was blowing, and rapid progress was made to the north towards Cape Crozier. A sail was hoisted on the sledge, and this assisted the dogs so much that three men were able to sit on the sledge, while a pace of about four miles an hour was maintained. Soon the area of crevasses, caused by the impinging of the Barrier ice on the land to the west, was reached again, and for thirty-seven miles the party twisted and turned in making a course past the obstacles; Joyce counted the crevasses that were passed, and he reported that he had seen one hundred and twenty-seven, ranging from two feet to thirty feet in width. The larger ones were open, and therefore easily detected, but the smaller ones had the usual snow-lids. On the 30th the men were held up by another blizzard, which completely buried the dogs and sledge, but they reached Hut Point at 11 p.m. on January 31.

A second load of stores was secured from the depot, including some luxuries, such as apples and fresh mutton, brought by a party from the ship, and on February 2 the party started south again. Joyce decided to take a new course in order to avoid the crevasses. He kept a course towards Cape Crozier for two days, and then marched south on the 5th and reached the depot without having seen any crevasses at all. I think that the crevasses run right across to Cape Crozier from the district around White Island, but they are evidently more snow covered along the outer course. When the party was close to the depot a blizzard came up from the south, and there was just time to get the tents up before the drift became thick. The tents were completely snowed up before the weather cleared, and the men had some difficulty in getting out again. The dogs were covered, but they seemed to be quite happy in their 'nests' deep in the drift. When dogs and sledge had been dug out the party started again, and at 2 a.m. on the 8th they reached the Bluff depot for the second time.

'We expected to find the Southern Party camped there, and to surprise them with the luxuries we had brought out for them,' wrote Joyce in his report, 'but they were not there. As our orders were to return on the 10th if the Southern Party did not turn up, we began to feel rather uneasy. It came on to blow again from the south, and presently the wind turned into a howling blizzard, and did not ease down until the 11th. During every lull we climbed the depot and looked round the horizon with the glasses, expecting every minute to see the Southern Party loom up out of the whiteness, but they did not appear. On the 11th after a consultation, we decided to lay depot flags in towards the Bluff, so that there would be no chance of the other party missing the food depot. We knew that they would be run out of provisions, as they were then eleven days overdue, and the position caused us great anxiety. After we had laid the flags, three miles and a half apart, with directions where to find the depot, we decided to march due south to look for the Southern Party. At every rest we would get on the sledge with the glasses, and look around, thinking that each snow hummock was a man or a tent. On the 13th Day sighted some marks in the snow that looked unusual, and on examination we found them to be the hoof-prints of the ponies, evidently made on the outward march of the Southern Party three months before. The tracks of the four sledges showed distinctly. We followed these tracks for seven hours, and then we lost them. We camped that night at 10 p.m., and early the next morning proceeded south again, thinking all the time that we would see something appear out of the loneliness. It is curious what things one can see in circumstances like these, especially with a bad light. We started back to the depot with all sorts of fears for the Southern Party.'

They reached the depot again at noon on the 16th, and Joyce states that as they approached the mound they were all sure that they could see a tent up and men walking about. When they got close, however, they found that everything was just as they had left it. They put all the provisions on top of the mound, lashed everything securely, and examined the flags to the eastward, and started on the march back to the coast, full of gloomy thoughts as to the fate of the Southern Party, which was now eighteen days overdue.

They proceeded first to the old *Discovery* depot found on the first journey, Joyce wishing to take some measurements in order to ascertain the movement of the Barrier ice, and the amount of the snowfall. The depot had been laid six years previously on bearings of the Bluff, and after its original position had been ascertained as exactly as possible, the distance to the bamboo pole was measured off by Day and Marston with a forty-foot length of rope, which had been measured of with a tape-measure. The distance was found to be 9600 ft., and the direction of the movement was about east-north-east. The Barrier ice at this point must therefore be moving forward at the rate of about 1500 ft. a year. The party then worked till 1 a.m. digging down in order to find what depth of snow had been deposited on top of the depot during the six years. It was found that the level at which the stays of the depot pole had been made fast was eight feet three inches down in hard compressed snow. A measured quantity of this snow was melted in order to ascertain the actual amount of the snowfall. The interesting points involved in these investigations will be dealt with in the reports on the scientific work of the expedition.

The party started north again on the following day, and covered a distance of thirty-three miles. The dogs pulled splendidly, and three men were able to ride on the sledge. On the second day crevasses were encountered again, and several times men fell through to the length of their harness. The general direction of the crevasses was east-south-east and west-south-west. The party had a narrow escape from complete disaster at this stage. 'We were going at a good trot over a very hard surface,' wrote Joyce, 'when I felt my foot go through. I called out "Crack!" and rushed the dogs over, and as the sledge touched the other side of the hard ridge, the whole snow-bridge over which we had passed fell in. Marston, who was running astern of the sledge, felt himself falling through space, but the pace of the dogs brought him over the crevasse, at the length of his harness. We found ourselves standing on the edge of a yawning gap that would easily have swallowed up sledge, dogs, and the whole party, and on the far side we could see our sledge tracks leading right up to the edge. It seemed almost a miracle how we had managed to escape. Day took a photograph, and we altered the course for Cape Crozier, getting out of the crevasses about 5 p.m. Then we camped for the night, having all had a good shaking up.'

A long march the next day over a good surface brought the party to Cape Armitage at midnight. Joyce found that the ice in the sound had gone out, and it was therefore necessary to climb through the gap at Observation Hill. A blizzard came up, and with great difficulty the party reached the old *Discovery* hut at Hut Point at 2 a.m. The distance covered during the day had been forty-five miles, an unusually good performance. The surface had been good, and the wind favourable, and the dogs had pulled splendidly. Joyce speaks very highly of the work of the dogs on this journey. They were pulling over 100 lb. per dog, and yet ran most of the time. They suffered a good deal from snow-blindness, and then they used to dig a hole in the snow and bury their faces right in; this method of treatment seemed to ease their eyes and they recovered from the attacks very quickly. 'One day I released Tripp, because he had a chafed leg,' wrote Joyce, 'and for the whole day he ran in his place in the team; as if he had been harnessed up. He slept about half a mile from camp that night, and when I tried to coax him over in the morning he would not come, but as soon as we got under way he came running up to his old place. I fed the dogs on one pound of biscuit a day each, and this seemed to satisfy them; as they went on their condition improved. The dog harness was generally satisfactory, but could have been improved with a few more swivels, in order to avoid tangling when the dogs jumped over their traces. I think that all dog teams should be taught to be driven, as a man cannot keep pace with dogs, and holding them back in order that a man may go ahead causes them to get fagged out. If they were let go at their best pace, one could, with a light load, say 80 lb. per dog, get forty miles a day out of them over a good surface.'

30

THE WESTERN JOURNEY

Meanwhile the Western Party, which had left the winter quarters for the second time on December 9, had been working in the western mountains. The three men (Armytage, Priestley and Brocklehurst reached the stranded moraines on December 13, and on this occasion succeeded in securing a large supply of skuas' eggs. The anticipated feast was not enjoyed, however, for only about a dozen of the eggs were 'good enough for eating', to quote the words of a member of the party. The other eggs were thrown on to the snow near the tent, and the result was an invasion of skuas, which not only ate the eggs, but also made themselves a general nuisance by pulling about the sledge harness and stores. At this time the men were troubled by patches of thin ice, about an eighth to a quarter of an inch thick, forming a lenticle, the top of the middle being sometimes as much as five or six inches from the actual surface. When these patches of ice were trodden on they broke down, and not infrequently disclosed a puddle of salt water an inch or two deep. Priestley thought that they were the final product of the thawing of snowdrifts, and owed their character to the fact that the salt water worked faster from below than did the sun from above.

On December 15 the party started to ascend the Ferrar Glacier, Priestley examining the rocks carefully on the way with a view to securing fossils if any were to be found. The surface was bad for the most part, soft snow being encountered where ice had been expected. On December 19 they were held up by a blizzard, and then they got on to very slippery crevassed ice. On December 20 they camped near the Solitary Rocks, at the spot at which Captain Scott had camped after leaving Dry Valley. The idea of getting to Depot Nunatak had to be abandoned, for a heavy snowfall made the travelling difficult, and the time at the disposal of the expedition was short. Priestley worked under the Bluff between Dry Valley and the east fork of the glacier without success, and then they moved over to Obelisk Mount. 'I have examined block after block of unfossiliferous-looking sandstone without any success,' wrote Priestley in his diary on the evening of the 21st. 'The only thing I can find different from the ordinary quartz grains are a few seams of conglomerate with quartz pebbles, and a few lenticles of a soft clayey substance. The other rock I have collected here is a junction between granite and porphyry, which is common. The sandstone is very weathered, dropping to pieces in many cases at a single blow. I am faced with the necessity of examining for fossils rocks which I should carefully avoid if I were at home or anywhere else. I have never seen a sedimentary rock that looked more unfossiliferous. Many of the boulders are coated with a hard crust of white, opaque salt (probably calcium carbonate), and if there was ever any lime in the sandstone it has probably been dissolved out long ago. There are numerous interesting rocks about here, but I am debarred from collecting much by the difficulty of transport. . . . There are evidently serious defects in the map near this point. The whole of the bluff opposite is marked as Beacon sandstone, and from the face of the cliff here it is easily seen, for at least 3000 feet, to be granite; the very grain in the stones can be seen. This granite is capped by the beacon sandstone on the tops of the hills, but the dolerite seems to have died out, with the exception of the upper flow. This formation is as it should be, taking into consideration the horizontal structure of the rocks, and it was the fact that I doubted the existence of Beacon sandstone so low down the series that brought me here, as much as the expectation of finding fossils if the mapping should be correct.'

At this time thawing was proceeding rapidly on the glacier. The party made for the north wall of the glacier, but was stopped by a precipice of ice, 200 to 300 feet in height, with a stream of water flowing at its foot. The deeper ripple-cracks and potholes were filled with water, and water was streaming down the convex face of the glacier to the stream which was roaring beneath the ice-face. The scene was a magnificent one, but the conditions were unpleasant from the point of view of the party. The ice was separated from the rock at the sides of the glacier by a thaw-gully about fifty feet deep, with a stream of water flowing at the bottom. Then came the lateral moraine, which was still within the region in which the rock-heat was felt, and formed a depression some three to six feet below the main surface of the glacier, commencing as an abrupt rise, almost perpendicular, but somewhat convex. After this came the ordinary billowy surface, and the next stones met with formed a sub-medial moraine not sufficiently thick to effect any lowering in the general level of the surface, although each stone was surrounded by its own hollow, filled with thaw water. Along the middle meandered a small stream, a few feet wide, with the bottom of its channel filled with morainic gravel matter. In the evening freezing commenced in the potholes that were sheltered from the rays of the sun.

Long needles of ice formed from the small grains of gravel, and crossed and recrossed in the most beautiful pattern. In some holes hexagonal plates of ice were being formed on the surface.

An examination of the Solitary Rocks proved that the map was incorrect at this point. The previous expedition had thought that the rocks formed an island, with the glacier flowing down on either side, but a close examination showed that the rocks were in reality a peninsula, joined to the main north wall by an isthmus of granite at least one thousand feet high. The glacier surged round the peninsula on its way down Dry Valley, and just below the isthmus was a lake of some size, fed by streams from a glacier opposite. These streams were yellow with silt, and another stream, also much discoloured, was running from the lake down to Dry Valley. The Solitary Rocks are at an altitude of about two thousand feet above sea-level. Priestley proceeded with geological and survey work in the neighbourhood of the east fork, and made an extensive examination of the spots known as Kurki Kills, Knob Head Mount and Windy Gully. On December 24, close to the camp, they found the bleached skeleton of a crabeater seal. It is rather curious that one of these animals should proceed so far up the glacier. A new camp was pitched at the foot of Knob Head Mountain, just below the second gully east of Windy Gully, and here Armytage and Priestley climbed up the slope behind to an altitude of 4200 ft., finding a yellow lichen at 3100 ft., a black lichen at 3800 ft. and a green lichen or moss at 4200 ft. The altitude of the camp was 2470 ft.

Christmas Day was spent at this camp, and, as was the case with the other sledging expeditions that were out at the time, a special feast was provided. For breakfast they had hoosh, sardines in tomato sauce and raisins; for lunch Garibaldi biscuits and jelly; and for dinner potted boneless chicken and a small plum pudding. Armytage picked up a piece of sandstone with fernlike markings, but Priestley was not hopeful of finding fossils in the greatly altered sandstone. The day was spent in geological work. 'We lose the sun here about 9.30 p.m.,' noted Priestley in his diary, 'and it is curious to observe the sudden change from bright light to darkness in the tent, while outside the thin surface of ice covering the thaw-water round the rocks immediately contracts with reports like a succession of pistol-shots, and sometimes breaks up and flies about in all directions, making a noise like broken glass. This is the effect of the quick cooling of the ice by the cold plateau wind immediately the sun's influence is withdrawn. The plum pudding was "top hole". Must remember to give one of the pot-holed sandstones to Wild for the New Zealand girl who gave him the plum pudding.'

On December 27 the men proceeded down the glacier again in order to see whether the Northern Party had arrived at Butter Point. Priestley studied the moraines on the way down, and made an extensive collection of specimens, and on January 1 they arrived at the depot. They had constant trouble with crevasses and 'potholes' on the way down the glacier, but met with no serious accident. The snow-bridges many times let them through up to their knees or waists, but never broke away entirely. The weather was unpleasantly warm for the sort of work they were undertaking, since the snow was thawing, and they were constantly wet.

They found no sign of the Northern Party at Butter Point, and after waiting there until the 6th they proceeded to the 'stranded moraines', a day's trek to the south, in order that geological specimens might be secured. The moraines, which were found by the *Discovery* expedition, and are relics of the days of more extensive glaciation, present a most varied collection of rocks, representative of the geological conditions to be found in the mountains to the west, and are of very great interest on that account. After spending two days at this spot, the party went back to Butter Point with about 250 lb. of specimens, and camped again till the 11th. Still there was no sign of the Northern Party, and on the 12th they went north to Dry Valley. There Priestley found a raised beach, about sixty feet above sea-level, and Brocklehurst climbed the mountain known as the Harbour Heights.

Numerous fragments of Pecten Colbecki, the shell at present common at Cape Royds, were found imbedded in the sand as far up as sixty feet, and Priestley thought that they would probably be found higher still. Writing of the moraines at this point, he said: 'In their chief characteristics they axe very similar to the stranded moraines. Large patches of gravel are mixed with boulders of every description and size, a chaos of sedimentary, volcanic, plutonic, hypabyssal and metamorphic rocks, segmented by watercourses, which are bordered by flats of gravel and spread out before reaching the sea over large, alluvial, fan-shaped mudflats. They differ from the stranded moraines in the presence of numerous specimens of now existing shells, imbedded in the gravel and sand of the moraines, but found in most cases under any steep declivity in a stream's bed where it has cut back through a gravel terrace. The remarkable part of the preservation of these shells is their extreme fragility. Of Pecten Colbecki I have seen thousands of specimens, and have secured many whole single valves. Of the Anataena so common at Cape Royds I came across several patches. At the head of one of the aluvial mudflats, about two feet above the present level of the sea-water, I secured many dried bodies of a small amphipod and a dried fish an inch long. The whole of the moraines so far as I have been are covered with seal bones, and I have seen two whole dried bodies, with the skin still on. One was a crabeater. Among several rock specimens secured was one of Beacon sandstone with the same curious markings as were found on two specimens secured by Armytage at Knob Head. The impression in the original stone was exactly as if the body of a wasp-like wingless insect several inches long had been pressed into clay.'

They went back to the depot on the 14th, and in accordance with the orders I had left, pitched camp in order to wait for the Northern Party until the 25th, when they were to make their way back to winter quarters, or signal for the ship by means of the heliograph. On January 24–25 this party had a very narrow escape from disaster. They were camped on the sea-ice at the foot of Butter Point, intending to move off on the return journey early on the morning of the 25th. Their position was apparently one of safety. Armytage had examined the tide-crack along the shore, and had found no sign of more than ordinary movement, and the ice in the neighbourhood seemed to be quite fast. At 7 a.m. on the 24th Priestley was first out of the tent, and a few minutes later he came running back to his companions to tell them that the ice they were on had broken away and was drifting away north to the open sea. The other two men turned out promptly, and found that his statement was only too true. There were two miles of open water between the floe and the shore, and they were apparently moving steadily out to sea. 'When we found that the ice had gone out,' wrote Armytage in his report to me, 'we struck camp, loaded up the sledge, and started away with the object of seeing whether we could get off the floe to the north. The position seemed to be rather serious, for we could not hope to cross any stretch of open water, there was no reasonable expectation of assistance from the ship, and most of our food was at Butter Point. We had not gone very far to the north before we came to an impassible lane of open water, and we decided to return to our original position. We went into camp, and had breakfast at 11 a.m. Then we held a consultation and agreed that it would be best to stop where we then were for a time, at any rate, on the off-chance of the ship coming along one of the lanes to pick us up on the following day, or of the current changing and the ice once more touching the shore. We waited till three o'clock in the afternoon, but there did not seem to be any improvement in the position. The Killer whales were spouting in the channels, and occasionally bumping the ice under us. Then we marched north again, but met with open water in every direction, and after we had marched right round the floe we got into camp at the old position at 10 p.m. We had a small meal of hoosh and biscuit. We had only four days' provisions on the floe with us, and I decided that we would have to go on short rations. We were encouraged by the fact that we had apparently ceased to move north, and were perhaps getting nearer the fast ice again. We got into our sleeping-bags in order to keep warm. At 11.30 p.m. Brocklehurst turned out to see whether the position had changed, and reported that we seemed to be within a few hundred yards of the fast ice, and still moving towards the land. I got out of my bag and put on my finnesko, and at midnight saw that we were very close to the fast ice, probably not more than two hundred yards away. I ran back as fast as I could, deciding that there was a prospect of an attempt to get ashore proving successful, and gave the other two men a shout. They struck the camp and loaded up within a very few minutes, while I went back to the edge of the floe at the spot towards which chance had first directed my steps. Just as the sledge got up to me, I felt the floe bump the fast ice. Not more than six feet of the edge touched, but we were just at that spot, and we rushed over the bridge thus formed. We had only just got over when the floe moved away again, and this time it went north to the open sea. The only place at which it touched the fast ice was that to which I had gone when I left the tent, and had I happened to go to any other spot we would not have escaped. We made our way to Butter Point, and at about three o'clock in the morning. camped and had a good meal. Then we turned in and slept. When we got up for breakfast, there was open water where we had been drifting on the floe, and I sighted the *Nimrod* under sail, ten or twelve miles out. We laid the heliograph on to the vessel, and after flashing for about an hour got a reply. The *Nimrod* came alongside the fast ice at three o'clock in the afternoon of January 26, and we went on board with our equipment and specimens. We left a depot of provisions and oil at Butter Point in case the Northern Party should reach that point after our departure.'

On January 22 and 23 a fresh wind blew from the south and commenced to break up the ice-sheet in the neighbourhood of Cape Royds, compelling the ship to refasten further to the southward. From this point Davis took a sledge-party to Hut Point with despatches that the supporting-party was to convey to me at the Bluff Depot. On the 25th the ice had broken up to such an extent that Captain Evans thought there would be a chance of getting far enough across McMurdo Sound to search the western coast-line for the party that had been exploring the western mountains, and also for the Northern Party, which might by that time have returned from the journey to the Magnetic Pole and reached Butter Point. The *Nimrod* stood out into the sound, and from a distance of ten or twelve miles a heliograph was seen twinkling near Butter Point. The ship was able to get right alongside the fast ice, and picked up Armytage, Priestley and Brocklehurst.

After this date fine weather was experienced only at short intervals, the season being advanced, and as a consequence the fast ice that remained in the sound commenced to break up rapidly, and took the form of pack trending northwards. When blizzards blew, as they did frequently, the *Nimrod* moored on the lee-side of a stranded iceberg in the neighbourhood of Cape Barne, with the object of preserving her position without the consumption of more coal than was absolutely necessary. After the ice had broken up sufficiently, shelter was found under Glacier Tongue.

The waiting was rather unpleasant for the remaining members of the shore-party and for those on board the ship, for the time was approaching when it would be necessary to leave for the north unless the *Nimrod* was to be frozen in for the winter, and two of the parties were still out. I had left instructions that if the Northern Party had not returned by February 1 a search was to be made along the western coast in a northerly direction. The party was three weeks overdue, and on February 1, therefore, the *Nimrod* went north, and Captain Evans proceeded to make a close examination of the coast. The ship did not get back to the hut until February 11. During this time Murray and Priestley found work of scientific interest. Priestley tramped the country, and now that the snow had in great measure disappeared, was enabled to see various interesting geological deposits previously covered up. Beds of sponge spicules, enclosing various other fossils, were evidence of recent elevation of the sea bottom. A thick deposit of salts was found on a mound between two lakes, and some curious volcanic formations were discovered. The smaller ponds were entirely melted, and gave a chance to find some forms of life not evident in winter. The penguins continued to afford Murray material for study.

The *Nimrod*'s search for the Northern Party was both difficult and dangerous. Captain Evans had to keep close to the coast, in order to guard against the possibility of overlooking a signal, which might consist only of a small flag, and the sea was obstructed by pack-ice. He was to go north as far as a sandy beach on the northern side of the Drygalski Barrier, and he performed his duty most thoroughly in the face of what he afterwards modestly described as 'small navigational difficulties'. The beach, which had been marked on the chart, was found to have no existence in fact, but the *Nimrod* reached the neighbourhood indicated, and then proceeded south again, still searching every yard of the coast. On the 4th a tent was sighted on the edge of the Barrier, and when a double detonator was fired the three men who had been to the Magnetic Pole came tumbling out and ran down towards the edge of the ice. Mawson was in such a hurry that he fell down a crevasse, and did not get out again until a party from the ship went to his assistance. 'They were the happiest men I have ever seen', said Davis in describing the finding of the party. Their sledge, equipment and specimens were taken on the *Nimrod*, which was able to moor right alongside the fast ice, and then Captain Evans proceeded back to the winter quarters.

In the chapters that follow Professor David tells the story of the Northern Party's journey.

31

PROFESSOR DAVID'S NARRATIVE

On September 19, 1908, Lieutenant Shackleton gave me his final instructions for the journey of the Northern Party to the Magnetic Pole. These he read over to me in the presence of Mawson and Dr Mackay. The instructions were as follows:

British Antarctic Expedition, 1907.
Cape Royds, *September* 19, 1908.

INSTRUCTIONS FOR NORTHERN SLEDGE-PARTY UNDER
COMMAND OF PROFESSOR E. DAVID.

Dear Sir,

The sledge-party which you have charge of consists of yourself, Douglas Mawson and Alistair Mackay.

You will leave winter quarters on or about October 1, 1908. The main objects of your journey are to be as follows:

(1) To take magnetic observations at every suitable point with a view of determining the dip and the position of the Magnetic Pole. If time permits, and your equipment and supplies are sufficient, you will try and reach the Magnetic Pole.

(2) To make a general geological survey of the coast of Victoria Land. In connection with this work you will not sacrifice the time that might be used to carry out the work noted in paragraph (1). It is unnecessary for me to describe or instruct you as to details re this work, as you know so much better than I do what is requisite.

(3) I particularly wish you to be able to work at the geology of the western mountains, and for Mawson to spend at least one fortnight at Dry Valley to prospect for minerals of economic value on your return from the north, and for this work to be carried out satisfactorily you should return to Dry Valley not later than the first week of January. I do not wish to limit you to an exact date for return to Dry Valley if you think that by lengthening your stay up north you can reach the Magnetic Pole,

but you must not delay, if time is short, on your way south again to do geological work. I consider that the *thorough* investigation of Dry Valley is of supreme importance.

(4) The *Nimrod* is expected in the Sound about January 15, 1909. It is quite possible you may see her from the west. If so, you should try to attract attention by heliograph to winter quarters. You should choose the hours noon to 1 p.m. to flash your signal, and if seen at winter quarters the return signal will be flashed to you, and the *Nimrod* will steam across as far as possible to meet you and wait at the ice-edge. If the ship is not in, and if she is and your signals are not seen, you will take into account your supply of provisions and proceed either to Glacier Tongue or Rut Point to replenish if there is not a sufficient amount of provision at Butter Point for you.

(5) *Re* Butter Point. I will have a depot of at least fourteen days' food and oil cached there for you. If there is not enough in that supply you ought to return as mentioned in paragraph (4).

(6) I shall leave instructions for the master of the *Nimrod* to proceed to the most accessible point at the west coast and there ship all your specimens. But before doing this, he must ship all the stores that are lying at winter quarters, and also keep in touch with the fast ice to the south on the look-out for the southern sledge-party. The Southern Party will not be expected before February 1, so if the ship arrives in good time you may have all your work done before our arrival from the south.

(7) If by February 1 after the arrival of the *Nimrod*, there is no evidence that your party has returned, the *Nimrod* will proceed north along the coast, keeping as close to the land as possible, on the look-out for a signal from you flashed by heliograph. The vessel will proceed very slowly. The ship will not go north of Cape Washington. This is a safeguard in event of any accident occurring to your party.

(8) I have acquainted both Mawson and Mackay with the main facts of the proposed journey. In the event of any accident happening to you, Mawson is to be in charge of the party.

(9) Trusting that you will have a successful journey and a safe return.

I am, yours faithfully,

(Sgd.) ERNEST H. SHACKLETON,
Commander

PROFESSOR DAVID,
CAPE ROYDS,
ANTARCTIC.

CAPE ROYDS,

BRITISH ANTARCTIC EXPEDITION, 1907.

PROFESSOR DAVID.

Dear Sir,

If you reach the Magnetic Pole, you will hoist the Union Jack on the spot, and take possession of it on behalf of the above expedition for the British nation.

When you are in the western mountains, please do the same at one place, taking possession of Victoria Land as part of the British Empire. If economic minerals are found, take possession of the area in the same way on my behalf as Commander of this expedition.

Yours faithfully,

(Sgd.) ERNEST H. SHACKLETON,
Commander.

We had a farewell dinner that night, given in honour of the Southern Depot Party, who were about to start to lay out a depot one hundred miles southerly from our winter quarters.

The following day, September 20, a strong southeasterly blizzard was blowing. In the afternoon the wind somewhat moderated, and there was less drift. Mackay had been making a sail for our journey to the Magnetic Pole, and we now tried the sail on two sledges lashed together on the ice at Backdoor Bay. We used the tent poles of one of the sledging-tents as a mast. The wind was blowing very strongly and carried off the two sledges with a weight on them of 300 lb., in addition to the weights of Mackay and myself, who were sitting on the sledges. We considered this a successful experiment.

The weather continued bad till the night of the 24th.

On September 25 we were up at 5.30 a.m., and found that the blizzard had subsided. Priestley, Day and I started in the motor-car, dragging behind us two sledges over the sea ice. One sledge, weighing altogether 606 lb. with its load, contained five of our fortnightly food-bags, six large tins of biscuits, and 60 lb. of oil. The other sledge, which with its load weighed about 250 lb., carried personal gear which we might have to use on the depot laying trip in the event of being surprised by a blizzard. At first Day travelled on his first gear; he then found that the engine became heated, and we had to stop for it to cool down. He discovered while we were waiting that one of the cylinders was not firing. This he soon fixed up all right. He then remounted the car and he put her on to the second gear. With the increased power given by the repaired cylinder we now sped over the floe-ice at fourteen miles an hour, much to the admiration of the seals and penguins. When, however, we had travelled about ten miles from winter quarters, and were some five miles westerly from Tent Island, we encountered numerous sastrugi of softish snow, the car continually sticking fast in the ridges. A little low drift was flying over the ice surface, brought up by a gentle blizzard. We left the heavy sledge ten miles out, and then with only the light sledge to draw behind us, Day found that he was able to travel on his third gear at eighteen miles an hour. At this speed the sledge, whenever it took one of the snow sastrugi at right angles, leapt into the air like a flying fish and came down with a bump on the surface of the ice. As we had occasionally to make sharp turns in order to avoid sastrugi and lumps of ice, our sledge had one or two capsizes. Meanwhile, the blizzard was freshening, and we tore along in hopes of reaching our winter quarters before it became very violent. We had just reached Flagstaff Point, and were taking a turn in towards the shore opposite the Penguin Rookery when the blizzard wind caught the side of the sledge nearly broadside on, and capsized it heavily. So violent was the shock that the aluminium cooking apparatus was knocked out of its straps, and the blizzard wind immediately started trundling this metal cylinder over the smooth ice. Day stopped his car as soon as possible, Priestley and I jumped off, and immediately gave chase to the runaway cooker. Meanwhile, the cooker had fallen to pieces so to speak; the tray part came away from the big circular cover; the melter and the supports for the cooking-pot and for the main outer covering also came adrift as well as the cooking-pot itself. The lid of the last-mentioned fell off, and immediately dumped on to the ice the three pannikins and our three spoons. These articles raced one another over the smooth ice-surface in the direction of the open water of Ross Sea. The spoons were easily captured, as also were the pannikins, which, being conical in shape, could not be bowled by the wind in a straight line, but described arcs of circles. Priestley and I recovered also the cooking-pot, and with Brocklehurst's help (for he had run down to meet us) the aluminium supports, but the large snow melter, the main outer casing, and the tray kept revolving in front of us at a speed which was just sufficient to outclass our own most desperate efforts. Finally, when we were nearly upon them, they took a joyous leap over the low cliff of floe-ice and disappeared one after another most exasperatingly in the black waters of the Ross Sea.

This was a shrewd loss, as aluminium cookers were, of course, very scarce. Priestley and I returned disconsolate, and very much winded after our mile's run in vain.

The following day we had intended laying out our second depot, but as some of the piston rings of the motor-car needed repair, we decided to postpone the departure until the day after. That afternoon, after the repairs had been completed, Day and Armytage went out for a little tobogganing before dinner. Late in the evening Armytage returned dragging slowly and painfully a sledge bearing the recumbent, though not inanimate form of Day. We crowded round to inquire what was the matter, and found that just when Armytage and Day were urging their wild career down a steep snow slope Day's foot had struck an unyielding block of kenyte lava, and the consequence had been very awkward for the foot. It was severely staved, so that he was quite unable to walk without assistance. As no one but Day could be trusted to drive the motor-car, this accident necessitated a further postponement of the laying of our second depot.

On September 28 it was blowing. On the 29th the day was fairly fine, but Day's foot was not well enough for him to start in the motor-car.

On September 30 a mild blizzard commenced blowing, and on October 1, the day on which Lieutenant Shackleton had intended that we should start, it was still raging with increased force. That day was spent chiefly in nailing strips of tin, painted blue, on all the geological specimen boxes, and double-labelling them.

On October 2 the weather was still bad, so that we were unable to start. On October 3, the weather having cleared, Day, Priestley, Mackay and I started with two sledges to lay our second depot. All went well for about eight miles out, then the carburetter played up. Possibly there was some dirt in the nozzle. Day took it all to pieces in the cold wind, and spent three-quarters of an hour in fixing it up. We then started off again gaily in good style. We crossed a large crack in the sea ice where there were numbers of seals and Emperor penguins. On the other side of this crack our wheels stuck fast in snow sastrugi. All hands got on to the spokes and started swinging the car backwards and forwards; when we got a good swing on, Day would suddenly snatch on the power and over we would go – that is, over one of the sastrugi – only to find, often, that we had just floundered into another one ahead. In performing one of these evolutions Priestley, who, as usual, was working like a Trojan, got his hand rather badly damaged through its being jammed between the spokes of the car wheel and the framework. Almost immediately afterwards one of my fingers was nearly broken, through the same cause, the flesh being torn off one of my knuckles; and then Mackay seriously damaged his wrist in manipulating what Joyce called the 'thumb-breaking' starter. Still we went floundering along over the sastrugi and ice cracks, Day every now and then getting out to lighten the car and limping alongside. At last we succeeded in reaching a spot amongst the snow sastrugi on the sea ice, fifteen miles distant from our winter quarters. Here we dumped the load intended for the Northern Party, and then Day had a hard struggle to extricate the car from the tangle of sastrugi and ice-cracks. At last, after two capsizes of the sledges, we got back into camp at 10 p.m., all thoroughly exhausted, all wounded and bandaged. Brocklehurst carried Day on his back for about a quarter of a mile from where we left the car up to our winter quarters. So thoroughly exhausted were we, that we had to take a day's rest on October 4, before making our final start.

The following are the details respectively of our permanent load and equipment and of our consumable load (food and oil) when we did eventually start:

NORTHERN PARTY'S PERMANENT LOAD

	Weight	
	lb	oz
2 11-ft. sledges	120	0
Tent, poles and floorcloth	30	0
Shovel	6	0
Primus and cooker	20	0
Three-man sleeping-bag	26	0
3 dozen plates	3	0
¼-plate camera and case	4	13
Legs of camera	1	14
Lloyd-Creak dip circle	23	0
Leas for dip circle	7	0
Spirit for primus stove	9	0
1 ready bottle for spirit	0	8
Sail and yard	11	0
Venesta board for table		
Centimetre rule		
Horn protractor	1	10
Pencils		
Hints to Travellers and *Nautical Almanac*		
3-in. theodolite and case	9	0
Legs of theodolite	5	4
Field-glasses	1	13
3 ice-axes, 3 lb. each	9	0
Rucksack and 60 ft. alpine rope	6	0
Haversack, hammer and chisel	a	0
Aneroid		
2 prismatic compasses	3	0
2 pairs of sledge thermometers in cases		
2 low-temperature thermometers	0	12
1 hypsometer in ease	1	0
Labels and small bags for specimens	1	0
Repair kit	2	0
Copper wire	0	4
Cod-line	1	0
Leather for repairs	2	0
1 pair shooting-boots for depot at Butter Point	3	8
1 pair ski boots (Mawson)	2	8
1 pair ski boots (David)	2	8

3 pairs ski boots	12	0
9 pairs finnesko, 2¼ lb each	20	4
Charts and tin case	1	0
Dram case of paper	1	0
30 lb. of personal gear ⎫ 6 lb. of bags ⎭	36	0
Prickers, nipples, and washers for primus	0	8
3 hanks sennegrass	4	8
3 bags for drying sennegrass	0	8
Medical bag	5	0
Depot flags, jack, and poles	4	0
Sledge harness.		
Sledge ropes and toggles.		
Small set of tools.		

Books:

Field note-books.

'Magnetic Memoir *of Discovery* Expedition.'

Sketch-book.

NORTHERN PARTY'S CONSUMABLE LOAD

Plasmon biscuit: 1 lb. per man per day = 3 lb. per day.
      93 days x 3 = 279 lb.
    Substitute for oatmeal, 1 lb. 3 oz. for 3 men per
      week x 13 = 14 lb. 10 oz.   = 294 0

Pemmican: 7.5 oz. per man per day x 3 x 93 = 2092 oz.   = 131 0

Emergency rations (checked by Marshall): 1½ oz. per
  man per day x 3 x 93 = 418½ oz.   = 26 0

Sugar (lumps): 3.8 oz. per man per day x 3 x 93   = 70 0

Tea (twice a day): a little less than half a tin per week = 9 0

Rowntree's Sweet Chocolate:
  8 oz. per man per week = normal allowance.
  4½ oz. per man per week = substitute for honey.
  12½ oz. per man per week
  12½ x 3 x 13½ = 487 oz.   = 32 0

Cocoa: 14½ oz. for three men per week (once a day for
  dinner). 14½ x 13 = 188 oz.   = 12 0
      Out of this plasmon cocoa available for 6 weeks.

Cheese: 2 oz. per man per day, 3 days per week
  18 oz. per week. 18 oz. x 13 2/7 = 239 1/7 oz.   = 5 0

Plasmon and dried milk   = 17 7

Salt: 2 oz. per week for 2 men = 4 oz. per week x 13 = 52 oz. = 3 4

Paraffiti oil in 10-lb. tins   100 0
                               —————
                                709 11

October 4 was a Sunday, and after the morning service we took the ponies out for exercise. In the evening the gramophone discoursed appropriate music, such as 'We parted on the Shore', 'I and my true love will never meet again by the bonnie, bonnie banks of Loch Lomond', concluding with the universal favourite, 'Lead, Kindly Light'.

Meanwhile, Mackay had his damaged wrist attended to, and I put the question to him as to whether or not he was prepared to undertake the long journey to the Magnetic Pole under the circumstances. He said that he was quite ready, provided Mawson and I did not object to his going with his wrist damaged and in a sling. We raised no objection, and so the matter was settled. All that night Mawson and I were occupied in writing final letters and packing little odds and ends.

The following morning, October 5, after an early breakfast, we prepared for the final start. It was quite wonderful what a lot of things had been forgotten until this last moment. The sledges were dragged down from our hut to the edge of the sea ice at the Penguin Rookery, a distance of a little over a quarter of a mile. Day was there with the motor-car, ready for the start. Every now and then some one of the pilgrims would remember that he had left something very important behind at the hut, and would go running back for it. These odd belongings had to be tied with bits of string on to the second sledge which we were going to take with us on our northern journey, consequently, by degrees, this sledge became hung over with boots, crampons, and all sorts of what Day called 'gadgets'. Murray, Brocklehurst and Armytage came down on the ice to bid us a final farewell. Brocklehurst took a photograph of us just before we started, then Day, Priestley, Roberts, Mackay, Mawson and I got aboard, some on the motor-car, some on the sledges. Those remaining behind gave us three cheers, Day turned on the power and away we went. A light wind was blowing from the south-east at the time of our start, bringing a little snow with it and another blizzard seemed impending.

After travelling a little over two miles, just beyond Cape Barne, the snow had become so thick that the coast-line was almost entirely hidden from our view. Under these circumstances I did not think it prudent to take the motor-car further, so Mackay, Mawson and I bid adieu to our good friends. Strapping on our harness we toggled on to the sledge rope, and with a one, two, three, and away, pulled off into the thick falling snow, which in a few minutes blotted out all view of the motor-car in our rear. As we slowly trudged along the signs of an approaching blizzard became more pronounced and we bore somewhat to our left so as to have Inaccessible Island as a lee under which to run for shelter, but after a time, as the threatened blizzard did not come up, we slewed our sledge more to the right, away from Inaccessible Island, heading up for our ten-mile depot. At last, towards evening, Mackay sighted the black flag over the depot about a mile distant.

We reached the depot about 7 p.m. and got up our tent. A fairly strong wind was still blowing from the south-east, raising low drift. We slept that night on the floe-ice, with about three hundred fathoms of water under our pillow.

The following morning, October 6, we started our relay work. We dragged the Christmas Tree sledge on first, as we were specially liable to lose parcels off it, for a distance of from one-third to half a mile. Then we returned and fetched up what we called the Plum Duff sledge, chiefly laden with our provisions. The light was dull, and a certain amount of soft, newly fallen snow made the sledging heavy. The weather may be described as thick, with snow falling at intervals. During the afternoon it cleared somewhat and the western mountains came into view at about 2 p.m. This was fortunate for us, as it enabled us later on to sight the flag over our fifteen-mile depot. We camped that night amongst screw pack-ice within less than a mile of this depot.

The following day, October 7, was beautifully fine and calm. We started about 9 a.m. and sledged over pressure ice ridges and snow sastrugi, reaching our fifteen-mile depot in three-quarters an of hour. Here we camped and repacked our sledges. We took the wholemeal plasmon biscuits out of two of the biscuit tins and packed them into canvas bags. This saved us a weight of about 8 lb.

We started again in the afternoon, relaying with the two sledges. The sledging again was heavy on account of the fresh, soft snow, and small sastrugi. We had a glorious view of the western mountains, crimsoned in the light of the setting sun. We camped that night close to a seal hole which belonged to a fine specimen of Weddell seal. We were somewhat disturbed that night, by the snorting and whistling of the seals as they came up for their blows. Evidently this seal hole was a syndicate affair. The sounds at times seemed right under our tent.

October 8 was a fine, clear day, with a beautiful sunset, and a magnificent mirage, in the direction of Beaufort Island. To the north of us, the curious hills, called by Captain Scott the 'Stranded Moraines', were now beginning to show out very plainly in the direction in which we were travelling.

On the morning of October 9 we got under way soon after eight o'clock. It was a lovely, calm day but cold, the thermometer registering minus 30° Fahr. at 8 p.m. The surface was fairly good for sledging, but in places we came on patches of soft snow, and a small, lumpy structure of the ice-surface, resembling a newly raked garden bed, evidently due to the thawing down and refreezing of 'ice flowers'. This made travelling very heavy. The 'Stranded Moraines' now showed up very clearly, and Butter Point itself became visible.

The following day, Saturday, October 10, we were awakened by the chatter of some Emperor penguins who had marched down on our tent during the night to investigate us. The sounds may be described as something between the cackle of a goose and the chortle of a kookaburra. On peeping out of the Burberry spout of our tent I saw four standing by the sledges. They were much interested at the sight of me, and the conversation between them became lively. They evidently took us for penguins of an inferior type, and the tent for our nest. They watched, and took careful note of all our doings, and gave us a good send-off when we started about 8.30 a.m.

On our journey that morning we passed close by a large bull seal of the Weddell species. A little further on we noticed a curious dark object on the ice in the distance, and on coming up to it found that it was a dead Weddell seal with its head, neck, and shoulders firmly frozen into the ice. Evidently it had stuck fast in a seal hole in the ice in trying to get down to the sea-water.

The sky was overcast, and light snow began to fall in the afternoon. A little later a mild blizzard sprang up from the south-east; we thought this a favourable opportunity for testing the sailing qualities of our sledges, and so made sail on the Plum Duff sledge. As Mackay put it, we 'brought her to try with main course.' As the strength of the blizzard increased, we found that we could draw both sledges simultaneously, which was, of course, a great saving in labour. We were tempted to carry on in the increasing strength of the blizzard rather longer than was wise, and consequently, when at last we decided that we must camp, had great difficulty in getting the tent up. We slipped the tent over the poles placed close to the ground in the lee of a sledge. While two of us raised the poles, the third shovelled snow on to the skirt of the tent, which we pulled out little by little, until it was finally spread to its full dimensions. We were glad to turn in and escape from the biting blast and drifting snow.

The following day, Sunday, October 11, a violent blizzard was still blowing, and we lay in our sleeping-bag until past noon, by which time the snow had drifted high upon the door side of our tent. As this drift was pressing heavily on our feet and cramping us, I got up and dug it away. The cooker and primus were then brought in and we all got up and had some hoosh and tea. The temperature, as usually happens in a blizzard, had now risen considerably, being 8.5° Fahr. at 1.30 p.m. The copper wire on our sledges was polished and burnished by the prolonged blast against it of tiny ice crystals, and the surface of the sea ice was also brightly polished in places. As it was still blowing we remained in our sleeping-bag for the rest of that day as well as the succeeding night.

When we rose at about 2 a.m. on Monday, October 12, the blizzard was over. We found very heavy snowdrifts on the lee side of our sledges, and it took us a considerable time to dig these away and get the hard snow raked out of all the chinks and crannies among the packages on the sledges. We made a start about 4 a.m., and all that day meandered amongst broken pack-ice. It was evident that the south-east blizzards drive large belts of broken floe-ice in this direction across McMurdo Sound to the western shore. The fractured masses of sea ice, inclined at all angles to the horizontal, are frozen in later, as the cold of winter becomes more intense, and of course, constitute a very difficult surface for sledging.

In order to make up for the time we had lost in our sleeping-bags during the blizzard, we travelled altogether fourteen hours, and succeeded in doing about six statute miles, that is, eighteen miles of relay work, and all felt much exhausted when we turned in that evening. As a result of this we did not wake until after 8 a.m. next morning.

We were now only about two miles from Butter Point. We got under way at 10 a.m., and a few hours later camped at the foot of a low ice cliff, about 600 yards south-south-east of Butter Point. Butter Point is merely an angle in this low ice cliff near the junction of the Ferrar Glacier valley with the main shore of Victoria Land. This cliff was from fifteen to twenty feet in height, and formed of crevassed glacier ice. It was covered by a hard snow crust, which every now and then gave way and let one down for a foot or so. This glacier ice was not part of the main Ferrar Glacier, but appeared to be simply a local piedmont glacier stretching along for some considerable distance between the base of the coast range and the sea ice, past the 'Stranded Moraines', until still further south it became confluent with that Mr H. G. Ferrar has described as the 'pinnacled ice'. It was evident that this piedmont ice was firmly attached to the land, as it was separated from the sea ice by a well-marked tide-crack. With the help of our ice axes we crossed over this crack and got up the little ice cliff on to the glacier ice, and selected there a suitable spot for our depot.

According to arrangements with Lieutenant Shackleton we were to leave a depot flag at Butter Point with a letter giving an account of our doings, and stating approximately by what date we hoped to return there. But the progress of our journey had been so much slower than we had originally anticipated that we decided before reaching Butter Point that it would be imperatively necessary, in order to make the Magnetic Pole in the time available, to lighten the load on our sledges by leaving a portion of our equipment and food.

During the latter part of this day Mawson and Mackay were busy making a mast and boom for the second sledge, it being our intention to use the tent floorcloth as a sail. Meanwhile I sorted out the material to be left at the depot.

The following day, Wednesday, October 14, we spent the morning in resorting the loads on our sledges. We depoted two tins of wholemeal plasmon biscuits, each weighing about 27 lb., also Mackay's mountaineering nail boots, and my spare head-gear material and mits. Altogether we lightened the load by about 70 lb. We sunk the two full tins of biscuits and a tin containing boots, &c., a short distance in the glacier ice to prevent the blizzards blowing them away. We then lashed to the tins a short bamboo flag-pole, carrying one of our black depot flags, and securely fastened to its base one of our empty air-tight milk tins, in which we placed our letters. In these letters for Lieutenant Shackleton and R. E. Priestley, respectively, I stated that in consequence of our late start from Cape Royds, and also on account of the comparative slowness of our progress thence to Butter Point, it was obvious that we could not return to Butter Point until January 12, at the earliest, instead of the first week of January, as was originally anticipated, We ascertained months later that this little depot survived the blizzards, and that Armytage, Priestley and Brocklehurst had no difficulty in finding it, and that they read our letters.

Leaving the depot about 9 a.m. on October 14, we started sledging across New Harbour in the direction of Cape Bernacchi. In the afternoon a light southerly wind sprang up bringing a little snow with it, the fall lasting from about 12.30 to 2.30 p.m. We steered in the direction of what appeared to us to be an uncharted island. On arriving at it, however, we discovered that it was a true iceberg, formed of hard blue glacier ice with a conspicuous black band near its summit formed of fine dark gravel. The iceberg was about a quarter of a mile in length, and thirty to forty feet high. In addition to the coarser bands of gravel there was a great quantity of dust, and fine dust bands, near the surface of the berg. This dust absorbing the heat of the sun had thawed its way deep down into the berg, thus forming numerous dust wells and dust grooves. There were several large cracks in the sea ice in the neighbourhood of this iceberg, and having taken the bearing of the trend of these by a compass they helped us to keep direction when the air was thick with falling snow.

The following day, October 15, was beautifully fine and calm; the sky was slightly cloudy with long belts of cirrus-stratus and alto-stratus. Erebus, now over fifty miles distant, was cloud capped. We had a glorious view up the magnificent valley of the Ferrar Glacier; the spurless hills on either side of the valley, strongly faceted in a direction parallel to each side of the valley, spoke eloquently of intense abrasive glacial action in the immediate geological past. The hills in the foreground, formed of gneissis granite, were of a rich chocolate brown to warm sepia hue, fading in the distance to exquisite tints of reddish purple and violet. Towards evening we had a wonderful vision of several large icebergs close ahead of us; it seemed as though they were only a mile or so distant, as one could see clearly the re-entering angles and bright reflected sides of the bergs lit up in the rays of the setting sun. Suddenly, as if by magic, they all vanished. They had been momentarily conjured up to our view by a wonderful mirage. In the departing rays of the setting sun Mount

Erebus and Mount Bird glowed with a glorious golden light. This was one of the most beautiful days we experienced during the whole of our journey. The cold was now less severe than it had been, the temperature being 9.5° Fahr. at 8 p.m.

32

PROFESSOR DAVID'S NARRATIVE
(CONTINUED)

On October 16 we were up at 3.30 a.m., and got under way at 5.30. A cold wind was blowing from the south, and after some trouble we set sail on both sledges, using the green floorcloth on the Christmas Tree sledge, and Mackay's sail on the Plum Duff sledge. A short time after we set sail it fell nearly calm; thick clouds gathered; a light wind sprang up from the south-east, veering to east-north-east, then back again to south-east in the afternoon. Fine snow fell for about three hours, forming a layer nearly a quarter of an inch in thickness. Towards evening we reached one of the bergs that had been miraged up the night before. It was four hundred yards long, and eighty yards wide, and was a true iceberg formed of glacier ice; Mackay, Mawson and I explored this. Like the previous iceberg its surface was pitted with numerous deep dust wells. It was wonderful to see what a very small amount of dust sufficed to dig these wells to a depth of several feet. The cliff of the berg which faced towards the north-west was deeply grooved, the appearance in the distance reminding one of a number of large parallel stalactites. Climbing up one of these deep grooves I found numbers of small angular rock pebbles, up to one and a half inches in diameter, adhering to the bottom of the groove, and it seemed as though these grooves, like the dust wells, were formed by the warmth of these small fragments of rock which, as the process of thawing of the ice cliff progressed, gradually settled down into long rows or strings as they crept gradually downwards under the influence of gravitation to the level of the sea ice below. As the shore was high and rocky, and seemed not more than half a mile distant, I went over towards it after our evening meal. It proved to be somewhat further than it appeared.

On the way, for the first time, I met with a structure in the sea ice known as pancake ice. The surface of the ice showed a rounded polygonal structure something like the tops of a number of large weathered basaltic columns. The edges of these polygons were slightly raised, but sufficiently rounded off by thawing or ablation to afford an easy surface for the runners of our sledge. Later on, in the autumn of the following year, we noticed this pancake ice in process of formation. If, as was often the case, there was any wind when the sea began to freeze over, the water at first commenced to look soupy; little by little the small ice particles which caused this appearance aggregated and formed myriads of small structures which may be likened to small open jam tarts. These would then coalesce in groups at their edges and form pancake ice. These pancakes were from one foot up to about three feet in diameter. Later, the pancakes would cohere and so a continuous hard ice crust would be formed over the sea surface; later freezing simply had the effect of strengthening and thickening this ice-sheet from below. Close in shore the pancake ice was traversed by deep tidal cracks. After climbing over these I reached the shore, which was composed of a well-marked terrace of coarse gravel and large and small erratic boulders. The smaller rock fragments were from three to six inches in diameter, the boulders being as much as five feet in diameter. The lower terrace was about twenty yards wide and as many feet in height above the sea; then followed a belt of coarsely crystalline white marble traversed by bands of grey gneiss and blackish rock. Capping this belt of ancient crystalline rocks was a terrace of angular gravel, from eighty to one hundred feet above sea-level, formed of small rock fragments from one to two inches in diameter. The belts of coarse marble, gneiss, &c., were stained green and reddish to ochreous brown in places, and appeared to have been much mineralised. The whole area seemed to promise well for economic minerals. One curious boulder specially attracted my attention; its large pinkish crystals were peppered over with small black crystals, the whole being enclosed in a greenish black base. A specimen of this boulder which we brought back with us will be described in detail in the geological notes.

On Saturday, October 17, Mawson, Mackay and I landed at Cape Bernacchi, a little over a mile north of our previous camp. Here we hoisted the Union Jack just before 10 a.m. and took possession of Victoria Land for the British Empire. Cape Bernacchi is a low rocky promontory, the geology of which is extremely interesting. The dominant type of rock is a pure white coarsely crystalline marble; this has been broken through by granite rocks, the latter in places containing small red garnets. The marble or tale schist contains graphite disseminated through it in small scales. A great deal of tourmaline and epidote are developed in the granite at its point of contact with the calcareous schists. It appeared that the granite had intruded the black tourmaline rocks.

After taking possession we resumed our sledging, finding the surface of pancake ice very good. The day being calm and clear and free from either falling or drifting snow, we were able, for the first time, to turn our sleeping-bag inside out and air it in the sun. Previous to this the reindeer fur inside the bag had become much encrusted with ice, chiefly the result of the freezing

of our breath. Although the heat of the sun was insufficient to actually thaw
the ice it evaporated it to a considerable extent, and we found the bag that
night much more comfortable to sleep in than it had been for many nights
previous.

The following day, one and a quarter miles north of our preceding camp,
we reached an interesting rocky headland. Here we found a mother seal
with a newly born baby seal, the latter about three and a half feet in length.
The mother seal at short intervals made a sound like 'Wa-a-a'. After a
close inspection the mother and baby were left undisturbed, and we turned
our attention to the rocks. These were most interesting, bearing a general
resemblance to those at Cape Bernacchi. Some of the quartz veins traversing
this point Mawson thought very favourable for gold.

When we left this point the wind had considerably freshened. We had
previously hoisted sail on both sledges, and the wind was now sufficiently
strong to admit of our pulling both sledges together. The total distance
travelled was seven statute miles. This was the most favourable wind we
experienced during the whole of our journey to and from the Magnetic Pole.

Shortly after leaving Baby Seal Point we encountered heavy belts of screw
pack-ice with high sastrugi between. The Christmas Tree sledge capsized
badly when being dragged over one of these high snow ridges. We were much
exhausted when we camped that night and had suffered somewhat from the
cold wind, the temperature being about 10° Fahr.

That night I experienced a rather bad attack of snow blindness, through
neglecting to wear my snow goggles regularly. Finding that my eyes were no
better next morning, and my sight being dim I asked Mawson to take my
place at the end of the long rope, the foremost position in the team. Mawson
proved himself on this occasion and afterwards so remarkably efficient at
picking out the best track for our sledges, and steering a good course that by
my request he occupied this position throughout the rest of the journey.

The next two days were uneventful, except for the fact that we occasionally
had extremely heavy sledging over screw pack-ice and high and long sastrugi.
The latter were from two to three feet high, bounded frequently by almost
perpendicular sides, and as they trended from west to east and our course
was from south to north they proved formidable obstacles to our progress,
and capsizes of the sledges were frequent.

On the night of October 20, we camped on the sea ice about three-
quarters of a mile off shore. To the north-east of us was an outward curve
of the shoreline, shown as a promontory on the existing chart. Early the
next morning I walked over to the shore to geologise, and found the
rocky headland composed of curious gneissic granite veined with quartz.
On ascending this headland I noticed to my surprise that what had been
previously supposed to be a promontory was really an island separated by

a narrow strait from the mainland. It was clear that by going through this strait we would save several miles. Accordingly, after breakfast we sledged into the strait. The western side of the strait was formed of glacier ice terminating eastward in an almost precipitous slope. Here and there masses of gneissic granite showed from beneath the ice. The eastern side of the strait was formed of terraced moraine gravels with large erratics embedded in the gravel of the top terrace, eighty feet above sea level.

While Mawson determined the position of this island by taking a round of angles with the theodolite, Mackay and I crossed the strait and explored the island, pacing and taking levels. The rocks of which the erratics and boulder-bearing gravels were formed were almost without exception of igneous origin. One very interesting exception was a block of weathered clayey limestone. This was soft and yellowish grey externally, but hard and blue on the freshly fractured surfaces inside. It contained traces of small fossils which appeared to be seeds of plants. Specimens of these were taken by us and were depoted later at another small island, which we called Depot Island. It is much to be regretted that we were unable later to reach this depot on account of dense belts of pack-ice, and so these very interesting specimens were lost. Two chips, however, of this rock were fortunately preserved, sufficient for chemical analysis and microscopic examination. There could be little doubt that this clayey limestone has been derived from the great sedimentary formation, named by H. T. Ferrar, the Beacon sandstone.

The island which we had been exploring we named provisionally Terrace Island. It was approximately triangular in shape, and the side facing the strait, down which we travelled, measured one mile 1200 yards in length.

The following day, October 22, we sighted the first skua gull we had seen that season. Snow fell in the afternoon between 2.30 and 5 p.m., forming a layer three-quarters of an inch deep. The temperature rose to plus 6.5° Fahr. at 7 p.m., and a blizzard seemed impending.

The following day, October 23, we held a serious council as to the future of our journey towards the Magnetic Pole. It was quite obvious that at our present rate of travelling, about four statute miles daily by the relay method, we could not get to the Pole and return to Butter Point early in January. I suggested that the most likely means of getting to the Pole and back in the time specified by Lieutenant Shackleton would be to travel on half rations, depoting the remainder of our provisions at an early opportunity. They both agreed, after some discussion, to try this expedient, and we decided to think the matter over for a few days and then make our depot.

We found, as the result of the fall of snow on the preceding day, that the runners of our sledge clogged, making it difficult to start the sledge after each halt. The temperature at 5 p.m. was now as high as plus 5° Fahr. There were numerous seals, mostly mother seals with young ones, on the ice near the course of our sledge, as many as seventeen seals being sometimes visible simultaneously.

The previous day we had observed a mother seal with twin baby seals. Mackay took up one of these in his arms and stroked it while it was nuzzling round. It somewhat resembled a large lizard. The mother snorted at him indignantly, meanwhile, but made no attempt to attack him.

We encountered some large cracks in the sea ice. The sea water between the opposite walls had been only recently frozen over so that the ice was not more than a few inches in thickness. One of these was eighteen feet wide, and we found that the ice bent under our weight when we tested it primarily. Mackay called it 'The Bridge of the Beresina'. We rushed the sledges over at a good speed, and although the ice bent under their weight it fortunately held. At about 3 p.m. the weather grew very thick and it began to snow; a mild blizzard developing later, we hoisted sail on both sledges.

The next day, October 24, we found it very warm in the sleeping-bag, the sky being thickly overcast with dense stratus cloud. A strong water sky showed up to the east of us, while over the mountains to the west it was moderately clear. The presence of this water sky, indicating open sea, warned us that it was unsafe to stand out far from the land. We reached that evening a long rocky point of gneissic granite, which we called Gneiss Point. After our evening hoosh we walked across to the point and collected a number of interesting geological specimens, including blocks of kenyte lava.

The following day, October 25, proved a very heavy day for sledging, as we had to drag the sledges over new snow from three to four inches deep. In places it had a tough top crust which we would break through up to our ankles. We met also several obstacles in the way of wide cracks in the sea ice, from six to ten feet in width, and several miles in length. The sea water between the walls of the cracks had only recently been frozen over, so that the ice was only just thick enough to bear the sledges. The vicinity of these great icecracks were perfect baby farms for young seals. It was a pretty sight to see one of these baby seals playing with its mother, whom it kept gently flicking over the nose with its small flippers, the mother every now and then gently boxing the baby's ear with one of her large flippers. One of these mothers charged down on Mackay, who was making an inspection of her baby at too close quarters to suit her fancy. Another mother was moaning in great distress over her baby, which had just died. Evidently the mother seal's affection for her young is very strong.

In pursuing our north-westerly course we were now crossing a magnificent bay, which trended westwards some five or six miles away from the course we were steering. On either side of this bay were majestic ranges of rocky mountains parted from one another at the head of the bay by an immense glacier with steep ice falls. On examining these mountains with a fieldglass it was evident that in their lower portions they were formed of granites and gneiss, producing reddish brown soils. At the higher levels, further inland, there were distinct traces of rocks showing horizontal stratification. The highest rock of all was black in colour, and evidently very hard, apparently some three hundred feet in thickness. Below this was some softer stratified formation, approximately one thousand feet in thickness. We concluded that the hard top layer was composed of igneous rock, possibly a lava, while the horizontal stratified formation belonged in all probability to the Beacon sandstone formation. Some fine nunataks of dark rock rose from the southeast side of the great glacier. On either side of this glacier were high terraces of rock reaching back for several miles from a modern valley edge to the foot of still higher ranges. It was obvious that these terraces marked the position of the floor of the old valley at a time when the glacier ice was several thousand feet higher than it is now, and some ten miles wider than at present. The glacier trended inland in a general south-westerly direction.

We longed to turn our sledges shorewards and explore these inland rocks, but this would have involved a delay of several days – probably a week at least – and we could not afford the time. Mawson took a series of horizontal and vertical angles with the theodolite to all the upper peaks in these ranges. We were much puzzled to determine on what part of the charted coast this wide bay and great glacier valley was situated. We speculated as to whether it was Granite Harbour, but decided that it could not be in view of the distance recorded by our sledge meter, for, according to this, we must still be some twenty miles south of Granite Harbour proper. We were to find out much later that the point opposite which we had now arrived was in reality Granite Harbour, and that its position was not shown correctly on the chart. Of course in pioneering work occasional mistakes such as these are inevitable.

The following day the sledge still proved very heavy on account of the soft snow – two to four inches deep – which was continually clogging the runners of our sledges. It was also difficult to steer a good course amongst the hummocky pack-ice on account of the day being dull and overcast. There was much low stratus cloud, and a light south-easterly wind.

The weather of October 27 was beautifully clear and sunshiny, and we had a glorious view of the great mountain ranges on either side of Granite Harbour. The rich colouring of warm sepia brown and terracotta in these rocky hills was quite a relief to the eye. Wind springing up in the south-east we made sail on both sledges, and this helped us a good deal over the soft snow and occasional patches of sharp-edged brash ice. Occasionally the runners of our sledge would catch on one of these sharp fragments, and there would be a harsh rasping sound as a shaving was peeled off the runner. We feared that the wind would develop into a true blizzard, but it proved to be only what Joyce used to call a 'carpet sweeper', driving along the newly fallen snow in white gossamer-like films over the sea ice.

Towards evening we fetched up against some high ice-pressure cracks with the ice ridged up six to eight feet high in huge tumbled blocks. We seemed to have got into a labyrinth of these pressure ridges from which there was no outlet. At last, after several capsizes of the sledges and some chopping through the ice ridges by Mackay, we got the sledges through, and camped on a level piece of ice. We were much helped in crossing the ridges by the long steep sastrugi of hardened snow. In places these ran like ramps up to the top of the pressure ridges, and were just wide enough and strong enough to bear our sledges. Mawson and I at this time were still wearing finnesko, while Mackay had taken to ski boots.

The following day, October 28, the sledging was again very heavy over sticky, soft snow alternating with hard sastrugi and patches of consolidated brash ice. Shavings of wood were being constantly rasped off the runners of our sledges. Mackay lost one of his finnesko off the sledge, but walked back a couple of miles in the evening and recovered it. Our course had taken us past a number of snowbergs; these were mostly about forty feet in height and from a quarter to half a mile in length. They were rigidly embedded in the sea ice. Occasionally we met with a true iceberg of blue ice amongst the snowbergs.

After our evening hoosh, Mawson and I went over to the shore, rather more than half a mile distant, in order to study the rocks. These we found were composed of coarse red granite; the top of the granite was much smoothed by glacier ice, and strewn with large erratic blocks. In places the granite was intersected by black dykes of basic rocks. One could see that the glacier ice, about a quarter of a mile inland from this rocky shore, had only recently retreated and laid bare the glaciated rocky surface. We found a little moss here amongst the crevices in the granite rock.

October 29 was beautifully fine, though a keen and fresh wind, rather unpleasantly cold, was blowing from off the high mountain plateau to our west. It blew from a direction west by south and caused a little low drift in the loose snow on the surface of the sea ice. There was still a great deal of deep, soft snow alternating with hard sastrugi and small patches of consolidated brash ice, so that the sledging was very heavy.

We were all thoroughly done up at night after completing our four miles of relay work. That evening we discussed the important question of whether it would be possible to eke out our food-supplies with seal meat so as to avoid putting ourselves on half rations, and we all agreed that this should be done. We made up our minds that at the first convenient spot we would make a depot of any articles of equipment, geological specimens, &c., in order to lighten our sledges, and would at the same time, if the spot was suitable, make some experiments with seal meat. The chief problem in connection with the latter was how to cook it without the aid of paraffin oil. We could not afford more paraffin for this purpose, as we estimated that even with the utmost care the supply for our primus, which we used for brewing tea, cocoa and hoosh, would become exhausted before we could hope to reach the Magnetic Pole, unless some kind of substitute for paraffin could be found.

The following day, October 30, was full of interest for us, as well as hard work. In the early morning, between 2.30 a.m. and 6.30 a.m., a mild blizzard was blowing. We got under way a little later and camped at about 10.30 a.m. for lunch alongside a very interesting rocky point. Mawson got a good set of theodolite angles from the top of this point. The point was formed of coarse porphyritic grey gneiss, traversed by black dykes of rock, apparently tinguaite, and another variety containing an abundance of sparkling black crystals of hornblende, which may be termed provisionally a hornblende lamporphyre.

After lunch we passed close by a mother seal and her baby. The mother charged us and we had to skid along quick and lively past her with the sledges. That day was the first occasion that we tried the experiment of strengthening the brew of the tea by using the old tea-leaves of a previous meal mixed with the new ones. This was Mackay's idea, and Mawson and I at the time did not appreciate the experiment. Later on, however, we were very glad to adopt it.

The sledging that afternoon was about the heaviest we had experienced up to date. The weather was now daily becoming warmer and the saline snow on the sea ice became sticky in consequence. It gripped the runners of the sledges like glue, and we were only able with our greatest efforts to drag the sledges over this at a snail's pace. We were all thoroughly exhausted that evening when we camped at the base of a rocky promontory about 180 ft. high. This cliff was formed of coarse gneiss, with numerous dark streaks, and enclosures of huge masses of greenish-grey quartzite.

After our evening hoosh we walked over to a very interesting small island about three-quarters of a mile distant. It was truly a most wonderful place geologically, and was a perfect elysium for the mineralogist. The island, which we afterwards called Depot Island, was accessible on the shoreward side, but rose perpendicularly to a height of 200 ft. above sea-level on the other three sides. There was very little snow or ice upon it, the surface being almost entirely formed of gneissic granite. This granite was full of dark enclosures of basic rocks, rich in black mica and huge crystals of hornblende. It was in these enclosures that Mawson discovered a translucent brown mineral, which he believed to be monazite, but which has since proved to be titanium mineral. Patches of a crystalline, milky-white mineral were to be seen amongst the large platy crystals of dark green hornblende. These white crystals we thought might be scapolite. We returned to camp and slept soundly after the severe work of the day.

We were up at 6 a.m. next morning, and after breakfast Mackay and Mawson went in pursuit of some seals which we had sighted further back on the previous day, while I climbed up an adjacent granite slope with the field-glasses, watching for a signal from them, if they were successful in their hunting, to bring up an empty sledge. They were, however, unsuccessful in their quest, and after some time returned to camp.

We packed up and made for the island at 9.30 a.m. The sledging was extremely heavy, and we fell into a tide-crack on the way, but the sledge was got over safely. Mackay sighted a seal about six hundred yards distant from the site of our new camp near the island, and just then we noticed that another seal had bobbed up in the tide-crack close to our old camp. Mackay and Mawson at once started off in the direction where the first seal had been sighted. It proved to be a bull seal in very good condition, and they killed it by knocking it on the head with an ice-axe. Meanwhile, I unpacked the Duff sledge and took it out to them. Returning to the site of our camp I put up the tent, and on going back to Mawson and Mackay found that they had finished fletching the seal. We loaded up the empty sledge with seal blubber, resembling bars of soap in its now frozen condition, steak and liver, and returned to camp for lunch.

After lunch we took some blubber and seal meat on to the island, intending to try the experiment of making a blubber fire in order to cook the meat. We worked our way a short distance up a steep, rocky gulley, and there built a fireplace out of magnificent specimens of hornblende rock. It seemed a base use for such magnificent mineralogical specimens, but necessity knows no laws. We had brought with us our primus lamp in order to start the fire. We put blubber on our iron shovel, warmed this underneath by means of the heat of the primus lamp so as to render down the oil from it, and then lit the oil. The experiment was not altogether successful. Mawson cooked for about three hours, closely and anxiously watched by Mackay and myself. Occasionally he allowed us to taste small snacks of the partly cooked seal meat, which were pronounced to be delicious.

While the experiment was at its most critical stage, at about 6 p.m., we observed sudden swirls of snowdrift high up on the western mountains, coming rapidly down to lower levels. For a few minutes we did not think seriously of the phenomenon, but as the drift came nearer we saw that something serious was in the air. Mackay and I rushed down to our tent, the skirt of which was only temporarily secured with light blocks of snow. We reached it just as it was struck by the sudden blizzard which had descended from the western mountains. There was no time to dig further blocks of snow, all we could do was to seize the heavy food-bags on our sledges, weighing sixty pounds each, and rush them on to the skirt of the tent. The blizzard struck our kitchen on the island simultaneously with our tent, and temporarily Mawson lost his mits and most of the tit-bits of seal meat, but these were quickly recovered, and he came rushing down to join us in securing the tent. While Mawson in frantic haste chopped out blocks of snow and dumped them on to the skirt of the tent, Mackay, no less frantically, struggled with our sleeping-bag, which had been turned insideout to air, and which by this time was covered with drift snow. He quickly had it turned right side in again, and dashed it inside the tent. At last everything was secured, and we found ourselves safe and sound inside the tent. The primus was quickly got going, and soon we had some hot cocoa and hot seal pottage, together with some small pieces of charred but delicious seal blubber. The blizzard continued until past our bedtime. We turned in with a determination of making further experiments on the cooking of seal meat on the following morning.

The following day, November 1, we breakfasted off a mixture of our ordinary hoosh and seal meat. After some discussion we decided that our only hope of reaching the Magnetic Pole lay in our travelling on half rations from our present camp to the point on the coast at the Drygalski Glacier, where we might for the first time hope to be able to turn inland with reasonable prospect of reaching the Magnetic Pole. Mawson was emphatic that we must conserve six weeks of full rations for our inland journey to and from the Pole. This necessitated our going on half rations from this island to the far side of the Drygalski Glacier, a distance of about one hundred statute miles. In order to supplement the regular half rations we intended to take seal meat.

While I was busy in calculating the times and distances for the remainder of our journey, and proportioning the food rations to suit our new programme, Mawson and Mackay conducted further experiments on the cooking of seal meat with blubber. While at our winter quarters, Mackay had made some experiments on the use of blubber as a fuel. He had constructed a blubber lamp, the wick of which kept alight for several hours at a time, feeding itself on the seal oil. He had tried the experiment of heating up water over this blubber lamp, and was partly successful at the time when we left winter quarters for our present sledging journey. But his experiments at the time were not taken very seriously, and the blubber lamp was left behind, a fact which we now much regretted. An effective cooking-stove was, however, evolved, as the result of a series of experiments this day, out of one of our large empty biscuit tins. The lid of this was perforated with a number of circular holes for the reception of wicks. Its edges were bent down, so as to form supports to keep the wick-holder about half an inch above the bottom of the biscuit tin. The wickholder was put in place; wicks were made of pieces of old calico food-bags rolled in seal blubber, or with thin slices of seal blubber enfolded in them, the calico being done up in little rolls for the purpose of making wicks, as one rolls a cigarette, the seal blubber taking the place of the tobacco in this case. Lumps of blubber were laid round the wick-holder. Then, after some difficulty, the wicks were lighted. They burned feebly at first, as seal blubber has a good deal of water in it. After some minutes of fitful spluttering, the wicks got fairly alight, and as soon as the lower part of the biscuit tin was raised to a high temperature, the big lumps of blubber at the side commenced to have the water boiled out of them and the oil rendered down.

This oil ran under the wick-holder and supplied the wicks at their base. The wicks, now fed with warm, pure seal oil, started to burn brightly, and even fiercely, so that it became necessary occasionally to damp them down with chips of fresh blubber. We tried the experiment of using lumps of salt as wicks, and found this fairly successful. We also tried small pieces of our brown rope for the same purpose, using the separated strands of these cut in pieces of about one and a half inches long. These made excellent wicks, but we could not spare much rope. We also tried the lampwick that we had brought with us for binding on our finnesko, but in this case also rigid economy was an absolute necessity. We decided to rely for wicks chiefly on our empty food-bags, and thought possibly that if these ran out we might have recourse to moss. But the empty food-bags supplied sufficient wick for our need.

That day, by means of galvanised iron wires, we slung the inner pot from our aluminium cooker over the lighted wicks of our blubber cooker, thawed down snow in it, added chips of seal meat and made a delicious bouillon. This had a rich red colour and seemed very nutritious, but to me was indigestible.

While Mawson was still engaged on further cooking experiments, Mackay and I ascended to the highest point of the island, selected a spot for a cairn to mark our depot, and Mackay commenced building the cairn. Meanwhile, I returned to camp and wrote a number of letters, including one to the commander of the *Nimrod*. The latter was accompanied by a sketch plan taken from the Admiralty chart to show the proper position of our final depot before we were to turn inland 'on the low sloping shore' to the north-west of the Drygalski Glacier. The other letters were to Lieutenant Shackleton and to my family.

The letter to the commander of the *Nimrod* contained the following statement of our plans:

Camp, Granite Harbour.*

Dear Sir,

I beg to inform you that we intend leaving here tomorrow in continuation of our journey towards the Magnetic Pole. We have to work our two sledges by relays, which, of course, means slow progress – only about four miles per day. At this rate we hope to reach the north side of the Drygalski Ice Barrier, at the point where 'low sloping shore' is marked on the Admiralty Chart of the Antarctic Sheet III. (please see sketch on opposite page), by about December 15. We propose to make a depot there marked by a black flag similar to the one we are leaving here at the island at south side of entrance to Granite Harbour. We propose to travel inland from the 'low sloping shore', and if possible reach the Magnetic Pole and return to depot. We estimate that this may take six weeks, so that we may not return to the coast at the low sloping shore depot until about January 25. We propose to wait there until the *Nimrod* calls for us at the beginning of February.'

The letter concluded with detailed instructions regarding the course to be pursued in searching for the party.

---

*At this time we were under the impression that this island was on the south side of Granite Harbour. We did not know that we had already left Granite Harbour about twelve miles to the south of us.

33
PROFESSOR DAVID'S NARRATIVE
(CONTINUED)

The old dragon under ground
In straiter limits bound,
Not half so far casts his usurped sway,
And wroth to see his kingdom fail,
Swinges the scaly horror of his folded tail.

MILTON

It had, of course, become clear to us before this letter was written, in view of our experience of the already cracking sea ice near the true Granite Harbour, as well as in view of our comparatively slow progress by relay, that our retreat back to camp from the direction of the Magnetic Pole would in all probability be entirely cut off through the breaking up of the sea ice. Under these circumstances we determined to take the risk of the *Nimrod* arriving safely on her return voyage at Cape Royds, where she would receive the instructions to search for us along the western coast, and also the risk of her not being able to find our depot and ourselves at the low sloping shore. We knew that there was a certain amount of danger in adopting this course, but we felt that we had got on so far with the work entrusted to us by our Commander, that we could not honourably now turn back. Under these circumstances we each wrote farewell letters to those who were nearest and dearest, and the following morning, November 2, we were up at 4.30 a.m. After putting all the letters into one of our empty dried-milk tins, and fitting on the air-tight lid, I walked with it to the island and climbed up to the cairn. Here, after carefully depoting several bags of geological specimens at the base of the flagstaff, I lashed the little post office by means of cord and copperwire securely to the flagstaff, and then carried some large slabs of exfoliated granite to the cairn, and built them up on the leeward side of it in order to strengthen it against the southerly blizzards. A keen wind was blowing, as was usual in the early morning, off the high plateau, and one's hands got frequently frost-bitten in the work of securing the tin to the flagstaff. The cairn was at the seaward end of a sheer cliff two hundred feet high.

On returning to camp I put some chopped seal meat into the cooking-pot on our blubber stove, which Mawson had meanwhile lighted, and about three-quarters of an hour later we partook of some nourishing, but no less indigestible seal bouillon. It was later than usual when we started our sledges, and the pulling proved extremely heavy. The sun's heat was thawing the snow surface and making it extremely sticky. Our progress was so painfully slow that we decided, after, with great efforts, doing two miles, to camp, have our hoosh, and then turn in for six hours, having meanwhile started the blubber lamp. At the expiration of that time we intended to get out of our sleeping-bag, breakfast, and start sledging about midnight. We hoped that by adopting nocturnal habits of travelling, we would avoid the sticky ice-surface which by daytime formed such an obstacle to our progress.

We carried out this programme on the evening of November 2, and the morning of November 3. We found the experiment fairly successful, as at midnight and for a few hours afterwards, the temperature remained sufficiently low to keep the surface of the snow on the sea ice moderately crisp.

On November 3 and 4 the weather was fine, and we made fair progress. At noon Mawson cleaned out the refuse from our blubber lamp. Amongst this were a few dainty bits; Mackay was what he called 'playing the skua', picking these over, when he accidentally transferred to his mouth and swallowed one of the salt wicks which we had been using in the blubber lamp. Mawson and I were unaware of this episode at the time. Later on, towards evening, he complained much of thirst, and proffered a gentle request, when the snow was being thawed down preparatory to making hoosh, that he might be allowed to drink some of the water before the hoosh was put into it; at the same time he gave us the plausible explanation above mentioned as the cause of his exceeding thirst. After debating the matter at some length, it was decided, in view of the special circumstances surrounding the case, and without creating a precedent – which otherwise might become a dangerous one – that he might be allowed on this occasion to take a drink. Mackay, however, considered that this water gift was given grudgingly, and of necessity, and accordingly he sternly refused to accept it. Just then, the whole discussion was abruptly terminated through the pot being accidentally capsized when being lifted off the blubber lamp, and the whole of the water was lost.

On the following day, November 5, we were opposite a very interesting coastal panorama, which we thought belonged to Granite Harbour, but which was really over twenty miles to the north of it. Magnificent ranges of mountains, steep slopes free from snow and ice, stretched far to the north and far to the south of us, and finished away inland, towards the heads of long glacier cut valleys, in a vast upland snow plateau. The rocks which were exposed to view in the lower part of these ranges were mostly of warm sepia brown to terracotta tint, and were evidently built up of a continuation of the gneissic rocks and red granites which we had previously seen. Above these crystalline rocks came a belt of greenish-grey rock, apparently belonging to some stratified formation and possibly many hundreds of feet in thickness; the latter was capped with a black rock that seemed to be either a basic plateau lava, or a huge sill. In the direction of the glacier valleys, the plateau was broken up into a vast number of conical hills of various shapes and heights, all showing evidence of intense glacial action in the past. The hills were here separated from the coast-line by a continuous belt of piedmont glacier ice. This last terminated where it joined the sea ice in a steep slope, or low cliff, and in places was very much crevassed. Mawson at our noon halts for lunch, continued taking the angles of all these ranges and valleys with our theodolite.

The temperature was now rising, being as high as 22° Fahr. at noon on November 5. We had a very heavy sledging surface that day, there being much consolidated brash ice, sastrugi, pie-crust snow, and numerous cracks in the sea ice. As an offset to these troubles we had that night, for the first time, the use of our new frying-pan, constructed by Mawson out of one of our empty paraffin tins. This tin had been cut in half down the middle parallel to its broad surfaces, and loops of iron wire being added, it was possible to suspend it inside the empty biscuit tin above the wicks of our blubber lamp. We found that in this frying-pan we could rapidly render down the seal blubber into oil, and as soon as the oil boiled we dropped into the pan small slices of seal liver or seal meat. The liver took about ten minutes to cook in the boiling oil, the seal meat about twenty minutes. These facts were ascertained by the empirical method. Mawson discovered by the same method that the nicely browned and crisp residue from the seal blubber, after the oil in it had become rendered down, was good eating, and had a fine nutty flavour. We also found, as the result of later experiments, that dropping a little seal's blood into the boiling oil produced eventually a gravy of very fine flavour. If the seal's blood was poured in rapidly into the boiling oil, it made a kind of gravy pancake, which we also considered very good as a variety.

We had a magnificent view this day of fresh ranges of mountains to the north of Depot Island. At the foot of these was an extensive terrace of glacier ice, a curious type of piedmont glacier. Its surface was strongly convex near where it terminated seawards in a steep slope or low cliff. In places this ice was heavily crevassed. At a distance of several miles inland, it reached the spurs of an immense coastal range, while in the wide gaps in this range the ice trended inland as far as the eye could see until it blended in the far distance with the skyline high up on the great inland plateau.

A little before 9 p.m. on November 5 we left our sleeping-bag, and found snow falling, with a fresh and chilly breeze from the south. The blubber lamp, which we had lighted before we had turned in, had got blown out. We built a chubby house for it of snow blocks to keep off the wind, and relighted it, and then turned into the sleeping-bag again while we waited for the snow and chips of seal meat in our cooking-pot to become converted into a hot bouillon; the latter was ready after an interval of about one hour and a half.

Just before midnight we brought the cooker alight into the tent in order to protect it from the blizzard which was now blowing and bringing much falling snow with it. Mawson's cooking experiments continued to be highly successful and entirely satisfactory to the party.

We waited for the falling snow to clear sufficiently to enable us to see a short distance ahead, and then started again, the blizzard still blowing with a little low drift. After doing a stage of pulling on both sledges to keep ourselves warm in the blizzard we set sail – always a chilly business – and the wind was a distinct assistance to us. We encountered a good deal of brash ice that day, and noticed that this type of ice surface was most common in the vicinity of icebergs, which just here were very numerous. The brash ice is probably formed by the icebergs surging to and fro in heavy weather like a lot of gigantic Yermaks, and crunching up the sea ice in their vicinity. The latter, of course, re-freezes, producing a surface covered with jagged edges and points.

We were now reduced to one plasmon biscuit each for breakfast and one for the evening meal, and we were unanimous in the opinion that we had never before fully realised how very nice these plasmon biscuits were. We became exceedingly careful even over the crumbs. As some biscuits were thicker than others, the cook for the week would select three biscuits, place them on the outer cover of our aluminium cooker, and get one of his mates to look in an opposite direction while the messman pointed to a biscuit and said, 'Whose?' The mate with averted face, or shut eyes, would then state the owner, and the biscuit was ear-marked for him, and so with the other two biscuits. Grievous was the disappointment of the man to whose lot the thinnest of the three biscuits had fallen. Originally, on this sledge journey, when biscuits were more plentiful, we used to eat them regardless of the loss of crumbs, munching them boldly, with the result that occasional crumbs fell on the floorcloth. Not so now. Each man broke his biscuit over his own pannikin of hoosh, so that any crumbs produced in the process of fracture fell into the pannikin. Then, in order to make sure that there were no loose fragments adhering to the morsel we were about to transfer to our mouths, we tapped the broken chip, as well as the biscuit from which it had been broken, on the sides of the pannikin, so as to shake into it any loose crumbs. Then, and then only, was it safe to devour the precious morsel. Mackay, who adopted this practice in common with the rest of us, said it reminded him of the old days when the sailors tapped each piece of broken biscuit before eating it in order to shake out the weevils.

Mawson and I now wore our ski boots instead of finnesko, the weather being warmer, and the ski boot giving one a better grip on the snow surface of the sea ice. The rough leather took the skin off my right heel, but Mackay fixed it up later in the evening, that is, my heel, with some 'Newskin'. As we found the sharp iron spikes of the ski boots made holes in our waterproof floorcloth we made a practice of always changing into our finnesko before entering the tent.

We sledged on uneventfully for the remainder of November 6, and during the 7th, and on November 8 it came on to blow again with fresh-falling snow. The blizzard was still blowing when the time came for us to pitch our tent. We had a severe struggle to get the tent up in the high wind and thick falling snow. At last the work was accomplished, and we were all able to turn into our sleeping-bag, pretty tired, at about 12.30 p.m.

The weather was still bad the following day, November 9. After breakfast of seal's liver, and digging out the sledges from the snow drift, we started in the blizzard, the snow still falling. After a little while we made sail on both sledges. The light was very bad on account of the thick falling snow, and we were constantly falling up to our knees in the cracks in the sea ice. It seemed miraculous that in spite of these very numerous accidents we never sprained an ankle.

That day we saw a snow petrel, and three skua gulls visited our camp. At last the snow stopped falling and the wind fell light, and we were much cheered by a fine, though distant view of the Nordenskjold Ice Barrier to the north of us. We were all extremely anxious to ascertain what sort of a surface for sledging we should meet with on this great glacier. According to the Admiralty chart, prepared from observations by the *Discovery* expedition, this glacier was between twenty-four and thirty miles wide, and projected over twenty miles from the rocky shore into the sea. We hoped that we might be able to cross it without following a circuitous route along its seaward margins.

We started off on November 10, amongst very heavy sastrugi and ridges of broken pack-ice. Cracks in the sea ice were extremely numerous. The morning was somewhat cloudy, but as the midnight sun got higher in the heavens, the clouds dispersed and the weather became comparatively warm, the temperature being up to plus 3° Fahr. at 8 a.m. That day when we pitched camp we were within half a mile of the southern edge of the Nordenskjold Ice Barrier.

The following day, November 11, as Mawson wished to get an accurate magnetic determination with the Lloyd-Creak dip circle, we decided to camp, Mackay and I exploring the glacier surface to select a suitable track for our sledges while Mawson took his observations. After breakfast we removed everything containing iron several hundred yards away from the tent, leaving Mawson alone inside it in company with the dip circle. We found that the ascent from the sea ice to the Nordenskjold Ice Barrier was a comparatively easy one. The surface was formed chiefly of hard snow glazed in places, partly through thawing and re-freezing, partly through the polishing of this windward surface by particles of fresh snow driven over it by the blizzards. Hummocky masses, apparently of the nature of large sastrugi, projected here and there to a height of six feet above the general level. The latter were something like elongated white ant's nests. In places the snow surface showed pie-crust structure, a bad surface for sledging. On the whole this Barrier was fairly free from crevasses, although Mackay and I crossed a few in our short pioneering excursion.

The surface ascended gradually to a little over one hundred feet above the level of the sea ice, passing into a wide undulating plain which stretched away to the north as far as the eye could see.

We returned to Mawson with the good news that the Nordenskjold Ice Barrier was quite practicable for sledging, and would probably afford us a much more easy surface than the sea ice over which we had previously been passing. Mawson informed us, as the result of his observations with the dip circle, that the Magnetic Pole was probably about forty miles further inland than the theoretical mean position calculated for it from the magnetic observations of the *Discovery* expedition seven years ago.

Early on the morning of November 12 we packed up, and started to cross the Nordenskjold Ice Barrier. We noticed here that there were two well-marked sets of sastrugi, one set, nearly due north and south, formed by the strong southerly blizzards, the other set, crossing nearly at right angles, coming from the west and formed by the cold land winds blowing off the high plateau at night on to the sea.

We were surprised to observe that this ice barrier was almost completely isolated from the shore by deep inlets, and for a time we speculated as to whether after all it might not be a gigantic tabular iceberg run aground. In view, however, of what we observed later there can be little doubt that it is of the nature of a large piedmont glacier, afloat at its seaward end and central portions. It is now practically inert, having no forward movement from the land towards the sea. It is just the vanishing remnant of what at one time was no doubt a large active glacier, vigorously pushed out seaward, the overflow ice from the vast snow-fields of the inland plateau. The supply, however, of ice near the coast has dwindled so enormously that there is no longer sufficient pressure to move this ice barrier.

This day, November 12, was an important one in the history of Mawson's triangulation of the coast, for he was able in the morning to sight simultaneously Mount Erebus and Mount Melbourne, as well as Mount Lister. We were fortunate in having a very bright and clear day on this occasion, and the round of angles obtained by Mawson with the theodolite were in every way satisfactory.

The following day, November 13, we were still on the Nordenskjold Ice Barrier. The temperature in the early morning, about 8 a.m., was minus 13° Fahr. Mawson had provided an excellent dish for breakfast consisting of crumbed seal meat and seal's blood, which proved delicious. We got under way about 2 a.m. It was a beautiful sunshiny day with a gentle cold breeze off the western plateau. When we had sledged for about one thousand yards Mawson suddenly exclaimed that he could see the end of the barrier where it terminated in a white cliff only about six hundred yards ahead. We halted the sledge, and while Mawson took some more theodolite angles Mackay and I reconnoitred ahead but could find no way down the cliff. We returned to the sledge and all pulled on for another quarter of a mile. Once more we reconnoitred, and this time both Mawson and I found some steep slopes formed by drifted snow which were just practicable for a light sledge lowered by an alpine rope. We chose what seemed to be the best of these; Mackay tied the alpine rope around his body, and taking his ice-axe descended the slope cautiously, Mawson and I holding on to the rope meanwhile. The snow slope proved fairly soft giving good foothold, and he was soon at the bottom without having needed any support from the alpine rope. He then returned to the top of the slope, and we all set to work unpacking the sledges. We made fast one of the sledges to the alpine rope, and after loading it lightly lowered it little by little down the slope, one of us guiding the sledge while the other two slacked out the alpine rope above. The man who went down the sledge to the bottom would unload it there on the sea ice and then climb up the slope, the other two meanwhile pulling up the empty sledge. This manoeuvre was repeated a number of times until eventually the whole of our food and equipment, including two sledges, were safely down on the sea ice below.

We were all much elated at having got across the Nordenskjold Ice Barrier so easily and so quickly. We were also fortunate in securing a seal; Mackay went off and killed this, bringing back seal steak, liver and a considerable quantity of seal blood. From the last Mackay said he intended to manufacture a black pudding. Usually, I believe, a black pudding is manufactured from the part of the blood which does not contain the fibrin, but on this occasion the black pudding was wholly formed of fibrin, so that it may be described as a negative rather than a positive black pudding. This fibrin was boiled up in seal oil, and though rather tasteless was at all events nourishing, and was certainly filling.

While Mackay had been in pursuit of the seal meat Mawson had taken a meridian altitude while I kept the time for him. After our hoosh we packed the sledges, and Mawson took a photograph showing the cliff forming the northern boundary of the Nordenskjold Ice Barrier. This cliff was about forty feet in height. We had some discussion as to whether or not there was a true tidal crack separating the sea ice from this ice barrier. Certainly, on the south side there was no evidence of the presence of any such crack, but on the north side there were small local cracks; yet it could hardly be said that these were of sufficient importance to be termed true tide-cracks. In one of these cracks most beautiful filagree ice crystals, fully one inch across, lined the sides of the walls of the crack in the sea ice. There can be little doubt I think, that the greater part of this Nordenskjold Ice Barrier is afloat.

The sun was so warm this day that I was tempted before turning in to the sleeping-bag to take off my ski boots and socks and give my feet a snow bath, which was very refreshing.

The following day, November 14, we were naturally anxious to be sure of our exact position on the chart, in view of the fact that we had come to the end of the ice barrier some eighteen miles quicker than the chart led us to anticipate we should. Mawson accordingly worked up his meridian altitude, and I plotted out the angular distances he had found respectively, for Mount Erebus, Mount Lister and Mount Melbourne. As the result of the application of our calculations to the chart it became evident that we had actually crossed the Nordenskjold Ice Barrier of Captain Scott's survey, and were now opposite what on his chart was termed Charcot Bay. This was good news and cheered us up very much, as it meant that we were nearly twenty miles further north than we previously thought we were.

The day was calm and fine, and the surface of the sea ice was covered with patches of soft snow with nearly bare ice between, and the sledging was not quite as heavy as usual. In the evening two skua gulls went for our seal meat during the interval that we were returning for the second sledge after pulling on the first sledge. It was wonderful how quickly these gulls made their appearance from distant parts of the horizon as soon as any fresh meat was available. The previous day one of them had actually attempted to eat the seal meat out of our frying-pan when the meat was being cooked in boiling oil. We could see as we came up from a distance that the heat of the savoury dish puzzled him a good deal, as each time he dipped his beak into our hot mince he jerked it out again very suddenly and seemed a very surprised bird.

We had a magnificent view of the rocky coast-line, which is here most impressive. The sea ice stretched away to the west of us for several miles up to a low cliff and slope of piedmont glacier ice, with occasional black masses of rock showing at its edge. Several miles further inland the Piedmont glacier ice terminated abruptly against a magnificent range of mountains, tabular for the most part but deeply intersected. In the wide gaps between this coast range were vast glaciers fairly heavily crevassed, descending by steep slopes from an inland plateau to the sea.

On November 15, there was a fresh wind from the west-south-west. The weather was overcast, and a few flakes of snow were falling. We killed two young seals to replenish our food-supply. Mackay took over the blubber cooking apparatus so as to set Mawson free for his theodolite observations. The sky was dull and leaden for most of the day, with occasional glimpses of light over the western mountains. On the whole it looked as if a blizzard were approaching.

We were still doing our travelling by night and sleeping during the afternoon. When we arose from our sleeping-bag at 8 p.m. on the night of November 15, we found that the signs of the blizzard had more or less passed away. There was a beautifully perfect 'Noah's Ark' in the sky; the belts of cirrus-stratus composing the ark stretched from south-south-west to north-north-east, converging towards the horizon in each of these directions. Fleecy sheets of frost smoke arose from over the open water on Ross Sea, and formed dense cumulus clouds. This, of course, was a certain indication to us that open water was not far distant, and impressed upon us the necessity of making every possible speed if we hoped to reach our projected point of departure on the coast for the Magnetic Pole before the sea ice entirely broke up.

This had been a truly glorious day, bright and sunny, and as this was the end of a food week and the messman for the week had kept a little food up his sleeve, so to speak, we fared sumptuously. The cocoa was extra strong, milky and sweet. Mackay's opinion was that such cocoa much reminded him of better days, and was absolutely uplifting.

The following day, November 17, after a very heavy sledging over loose powdery snow six inches deep we reached a low glacier and ice cliff. We were able to get some really fresh snow from this barrier or glacier, the cliffs of which were from thirty to forty feet high. It was a great treat to get fresh water at last, as since we had left the Nordenskjold Ice Barrier the only snow available for cooking purposes had been brackish.

The following day was also bright and sunny, but the sledging was terribly heavy. The sun had thawed the surface of the saline snow and our sledge runners had become saturated with soft water. We were so wearied with the great effort necessary to keep the sledges moving that at the end of each halt we fell sound asleep for five minutes or so at a time across the sledges. On such occasions one of the party would wake the others up, and we would continue our journey. We were even more utterly exhausted than usual at the end of this day.

By this time, however, we were in sight of a rocky headland which we took to be Cape Irizar, and we knew that this cape was not very far to the south of the Drygalski Glacier. Indeed, already, a long line was showing on the horizon which could be no other than the eastward extension of this famous and, as it afterwards proved, formidable glacier.

On November 19, we had another heavy day's sledging, ankle deep in the soft snow with occasional thin patches of sludgy saline ice from which ice flowers had recently disappeared through thawing. We only did two miles of relay work this day and yet were quite exhausted at the end of it.

The following day, November 20, being short of meat we killed a seal calf and cow, and so replenished our larder. At the end of the day's sledging I walked over about two miles to a cliff face, about six miles south of Cape Irizar. The rocks all along this part of the shore were formed of coarse gneissic granite, of which I was able to collect some specimens. The cliff was about one hundred feet high where it was formed of the gneiss, and above this rose a capping of from seventy to eighty feet in thickness of heavily crevassed blue glacier ice. There were here wide tidecracks between the sea ice and the foot of the sea cliff. These were so wide that it was difficult to cross them. The whole shore line was literally alive with seals and seal calves; there were over fifty of them in a stretch of about three hundred yards. At a distance of two miles our tent was, of course, quite out of sight, and one had to be guided back, on this as on other similar occasions, chiefly by one's footprints.

The following day, November 21, the sledging was painfully heavy over thawing saline snow surface, and sticky sea ice. We were only able to do two and two-third miles.

On November 22, on rounding the point of the low ice barrier, thirty to forty feet high, we obtained a good view of Cape Irizar, and also of the Drygalski Ice Barrier.

On November 23 we found that a mild blizzard was blowing, but we travelled on through it as we could not afford to lose any time. The blizzard died down altogether about 3 a.m., and was succeeded by a gentle westerly wind off the plateau. That evening, after our tent had been put up and we had finished the day's meal, I walked over a mile to the shore. The prevailing rock was still gneissic granite with large whitish veins of aplitic granite. A little bright green moss was growing on tiny patches of sand and gravel, and in some of the cracks in the granite. The top of the cliff was capped by blue glacier ice. With the help of steps cut by my ice-axe I climbed some distance up this in order to try and get some fresh ice for cooking purposes, but close to the top of the slope I accidentally slipped and glissaded most unwillingly some distance down before I was able to check myself by means of the chisel edge of the ice-axe. My hands were somewhat cut and bruised, but otherwise no damage was done. The whole of this ice was slightly bitter; no doubt sea spray in heavy weather when the sea was open during summer time, had dashed over the headland, and so flavoured the ice with sea salts. At last I obtained some fairly fresh ice in the form of large ice stalactites depending from an overhanging cliff of glacier ice. With these and my geological specimens I trudged back to the camp.

On November 24, a strong keen wind was blowing off the plateau from the west-south-west. This died down later on in the morning at about 2 a.m. and the temperature at 9 a.m. rose as high as plus 20° Fahr. We were all suffering somewhat from want of sleep, and although the snow surface was better than it had been for some little time we still found the work of sledging very fatiguing. A three-man sleeping-bag, where you are wedged in more or less tightly against your mates, where all snore and shin one another and each feels on waking that he is more shinned against than shinning, is not conducive to real rest; and we rued the day that we chose the three-man bag in preference to the one-man bags. That afternoon and evening we slept a little longer than usual, and felt much refreshed on the early morning of November 25.

It was interesting to watch at lunch time the anxious face of the messman for the week as he sat with his nose close to the outer cover of the aluminium cooker in order to catch the first whiff of the delicious aroma which told that the tea in the water of the inner cookingpot had been just brought to the boil. With the first sniff of the aroma the messman would immediately unscrew the brass valve of the primus, so as to let the air in and the primus lamp down, with a view to saving paraffin oil.

34

PROFESSOR DAVID'S NARRATIVE (CONTINUED)

On the following day, November 26, we saw on looking back that the rocky headland, where I had collected the specimens of granite and moss, was not part of the mainland but a small island. This day was rather a memorable one in our journey, as we reached a large rocky promontory, which we supposed at the time to be Cape Irizar. Subsequent observations, however, proved that we must already have passed Cape Irizar, which was in all probability the small island just referred to.

We had some good sledging here over pancake ice nearly free from snow and travelled fast. While Mackay secured some seal meat Mawson and I ascended the rocky promontory, climbing at first over rock, then over glacier ice, to a height of about six hundred feet above the sea. The rock was a pretty red granite traversed by large dykes of black rocks, apparently of an alkaline character, belonging to the phonolites or tinguaites.

From the top of the headland to the north we had a magnificent view across the level surface of sea ice far below us. We saw that at a few miles from the shore an enormous iceberg, frozen into the floe, lay right across the path which we had intended to travel in our northerly course on the morrow. To the north-west of us was Geikie Inlet and beyond that stretching as far as the eye could follow was the great Drygalski Glacier. Beyond the Drygalski Glacier were a series of rocky hills. One of these was identified as probably being Mount Neumayer. Several mountains could be seen further to the north of this, but the far distance was obscured from view by cloud and mist so that we were unable to make out the outline of Mount Nansen. It was evident that the Drygalski Glacier was bounded landwards on the north by a steep cliff of dark, highly jointed rock, and we were not a little concerned to observe with our field-glasses that the surface of the Drygalski Glacier was wholly different to that of the Nordenskjold Ice Barrier. It was clear that the surface of the Drygalski Glacier was formed of jagged surfaces of ice very heavily crevassed, and projecting in the form of immense *séracs* separated from one another by deep undulations or chasms. It at once suggested to my mind some scaly dragon-like monster and recalled the lines of Milton quoted at the commencement of the previous chapter. The 'Scaly horror of his folded tail' did not seem enchanting even at this distance of ten to fifteen miles. We could see that much of this glacier was absolutely impossible for sledging, but it appeared that further eastward the inequalities of the ice-surface became less pronounced, and, at the extreme eastward extension, at a distance of some twenty-five to thirty miles from where we stood, the surface appeared fairly smooth. After taking these observations from our point of vantage we retraced our steps. Mawson, in his spiked:ski boots, got down the sloping ice-surface with comparative ease, but as I had finnesko on I found it necessary to cut steps with my ice-axe all the way down the glacier ice.

It was obvious from what we had seen looking out to sea to the east of our camp that there were large bodies of open water trending shorewards in the form of long lanes at no great distance. The lanes of water were only partly frozen over, and some of these were interposed between us and the Drygalski Glacier. Clearly not a moment was to be lost if we were to reach the Drygalski Glacier before the sea ice broke up. A single strong blizzard would now have converted the whole of the sea ice between us and the Drygalski Glacier into a mass of drifting pack. We obtained from this rocky promontory a fine collection of geological specimens, and here, as elsewhere, got abundant evidence of former much greater extension of the inland ice sheet.

The following day, November 27, we decided to run our sledges to the east of the large berg which we had observed on the previous day, and this course apparently would enable us to avoid a wide and ugly looking tide-crack extending northwards from the rocky point at our previous camp. The temperature was now as high as from plus 26° to plus 28° Fahr. at mid-day, consequently, the saline snow and ice were all day more or less sticky and slushy. We camped near the large berg.

On the morning of November 28, a mother seal with a well-grown baby came up to our tent and sniffed and snorted around its skirt. It seemed about to enter the tent when I hunted it off, and mother and baby, meanwhile, made tracks, in every sense of the word, for the open water. Then we packed up and started our sledges, and pulled them over a treacherous slushy tide-crack, and then headed them round an open lead of water in the sea ice. At 3 a.m. we had lunch near the east end of the big berg. Near here Mackay and Mawson succeeded in catching and killing an Emperor penguin, and took the breast and liver. This bird was caught close to a lane of open water in the sea ice. We found that in the direction of the berg this was thinly frozen over, and for some time it seemed as though our progress further north was completely blocked. Eventually we found a place where the ice might just bear our sledges. We strengthened this spot by laying down on it slabs

of sea ice and shovelfuls of snow, and when the causeway was completed –
not without Mackay breaking through the ice in one place and very nearly
getting a ducking – we rushed our sledges over safely, although the ice was
so thin that it bent under their weight. We were thankful to get them both
safely to the other side.

We now found ourselves amongst some very high sastrugi of hard tough
snow. We had to drag the sledges over a great number of these, which were
nearly at right angles to our course. This work proved extremely fatiguing.
The sastrugi were from five to six feet in height. As we were having dinner
at the end of our day's sledging we heard a loud report which we considered
to be due to the opening of a new crack in the sea ice. We thought it was
possible that this crack was caused by some movement of the great active
Drygalski Glacier, now only about four miles ahead of us to the north.

We got out of our sleeping-bag soon after 8 p.m. on the evening of the
28th, and started just before midnight. The ice-surface over which we were
sledging this day had a curious appearance resembling rippling stalagmites,
or what may be termed ice marble. This opacity appeared to be due to a
surface enamel of partly thawed snow. This surface kept continually cracking
as we passed over it with a noise like that of a whip being cracked. It was
evidently in a state of tension, being contracted by the cold which attained
its maximum soon after midnight, for, although of course we had for many
weeks past been having the midnight sun it was still so low in the heavens
towards midnight that there was an appreciable difference in the temperature
between midnight and the afternoon. This difference in our case was further
accentuated by the cold nocturnal wind from the high plateau to our west.
This wind was of the nature of a land breeze on a large scale.

There were here two sets of sastrugi, the principal set parallel to the
plateau wind and trending here from nearly north-west to south-east; the
other set, caused by the blizzard winds, trended from south to north. We
were now getting very short of biscuits, and as a consequence were seized
with food obsessions, being unable to talk about anything but cereal foods,
chiefly cakes of various kinds and fruits. Whenever we halted for a short rest
we could discuss nothing but the different dishes with which we had been
regaled in our former lifetime at various famous restaurants and hotels.

The plateau wind blew keenly and strongly all day on November 29. As
we advanced further to the north the ice-surface became more and more
undulatory, rising against us in great waves like waves of the sea. Evidently
these waves were due to the forward movement, and consequent pressure of
the Drygalski Glacier. We had a fine view from the top of one of these ridges
over the surface of the Drygalski Glacier, to the edge of the inland plateau.
Far inland, perhaps forty or fifty miles away, we could see the great névé
fields, which fed the Drygalski Glacier, descending in conspicuous ice falls,

and beyond these loomed dim mountains. At the end of this day we hardly knew whether we were on the edge of the sea ice or on the thin edge of the Drygalski Glacier. Probably, I think, we were on very old sea ice, perhaps representing the accumulations of several successive seasons.

It fell calm at about 9 p.m., but just before midnight, November 29–30, the plateau wind returned, blowing stronger than ever. As the sun during the afternoon had now considerable heating power we tried the experiment of putting snow into our aluminium cookingpot, the exterior of which by this time was permanently coated with greasy lamp-black from the blubber lamp, and leaving the pot exposed in the evening to the direct rays of the sun. The lamp-black, of course, formed an excellent absorbent of the sun's heat-rays. On getting out of the sleeping-bag at 9 p.m. on November 29 I found that about half the snow I had put into the cooking-pot had been thawed down by the sun's heat. This, of course, saved both paraffin and blubber. It takes, of course, as much energy to thaw ice or snow at a temperature of 32° Fahr. to form a given volume of water as it does to raise that water from 32° Fahr. up to boiling-point. As our snow and ice used for domestic purposes frequently had a temperature of many degrees below zero, the heat energy necessary to thaw it was greater than that required to raise the water from freezing-point to boiling-point.

As we advanced with our sledge on the early morning of November 30, the ice ridges fronting us became higher and steeper, and we had much ado straining with all our might on the steep ice slopes to get the sledges to move, and they skidded a good deal as we dragged them obliquely up the slopes. The plateau wind, too, had freshened, and was now blowing on our port bow at from fifteen to twenty miles an hour, bringing with it a good deal of low drift. At last, about 10 a.m., the plateau wind dropped and with it the drift, and the weather became warm and sunny.

The glacier now spread before us as a great billowy sea of pale green ice, with here and there high embankments of marble-like névé resembling railway embankments. Unfortunately for our progress, the trend of the latter was nearly at right angles to our course. As we advanced still further north the undulations became more and more pronounced, the embankments higher and steeper. These embankments were now bounded by cliffs from forty to fifty feet in height, with overhanging cornices of tough snow. The cliffs faced northwards. The deep chasms which they produced formed a very serious obstacle to our advance, and we had to make some long *détours* in order to head them off. On studying one of these chasms it seemed to me that their mode of origin was somewhat as follows: In the first place the surface of the ice had become strongly ridged through forward movement of the glacier, with perhaps differential frictional resistance; the latter causing a series of undulations, the top of each ice undulation would then be further raised by

THE SOUTHERN PARTY ON BOARD THE *NIMROD*. LEFT TO RIGHT: WILD, SHACKLETON, MARSHALL, ADAMS.

THE NORTHERN PARTY AT THE SOUTH MAGNETIC POLE
FROM LEFT: DR. MACKAY, PROFESSOR DAVID,
DOUGLAS MAWSON

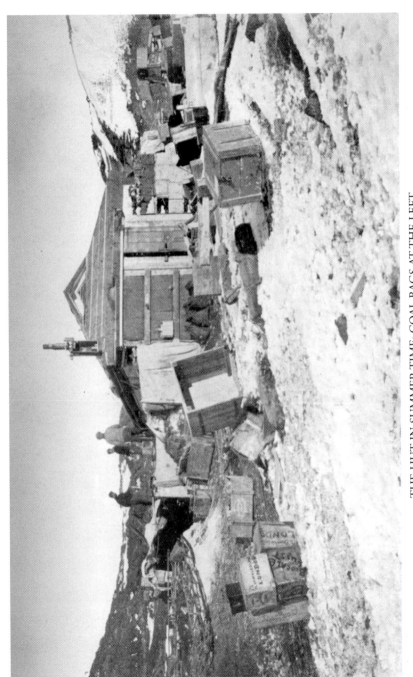

THE HUT IN SUMMER TIME; COAL BAGS AT THE LEFT

THE MOTOR-CAR IN SOFT SNOW, AFTER THE RETURN OF THE SHIP

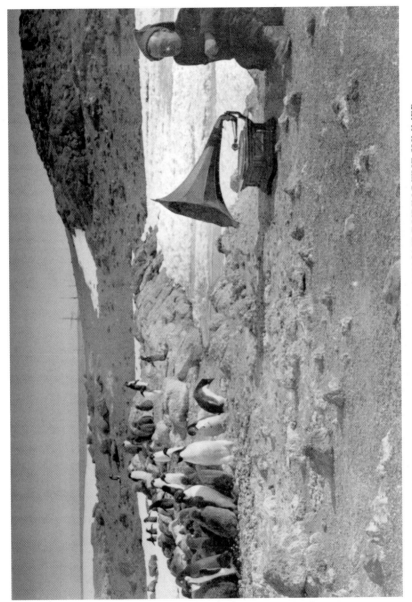

PENGUINS LISTENING TO THE GRAMOPHONE DURING THE SUMMER

A SEAL DESTINED FOR THE LARDER

FETCHING SNOW FOR COOKING PURPOSES

START OF WESTERN PARTY FROM CAPE ROYDS

THE MOTOR NEAR THE WINTER QUARTERS

A HAUL OF FISH

GROUP IN THE HUT IN THE SUMMER: JOYCE AT THE SEWING MACHINE

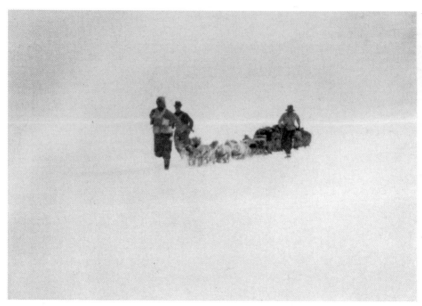

A DOG TEAM WITH LOADED SLEDGE GOING SOUTH TO LAY A DEPOT
FOR THE RETURN OF THE SOUTHERN PARTY

DEPOT PARTY PITCHING A TENT

THE BLUFF DEPOT

DIGGING TO ASCERTAIN THE DEPTH OF SNOW COVERING A DEPOT
LEFT BY THE *DISCOVERY* EXPEDITION

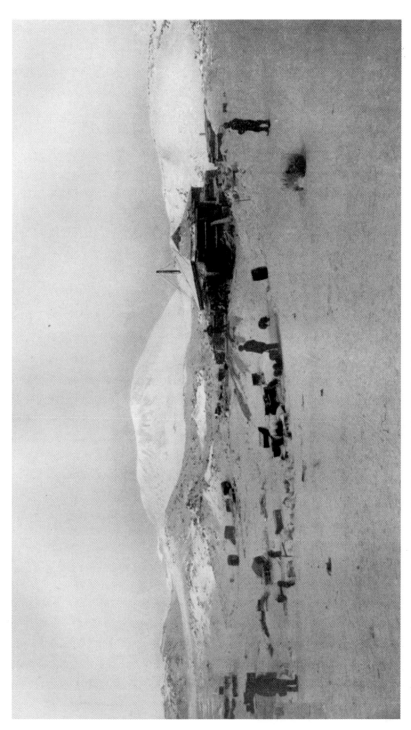

THE WINTER QUARTERS, WITH MOUNT EREBUS IN THE BACKGROUND. THE DOG-KENNELS ARE SEEN ON THE LEFT.

CAMP ON DECEMBER 17 ON THE FERRAR GLACIER BELOW
SENTINEL ROCK

ROUGH ICE SURFACE NEAR WINDY GULLY

THE WESTERN PARTY CAMPED ON THE FERRAR GLACIER ON DECEMBER 18.
HEAVY HANGING GLACIERS ON THE HILLS.

WESTERN PARTY'S CAMP ON DECEMBER 28 BELOW A HANGING GLACIER AT THE CATHEDRAL ROCKS an accumulation of snow partly carried by the west-north-west plateau wind, partly by the southerly blizzard wind. These two force components produced these overhanging cliffs facing the north. For some reason the snow would not lie at the bottoms of the troughs between the undulations. Probably they were swept bare by the plateau wind. It was hardly to be wondered at that we were unable to advance our sledges more than about one mile and a half that day.

The next day, December 1, the hauling of our sledges became much more laborious. For half a day we struggled over high sastrugi, hummocky ice ridges, steep undulations of bare blue ice with frequent chasms impassable for a sledge, unless it was unloaded and lowered by alpine rope. After struggling on for a little over half a mile we decided to camp, and while Mawson took magnetic observations and theodolite angles, Mackay and I reconnoitred ahead for between two and three miles to see if there was any way at all practicable for the sledge out of these mazes of chasms, undulations and *séracs*. Mackay and I were roped together for this exploratory work, and fell into about a score of crevasses before we returned to camp, though in this case we never actually fell with our head and shoulders below the lids of the crevasses, as they were mostly filled at the surface with tough snow. We had left a black signal flag on top of a conspicuous ice mound as a guide to us as to the whereabouts of the camp, and we found this a welcome beacon when we started to return, as it was by no means an easy task finding one's way across this storm-tossed ice sea, even when one was only a mile or two from the camp. On our return we found that Mawson was just completing his observations. He found that the dip of the needle here was 2½° off the vertical. We brought the tent down from where he had been taking magnetic observations, and treading warily, because of crevasses, set it up again close to our sledge, and had lunch.

We noticed in the case of the snow lids over crevasses that they were covered by a very pretty moss-like growth of pointed ice crystals. This growth was apparently due to a slow upward steaming of moist air from the spaces between the walls of the crevasses below. Possibly during the day the air beneath the snow lids may become slightly warmed, and as the temperature falls at night, particularly under the influence of the plateau wind, a slow percolation of the warm air through the snow lid may take place, and the small amount of moisture in it is deposited on the surface of the lid on coming in contact with the colder air outside. This process, continued from day to day, gradually builds up these moss-like crystals.

That afternoon we discussed the situation at some length. It appeared that the Drygalski Glacier must be at least twenty miles in width. If we were to cross it along the course which we were now following at the rate of half a mile every half day it would obviously take at least twenty days to get to the other side, and this estimate did not allow for those unforeseen delays which experience by this time had taught us were sure to occur. The view which Mackay and I had obtained of the glacier ice ahead of us showed that our difficulties, for a considerable distance, would materially increase. Under these circumstances we were reluctantly forced to the conclusion that our only hope of ultimate success lay in retreat. We accordingly determined to drag the sledges back off the glacier on to the sea ice by the way along which we had come.

Early on the morning of December 2 the retreat began. Just before midnight it had been clear and sunny, but as midnight approached a thick fog suddenly came up and obscured everything. Consequently we had great difficulty in picking up our old sledge tracks as we retreated over the glacier ice. The weather was still very thick and foggy at 3 a.m., but a little before 6 a.m. the fog cleared off and the sun shone through. We had now reached the southern edge of the glacier, and were back on the old undulating sea ice. We turned our sledges eastwards following parallel with the glacier edge. Immediately on our left rose large rounded hummocky masses of ice belonging to the Drygalski Glacier, and from fifty to sixty feet in height. The sky, meanwhile, had become again overcast with dense cumulus which drifted across rapidly from a south-easterly direction.

The following day we still travelled eastwards parallel to the southern edge of the Drygalski Glacier. The sledging was chiefly over soft snow, ankle deep, with occasional high snow sastrugi, and here and there a patch of rippled sea ice. There could be no doubt about it being sea ice this time because in one place, at the foot of one of these steep snow ridges, we noticed a pool of water only thinly frozen over, and on breaking the ice I tasted the water and found it was very salt.

Towards the end of this day's sledging we passed a long inlet trending north-westerly. This inlet was floored with sea ice, and made a long, deep indentation in the glacier ice. After our hoosh, and before turning into the sleeping-bag, Mawson and I went on to the north over some high hummocky ridges of the Drygalski Glacier to look ahead. Mawson, after a while, returned to camp, while I turned north-westwards to explore the inlet. After falling into a few crevasses which traversed the great billowy hummocks of blue glacier ice in all directions, I got down into the inlet, and on following it north-westwards, found that it gradually passed into a definite glacial river channel, and became quite impracticable for sledging. It was quite clear from the steep banks of this channel, cut out of the hard snow, névé and glacier ice, that during the few weeks of thaw in this part of the Antarctic, great volumes of thaw water must rush down off the higher parts of the glacier towards the sea, and in their passage they tear out deep cañon-like channels in the glacier ice and névé. This channel trended at first exactly in the direction in which we wished to make, but it was obvious that it was an impossible route for the sledges.

We decided on December 4 that we had better go on an extended reconnoitring expedition before we again risked landing our sledge in a labyrinth of pressure ridges and crevasses. After hauling our sledges for a little less than a mile, and meeting with steep slopes of snow dunes, we halted. While Mackay sewed one of the tent-poles, which had become loosened, back into its place in the canvas crown which held the tops of the tent-poles together, Mawson and I climbed on to some hummocks a little north of the camp to see which route would be best to follow on our reconnoitring journey. After lunch we all three started with our ice-axes and the alpine rope. We travelled up a broad bottomed snow valley for about two miles trending in the direction of Mount Larsen. Then for a little over a mile beyond it trended more to the right in the direction of Mount Nansen. Here we got into difficult country, the snow surface being succeeded by steep-sided hummocks, rolls and ridges of blue glacier ice, with occasional deep chasms and very numerous crevasses. We fell into numbers of the latter up to our thighs, but the snow lids as yet were just strong enough to stop us going deeper. Mawson opened up one of these snow lids with his ice-axe, and we noticed that the lid was from one to one and a half feet thick, while the crevasse was thirty feet wide and of vast depth. Much of the ground over which we were travelling rang hollow, and was evidently only roofed over by a thin layer of tough snow. Altogether we travelled about four miles to the north of our camp but could see no sign from there of any sea to the north of us. Meanwhile, Mackay diverged somewhat to the west, climbed on the top of a high ice pyramid, but was unable to see any trace of the sea beyond. We now returned at a smart pace back to camp, arriving about 9 a.m. We were all pretty tired, and, as usual before entering the tent, we took off our spiked ski boots so as to avoid puncturing the waterproof floorcloth, and put on finnesko. Hoosh was prepared, and we had a good meal of it, as well as of fried seal meat with blubber and seal oil.

It was evident now that even if we were to succeed in crossing the Drygalski Glacier, the passage would occupy a good many days, even under the most favourable circumstances, and our provisions were running very short. After we finished our hoosh, Mawson, with the field-glasses, sighted a seal near to the big berg to the south of us, which we had passed some five days previously. We decided that we would go after this seal the next day; meanwhile, the seal disappeared. Fearing that a blizzard might spring up on the following day, I proposed to go that evening out to the berg in search of seals, but Mackay kindly volunteered instead and started off with his ruck-sack and ice-axe and a small allowance of provisions, consisting of some cooked seal meat, biscuits and chocolate. He had a long journey before him.

While he was gone I was chiefly occupied in dividing up our rations into half-ration lots. At 5 p.m. I was attracted by the notes of a penguin behind an ice mound at no great distance. Rousing Mawson, we both went in pursuit and after a long and severe chase, captured an Adelie penguin.

At about midnight, December 4–5, Mackay returned to camp after his fourteen miles' tramp over the sea ice. He brought back with him a most welcome addition to our larder in the shape of over thirty pounds of seal meat, liver and seal blubber. He reported that he had had great difficulty in crossing the large icecrack where we had constructed the causeway for our sledge some five days previously, and he said that it would now have been impossible to have got the sledge over it. Mackay had been up over seventeen hours, and had been sledging, travelling over heavy ice, and carrying his heavy load of seal meat with only short intervals for meals. He had travelled a distance of about twenty-four miles, and of course under the circumstances was much exhausted and badly in need of a long rest. By securing the so much needed additional food-supply, he had rendered us an extremely important service. It now, of course, became necessary to give him the needed rest on the following day. Accordingly, the earlier part of December 5 we spent in the sleeping-bag.

Soon after midnight, December 5–6, we left our camp on the south side of the Drygalski Glacier, and struck across the high ridges of blue ice into the small valley in the glacier which we had prospected two days previously. As usual a keen wind was blowing off the plateau at this time of the morning, but the temperature soon rose to plus 23° Fahr. at 7.15 a.m. The sky was overcast with heavy stratus and cumulus clouds, especially in the direction of Cape Washington. We passed over a considerable number of crevasses without any serious accident. The day's sledging was heavy on account of the strongly undulating surface of the ice and the quantity of soft snow in the ice valley on the surface of the Drygalski Glacier.

The following day, December 7, was also dull and lowering with very dense cumulus clouds over Cape Washington and Mounts Melbourne and Nansen. We inferred that this dense cumulus was due to the presence of open water between the Drygalski Glacier and Cape Washington, and were not a little anxious as to whether, in the event of the sea ice having all drifted out on the north side of the Drygalski Glacier, it would be possible for us to travel shorewards on the surface of the glacier itself, when we got to the other side. We encountered many precipitous slopes from thirty to forty feet deep, often with overhanging cornices, barring our northward progress like those already met with in the part of the glacier from which we had retreated. These overhanging cliffs, however, were not quite as serious as those which we had left behind, and by making considerable *détours* we managed to circumvent them. At last we seemed to have got amongst an impassable belt of high crevassed ice ridges with precipitous chasms between. After a good deal of reconnoitring ahead a clue out of the labyrinth was discovered in the form of a series of high snow ridges which led backwards and forwards, in and out, amongst the high-pressure ridges, and eventually enabled us to land our sledges in a broad crevassed valley on the glacier surface.

After the hoosh at the end of our day's sledging, Mawson and I walked about two miles, looking out for a track for the next morning. The outlook was by no means encouraging, as the surface still bristled with huge ice undulations as far as the eye could reach. It was just as though a stormy sea had suddenly been frozen solid, with the troughs between its large waves here and there partly filled with snow, while the crests of the waves were raised by hard ridges of drift snow, terminating in overhanging cliffs facing the north. It was obvious, too, that the glacier ice over which we would have to travel, was still very heavily crevassed. As we returned, a mild blizzard sprang up from the south-south-west, bringing low drift with it. The blizzard cleared off in about an hour and a half, and the sun came out strong and hot, and rapidly thawed the snow on our tent and on the food-bags stored on our sledges.

The following day, December 8, we dug away the drift snow piled by the blizzard against our sledges, and were pleased to find that the day was beautifully fine and sunny with a light breeze from the west-south-west. The sledging was very heavy up and down steep ice slopes with much soft snow between.

Mawson had a slight attack of snow blindness on December 9. The day was so warm that we even felt it oppressive, the temperature at midnight being as high as plus 19° Fahr. The glacier ice kept cracking from time to time with sharp reports. Possibly this may have been due to the expansion of the ice under the influence of the hot sun. At one spot the sledges had to be dragged up a grade of 1 in 3 over smooth blue glacier ice. This was exceedingly heavy work. At last, when we were near to our time for camping, Mackay, on going on a short distance ahead to reconnoitre with the field-glasses, sighted open water on the northern edge of the Drygalski Ice Barrier, about three to four miles distant. He announced his discovery with shouts of 'θαλαττα, θαλαττα', which thrilled us now as of old they thrilled the Ten Thousand. It was no sparkling waters of the Euxine that had met his gaze, but a Black Sea nevertheless, for so it appeared as its inky waves heaved under the leaden sky. But what a joy to have reached once more that friendly water world that went up by many a creek and river to our homes. It was now clear to us that we could not hope for sea ice over which to sledge westwards to the shore, where we proposed to make our final depot before attempting the ascent of the great inland plateau in order to reach the Magnetic Pole.

During the day we were cheered by a visit from several snow petrels, which flew around our camp, as well as from three skua gulls. Mawson managed to snare one of the skuas with a fishing-line, but it got away when he was hauling in the line. Our sledging that day was not quite so heavy; the ice undulations were less formidable, and the belts of snow between became wider and firmer. Just after lunch a beautiful Wilson's petrel flew around us.

December 10 saw us still struggling to cross the Drygalski Glacier. We could see that we were now on a pretty high ridge, but the highest part of the glacier now lay to the south and therefore behind us. We were much rejoiced towards the end of the day's sledging to find ourselves at last off the true glacier type of surface, and on to what may be described as an undulating barrier type. This improvement of the surface to our west enabled us to do what we had been longing to do for the last six days, turn our sledge westwards. At first we had to incline somewhat to the north-west in order to skirt round some high ice ridges. Then, after making some northing, we were able to go nearly due west. The snow surface was largely of the pie-crust type; our ski boots broke through it at every step and we sank in up to our ankles. At intervals we still crossed low ridges of solid glacier ice, traversed by crevasses. All the crevasses were more or less roofed over with tough snow lids. These lids sometimes were slightly in relief, or sometimes showed slight depressions in the general surface. In such areas the snow lids rung hollow as the sledges travelled over them. We found the snow lids always most treacherous close to either wall of the crevasse, and we frequently fell partially through at such spots, but had no very bad falls in this part of the glacier.

The following day, December 11, we had a fine view of 'Terra Nova' Bay, and as far as could be judged the edge of the Drygalski Ice Barrier on the north was now scarcely a mile distant. We were much surprised at the general appearance of the outline of the Ice Barrier coastal ice and coast-line ahead of us. It did not agree, as far as we could judge, with the shape of this region as shown on the Admiralty chart, and we could see no certain indication whatever of what was called, on the chart, 'the low, sloping shore'. Accordingly we halted a little earlier than usual in order to reconnoitre. There was a conspicuous ice mound about half a mile to the north-west of this camp. Mackay started off with the field-glasses for a general look round from this point of vantage. Mawson started changing his plates in the sleeping-bag, while I prepared to go out with my sketch-book and get an outline panoramic view of the grand coast ranges now in sight. Crevasses of late had been so few and far between that I thought it was an unnecessary precaution to take my ice-axe with me, but I had scarcely gone more than six yards from the tent when the lid of a crevasse suddenly collapsed under me at a point where there was absolutely no outward or visible sign of its existence, and let me down suddenly nearly up to my shoulders. I only saved myself from going right down by throwing my arms out and staying myself on the snow lid on either side. The lid was so rotten that I dared not make any move to extricate myself, or I might have been precipitated into the abyss. Fortunately Mawson was close at hand, and on my calling to him, he came out of our sleeping-bag, and bringing an ice-axe, chipped a hole in the firm ice on the edge of the crevasse nearest to me. He then inserted the chisel edge of the ice-axe in the hole and holding on to the pick point, swung the handle towards me: grasping this, I was able to extricate myself and climbed out on to the solid ice.

It was a beautiful day, the coast-line showing up very finely, and I was able to get from the ice mound a sketch of the mountains. Mawson also took three photographs, making a panoramic view of this part of the coast. He was able, also, to get a valuable series of angles with the theodolite, which showed that the shape of the coast-line here necessitated serious modification of the existing chart.

35
PROFESSOR DAVID'S NARRATIVE
(CONTINUED)

Die schönste Jungfrau sitzet
Dort oben wunderbar,
Ihr goldnes Geschmeide blitzet,
Sie Kämmt ihr goldnes Haar.

Sie Kämmt es mit goldenem Kamme,
Und singt ein Lied dabei
Das hat ein wundersame,
Gewaltige melodei.

HEINE

Far beyond the golden mountains to the north and west lay our goal, but as yet we knew not whether we were destined to fail or succeed. Meanwhile no time was to be lost in hurrying on and preparing for a dash on to the plateau, if we were to deserve success.

The following day, December 12, we sledged on for half a mile until we were a little to the west of the conspicuous ice mound previously described. We concluded that as this ice mound commanded such a general view of the surrounding country, it must itself be a conspicuous object to any one approaching the Drygalski Glacier by sea from the north; and so we decided that as there was still no trace of the 'low, sloping shore' of the chart, and that as the spot at which we had now arrived was very near to the area so named on the chart, we would make our depot here.

We intended to leave at this depot one of our sledges with any spare equipment, a little food, and all our geological specimens, and proceed thence shorewards and inland with one sledge only. We estimated that we still had fully 220 miles to travel from this depot on the Drygalski Glacier to the Magnetic Pole. It was, therefore, necessary now to make preparations for a journey there and back of at least 440 miles. We thought that with *détours* the journey might possibly amount to 500 miles.

We could see, even from our distance of from twenty to thirty miles from the shore-line, that we had no light task before us in order to win a way on to the high inland plateau. Before we knew that the whole of the sea ice had gone out between us and Mount Melbourne, we had contemplated the possibility of travelling further northwards along the coast on sea ice, down to a spot marked on the chart as Gerlache Inlet. This inlet we now saw was situated amongst a wilderness of high sharp jagged mountain peaks, rising to heights of from 6000 to 8000 ft. above sea-level, and as it could now be approached only from the land, it was now practically inaccessible. Nearer to us, and to the north-west of our position on the Drygalski Ice Barrier, was the giant form of Mount Nansen, one of the grandest and most imposing of all the mountains seen by us in the Antarctic. Further to the left and nearly due west of us was another fine dark mountain massif, Mount Larsen. Between Mount Larsen and Mount Nansen was a vast glacier with a rugged surface, steep ice falls and large crevasses. About midway between Mounts Larsen and Nansen was a huge nunatak of black rock, rising abruptly from the ice surface at a point several miles inland from the shore-line. Further to the left of Mount Larsen was another glacier less formidable in appearance and smaller in size than the Mount Nansen Glacier. This terminated near the coast in rather a steep slope, and gradually became confluent with the Drygalski Glacier. To the south of this glacier, which may be termed the Mount Larsen Glacier, was another great mountain massif with Mount Bellingshausen on the north and Mount Neumayer on the south. The foot-hills of Mount Neumayer terminated in steep precipices forming the northern wall of the Drygalski Glacier.

Our first business was to lay in a stock of provisions sufficient to last us for our 500 miles of further journeying. Mackay started for a small inlet about a mile and a half distant from our camp, where he found a number of seals and Emperor and Adelie penguins. He killed some seals and Emperor penguins, and loaded a good supply of seal steak, blubber, liver and penguin steak and liver on to the sledge. In the course of his hunting, he fell through an ice bridge, at a tide-crack, up to his waist in the water. Mawson and I went out to meet him when the sledge was loaded, and helped to drag it back to camp. We found it very hot in the tent, the weather being fine and sunny. It was delightful to be able at last to rest our weary limbs after the many weeks of painful toil over the sea ice and the Drygalski Glacier.

We started cooking our meat for the sledging trip on the following day, December 13, our intention being to take with us provisions for seven weeks, in addition to equipment, including scientific instruments, &c. We estimated that the total weight would amount to about 670 lb. We were doubtful, in our then stale and weakened condition, whether we should be able to pull such a load over the deep loose snow ahead of us, and then drag it up the steep ice slopes of the great glaciers which guarded the route to the plateau.

The sun was so hot that it started melting the fat out of our pemmican bags, so that the fat actually oozed through not only the canvas of the bags themselves, but also through the thick brown canvas of the large fortnightly food-bags, which formed a sort of tank for containing the pemmican bags, and we found it necessary at once to shade the food-bags from the sun by piling our Burberry garments over them. Leather straps, tar rope, tins, sledge harness, lamp-black off the blubber cooker, warmed by the rays of the sun, all commenced to sink themselves more or less rapidly into the névé.

We unpacked and examined both sledges, and found that of the two, the runners of the Duff Sledge were the less damaged. As the result of the rough treatment to which it had recently been subjected, one of the iron brackets of this sledge was broken, but we replaced it with a sound one from the discarded Christmas Tree Sledge.

The following day, December 14, we were still busy preparing for the great trek on the morrow. Mackay was busy cooking Emperor penguin and seal meat for the plateau journey; Mawson was employed in transferring the scientific instrument boxes and the Venesta boxes in which our primus lamp and other light gear were packed from the Christmas Tree sledge on to the Duff sledge. He also scraped the runners of the sledge with pieces of broken glass in order to make their surfaces as smooth as possible. I was busy fixing up depot flags, writing letters to the Commander of the *Nimrod*, Lieutenant Shackleton, and my family, and fixing up a milk tin to serve as a post office on to the depot flag-pole. When all our preparations were completed we drew the Christmas Tree sledge with some of our spare clothing, our blubber cooker, a biscuit tin with a few broken biscuits, and all our geological specimens to the top of the ice mound, about a quarter of a mile distant. On reaching the top of the mound we cut trenches with our ice-axes in which to embed the runners of the sledge, fixed the runners in these grooves, piled the chipped ice on top, then lashed to the sledge, very carefully, the flag-pole about six feet high, with the black flag displayed on the top of it. The wind blew keenly off the plateau before our labours were completed. We all felt quite sorry and downcast at parting with this sledge, which by this time seemed to us like a bit of home. We then returned to camp. Just previous to depoting this sledge, Mackay fixed another small depot flag close to the open sea a few yards back from the edge of the ice cliff.

Soon after we had turned into our sleeping-bag, a gentle blizzard started to blow from west by south. This continued all night, increasing in intensity in the morning. We were able to see great whale-backed clouds, very much like those with which we had been familiar over Mount Erebus, forming over Mount Nansen. As this blizzard wind was blowing partly against us, we decided that we would wait until it had either slackened off, or decreased in force.

The whole of the next day, unfortunately, the blizzard continued. The sun was very hot, and as the result of its heat we were today, for the first time, subjected to a new trouble. The blizzard, of course, drifted snow all over our tent; and a strong thaw set in on the side of it which faced the sun. The wind, flapping the canvas of the tent against the tent-poles, brought the thaw water through on to the poles facing the sun. Inside the tent, however, the temperature was just below freezing-point, and as the water started to trickle down the poles it froze. With the flapping of the tent backwards and forwards against the tentpoles, the small ridge of ice on the upper surface of each tent-pole became drawn out into sharp, saw-like teeth, and these started cutting through the canvas. All through this day, consequently, we had to be continually getting out of the sleeping-bag and running our hands down the tent-poles so as to rub off the ice teeth.

The blizzard continued till midnight of December 15–16, when its force markedly decreased. We breakfasted accordingly just after midnight. I dug out the sledge from the snow which had drifted over it, and Mackay cached some seal meat in an adjoining ice mound. At last, about 7 a.m., we made a start, and were delighted to find that, chiefly as the result of the three days' rest in camp, we were able to pull our sledgeweighing about 670 lb. with comparative ease. The snow, though soft, had become crusted over the surface through the thaw brought on by the blizzard, followed by freezing during the succeeding cold night. The sledging was certainly heavy, but not nearly so distressing as that which we had recently experienced in crossing the Drygalski Glacier. The 'tablecloth was being laid' on the top of Mount Nansen in the form of a remarkable flattish thin white fleecy cloud. It looked as though a high-level blizzard was blowing over the summit. We steered towards the great black nunatak midway between Mount Nansen and Mount Larsen, as Mawson and Mackay both considered that in this direction lay our chief hope of finding a practical route to the high plateau.

On December 17 we had a very interesting day. The sledging was rather heavy, being chiefly over soft snow and pie-crust snow. It was difficult to decide sometimes whether we were on fresh-water ice or on sea ice. Here and there we crossed ice ridges, evidently pressure ridges of some kind. These would be traversed by crevasses which showed the ice in such places to be at least thirty to forty feet in thickness. Close to our final camping-ground for the day was a long shallow valley or barranca; it was from one hundred and twenty to one hundred and thirty yards in width. The near side was steep, though not too steep for us to have let our sledge down; but the far side was precipitous, being bounded by an overhanging cliff from twenty to thirty feet high. The floor of this valley was deeply and heavily crevassed. This sunken valley, therefore, formed a serious obstacle to our advance.

While Mackay was preparing the hoosh Mawson travelled to the right, and I to the left along this valley seeking for a possible crossing place. At last Mawson found a narrow spot where there had been an ice bridge over the valley, but this had become cracked through at the centre. It was nevertheless strong enough to bear our sledge. Near this ice bridge Mawson stated that he noticed muddy material containing what appeared to be foraminifera, squeezed up from below. The day had been calm and clear, and we were able to get detailed sketches of this part of the coast range.

The following day we made for the ice bridge with our sledge, and found that the crack crossing it had opened to a width of eighteen inches during the night. The far side had become, too, somewhat higher than the near side. We had little difficulty in getting the sledge over, and after crossing several other cracks in the ice and névé without mishap reached once more a fairly level surface. A light plateau wind was now blowing from off the Mount Nansen glacier. The hard snow surface was furrowed by two very definite sets of sastrugi, one set coming from a south-westerly direction, and apparently caused by blizzard wind, the other from nearly north-west. The latter were evidently due to strong rushes of cold air from the high plateau down the broad valley occupied by the Mount Nansen glacier. That day we passed over a series of pressure ridges with their steeper sides directed towards the north-west. At the bottom of these steep slopes the ice was often crevassed, and sometimes we had some little difficulty in crossing them. They were probably due to pressure from the Drygalski Glacier.

At lunch time, soon after midnight, we reached some very interesting glacial moraines in the form of large to small blocks, mostly of eruptive rock, embedded in the ice. It was probable, from their general distribution, that they formed part of an old moraine of Mount Nansen, though now about fifteen miles in advance of the present glacier front. A conspicuous rock amongst the boulders was a greenish-grey to greenish-black diorite, very rich in sphene. The brown crystals of sphene were frequently intercrystallised with the felspars, and gave the rock a very pretty appearance. Small fragments of sandstone and clay shale were also represented in these moraines. The larger blocks were up to seven feet in diameter, and formed chiefly of reddish porphyritic granite. We collected a number of specimens from this moraine.

Fine rolls of cumulus clouds were gathering to our north-east. The day was calm with occasional gleams of sunshine. After the plateau wind had died down about 2p.m. it commenced to snow a little, the snow coming from between south-west and west-south-west.

At midnight on December 19 we started sledging in the falling snow, guided partly by the direction of the wind, partly by that of the pressure ridges and crevasses, occasionally taking compass bearings. Before we had gone far we reached a tide-crack with open water three to four feet wide. There was also a width of about eighteen feet of recently formed thin ice at this tide-crack. We tasted the water in this crack and found that it was distinctly salt. It was clear then that at this part of our journey we were travelling over sea ice. About half a mile further on we reached another open tide-crack, and had to make a considerable *détour* in order to get over it. The surface of the ice was now thawing, and we trudged through a good deal of slushy snow, with here and there shallow pools of water as blue as the Blue Grotto of Capri. On the far side of this second tide-crack, and beyond the blue pools, we reached a large pressure ridge forming a high and steep scarped slope barring our progress. Its height was about eighty feet. There was nothing for it, if we were to go forward, but to drag our heavy sledge up this steep slope. It was extremely exhausting work, and we were forced to halt a few times, and had to take the sledge occasionally somewhat obliquely up the slope where it was very steep. In such cases the sledge frequently skidded. Our troubles were increased by the fact that this ice slope was traversed by numerous crevasses, which became longer and wider the further we advanced in this direction.

At last we got to the slope, only to see in the dim light that there were a succession of similar slopes ahead of us, becoming continually higher and steeper. The ice, too, became a perfect network of cravasses, some of which were partly open, but most of them covered over with snow lids. Suddenly, when crossing one of these snow lids, just as he was about to reach the firm ice on the other side, there was a slight crash and Mawson instantly disappeared from sight. Fortunately the toggle at the end of his sledge rope held, and he was left swinging in the empty space between the walls of the crevasse, being suspended by his harness attached to the sledge rope. Mackay and I hung on to the rope in case it should part at the toggle, where it was somewhat worn. Meanwhile, Mawson called out from below to pass him down the alpine rope. Leaving Mackay to keep hold of the toggle end of Mawson's harness rope, I hurried back to the sledge, which was about ten feet behind, and just as I was trying to disengage a coil of rope Mawson called out that he felt he was going. I ran back and helped Mackay to keep a strain on Mawson's harness rope. Mawson then said that he was all right. Probably at the time he felt he was going the rope had suddenly cut back through the lid of the crevasse and let him down for a distance of about a couple of feet. Altogether he was about eight feet down below the level of the snow lid. While I now held on to Mawson's harness rope Mackay hurried back to the sledge, and with his Swedish knife, cut the lashing around the alpine rope, and started uncoiling it, making a bowline at the end in which Mawson could put his foot. Meanwhile Mawson secured some ice crystals from the side of the crevasse, and threw them up for examination. The alpine rope having been lowered, Mawson put his foot into the bowline and got Mackay to haul his leg up as high as his bent knee would allow it to go, then, calling to him to hold tight the rope, Mawson, throwing the whole weight of his body on to it, raised himself about eighteen inches by means of his arms so as to be able to straighten his right leg. Meanwhile, I took in the slack of his harness rope. He then called to me to hold tight the harness rope, as he was going to rest his whole weight on that, so as to take the strain off the alpine rope. Mackay then was able to pull the alpine rope up about eighteen inches, which had the effect of bending up Mawson's right leg as before. Mackay then held fast the alpine rope, and Mawson again straightened himself up on it, resting his whole weight on that rope. Thus little by little he was hoisted up to the under surface of the snow lid, but as his harness rope had cut back a narrow groove in this snow lid several feet from where the snow gave way under him Mawson now found his head and shoulders pressing against the under side of the snow lid, and had some difficulty in breaking through this in order to get his head out. At last the top of his head emerged, a sight for which Mackay and I were truly thankful, and presently he was able to get his arms up, and soon his body followed, and he got safely out on the near side of the crevasse. After this episode we were extra cautious in crossing the crevasses, but the ice was simply seamed with them. Twice when our sledge was being dragged up ice-pressure ridges it rolled over sideways with one runner in a crevasse, and once the whole sledge all but disappeared into a crevasse, the snow lid of which had partly collapsed under its weight. Had it gone down completely it would certainly have dragged the three of us down with it, as it weighed nearly one-third of a ton. It was clear that these high-pressure ridges and numerous crevasses were caused now, not by the Drygalski, but by the Nansen Glacier.

It was now somewhat foggy, but occasionally the fog and mist lifted, and in the distance one caught glimpses of magnificent cliffs of reddish brown granite, with wisps and wreathes of white mist hanging around the summits. The view reminded me of the Grampians in Scotland near Ossian's Cave at the Pass of Glencoe. Later on in the day we saw in the dim light that we had before us a long steep descent into an ice valley, which appeared to be heavily crevassed at the bottom. As we were uncertain whether we could get across it at this spot we left our tent and sledge, and reconnoitred ahead, taking with us the alpine rope and our ice-axes. We found a way of crossing this valley, but could see that the ice-surface ahead of us was apparently worse than ever. We returned to our tent and sledge, and put up the tent, and chopped lumps of ice off the glacier with which to load the skirt, as no snow was available at the time. It was just commencing to snow, and wind was freshening from the south-west. We were now in a perfect labyrinth of crevasses and pressure ridges. Snow continued falling heavily accompanied by a blizzard wind for the rest of that day and the whole of the succeeding night. Inside the tent we experienced some discomfort through the dripping of water caused by the thawing snow. As usual during a blizzard the temperature rose, and although the sun's heat rays were partly intercepted by the falling snow quite sufficient warmth reached the side of the tent nearest the sun to produce this thaw. Pools of water lodged on the foot of our sleeping-bag, but we were able to keep the head of it fairly dry by fixing up our Burberry blouses and trousers across the poles on the inside of the tent so as to make a temporary waterproof lining just above our heads. We were all thoroughly exhausted, and slept until about 7 a.m. the following day, December 20. By that time the snow cleared off.

About six inches of snow had fallen, and was lying deeply drifted in places. We dug away the drift snow from around the sledges, and after the morning hoosh held a council of war. The question was whether we should continue pulling on in the direction of the nunatak rising from the Mount Nansen Glacier, or whether we should retreat and try some other way which might lead us to the plateau. Mackay was in favour of hauling ahead over the Mount Nansen Glacier, while Mawson and I favoured retreat, and trying a passage in some other direction.

At last we decided to retreat. Our fortunes now, so far as the possibility of reaching the Magnetic Pole were concerned, seemed at a low ebb. It was already December 20, and we knew that we had to be back at our depot on the Drygalski Glacier not later than February 1 or 2, if there was to be a reasonable chance of our being picked up by the *Nimrod*. We had not yet climbed more than 100 ft. or so above sea-level, and even this little altitude was due to our having climbed ice-pressure ridges, which from time to time dipped down again to sea-level. We knew that we had to travel at least 480 to 500 miles before we could hope to get to the Magnetic Pole and back to our depot, and there remained only six weeks in which to accomplish this journey, and at the same time we would have yet to pioneer a road up to the high plateau. Now that everything was buried under soft snow it was clear that sledging would be far slower and more laborious than ever. We soon proved that this was the case, for after starting the sledge it gathered masses of soft snow around it and under it as it went, and at the end of 200 yards we had to halt for a temporary rest, hoist the sledge up on one side and knock away the masses of clogged snow from underneath it. This had to be repeated every few hundred yards, and after we had gone half a mile we decided to leave the sledge and go ahead with ice-axes and alpine rope to reconnoitre.

We started off in a south-westerly direction with the intention of seeing whether the Mount Bellingshausen Glacier slope would be more practicable for our sledges than the Mount Nansen Glacier. We trudged through soft thawing snow with here and there shallow pools of water on the surface of the ice. This, of course, saturated our socks, which froze as the temperature fell during the night. After proceeding about two and a half miles we observed with the field-glasses that the foot of the Mount Bellingshausen Glacier was not only steep but broken and rugged. We decided to examine what appeared to be a narrow stretch of snow mantling around the base of a granite mountain, one of the offshoots from the Mount Larsen massif. After crossing a good deal of pressure ice and crevasses, and floundering amongst the boulders of old moraines we reached some shallow lakes of thawed snow near the junction between the sea ice and the foot of the snow slope for which we had been steering. In the neighbourhood of the moraines, which here consisted of great blocks of eruptive rock partly or wholly imbedded in ice, the blocks became so warmed up by the sun's heat that they partially thawed the ice around, and in some cases above them: and so when one stepped, near one of these blocks, or over a concealed block, the ice gave way with a crash letting one down a depth of from one to three feet. At one place, before reaching the shallow lakes, we found quite a strong stream of water flowing just under the surface of the ice. This was evidently supplied from thaw water from the slopes near the shore-line.

After paddling, unwillingly, in the shallow lakes we reached the foot of what proved now to be not a snow slope but a small branch glacier. This was covered with a considerable depth of soft newly drifted snow, and we found the ascent in consequence very tiring as we sunk at each step in the soft snow over our knees. At last we attained an altitude of 1200 ft. above sea-level, and were then high enough to see that the upper part of this branch glacier joined the Mount Bellingshausen Glacier at about 800 ft. higher and some half mile further on. We were well pleased with this discovery, but as the glacier front ascended about 1500 ft. in less than a mile we did not look forward to the task of getting our heavy sledge up this steep slope, encumbered as it was with soft deep thawing snow.

On our return to the shore-line down the glacier slope we discovered that it was slightly crevassed in places, though not heavily so. At the foot of the glacier, and a short distance towards our camp, we found a moraine gravel. This was intermixed with a dark marine clay containing numerous remains of serpulae, pecten shells, bryozoa, foraminifera, &c. Mackay also found a perfect specimen of a solitary coral, allied to Delto-cyathus, and also a Waldheimia. All these specimens were carefully preserved and brought into camp. While we were collecting these specimens we could hear the roar of many mountain torrents descending the steep granite slopes of the great mountain mass to the south of our branch glacier. Occasionally, too, we heard the boom and crash of an avalanche descending from the high mountain top. Such sounds were strange to our ears, accustomed so long to the almost perfect solitude and silence of the Antarctic, hitherto broken only by the bleating of baby seals and the call of the penguins.

Mawson discovered in another part of the moraine, nearer to our camp, a bright green mineral forming thin crusts on a very pretty quartz and felspar porphyry. These we decided to examine more carefully on the morrow. We were all thoroughly exhausted after the day's work, and Mackay had a rather bad attack of snow blindness. For some time after we got into the sleeping-bag, and before we dozed off, we could still hear the intermittent roar of avalanches like the booming of distant artillery.

The following day, December 22, we picked our way with our sledge cautiously amongst the crevasses and over the pressure mounds, the traversing of which gave us some trouble in places, and eventually reached a fairly good track along the ice parallel to the moraine from which we had been collecting the day previous. We found a large pool of thaw water on the surface of the ice. This was fed by a sub-glacial stream coming from an old rock moraine. We could hear this stream rolling the pebbles along in its channel. At another point the moraine showed a remarkable cone, which at first sight we took for a typical esker, but a nearer examination revealed the fact that the whole cone, with the exception of the exterior, was formed of solid ice with only an outer coating of sand, mud and gravel associated with abundant marine organisms similar to those collected by us the previous day. We halted when we arrived opposite the green mineral observed by Mawson the previous day. We collected a good deal of this. At first sight we thought it was the common mineral epidote, but its hardness and the fact that it had turned yellow, where it was weathered, made this hypothesis untenable. The green crusts formed by it were about one-fortieth to one-sixteenth of an inch in thickness, and it was evidently fairly widely distributed in that locality, as numerous large joint faces of the quartz and felspar porphyry were completely coated with it. A little further on we came upon an enormous silicious sponge, eighteen inches by two feet in diameter, adhering firmly to one of the moraine boulders. We secured specimens of this.

Altogether the locality was most fascinating, and we longed to have been able to spend more time there. Amongst other interesting problems was the question as to how the material of the sea floor came to be uplifted here to a height of twenty to thirty feet or more above sea-level, and as to how the marine sediments came to be resting on an old conical surface of dense ice. We tested the latter to see whether it was of salt or of fresh-water origin; it was not distinctly saline, though slightly so – much as glacier ice would be if it were sprayed by the sea. None of us could account for this curious phenomenon. It seemed as though the marine muds had been subjected to considerable pressure, as numbers of the fossils in it were triturated and shattered. It is of course just possible that in the forward movement of the Mount Nansen Glacier it may have pushed up some of the sea bottom above sea-level, and still there remains the question as to how masses of ice came to find their way under the moraine sediments. It is possible that after an extensive glaciation of this region the glacier ice from inland spread over the spot where this moraine is now situated, but on the retreat of the ice inland, while still a small thickness of ice was left in this bay, a submergence ensued, and during that submergence a marine mud was deposited over the ice together with the larger organisms found in association with the mud. Then there was an advance of the ice once more, and moraines of large blocks of rock were laid down over the top of the moraine muds and the relics of the ancient glacier ice. Then once more the ice retreated to its present position leaving the moraine blocks and moraine muds of the old ice in the relative situations mentioned.

As we skirted the foot of the small branch glacier we noticed several small puffs of snow near the top angle of the snow slope which we proposed to escalade. Just as we were pulling our sledge to the foot of this slope the puff of wind with drift snow developed suddenly into a strong blizzard. We pulled in against this with great difficulty for half an hour, then camped at the foot of the slope. The blizzard with its heavy drift snow and the occasional gleams of warm sunshine cast much drift over our tent with accompanying thaw. Consequently inside the tent water dripped heavily all over our clothing and sleeping-bag. Fortunately we were just above the level of the thaw water of the small lakes, but we could hear water trickling close underneath our tent amongst the granite boulders of the moraines just under the ice.

We were able now to economise fuel, as we could bale the water out of these rock pools and streams for making our hoosh, tea and cocoa. All that night the blizzard raged, and we thought any moment that the tent would be ripped up from top to bottom. It was getting very thin by this time and had already been frequently repaired by Mackay and Mawson. On this occasion several new rents started from near the top of the tent and spread downwards. Moreover, the canvas cap of our tent was broken by the force of the wind and the pressure of the drift snow.

The following day, about 7 a.m., I got up and dug away the drift snow from the lee side of the tent, which was cramping our feet and legs, and found that it was still snowing heavily outside, and blowing hard as well. In the afternoon the blizzard slacked off somewhat, and the drift nearly ceased. We got up accordingly and had a meal. We halved our sledge load, repacked the sledge, and by dint of great exertions, dragged it up the steep snow and ice slope to a height of 800 ft. above the sea. This was done in the teeth of a mild but freshening blizzard. The blizzard at last got too strong for us, so that we left the load at the altitude mentioned and returned back to our tent with the empty sledge.

We had been pleased to find that the blizzard, although it had delayed us and damaged our tent, had proved a blessing in disguise. It had not brought with it much fresh snow, but had blown away most of the loose snow left by the preceding blizzard, leaving behind it now a fairly hard snow surface suitable for sledging.

Mackay's eyes, still suffering from the effects of snow-blindness, were treated with a solution of thin tabloids (laminae) of sulphate of zinc and cocaine, with the result that his eyes were much better the following day, December 25. This day there was still a strong breeze coming off the plateau, and sweeping over our tent. A little later in the morning the weather became calm, and a glorious sunny day smiled upon us. Mawson and Mackay repaired the rents in the tent, while I saw to repacking of the sledge with the remaining half load, and collected some geological specimens.

We started shortly before noon and commenced dragging up the second part of our load to the accompaniment of the music of murmuring streams. During our interval for lunch, Mawson was able to get some theodolite angles. We had the great satisfaction, when we turned in at 10 p.m. on Christmas Eve, to find that we were above the uncomfortable zone of thaw, and everything around us was once more crisp and dry, though cold. Our spirits, too, mounted with the altitude. We were now over 1200 ft. above sea-level.

36
PROFESSOR DAVID'S NARRATIVE
(CONTINUED)

The following day, December 25, was Christmas Day. When I awoke, I noticed a pile of snow on top of the sleeping-bag close to my head. At first, before I was fully awake, I imagined that it was the moisture condensed from Mawson's breath. Then I heard the gentle patter of snow-flakes, and, on turning my head in the direction in which the rustling proceeded, saw that the wind had undermined the skirt of our tent, and was blowing the snow in through a small opening it had made. Accordingly, I slipped out and snowed up the skirt again, trampling the snow down firmly. A plateau wind was now blowing with almost blizzard force.

About two hours later we got up, and after some trouble with the primus lamp on account of the wind, had our breakfast, but as the wind was blowing dead against us, we turned into the sleeping-bag for a short time. It was nearly noon before the wind died down, and we started off with our sledge, still relaying with hall loads, the day being now beautifully clear and sunny. At the 1800 ft. level we started our sledge meter again, having lifted it off the ice while we were going up the steep slope. A little further on we were able to put the whole of our load again on to the sledge and so dispense with further relay work. This, too, was a great blessing.

When we arrived at our spot for camping that night we had the satisfaction of finding that we were over 2000 ft. above sea-level, and that we had, in addition to the climbing, travelled that day about four miles. The plateau wind had almost gone, and once more we revelled in being not only high, but dry. Having no other kind of Christmas gift to offer, Mawson and I presented Mackay with some sennegrass for his pipe, his tobacco having long ago given out. We slept soundly that Christmas night.

On December 26 we observed dense dark snow clouds to the north-east, and a little light snow commenced to fall, but fortunately the weather cleared towards the afternoon. Mawson lost one of his blue sweaters off the sledge, but he and Mackay went back some distance and recovered it. Towards the afternoon we found it necessary to cross a number of fairly large crevasses. These were completely snowed over, and although we frequently fell through up to our knees, we had no serious trouble from them on this occasion. Some of them were from twenty to thirty feet in width, and it was fortunate for us that the snow lids were strong enough to carry safely the sledge and ourselves. Mackay suggested, for greater security, fastening the alpine rope around Mawson, who was in the lead, and securing the other end of it to the sledge. The rope was left just slack enough to admit of the strain of hauling being taken by the harness rope, hence Mawson had two strings to his bow in case of being suddenly precipitated into a crevasse. This was a good system, which we always adopted afterwards in crossing heavily crevassed ice.

The following day, December 27, we decided to make a small depot of our ski boots (as by this time it appeared we were getting off the glacier ice on to hard snow and névé where we should not require them) and also of all our geological specimens, and about one day's food-supply, together with a small quantity of oil – a supply for about two days in one of our oil-cans. The following is a list of the provisions:

> Powdered cheese (enough for two meals).
> Tea (for four meals).
> Twenty-five lumps of sugar.
> Hoosh for one meal.
> Chocolate (for one and a half meals).
> Twelve biscuits.

We also left an empty biscuit tin into which we crammed our ski boots, and our three ice-axes, using one of them stuck upright as a staff for a small blue flag to mark the depot. Mawson took some good bearings with the prismatic compass, and we then proceeded on our way. This depot we called the Larsen Depot, as it was close to one of the southern spurs of Mount Larsen.

All eyes were now strained, as we advanced with our sledge, to see whether there was still any formidable range of mountains ahead of us barring our path to the plateau. At one time it seemed as though there was a high range in the dim distance, but a careful examination with the field-glasses showed that this appearance was due only to clouds. Our joy and thankfulness was unbounded when we at last realised that apparently there was now a fairly easy ascent of hard névé and snow on to the plateau. That day we sledged a little over ten miles. During the night there was a very strong radiant in the sky from about south-west to north-east, with a movement of altro-stratus cloud from north-west to south-east. Therefore, probably, this radiant was due to formation of great rolls of cloud curled over by the anti-trade wind as it pressed forward in a south-easterly direction. The rolls of clouds were distinctly curved convexly towards the south-east.

The following day, December 28, we travelled on north-westwards in thick cloudy weather, at first quite calm. At about 10 a.m. a breeze set in from the sea, spreading westwards over the top of Mount Nansen over 8000 ft. above sea-level. Above Nansen it met the upper current wind and was obviously deflected by it in a south-easterly direction. Meanwhile, in the direction of the coast the sky was very dark and lowering, and probably snow was falling there. Remarkable pillars of cloud formed over the Mount Larsen group. These were photographed by Mawson. We passed over occasional patches of nearly bare glacier ice, alternating with stretches of hard névé. When we camped that evening we had sledged a little over ten miles, and a keen, cold wind was blowing gently off the high plateau to our west.

The following day, December 29, was clear, calm, and cold. At noon a pretty strong wind was blowing off the plateau. The surface of the snow was fairly strongly ridged with sastrugi. One set was made by winds coming from between west-south-west and west by north, the other by winds nearly north-westerly, or between west-30°-north and west-40°-north. As this latter bearing was not far off the direction in which we were travelling, we were able from time to time to follow these minor sastrugi, which were thus of considerable help to us in bringing over the sastrugi more oblique to the direction in which we were travelling.

The following day, December 30, Mounts Larsen and Bellingshausen were disappearing below the horizon, and several mountains were showing up clearly and sharply to the north of us, the principal peaks of which were at first identified by us as Mount New Zealand and Mount Queensland of Captain Scott's chart. Later Mawson concluded that the western of the two at any rate was new and unnamed.

There was still a strong plateau wind. We were now at an altitude of about 4500 ft. Once more, as in winter time, our breath froze into lumps of ice, cementing our Burberry helmets to our beards and moustaches. In putting up the tent for lunch in the strong plateau wind, it became badly torn near the cap piece. This wind had started before midnight on the previous night, and was blowing strongly until the afternoon, at from twelve to about fifteen miles an hour. It carried along with it a little low drift. The plateau wind did not die down until the evening. Our distance travelled was eleven miles, and we were still travelling on an up grade, being now nearly 5000 ft. above sea-level.

December 31 passed off without any special event other than that after Mackay had repaired the tent in the morning, it became torn again at lunch-time when we were fitting it over the tent-poles. Mawson took a fresh set of magnetic observations. We camped for this purpose at the bottom of a wide undulation in the névé surface. We were disappointed at his announcement that he made out that the Magnetic Pole was further inland than had been originally estimated. What with the observations with the Lloyd-Creak dip circle, and the time occupied in repairing the rents in the tent, we ran ourselves somewhat short of time for our sledging that day, and did not camp until a little before midnight. We were still dragging the sledge on an up grade; the surface was softer and more powdery than before, and the sastrugi heavier. Also since the previous Tuesday we had been obliged to put ourselves on somewhat shorter rations than before, as we had to take one-eighth of our rations out in order to form an emergency food-supply in the event of our journey to and from the Magnetic Pole proving longer than we originally anticipated.

That night, about a mile before reaching camp, we sighted to the west of us, much to our surprise, some distinct ice falls. This showed us that the snow desert over which we were travelling had still some kind of creeping movement in it. A skua gull came to visit us this New Year's Eve. He had been following us up for some time in the distance, mistaking us, perhaps, for seals crawling inland to die, as is not infrequently the habit of these animals. We were now about eighty miles inland from the nearest open water. Being disappointed of his high hopes, he left us after that day and we saw him again no more. The run for the day was about ten miles. We felt very much exhausted when we turned into our sleeping-bag that night.

January 1, 1909 (New Year's Day), was a beautiful calm day with a very light gentle plateau wind, with fairly high temperature. The sky was festooned in the direction of Mount Nansen with delicate wispy cirrus clouds converging in a north-east direction. Later on, towards the evening, it was evident that these cirrus clouds were strongly bent round from south-west in a northerly direction. Possibly this bending with the concave side to the west-north-west was due to the pressure at a high level of the anti-trade wind blowing towards the east-south-east. Mawson took observations for latitude and for magnetic deviation at noon. He made our latitude at noon to be 74° 18′. That night Mawson gave us a grand hoosh and a rich pot of cocoa in celebration of New Year's Day. We all thoroughly enjoyed this meal after our exhausting march.

On January 2 we noticed that the sastrugi were gradually swinging round into a direction a little north of west. The snow was frequently soft in large patches, which made sledging very heavy. We ascended altogether about 290 ft., but we crossed a large number of broad undulations, the troughs of which were from thirty to forty feet below their crests. These undulations considerably increased the work of sledging, and the loose patches of snow were so very soft and powdery that the runners of our sledge sunk deeply into them, so that it was only with our utmost efforts that we were able that day to finish our usual ten miles. Again we were much exhausted when the time came for camping. We were beginning to suffer, too, from hunger, and would have liked more to drink if we could have afforded it. We talked of what we would have drunk if we had had the chance. Mackay said he would have liked to drink a gallon of buttermilk straight off; Mawson would have preferred a big basin of cream; while I would have chosen several pots of the best coffee with plenty of hot milk.

We were still climbing on January 8, having ascended another 500 ft. It proved the heaviest day's sledging since we reached the plateau. The snow was still softer than on the previous day, and the surface was more undulating than ever, the troughs of the undulations being about fifty feet below the crests. The sastrugi themselves were from two to three feet in height. The crests of the large undulations were usually formed of hard snow, the strong winds having blown any loose material off them. This loose material had accumulated to some depth in the troughs, and hence made the wide patches of soft snow which made our sledge drag so heavily as we crossed them. By dint of great efforts we managed to finish our ten miles for that day.

The next day, January 4, we were pleased to find that there was less up grade than on the previous day. We were now at an altitude of over 6000 ft., and found respiration in the cold, rarified air distinctly trying. It was not that we suffered definitely from mountain sickness, but we felt weaker than usual as the result, no doubt, of the altitude combined with the cold. Towards evening, large clouds developed, much like the whaleback clouds which we had often observed forming over Erebus about the time of blizzards. Great rolls of cumulus spread rapidly from the northwest towards the south-east, and we feared that a blizzard was impending. On the whole the sledging was a little easier today than the preceding day, and again we managed to do our ten miles.

On the morning of January 5 we found the sky thickly overcast, except to the south and the south-east where clear strips of blue were showing. We thought that snow was coming. The weather was perfectly calm, comparatively warm, but the light dull. We could still see the new inland mountain and Mount New Zealand distinctly. The sun was so oppressively hot when it peeped out from behind the clouds that one could feel it burning the skin on one's hands.

The surface was more marked by sastrugi than ever, but on the whole firm. We sledged ten miles. I will quote from my diary the notes regarding some succeeding days.

January 3. Today the weather was gloriously fine. Bright, warm sunshine with a crisp, cold air in the early morning and the weather almost calm. The pulling was rather heavy during the afternoon; possibly the hot sun may have somewhat softened the surface of the snow. This morning I left off my crampons and put on a new pair of finnesko. These latter proved somewhat slippery, and in falling heavily this afternoon over one of the sastrugi I slightly strained some muscles on the inner side of my left leg, just below the knee. This gave me a considerable amount of pain for the rest of the journey. Mackay lost all his stockings and socks off the bamboo pole of the sledge, but was fortunate enough to recover them after walking back over a mile on our tracks.

January 7. We were up at 5 a.m., when the temperature was minus 13° Fahr. We were anxious to arrive at the end of our first five miles in good time for Mawson to get a meridian altitude, and take theodolite angles to the new mountain and Mount New Zealand, which were now almost disappearing from view below the horizon. Mawson made our latitude today 73° 43′. This was one of the coldest days we had as yet experienced on the plateau, the wind blowing from west by north. We all felt the pulling very much today, possibly because it was still slightly uphill, and probably partly on account of mountain lassitude. The distance travelled was ten miles.

Friday, January 8. Today, also, was bitterly cold. The wind blew very fresh for some little time before noon from a direction about west by north, raising much low drift. Our hands were frost-bitten several times when packing up the sledge. The cold blizzard continued for the whole day. At lunch time we had great difficulty in getting up the tent, which became again seriously torn in the process. Our beards were frozen to our Burberry helmets and Balaclavas, and we had to tear away our hair by the roots in order to get them off. We continued travelling in the blizzard after lunch. Mawson's right cheek was frostbitten, and also the tip of my nose. The wind was blowing all the time at an angle of about 45° on the port bow of our sledge. We just managed to do our ten miles and were very thankful when the time came for camping.

The following day, January 9, a very cold plateau wind was still blowing, the horizon being hazy with low drift. We were now completely out of sight of any mountain ranges, and were toiling up and down amongst the huge billows of a snow sea. The silence and solitude were most impressive. About 10.30 a.m. a well-marked parphelion, or mock sun, due to floating ice crystals in the air, made its appearance. It had the form of a wide halo with two mock suns at either extremity of the equator of the halo parallel to the horizon and passing through the real sun. Mawson was able to make his magnetic deviation observation with more comfort, as towards noon the wind slackened and the day became gloriously bright and clear. In the afternoon it fell calm.

We were feeling the pinch of hunger somewhat, and as usual our talk under these circumstances turned chiefly on restaurants, and the wonderfully elaborate dinners we would have when we returned to civilisation. Again we accomplished our ten miles, and were now at an altitude of over 7000 ft.

January 10 was also a lovely day, warm and clear; the snow surface was good and we travelled quickly. There was a strong 'Noah's Ark' structure in the high-level cirrus clouds, there being a strong radiant point respectively in the north-west and south-east, and this made us somewhat apprehensive that we were in for another blizzard. These cirrus clouds were also strongly curved with the concave side of the curve facing the north-east. We thought this curve was, perhaps, due to the anti-trade wind bending round in a direction following that of the curve in the wisps of cirrus.

January 11. We were up about 7 a.m., the temperature at that time being minus 12° Fahr. It was a cold day today, and we had a light wind nearly southerly. At first it blew from between south and south-south-east; this gradually freshened at lunch time and veered towards the west. It then returned again more towards the south-south-east. Mawson had a touch of snow-blindness in his right eye. Both he and Mackay suffered much through the skin of their lips peeling off, leaving the raw flesh exposed. Mawson, particularly, experienced great difficulty every morning in getting his mouth opened, as his lips were firmly glued together by congealed blood.

That day we did eleven miles, the surface being fairly firm, and there being no appreciable general up grade now, but only long-ridged undulations, with sastrugi. We noticed that these sastrugi had now changed direction, and instead of trending from nearly west, or north of west, eastwards, now came more from the south-east directed towards the north-west. This warned us that we might anticipate possibly strong head winds on our return journey, as our course at the time was being directed almost north-west, following from time to time the exact bearing of the horizontal magnetic compass. The compass was now very sluggish, in fact the theodolite compass would scarcely work at all. This pleased us a good deal, and at first we all wished more power to it: then amended the sentiment and wished less power to it. The sky was clear, and Mawson got good magnetic meridian observations by means of his very delicately balanced horizontal moving needle in his Brunton transit instrument.

January 12. The sky today was overcast, the night having been calm and cloudy. A few snowflakes and fine ice crystals were falling. The sun was very hot and it somewhat softened the snow surface, thereby increasing of course the difficulty of sledging. We sledged today ten and three-quarter miles.

That evening, after hoosh, Mawson, on carefully analysing the results set forth in the advance copy of the *Discovery* Expedition Magnetic Report, decided that although the matter was not expressly so stated, the Magnetic Pole, instead of moving easterly, as it had done in the interval between Sabine's observations in 1841 and the time of the *Discovery* expedition in 1902, was likely now to be travelling somewhat to the north-west. The results of dip readings taken at intervals earlier in the journey also agreed with this decision. It would be necessary therefore to travel further in that direction than we had anticipated in order to reach our goal. This was extremely disquieting news, for all of us, as we had come almost to the limit of our provisions, after making allowance for enough to take us back on short rations to the coast. In spite of the anxiety of the situation extreme weariness after sledging enabled us to catch some sleep.

The following morning, January 13, we were up about 6 a.m. A light snow was falling, and fine ice crystals made the sky hazy. There was a light wind blowing from about south-south-east. About 8 a.m. the sun peeped through with promise of a fine day. We had had much discussion during and after breakfast as to our future movements. The change in the position of the Pole necessitated of course a change in our plans. Mawson carefully reviewed his observations as to the position of the Magnetic Pole, and decided that in order to reach it we would need to travel for another four days. The horizontally moving needle had now almost ceased to work. We decided to go on for another four days and started our sledging. It was a cold day with a light wind. The temperature at about 10.30 a.m. being minus 6° Fahr. At noon Mawson took a magnetic reading with the Lloyd-Creak dip circle, which was now fifty minutes off the vertical, that is, 89° 10'. At noon the latitude was just about 73° South. The sastrugi were now longer and higher than usual, and there were two distinct sets. The strongest sastrugi trended from south to north; a subordinate set from south-east to north-west. That day we sledged thirteen miles.

January 14. The day was gloriously clear and bright with a warm sun. A gentle wind was blowing from about south-south-east, and there was a little cumulus cloud far ahead of us over the horizon. The surface of the snow over which we were sledging was sparkling with large reconstructed ice crystals, about half an inch in width and one-sixteenth of an inch in thickness. These crystals form on this plateau during warm days when the sun's heat leads to a gentle upward streaming of the cold air with a small amount of moisture in it from beneath. Under these influences combined with the thawing of the surface snow, these large and beautiful ice crystals form rapidly in a single day. We observe that after every still sunny day a crop of these crystals develops on the surface of the névé, and remains there until the next wind blows them off. They form a layer about half an inch in thickness over the top of the névé. In the bright sunlight the névé, covered with these sheets of bright reflecting ice crystals, glittered like a sea of diamonds.

The heavy runners of our sledge rustled gently as they crushed the crystals by the thousand. It seemed a sacrilege. The sastrugi were large and high, and our sledge bumped very heavily over them with a prodigious rattling of our aluminium cooking-gear. It was clear that the blizzard winds blow over this part of the plateau at times with great violence. Apparently all the winds in this quarter, strong enough to form sastrugi, blow from south or west of south or from the south-east. Our run today was twelve miles one hundred and fifty yards.

January 15. We were up today at 6 a.m. and found a cold southerly breeze blowing, the temperature being minus 19° Fahr. at 6.30 a.m. Mawson got a good latitude determination today, 72° 42′.

At about twenty minutes before true noon Mawson took magnetic observations with the dip circle, and found the angle now only fifteen minutes off the vertical the dip being 89° 45′. We were very much rejoiced to find that we were now so close to the Magnetic Pole. The observations made by Bernacchi, during the two years of the *Discovery* expedition's sojourn at their winter quarters on Ross Island, showed that the amplitude of daily swing of the magnet was sometimes considerable. The compass, at a distance from the Pole, pointing in a slightly varying direction at different times of the day, indicates that the polar centre executes a daily round of wanderings about its mean position. Mawson considered that we were now practically at the Magnetic Pole, and that if we were to wait for twenty-four hours taking constant observations at this spot the Pole would, probably, during that time, come vertically beneath us. We decided, however, to go on to the spot where he concluded the approximate mean position of the Magnetic Pole would lie. That evening the dip was 89° 48′. The run for the day was fourteen miles.

From the rapid rate at which the dip had been increasing recently, as well as from a comparison of Bernacchi's magnetic observations, Mawson estimated that we were now about thirteen miles distant from the probable mean position of the South Magnetic Pole. He stated that in order to accurately locate the mean position possibly a month of continuous observation would be needed, but that the position he indicated was now as close as we could locate it. We decided accordingly, after discussing the matter fully that night, to make a forced march of thirteen miles to the approximate mean position of the Pole on the following day, put up the flag there, and return eleven miles back on our tracks the same day. Our method of procedure on this journey of twenty-four miles is described in the journal of the following day.

Saturday, January 16. We were up at about 6 a.m. and after breakfast we pulled on our sledge for two miles. We then depoted all our heavy gear and equipment with the exception of the tent, sleeping-bag, primus stove, and cooker, and a small quantity of food, all of which we placed on the sledge together with the legs of the dip circle and those of the theodolite to serve as marks. We pulled on for two miles and fixed up the legs of the dip circle to guide us back on our track, the compass moving in a horizontal plane being now useless for keeping us on our course. At two miles further we fixed up the legs of the theodolite, and two miles further put up our tent, and had a light lunch. We then walked five miles in the direction of the Magnetic Pole so as to place us in the mean position calculated for it by Mawson, 72° 25′ South latitude, 155° 16′ East longitude. Mawson placed his camera so as to focus the whole group, and arranged a trigger which could be released by means of a string held in our hands so as to make the exposure by means of the focal plane shutter. Meanwhile, Mackay and I fixed up the flag-pole. We then bared our heads and hoisted the Union Jack at 3.30 p.m. with the words uttered by myself, in conformity with Lieutenant Shackleton's instructions, 'I hereby take possession of this area now containing the Magnetic Pole for the British Empire.' At the same time I fired the trigger of the camera by pulling the string. Thus the group were photographed in the manner shown on the plate. The blurred line connected with my right band represents the part of the string in focus blown from side to side by the wind. Then we gave three cheers for his Majesty the King.

There was a pretty sky at the time to the north of us with low cumulus clouds, and we speculated at the time as to whether it was possible that an arm of the sea, such as would produce the moisture to form the cumulus, might not be very far distant. In view of our subsequent discovery of a deep indent in the coast-line in a southerly direction beyond Cape North, it is possible that the sea at this point is at no very considerable distance.

The temperature at the time we hoisted the flag was exactly 0° Fahr. It was an intense satisfaction and relief to all of us to feel that at last after so many days of toil, hardship and danger we had been able to carry out our leader's instructions, and to fulfil the wish of Sir James Clarke Ross that the South Magnetic Pole should be actually reached, as he had already in 1831 reached the North Magnetic Pole. At the same time we were too utterly weary to be capable of any great amount of exultation. I am sure the feeling that was uppermost in all of us was one of devout and heartfelt thankfulness to the kind Providence which had so far guided our footsteps in safety to that goal. With a fervent 'Thank God' we all did a right-about turn, and as quick a march as tired limbs would allow back in the direction of our little green tent in the wilderness of snow.

It was a weary tramp back over the hard and high sastrugi and we were very thankful when at last we saw a small dark cone, which we knew was our tent, rising from above the distant snow ridges. On reaching the tent we each had a little cocoa, a biscuit and a small lump of chocolate. We then sledged slowly and wearily back, picking up first the legs of the theodolite, then those of the dip circle, and finally reached our depot a little before 10 p.m.

In honour of the event we treated ourselves that night to a hoosh, which though modest was larger in volume than usual, and was immensely enjoyed. Mawson repacked the sledge after hoosh time, and we turned into the sleeping-bag faint and weary, but happy with the great load of apprehension of possible failure, that had been hanging over us for so many weeks, at last removed from our minds. We all slept soundly after twenty-four miles of travel.

37

PROFESSOR DAVID'S NARRATIVE
(CONTINUED)

Coldly thy rosy shadows bathe me, cold
Are all thy lights, and cold my wrinkled feet.

TENNYSON

I called the camp a little before 10 a.m. the following morning. We now discussed the situation and our chances of catching the *Nimrod*, if she came in search of us along the coast in the direction of our depot on the Drygalski Glacier. We had agreed, before we decided to do the extra four days' march to the shifted position of the Magnetic Pole, that on our return journey we would do not less than thirteen miles a day. At the Magnetic Pole we were fully 260 statute miles distant, as the skua flies, from our depot on the Drygalski Glacier. As we had returned eleven of these miles on the day previous we still had 249 miles to cover. It was now January 17, and the *Nimrod* was due to start to search for us on February 1. As there was of course plenty of sunlight day and night, we thought it quite possible that she might be up to the Drygalski Glacier on February 2 – possibly on the morning of that day. We accordingly decided to try and make back to our Drygalski depot by February 1. This gave us fifteen days. Consequently we would have to average sixteen and two-third miles a day in order to reach the coast in the time specified. This of course did not allow of any delay on account of blizzards, and we had seen from the evidence of the large sastrugi that blizzards of great violence must occasionally blow in these quarters, and from the direction of the sastrugi during our last few days' march it was clear that the dominant direction of the blizzard would be exactly in our teeth. The prospect, therefore, of reaching our depot in the specified time did not appear bright. Providentially we had most beautiful and glorious weather for our start on January 17. It remained fine for the whole day, and we were greatly favoured by a light wind which now blew from between north-west and west-north-west – a perfectly fair wind for our journey. In fact the wind changed direction with us. It had helped us by blowing from the south-east, just before we reached the Magnetic Pole, and now it was blowing in the

352

opposite direction, helping us home. That day, in spite of the late start, we sledged sixteen miles.

On January 18 the weather again was fine, and we had a hard day's sledging. Unfortunately Mawson's left leg became very lame and pained him a good deal. There was a strong radiant in the clouds towards the north-west, and we were a little apprehensive of the wind in consequence. Our run for the day was sixteen miles two hundred yards. This was the end of my week's cooking, and we were able to indulge that night in a fairly abundant hoosh, also in very milky and sweet cocoa, and Mackay admitted that he actually felt moderately full after it for the first time since we had left the Drygalski Depot.

The following day, January 19, we boiled the hypso-meter at our camp, and found the level to be about 7350 ft. above the sea. The boiling-point was 196.75° Fahr. There was a cold fresh wind blowing from the south-east, a head wind for us, the temperature at the time being minus 11° Fahr. There were still low cumulus clouds to the north of us. The wind freshened in the afternoon to a mild blizzard, and we found pulling against it very severe work. That morning we had quite an unusual diversion. Mawson, who is a bold culinary experimenter, being messman for the week, tried the experiment of surreptitiously introducing a lump of sugar into the pemmican. Mackay detected an unusual flavour in the hoosh, and cross-questioned Mawson severely on the subject. Mawson admitted a lump of sugar. Mackay was thereupon roused to a high pitch of indignation, and stated that this awful state of affairs was the result of going out sledging with 'two foreigners'. This mild blizzard partly obliterated our old sledge tracks by piling over them new sastrugi of fine hard snow. We had a great struggle that day to make our sixteen miles, but fortunately the blizzard slackened off towards 9 p.m., and we just managed it.

Owing to some miscalculation, for which I was responsible, we discovered that we had no tea for this week, our sixth week out, unless we took it out of the tea-bag for the seventh week. Accordingly we halved the tea in the seventh week bag, and determined to collect our old tea-bags at each of our old camps as we passed them, and boil these bags together with the small pittance of fresh tea. And here I may mention the tastes of the party in the matter of tea somewhat differed. Mackay liked his tea thoroughly well and long boiled, whereas Mawson and I liked it made by just bringing the water to the boil; as soon as we smelt the aroma of tea coming from underneath the outer lid of the cooker we used to shut off the primus lamp immediately and decant the tea into the pannikins. Mackay had always objected to this procedure when we were sledging along the sea ice where water boils at about 212° Fahr.; now, however, he had a strong scientific argument in his favour for keeping the pot boiling for a few minutes after the tea had been put in. He pointed out that at our present altitude water boiled at just over 196° Fahr., a temperature which he maintained was insufficient to extract the proper juices and flavour from the tea, unless the boiling was very much prolonged. Mawson, however, averred – on chemical and physical grounds – that with the diminished atmospheric pressure certain virtuous constituents of the tea could be extracted at a lower temperature. The discussion was highly scientific and exhilarating, though not very finite. It was agreed as a compromise to allow the boiling to continue for three or four minutes after the water had come to the boil before the tea was poured out. As in our progress coastwards we were continually coming upon more old tea-bags at our old camps, and always collected these and did not throw away any that had been used before we soon had quite an imposing collection of muslin bags with old tea leaves, and with the thorough boiling that they now got there was a strong flavour of muslin superadded to that of old tea. Nevertheless this drink was nectar.

January 20. We were still able today to follow our sledge tracks, which was a great blessing, the magnetic needle being of so little use to us. We had the wind slightly against us bringing up a little low drift. Again we made our sixteen-mile run, though with great difficulty, for the wind had been blowing freshly all day on our starboard bow.

In view of the good progress that we had made, and after carefully calculating out the provisions left over, Mawson, who was at this time messman, proposed that we should return to nearly full rations, as we were becoming much exhausted through insufficient food. This proposal was, of course, hailed with delight.

On January 21 there was a light wind with low temperature, clear sky and hot sun, which combined to consolidate the surface over which we were sledging. By this time Mackay and Mawson's raw lips, which had been cracked and bleeding for about a fortnight previously, were now much better. Mawson's lame leg had also improved. Again we did our sixteen-mile run.

January 22. We were up soon after 7 a.m. It was a clear day with bright sunshine. The wind started soon after 5 a.m., constantly freshening, as it usually did in this part of the plateau, till about 3 p.m. Then it gradually died down by about 10 p.m. The temperature at 7.15 a.m. was minus 20° Fahr., and at this altitude we found the wind at this temperature very trying. Today we had to sledge over a great deal of pie-crust snow, which was very fatiguing. Again we did sixteen miles. We had since the day before yesterday lost our old sledge tracks. Mackay earned a pound of tobacco, to be given him when we returned to civilisation, by being the first to make the 'land fall' – new mountain, west of Mount New Zealand – which showed out now in the far distance very faintly a little to the left of our course. It was a welcome sight to all of us. Today we sledged fifteen miles.

LOOKING DOWN THE EASTERN ARM OF THE FERRAR GLACIER TOWARDS
DRY VALLEY FROM SOLITARY ROCKS

DRY VALLEY

PICKING UP THE WESTERN PARTY

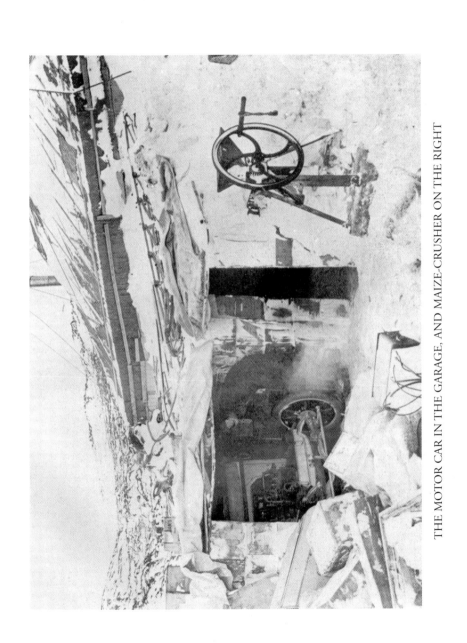

THE MOTOR CAR IN THE GARAGE, AND MAIZE-CRUSHER ON THE RIGHT

MARSTON AND MURRAY AT THE DOOR OF THE HUT

DAISY'S THIRD LITTER AT THE WINTER QUARTERS

THE MOTOR HAULING STORES FOR A DEPOT

ADELIE PENGUINS VISIT A CAMP

SEALS AT THE ICE-EDGE

THE NORTHERN PARTY ON THE PLATEAU

POOL OF THAW WATER FORMED BY THE EMERGENCE OF A SUB-GLACIAL
STREAM SOUTH-EAST OF MOUNT LARSEN

NIMROD PICKING UP THE NORTHERN PARTY AT THE EDGE OF THE DRYGALSKI BARRIER

CAPTAIN EVANS AND THE *NIMROD* AFTER A BLIZZARD

THE DECK OF THE *NIMROD* AFTER A BLIZZARD

THE SHIP OFF PRAM POINT, JUST BEFORE LEAVING FOR THE NORTH

MURRAY HOLDING YOUNG PENGUINS

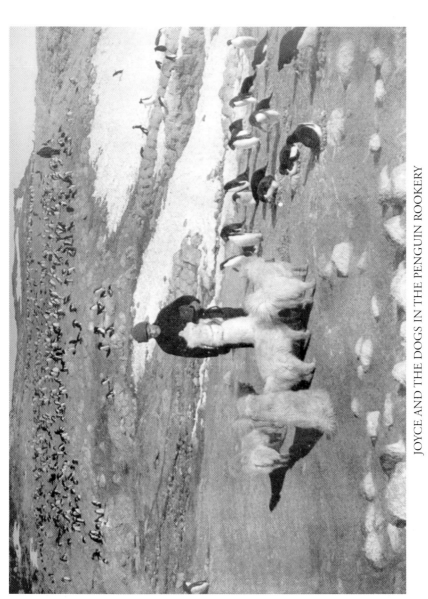

JOYCE AND THE DOGS IN THE PENGUIN ROOKERY

ICE CRYSTALS FORMED ON THE LINE OF A FISH TRAP

January 23. The weather was bright and cold with a light southerly wind. This day was very fatiguing, the sledging being over patches of soft snow and pie-crust snow. At the same time we were conscious now that although we were sledging up and down wide undulations we were on the whole going down hill, and the new mountain was already showing up as an impressive massif. The air was cold and piercing. Mawson's right leg was still painful. That night we were all very much exhausted, and were obliged to allow ourselves fully eight hours sleep. Our run was sixteen miles.

January 24. Today we had more heavy sledging over a lot of pie-crust snow and soft snow. The wind was blowing somewhat against us at about twelve miles an hour, the temperature being minus 4° Fahr. in the afternoon. A low drift was sweeping in waves over the snow desert; it was a desolate scene. Later in the day we were cheered by the sight of Mount Baxter.

Towards evening we had some discussion as to whether we were following approximately our old outgoing tracks. Mackay thought we were nearer to the new mountain than before, I thought we were further to the south-west, Mawson, who was leading, contended that we were pretty well on our old course. Just then I discovered that we were actually on our old sledge tracks, which showed up plainly for a short distance between the newly formed sastrugi. This spoke volumes for Mawson's skill as a navigator. Distance sledged sixteen miles.

January 25. It was blowing a mild blizzard. We estimated at lunch time that we were about eighty and a half miles distant now from our Mount Larsen Depot. The temperature during the afternoon was minus 3° Fahr. We all felt, as usual, much fatigued after the day's sledging. For the past four or five days we each took an Easton syrup tabloid for the last stage but one before reaching camp, and this certainly helped to keep us going. This evening the blizzard died down about 8 p.m., and Mount Nansen was sighted just before we camped.

January 26. We lost our old sledge tracks again today. The weather turned cloudy in the afternoon, and the light was very bad. We now reached a surface of hard marble-like névé, which descended by short steep slopes. We did not at first realise that we were about to descend what we had termed the Ice Falls on the outward journey. Every now and then the sledge would take charge and rush down this marble staircase, bumping very heavily over the steps. Mawson and I frequently came heavy croppers. Mawson put on crampons outside his finnesko to enable him to get a grip of the slippery surface, but my crampons were frozen so hard and so out of shape that I was unable to get them on, so I followed behind and steadied the sledge as it continued bumping its way down the marble steps. At last we reached once more a flattened surface and camped. Our run for the day was fourteen and a half miles.

January 27. This morning we all felt very slack after the night spent in the closely covered sleeping bag, the sky at the time being cloudy. Under these circumstances, as we now had come down from our highest altitude by about 4000 ft., and the temperature, of course, had somewhat risen, we felt stifled and depressed. During the morning fine snow fell and the weather was quite thick to the south and east of us. Mawson steered us by the trend of the sastrugi. As the day wore on, the weather cleared up and we had a good view of the new mountain, Mount New Zealand, and Mount Baxter. The pulling at first was very hard work, being up-hill, but later we had a good run down hill to the spot where we camped for lunch. After lunch we sledged down a still steeper slope, the sledge occasionally taking charge. At this spot Mackay partially fell into a crevasse. Today we were much cheered by the sight at last of Mount Larsen. By the time we reached the spot where we camped that night we had a good clear view of Larsen. The distance travelled was sixteen miles. We were now only about forty miles from our Mount Larsen Depot.

January 28. We turned out of the sleeping-bag today at about 6.30 a.m. A blizzard was blowing, and after breakfast we had much difficulty in the cold wind in getting up the mast and sail. Mackay, who usually did the greater part of this work, got his hands rather badly frost-bitten before our preparations were completed. We used the thick green canvas floorcloth as a sail; the tent-poles served us for a mast, and a piece of bamboo did duty as a yard.

The wind was blowing at, perhaps, about twenty-five miles an hour, and as soon as we started the sledge, it began to travel at such a hot pace that Mackay and Mawson, with their long legs, were kept walking at the top of their speed, while I, with my shorter ones, was kept on a jog trot. Occasionally, in an extra strong puff of wind, the sledge took charge. On one of these occasions it suddenly charged into me from behind, knocked my legs from under me, and nearly juggernauted me. I was quickly rescued from this undignified position under the sledge runners by Mawson and Mackay. We had now arrived at a part of the plateau where the monotonous level or gently undulating surface gave place to sharp descents. It was necessary in these cases for one of us to untoggle from the front of the sledge and to toggle on behind, so as to steer and steady it. About noon, when we were in full career, the bow of the sledge struck one of the high sastrugi obliquely and the sledge was capsized heavily, but fortunately nothing was broken. After righting the sledge, we camped for lunch.

At lunch, with a faint hope of softening the stern heart of our messman for the week – Mackay – and inducing him to give us an extra ration of food, I mildly informed him that it was my birthday. He took the hint and we all fared sumptuously at lunch and dinner that day. The day's run was twenty miles. It had been one of the most fatiguing days that we had as yet experienced, and we were all utterly exhausted when we turned into our sleeping-bag at 8.30 p.m.

January 29. We were up at about 8 a.m., and found that the plateau wind was still blowing at a speed of about fifteen miles an hour. After our experience of the preceding day we decided that we would not make sail on the sledge, and as a matter of fact, found that pulling the sledge in the ordinary way was far less wearying than the sailing had proved the preceding day. We pulled on steadily hour after hour, and Mounts Nansen and Larsen grew every moment clearer and larger, and we began to hope that we might be able to reach our depot at Mount Larsen that night. After we had sledged about ten miles, descending at a gentle grade all the way, we found that there was a slight up grade in the snow surface towards the foot of Mount Larsen, but it was not steep enough to cause us any trouble. But later in the day, Mawson's sprained leg caused him a good deal of pain, and we had almost decided to camp at a point nearly twenty miles from our preceding camp, when Mackay's sharp eyes sighted, at a distance of about a mile, our little blue flag, tied to the ice-axe at our depot. We soon reached the depot, fixed up the tent, had a good hoosh, and turned into the sleeping-bag past midnight.

We were up at 9 a.m. on January 30. The day was sunny, but ominous clouds were gathering overhead as well as to the south. After breakfast we collected the material at our depot, chiefly ski boots, ice-axes, oil, a little food, and geological specimens, and loaded these on to our sledge. We found that, owing to the alternate thawing and freezing of the snow at our depot, our ski boots were almost filled with solid ice. The work of chipping out this ice proved a slow and tedious job, and we did not get started until about 11 a.m. Soon after we got going we found ourselves for a time in a meshwork of crevasses. These were from a foot up to about twenty feet in width. Nearly all of them were roofed over with a hard layer of snow. The only visible evidence of the existence of a crevasse was a slight depression in the snow surface at the inner edges of the two walls bounding the crevasses, the whole of the snow roof or lid being slightly counter-sunk below the general level of the surrounding snow surface.

This, however, was not always the case, and crevasses not infrequently existed entirely concealed from view under a perfectly smooth hard snow surface. On account of the fact, as already explained, that the snow lids were thinner next to the walls of the crevasse, and thicker towards a position central between the walls, we always used to take care, if we could see the little depression in the snow surface – a sure indication of a crevasse – not to put our foot down near the edge of the depression, but to alight on the snow lid some feet away from the crevasse wall.

On stepping out on to one of these snow lids a large piece suddenly gave way under me, and I was instantly precipitated into the chasm below, but fortunately caught the alpine rope under my arm as I was falling; this broke the force of the jerk on my sledge harness. I was down about six feet below the snow lid, and Mawson and Mackay holding on to the harness and alpine ropes which were supporting me, I was able to climb out quickly, and we resumed our journey. Shortly after this, and after crossing a number of other crevasses, we discovered that the wheel of our sledge meter had disappeared. Probably it had got into one of the crevasses, and gone to the bottom. As we were now so close to the end of our journey, the loss of this, which earlier in our travels would have been a serious disaster, was not of much importance. We had run about eight miles before this lunch, previous to the loss of our sledge meter wheel. At lunch-time Mawson compounded a wonderful new hoosh made out of seal liver, pounded up with a geological hammer, and mixed with crushed biscuit.

We had some discussion as to whether it would be better to descend on to the sea ice by the old track up which we had come, which we termed Backstairs Passage, or make down the main Larsen Glacier to the point where it junctioned with the Drygalski Glacier. Mackay was in favour of the former, Mawson and I of the latter. Mackay thought the devil one knew was better than the devil one didn't know, while Mawson and I feared that during the thaw, which was rapidly breaking up the sea ice at the time when we were ascending the plateau, the ice might have gone away from the base of Backstairs Passage right up to the steep granite cliffs of the coast. Had this been the case, and had we descended by our old route, we should have had to retrace our steps and become involved in a very arduous uphill piece of sledging necessitating an ascent of at least 1000 to 1500 ft. in a distance of a little over a mile. As subsequent events proved, Mackay was right and we were wrong.

We held on down the main glacier with the imposing cliffs and slopes of dark-red granite and blackish eruptive rock intermixed with it close on our left Mawson's leg was now so bad that it was only with considerable pain and difficulty that he could proceed, and both Mackay's and my eyes were affected a good deal by snow blindness and were painful. We found as we advanced that at about six miles easterly from our lunch camp, the surface of the Mount Larsen Glacier descended at a very steep angle. Somewhat ahead to the right it was clear that, where it junctioned with the Drygalski Glacier, it was seamed by enormous crevasses and traversed by strong pressure ridges. We held on with our sledge on a course which took us close to the north side of the glacier. At last the descent became so steep that it was with the utmost difficulty that we could hold the sledge back and prevent its charging down the slope. We halted here and Mackay went ahead to reconnoitre. Presently he came back and said that the narrow strip of snow covering the glacier ice, near its contact with the rocky cliffs on our left, was continuous right down to the bottom of the slope, and he thought it was practicable, if we made rope brakes for the runners on our sledge, to lower it down this steep slope in safety. He fixed on some brakes of brown tarred rope by just twisting the rope spirally around the sledge runners. We then cautiously started the sledge down the steepest bit of the slope, all of us ready to let go in case the sledge took charge. The rope brake worked wonders, and it was even necessary to put a slight pull on the sledge in places in order to get it down the steep snow surface. We had left the great crevasses and ice falls near the junction of the Mount Larsen and Drygalski Glaciers a little to our right.

We now found ourselves on an ice-surface quite unlike anything which we had hitherto experienced. In the foreground were some small frozen lakes close to the foot of the granite hills; on the far side of the lakes were beautiful glacial moraines. All around the lakes, and for a considerable distance up the ice slopes descending towards them, the surface of the ice was formed of a series of large thin anastomosing curved plates of ice. These were pieced together in such a way as to form a pattern on a large scale resembling the cups of some of the recent compound corals, or the ancient extinct form known to geologists as *Alveolites*. These curved ice plates or tiles sloped at an angle of about 45°, and formed, of course, an immense obstruction to sledging, as their sharp edges caught and held our sledge runners. We found, too, that it was very distressing travelling over this extraordinary surface, which, from a scenic point of view, was exquisitely beautiful. As we stepped forwards, our feet usually crashed through the ice tiles, and our legs were imbedded in the formation up to our knees. Frequently, under these circumstances, we would stumble forwards, and had some difficulty in dragging our legs out. It was like sledging over a wilderness of glass cucumberframes set up at an angle of 45°. Another moment one would find the tiles thick enough and strong enough to support one, but their surfaces being at an angle of 45° to the horizontal, our feet would slip down them sideways and we ran an imminent risk of spraining our ankles. At every step we took we did not know until after the event which of the above two experiences would follow.

After sledging for a short distance over surfaces of this kind, sloping somewhat steeply to the small lakes, we decided to camp on the pale green ice of one of these lakes. Mawson tested this ice and found that it was strong enough to hold, though evidently of no great thickness. We sledged along this lake for a few hundred yards to its north-east end. There was a little snow here which would do for loading the skirt of our tent. By this time the sky was thickly overcast. We fixed up the tent, chopping little holes in the surface of the smooth ice, in which to socket the ends of the tent-poles, and while Mackay cooked, Mawson and I snowed the skirt. This was subsequent to a little reconnoitring which we each did. It was 2 a.m. before we camped on the lake ice, and 4 a.m. before we turned into our sleeping-bag.

Close to our tent was the most beautiful lateral moraine which we had yet discovered. It was formed of blocks of bright red granite, together with quartz porphyries with much rusty stain due to oxidation of iron pyrites, and masses of dark brown rocks, more basic, perhaps of an intermediate character between granite and diorite. We found that immediately to the right of us, in an easterly direction – that is, directly between us and our depot on the Drygalski Glacier – were great pressure ridges of ice, and a vast entanglement of crevasses. In fact, in that direction the glacier seemed impassable. The only possible outlet for us with our sledge appeared to be close alongside of the lateral moraine at the point where the glacier ice joined it. Even this route was obviously a very difficult one, and we decided before we turned in that on the morrow we should have to unload our sledge and make a portage, or a plurality of portages. The ice on the small lake on which we were camped was only between two and three inches thick, and had obviously formed quite recently after the thaw. It commenced to thaw now under the influence of the warmth of our sleepingbag, as we lay in it, and we found shallow pools of water all around us when we awoke the next morning.

January 31. We were up about 11 a.m., having slept soundly after the very exhausting work of our previous day's sledging. During the night it had snowed heavily, there being fully from three to four inches of newly fallen snow covering everything around us, and it was still snowing while we were having breakfast. After breakfast the snow nearly ceased, and we took half the load off our sledge and started with the remainder to try and work a passage out of the ice-pressure ridges of the combined Drygalski and Larsen Glaciers on to the smoother sea ice, and eventually on to the Drygalski Ice Barrier. While Mawson and Mackay pulled, I steadied the sledge on the lower side in rounding the steep sidelings. We were still sledging over the leafy or tile ice, which mostly crunched underfoot with a sharp tinkling sound. We skirted the lateral moraine for a distance of over half a mile, following a depression in the ice-surface apparently produced by a stream, the outlet of the waters of the small lakes. At one spot Mawson crashed right through into the water beneath, and got wet up to his thighs. In spite of my efforts to keep it on even keel, the sledge frequently capsized on these steep sidelings. At last, after struggling up and down heavy slopes, and over low-lying areas of rotten ice, which every here and there let us through into the water beneath, we arrived at the foot of an immense ice-pressure ridge. It was a romantic-looking spot, though at the time we did not exactly appreciate its beauties. To our left was a huge cliff of massive granite rising up steeply to heights of about 2000 ft. The combined pressure of the Drygalski and Mount Larsen Glaciers had forced the glacier ice up into great ridges, trending somewhat obliquely to the coast cliff.

We went back to the tent where we got some hot tea, of which Mawson, particularly, was very glad, as he was somewhat cooled down as the result of his wetting. Then we packed up the remainder of our belongings on the sledge and dragged it down to where we had dumped the half load on the near side of the pressure ridge. Mackay reconnoitred ahead, and found that the large-pressure ridge, which appeared to bar our progress towards our depot, gradually came nearer and nearer in to the granite cliff, until it pressed hard against the cliff face. Obviously, then, we were impounded by this huge pressure ridge, and would have to devise some means of getting over it. Taking our ice-axes we smoothed a passage across part of the ridge. This proved a very tough piece of work. We then unloaded the sledge and passed each one of our packages over by hand. Finally we dragged the sledge up and hoisted it over and lowered it down safely on the other side. After this we reloaded the sledge and dragged it for some considerable distance over more of the leafy ice-surface alternating with flattish depressions of rotten ice and snow, with water just beneath. We were now troubled, not only by the tile-ice surface, but also by small channels with steep banks, apparently eroded by glacial streams which had been flowing as the result of the thaw while we were on the Magnetic Pole plateau. We were also worried from time to time as to how to get over the vast number of intersecting crevasses which lay in our path.

Little by little the surface improved as we sledged towards our depot. The platy structure on the ice became less and less pronounced, giving place to a surface like that of innumerable frozen wavelets with sharp crests. By lunchtime we arrived at a grand old glacial moraine. Amongst its boulders was a handsome coarsely crystalline red granite of which Mackay secured a good specimen. Numbers of boulders projected a few feet above the surface of the ice, but most of them were wholly encased in ice. After lunch, the sledging surface, though still heavy, owing to the newly fallen snow, improved a little, but we soon found our progress barred by what may be termed an ice donga, apparently an old channel formed by a river of thaw water. We encountered three such dongas that afternoon. They were from a few feet up to fifty or a hundred feet or more in width, and from ten to twenty feet deep, and bounded by precipitous or overhanging sides.

After a considerable amount of reconnoitring by Mackay and Mawson, and often making considerable *détours* with our sledge, we managed to cross them. Our difficulties were increased by the innumerable crevasses and steep ice ridges. Some of these crevasses were open, while others were roofed over with tough snow. We fell into these crevasses from time to time, and on one occasion, Mackay and I fell into the same crevasse simultaneously, he up to his shoulders and I up to my waist. Fortunately we were able, by throwing out our arms, to prevent ourselves from falling right through the snow lid. While we were sledging on through the night amongst this network of crevasses, the sky became heavily overcast, and it commenced to snow. At last we succeeded in getting within less than a mile of the moraine containing the boulders of remarkable sphene-diorite, specimens of which we had collected at that spot on our outward journey. Here we camped and turned into our sleeping-bag at 7 a.m. on February 1.

It continued snowing heavily during the day, the fall being about six inches in depth. The snow on the side of the tent facing the sun thawed rapidly, and the thaw water dripped through and formed pools on top of our sleeping-bag. Mawson's sprained leg pained him a great deal. We estimated that we were now only about sixteen miles, as the skua flies, from our depot on the Drygalski Glacier, but as we had only two days' food left, it became imperative to push on without delay. We started sledging in the thick driving snow on the evening of February 1. The surface was covered with a layer of soft snow, nine inches in thickness, but in the drifts it was, of course, deeper. The work of sledging under these circumstances was excessively laborious and exhausting, and besides it was impossible to keep our proper course while the blizzard lasted. Accordingly, we camped at 8 p.m., and after our evening meal we rolled into our sleeping-bag and slid into the dreamless sleep that comes to the worn and weary wanderer.

At 3 a.m. on February 2 we were rejoiced to find the sun shining in a clear sky. We intended making a desperate attempt this day to reach our depot, as we knew that the *Nimrod* would be due – perhaps overdue – by the night. We saw as we looked back that our track of yesterday was about as straight as a corkscrew. Once more we pulled out over the soft snow, and although refreshed somewhat by our good sleep we found the work extremely trying and toilsome. We crossed an ice donga, and about four miles out reached the edge of a second donga. Here we decided to leave everything but our sledge, tent, sleeping-bag, cooking-apparatus, oil and food, and make a forced march right on to the Drygalski Depot. Accordingly we camped, had tea and two biscuits each, and fixed up our depot, including the Lloyd-Creak dip circle, theodolite and legs, geological collections, &c., and marked the spot with a little blue flag tied on to an ice-axe.

We now found the sledge, thus lightened, distinctly easier to pull, and after making a slight *détour*, crossed the donga by a snow bridge. Soon we reached another donga, and successfully crossed it. At three and a half miles further at 8 p.m. we camped again and had a little cheese and biscuit. After this short halt we pulled on again, steering north-8°-east magnetic. Mawson occasionally swept the horizon with our excellent field-glasses in hopes of sighting our depot. Suddenly he exclaimed that he saw the depot flag distinctly on its ice mound, apparently about seven miles distant, but it was well round on the starboard bow of our sledge on a bearing of south-

38°-west magnetic. Mackay and I were much excited at Mawson's discovery. Mackay seized the field-glasses as soon as Mawson put them down and directed them to the spot indicated, but could see no trace of the flag; then I looked through the glasses with equally negative results. Mawson opined that we must both be snow-blind. Then he looked through them again, and at once exclaimed that he could see no trace of the flag now. The horizon seemed to be walloping up and down, just as though it was boiling, evidently the result of a mirage. Mawson, however, was so confident that he had seen the flag when he first looked, that we altered course to south-38°-west magnetic, and after we had gone a little over a mile, and reached the top of a slight eminence in the ice-surface, we were rejoiced to hear the announcement that he could now see the depot flag distinctly. We kept on sledging for several miles further. At midnight, when the temperature had fallen to zero, I felt that the big toe of my right foot was getting frostbitten. My ski boots had all day been filled with the soft snow and the warmth of my foot had thawed the snow, so that my socks were wet through; and now, since the springing up of the wind and the sudden fall in temperature, the water in the socks had turned to ice. So we halted, got up the tent, started the primus and prepared for a midnight meal, while, with Mawson's assistance, I got off my frozen ski boots and socks and restored the circulation in my toe, and put on some socks less icy than those I had just taken off.

We were much refreshed by our supper, and then started off again, thinking that at last we should reach our depot, or at all events, the small inlet a little over a mile distant from it, but 'the best laid schemes of mice and men gang aft agley'. There was an ominous white streak ahead of us with a dark streak just behind it, and we soon saw that this was due to a ravine or barranca in the snow- and ice-surface interposing itself between ourselves and our depot. We soon reached the near cliff of the barranca.

The barranca was about two hundred yards in width, and from thirty to forty feet deep. It was bounded by a vertical cliff or very steeply inclined slope on the near side, the north-west side, and by an overhanging cliff festooned with stalactites on the south-east side. To the north-east a strip of dark sea-water was visible between the walls of the barranca, which evidently communicated by a long narrow channel with the ocean outside, some three miles distant. Inland, the barranca extended for many miles as far as the eye could reach. The bottom of the barranca immediately beneath us was floored with sea ice covered with a few inches of snow. This ice was traversed by large tide-cracks, and we were much excited to see that there were a number of seals and Emperor penguins dotted over the ice floor. We determined to try and cross the barranca. We looked up and down the near cliff for a practicable spot where we could let down our sledge, and soon found a suitable slope, a little to the north-east of us, formed by a steep snow drift.

We sledged on to this spot, and making fast the alpine rope to the bow of the sledge, lowered it cautiously, stern first, to the bottom. The oil-cans in the rear of the sledge were rattled up somewhat when it struck bottom, but no harm was done. At the bottom we had some trouble in getting the sledge over the gaping tide-cracks, some ten to fifteen feet deep and three to five feet wide.

Arrived at the middle of the floor of the barranca, Mackay killed two Emperor penguins, and took their breasts and livers to replenish our exhausted larder. Meanwhile, Mawson crossed to the far side of the floor of the barranca on the look-out for a possible spot where we might swarm up. I joined him a few minutes later, and as I was feeling much exhausted after the continuous forced marches back from the Magnetic Pole, asked him to take over the leadership of the expedition. I considered that under the circumstances I was justified in taking this step. We had accomplished the work assigned to us by our leader, having reached the Magnetic Pole. We were within two or three miles of our Drygalski Depot, and although the only food left there was two days' supply of broken biscuits with a little cheese, we had a good prospect of meat-supply, as the barranca abounded in seals and penguins, so that for the present we had no reason to apprehend the danger of starvation. On the other hand, as regards our ultimate personal safety, our position was somewhat critical. We were not even certain that the *Nimrod* had arrived at all in Ross Sea that season, though we thought it, of course, very probable that she had. In the next case, on the assumption that she had arrived, it was very possible that in view of the great difficulties of making a thorough search along the two hundred miles of coast, at any part of which we might have been camped – difficulties arising from heavy belts of pack-ice and icebergs, as well as from the deeply indented character of that bold and rugged coast – it was quite possible that the *Nimrod* would miss sighting our depot flags altogether. In the event of the *Nimrod* not appearing within a few days, it would be necessary to take immediate and strenuous action with a view either to wintering at the spot, or with a view to an attempt to sledge back around the great mountain massifs and over the many steeply crevassed glaciers for over two hundred miles to our winter quarters at Cape Royds. Even now, in the event of some immediate strenuous action being necessary, if the *Nimrod* were to suddenly appear at some point along the coast, I thought it would be best for Mawson, who was less physically exhausted than myself, to be in charge. He had, throughout the whole journey, shown excellent capacity for leadership, fully justifying the opinion held of him by Lieutenant Shackleton when providing in my instructions that in the event of anything happening to myself Mawson was to assume the leadership. When I spoke to him on the subject, he at first demurred, but finally said that he would act for a time, and would think the matter over at his leisure before definitely deciding to become permanently the leader. I offered to give him authority in writing as leader, but this he declined to receive.

Meanwhile, the examination of the cliff face on the south-east side of the barranca showed that there was one very difficult but apparently possible means of ascent. We returned to where we had left Mackay, and then we three dragged the sledge around to the edge of a rather formidable tide-crack, behind which lay the mound of snow up which we hoped to climb; our idea being to unpack our sledge, drag it to the top of this steep mound, and rearing it on end at the top of the mound, use it as a ladder for scaling the overhanging cliff above.

Mackay managed to cross the tide-crack, using the bamboo poles of our tent as a bridge, and after some difficulty, reached the top of the snow mound under the overhanging cliff. Much to our disappointment, however, he discovered that the mound was formed of very soft snow, his ice-axe sinking in to the whole depth of the handle directly he placed it on top of the mound. It was obvious that as our sledge would sink in to at least an equal depth, the top of it would then be too short to enable any of us to scale the overhanging cliff by its means. We were, therefore, reluctantly compelled to drag our sledge back again over the tide-cracks to the north-west side of the barranca down which we had previously lowered our sledge. We then discovered that, as in classical times, while the descent to Avernus was easy, it was difficult and toilsome to retrace one's steps. With Mawson ahead with the ice-axe and towing rope, and Mackay and I on either side of the sledge in the rear, we managed by pulling and pushing together to force the sledge up a few inches at a time. At each short halt, Mawson would stick in the ice-axe, take a turn of the leading rope around it, and support the sledge in this way for a brief interval while we all got our breath. At last the forty feet of steep slope was successfully negotiated, and we found ourselves once more on the level plain at the top of the barranca, but of course, on the wrong side in reference to our depot. As we were within three miles of the open sea we thought it would be safe to camp here, as had the *Nimrod* sighted our depot flag and stood in to the coast, we could easily have hurried down to the entrance of the inlet and made signals to her.

We had now been up since 8 a.m. on the previous day, and were very thankful to be able to enter our tent, and have a meal off a stew of minced penguin liver. We then turned into the sleeping-bag at about 7 a.m. Just about a quarter of an hour after we had turned in, as we learnt later, the *Nimrod* must have passed, bound north towards Mount Melbourne, within three miles of the ice cliff on which our tent was now situated. Owing, however, to a light wind with snow drift, she was unable to sight either our depot flag or tent.

38
PROFESSOR DAVID'S NARRATIVE
(CONCLUDED)

February 3. After sleeping in the bag from 7 a.m. until 11 a.m. we got up and had breakfast, packed our sledge, and started along the north bank of the snow cañon. The snow and ice at the bottom were dotted with basking seals and moulting Emperor penguins. Fully a hundred seals could be counted in places in a distance of as many yards along the cañon. At about one mile from the camp we reached a small branch cañon, which we had to head off, by turning to our right. We now proceeded about one and a half miles further along the edge of the main cañon, and in our then tired and weak state were much dispirited to find that it still trended inland for a considerable distance. We now halted by the sledge while Mackay went ahead to try and find a crossing, and presently Mawson and I were rejoiced to hear him shout that he had discovered a snow bridge across the cañon. Presently he rejoined us, and together we pulled the sledge to the head of the snow bridge. It was a romantic spot. A large slice of the snow or névé cliff had fallen obliquely across the cañon, and its surface had then been raised and partially levelled up with soft drift snow. There was a crevasse at both the near and far ends of the bridge, and the middle was sunk a good deal below the abutments. Stepping over the crevasse at the near end we launched the sledge with a run down to the centre of the bridge, then struggled up the steep slope facing us, Mackay steadying the sledge from falling off the narrow causeway, while we all three pulled for all we were worth. In another minute or two we were safely across with our sledge, thankful that we had now surmounted the last obstacle that intervened between us and our depot.

While heading for the depot we sighted an Emperor penguin close to our track. Mackay quickly slew him, and took his flesh and liver for our cooking-pot. Two miles further on we camped. Mawson minced the Emperor's flesh and liver, and after adding a little snow, I boiled it over our primus so as to make one and a half pots of soupy mincemeat for each of us. This was the most satisfying meal we had had for many a long day. After lunch we sledged on for over one and a half miles further towards the depot, and at about 10.30 p.m. reached an ice mound on the south side of the inlet in which the snow cañon terminated seawards. This camping spot was a little over a mile distant from our depot. We were now all thoroughly exhausted and decided to camp. The spot we had selected seemed specially suitable, as from the adjacent ice mound we could get a good view of the ocean beyond the Drygalski Barrier. While Mawson and I got up the tent, Mackay went to kill a seal at the shore of the inlet. He soon returned with plenty of seal meat and liver. He said that he had found two young seals, and had killed one of them; that they had both behaved in a most unusual manner, scuttling away quickly and actively at his approach, instead of waiting without moving, as did most of the Weddell seals, of which we had hitherto had experience. We discovered later that these two seals belonged to the comparatively rare variety known as Ross seal. After a delicious meal of seal blubber, blood and oil, with fried meal and liver, cooked by Mawson, Mawson and I turned into the sleeping-bag, leaving Mackay to take the first of our four-hour watches on the look-out for the *Nimrod*. During his watch he walked up to our depot and dug out our biscuit tin, which had served us as a blubber lamp and cooker, together with the cut-down paraffin tin which we had used as a frying-pan. Both these he carried down to our tent. There he lit the blubber lamp just outside the tent and cooked some penguin meat, regaling himself at intervals, during his four hour's watch, with dainty morsels from the savoury dish. When he called me up at 4 a.m. I found that he had thoughtfully put into the frying-pan a junk of Emperor's breast, weighing about two pounds, for me to toy with during my watch. A chilly wind was blowing off the plateau, and I was truly thankful for an occasional nibble at the hot penguin meat. After cooking some more penguin meat I called up Mawson soon after 8 a.m. on February 4, and immediately afterwards turned into the bag, and at once dropped off sound asleep.

Mawson did not call Mackay and myself until after 2 p.m. We at once rolled up the sleeping-bag, and Mawson cooked a generous meal of seal and penguin meat and blubber, while Mackay made a thin soupy broth on the primus. Meanwhile, I went on to the ice mound with the field-glasses, but could see nothing in the way of a ship to seaward and returned to the tent. We all thoroughly enjoyed our liberal repast, and particularly relished the seal's blood, gravy and seal oil.

After the meal we discussed our future plans. We decided that we had better move the tent that afternoon up to our old depot, where it would be a conspicuous object from the sea, and where, too, we could command a more extensive view of the ocean. We also talked over what we had best do in the event of the *Nimrod* not turning up, and decided that we ought to attempt to sledge overland to Hut Point, keeping ourselves alive on the way, as best we might, with seal meat. It must be admitted that the prospect of tackling two hundred miles of coast, formed largely of steep rocky foreshores, alternating with heavily crevassed glacier ice, was not a very bright one. We also discussed the date at which we ought to start trekking southwards. Mackay thought we ought to commence making our preparations at once, and that unless the *Nimrod* arrived within a few days we ought to start down the coast with our sledge, tent, sleeping-bag, cooker and seal meat, leaving a note at the depot for the *Nimrod*, in case she should arrive later asking her to look out for us along the coast, and if she couldn't sight us, to lay depots of food and oil for us at certain specified spots. He considered that by this method we could make sure of beginning the long journey in a sound state of health, and, if fortunate, might reach Hut Point before the beginning of the equinoctial gales in March. Mawson and I, on the other hand, thought that we ought to wait on at our present camp until late in February.

From whatever point of view we looked at it, our present lot was not a happy one. The possibility of a long wait in the gloomy region of the Drygalski Glacier, with its frequent heavy snows at this season of the year, and leaden sky vaulted over the dark sea, was not pleasing to contemplate. Still less cheerful was the prospect of a long, tedious and dangerous sledge journey towards Hut Point. Even the diet of seal and penguin, just for the moment so nice, largely because novel, would soon savour of *toujours perdrix*.

Dispirited by forebodings of much toil and trouble, we were just preparing to set our weary limbs in motion to pack up our belongings for the short trek up to the depot, when Bang! went something, seemingly close to the door of our tent; the sound thrilled us; in another instant the air reverberated with a big boom! much louder than the first sound. Mawson gave tongue first, roaring out, 'A gun from the ship!' and dived for the tent door. As the latter was narrow and funnel-shaped there was for the moment some congestion of traffic. I dashed my head forwards to where I saw a small opening, only in time to receive a few kicks from the departing Mawson. Just as I was recovering my equilibrium, Mackay made a wild charge, rode me down and trampled over my prostrate body. When at length I struggled to my feet, Mawson had got a lead of a hundred yards, and Mackay of about fifty. 'Bring something to wave', shouted Mawson, and I rushed back to the tent and seized Mackay's ruck-sack. As I ran forward this time, what a sight met my gaze. There was the dear old *Nimrod*, not a quarter of a mile away, steaming straight towards us up the inlet, her bows just rounding the entrance. At the sight of the three of us running frantically to meet the ship, hearty ringing cheers burst forth from all on board. How those cheers stirred every fibre of one's being! It would be hard, indeed, for any one, not situated as we had been, to realise the sudden revulsion of our feelings. In a moment, as dramatic as it was heavenly, we seemed to have passed from death into life. My first feelings were of intense relief and joy; then of fervent gratitude to the kind Providence which had so mercifully led our friends to our deliverance.

A sudden shout from Mackay called me back to earth, 'Mawson's fallen into a deep crevasse. Look out, it's just in front of you!' I then saw that Mackay was kneeling on the snow near the edge of a small oblong sapphire-blue hole in the névé. 'Are you all right, Mawson?' he sang out, and from the depth, came up the welcome word, 'Yes'. Mackay then told me that Mawson was about twenty feet down the crevasse. We decided to try and pull him up with the sledge harness, and hurried back to the sledge, untoggled the harness, ran back with it to the crevasse, and let one end down to Mawson. We found, however, that our combined strength was insufficient to pull him up, and that there was a risk, too, of the snow lid at the surface falling in on Mawson, if weight was put upon it, unless it was strengthened with some planking. Accordingly, we gave up the attempt to haul Mawson up, and while I remained at the crevasse holding one end of the sledge harness Mackay hurried off for help to the *Nimrod*, which was now berthing alongside of the south wall of the inlet, about two hundred yards distant. Mackay shouted to those on board, 'Mawson has fallen down a crevasse, and we got to the Magnetic Pole.' The accident had taken place so suddenly that those on board had not realised in the least what had happened. A clear, firm, cheery voice, that was strange to me, was now heard issuing prompt orders for a rescue party. Almost in less time than it takes to write it, officers and sailors were swarming over the bows of the *Nimrod*, and dropping on to the ice barrier beneath. I called down to Mawson that help was at hand. He said that he was quite comfortable at present; that there was sea water at the bottom of the crevasse, but that he had been able to sustain himself a couple of feet above it on the small ledge that had arrested his fall. Meanwhile, the rescue party, headed by the first officer of the *Nimrod*, J. K. Davis, had arrived on the scene.

The crevasse was bridged with a suitable piece of sawn timber, and Davis, with that spirit of thoroughness which characterises all his work, promptly had himself lowered down the crevasse. On reaching the bottom he transferred the rope by which he had been lowered to Mawson, and with a long pull and a strong pull and a pull altogether, the company of the *Nimrod* soon had Mawson safe on top, none the worse for the accident with the exception that his back was slightly bruised. As soon as the rope was cast free from Mawson, it was let down again for Davis, and presently he, too, was safely on top.

And now we had a moment of leisure to see who constituted the rescue party. There were the dear old faces so well known on our voyage together the previous year, and interspersed with them were a few new faces. Here were our old comrades Armytage and Brocklehurst, Dr Michell, Harbord (the officer who – as we learned later – had sighted our depot flag), our good stewards Ansell and Ellis, the genial boatswain Cheetham, Paton, and a number of others. What a joyous grasping of hands and hearty all-round welcoming followed. Foremost among them all to welcome us was Captain Evans, who had commanded the SS *Koonya*, which towed the *Nimrod* from Lyttelton to beyond the Antarctic Circle, and it goes without saying that the fact that the *Nimrod* was now in command of a master of such experience, so well and favourably known in the shipping world of New Zealand and Australia, gave us the greatest satisfaction. He hastened to assure me of the safety and good health of my wife and family. While willing hands packed up our sledge, tent and other belongings, Captain Evans walked with us to the rope ladder hanging over the bows of the *Nimrod*.

Quickly as all this had taken place, Mackay had already found time to secure a pipe and some tobacco from one of our crew, and was now puffing away to his heart's content. We were soon all on the deck of the *Nimrod* once more, and were immediately stood up in a row to be photographed. As soon as the cameras had worked their wicked will upon us, for we were a sorry sight, our friends hurried us off for afternoon tea. After our one hundred and twenty-two days of hard toil over the sea ice of the coast and the great snow desert of the hinterland, the little ship seemed to us as luxurious as an ocean liner. To find oneself seated once more in a comfortable chair, and to be served with new-made bread, fresh butter, cake and tea, was Elysium.

We heard of the narrow escape of Armytage, Priestley and Brocklehurst, when they were being carried out to sea, with only two days' provisions, on a small ice-floe surrounded by killer-whales; and how, just after the momentary grounding of the floe, they were all just able to leap ashore at a spot where they were picked up later by the *Nimrod*. We also heard of the extraordinary adventures and escape of Mackintosh and MacGillan in their forced march overland, without tent or sleeping-bag, from Mount Bird to Cape Royds; of the departure of the supporting-party to meet the Southern Party; and, in short, of all the doings at Cape Royds and on the *Nimrod* since we had last heard any news. Pleasantly the buzz of our friend's voices blended itself with the gentle fizzing of steam from the *Nimrod*'s boiler, and surely since the days of John Gilpin 'were never folk so glad' as were we three.

Here it may not perhaps be out of place to quote from Captain Evans' private log in reference to the relief of our Northern Party by the *Nimrod*. After hearing from the Western Party under Armytage that we were long overdue at Butter Point, and after consulting with Murray at Cape Royds, he decided to commence to search for us, as ordered in Lieutenant Shackleton's instructions, on February 1. He left accordingly at that date, and after looking for us in vain at the Butter Point depot, and at Granite Harbour he sailed northwards for the Drygalski Ice Barrier Tongue, and when about three miles off our depot island had sighted our little flag and cairn, but was not certain that it was a depot. Nearer approach was precluded at the time by the pack-ice.

Captain Evans' private log reads as follows:

February 3, 1.30 a.m. Cleared belt of pack proceeded westward along Drygalski Barrier edge. Moderate to strong south-west wind, force four to eight with snow drift; 7.30 a.m. to 9.30 a.m. off Barrier. (At this time the *Nimrod* must have passed within about three miles of the spot where we were at our last camp before reaching the inlet, and had it not been for a little falling snow our flag and tent would probably have been sighted on this occasion); 10 a.m. to 2.15 p.m.: coasted along the beach at distances of from one-fifth of a mile to three-quarters of a mile in water from ten to fifty fathoms; 1 p.m. wind dropped to calm; 2.15 p.m. bearing true north-20°-east, distant twenty-four miles Mount Melbourne. Came to top of bight (Gerlache Inlet) full of pack; sounded in sixty-four fathoms; took bearings and stood eastward to search Cape Washington; 3.30 p.m. entered the pack-ice.

Midnight: rounded Cape Washington at a distance of one and a half cables in eleven to twenty fathoms, both sides of the cape quite inaccessible – awful-looking ice cliffs northern side – crevassed ice slopes south side. Fresh south-south-west wind, force 5–6 . . . No sign of party or record anywhere.

February 4, 1909, 10 a.m. Pack-ice stretching east and west to northward – turned back to try coast again to the southward. Fresh southerly wind, force 6 – clear and fine, barometer 28.86, thermometer 17° . . . Proceeding again along Drygalski Barrier; 3 p.m. sighted two flags on Barrier edge and a little back of it – small inlet developing. (The third officer, Mr A. Harbord, first sighted these flags, and came to the captain and said, 'I think, sir, I see a flag,' and then Armytage, bringing his powerful deer-stalking telescope to bear on the object, said to the captain, 'It's a dead sitter, sir.' T.W.E.D.) 3.40 p.m. arrived at upper end of inlet – picked up Professor David, Mawson and Mackay, just arrived back from Magnetic Pole; 5 p.m. killed first Ross seal; 2 p.m. great depression, 4 p.m. great elation . . . At 3.30 p.m., upon sighting the top of the Northern Party's tent, we fire a distress double detonator. Upon hearing this in the tent we learn that they all jumped up, and upset each other, and everything, including the tin of seal blubber and blood which they were drinking, and which Professor David pronouces good when you get used to it, and rushed out, Mawson first, who almost immediately went down a crevasse, from which Mr Davis and a party from the ship soon pulled him up. A great meeting – a tremendous relief.'

After afternoon tea came the joy of reading the home letters, and finding that the news was good. Later we all three had a novel experience, the first real wash for over four months. After much diligent work with hot water, soap and towel some of the outer casing of dirt was removed, and bits of our real selves began to show through the covering of seal oil and soot.

Dinner followed at 6 p.m. and it is scarcely necessary to add that with our raging appetites, and all the new types of dainty food around us we over-ate ourselves. This did not prevent us from partaking liberally of hot cocoa and gingerbread biscuits before turning in at 10 p.m. None but those whose bed for months has been on snow and ice can realise the luxury of a real bunk, blankets and pillow in a snug little cabin. A few minutes' happy reverie preceded sound sleep. At last our toilsome march was over, the work that had been given us to do was done, and done just in the nick of time; the safety of those nearest and dearest to us was assured, and we could now lay down our weary limbs to rest.

Under Providence one felt one owed one's life to the patient and thorough search, sound judgment and fine seamanship of Captain Evans, and the devotion to duty of his officers and crew and no pen can describe how that night one's heart overflowed with thankfulness for all the blessings of that day. One's last thought in the twilight that comes between wakefulness and sleep is expressed in the words of our favourite record on the gramophone, the hymn so grandly sung by Evan Williams:

So long Thy power hath blest me, sure it still will lead me on.

If one may be permitted to take a brief retrospect of our journey the following considerations present themselves: The total distance travelled from Cape Royds to the Magnetic Pole and back to our depot on the Drygalski Glacier was about 1260 miles. Of this, 740 miles was relay work, and we dragged a weight of, at first, a little over half a ton, and finally somewhat under half a ton for the whole of this distance.

For the remaining 520 miles from the Drygalski Depot to the Magnetic Pole and back we dragged a weight at first, of 670 lb., but this finally became reduced to about 450 lb., owing to consumption of food and oil, by the time that we returned to our depot.

We were absent on our sledge journey for one hundred and twenty-two days, of which five days were spent in our tent during heavy blizzards, and five days partly in experimenting in cooking with blubber and partly in preparing supplies of seal meat for the journey from the sea ice over the high plateau, and three days in addition were taken up in reconnoitring, taking magnetic observations, &c. We therefore covered this distance of 1260 miles in 109 travelling days, an average of about eleven and a half miles a day.

We had laid two depots before our final start, but as these were distant only ten miles and fifteen miles respectively, from our winter quarters they did not materially help us. We had no supporting-party, and with the exception of help from the motor-car in laying out these short depots we pulled the sledges for the whole distance without assistance except, on rare occasions, from the wind.

The travelling over the sea ice was at first pretty good, but from Cape Bernacchi to the Nordenskjold Ice Barrier we were much hampered by screwed pack-ice with accompanying high and hard snow ridges. Towards the latter part of October and during November and part of December the thawing surface of saline snow, clogging and otherwise impeding our runners, made the work of sledging extremely laborious. Moreover, on the sea ice – especially towards the last part of our journey over it – we had ever present the risk of a blizzard breaking the ice up suddenly all around us, and drifting us out to sea. There can be no doubt, in view of the wide lanes of open water in the sea ice on the south side of the Drygalski Glacier, when we reached it on November 30, that we got to glacies firma only in the nick of time.

Then there was the formidable obstacle of the Drygalski Glacier, with its wide and deep chasms, its steep ridges and crevasses, the passage of this glacier proving so difficult that although only a little over twenty miles in width it took us a fortnight to get across. On the far side of the Drygalski was the open sea forcing us to travel shorewards over the glacier surface. Then had come the difficult task of pioneering a way up to the high plateau – the attempt to force a passage up the Mount Nansen Glacier – our narrow escapes from having our sledge engulphed in crevasses – the heavy blizzard with deep new fallen snow and then our retreat from that region of high-pressure ridges and crevasse entanglements – our abandonment of the proposed route up the snout of the Bellingshausen Glacier, and finally our successful ascent up the small tributary glacier, the 'backstairs passage', to the south of Mount Larsen.

On the high plateau was the difficulty of respiration, biting winds with low temperatures, difficult sledging – sometimes against blizzards – over broad undulations and high sastrugi, the cracking of our lips, fingers and feet, exhaustion from insufficient rations, disappointment at finding that the Magnetic Pole had shifted further inland than the position previously assigned to it. Then, after we had just succeeded by dint of great efforts in reaching the Pole of verticity, came the necessity for forced marches, with our sledge, of from sixteen to twenty miles a day in order to reach the coast with any reasonable prospect of our being picked up by the *Nimrod*.

Then came our choice of the difficult route down the snout of the Bellingshausen Glacier, and our consequent difficulties in surmounting the ice-pressure ridges; then the difficulty of sledging over the 'tile-ice' surface, the opposing ice barrancas formed by the thaw water while we were on the high plateau; the final heavy snow blizzard; our loss of direction when sledging in bad light and falling snow, and finally our arrest by the deep barranca of what afterwards was known as Relief Inlet.

But ours were not the only, nor the greatest, difficulties connected with our journey. There were many disappointments, dangers and hardships for the captain, officers and crew of the *Nimrod* in their search for us along that two hundred miles of desolate and, for a great part, inaccessible coast-line. How often black spots ashore, proving on nearer view to be seals or penguins, had been mistaken for depot flags; how often the glint of sunlight off brightly reflecting facets of ice had been thought to be 'helios', only the disappointed ones can tell; how often, too, the ship was all but aground, at other times all but beset in the ice-pack in the efforts to get a clearer view of the shore-line in order to discover our depot! This is a tale that the brave men who risked their lives to save ours will scorn to tell, but is nevertheless true.

As the result of our journey to the Magnetic Pole and back, Mawson was able to join up in his continuous triangulation survey, Mount Erebus with Mount Melbourne, and to show with approximate accuracy the outline of the coast-line, and the position and height of several new mountains. He and I obtained geological collections, sketches and notes – especially on glacial geology – along the coast-line, and he also took a series of photographs; while Mackay determined our altitudes on the plateau by means of the hypsometer. Mawson also made magnetic determinations, and I was able to gather some meteorological information. A summary of this work is given in the Scientific Memoirs of the expedition.

Unfortunately the time available during our journey was too short for detailed magnetic, geological or meteorological observations. Nevertheless, we trust that the information obtained has justified the journey. At all events we have pioneered a route to the Magnetic Pole, and we hope that the path thus found will prove of use to future observers.

It is easy, of course, to be wise after the event, but there is no doubt that had we known that there was going to be an abundance of seals all along the coast, and had we had an efficient team of dogs we could have accomplished our journey in probably half the time that it actually occupied. Future expeditions to the South Magnetic Pole would probably do well to land a strong and well-equipped party, either at Relief Inlet, or better, as near to Backstairs Passage as the ship can be taken, and as early in December as the state of the sea ice makes navigation possible. A party of three, with a supporting-party also of three, with good dog teams and plenty of fresh seal meat, could travel together for about seventy miles inland; then the supporting-party might diverge and ascend Mount Nansen from its inland extremity. The other party, meanwhile, might proceed to the Magnetic Pole at not less than fifteen miles a day. This should admit of their spending from a week to a fortnight at the Pole, and they should then be able to return to the coast early in February. Meanwhile, there would be plenty of scope for a third party to explore the foot-hills of Mount Larsen and Mount Nansen, search and map their wonderful moraines, and examine the deeply indented rocky coast-line from Nansen to the as yet untrod volcano Mount Melbourne.

39

ALL ABOARD: THE RETURN TO NEW ZEALAND

The *Nimrod*, with the members of the Northern Party aboard, got back to the winter quarters on February 11 and landed Mawson. The hut party at this period consisted of Murray, Priestley, Mawson, Day and Roberts. No news had been heard of the Southern Party, and the Depot Party, commanded by Joyce, was still out. The ship lay under Glacier Tongue most of the time, making occasional visits to Hut Point in case some of the men should have returned. On February 20 it was found that the Depot Party had reached Hut Point, and had not seen the Southern Party. The temperature was becoming lower, and the blizzards were more frequent.

The instruction left by me had provided that if we had not returned by February 25, a party was to be landed at Hut Point, with a team of dogs, and on March 1 a search-party was to go south. On February 21 Murray and Captain Evans began to make preparations for the landing of the relief party. The ship proceeded to Cape Royds where Mawson was picked up. In accordance with my expressed wish he was offered the command of the relief party, and accepted it. If it became necessary to go south in search of the Southern Party the men landed at Hut Point would have to spend another winter in the south, as the ship could not wait until their return. It was therefore a serious matter for those who stayed, but there was no lack of volunteers. These arrangements being completed, most of the members of the expedition then on board went ashore at Cape Royds to get the last of their property packed ready for departure. The ship was lying under Glacier Tongue when I arrived at Hut Point with Wild on February 28, and after I had been landed with the relief party in order to bring in Adams and Marshall, it proceeded to Cape Royds in order to take on board the remaining members of the shore-party and some specimens and stores.

The *Nimrod* anchored a short distance from the shore, and two boats were launched. The only spot convenient for embarkation near the ship's anchorage was at a low ice cliff in Backdoor Bay. Everything had to be lowered by ropes over the cliff into the boats. Some hours were spent in taking on board the last of the collections, the private property, and various stores.

A stiff breeze was blowing, making work with the boats difficult, but by 6 a.m. on March 2 there remained to be taken on board only the men and dogs. The operation of lowering the dogs one by one into the boats was necessarily slow, and while it was in progress the wind freshened to blizzard force, and the sea began to run dangerously. The waves had deeply undercut the ice-cliff, leaving a projecting shelf. One boat, in charge of Davis, succeeded in reaching the ship, but a second boat, commanded by Harbord, was less fortunate. It was heavily loaded with twelve men and a number of dogs, and before it had proceeded many yards from the shore an oar broke. The Nimrod was forced to slip her moorings and steam out of the bay, as the storm had become so severe that she was in danger of dragging her anchors and going on the rocks. An attempt to float a buoy to the boat was not successful, and for some time Harbord and the men with him were in danger. They could not get out of the bay owing to the force of the sea, and the projecting shelf of ice threatened disaster if they approached the shore. The flying spray had encased the men in ice, and their hands were numb and half-frozen. At the end of an hour they managed to make fast to a line stretched from an anchor a few yards from the cliff, the men who had remained on shore pulling this line taut. The position was still dangerous, but all the men and dogs were hauled up the slippery ice-face into safety before the boat sank. Hot drinks were soon ready in the hut, and the men dried their clothes as best they could before the fire. Nearly all the bedding had been sent on board, and the temperature was low, but they were thankful to have escaped with their lives.

The weather was bitter on the following morning (March 3), and the Nimrod, which had been sheltering under Glacier Tongue, came back to Cape Royds. A heavy sea was still running, but a new landing-place was selected in the shelter of the Cape, and all the men and dogs were got aboard. The ship went back to the Glacier Tongue anchorage to wait for the relief Party.

About ten o'clock that night Mackintosh was walking the deck engaged in conversation with some other members of the expedition. Suddenly he became excited and said, 'I feel that Shackleton has arrived at Hut Point.' He was very anxious that the ship should go up to the Point, but nobody gave much attention to him. Then Dunlop advised him to go up to the crow's-nest if he was sure about it, and look for a signal. Mackintosh went aloft, and immediately saw our flare at Hut Point. The ship at once left for Hut Point, reaching it at midnight, and by 2 a.m. on March 4 the entire expedition was safe on board.

There was now no time to be lost if we were to attempt to complete our work. The season was far advanced, and the condition of the ice was a matter for anxiety, but I was most anxious to undertake exploration with the ship to the eastward, towards Adelie Land, with the idea of mapping the coast-line in that direction. As soon as all the members of the expedition were on board the *Nimrod*, therefore, I gave orders to steam north, and in a very short time we were under way. It was evident that the sea in our neighbourhood would be frozen over before many hours had passed, and although I had foreseen the possibility of having to spend a second winter in the Antarctic when making my arrangements, we were all very much disinclined to face the long wait if it could be avoided. I wished first to round Cape Armitage and pick up the geological specimens and gear that had been left at Pram Point, but there was heavy ice coming out from the south, and this meant imminent risk of the ship being caught and perhaps 'nipped'. I decided to go into shelter under Glacier Tongue in the little inlet on the north side for a few hours, in the hope that the southern wind, that was bringing out the ice, would cease and that we would then be able to return and secure the specimens and gear. This was about two o'clock on the morning of March 4, and we members of the Southern Party turned in for a much needed rest.

At eight o'clock on the morning of the 4th we again went down the sound. Young ice was forming over the sea, which was now calm, the wind having entirely dropped, and it was evident that we must be very quick if we were to escape that year. We brought the *Nimrod* right alongside the pressure ice at Pram Point, and I pointed out the little depot on the hillside. Mackintosh at once went off with a party of men to bring the gear and specimens down, while another party went out to the seal rookery to see if they could find a peculiar seal that we had noticed on our way to the hut on the previous night. The seal was either a new species or the female of the Ross Seal. It was a small animal, about four feet six inches long, with a broad white band from its throat right down to its tail on the underside. If we had been equipped with knives on the previous night we would have despatched it, but we had no knives and were, moreover, very tired, and we therefore left it. The search for the seal proved fruitless, and as the sea was freezing over behind us I ordered all the men on board directly the stuff from the depot had been got on to the deck, and the *Nimrod* once more steamed north. The breeze soon began to freshen, and it was blowing hard from the south when we passed the winter quarters at Cape Royds. We all turned out to give three cheers and to take a last look at the place where we had spent so many happy days. The hut was not exactly a palatial residence and during our period of residence in it we had suffered many discomforts, not to say hardships, but, on the other hand, it had been our home for a year that would always live in our memories. We had been a very happy little party within its walls, and often when we were far away from even its measure of civilisation, it had been the Mecca of all our hopes and dreams. We watched the little hut fade away in the distance with feelings almost of sadness, and there were few men aboard who did not cherish a hope that some day they would once more live strenuous days under the shadow of mighty Erebus.

I left at the winter quarters on Cape Royds a supply of stores sufficient to last fifteen men for one year. The vicissitudes of life in the Antarctic are such that such a supply might prove of the greatest value to some future expedition. The hut was locked up and the key hung up outside where it would be easily found, and we readjusted the lashing of the hut so that it might be able to withstand the attacks of the blizzards during the years to come. Inside the hut I left a letter stating what had been accomplished by the expedition, and giving some other information that might be useful to a future party of explorers. The stores left in the hut included oil, flour, jams, dried vegetables, biscuits, pemmican, plasmon, matches and various tinned meats, as well as tea, cocoa, and necessary articles of equipment. If any party has to make use of our hut in the future, it will find there everything that it requires.

The wind was still freshening as we went south under steam and sail on March 4, and it was fortunate for us that this was so, for the ice that had formed on the sea water in the sound was thickening rapidly, assisted by the old pack, of which a large amount lay across our course. I was anxious to pick up a depot of geological specimens on Depot Island, left there by the Northern Party, and with this end in view the *Nimrod* was taken on a more westerly course than would otherwise have been the case. The wind, however, was freshening to a gale, and we were passing through streams of ice, which seemed to thicken as we neared the shore. I decided that it would be too risky to send a party off for the specimens, as there was no proper lee to this small island, and the consequences of even a short delay might be serious. I therefore gave instructions that the course should be altered to due north. The following wind helped us, and on the morning of March 6 we were off Cape Adare. I wanted to push between the Balleny Islands and the mainland, and make an attempt to follow the coastline from Cape North westward, so as to link it up with Adelie Land. No ship had ever succeeded in penetrating to the westward of Cape North, heavy pack having been encountered on the occasion of each attempt. The *Discovery* had passed through the Balleny Islands and sailed over part of the so-called Wilkes Land of the maps, but the question of the existence of this land in any other position had been left open.

We steamed along the pack-ice, which was beginning to thicken, and although we did not manage to do all that I had hoped, we had the satisfaction of pushing our little vessel along that coast to longitude 166° 14′ East, latitude 69° 47′ South, a point further west than had been reached by any previous expedition. On the morning of March 8 we saw, beyond Cape North, a new coast-line extending first to the southwards and then to the west for a distance of over forty-five miles. We took angles and bearings, and Marston sketched the main outlines. We were too far away to take any photographs that would have been of value, but the sketches show very clearly the type of the land. Professor David was of opinion that it was the northern edge of the polar plateau. The coast seemed to consist of cliffs, with a few bays in the distance. We would all have been glad of an opportunity to explore the coast thoroughly, but that was out of the question; the ice was getting thicker all the time, and it was becoming imperative that we should escape to clear water without further delay. There was no chance of getting further west at that point, and as the new ice was forming between the old pack of the previous year and the land, we were in serious danger of being frozen in for the winter at a place where we could not have done any geological work of importance. We therefore moved north along the edge of the pack, making as much westing as possible, in the direction of the Balleny Islands. I still hoped that it might be possible to skirt them and find Wilkes Land. It was awkward work, and at times the ship could hardly move at all.

Finally, about midnight on March 9, I saw that we must go north, and the course was set in that direction. We were almost too late, for the ice was closing in and before long we were held up, the ship being unable to move at all. The situation looked black, but we discovered a lane through which progress could be made, and in the afternoon of the 10th we were in fairly open water, passing through occasional lines of pack. Our troubles were over, for we had a good voyage up to New Zealand, and on March 22 dropped anchor at the mouth of Lord's River, on the south side of Stewart Island. I did not go to a port because I wished to get the news of the expedition's work through to London before we faced the energetic newspaper men.

That was a wonderful day to all of us. For over a year we had seen nothing but rocks, ice, snow and sea. There had been no colour and no softness in the scenery of the Antarctic; no green growth had gladdened our eyes, no musical notes of birds had come to our ears. We had had our work, but we had been cut off from most of the lesser things that go to make life worth while. No person who has not spent a period of his life in those 'stark and sullen solitudes that sentinel the Pole' will understand fully what trees and flowers, sun-flecked turf and running streams mean to the soul of a man. We landed on the stretch of beach that separated the sea from the luxuriant growth of the forest, and scampered about like children in the sheer joy of being alive. I did not wish to despatch my cablegrams from Half Moon Bay until an hour previously arranged, and in the meantime we revelled in the warm sand on the beach, bathed in the sea and climbed amongst the trees. We lit a fire and made tea on the beach, and while we were having our meal the wekas, the remarkable flightless birds found only in New Zealand, came out from the bush for their share of the good things. These quaint birds, with their long bills, brown plumage and quick, inquisitive eyes have no fear of men, and their friendliness seemed to us like a welcome from that sunny land that had always treated us with such open-hearted kindliness. The clear, musical notes of other birds came to us from the trees, and we felt that we needed only good news from home to make our happiness and contentment absolutely complete. One of the scientific men found a cave showing signs of native occupation in some period of the past, and was fortunate enough to discover a stone adze made of the rare pounamu, or greenstone.

Early next morning we hove up the anchor, and at 10 a.m. we entered Half Moon Bay. I went ashore to despatch my cablegram, and it was strange to see new faces on the wharf after fifteen months during which we had met no one outside the circle of our own little party. There were girls on the wharf, too, and every one was glad to see us in the hearty New Zealand way. I despatched my cablegrams from the little office, and then went on board again and ordered the course to be set for Lyttelton, the port from which we had sailed on the first day of the previous year. We arrived there on March 25 late in the afternoon.

The people of New Zealand would have welcomed us, I think, whatever had been the result of our efforts, for their keen interest in Antarctic exploration has never faltered since the early days of the *Discovery* expedition, and their attitude towards us was always that of warm personal friendship, but the news of the measure of success we had achieved had been published in London, and flashed back to the southern countries, and we were met out in the harbour and on the wharves by cheering crowds. Enthusiastic friends boarded the *Nimrod* almost as soon as she entered the heads, and when our little vessel came alongside the quay the crowd on deck became so great that movement was almost impossible. Then I was handed great bundles of letters and cablegrams. The loved ones at home were well, the world was pleased with our work, and it seemed as though nothing but happiness could ever enter life again.

EPILOGUE

Shackleton's subsequent expedition and the famous boat journey demands to be read and not retold. But there was to be a long epilogue of bizarre financial schemes and ill thought through plans before Shackleton was to return on his last expedition in 1922. In every way the world had changed. The First World War had ripped open people's dreams and hopes. And in this new, grey world Shackleton was like a man out of time. Repeatedly unfaithful, he drank and smoked more and more, and gradually those who had once idolised him began to fall away. He still had no money and still chased after those dreams of riches and fame that had haunted him all his life: there was a surreal scheme involving Hungarian gold, frustrated by endless Balkan evasiveness; he tried to make money out of the White Russian cause in Arkhangel, but the rise of Soviet power was to dash hopes there. And so it went on.

Shackleton sailed again on 17 September 1921. He had no real plans. His ship was totally unsuitable. It was all too obviously a means of escape. In Rio he had a massive heart attack, yet refused to be properly examined and still insisted on continuing. He seemed a shadow of his former self. At South Georgia, by the same whaling station he had tramped into all those years before at the end of the Boat Journey, he had another heart attack. This time it was fatal. He was forty-nine years old. Emily, his wife, turned his body back at Montevideo and it is at Grytviken in South Georgia that he is buried.

Shackleton left debts in today's money of over £500,000, and yet somehow that is all forgotten. Forgotten too is the fact that all his expeditions failed. What is left is the memory of an utterly inspiring leader of men; a man of indomitable courage and iron will who led where many another would have fallen by the wayside; a man who today stands as the touchstone of courage and leadership against impossible odds. It is against this backdrop that his failings and weaknesses seem somehow to shrink.

The last word should be left to two men. One is Roald Amundsen: 'Sir Ernest Shackleton's name will for evermore be engraved with letters of fire in the history of Antarctic exploration. Courage and willpower can make miracles. I know of no better example than what that man has accomplished.' The other is Sir Arthur Conan Doyle, who, in a speech on British rearmament remarked: 'We can pass the eight *Dreadnoughts*, if we are sure of the eight Shackletons.'

Hugh Andrew
October 2000